Brief Contents

P9-DHL-595

Critical Thinking, Thoughtful Writing

A Rhetoric with Readings

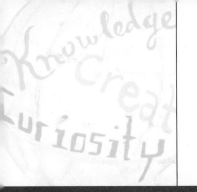

Critical Thinking, Thoughtful Writing

A Rhetoric with Readings

FOURTH EDITION

John Chaffee, PH.D.

Director, NY Center for Critical Thinking and Language Learning
LaGuardia College, City University of New York

Christine McMahon
Barbara Stout

English Department, Montgomery College

Houghton Mifflin Company

Boston   New York

For Jessie and Joshua

Publisher: Patricia A. Coryell
Editor-in-Chief, English: Carrie Brandon
Senior Sponsoring Editor: Lisa Kimball
Senior Development Editor: Judith Fifer
Senior Marketing Manager: Tom Ziolkowski
Senior Project Editor: Carol Newman
Art and Design Manager: Jill Haber
Cover Design Director: Tony Saizon
Senior Photo Editor: Jennifer Meyer Dare
Composition Buyer: Chuck Dutton
New Title Manager: James Lonergan
Editorial Assistant: Katilyn Crowley
Marketing Assistant: Bettina Chiu
Editorial Assistant: Paola Moll

Cover image: Illustration © Andy Powell.

Text and photo credits begin on page 570.

Copyright © 2008 by John Chaffee. All rights reserved.

No part of this work may be reproduced or transmitted in any form or by any means, electronic or mechanical, including photocopying and recording, or by any information storage or retrieval system without the prior written permission of the copyright owner unless such copying is expressly permitted by federal copyright law. With the exception of nonprofit transcription in Braille, Houghton Mifflin is not authorized to grant permission for further uses of copyrighted selections reprinted in this text without the permission of their owners. Permission must be obtained from the individual copyright owners as identified herein. Address requests for permission to make copies of Houghton Mifflin material to College Permission, Houghton Mifflin Company, 222 Berkeley Street, Boston, MA 02116-3764.

Printed in the U.S.A.

Library of Congress Catalog Number: 2007924858

Instructor's Exam Copy:
ISBN 13: 978-0-618-83296-5
ISBN 10: 0-618-83296-3

For orders, use student text ISBNs:
ISBN 13: 978-0-618-78348-9
ISBN 10: 0-618-78348-2

1 2 3 4 5 6 7 8 9-VH-11 10 09 08 07

Contents

CHAPTER 3   Thinking Critically, Writing Thoughtfully   **50**

CHAPTER 4   Viewing Critically, Thinking Creatively   **84**

**Part Two
Thinking and Writing to
Shape Our World   183**

CHAPTER **12** Solving Problems: Writing to Propose Solutions   **397**

Preface

Leo Tolstoy eloquently observed that "the relations of word to thought, and the creation of new concepts, is a complex, delicate, and enigmatic process unfolding in our soul." Writers and teachers of writing have long recognized intricate relationships between the extraordinary human processes of thought and language. This insight, which helps beginning college students become thoughtful writers, informs the comprehensive approach of *Critical Thinking, Thoughtful Writing: A Rhetoric with Readings,* Fourth Edition. The synergy between what experts in the thinking process (philosophers and psychologists, for example) understand about learning can be powerfully integrated with the critical thinking process as understood by teachers of writing and composition, especially in an age of increasingly complex channels of information and media.

Critical Thinking, Thoughtful Writing: A Rhetoric with Readings, Fourth Edition, presents an integrated approach to teaching the thinking, writing, and reading skills—of both verbal and visual texts—that first-year composition students need in order to successfully meet the challenges of academic work as well as the professional workplace. As students develop higher-order thinking abilities, they learn to articulate their ideas through writing and the creation of multimodal texts. And as they develop their abilities to navigate the writing process, students learn to think coherently, precisely, and creatively. This approach integrates the development of thinking skills with composing skills so they not only reinforce each other but also become inseparable.

This book stimulates and guides students to think deeply and beyond superficialities, to refuse to be satisfied with the first idea they have, to look objectively at multiple perspectives on complex issues, and to formulate their own informed conclusions. It encourages students to develop an interest in research and in delving into possibilities rather than settling for easy answers. It challenges students to be independent in their thinking and courageous in their convictions. And it shows them how to organize information, interpret different perspectives, solve challenging problems, analyze complex issues, and communicate their ideas clearly.

Advantages of a Critical Thinking Framework

The critical thinking framework of this text helps instructors and students in the following ways:

- **By providing an intellectual and thematic framework** that helps writing teachers place rhetorical concerns in a meaningful context. *Critical Thinking,*

Thoughtful Writing challenges and guides students to think and write about important topics that build on their cognitive activities and critical explorations. This process enables students to improve both the technical aspects of their writing (coherence, organization, detail, grammar, and mechanics) and the quality of their writing (depth, insight, sophistication).

- **By leading students to understand the reciprocal relationship** between the process of thinking and the process of writing. The text stimulates students to explore their own composing processes, gradually mastering the forms of thought and critical thinking that are the hallmark of mature and thoughtful writing.

- **By helping students to appreciate that reading is a thinking activity** rather than a series of decoding skills. This understanding accelerates and enhances reading development. Students are better able to understand and develop the interrelated thinking abilities that the reading process comprises, including problem solving, forming and applying concepts, and relating ideas to larger conceptual frameworks.

Content and Organization

Movement from the Personal to the Social

The book moves logically from introducing creative and critical thinking to explaining how these tools can be used in different kinds of writing. Part One helps students understand themselves as thinkers and writers; the Writing Projects in this section ask them to write from their own experiences and observations. Part Two explores important thinking patterns and language issues; here, the Writing Projects ask them to incorporate ideas and perspectives from others into their expository writing. Part Three uses an increasing number of sources as students work with problem solving, argumentation, and research. This logical progression pulls students beyond their personal experiences and pushes them to think and write about challenging issues and concepts, while seeing how social issues are connected with their own lives. The practical strategies will help students address writing assignments in other academic classes and in the workplace.

Four Integrated Elements to Each Chapter

1. **Critical Thinking Focus** examines the thinking skill central to each chapter. Examples of critical thinking skills are thinking about thinking, creative thinking, decision-making, evaluating perspectives, causal reasoning, conceptualizing, constructing knowledge, problem solving, and developing reasoned arguments.
2. **Writing Focus** provides strategies and Thinking-Writing Activities that draw upon the chapter's critical thinking skill.

3. **Reading Focus** comprises 45 professional readings (essays, articles, or book chapters) and 14 student essays, on themes including creativity, decision-making, politics and culture, gender, language, problem solving, and arguments on timely and provocative topics. Each chapter offers three or more pieces of professional writing (such as essays, investigative reporting, and editorials, as well as some imaginative genres) and at least one student essay. The readings reflect the critical thinking focus in each chapter and provide the basis for assignments that initiate students' writing.

4. **Writing Project** builds on the reading themes and skills developed through the chapter's activities. These carefully structured projects move systematically through stages toward a finished project, providing guidance for each stage of the writing process. Each chapter includes at least one student example of the completed Writing Project.

Special Features

Practical Critical Thinking Strategies for Writing and for Evaluating Images   This book introduces the process of thinking critically as a practical and powerful approach to writing, to critically evaluating electronic and visual media, and to life in general. For example, in learning a thoughtful approach for making decisions, students apply the decision-making process to revising drafts as well as to making important decisions in other areas of their lives. By developing their problem-solving abilities, students become able both to compose a problem-solving essay and to be more effective in solving problems beyond the classroom.

Comprehensive Thinking-Writing Model   The Thinking-Writing Model introduced in Chapter 1 (pages 7–9) and reinforced throughout the book provides a clear graphic representation of the writing process and of the connections between critical thinking and thoughtful writing, as well as creative thinking and inventive writing.

Creative Thinking to Enrich the Writing Process   The book shows that creative thought can and should be an integral part of academic writing. All aspects of the writing process can be approached creatively, including topic selection, generating ideas and drafting, using specific details, and writing introductions and conclusions. In learning to think creatively, students discover strategies to make their writing more inventive, while also infusing creative energy into other areas of their lives.

Emphasis on Collaboration   The value of collaboration in thinking and writing is emphasized throughout, with this special icon highlighting Thinking-Writing Activities and other material specifically designed for collaboration and peer review. Critical thinking is emphasized in the active exploration of ideas, listening to others, and carefully evaluating opinions and arguments, and provides a context for collaborative learning. Students learn to examine their own opinions more analytically and relate these opinions to the world at large. They learn to assess alternative points of view in dialogue with others, contributing to their development into a community of concerned thinkers and writers.

Cross-Disciplinary Approach   Recognizing that first-year composition courses prepare students to write in all of their courses and after college, this book presents examples, selections, and assignments from sociology, psychology, linguistics, history, business, cultural studies, economics, and the natural and hard sciences.

Critical Thinking as a Tool for Living   The book views learning to think, write, and read as integral dimensions of an individual's personal growth and transformation. It aims to help students grow. While learning how to think and write, students are encouraged to apply these critical and creative thinking skills to all facets of their lives, enabling them to make enlightened decisions, solve challenging problems, analyze complex issues, communicate effectively, nurture creative talents, and become more thoughtful and socially aware citizens.

New to the Fourth Edition

The fourth edition of *Critical Thinking, Thoughtful Writing* makes even clearer the connections between critical thinking, thoughtful writing, and active reading. New chapters, features, and content include the following:

- **NEW: Thinking Critically About Images.** Two four-color inserts (in Chapter 4 and Chapter 13) challenge students to see how the "evidence" of seemingly objective photojournalism can tell startlingly different stories about the same phenomenon, as well as evaluate how effective combinations of text and image can create compelling persuasive messages. Additional discussion of how images (from photojournalism to advertising) are created, how to interpret their messages, and how to incorporate them within students' own work appears in Chapters 4, 9, 10, 13, and 14.

- **NEW: Four Qualities of a Critical Thinker.** Adapted from John Chaffee's best-selling text *Thinking Critically*, these four characteristics—open-mindedness, creativity, curiosity, and knowledge—are woven consistently throughout the newly revised writing and reading pedagogy. Each chapter begins with a brief profile of someone who exemplifies these four qualities—writers, geneticists, explorers, and others who have made significant achievements in a range of disciplines. These four characteristics are both easily recognizable by students and achievable as goals inside and outside the classroom.

- **NEW: Online Study Center icons.** New icons refer students to the companion student web site, the Online Study Center for *Critical Thinking, Thoughtful Writing*, where they will find additional writing prompts and research sources.

- **NEW: Casebook on Hurricane Katrina.** Chapter 10, "Exploring Cause and Effect: Writing to Speculate" now includes four essays in which journalists interrogate and examine the coverage of 2005's Hurricane Katrina, determining how issues of race and class influenced the ways in which stories were told—and, often, just as rapidly disproved. In addition, two brief reflections by photojournalists assigned to cover the storm and its aftermath offer additional insight into the production of visual evidence. Each essay serves as a model of causal reasoning as well as demonstrating how writers work to avoid causal fallacies— while challenging the apparent "truths" of official sources.

- **NEW: More models of persuasive writing and writing from sources.** In response to reviewer suggestions, the fourth edition of *Critical Thinking, Thoughtful Writing* now moves more quickly from first-person personal or "expressivist" writing to source-based, objective, and investigative writing. Without sacrificing the fundamental pedagogy of *Critical Thinking, Thoughtful Writing*, which is based on John Chaffee's three decades of classroom teaching, this new edition provides more diverse rhetorical models for today's composition classrooms.

- **REVISED: Audience, purpose, and subject**—the cornerstones of the rhetorical triangle—have been reinforced and highlighted throughout this edition. Look for these key words in chapter headings to help students continually redirect and refine their understanding of "The Thinking-Writing Model" introduced in Chapter 1.

- **REVISED: Enhanced discussion of plagiarism**—what it is and how to avoid it—with critical thinking exercises and specific guidelines for detecting and averting the common errors in research that can lead to plagiarism, now that so much material can be accessed and copied easily.

Supplements

Online Teaching Center   The Houghton Mifflin *Online Teaching Center for Critical Thinking, Thoughtful Writing,* Fourth Edition, is found at **college.hmco.com/pic/ chaffeeCTTW4e.** The Instructor Resources found on the site are password-protected and include a revised edition of the **Instructor's Resource Manual,** which offers thoughtful suggestions for teaching the fourth edition, including recent scholarship; discussion of collaborative learning and peer review; sample syllabi; teaching suggestions (including suggestions for teaching the new material on Thinking Critically About Images); handouts and transparency masters for key processes and diagrams; as well as a writing inventory and reader response guidelines; and suggestions for additional readings, films, and videos.

Online Study Center   Throughout the student text, this icon *Online Study Center* directs students to the text's accompanying web site, at **college.hmco.com/pic/ chaffeeCTTW4e.** This enriched learning center includes further information on the innovators profiled in the "Four Characteristics of a Critical Thinker" feature;

additional resources on visual rhetoric; further exercises and inspiration for critical thinking, creativity, and research, and many of the topics discussed in the readings as well as interactive step-by-step directions for completing each of the Writing Projects. Students will enjoy working with "Tom Randall's Halloween Party," an interactive court case that allows them to analyze evidence, devise cross-examination questions, and serve as judge and jury evaluating the case of a college student charged with serving alcohol to an underage guest.

The Authors

Critical Thinking, Thoughtful Writing is the result of collaboration of three authors. John Chaffee is Director of the New York Center for Critical Thinking and Language Learning, and Professor of Philosophy at The City University of New York. His best-selling textbook *Thinking Critically,* going into its Ninth Edition, presents a comprehensive, language-based approach to learning that helped define the field of critical thinking. His introduction to philosophy text, *The Philosopher's Way,* has been acclaimed as a genuinely innovative contribution to the field. Barbara Stout and Christine McMahon, both former English professors at Montgomery College, used *Thinking Critically* in their composition courses for seven years, which made them ideally suited to adapt its critical thinking approach to the teaching of writing, resulting in this text.

Acknowledgments

The following reviewers offered wise insights to and suggestions for the manuscript over this or earlier editions: Catherine Amdahl, Harrisburg Area Community College; Sonya Alvarado, Eastern Michigan University; Kathryn Bartle Angus, California State University, Fullerton; Jeanelle Barrett, Tarleton State University; Sally M. Baynton, San Antonio College; Larry Beason, University of South Alabama; Bruce Beckum, Colorado Mountain College; Patricia Bizzel, College of the Holy Cross; Bradley W. Bleck, Spokane Falls Community College; Paul Bodmer, Bismark State College; Stephanie Byrd, Cleveland State University; Christine Caver, University of Texas, San Antonio; Frankie Chadwick, University of Arkansas at Little Rock; Gina Claywell, Murray State University; Huey Crisp, University of Arkansas at Little Rock; Sarah Dangelantonio, Franklin Pierce College; Charlie Davis, Boise State University; Damian Doyle, University of Colorado at Boulder; Thomas Fink, LaGuardia College; Adam Fischer, Bowie State University; Kim Grewe, Wor-Wic Community College; Judith A. Hinman, College of the Redwoods; Martha M. Holder, Wytheville Community College; Elizabeth Hooper, University of Texas, San Antonio; Frederick T. Janzow, Southeast Missouri State University; Margaret Johnson, Idaho State University; John H. Jones, Jacksonville State University; Dipo Kalejaiye, Prince George's Community College; John Kinkade, University of Southern Indiana;

Chikako D. Kumamoto, College of DuPage; Anna M. Lang, University of Indianapolis; Shirley Wilson Logan, University of Maryland; Cheryl R. Lyda, Idaho State University; Linda McHenry, Fort Hays State University; Paul J. Morris, II, Pittsburgh State University; Joan Mullin, University of Toledo; Lisa Nicholas, University of Southern Indiana; Elizabeth A. Nist, Anoka-Ramsey Community College; John Regan, Boston University; Shirley Roberts, Brookhaven College; Jeffrey Roessner, Mercyhurst College; Denise Rogers, University of Louisiana at Lafayette; Kenneth Rosenauer, Missouri Western State College; Nicholas Schevera, College of Lake County; Isaiah Smithson, Southern Illinois University; Byrin Stay, Mount St. Mary's College; Judith L. Steele, Mid-America Christian University; Kay Stokes, Hanover College; Leslie Stoupas, Colorado Mountain College; John T. Stovall, National-Louis University; Michael Thomas, College of the Redwoods; William Vaughn, Central Missouri State University; Elizabeth Wahlquist, Brigham Young University; Jane Armstrong Woodman, Northern Arizona University.

John Chaffee would also like to thank Christine McMahon and Barbara Stout for the dedication and expertise they brought to the unique project of extending his work in critical thinking to the field of composition. Their approaches to teaching writing and their active involvement in the composition field have contributed significantly to a text that is practical, effective, and adaptable to a variety of instructional contexts.

As has been the case for the last several decades, John has been privileged to work with a stellar team of individuals at Houghton Mifflin Company who are exemplary professionals and also good friends. Judy Fifer is the Senior Development Editor on this edition, and she is a joy to work with, integrating an insightful vision for the book with a conscientious attention to detail and an unwavering commitment to excellence. In her role as Senior Sponsoring Editor, Lisa Kimball provided the comprehensive direction and support for the book that is so crucial for its success. Carol Newman, Senior Project Editor, continues to delight both personally and professionally, with her distinctive brand of absolute professionalism, dedicated work ethic, and a sense of humor served very dry. I am also grateful to Tom Ziolkowski, the Senior Marketing Manager, for his talented efforts on behalf of the book now and in the future.

A special acknowledgment goes to Joyce Neff at Old Dominion University for her superb work in writing the earlier editions of the Instructor's Resource Manual. John is particularly indebted to the members of the English Department at LaGuardia College for their creative collaboration in linking the writing and critical thinking programs, a process that was initially supported with funding from the National Endowment for the Humanities.

John's children, Jessie and Joshua, and his wife, Heide Lange, have provided ongoing love, support and guidance that have enhanced this book and brought purpose and meaning to his life.

Christine McMahon gratefully acknowledges the W. K. Kellogg Foundation, whose Beacon College Project supported the Critical Literacy Institute at Oakton College, and the faculty at Oakton who invited Montgomery College to be an associate college; she came to know John Chaffee's work through them. She is indebted to the administrators at Montgomery College who chose her as the Project Director for the grant and who continue to provide generous support for Montgomery's critical literacy program. Barbara and John have been wonderful co-authors. The students Christine has taught, some of whose work appears in this book, helped her learn how to teach and motivated her to share what she knows. Her husband, Michael, helped her in every way, while her grownup children, Gregory and Beth, provided love and support, and her granddaughter, Brooke, kept her spirits up.

Barbara Stout is grateful to countless colleagues from many colleges and universities whose scholarship in composition, rhetoric, and writing across the curriculum is the foundation for informed teaching, programs, and textbooks. She is grateful to the Conference on College Composition and Communication, the Two-Year College English Association, and the national Writing Project for providing opportunities for sharing information and ideas. Her thanks also extend to the faculty and administrators in Montgomery College's Critical Literacy Project, to the English Department's office staff and faculty colleagues, and to her students, from whom she always learns more than she can teach. She greatly appreciates John's and Chris's friendship and sound thinking. Of course, her most heartfelt thanks are to her family: David, Richard, Rebecca, Sally, Lyn, Mitch, Roxanne, Patrick, Kathleen, Sean, and Florence.

Critical Thinking, Thoughtful Writing

A Rhetoric with Readings

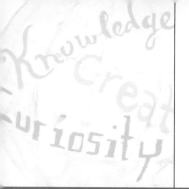

Tools for Thinking, Reading, and Writing

Writing, reading, and creating text and images are how our minds explore and explain our world. The use of language and images is what makes us human; it is how we argue, how we tell stories, how we learn, how we creatively and politically express ourselves. To write is to use language thoughtfully, with a sense of audience and purpose. When you write, you pay close attention to the words that you choose, the structure of your paragraphs, the images you create. You contemplate your subject, search for exactly the right word to describe an observation, draw together different pieces of evidence to persuade a reader to think as you do. Writing helps you make sense of yourself and your world by illuminating your thought processes; writing is your mind in motion, working to clarify and understand. Learning to read critically helps you to become more aware of the strategies available to thoughtful writers. Reading texts and critically viewing images engage your mind with other conversations and open up additional perspectives.

Thinking clearly and critically about your reading strategies and your writing process will greatly enhance your ability to express yourself in all areas of your life. Part One of this book sharpens your awareness of the relationships among thinking, reading, writing, and creating texts and images and introduces you to ways of becoming a critical thinker and reader and a thoughtful writer.

Thinking Through Writing

Knowledge Creativity Curiosity

> 66 *I write to understand as much as to be understood.* 99
>
> —*Elie Wiesel*

Critical Thinking Focus: Thinking through writing

Writing Focus: The writing process

Reading Themes: Writing as self-expression

Writing Activity: Reflecting on past critical thinking

Thinking and Writing in College

The writer E. M. Forster once remarked, "How do I know what I think until I see what I say?" What did he mean by this? That you can't write better than you think! In many ways college is a whole new world. Not only are you expected to do more work in your courses, but you also are expected to work at a higher level: to *write more analytically,* to *think more conceptually,* and to *read more critically* than ever before. As a college writer, a citizen, or a member of a profession, you are expected to write with depth, insight, and analytical understanding. In order to achieve this level of sophistication in writing, you need to develop comparably advanced thinking abilities.

Becoming an effective writer enables you to represent your experience with clarity and precision. As you may have learned from your communication experiences thus far, the very process of using language serves to generate ideas. As a vehicle for creating and communicating your ideas, writing can be thought of as a catalyst that stimulates your personal and intellectual development. Since the writing process also enlarges your understanding of the world, becoming an effective writer is at the heart of your education.

To improve your writing abilities, you need to write on a regular basis, integrating writing into your life as a vital and natural element. Therefore, this book offers you Thinking-Writing Activities. These can be done in various ways: out of class or in, individually or in pairs or groups, and in whatever format your instructor specifies. Your instructor might ask you to record your responses in a journal to be reviewed periodically or in a class web site or on-line forum. Your writing may also be shared with classmates or used as a basis for discussion. The work you do for the Thinking-Writing Activities will help to prepare you for the Writing Projects that conclude each chapter. These will give you an opportunity to think deeply about important subjects, to express your own distinctive point of view in a thoughtful and organized fashion, and to analyze the ideas of others from a variety of sources. Collaborative Activities provide the opportunity to enrich your writing by working with other students.

THINKING-
WRITING
ACTIVITY

Recalling a Learning Experience

Recall a memorable learning experience that you have had, either in school or outside. Describe that experience and explain why it has had a lasting impact on you. Discuss how the experience has contributed to your development as a thinker and writer.

Becoming a Critical Thinker and Thoughtful Writer

Who is a critical thinker, and how do you become one? Traditionally, when people refer to a critical thinker, they mean someone who has developed an understanding of today's complex world, a thoughtful perspective on ideas and issues, the capacity for insight and good judgment, and sophisticated reasoning and language abilities. Critical thinkers are able to

- Articulate their ideas clearly and persuasively in writing
- Understand and evaluate what they read
- Discuss ideas in an informed, productive fashion

By questioning and analyzing, by evaluating and making sense of information, you examine your own thinking and that of others. And by clearly expressing your ideas in writing, you enter a larger community of thinkers and writers who enrich and sharpen your own thoughts through their responses. These thinking and writing activities help you reach the best possible conclusions and decisions.

Qualities of a Thoughtful Writer

A thoughtful writer is a person who thinks critically while moving through the process of writing. This writer reflects deeply on the ideas to be expressed and thinks carefully about the language and organization needed to meet the goals of the writing situation. In short, a thoughtful writer is a critical thinker. No collection of writing tips and strategies will ever enable you to write thoughtfully if you're not thinking critically.

Throughout this text, we focus on four qualities that characterize critical thinkers and thoughtful writers, and we will tie these thinking-writing qualities into specific stages of the writing process.

- Curious
- Open-minded
- Knowledgeable
- Creative

Let's explore these qualities in greater depth.

Curious   Thoughtful writers explore situations with probing questions that penetrate beneath the surface of issues, instead of being satisfied with superficial explanations. (They *want* to learn, to discover . . .)

Open-minded   Thoughtful writers explore their subjects from many different perspectives, willing to listen carefully to every viewpoint and evaluating each perspective carefully and fairly. Rather than being locked in to one point of view or a single limited framework, they strive to understand and communicate the complex dimensions of their themes. For example, if they are writing about a social issue, they strive to present different perspectives on the issue as they reason their way to an informed conclusion.

Knowledgeable   Thoughtful writers always work to support their opinions with facts, evidence, and reasons. They recognize that opinions have value only to the extent that they are *informed* opinions. On the other hand, if they lack knowledge of the subject, they acknowledge this and set out to research what they need to know.

Creative   Thoughtful writers strive to develop inventive approaches to subjects; their writing is fresh and imaginative, avoiding clichés and tired conventions. They seek to break out of established patterns of thinking and approach themes and ideas from innovative directions.

Thinking critically by carefully exploring your thinking process is one of the most satisfying aspects of being a mature, educated human being. Analogously, *writing thoughtfully* involves thinking critically as you move through the process of writing so that you can express your ideas effectively. In each chapter of this book, we will meet scientists, explorers, artists, activists, and others who reflect these four qualities in their writing as well as in their work.

The Thinking-Writing Model

The paradox of acquiring any complex ability is that in the best of all possible worlds, you would learn all the component parts of the activity at the same time. For example, learning to drive a car requires you to master a variety of component skills that operate simultaneously: watching the road ahead, steering, applying the appropriate pressure on the gas pedal, braking, keeping a proper distance from other vehicles, watching for traffic signs and traffic lights, keeping an eye open for pedestrians, and so on. Yet a book on driving, or a video, focuses on one skill at a time because that is how information is presented most easily. Somehow you have to make the leap from learning all of the skills separately in a linear, step-by-step fashion to using them all at the same time, in complex relationships with one another.

Learning the complex skills of thinking critically and writing thoughtfully poses a similar dilemma. Although it is essential to learn each of the component parts of these processes, what distinguishes critical thinkers and thoughtful writers is that they can use all of these individual skills simultaneously.

The visual Thinking-Writing Model (Figure 1.1) presents each of these processes in relationship to each other. As you work on the various chapters and activities in this book, you will become more familiar with the different dimensions of the thinking-writing process.

As you examine the model, the writing process typically begins with a question. What is the *Purpose* of this communication? What is the *Subject?* Who is the *Audience?* Who is the *Writer,* and what is the writer's perspective? Engaging these questions utilizes our core abilities to *Think Creatively* about ideas we want to communicate, *Think Critically* in order to organize and clarify these ideas, and *Write Thoughtfully* by using the appropriate vocabulary and language forms to communicate our ideas.

The writing process itself is dynamic and holistic. The key elements of the process are *Generating* ideas, *Defining* a focus, *Drafting, Organizing, Revising,* and *Proofreading.* For most writers, these activities rarely occur in a neat, orderly sequence: the process is much more organic and recursive. Effective writers also *Collaborate* with other people in order to help them produce the highest quality of writing, and their assistance can occur at any stage in the writing process.

At the very center of the model is *Communicating,* the process by which we share our thoughts, feelings, and experiences. Communication creates miraculous moments when our minds touch and engage other minds. The word *communicating* comes from the Latin word *communicare,* which means "to share, to impart, to make common." As members of a social species, we need to share thoughts and feelings with other human beings. As technologies allow speedier and speedier communication throughout the world, critical thinking and thoughtful writing are evermore vital to the survival and progress of humanity.

This book is designed to offer you opportunities to build on the strengths you have and to grow as a critical thinker and thoughtful writer. The following Thinking-Writing Activity asks you to reflect on your own thinking-writing process as a starting point.

FIGURE 1.1   The Complete Thinking-Writing Model

THINKING-
WRITING
ACTIVITY

Analyzing a Writing Experience

Describe in detail a writing experience that you found particularly satisfying or successful: for example, a paper you wrote for school, a market analysis you created for your company, or a letter in which you expressed important thoughts and feelings. After completing your description, answer the following questions in your journal or notebook.

- What was your goal or purpose in writing?
- What was the reaction of the people who read it—your audience?
- How did you think of the key ideas you included?
- How did you organize your ideas?
- Did you use other sources (such as readings) to provide support and context for your writing?
- In what ways did you revise your writing?
- How did you feel after completing your writing?

Your analysis will probably demonstrate that you already use many of the abilities that are integral to the Thinking-Writing Model. Carefully examine the Thinking-Writing Model in Figure 1.1. Before long, the model will become familiar, and you will be able to use it as a powerful guide to strengthen and clarify your thinking and writing. Let's explore the various dimensions of the Thinking-Writing Model and see how they work together to produce clear thinking and effective writing.

Rhetoric and the Writing Situation

Writing always occurs in a situation within which the act of writing takes place. Writers have reasons to write, someone to whom they wish to write, a subject about which they have something important to say, and a sense of self as a writer that they want to project. Although these ideas are of great importance today, they are not new. They come from the study of *rhetoric*, the principles developed in ancient times for speaking and writing effectively. Rhetoric is the art of inventing or discovering your ideas, arranging them in the most persuasive way, and then expressing them in suitable language in order to have the desired effect on their audiences. Today the word *rhetoric* has both a negative and a positive meaning: language that is insincere and not to be taken seriously—"mere rhetoric"—and the positive meaning with which this book is concerned, the study of the principles and rules for effective writing.

FIGURE 1.2   The Writing Situation

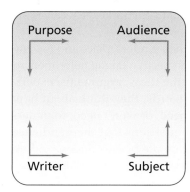

We begin our study of rhetoric with the components of the writing situation: purpose, audience, subject, and writer. In Figure 1.2, these four components appear in the first part of the model because they need to be considered when the writer begins to write, but they also need to be thought about at every stage of writing and communicating. To help you develop your rhetorical skills, these components are discussed individually at the beginning of each of the Writing Projects in subsequent chapters.

Online Study Center

Classical Rhetoric
Visit the Online Study Center for *Critical Thinking, Thoughtful Writing* at *college.hmco.com/pic/chaffeeCTTW4e* to learn more about classical rhetoric.

Purpose

Every act of writing has a *purpose*. When you complete a paper for a college course, you hope to show your instructor that you have understood and can both apply and communicate concepts relevant to the class. In a business setting, your aim is to transmit information or requests in a memo or a report; in your civic life, you want to advocate for community interests through letters or petitions; in your private life, you write in your journal and email your friends so that you can later recall your activities and feelings. A crucial part of becoming a thoughtful writer is maintaining a clear sense of the specific audience and purpose for whatever subject you are writing on.

Audience

Thoughtful writers shape their work by consideration of their *audience,* the intended reader or readers. Although there are some instances when you write only for yourself (a diary entry, for example); you probably intend most of your writing to be read by someone else: the person receiving your letter, the coworkers reading your memo, the friend enjoying your blog, or the instructor grading your paper. The more you think about your audience, the more concerned you will be about using language and visuals to make yourself clear, and the better your writing will become. The real skill lies in writing so clearly and coherently that your audience receives exactly the same message that you intended to send.

Thoughtful writers are able to put themselves in their readers' place and to view their own writing through their readers' eyes. This perspective-taking helps them to craft their writing so that it will best communicate the ideas, arguments, experiences, and emotions they seek to convey. In other words, they think about how much background information their audience will need, or won't need, to understand the intended message. Anticipating possible questions that their audience may have, they try to answer such questions at appropriate places. Understanding that the audience may have strong feelings about certain controversial topics, they consider those feelings as they write.

Subject

Writing has to be about someone or something—a *subject*. Sometimes the subject originates in your own experience, but often it comes from ideas and information provided by others. Much of college writing involves responding to ideas and concepts presented in textbooks, lectures, or research sources. Today, much of the research you will do for college begins on the Internet, so the ability to find and evaluate online sources is crucial. Your writing task is usually to demonstrate your understanding of the ideas presented and also to apply, analyze, synthesize, or evaluate the ideas being expressed. The quality of your writing depends on the quality of your thinking as you process ideas and present them in order to communicate your own informed perspective on the subject.

Writer

Of course, any writing situation calls for a *writer,* and the characteristics of the writer affect what is written and how it is produced. A writer's identity as a woman or a man or as a member of an ethnic or other social group often influences approaches and attitudes. The relationship of the writer to the language or dialect being used makes a difference; whether the writer is tired or energetic, happy or sad, and so forth, makes a difference, too.

The relationship of the writer to the intended audience also makes a difference. When writing email or blogs for friends, casual style and the admission of a lack of information on a subject are permissible. But college writers are expected to write with some authority as they join in a larger conversation of educated authors. If a piece of writing is about your own life and experiences, you automatically have that authority since no one knows your life better than you do. But many college assignments call for subjects related to class material, and you are still expected to write with authority. That is why the library and the Internet are so important to you; by gathering information you can become knowledgeable on almost any subject. One of the worst ways for a college writer to begin is, "I don't know much about this subject, but here goes."

FROM *My American Journey*

BY COLIN POWELL (b. 1937)

In the following excerpt from his best-selling autobiography *My American Journey*, former Secretary of State Colin Powell writes with authority about his life. Powell was born in New York City to immigrant parents from Jamaica. He attended public schools in the city, graduating from the City College of New York with a degree in geology. As a student at CCNY, he participated in ROTC, receiving a commission as an Army second lieutenant upon graduation. Powell served for thirty-five years, rising to the rank of four-star General and holding, from 1989 through 1993, the position of Chairman of the Joint Chiefs of Staff, the highest military position in the Department of Defense.

Powell's name has often been mentioned as a candidate for public office. He has been awarded two Presidential Medals of Freedom and the Congressional Gold Medal, among other military honors and decorations.

I have made clear that I was no great shakes as a scholar. I have joked over the years that the CCNY [City College of New York] faculty handed me a diploma, uttering a sigh of relief, and were happy to pass me along to the military. Yet, even this C-average student emerged from CCNY prepared to write, think, and communicate effectively and equipped to compete against students from colleges that I could never have dreamed of attending. If the Statue of Liberty opened the gateway to this country, public education opened the door to attainment here. Schools like my sister's Buffalo State Teachers College and CCNY have served as the Harvards and Princetons of the poor. And they served us well. I am, consequently, a champion of public secondary and higher education. I will speak out for them and support them for as long as I have the good sense to remember where I came from.

Shortly before the commissioning ceremony in Aronowitz Auditorium, Colonel Brookhart called me into his office in the drill hall. "Sit down, Mr. Powell," he said. I did, sitting at attention. "You've done well here (in ROTC). You'll do well in the Army. You're going to Fort Benning soon."

He warned me that I needed to be careful. Georgia was not New York. The South was another world. I had to learn to compromise, to accept a world I had not made and that was beyond my changing. He mentioned the black general Benjamin O. Davis, who had been with him at West Point, where Davis was shunned the whole four years by his classmates, including, I assumed, Brookhart. Davis had gotten himself into trouble in the South, Brookhart said, because he had tried to buck the system. The colonel was telling me, in effect, not to rock the boat, to be a "good Negro." . . .

The Army was becoming more democratic, but I was plunged back into the Old South every time I left the post. I could go into Woolworth's in Columbus, Georgia, and buy anything I wanted, as long as I did not try to eat there. I could go into a department store and they would take my money, as long as I did not try to use the men's room. I could walk along the street, as long as I did not look at a white woman. . . .

5   One night, exhausted and hungry, I locked up the house and headed back toward the post. As I approached a drive-in hamburger joint on Victory Drive, I thought, okay, I know they won't serve me inside, so I'll just park outside. I pulled in, and after a small eternity, a waitress came to my car window. "A hamburger, please," I said.

She looked at me uneasily. "Are you Puerto Rican?" she asked.

"No," I said.

"Are you an African student?" She seemed genuinely trying to be helpful.

"No," I answered. "I'm a Negro. I'm an American. And I'm an Army officer."

10   "Look, I'm from New Jersey," the waitress said, and "I don't understand any of this. But they won't let me serve you. Why don't you go behind the restaurant, and I'll pass you a hamburger out the back window."

Something snapped. "I'm not that hungry," I said, burning rubber as I backed out. As I drove away, I could see the faces of the owner and his customers in the restaurant windows enjoying this little exercise in humiliation. . . .

Racism was still relatively new to me, and I had to find a way to cope psychologically. I began by identifying my priorities. I wanted, above all, to succeed at my Army career. I did not intend to give way to self-destructive rage, no matter how provoked. If people in the South insisted on living by crazy rules, then I would play the hand dealt me for now. If I was to be confined to one end of the playing field, then I was going to be a star on that part of the field. Nothing that happened off-post, none of the indignities, none of the injustices, was going to inhibit my performance. I was not going to let myself become emotionally crippled because I could not play on the whole field. I did not feel inferior, and I was not going to let anybody make me believe I was. I was not going to allow someone else's feelings about me to become my feelings about myself. Racism was not just a black problem. It was America's problem. And until the country solved it, I was not going to let bigotry make me a victim instead of a full human being. I occasionally felt hurt; I felt anger; but most of all I felt challenged. I'll show you!

QUESTIONS FOR ACTIVE READING

1. What purpose or purposes do you think Powell had in mind while writing? How does he try to achieve his purpose(s)? List two specific examples from the reading to support your answer.

2. What audience do you think Powell had in mind while writing? Identify a specific audience, either one person or a group of persons, to whom you would recommend this reading.

3. Describe the writer as specifically as you can. What is your attitude toward him, now that you have read this? Does this represent any change in your attitude toward Powell?

QUESTIONS FOR THINKING CRITICALLY

1. Describe an experience in which you were the victim of discrimination or prejudice. How did it make you feel? How did you deal with it?

2. Colin Powell was determined to achieve his goals, despite many obstacles. Describe in your own words the thinking approach he used to deal with the pervasive racism that he encountered.

3. Powell concludes his autobiography with an affirmation regarding the United States that seems particularly relevant in these perilous times: "We will come through because our founders bequeathed us a political system of genius, a system flexible enough for all ages and inspiring noble aspirations for all time. We will continue to flourish because our diverse American society has the strength, hardiness, and resilience of the hybrid plant we are."

Explain whether you agree with Powell that America's ethnic diversity is a source of strength and resilience, and list the reasons why or why not.

Writing Thoughtfully, Thinking Creatively, Thinking Critically

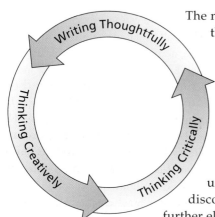

FIGURE 1.3   Core Abilities

The next part of the Thinking-Writing Model, Figure 1.3, indicates the reciprocal relationships among writing thoughtfully, thinking creatively, and thinking critically. The ability to be creative is one of the four qualities that distinguish critical thinkers and thoughtful writers. When you first decide to write something, you need to come up with some initial ideas to write about. Your ability to *think creatively* makes producing such ideas possible. When you think creatively, you discover ideas—and connections among ideas—that are illuminating, useful, often exciting, sometimes original, and usually worth developing. We can define *thinking creatively* as discovering and developing ideas that are unusual and worthy of further elaboration.

Simultaneously (or *almost* simultaneously), these beginning ideas find form in language expressed in writing. Yet the process of writing thoughtfully elaborates and shapes the ideas that you are trying to express, especially if you are to bring your critical thinking abilities to bear on this evolving process. This extraordinarily complex process typically takes place in a very natural fashion as creative thinking and critical thinking work together to produce thoughtful writing, which in turn gives form to your ideas and communicates them to others.

Effective writers not only use each of these processes but also are able to integrate them. For example, it is impossible to write thoughtfully without creating ideas that reflect your vision of the world or without using your critical thinking abilities to evaluate the accuracy and intelligibility of your writing. Unfortunately, these essential abilities are not always taught explicitly. Too often, writing is emphasized as a way of putting words together in conventional forms, not as a dynamic means of personal expression that liberates us to articulate our creative perspectives—tempered by critical evaluation.

The Writing Process

The Recursive Nature of the Writing Process

Despite the many different writing forms and contexts, the basic elements of the writing process remain constant:

* Generating ideas
* Defining a focus (main idea or *thesis*)

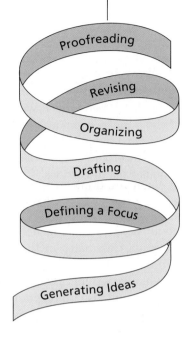

FIGURE 1.4   The Writing Process

- Organizing ideas into various thinking patterns
- Drafting
- Revising, editing, and proofreading
- Collaborating, which can weave through all these activities

These elements of the writing process occur within the writing situation as a result of creative and critical thinking, and they are depicted in the third part of the Thinking-Writing Model (Figure 1.4). For most writers, these activities rarely occur in a neat, orderly sequence. Instead, writers move in different ways, from generating ideas to drafting to more generating to organizing to revising to generating to editing—around and around—as they develop ideas and clarify them. And each element of the writing process depends upon the writer's awareness of subject, audience, and purpose.

You have probably discovered that the process of writing does not merely express your thinking; it also stimulates your thoughts, bringing to the surface new ideas and ways to explore them. So although you may begin a writing project by generating some ideas, you may find yourself returning to generate more ideas later on as you work to organize and draft your thoughts, developing new or refined concepts to write about. And as you gain more experience with collaboration, you may find yourself turning to others more frequently to benefit from their ideas and perspectives, which may send you back to generating, focusing, drafting, or organizing.

Generating Ideas

We have seen that most writing efforts begin with identifying something to write about—a subject. Since ideas are not created in isolation but are almost always related to a particular subject, you expand ideas by exploring that subject. Some writing projects have very specific requirements; others may be more open-ended. In most cases, however, you will be expected to come up with your own ideas. Even when you are responding to an assigned subject or a reading selection, you are typically expected to offer an original insight or viewpoint. As a thoughtful writer, you are expected to be open-minded, creative, and curious. At this stage of generating ideas, a number of strategies are useful, such as brainstorming, creating mind maps, freewriting, and asking key questions to stimulate your creative thinking. These strategies will be explored in depth in a later chapter.

Keeping a Journal or Blog

Keeping a journal or blog is rewarding in several ways. First, as you already know, the process of writing stimulates your mind and helps shape your thinking. Also, writing creates a record of your thoughts and feelings that you can return to and perhaps use as the starting place for a finished piece of writing. Journal entries should be freely written, with no concern for punctuation or polished prose. Nor should you evaluate your ideas. Just let them flow, write them in a notebook or a computer file, and make journal keeping a part of your daily life. A blog, or online journal, allows you to incorporate visuals and audio into your writing as well as join larger virtual communities and discussions.

Defining a Focus

After generating a number of possible ideas to write about, academic writers need to define a focus. Academic writing is *expected* to have a focus; classmates, instructors, and others interested in your subject expect more than a list of facts. Once selected, your main idea—known as a thesis or, for argumentative writing, a claim—will organize and direct your thinking. Your thesis or claim will also guide your exploration of the subject and suggest new ideas. Of course, a variety of main ideas can develop out of any particular situation, and your initial working thesis will probably need redefining as you draft your paper.

Sometimes you will need to do some drafting and organizing before you are ready to define your focus. And sometimes you will need to refocus your thesis as you do further drafting.

Organizing Ideas

Once you have a tentative thesis or claim, you may be ready to plan the organization of your paper. But at this point or even earlier, you may realize that you don't have enough information on your subject to fulfill your purpose. Remembering that a thoughtful writer is knowledgeable, you may need to generate more ideas or to consult other sources of information in order to write with authority. When you are ready to begin organizing, ask yourself, "What are my main points, and how should they be presented to my audience?" You can use a variety of thinking patterns as you organize your writing, such as reporting chronologically, comparing and contrasting, or dividing and classifying. Your choice of thinking pattern will depend on the subject you are exploring, your purpose, and your audience. We will examine these patterns in later chapters.

It usually helps to have a tentative organization to guide your drafting, but often your organization changes as you draft and revise. This is a natural and productive part of most people's writing processes.

Drafting

Drafting begins when you actually begin to write. *What* you write reflects your previous work from the initial stages of the writing process: generating ideas, defining a focus, and thinking about an organizational structure. Your writing expresses how far your thinking on the subject has progressed to that point. It is unlikely that your draft will emerge in finished form. In fact, your initial draft should undergo substantial revision until it finally represents your mind's best work. So don't get obsessed with trying to craft the perfect sentence, fashion the ideal metaphor, or secure the optimal word. You'll have time to do that later on. The most important goal in drafting is to get *started*. Get those vague and evolving ideas onto paper, where they can be examined, reflected upon, and refined.

Often you will find it useful to draft in sections, according to the plan you established. But be prepared to let the writing process take you to new places that you didn't anticipate. The process of writing is a catalyst for your thinking process, creating new ideas and leading in unexpected directions. Trusting your writing/ thinking process leads to creative breakthroughs that will enrich your original plan.

Naturally, what you are drafting—a summary, an argument, a report—influences the way you express and organize your thinking. Much of your academic writing will be in the form of essays in which you are expected to take a position, analyze a concept, or interpret a subject. The structure normally used to organize ideas in an essay typically reflects the basic questions raised when you discuss ideas with others. As you draft, keep in mind the questions of a hypothetical audience (from Mina Shaughnessey's book *Errors and Expectations*):

What is your point? (stating the main idea)

I don't quite get your meaning. (explaining the main idea)

Prove it to me. (providing examples, evidence, and arguments to support the main idea)

So what? (drawing a conclusion)

Revising, Editing, and Proofreading

Because thinking and writing are recursive processes, you are continually revising your thinking and writing as you work on almost any paper. Whatever your drafting style, though, once you have expressed your thinking in language, you must be able to go back and "re-see" (the origin of the word *revise*) your drafts as clearly as possible.

Most writers have a hard time looking objectively at their own writing. They know what they mean; they sometimes like certain words, sentences, or clever ideas and don't want to change them. But thoughtful writers have acquired the ability to be critical readers of their own work and to accept the fact that they may need to make major changes in their drafts. Writers and researchers in many disciplines share their drafts with colleagues for feedback and additional perspective, a collaborative process called *peer review*. We will explore strategies for peer review in Chapter 3.

As they revise, they are aware of a second voice in their heads, their Reader/ Editor. This voice asks useful questions, not unlike those listed previously under Drafting:

Have you made your main point clear?

Have you proved your point to your audience by giving enough information and examples?

Could you reorganize any of your ideas to help your audience understand more easily?

Many writers wait until they are satisfied with the content and organization before they *edit* smaller components, such as paragraph division, topic sentences, sentence variety, connections, and transitions. Then they *proofread,* checking spelling and punctuation. And sometimes while they are editing or proofreading, they see content and organization problems that require more revision!

"Writing Is Not a McDonald's Hamburger"

BY NATALIE GOLDBERG
FROM *Writing Down the Bones*

Acclaimed as much for her intuitive, compassionate teaching of writing as she is for her own well-received prose, Natalie Goldberg's 1986 book *Writing Down the Bones* (from which "Writing Is Not a McDonald's Hamburger" is excerpted) has become a touchstone not only for aspiring writers but also for anyone wishing to live more creatively. Goldberg has continued to mine her personal life, her deeply engaged study of Zen Buddhism, and her painterly observations of the natural world (particularly the landscape around her home in Taos, New Mexico) in such books as *Wild Mind: Living the Writer's Life* (1990), *Long Quiet Highway: Waking up in America* (1993), and *Thunder and Lightning: Cracking Open the Writer's Craft* (2000). Goldberg lives with her partner in Taos, New Mexico; and St. Paul, Minnesota.

Sometimes I have a student who is really good right from the beginning. I'm thinking of one in particular. The air was electric when he read, and he was often shaking. The writing process split him open; he was able to tell about being fourteen years old in a mental hospital, about walking the streets of Minneapolis tripping on LSD, about sitting next to the dead body of his brother in San Francisco. He said he had wanted to write for years. People told him he should be a writer, but anytime he sat down to write he couldn't connect the words on paper with the event or his feelings.

That is because he had an idea of what he wanted to say before he came to paper. Of course, you can sit down and have something you want to say. But then you must let its expression be born in you and on the paper. Don't hold too tight; allow it to come out how it needs to rather than trying to control it. Yes, those experiences, memories, feelings, are in us, but you can't carry them out on paper whole the way a cook brings out a pizza from the oven.

Let go of everything when you write, and try at a simple beginning with simple words to express what you have inside. It won't begin smoothly. Allow yourself to be awkward. You are stripping yourself. You are exposing your life, not how your ego would like to see you represented, but how you are as a human being. And it is because of this that I think writing is religious. It splits you open and softens your heart toward the homely world.

When I'm cranky now, miserable, dissatisfied, pessimistic, negative, generally rotten, I recognize it as a feeling. I know the feeling can change. I know it is energy that wants to find a place in the world and wants friends.

5   But yes, you can have topics you want to write about—"I want to write about my brother who died in San Francisco"—but come to it not with your mind and ideas, but with your whole body—your heart and gut and arms. Begin to write in the dumb, awkward way an animal cries out in pain, and there you will find your intelligence, your words, your voice.

People often say, "I was walking along [or driving, shopping, jogging] and I had this whole poem go through my mind, but when I sat down to write it, I couldn't get it to come out right." I never can either. Sitting to write is another activity. Let go of walking or jogging and the poem that was born then in your mind. This is another moment. Write another poem. Perhaps secretly hope something of what you thought a while ago might come out, but let it come out however it does. Don't force it.

The same student mentioned above was so excited about writing that he immediately tried to form a book. I told him, "Take it slow. Just let yourself write for a while. Learn what that is about." Writing is a whole lifetime and a lot of practice. I understood his urgency. We want to think we are doing something useful, going someplace, achieving something—"I am writing a book."

Give yourself some space before you decide to write those big volumes. Learn to trust the force of your own voice. Naturally, it will evolve a direction and a need for one, but it will come from a different place than your need to be an achiever. Writing is not a McDonald's hamburger. The cooking is slow, and in the beginning you are not sure whether a roast or a banquet or a lamb chop will be the result.

QUESTIONS FOR ACTIVE READING

1. What purpose or purposes do you think Goldberg had in mind while writing? Specify any one thing in the reading that helps you to identify her purpose.

2. What audience do you think she had in mind while writing? What other audiences might benefit from reading his? What audiences might not benefit?

3. What is her subject? Be as specific as you can in describing it. What is her attitude toward her subject?

QUESTIONS FOR THINKING CRITICALLY

1. Goldberg, a Zen Buddhist, claims in paragraph 3 that she believes "writing is religious." How does she define and understand "religious," and what specific qualities of writing make it a "religious" activity or experience? Do you agree with her definition of *religious?* Compare your own definition of a "religious" activity or mindset with Goldberg's.

2. Athletes often describe their feeling at peak performance as being "in the flow." Goldberg describes something similar about the process of inspiration. Describe a time when you felt like you were "in the flow" of an activity (physical, artistic, or intellectual). How did you get "in the flow"? Is there a specific strategy or ritual that you use to help you get "in the flow"?

3. Goldberg uses an amusing metaphor to describe what writing is *not*. Do you agree with her metaphor? Create other metaphors that describe your feeling about writing (especially academic writing).

Collaborating

When you work with other people in the writing process, you participate in collaboration. You can collaborate with others at every stage of the thinking and writing process. People can help one another generate ideas, identify a main idea to pursue, or suggest possible approaches and ways of organizing. Some entire pieces of writing, especially in business, are produced collaboratively by a team of writers. Since collaborating can occur in all writing process activities, the line representing collaboration circles around them in the model in Figure 1.1.

Writers often discover new perspectives when others review drafts of their writing. This is the moment when writers get a sense of how effective their efforts at communication are. No matter how clearly you try to keep your audience in mind as you write, you may not succeed at first. There is no substitute for having your audience (or people like your intended audience) let you know what you have and have not communicated clearly. With their suggestions, you can improve and refine your writing so that it will better convey what you intended. As a critical thinker and informed writer, you will learn to work with others in developing your thinking and writing, welcoming their advice when you are the sole author and contributing well when you are part of a writing team. Opportunities for collaborating are marked throughout the book with the icon to the left of this section.

Of course, in writing collaboratively, you also have a responsibility to respond critically to the writing of others. *Critical* is related to *criticize*, which means "to question and evaluate." Unfortunately, the ability to criticize is often used destructively to tear down someone else's thinking. Criticism, however, should be *constructive*—analyzing for the purpose of developing better understanding. To develop your abilities to think critically and write thoughtfully, it is important to offer and receive constructive criticism.

Becoming a critical thinker and a thoughtful writer does not simply involve mastering certain life skills; it affects the entire way that you view the world and live your life. You already use critical thinking in many aspects of your life: how you make decisions, how you relate to others, and how you deal with controversial issues. These abilities can be improved with information, strategies, and practice, and you will continue to develop them as you move forward through college and your career.

THINKING-
WRITING
ACTIVITY

Expressing a Deeper Meaning

This Thinking-Writing Activity gives you an opportunity to apply some of the ideas we have been exploring in this chapter. Think of a place—or, if you can, go and visit a place—that has special meaning for you, a place that led you to a realization about life. Write a description that effectively communicates *where* you are as well as expressing a deeper kind of meaning. What kind of meaning, exactly, is up to you, and depends on the feelings that the place evokes. Reach deep within yourself and discover an analogous feeling to articulate in your writing.

- Consider the audience for whom you are writing and the purpose you would like to accomplish.

- After writing your first draft, *rewrite* your paper to more fully express your feelings and ideas.

- Add details that communicate your meaning as specifically as possible.

- Craft your sentences so that they flow together and create a consistent "picture" of the place you are describing.

- Share your paper with your classmates. Ask them what feelings and ideas your description communicated to them.

- As a group, discuss which steps of the writing process for this assignment came easily and which required more effort.

2

Reading Actively, Reading Critically

"
Read not to contradict nor to believe, but to weigh and consider
"

—*Francis Bacon*

Critical Thinking Focus: Reflecting on reading and making meaning

Writing Focus: Thinking about rhetorical choices and writing in response to reading

Reading Themes: Using your response to reading as a subject for writing

Reading in College

Let's begin this chapter with a question: What does it mean to read? Not so long ago, to "read" meant to turn the pages of a book, a newspaper, or an owner's manual. Reading was a physical activity that required lamplight or daylight, and texts were physical objects that you carried around in a backpack or briefcase. When you went to the library, it was usually to borrow a book that you would read and then return two weeks later. When you woke up in the morning, you read a newspaper as you drank your coffee. And when you got home from classes, you stayed up late into the night with your textbooks and a dictionary.

The physical act of reading—of opening, turning, flipping back and forth, underlining, inserting a bookmark— seems at times to be almost quaint, like rollerskating instead of rollerblading, or using a dial-up modem instead of a high-speed digital connection. And yet reading—the deciphering of, and interacting with, ideas and language— is at the core of a liberal education. You read to be entertained, to be informed, to learn. Even though most of us might do most of our "reading" without ever getting near a book, the fundamental skills of deciphering and interacting are equally applicable to the screen and the page. And whatever, however, or wherever you plan to communicate in your professional life, those fundamental reading skills will make you a better writer in any medium.

Reading Actively

To read actively is to work at deciphering the many layers of a text. An active reader has a dictionary (online or print) at hand, along with annotating tools, plenty of time, and the will to jot down questions and comments either on the printed page (or printout), in a reading journal, or in a word processing document. When you read actively, you give your full concentration and attention to the text. (Passive reading, on the other hand, is usually marked by boredom and daydreaming. If you look up from the page or screen and can't remember what you were just "reading," you weren't really reading at all—you were just looking at words.)

Active reading is also productive reading. You have a sense, as you begin to read, of what you might expect to discover. Active—and critical—reading also imply *re-*reading; the following strategies will require you to work through a new text at least twice, becoming familiar with its structure as you delve into its content.

The following strategies for active reading will help to make any reading task—academic, professional, or even leisurely—more productive. They also apply equally to print texts and web sites.

Review the Table of Contents or Chapter Outlines

The table of contents and chapter outlines of a book or web site provide you with the general structure and organization of a text. By beginning with these elements, you can develop an overall understanding of the reading, the organization of its major ideas, and the way specific details fit into this organization. It's as if you are taking an aerial view of the territory you are going to explore, looking for key landmarks, examining the patterns of connecting roads, and developing a sense of the terrain.

Review the table of contents in this book, taking particular note of the topics that are covered and the way these topics are organized. Now look at where this chapter fits in relation to the overall design of the book. How do the topics of this chapter relate to the other topics in the book?

THINKING-
WRITING
ACTIVITY

Taking a Reading Inventory

In your journal, respond to any or all of these questions. Your teacher may ask you to share and discuss your responses with other students.

1. Is there anyone in your life to whom you read—a child, an older person, a friend? (Or perhaps you read aloud as part of a religious service or a professional presentation.) In what context do you read aloud? How does reading aloud define or contribute to your relationship to your audience?

2. Who taught you to read? Do you remember learning to read? Have you helped anyone else learn to read?

3. What was the last thing you read out of sheer curiosity or pleasure? Were you surprised by your response to that text? Would you recommend it to a friend, or was this purely a "guilty" pleasure?

Read the Introductory Paragraphs and the Concluding Paragraphs or Summary

After reviewing the table of contents or chapter outline, review next the opening and closing paragraphs or summary. In academic textbooks, authors generally explain the major goals of the chapter in the introduction and then conclude by reviewing the key topics that have been explored. Reviewing these sections should help you fill in the mental map you are creating of the reading assignment and help you develop a plan for exploring the material.

Other kinds of writing—essays, journalism, blogs—often include a thesis statement in the opening paragraph and summarize the overall argument or problem in the concluding paragraph. Note the topic sentence of each paragraph, which will give you an overall sense of the text's structure and organization.

Review the opening and concluding sections of this chapter. What additional information have you gathered about the chapter?

Scan the Reading Assignment, Taking Particular Note of Section Headings, Illustrations, and Diagrams

The next step is to scout the territory by completing a rapid scan of what lies ahead. Move quickly through the material, focusing on the section headings, boxed or shaded areas, illustrations, diagrams, and other defining features. This should help you continue to fill in and elaborate your mental map, noting key points, concepts, definitions, and relationships.

Quickly scan this chapter, noting the features mentioned above. What new information have you gathered as a result of this scouting process?

FOUR QUALITIES OF A CRITICAL THINKER

Writer Julia Alvarez

Curious   Thoughtful, active readers are motivated by a genuine desire to know more, to learn something different, and to expand their world-view. In her essay "Grounds for Fiction" (p. 36), writer and teacher Julia Alvarez describes her collection of random notes, newspaper clippings, titles of scientific articles, and other texts that pique her interest as a writer and inspire her to explore a subject, an idea, or a life.

Open-minded   A reader who thinks critically welcomes the challenge of a difficult text. For Alvarez, who immigrated to New York City with her family from the Dominican Republic, the challenge of learning a new language strengthened both her writing and her storytelling. "When I'm asked what made me into a writer, I point to the watershed experience of coming to this country," she has said. "Not understanding the language, I had to pay close attention to each word— great training for a writer."

Knowledgeable   When you come to an unfamiliar phrase, allusion, or word in a reading, what do you do? Whether

THINKING-
WRITING
ACTIVITY

Previewing a Reading Assignment

Select a reading assignment from one of your courses, and before beginning to read, apply the previewing strategies that we have been considering:

- Examine the table of contents or chapter outline.
- Read the introductory paragraphs and the concluding paragraphs or summary.
- Scan the reading assignment, taking particular note of section headings, illustrations, and diagrams.

Then write a short paragraph, reporting specifically what each of the three strategies showed you about the assignment.

Annotating

Annotation is one of the most productive techniques that you will use in your college reading. It involves writing, or entering, your reactions to a text as you are reading, either with pen or pencil on paper or with your computer's graphic tools to annotate something that you have downloaded. When annotating, you are talking *with* the text, not allowing it to talk *at* you.

Your annotations will reflect your agreement and disagreement with what you read, your questions, what you see as important ideas, where you see relationships among parts of the texts, and where you see connections with additional ideas. Some methods are

- Underlining and numbering key points
- Circling key words and drawing lines to show relationships—for example, between a main idea and support for it

you are learning a new language, like Alvarez, or exploring a new academic concept, as a thoughtful reader you should either go immediately to a dictionary or a search engine for clarification, or jot it down to look up later. The knowledge to be gained from reading is not solely from the overall subject matter but also from the writer's use of language and store of general knowledge (historical, cultural, political, etc.).

Creative   Alvarez has drawn on her rich life's experiences for her essays, novels, memoirs, and poetry. She reaches out to diverse populations of readers and writers, publishing books for children and young adults and teaching writing in bilingual elementary schools and workshops for senior

citizens. When you read creatively, you think about how to incorporate the text's viewpoint or information into your own context—either in your writing or in your life.

Online Study Center
Julia Alvarez
Visit the Online Study Center for *Critical Thinking, Thoughtful Writing* at *college.hmco.com/pic/ chaffeeCTTW4e* to learn more about Julia Alvarez.

- Using question marks to indicate parts that you do not understand
- Commenting on the author's ideas or language or writing techniques
- Noting connections with your life or with other texts

Most word processing programs include annotation features such as high-lighting, changing a font color, or inserting comments and questions. To annotate an online source, either save the online text in your word processing file or simply print out the page and highlight it on paper. (Many web sites for periodicals, newspapers, and journals offer a "printer-friendly" option for articles, which allows you to print only the text, on continuous pages, without having to "click" through each separate page or print out banner advertisements.)

Summarizing

When you summarize a text, you use your own language to briefly and succinctly restate the author's main point. A summary follows the structure and organization of the original text, and might directly quote (using quotation marks) particularly interesting or apt words and phrases. When you summarize, you do not comment on or evaluate the text (that comes later); instead, writing the summary is a cognitive tool to ensure that you understand both the content and the structure of the text.

Summarizing is a strategy that is most effective at your second or third reading of a text, after you have annotated the text and looked up any unfamiliar terms or concepts.

Reading Critically

After reading actively in order to understand the content of a text, a thoughtful reader looks at it again, this time to read it critically. As a critical reader, you will analyze the text and evaluate its ideas and methods of presenting them. You will think of other subjects or issues to which the text might be connected.

Asking Questions

Asking questions will help you read critically. One set of useful questions is based on the components of writing that you learned in Chapter 1: purpose, audience, subject, writer, and context.

1. What is the *purpose* of the selection, and how is the author trying to achieve it?

2. Who is the intended *audience,* and what assumptions is the writer making about it?

3. What is the *subject* of the selection, and how would you evaluate its cogency and reliability?

4. Who is the *writer,* and what perspective does she bring to the writing selection?

5. What is the larger *context* in which this selection appears? Is the writer responding to a particular event or participating in an ongoing debate?

Some questions often used to generate writing also help with critical reading.

Questions of Interpretation   Questions of interpretation probe for relationships among ideas.

   Is a *time sequence* given in this text? If so, what is its importance?

   Is a *process of growth or development* explained in this text? If so, what is its importance?

   What is *compared or contrasted* in this text? What are the purposes of any comparisons?

   What is the *context* of the selection, and what contextual components might be significant? (For example, the time of its writing, characteristics of that time, the relationship to other works by the same author, whether or not it is a translation)

   Are *causes* discussed in this text? If so, what is suggested about those causes and their effects?

Questions of Analysis   Questions of analysis look at parts of a text and the relationship of those parts to the whole, and at the reasoning being presented.

   Is this text divided into identifiable *sections?* What are they? Are sections arranged logically?

   What *evidence* or *examples* support the ideas presented in the text?

   Does the text give *alternatives* to the ideas presented?

Questions of Evaluation   Questions of evaluation establish the truth, reliability, applicability—the value of the text. They usually address the effectiveness of the writing as well.

   What is the *significance* of the ideas in this text?

   What is the apparent level of *truth* in this text? What criteria for truth does it meet?

   What are the sources of information in this text? Are they *reliable?* Why?

   Can the ideas in this text be *applied* to other situations?

   What is *effective* about the writing in this text? Clarity?

   The right tone? Appropriate—or imaginative—word choices? Organization?

Of course, you are not likely to ask all these questions about everything you read, and you will find other questions to ask as well.

Using a Problem-Solving Approach

Successful readers often approach difficult reading passages with a problem-solving approach.

Step 1: What is the problem? What don't I understand about this passage? Are there terms or concepts that are unfamiliar? Are the logical connections between the concepts confusing? Do some things just not make sense?

Step 2: What are the alternatives? What are some possible meanings of the terms or concepts? What are some potential interpretations of the central meaning of this passage?

Step 3: What is the evaluation of the possible alternatives? What are the "clues" in the passage, and what alternative meanings do they support? What reasons or evidence support these interpretations?

Step 4: What is the solution? Judging from my evaluation and what I know of this subject, which interpretation is most likely? Why?

Step 5: How well is the solution working? Does my interpretation still make sense as I continue my reading, or do I need to revise my conclusion?

Of course, expert readers go through this process very quickly, much faster than it takes to explain it. Although this approach may seem a little cumbersome at first, the more you use it, the more natural and efficient it will become. Let's begin by applying it to a sample passage. Carefully read the following passage from the French philosopher Jean-Paul Sartre's "Existentialism Is Humanism," and use the problem-solving approach to determine the correct meanings of the italicized concepts and the overall meaning of the passage.

> *Existentialism,* of which I am a representative, declares with greater consistency that if God does not exist there is at least one being whose existence comes before its essence, a being which exists before it can be defined by any conception of it. That being is man or, as Heidegger has it, the human reality. What do we mean by saying that existence precedes essence? We mean that man first of all exists, encounters himself, surges up in the world—and defines himself afterwards. If man as the existentialist sees himself as not definable, it is because to begin with he is nothing. He will not be anything until later, and then he will be what he makes of himself. Thus, there is no human nature, because there is no God to have a conception of it. Man simply is. Not that he is simply what he conceives himself to be, but he is what he wills, and as he conceives existence. Man is nothing else but that which he makes of himself. This is the first principle of existentialism. . . . If, however, it is true that existence is prior to essence, man is responsible for what he is. Thus, the first effect of existentialism is that it puts every man in possession of himself as he is, and places the entire responsibility for his existence squarely upon his own shoulders. . . . That is what I mean when I say that man is condemned to be *free.* Condemned, because he did not create himself, yet is nevertheless at liberty, and from the moment that he is thrown into this world he is responsible for everything he does. . . . In life, a man commits himself, draws his own portrait and there is nothing but that portrait.

THINKING-
WRITING
ACTIVITY

A Problem-Solving Approach to Reading

Step 1: What parts (if any) of this passage do you find confusing?

Step 2: What are some possible definitions of the italicized words, and what are some potential interpretations of this passage?

Existentialism: (a) _____

(b) _____

Free: (a) _____

(b) _____

Overall Meaning: (a) _____

_____

Overall Meaning: (b) _____

_____

Step 3: What contextual clues can you use to help you define these concepts and determine the overall meaning? What knowledge of this subject do you have, and how can this knowledge help you understand this passage?

Step 4: Judging from your evaluation in Step 3, which of the possible definitions and interpretations do you think are most likely? Why?

Step 5: How do your conclusions compare with those of the other students in the class? Should you revise your definitions or interpretation?

Select a challenging passage from a course textbook and apply the preceding problem-solving approach.

Online Study Center
A Problem-Solving Approach to Reading
Visit the Online Study Center for *Critical Thinking, Thoughtful Writing* at *college.hmco.com/pic/ chaffeeCTTW4e* to learn more about the problem-solving approach to reading.

Practicing Active and Critical Reading: One Student's Approach

Here is how one student, Joshua Bartlett, used previewing, problem solving, annotating, and summarizing with an essay that his philosophy professor assigned to show students how ideas from more than 2,500 years ago can apply to their lives today.

Previewing Because this was an instructor's handout, Joshua's previewing started with a look at the title, the first two paragraphs, and the concluding paragraph. Because this is a short essay, Joshua moved quickly to scanning, reading through, and annotating. He was a bit confused when he read the first paragraph since the class had not yet begun studying Plato.

Problem solving Joshua realized that his major *problem* with this text was his lack of knowledge about Plato and Socrates. He decided that his *alternatives* were (1) to look them up in his philosophy class book or the encyclopedia or (2) to go on reading. He quickly *evaluated* the alternatives. Consulting his book or the encyclopedia would take some time, and he wanted to finish this assignment before he had to go to work. He knew that he would learn about Plato and Socrates next week in his class. His previewing had shown him that these problem paragraphs would be explained later in the essay. He *solved the problem* by deciding to go on reading. He felt that his solution *worked well* when he was able to summarize the essay.

Annotating Joshua gave Tanner's essay a second and then a third reading, each time using a colored pen to draw his attention to specific points in the text. He underlined important points, placed question marks next to parts he did not understand, and commented on the writer's rhetorical strategies to better help him understand the writer's argument.

Summarizing Joshua's philosophy professor asked the students to prepare a summary of the essay and be ready to share it with the class. She did this so that class discussion would be focused. Joshua took his annotations to class, too, so he was able to participate effectively. Here is his summary:

"On Plato's Cave" claims that much of what we see, hear, and read may give us inaccurate images and projections of points of view and that we need to try to discover what is really solid, rather than believe what might not be. This essay begins by quoting Plato's description of human beings chained in a cave, seeing only reflections of people, animals, and material items. The essay connects this fantasy situation with our experiences with the media, and even with what parents and teachers tell us. The essay says that Plato tells of a person escaping from the cave and seeing the real world. It says that we, too, can climb out of darkness by understanding how received information and our resulting beliefs need to be examined so that we can have "substantiated knowledge."

On Plato's Cave

By Sonja Tanner

In the seventh book of Plato's dialogue *The Republic,* he offers an image of education in which humans are likened to prisoners in a cave. To understand this fully, we can attempt to render this image.

"Next, then," (Socrates) said, "make an image of our nature in its education and (want) of education, likening it to a condition of the following kind. See human beings as though they were in an underground cave-like dwelling with its entrance, a long one, open to the light across the whole width of the cave.

I guess we'll learn about Socrates next week—then I'll get this funny use of word.

They are in it from childhood with their legs and necks in bonds so that they are fixed, seeing only in front of them, unable because of the bond to turn their heads all the way around. Their light is from a fire burning far above and behind them. Between the fire and the prisoners there is a road above, along which we see a wall, built like the partitions puppet-handlers set in front of the <u>human beings</u> and over which they show the puppets."

"I see," (Glaucon) said.

"Then also see along this wall human beings carrying all sorts of artifacts, which project above the wall, and statues of men and other animals wrought from stone, wood, and every kind of material. . . ." (514a1–515a2, Allan Bloom, trans.)

We see persons at the bottom of a cave, <u>chained so as</u> to prevent them from leaving the cave and from turning around to see what is behind them. Positioned in this way, they can only watch the shadows projected onto the back wall of the cave, by the passing of the artifacts in front of the fire. Behind the prisoners is a low wall which obscures the persons carrying these artifacts. This projection is like those we create around campfires, or in front of slide projectors, where a set of hands may look like a barking dog or a flying bird. A similar distortion takes place in the cave. Further up the cave is a fire and beyond that lies the cave's opening to the sunlight.

Having sketched what is happening within the cave literally, we must now try to <u>interpret what this image means figuratively</u>. When Glaucon remarks upon how strange these prisoners are, Socrates tells him <u>that they are like us</u>. How are we like these passive and helpless prisoners? <u>Do we ever receive information or entertainment without thinking about where it actually comes from?</u> Although Plato was writing over two thousand years before the invention of cathode ray tubes, the modern example of television may show us what he meant. If the projected images are analogous to those televised to us, then what might the <u>persons behind the wall represent? Acting as filters of information, they might be seen as television networks, advertisers, or the media in general.</u> They and their motivations for presenting information about the world to us through their particular perceptual lenses are obscured from view like the persons who pass behind the wall in the cave. As the chains prevent the prisoners from turning to see

---

Margin annotations:

spooky

? the ones in the cave? no

who?

Ok—clearer than bonds

—or with a flashlight

aha! where?

important point
now it's making sense

important point

This whole paragraph is important

maybe the thesis

what is causing the images they watch, we are sometimes prevented by ignorance or uncritical thinking from recognizing the interests and persons served by the way in which information is presented to us. When we are unaware as to how perceptual lenses shape what it is we then believe, the information we receive and the beliefs we build upon this information may

They sure do!

be distorted, like the shadows projected onto the wall. Many other persons shape the information we receive and the beliefs we hold. Authorities of all sorts fulfill this function—politicians, journalists, parents, teachers, writers and sometimes even ourselves.

!!

Plato does not think us <u>doomed to</u> this unreflective state, however. Escape from the cave, though mysterious, is possible. Someone is apparently released from their bonds, turns around, and despite the confusion and pain from the dazzling light and arduous ascent, both of which they are unaccus-

good comparison

tomed to, is able to leave the cave. Just as when we leave a <u>matinee movie and enter</u> bright sunlight, we are at first dazzled and our eyes need a few moments to adjust to the light, the ascendant may experience disorientation or confusion upon first turning around. Turning from the shadows, this person discovers the objects causing these projections and the persons carrying them and, once outside the cave, the beings which these artifacts are made to resemble. <u>The journey upwards is one of turning from images to their originals, ending ultimately in one's view of the sun itself</u>, which,

!

as the earth's <u>source of heat and light</u>, is a cause of all of the beings described in this allegory.

But how is <u>escape</u> from chains which bind at the neck and legs possible? Does someone release the prisoner and force them up into the light, and if so, who is this and why do they do it? Perhaps we are taking this image too literally in seeing this as a physical journey. Taking a cue from the aforementioned example in which the <u>projections represent beliefs and</u>

escape → journey

another explanation

<u>information we take on uncritically</u>, perhaps this journey is not <u>physical but mental</u>. The chains <u>may signify</u> ignorance and the uncritical taking over of second-hand opinions or beliefs and, as such, the chains themselves may even be self-imposed. Such an <u>intellectual journey</u> begins with a recognition that what we see and believe are only images, and by turning away from such appearances towards reality.

repeats

If the ascent <u>is intellectual</u>, rather than <u>physical</u>, a problem presents itself. Although Plato describes the release of a prisoner as though she or he were dragged up and out of the cave by the scruff of their neck, this type of force seems unlikely to guide an intellectual journey. Could one truly be

probably not

<u>forced or compelled to think independently?</u> What else would motivate the journey? This is a particularly difficult question given the description of both ascent and return back into the cave as arduous, painful, and as subjecting one to derision and danger from the prisoners. What benefit could make good of undergoing such difficulties to leave the cave? We have been assuming here that the compulsion Plato describes as motivating the

hard to understand (read slow!)

ascent is a force external to the ascendant, but internal forces motivate us as well. Why take the treacherous journey out of the cave? Perhaps sim-

!

Aha—again!

This sounds like my dad!

ply because we <u>want</u> to. Our motivation upwards may be a desire for knowledge, as opposed to mere beliefs. If desire is the impetus for the <u>ascent</u>, this places <u>responsibility</u> for one's <u>education squarely on the shoulders of</u>

The cave makes sense here

<u>the individual.</u> We may have <u>assistance, encouragement</u> and <u>sometimes</u> even external forces compelling us upwards, but ultimately, our success depends <u>upon</u> our own <u>desire</u> for <u>knowledge and truth</u>, and our willingness to give up what we are accustomed to—the passive life and familiar comforts of cave-dwelling—for the rewards of rational and grounded knowledge.

important phrase

We are now able to locate ourselves on the (trajectory of enlightenment.) Looking at and discussing images are a first stage in education according to

Here's the main point

Plato and indeed that is precisely what we have done here thus far. The next step then seems to be turning away from the images we accept unre-

One of those essays that leads up to it—doesn't state it at the beginning the way my English teacher wants us to do

flectively and towards questions as to why we believe what we do, who or what are the sources of these beliefs, and how reliable are these sources, which can distinguish unfounded beliefs from substantiated knowledge. Maybe this ascent is undertaken by us on a regular basis, rather than simply once, in our lives.

Using Metacognitive Strategies

Metacognition is a process we have been working on throughout this book. While *cognition* refers to the process of thinking, *metacognition* refers to a form of thinking *about* the thinking process. For example, think about what you will be doing this

THINKING-
WRITING
ACTIVITY

Your Reactions

1. Write your reactions to the strategies for active and critical reading in this chapter. Which have you used before? How do they work for you? Which do you want to try now as you do your college reading?

2. How would you annotate "On Plato's Cave"?

3. Do you think that Joshua wrote an accurate summary of it? Would you summarize it differently?

If you can, share your reactions with classmates and notice agreements and disagreements.

evening, and as you are thinking about this, make a special effort to stand outside your thinking process and observe it while it is going on. This process of becoming an observer to your own thinking process—"reflecting" on your thinking—may feel strange, but it is well within your power if you concentrate. In the following space, describe some of the characteristics of the thinking process that you observed yourself engaging in. For instance, did you find you were talking to yourself? Did your thinking make use of still or moving visual images? Did you feel ideas were rushing through your mind like a river, or were your thoughts organized in an orderly fashion? Did you find one idea led to another idea, which led to another idea, through a series of associations?

Characteristics of My Thinking Process:

1. _____

2. _____

3. _____

By participating in this activity you were actually engaging in the process of *metacognition*, working to become aware of the process you use to think about something.

While the process of reading is a thinking (cognitive) activity, expert readers also engage in metacognition while they are reading. In other words, they are aware of their thinking process as they are reading, and they use this awareness to improve their thinking. This awareness can be expressed as a variety of questions:

Goals What are my goals in reading this passage? How well am I meeting these goals?

Comprehension How well do I understand what I am reading? What parts do I understand, and what parts am I confused about?

Anticipation What events are going to take place following the ones I am reading about? How will the author develop and elaborate on these ideas?

Author's Purpose What is the author's point of view, and why did she adopt this particular perspective? How has her point of view affected the information she selected and the manner in which she presented this information?

Evaluation Is this information accurate? Do the ideas make sense? What evidence and reasons does the author provide to support her perspective?

As you work to answer these questions, you are likely to find that you are *rereading* key sections, and this rereading is an essential part of the process of reading effectively.

THINKING-
WRITING
ACTIVITY

Practicing Metacognition

Although developing metacognitive reading abilities is a complex process that takes place over time, you can begin using these strategies immediately. Select a chapter from one of your textbooks. As you read, make a conscious effort to ask— and to answer—the metacognitive questions noted above. Record your experience, identifying the questions that you found yourself asking, and how the process of asking—and trying to answer—these questions while you were reading affected your understanding of the material. The metacognitive questions are part of a reading worksheet located below that you can use for reference later.

Reading Worksheet

Reading Assignment: _____

Reading Environment: _____

Reading Schedule: _____

Date Due: _____

Day   *Time Planned for Reading*

_____   _____

_____   _____

Reading Strategies

Problem Solving

Step 1: What is the problem in understanding the reading?
Step 2: What are the possible meanings and interpretations?
Step 3: What are the contextual clues, reasons, or evidence?
Step 4: What meaning or interpretation is most likely?
Step 5: How well is my conclusion working?

Metacognition

What are my *goals* in reading this passage, and how well am I meeting these goals?
What parts do I *understand,* and what parts are *confusing*?
How will the author *elaborate* and *develop* ideas I am reading about?
What is the author's *point of view,* and why did she adopt this particular perspective?
Do the ideas *make sense*? What *evidence* and *reasons* support the ideas presented?

Annotation

"Grounds for Fiction"

BY JULIA ALVAREZ (b. 1950)

Poet, novelist, and teacher Julia Alvarez was born in New York City but raised in the Dominican Republic. Her novel *In the Time of the Butterflies* (1994) is based on the true story of the four Mirabal sisters who fought against the brutal Trujillo dictatorship, and her enormously popular *How the Garcia Girls Lost Their Accents* (1991) deftly explores the relationships among sisters. Both novels were critically acclaimed, nominated for and winning several important prizes. Her most recent novel, *Saving the World,* was published in 2006.

In recent years, Alvarez and her husband have started an organic coffee farm in the Dominican Republic; she recently brought a group of her American college students to the farm to work alongside local farmers and teach literacy classes in the community.

Every once in a while after a reading, someone in the audience will come up to me. *Have I got a story for you!* They will go on to tell me the story of an aunt or sister or next-door neighbor, some moment of mystery, some serendipitous occurrence, some truly incredible story. "You should write it down," I always tell them. They look at me as if they've just offered me their family crown jewels and I've refused them. "I'm no writer," they tell me. "You're the writer."

"Oh, you never know," I reply, so as to encourage them. What I should tell them is that writing ideas can't really be traded in an open market. If they could be, writers would be multimillionaires. Who knows what mystery (or madness) it is that drives us to our computers for two, three, four years, in pursuit of some sparkling possibility that looks like dull fact to everyone else's eyes. One way to define a writer is she who is able to make what obsesses her into everyone's obsession. I am thinking of Goethe, whose *Sorrows of Young Werther,* published in 1774, caused a spate of suicides in imitation of its young hero. Young Werther's blue frock coat and yellow waistcoat became the fad. We have all been the victims of someone's too-long slide show of their white-water rafting trip or their recounting of a convoluted, boring dream. But a Mark Twain can turn that slide show into the lively backdrop of a novel, or a Jorge Luis Borges can take the twist and turn of a dream and wring the meaning of the universe from it.

But aside from talent—and granted, that is a big aside, one that comes and goes and shifts and grows and diminishes, so it is also somewhat unpredictable—how can we tell when we've got it: that seed of experience, of memory, that voice of a character or fleeting image that might just be grounds for fiction? The answer is that we can never tell. And so another way to define a writer is someone who is willing to find out. As James Dickey once explained to an audience, "I work on the process of refining low-grade ore. I get maybe a couple of nuggets of gold out of fifty tons of dirt. It is tough for me. No, I am not inspired."

"Are you all here because you want to muck around in fifty tons of dirt?" I ask my workshop of young writers the first day. Not one hand goes up unless I've told them the Dickey story first.

5 In fact, my students want to know ahead of time if some idea they have will make a good story. "I mean, before I spend hours and hours on it," one young man explained. I told my students what Mallarmé told his friend the painter Degas, when Degas complained that he couldn't seem to write well although he was "full of ideas." Mallarmés's famous answer was, "My dear Degas, poems are not made out of ideas. Poems are made out of words." I told my student that if a young writer had come up to me and told me that he was going to write a story about a man who wakes up one morning and finds out that he has been turned into a cockroach, I would have told him to forget it. That story would never work. "And I would have stopped Kafka from writing his 'Metamorphosis,'" I concluded, smiling at my student, as if he might be a future Kafka.

"Well, it's just two pages," he grumbled. "And I have this other idea that might be better. About a street person who is getting Alzheimer's."

"Write both stories, and I'll read them and tell you what I think of them," I said. He looked alarmed. So I leveled with him. I told him that if he didn't want to spend hours and hours finding out if the kernel of an idea, the glimmer of an inspiration, the flash of a possibility would make a good story, he should give up the *idea* of wanting to be a writer.

As much as I can break down the process of writing stories, I would say that this is how it begins. I find a detail or image or character or incident or cluster of events. A certain luminosity surrounds them. I find myself attracted. I come forward. I pick it up, turn it around, begin to ask questions, and spend hours and weeks and months and years trying to answer them.

I keep a folder, a yellow folder with pockets. For a long time it had no label because I didn't know what to label it: WHATCHAMACALLITS, filed under *W*, or also under *W*, STORY-POEM-WANNABES. Finally, I called the folder CURIOSIDADES, in Spanish so I wouldn't have to commit myself to what I was going to do in English with these random little things. I tell my students this, too, that writing begins before you ever put pen to paper or your fingers down on the keyboard. It is a way of being alive in the world. Henry James's advice to the young writer was to be someone on whom nothing is lost. And so this is my folder of the little things that have not been lost on me; news clippings, headlines, inventory lists, bits of gossip that I've already sensed have an aura about them, the beginnings of a poem or a short story, the seed of a plot that might turn into a novel or a query that might needle an essay out of me.

10 Periodically, when I'm between writing projects and sometimes when I'm in the middle of one and needing a break, I go through my yellow folder. Sometimes I discard a clipping or note that no longer holds my attention. But most of my curiosidades have been in my folder for years, though some have migrated to new folders, the folders of stories and poems they have inspired or found a home in.

Here's one of these curiosidades that is now in a folder that holds drafts of a story that turned into a chapter of my novel ¡YO! This chapter is in the point of view of Marie Beaudry, a landlady who, along with other narrators, gets to tell a story on Yolanda García, the writer. The little curiosity that inspired Marie's voice was a note

I found in the trash of an apartment I moved into. It has nothing at all to do with what happens in my story.

> Re and Mal: Here's the two keys to your father's apt. Need I say more excepting that's such a rotten thing you pulled on him. My doing favors is over as of this morning. Good luck to you two hard-hearted hannahs. I got more feeling in my little finger than the two of you got in your whole body.
>
> Jinny

I admit that when I read this note, I wanted to move out of that apartment. I felt the place was haunted by the ghost of the last tenant against whom some violation had been perpetrated by these two hard-hearted hannahs, Re and Mal. Over the years that handwritten note stayed in my yellow folder and eventually gave me the voice of my character Marie Beaudry.

Here's another scrap from deep inside one of the pockets. It's the title of an article in one of my husband's ophthalmological journals: "Treatment of Chronic Post-filtration Hypotony by Intrableb Injection of Autologous Blood." I think I saved that choice bit of medical babble because of the delight I took in the jabberwocky phenomenon of that title.

> 'Twas brillig and the slithy toves
> Did gyre and postfiltrate the wabe;
> All hypotonious was the blood,
> And autologous the intrableb.

I have not yet used it in a story or poem, but who knows, maybe someday you will look over the shoulder of one of my characters and see that he is reading this article or writing it. I can tell you that this delight in words and how we use and misuse them is a preoccupation of mine.

Maybe because I began my writing life as a poet, the naming of things has always interested me:

> Mother, unroll the bolts and name
> the fabrics from which our clothing came,
> dress the world in vocabulary:
> broadcloth, corduroy, denim, terry.

Actually, that poem, "Naming the Fabrics," besides being inspired, of course, by the names of fabrics, was also triggered by something I picked up while reading *The 1961 Better Homes and Garden Sewing Book,* page 45: "During a question and answer period at a sewing clinic, a woman in the audience asked this question: 'I can sew beautifully; my fitting is excellent; the finished dress looks as good as that of any professional—but how do I get up enough courage to cut the fabric?'" I typed out this passage and put it away. A few months later, this fear found its way from my yellow folder to my poem, "Naming the Fabrics":

> I pay a tailor to cut his suits
> from seersucker, duck, tweed, cheviot,
> those names make my cutting hand skittish—
> either they sound like sex or British.

Since I myself have no sewing skills to speak of, I didn't know about this fear that seamstresses experience before cutting fabric. Certainly, the year 1961, when this sewing book was published, brings other fears to mind: the Berlin Wall going up; invaders going down to the Bay of Pigs; Trujillo, our dictator of thirty-one years, being assassinated in the Dominican Republic. But this housewife in Indiana had her own metaphysical fears to work out on cloth. "How do I get up enough courage to cut the fabric?" Her preoccupation astonished me and touched me for all kinds of reasons I had to work out on paper.

15 You might wonder what a "serious writer" was doing reading *The 1961 Better Homes and Garden Sewing Book.* Wouldn't my time have been better spent perusing Milton or Emily Dickinson or even the *New York Review of Books* or *The Nation?* All I can say in my defense is that I believe in Henry James's advice: be someone on whom nothing is lost. Or what Deborah Kerr said in *Night of the Iguana,* "Nothing human disgusts me." I once heard a writer on *Fresh Air* tell Terry Gross that one of the most important things he had ever learned in his life was that you could learn a lot from people who were dumber than you. You can also learn a lot from publications that are below your literary standards: housekeeping books, cookbooks, manuals, cereal boxes, and the local newspapers of your small town.

These last are the best. Even if some of this "news" is really glorified gossip—so what? Most of our classics are glorified gossip. Think of the Wife of Bath's inventory of husbands or the debutante's hair-rape in "The Rape of the Lock." How about Madame Bovary's steamy affair? Is what happened to Abelard over his Héloïse or to Jason for pissing off Medea any less infamous than the John and Lorena Bobbit story of several years ago? The wonderful Canadian writer Alice Munro admits that she likes reading *People* magazine, and "not just at the checkout stand. I sometimes buy it." She goes on to say that gossip is "a central part of my life. I'm interested in small-town gossip. Gossip has that feeling in it, that one wants to know about life."

I've gotten wonderful stories from the *Addison Independent,* the *Valley Voice,* even the *Burlington Free Press* that would never be reported in the *Wall Street Journal* or the *New York Times:*

11-Year-Old Girls Take Car on Two-State Joyride

Two 11-year-old girls determined to see a newborn niece secretly borrowed their grandfather's car, piled clothes on the front seat so they could see over the steering wheel and drove more than 10 hours.

Neither one of them had ever driven a car before, said Michael Ray, Mercer County's juvenile case worker. The youngsters packed the Dodge Aries with soda, snacks, and an atlas for their trek from West Virginia to the central Kentucky town of Harrodsburg. "They were determined to see that baby," said caseworker Ray.

You could write a whole novel about that. In fact, in Mona Simpson's latest novel, *A Regular Guy,* eleven-year-old Jane di Natali is taught by her mother to drive their pickup with wood blocks strapped to the pedals so her short legs can reach them. Little Jane takes off on her own to see her estranged father hundreds of miles away. I wonder if Mona Simpson got her idea for Jane's odyssey from reading about these two eleven-year-olds.

Here's another article I've saved in my yellow folder:

Misdiagnosed Patient Freed After 2 Years

A Mexican migrant worker misdiagnosed and kept sedated in an Oregon mental hospital for two years because doctors couldn't understand his Indian dialect is going home.

Adolfo Gonzales, a frail 5-foot-4-inch grape picker who doesn't speak English or Spanish, had been trying to communicate in his native Indian dialect of Trique.

Gonzales, believed to be in his 20s, was born in a village in Oaxaca, Mexico. He was committed in June 1990 after being arrested for indecent exposure at a laundromat. Charges later were dropped.

I couldn't get this story out of my head. First, I was—and am—intensely interested in the whole Scheherazade issue of how important it is to be able to tell our stories to those who have power over us. Second, and more mundanely, I was intensely curious about those charges that were later dropped: indecent exposure at a laundromat. What was Adolfo Gonzales doing taking his clothes off in a laundromat? Why was he in town after a hard day of grape picking? I had to find answers to these questions, and so I started writing a poem. "It's a myth that writers write what they know," the writer Marcie Hershman has written. "We write what it is that we need to know."

The next payday you went to town
to buy your girl and to wash your one
set of working clothes.
In the laundromat, you took them off
to wring out the earth you wanted
to leave behind you.
    from "Two Years Too Late"

20   Of course, you don't even have to go to your local paper. Just take a walk downtown, especially if you live in a small town, as I do. All I have to do is have a cup of coffee at Steve's Diner or at Jimmy's Weybridge Garage and listen to

my neighbors talking. Flannery O'Connor claimed that most beginners' stories don't work because "they don't go very far inside a character, don't reveal very much of the character. And this problem is in large part due to the fact that these characters have no distinctive speech to reveal themselves with." Here are some examples of my fellow Vermonters talking their very distinctive and revealing speech.

> He's so lazy he married a pregnant woman.
>
> I'm so hungry I could eat the north end out of a southbound skunk.
>
> The snow's butt-high to a tall cow.
>
> More nervous than a long-tailed cat in a room full of rocking chairs.
>
> I'm so sick that I'd have to get well to die.

Of course if, like Whitman, you do nothing but listen, you will also hear all kinds of bogus voices these days, speaking the new doublespeak. In our litigious, politically overcorrected, dizzily spin-doctored age, politicians and public figures have to use language so that it doesn't say anything that might upset anyone. Here's a list of non-terms and what they really stand for:

Sufferer of fictitious disorder syndrome:	Liar
Suboptimal:	Failed
Temporarily displaced inventory:	Stolen
Negative gain in test scores:	Lower test scores
Substantive negative outcome:	Death

We're back to "Treatment of Chronic Postfiltration Hypotony by Intrableb Injection of Autologous Blood," what Ken Macrorie in his wonderful book about expository writing, *Telling Writing,* calls "Engfish"—homogenized, doctored-up, approximate language that can't be traced to a human being.

I tend to agree with what Dickinson once said about poetry, "There are no approximate words in a poem." Auden even went so far as to say that he could pick out a potential poet by a student's answer to the question, "Why do you want to write poetry?" If the student answered, "I have important things to say," then he was not a poet. If he answered, "I like hanging around words listening to what they say," then maybe he was going to be a poet.

I got enmeshed in one such string of words when I visited the United Nations to hear my mother give a speech on violation of human rights. At the door an aide handed me the list of voting member countries and the names caught my eye: Dem Kampuchea, Dem Yemen, Denmark, Djibouti, Dominica, Dominican Republic, Ecuador, Egypt. . . . When I got home, I started writing a poem, ostensibly about hearing my mother give that speech, but really because I wanted to use the names of those countries:

> I scan the room for reactions,
> picking out those countries
> guilty of her sad facts.
> Kampuchea is absent,
> absent, too, the South African delegate.
> I cannot find the United States.
> Nervous countries predominate,
> Nicaragua and Haiti,
> Iraq, Israel, Egypt.
>   *from* "Between Dominica and Ecuador"

But of course, it's not just words that intrigue writers, but the stories, the possibilities of human character that cluster around a bit of history, trivia, gossip.

For instance, Anne Macdonald's book, *Feminine Ingenuity,* inspired a character trait of the mother in *How the García Girls Lost Their Accents.* According to Macdonald, at the beginning of the twentieth century, 5,535 American women were granted patents for inventions, including a straw-weaving device, an open-eye needle for sewing hot-air balloons, and special planking designed to discourage barnacles from attaching themselves to warships. These intriguing facts gave me a side of the mother's character I would never have thought up on my own. Inspired by the gadgetry of her new country, Laura García sets out to make her mark: soap sprayed from the nozzle head of a shower when you turn the knob a certain way; instant coffee with creamer already mixed in; time-released water capsules for your potted plants when you were away; a key chain with a timer that would go off when your parking meter was about to expire. (And the ticking would help you find your keys easily if you mislaid them.)

Sometimes the inspiration is history. History . . . that subject I hated in school because it was so dry and all about dead people. I wish now my teachers had made me read novels to make the past spring alive in my imagination. For years, I wanted to write about the Mirabal sisters, but I admit I was put off by these grand historical abstractions. It wasn't until I began to accumulate several yellow folders' worth of vivid little details about them that these godlike women became accessible to me. One of my first entries came from my father, who had just returned from a trip to the Dominican Republic: "I met the man who sold the girls pocketbooks at El Gallo before they set off over the mountain. He told me he warned them not to go. He said he took them out back to the stockroom supposedly to show them inventory and explained they were going to be killed. But they did not believe him." I still get goosebumps reading my father's letter dated June 5, 1985. It went in my yellow folder. That pocketbook-buying scene is at the end of the novel I published nine years later.

25   So what are you to conclude from this tour of my yellow folder? That this essay is just an excuse to take you through my folder and share my little treasures with you? Well, one thing I don't want you to conclude is that this preliminary woolgathering is

a substitute for the real research that starts once you have a poem or story going. In "Naming the Fabrics," for instance, though I was inspired by the plaintive question asked at a sewing clinic, I still had to go down to the fabric store and spend an afternoon with a very kind and patient saleslady who taught me all about gingham and calico, crepe and gauze. I spent days reading fabric books, and weeks working on the poem, and years going back to it, revising it, tinkering with it. For my story, "The Tent," I had to call up the National Guard base near Champaign, Illinois, and get permission from the base commander to go observe his men setting up a tent. ("What exactly do you need this for?" he asked at least half a dozen times.) Sometimes I think the best reason for a writer to have a reputable job like being a professor at a university or a vice president of Hartford Insurance Company is so you can call up those base commanders or bother those salesladies in fabric stores as if you do have a real job. Otherwise, they might think you are crazy and lock you up like poor Adolfo Gonzales.

On the whole, I have found people to be kind and generous with their time, especially when you ask them to talk about something they know and care about. Many people have actually gone beyond kindness in helping me out. I remember calling up the local Catholic priest, bless his heart, who really deserves, I don't know, a plenary indulgence for tolerance in the face of surprise. Imagine getting an early-morning call (my writing day starts at 6:30, but I really don't do this kind of phone calling till about 7:30 since I do want my sources to be lucid). Anyhow, imagine an early-morning call at your rectory from a woman you don't know who asks you what is the name of that long rod priests have with a hole on one end to sprinkle people with holy water? I'd be lying if I tried to make drama out of the phone call and say there was a long pause. Nope. Father John spoke right up, "Ah yes, my aspergill."

One thing I should add—the bad news part of all this fun, but something writers do have to think about in this litigious age—what is grounds for fiction can also be, alas, grounds for suing. All three of my novels have been read by my publisher's lawyer for what might be libelous. Thank goodness Algonquin's lawyer is also a reader who refuses to vacuum all the value out of a book in order to play it safe. Still, I have had to take drinks out of characters' hands and make abused ladies disabused and make so many changes in hair coloring and hairstyle that I could start a literary beauty parlor.

But even if your fictional ground is cleared of litigious material, there might still be grounds for heartache. Your family and friends might feel wounded when they can detect—even if no one else can—the shape of the real behind the form of your fiction. And who would want to hurt those very people you write for, those very people who share with you the world you are struggling to understand in your fiction for their sake as well as your own?

I don't know how to get around this and I certainly haven't figured out what the parameters of my responsibility are to the real people in my life. One of my theories, which might sound defensive and self-serving, is that there is no such thing as straight-up fiction. There are just levels of distance from our own life experience, the thing that drives us to write in the first place. In spite of our caution and precaution, bits of our lives will get into what we write. I have a friend whose mother finds herself in all his novels, even historical novels set in nineteenth-century Russia or islands in the Caribbean where his mother has never been. A novelist writing about Napoleon might convey his greedy character by describing him spooning gruel into his mouth, only to realize that her image of how a greedy man eats comes from watching her fat Tío Jorge stuff his face with sweet habichuelas.

30   I think that if you start censoring yourself as a novelist—*this is out of bounds, that is sacrosanct*—you will never write anything. My advice is to write it out, and then decide, by whatever process seems fair to you—three-o'clock-in-the-morning insomniac angst sessions with your soul, or a phone call with your best friend, or a long talk with your sister—what you are going to do about it. More often than not, an upset reaction has more to do with people's wounded vanity or their own unresolved issues with *you* rather than what you've written. I'm not speaking now of meanness or revenge thinly masquerading as fiction, but of a writer's serious attempts to render justice to the world she lives in, which includes, whether she wants it to or not, the people she loves or has tried to love, the people who have been a part of the memories, details, life experiences that form the whole cloth of her reality—out of which, with fear and a trembling hand, she must perforce cut her fiction.

But truly, this is a worry to put out of your head while you are writing. You'll need your energy for the hard work ahead: tons and tons of good *ideas* to process in order to get those nuggets of pure prose. What Yeats once said in his poem "Dialogue of Self and Soul" could well be the writer's pledge of allegiance:

> I am content to follow to its source,
> every event in action or in thought.

And remember, no one is probably going to pay you a whole lot of money to do this. You also probably won't save anyone's life with anything you write. But so much does depend on seeing a world in a grain of sand and a heaven in a wildflower. Maybe we are here only to say: house, bridge, aspergill, gingham, calico, gauze. "But to say them," as Rilke said, "remember oh, to say them in a way that the things themselves never dreamed of existing so intensely."

But this is too much of an orchestral close for the lowly little ditty that starts with a newspaper clipping or the feel of a bolt of gingham or a cup of coffee at the Weybridge Garage. The best advice I can give writers is something so dull and simple you'd never save it in your yellow folder. But go ahead and engrave it in your writer's heart. If you want to be a writer, anything in this world is grounds for fiction.

QUESTIONS FOR ACTIVE READING

1. In rereading the essay, highlight all the cultural allusions Alvarez makes—the writers she cites, the paintings she mentions, the literary characters who obsess her,

even the tabloid news stories she finds entertaining. Using the Internet (and working with partners, if you like), look up any allusions that are unfamiliar, and annotate your text by writing explanations of those allusions in the margins. What is Alvarez's purpose for all these allusions? How do you, as a reader, respond to the breadth of her interests?

2. How does Alvarez demonstrate the four qualities of an active, thoughtful, and critical reader? In what ways is she curious, open-minded, knowledgeable, and creative in her reading and her use of what she reads?

3. After you have annotated the essay to clarify any unfamiliar allusions, respond to any or all of the previous metacognitive reading questions. Do any portions of the essay resist your questioning? Compare notes with your classmates—what is most difficult about Alvarez's essay, and why?

QUESTIONS FOR THINKING CRITICALLY

1. An *apologia* is a kind of argument, a defense that someone writes to explain and justify his or her actions, beliefs, or opinions. It's different from an *apology,* in which someone admits wrongdoing. In what ways does Alvarez present an apologia for herself as a writer? How, conversely, would she respond to a writer who might feel compelled to offer an apology for something he or she had written?

2. What does it mean to be *inspired*? (Look the word up; are you surprised by its etymology?) Where does Alvarez find inspiration? Look into the creative habits of another artist (in any medium) whose work you admire. From where does she draw her inspiration?

3. Get an empty folder. For one week, make an effort to put anything in that folder that catches your interest—an email from a friend, a photograph from the newspaper, the menu from a coffee shop, the stub from a movie ticket. At the end of the week, dump the contents of the folder on your desk. What story do these scraps tell you about yourself? about your life? Can you arrange them into any sort of "narrative," either creative or very close to true?

You could also exchange folders with a classmate. What stories could you tell about your classmate based on what's in his folder?

Making Meaning

Words are not simple entities with one clear meaning that everyone agrees on. Instead, most words are complex, multidimensional carriers of meaning; their exact meaning often varies from person to person. These differences in meaning can lead to disagreements and confusion. To understand how words function, you have to examine the way that words serve as vehicles to express meaning.

Words arouse a variety of ideas, feelings, and experiences. Taken together, these responses express the total meaning of the words for each individual. Linguists believe that this total meaning is actually composed of four different types of meaning:

- semantic meaning
- perceptual meaning
- syntactic meaning
- pragmatic meaning

Let us examine each of them in turn.

Semantic Meaning (Denotation)

The *semantic meaning* of a word expresses the relationship between a *linguistic event* (speaking or writing) and a *nonlinguistic event* (an object, idea, or feeling). For example, saying "chair" relates to an object you sit in while saying "college education" relates to the experience of earning an academic degree through post-secondary study.

The semantic meaning of a word, also referred to as its *denotative meaning,* expresses the general properties of the word, and these properties determine how the word is used within its language system. How do you discover the general properties that determine word usage? Besides examining your own knowledge of the meaning and use of words, you can check dictionary definitions. They tend to focus on the general properties that determine word usage. For example, a dictionary definition of *chair* might be "a piece of furniture consisting of a seat, legs, and back, and often arms, designed to accommodate one person."

However, to understand a word's semantic meaning fully, you often need to go beyond defining its general properties to identifying examples that embody those properties. If you are sitting in a chair or can see one from where you are, examine its design. Does it embody all the properties identified in the definition? (Sometimes unusual examples embody most, but not all, the properties of a word's dictionary definition—for example, a beanbag chair lacks legs and arms.) If you are trying to understand the semantic meaning of a word, it is generally useful to see both the word's general properties and examples that illustrate them.

Perceptual Meaning (Connotation)

The total meaning of a word also includes its *perceptual meaning,* which expresses the relationship between a linguistic event and an individual's consciousness. For each of us, words elicit personal thoughts and feelings based on previous experiences and past associations. A person might relate saying "chair" to his favorite chair in his living room or the small chair that he built for his daughter. Perceptual meaning also includes an individual's positive and negative responses to the word.

When you read or hear the word *book,* what positive or negative feelings does it arouse? What about *textbook? mystery book? comic book? cookbook?* In each case, the word probably elicits distinct feelings, and these contribute to the meaning each word has for you. For this reason, perceptual meaning is also sometimes called *connotative meaning,* the literal or basic meaning of a word plus all it suggests or connotes to you.

Syntactic Meaning

A third component of a word's total meaning is its *syntactic meaning,* which defines its relation to other words in a sentence. The syntactic meaning defines three relationships among words:

- *Content:* words that express the major message of the sentence
- *Description:* words that elaborate or modify the major message of the sentence
- *Connection:* words that join the major message of the sentence

For example, in the sentence "The two novice hikers crossed the ledge cautiously," *hikers* and *crossed* represent the content, or major message, of the sentence. *Two* and *novice* describe *hikers,* and *cautiously* elaborates on *crossed.*

At first, you may think that this sort of relationship among words involves nothing more than semantic meaning. The following sentence, however, clearly demonstrates the importance of syntactic meaning in language: "Invisible fog rumbles in on lizard legs." Although *fog* does not *rumble,* and it is not *invisible,* and the notion of moving on *lizard legs* seems incompatible with *rumbling,* the sentence does "make sense" at some level of meaning—namely, at the syntactic level. One reason it does is that there are three basic content words—*fog, rumbles,* and *legs*—and two descriptive words—*invisible* and *lizard.*

The third major syntactic relationship is connection. Connective words join ideas, thoughts, or feelings being expressed. For example, you could connect content meaning to either of the two sentences in the following ways:

> The two novice hikers crossed the ledge cautiously *after* one of them slipped.
> Invisible fog rumbles in on lizard legs, *but* acid rain doesn't.

When you add the content words *one slipped* and *rain doesn't,* you join the ideas, thoughts, and feelings they represent to the ideas, thoughts, or feelings expressed earlier (*hikers crossed* and *fog rumbles*) by using the connective words *after* and *but.*

The second reason that "Invisible fog rumbles in on lizard legs" makes sense at the syntactic level of meaning is that the words of that sentence obey the syntax, or order, of English. Most English speakers would have trouble making sense of "Invisible rumbles legs lizard on fog in"—or of "Barks big endlessly dog brown the," for that matter. Because of syntactic meaning, each word in the sentence derives part of its total meaning from the ways in which it is combined with the other words in that sentence.

THINKING-
WRITING
ACTIVITY

Syntactic Meaning

Look at the following sentences and explain the difference in meaning between the two in each pair.

1. a. The process of obtaining an *education at college* changes a person's future possibilities.

   b. The process of obtaining a *college education* changes a person's future possibilities.

2. a. She felt *happiness* for her long-lost brother.

   b. She felt the *happiness* of her long-lost brother.

3. a. The most important thing to me is *freedom from* the things that restrict my choices.

   b. The most important thing to me is *freedom* to make my choices without restrictions.

4. a. Michelangelo's painting of the Sistine Chapel ceiling represents his *creative* genius.

   b. The Sistine Chapel ceiling represents the *creative* genius of Michelangelo's greatest painting.

5. a. I *love* the person I have been involved with for the past year.

   b. I am *in love* with the person I have been involved with for the past year.

Pragmatic Meaning

The fourth element that contributes to the total meaning of a word is its *pragmatic meaning.* The pragmatic meaning of a word involves the person who is writing and the situation in which the word is written. For example, the statement "That student likes to borrow books from the library" allows a number of pragmatic interpretations:

1. Was the writer outside looking at *that student* carrying books out of the library?

2. Did the writer have this information because he or she is a classmate of *that student* but did not actually see the student carrying books?

3. Was the writer in the library watching *that student* check the books out?

The correct interpretation or meaning of the sentence depends on what was actually taking place in the situation—in other words, its pragmatic meaning, which is also called its *situational meaning.*

The four types of meanings you just examined—semantic, perceptual, syntactic, and pragmatic—create the total meaning of a word. That is, all the dimensions of a word—all the relationships that connect linguistic events with nonlinguistic events, with your consciousness, with other linguistic events, and with situations in the world—make up the meaning you assign to the word. Later, we will build on the ideas of this section.

THINKING-
WRITING
ACTIVITY

Pragmatic Meaning

For each of the following sentences, try describing a pragmatic context that identifies the person writing and the situation for which it is being written.

1. A *college education* is currently necessary for many careers that formerly only required high school preparation.

2. The utilitarian ethical system is based on the principle that the right course of action is that which brings the greatest *happiness* to the greatest number of people.

3. The laws of this country attempt to balance the *freedom* of the individual with the rights of society as a whole.

4. "You are all part of things, you are all part of *creation*, all kings, all poets, all musicians, you have only to open up, to discover what is already there."—Henry Miller

5. "If music be the food of *love*, play on."—Shakespeare

After completing the activity, compare your answers with those of your classmates. In what ways are the answers similar or different? Analyze the ways in which different pragmatic contexts (persons speaking and situations) affect the meanings of the italicized words.

Thinking Critically, Writing Thoughtfully

> *The mere process of writing is one of the most powerful tools we have for clarifying our own thinking.*
>
> —*James Van Allen*

Critical Thinking Focus: Thinking about thinking

Writing Focus: Reflecting on experiences

Reading Theme: Experiences that have affected beliefs

Writing Project: Recalling the impact of experience on a belief

From Insight to Writing to Informed Beliefs (and Back Again)

Thinking, writing, reading—these are the tools you use to understand your world, develop relationships with others, and make intelligent decisions in your quest to live a meaningful life. The underlying theme of this book is the way these potentially powerful tools are intrinsically related to one another. Every day you make choices in many areas of your life, choices that are guided by the beliefs you have developed. Successful choices are generally the product of enlightened beliefs that we have developed as a result of thinking critically, reading actively, and writing thoughtfully, as well as through lived experience. Whether the choices involve how best to write a research paper, enliven your social life, or pursue a challenging career, these fundamental abilities provide you with the means to construct beliefs that will guide your choices.

Using these four core qualities as a framework, this chapter extends and deepens them by exploring other related qualities that characterize critical thinkers, active readers, and thoughtful writers, including the following:

- Thinking actively
- Thinking independently
- Viewing a situation from different perspectives
- Supporting diverse perspectives with evidence and reasons

The chapter then presents readings in which authors think critically by reflecting on experiences that have affected their beliefs. Concluding the chapter is a Writing Project which asks you to think critically and write thoughtfully about an experience that had an important impact on a belief that you held or hold. You should keep this Writing Project in mind as you read the chapter and work on Thinking-Writing Activities.

Thinking Actively and Writing

When you think critically, you are *actively* using your intelligence, knowledge, and abilities to deal effectively with life's situations. Similarly, when you write thoughtfully, you act in the following ways:

- You *become involved* in the subject you are writing about, and because the writing process stimulates your thinking, you often discover ideas that you were unaware of until you started writing. Also, if you keep a journal or notebook and make writing part of your daily life, you find yourself more involved in and more reflective about your world.
- You *take initiative* as you develop confidence in your writer's voice, so you express your own perspectives instead of imitating the ideas of others.
- You *follow through* as you revise and edit in order to produce your best effort.
- You *take responsibility* for your work. That is, you begin assignments promptly and schedule enough time to complete them. Though your professors will guide you, and your classmates and writing center tutors will make suggestions about your drafts, you are in charge of your writing, and it is up to you to complete it honestly and well.

When you are thinking actively, you are not just waiting for something to happen. You are engaged in the process of achieving goals, making decisions, analyzing issues, and writing thoughtfully.

Influences on Your Thinking

As our minds grow and develop, we are exposed to influences that encourage us to think actively. We also, however, have many experiences that encourage us to think passively. For example, some analysts believe that when people, especially children, spend much of their time watching television or playing video games instead of reading and writing, they are being encouraged to think passively, thus inhibiting their intellectual growth.

You are influenced to think passively if an employer gives you detailed instructions for performing every task that permit no exception or deviation. On the other hand, when an employer gives you general areas of responsibility within which you are expected to make thoughtful and creative decisions, you are being stimulated to think actively and independently. Of course, certain people or activities can act as either active or passive influences, depending on specific situations and your individual responses. For example, consider employers. If you are performing a routine, repetitive task— such as a summer job in a peanut-butter cracker plant, hand-scooping 2,000 pounds of peanut butter a day—the very nature of the work encourages passive, uncritical thinking (although it might also lead to creative daydreaming!).

In college, you will find that your course work and teachers encourage you to think actively by expecting you to apply, analyze, synthesize, and evaluate the information you are acquiring. Professors may assign independent research projects, give essay exams, and require you to write papers in which you must bring your informed perspective to the course material.

Thinking Independently

Answer the following questions on the basis of what you believe to be true.

	Yes	No	Not Sure
1. Is the earth flat?			
2. Is the soul immortal?			

(Continued on page 54)

FOUR QUALITIES OF A CRITICAL THINKER

Biologist Charles Darwin

Curiosity   Without curiosity, you become complacent and limited in your understanding, resulting in beliefs that are misdirected, inadequate, and mistaken. The son and grandson of scientists, Charles Darwin (1809–1882) came of age at a time when many discoveries about nature and technology were being made. At the age of twenty-two, as a theology student, Darwin was invited to join a five-year official voyage on the British sailing ship the *Beagle*. His scientific interest piqued, Darwin joined the dangerous expedition as a naturalist, botanist, and zoologist. There are few such adventures left to young scientists and students these days, but that same spirit of inquiry can lead you to make personally significant discoveries of your own.

Open-minded   Informed beliefs result from actively exploring diverse ideas and perspectives. Darwin, as a scientist,

also relied on close and careful study of the empirical evidence. As he writes in *The Origin of Species* (1859), upon his return to England, it "occurred" to Darwin "that something might perhaps be made out on this question [the origin of species] by patiently accumulating and reflecting on all sorts of facts which could possibly have any bearing on it." He notes, "I have not been hasty in coming to a decision." Wrestling with his own religious faith in light of his scientific observations, Darwin recognized the enormous cultural and philosophical impact his work would have on his audience. In recent years, the battle over the teaching of "intelligent design" in science classrooms has forced many people of good will to reconsider the boundary between being open-minded and being forced to consider ideas that they may feel are either morally repugnant or scientifically unjustified. Your own writing and thinking will have greater significance and

Active and Passive Influences

Here is a list of some of the influences we all experience in our lives, along with space for adding others you are aware of. As you read through the list, place an *A* next to items that you believe influence you to think actively and a *P* next to items that make you more passive.

Activities	*People*
Reading	Family members
Writing	Friends
Watching television	Employers
Surfing the Internet	Advertisers
Drawing and painting	Teachers
Playing video games	Police officers
Playing sports	Religious leaders
Listening to music	Politicians
_____	_____
_____	_____

Identify one important influence in your life that stimulates you to think actively; then identify one that encourages you to think passively. Write explanations of how each has affected your thinking. Provide at least two specific examples for each influence.

meaning to you as you push the limits of your own understanding.

Knowledgeable   By his own admission, in his brief autobiography (1876), Darwin describes himself as at best an indifferent student in school ("my time was sadly wasted there," he writes of his college days). What inspired him as a child and as a young man were long walks through the countryside, fishing, collecting unusual plants and minerals, and talking with friends and interesting people. Contemporary scientists gain knowledge through years of laboratory work, reading professional journals, and attending conferences with colleagues. And yet their knowledge, especially for biologists following in Darwin's footsteps, is also tested and expanded by forays into the natural world. As you have probably observed in your own life, your academic and professional interests are just as likely to be encouraged by "real-life" experience as by classroom experiences. Your personal experiences and insights can be incorporated into your college writing in assignments ranging

from personal essays through research papers based on your observations and fieldwork.

Creative   Breakthroughs in thinking lead to vital, lively writing and insightful, informed beliefs. It was rare enough in Darwin's day for a scientist to be included on an official voyage of exploration (such voyages had primarily military and commercial purposes). That Darwin was also a widely read scholar with a wide range of allusions, references, and descriptive techniques made his books not only scientific and philosophically important but also commercial bestsellers.

Online Study Center
Charles Darwin
Visit the Online Study Center for *Critical Thinking, Thoughtful Writing* at *college.hmco.com/pic/ chaffeeCTTW4e* for more on Charles Darwin.

	Yes	No	Not Sure

3. Should marijuana be legalized?

4. Should music lyrics and videos be censored?

5. Should we always follow "the Golden Rule" ("do unto others as you would have them do unto you")?

Your responses to these questions reveal aspects of the way your mind works, beliefs you have developed that you express in your speaking and writing. How did you arrive at these conclusions? Your views on these and many other issues probably had their beginnings with your family, especially your parents or other adults who raised you. When you were little, you were very dependent on those adults, and you were influenced by the way they saw the world. As you grew up, you learned how to think, feel, and behave in various situations. Very likely your teachers included your brothers and sisters, friends, religious leaders, instructors, books, and the media. You absorbed most of what you learned passively, without even being aware of doing so. Many of your ideas about the issues raised in the five questions you just answered probably were shaped by experiences you had while growing up.

As a result of your ongoing experiences, however, your mind—and your thinking—have continued to mature. Instead of simply accepting the views of others, you have gradually developed the ability to examine your earlier thinking and to decide how much of it still makes sense to you and whether you should accept it. Now, when you think through important ideas, use this standard when making a decision: Are there good reasons or evidence that support this thinking? If there are, you can actively decide to adopt the ideas. If not, you can modify or reject them.

"I keep my core beliefs written on my palm for easy reference."

Of course, you may not *always* examine your own thinking or the thinking of others so carefully. In fact, people often continue to believe the same ideas they were brought up with, without ever examining and deciding for themselves what to think. Or they may blindly reject the beliefs they were brought up with, without really examining them.

How do you know when you have examined and adopted beliefs yourself instead of simply borrowing them from others? One indication of having thought your beliefs through is being able to explain why you believe in them, giving the reasons that led you to your conclusions.

Still, not all reasons and evidence are equally strong or accurate. For example, in Europe before the fifteenth century, the common belief that the earth was flat was supported by the following reasons and evidence:

> *People of Authority:* Many educational and religious authorities taught that the earth was flat.

> *Recorded References:* The written opinions of scientific experts supported belief in a flat earth.

> *Observed Evidence:* No person had ever circumnavigated the earth.

> *Personal Experience:* From a normal vantage point, the earth *looks* flat.

THINKING-
WRITING
ACTIVITY

Evaluating Beliefs

For each of the five beliefs you expressed at the beginning of this section, explain how you arrived at it and state the reasons and evidence that you believe support it.

1. *Example:* Is the earth flat?

    Belief: No, it is round.

    Reasons/Evidence:

    a. People of Authority: My parents and teachers taught me this.

    b. Recorded References: What references support your beliefs? I read about the earth in science textbooks and saw films and videos.

    c. Observed Evidence: I have seen a sequence of photographs taken from outer space that show the earth as a globe.

    d. Personal Experience: When I flew across the country, I could see the horizon line changing.

2. Is the soul immortal?

3. Should marijuana be legalized?

4. Should music lyrics and videos be censored?

5. Should we follow "the golden rule" in our relationships with others?

(*Continued*)

To evaluate the strengths and accuracy of the reasons and evidence you identified for holding your beliefs on the five issues, address questions such as the following:

People of Authority: Are the authorities knowledgeable in this area? Are they reliable? Have they ever given inaccurate information? Do other authorities disagree with them?

Recorded References: What references support your belief? What are the credentials of the authors? Do other authors disagree with their opinions? On what reasons and evidence do the authors base their opinions?

Observed Evidence: What is the source and foundation of the evidence? Can the evidence be interpreted differently? Does the evidence support the conclusion?

Personal Experience: What were the circumstances under which the experiences took place? Were distortions or mistakes in perception possible? Have other people had either similar or conflicting experiences? Are there other explanations for your experiences?

As a college writer, you are going to apply these questions to material you encounter while gathering information for essays, projects, or reports. The opposite of thinking for yourself is simply accepting the thinking of others without examining or questioning it. Learning to become an independent thinker is a complex, ongoing process.

Viewing a Situation from Different Perspectives

Critical thinkers listen to other views and new ideas and examine them carefully. No one person has *all* the answers! Your beliefs represent just one perspective on whatever problem you want to solve or situation you are trying to understand. In addition to your own particular viewpoint, there may be others, equally important, that you need to consider if you are to develop a more complete understanding of the problem or situation. Learning to think critically and write thoughtfully, in fact, requires this.

Audience and Perspective   Effective writing depends on always having a clear sense of your readers, the audience for whom you are writing. The ability to remain focused on that audience includes being able to see things from their point of view, to think empathetically within their frame of reference, and to understand their perspective. Perspective taking is essential to becoming a thoughtful writer. To begin with, exploring topics from a variety of vantage points is often the best way to present a comprehensive analysis of the subject you are writing about. When you are tied to only one perspective, your writing tends to be one-sided and superficial. In order to produce your most accomplished writing, you need to be open to the informed comments and suggestions of others and flexible enough to use that feedback to refine your writing.

For most of the issues and problems you will explore and write about in college, one viewpoint is simply not adequate to provide a full and satisfactory understanding. To increase and deepen your knowledge, you must seek other perspectives. In academic and professional writing, you will be expected to seek actively (and *listen to*) other people's viewpoints. It is often very difficult to see things from points of view other than your own; if you are not careful, you can make the serious mistake of assuming that the way you see things is the way they really are.

In order to identify with perspectives other than your own, then, you also have to work to grasp the reasons for these alternate viewpoints. This approach, which stimulates you to evaluate your beliefs critically, is enhanced by writing. Writing about beliefs encourages people to explain their reasons for holding them and provides a vehicle for sharing their thinking with those who have contrasting points of view.

THINKING-
WRITING
ACTIVITY

Two Sides of a Belief

Describe in detail a belief about which you feel very strongly. Then explain the reasons or experiences that led you to this belief. Next, describe a point of view that differs from your belief. Identify some of the reasons someone would have that point of view.

Purpose and Perspective   Being open to new ideas and different viewpoints means being *flexible* enough to change or modify one's own ideas in the light of new information or better insight. People do have a tendency to cling to the beliefs they were brought up with and the conclusions they have arrived at. If you are going to continue to grow and develop as a thinker, however, you have to be willing to change or modify your beliefs when evidence suggests that you should.

In contrast to open and flexible thinking, *un*critical thinking tends to be one-sided and close-minded. People who think uncritically are convinced that they alone see things as they really are and that everyone who disagrees with them is wrong. It is very difficult for them to step outside their own viewpoints and look at issues from other people's perspectives. Words often used to describe this type of person include *dogmatic, subjective,* and *egocentric.*

Supporting Diverse Perspectives with Reasons and Evidence

When you are thinking critically, you can offer sound reasons for your views. As a thoughtful writer, you cannot simply take a position on an issue or make a claim; you have to back up your views, reinforce them with information that you feel supports your position. There is an important distinction between *what* you believe and *why* you believe it.

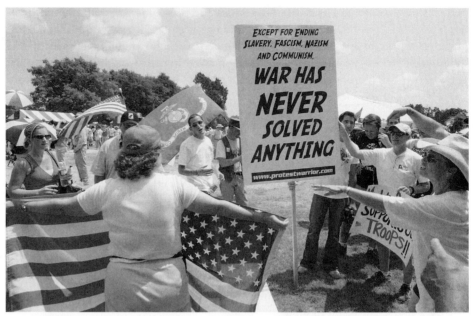

As critical thinkers and thoughtful writers we have an obligation to appreciate diverse perspectives on complex issues and develop informed opinions that are supported by compelling reasons.

If you want to know all sides of an issue, you have to be able to give supporting reasons and evidence not just for your own views but also for the views of others.

Consider the issue of whether side air bags should be standard equipment for cars. As you try to make sense of this issue, you should attempt to identify not just the reasons for your view but also the reasons for other views. Following are reasons that support each view of this issue.

Issues

Side air bags should be standard equipment.	Side air bags should not be standard equipment.

Supporting Reasons

1. Studies show that side air bags save lives in accidents.

2. Studies show that side air bags reduce injury in accidents.

Supporting Reasons

1. Side air bags sometimes injure and even kill children and small adults.

2. Side air bags should not be forced on citizens of a free country.

Now see if you can identify additional supporting reasons for each position on making air bags standard equipment. For each of the following issues, identify reasons that support each side.

Issues

1. Multiple-choice and true/false exams should be given in college-level courses.
2. It is better to live in a society in which the government plays a major role in citizens' lives.
3. The best way to deal with crime is to impose long prison sentences.
4. When a couple divorce, the children should choose the parent with whom they wish to live.

1. Multiple-choice and true/false exams should *not* be given in college-level courses.
2. It is better to live in a society that minimizes the role of the government in citizens' lives.
3. Long prison sentences will not reduce crime.
4. When a couple divorce, the court should decide all custody issues regarding the children.

THINKING-
WRITING
ACTIVITY

Viewing Different Perspectives

Seeing different perspectives is crucial to getting a more complete understanding of ideas expressed in passages you read. Read the two passages that follow. Then, for each passage, do these four things:

1. Identify the main idea of each passage.
2. List the reasons that support the main idea.
3. Develop another view of the main issue.
4. List the reasons that support the other view.

If we want auto safety but continue to believe in auto profits, sales, styling, and annual obsolescence, there will be no serious accomplishments. The moment we put safety ahead of these other values, something will happen. If we want better municipal hospitals but are unwilling to disturb the level of spending for defense, for highways, or for household appliances, hospital service will not improve. If we want peace but still believe that countries with differing ideologies are threats to one another, we will not get peace. What is confusing is that up to now, while we have wanted such things as conservation, auto safety, hospital care, and peace, we have tried wanting them without changing consciousness, that is, while continuing to accept those underlying values that stand in the way of what we want. The machine can be controlled at the "consumer" level only by people who change their whole value system,

(Continued)

their whole worldview, their whole way of life. One cannot favor saving our wildlife and wear a fur coat.

Most wicked deeds are done because the doer proposes some good to himself. The liar lies to gain some end; the swindler and thief want things which, if honestly got, might be good in themselves. Even the murderer may be removing an impediment to normal desires or gaining possession of something his victim keeps from him. None of these people usually does evil for evil's sake. They are selfish or unscrupulous, but their deeds are not gratuitously evil. The killer for sport has no such comprehensible motive. He prefers death to life, darkness to light. He gets nothing except the satisfaction of saying, "Something which wanted to live is dead. There is that much less vitality, consciousness, and, perhaps, joy in the universe. I am the Spirit that Denies." When a human wantonly destroys one of humankind's own works, we call him Vandal. When he wantonly destroys one of the works of God, we call him Sportsman.

Developing Informed Beliefs

The process of developing informed beliefs is ongoing and lifelong. It is also a process that is essential for you to achieve success and happiness since your beliefs constitute the "map" you use to guide your choices. If your belief map is accurate, your choices will reflect a clear understanding of the world. However, if your belief map is inaccurate or incomplete, you are in jeopardy of making ineffective or wrongheaded choices.

Developing informed beliefs involves the core qualities of a critical thinker and thoughtful writer to which we have been referring: *curious, open-minded, knowledgeable, creative*. The themes of this chapter complement these qualities:

- *Thinking actively* provides the impetus for asking questions, keeping an open mind, seeking knowledge, and being inventive.
- *Thinking independently* is achieved by being curious, going beyond familiar points of view, engaging in research to develop one's own informed opinions, and transcending conventional norms to achieve creative insights.
- *Viewing situations from different perspectives* is the essence of questioning narrow points of view in order to become truly open-minded. Perspective taking is also the vehicle one uses to develop genuine knowledge and achieve creative insights.
- *Supporting diverse perspectives with reasons and evidence* is the outgrowth of questioning, open-minded explorations, and utilizing one's knowledge.

Creating a Belief Map

Just as maps help you to navigate your way through unfamiliar territory, belief mapping is a creative strategy for visualizing a path through new and challenging ideas. You can use belief mapping to help you better understand the origins of your own beliefs and positions as well as to plan ways to become a more active and independent thinker. In Chapter 4, we will explore how to use mapping and other visual strategies to help plan writing assignments.

To create a belief map, return to the topics in the Thinking-Writing Activity on page 53 and follow these guidelines:

- Select a topic (either an activity or a person) that has had a *passive* influence on your thinking. This is the starting point of your journey.

- Next, select a topic (again, an activity or a person) that has had an *active* influence on your thinking. This is the route you will travel.

- Finally, select a personal, academic, or career goal. This is your destination.

- Using any visual or artistic medium that appeals to you (such as a simple pencil sketch, a collage, or graphic-arts software), create a map that shows how the active influences on your thinking will help you navigate from your starting point to your goal. What kinds of obstacles might you expect along the way? How would you visually represent those obstacles? How would you describe them to someone on a similar journey?

Experiences That Affected Beliefs

In the following narratives, three writers reflect on learning experiences that caused them to evaluate and in some cases revise beliefs about themselves, the world in which they live, other people, and ways to live their lives.

As you read the selections, keep in mind one set of critical reading questions that we identified in Chapter 2.

- Who is the *writer*, and what perspective does he or she bring to the writing selection?
- What is the *subject* of the selection, and how would you evaluate its cogency and reliability?
- Who is the intended *audience*, and what assumptions is the writer making about it?
- What is the *purpose* of the selection, and how is the author trying to achieve it?

Following each selection are questions designed to stimulate and guide your critical thinking, active reading, and thoughtful writing.

FROM *An American Childhood*
BY ANNIE DILLARD (b. 1945)

Annie Dillard's engagement with nature and its reflection of the spiritual life informs her extensive creative and nonfiction writing. A poet, novelist, and essayist, Dillard won the Pulitzer Prize for her memoir *Pilgrim at Tinker Creek* (1974). Her close observations of the environment and her ongoing spiritual quests combine in her views on writing, as in this passage from "Write Till You Drop": "The sensation of writing a book is the sensation of spinning, blinded by love and daring. It is the sensation of a stunt pilot's turning barrel rolls, or an inchworm's blind rearing from a stem in search of a route. At its worst, it feels like alligator wrestling, at the level of the sentence." In the following memoir, she describes how her parents encouraged her early explorations of the natural world.

After I read *The Field Book of Ponds and Streams* several times, I longed for a microscope. Everybody needed a microscope. Detectives used microscopes, both for the FBI and at Scotland Yard. Although usually I had to save my tiny allowance for things I wanted, that year for Christmas my parents gave me a microscope kit.

In a dark basement corner, on a white enamel table, I set up the microscope kit. I supplied a chair, a lamp, a batch of jars, a candle, and a pile of library books. The microscope kit supplied a blunt black three-speed microscope, a booklet, a scalpel, a dropper, an ingenious device for cutting thin segments of fragile tissue, a pile of clean slides and cover slips, and a dandy array of corked test tubes.

One of the test tubes contained "hay infusion." Hay infusion was a wee brown chip of grass blade. You added water to it, and after a week it became a jungle in a drop, full of one-celled animals. This did not work for me. All I saw in the microscope after a week was a wet chip of dried grass, much enlarged.

Another test tube contained "diatomaceous earth." This was, I believed, an actual pinch of the white cliffs of Dover. On my palm it was an airy, friable chalk. The booklet said it was composed of the silicaceous bodies of diatoms—one-celled creatures that lived in, as it were, small glass jewelry boxes with fitted lids. Diatoms, I read, come in a variety of transparent geometrical shapes. Broken and dead and dug out of geological deposits, they made chalk, and a fine abrasive used in silver polish and toothpaste. What I saw in the microscope must have been the fine abrasive—grit enlarged. It was years before I saw a recognizable, whole diatom. The kit's diatomaceous earth was a bust.

5   All that winter I played with the microscope. I prepared slides from things at hand, as the books suggested. I looked at the transparent membrane inside an onion's skin and saw the cells. I looked at a section of cork and saw the cells, and at scrapings from the inside of my cheek, ditto. I looked at my blood and saw not much; I looked at my urine and saw long iridescent crystals, for the drop had dried.

All this was very well, but I wanted to see the wildlife I had read about. I wanted especially to see the famous amoeba, who had eluded me. He was supposed to live in the hay infusion, but I hadn't found him there. He lived outside in warm ponds and streams, too, but I lived in Pittsburgh, and it had been a cold winter.

Finally late that spring I saw an amoeba. The week before, I had gathered puddle water from Frick Park, it had been festering in a jar in the basement. This June night after dinner I figured I had waited long enough. In the basement at my microscope table I spread a scummy drop of Frick Park puddle water on a slide, peeked in, and lo, there was the famous amoeba. He was as blobby and grainy as his picture; I would have known him anywhere.

Before I had watched him at all, I ran upstairs. My parents were still at table, drinking coffee. They, too, could see the famous amoeba. I told them, bursting, that he was all set up, that they should hurry before his water dried. It was the chance of a lifetime.

Father had stretched out his long legs and was tilting back in his chair. Mother sat with her knees crossed, in blue slacks, smoking a Chesterfield. The dessert dishes were still on the table. My sisters were nowhere in evidence. It was a warm evening; the big dining-room windows gave onto blooming rhododendrons.

10

Mother regarded me warmly. She gave me to understand that she was glad I had found what I had been looking for, but that she and Father were happy to sit with their coffee, and would not be coming down.

She did not say, but I understood at once, that they had their pursuits (coffee?) and I had mine. She did not say, but I began to understand then, that you do what you do out of your private passion for the thing itself.

I had essentially been handed my own life. In subsequent years my parents would praise my drawings and poems, and supply me with books, art supplies, and sports equipment, and listen to my troubles and enthusiasms, and supervise my hours, and discuss and inform, but they would not get involved with my detective work, nor hear about my reading, nor inquire about my homework or term papers or exams, nor visit the salamanders I caught, nor listen to me play the piano, nor attend my field hockey games, nor fuss over my insect collection with me, or my poetry collection or stamp collection or rock collection. My days and nights were my own to plan and fill.

When I left the dining room that evening and started down the dark basement stairs, I had a life, I sat with my wonderful amoeba, and there he was, rolling his grains more slowly now, extending an arc of his edge for a foot and drawing himself along by that foot, and absorbing it again and rolling on. I gave him some more pond water.

I had hit pay dirt. For all I knew, there were paramecia, too, in that pond water, or daphniae, or stentors, or any of the many other creatures I had read about and never seen: volvox, the spherical algal colony; euglena with its one red eye; the elusive glassy diatom; hydra, rotifers, water bears, worms. Anything was possible. The sky was the limit.

QUESTIONS FOR ACTIVE READING

1. Examine the structure of Dillard's essay. How much time passes over the course of the essay, and how can you tell? When does she "pause" in her narrative, and why?

2. Compare the vocabulary of the final paragraph with the rest of the essay. Why do you think Dillard concludes her essay with this kind of language?

3. In paragraph 11, Dillard asks a rhetorical question (a question that a writer does not answer, but leaves to the reader). Although it's just one word, what is the full meaning of that question? How would you, as a reader, answer it, based on what you know of Dillard's parents? based on your own parents, or your own experience as a parent?

QUESTIONS FOR THINKING CRITICALLY

1. When Annie Dillard rushed to share her discovery of the amoeba with her parents, they politely declined. What reaction had she expected, and what did this reveal about her beliefs regarding her relationship with her parents?

2. Her parents' lack of interest in this and other passions in her life led her to a conclusion: "I had essentially been handed my own life." Explain why you think she reached this conclusion.

3. Based on your own experience, do you believe that the best way to achieve "your own life" is through your parents' lack of involvement in your life?

4. The author states that "you do what you do out of your private passion for the thing itself." This "private passion" is a kind of curiosity, a key characteristic of a critical thinker. Describe a "private passion" of your own that you pursue not to please others but because of your personal curiosity and enthusiasm.

"Reversing Established Orders"

BY STEPHEN JAY GOULD (1941–2002)
FROM *Leonardo's Mountain of Clams and the Diet of Worms: Essays on Natural History*

Stephen Jay Gould started his academic career as a professor of geology at Harvard University but expanded his interests into evolutionary biology. He was curator of invertebrate paleontology at Harvard's Museum of Comparative Zoology and a writer with a gift for translating complex scientific theories into informed, but witty, prose that nonscientists can understand and enjoy. His essays appeared in magazines such as *Natural History* and *Discover* and were collected in the books *Ever Since Darwin*, *The Panda's Thumb*, *The Flamingo's Simile*, and *Leonardo's Mountain of Clams and the Diet of Worms*, in which the following essay appears. This essay illustrates the ongoing process by which natural scientists use inferences to discover factual information and to construct theories explaining that information.

We all know how the world works. A fisherman asks his boss in Shakespeare's *Pericles*: "Master, I marvel how the fishes live in the sea," and receives the evident response, "Why, as men do a-land; the great ones eat up the little ones." Consequently, when humorists invent topsy-turvy worlds, they reverse such established orders and then emphasize the rightness of their absurdity. Alice's Wonderland works on the principle of "sentence first—verdict afterwards." In Gilbert and Sullivan's town of Titipu, the tailor Ko-ko, condemned to death by decapitation, is elevated instead to the rank of Lord High Executioner because—it is so obvious; after all—a man "cannot cut off another's head until he's cut his own off." Pish-tush explains all this in a spirited song with a rousing chorus: "And I am right, and you are right, and all is right too-loora-lay."

Social and literary critics of the so-called postmodernist movement have emphasized, in a cogent and important argument often buried in the impenetrable jargon of their discourse, that conventional support for established orders usually relies upon claims for the naturalness of "dualisms" and "hierarchies." In creating dualisms, we divide a subject into two contrasting categories; in imposing hierarchy upon these dualisms, we judge one category as superior, the other as inferior. We all know the dualistic hierarchies of our social and political lives—from righteous versus infidel of centuries past to the millionaire CEOs who deserve tax cuts versus single mothers who should lose their food stamps in our astoundingly mean-spirited present. The postmodernists correctly argue that such dualisms and hierarchies represent our own constructions for political utility (often nefarious), rather than nature's factual and inevitable dictate. We may choose to parse the world in many other ways with radically different implications.

Our categorizations of nature also tend to favor dualistic hierarchies based upon domination. We often divide the world ecologically into predators and prey, or anatomically into complicated and dominant "higher" animals versus simpler and subservient "lower" forms. I do not deny the utility of such parsings in making predictions that usually work—big fish do generally eat little fish, and not vice versa. But the postmodernist critique should lead us to healthy skepticism, as we scrutinize the complex and socially embedded reasons behind the original formulations of our favored categories. Dualism with dominance may primarily record a human imposition upon nature, rather than a lecture directed to us by the birds and bees.

Natural historians tend to avoid tendentious preaching in this philosophical mode (though I often fall victim to such temptations in these essays). Our favored style of doubting is empirical: if I wish to question your proposed generality, I will search for a counterexample in flesh and blood. Such counterexamples exist in abundance, for they form a staple in a standard genre of writing in natural history—the "wonderment of oddity" or "strange ways of the beaver" tradition. (Sorry to be so disparaging—my own ignoble dualism, I suppose. The stories are terrific. I just often yearn for more intellectual generality and less florid writing.)

5   Much of our fascination with "strange cases" lies in their abrogation of accepted dualisms based on dominance—the "reversing established orders" of my title. As an obvious example, and paragon of this literature, carnivorous plants have always elicited primal intrigue—and the bigger and more taxonomically "advanced" the prey, the more we feel the weirdness. We yawn when a Venus's flytrap ensnares a mosquito, but shiver with substantial discomfort when a large pitcher plant devours a bird or rodent.

I keep a file marked "Reversals" to house such cases. I have long been on the lookout for optimal examples, where all three of the most prominent dualisms based on dominance suffer reversal: predator and prey, high and low, large and small—in other words, where a creature from a category usually ranked as small in body, primitive in design, and subject to predation eats another animal from a category generally viewed as bigger, anatomically superior, and rapacious. I now have four intriguing examples, more than enough for an essay. Since we postmodernists abjure hierarchical ranking, I will simply present my stories in the nonjudgmental chronological order of their publication (though postmodernism in this sense—and truly I am not a devotee of this movement—may be a cop-out and an excuse, for not devising a better logical structure for this essay!)

· · · · ·

1. Frogs and flies. Frogs eat flies. If flies eat frogs, then we might as well be headed for bedlam or the apocalypse. My colleague Tom Eisner of Cornell University is revered throughout our profession as the past master of natural oddities with important and practical general messages. One day in August 1982, at a small pond in Arizona, Eisner and several colleagues noted thousands of spadefoot toads congregating on the muddy shore as they emerged to adulthood in near synchrony from their tadpole stage. Eisner and colleagues described their discovery in a technical publication:

> Space only centimeters apart in places, they were all of minimal adult size (body length, 1.5 to 2 cm [less than an inch]). Conspicuous among them were toads that were dead or dying, apparently having been seized by a predator in the mud and drawn partly into the substrate, until only their head, or head and trunk, projected above ground. We counted dozens of such semisubmerged toads.

They then dug deeper and to their great surprise, found the predator "a large grublike insect larva, subsequently identified as that of the horsefly *Tabanus punctifer*." In other words, flies can eat toads! (Although astonishment may be lessened in noting that the tiny toads are much smaller than enormous fly larvae.) Unusually large insects and maximally small vertebrates have also been featured in the few other recorded cases of such reversals—frogs, small birds, even a mouse, consumed by praying mantids, for example.

The fly larvae force themselves into the mud, rear end first, until their front end, bearing the mouthparts, lies flush with the surface. The larvae then catch toads by hooking their pointed mandibles into the hind legs or belly, and then dragging the toad partway into the mud. The larvae—please remember that many tales in natural history are not pleasant by human standards—then suck the toad dry (and dead) by ingesting blood and body fluids only.

I loved the wry last sentence of the paper by Eisner and his colleagues—unusual in style for a technical article, but odd stories have always permitted some literary license:

> The case we report is a reversal of the usual toad-eats-fly paradigm, although . . . the paradigm may also prevail in its conventional form. Adult *Scaphiopus* [the spadefoot

toad] might well on occasions have predatory access to the very *Tabanus* flies that as larvae preyed upon their conspecifics.

J. Greenberg, reporting for *Science News* (November 5, 1983), began his commentary with the emotional impact of such reversals:

> This is the Okeechobee Fla. Little League team thrashing the New York Yankees; this is Wally Cox beating out Burt Reynolds for the girl; this is Grenada invading the United States. "This is unlike anything I've ever seen," says Thomas Eisner.

· · · · ·

2. LOBSTERS AND SNAILS. Decapod crustaceans (lobsters, crabs, shrimp) eat snails, as all naturalists know. In fact, the classic case of an extended evolutionary "arms race," elegantly documented over many years by my colleague Geerat Vermeij, involves increased strength of crab claws correlated with ever more efficient protective devices (spines, ribs, thicker and wavier shells) in snails over geological time. Land crabs are the overwhelmingly predominant predator of my own favorite subject for research, the Caribbean land snail *Cerion*. If snails eat decapods, we might as well retire.

Amos Barkai and Christopher McQuaid studied rock lobsters and whelks (snails of middling size) in waters around two islands, Marcus and Malgas, located just four miles apart in the Saldanha Bay area of South Africa. On Malgas, as all God-fearing folk would only rightly suspect, rock lobsters eat mollusks, mostly mussels and several species of whelks. Barkai and McQuaid write in their 1988 account: "The rock lobsters usually attacked the whelks by chipping away the shell margin with their mouth parts."

The local lobstermen report that, twenty years ago, rock lobsters were equally common on both islands. But lobsters then disappeared from Marcus Island, for unclear reasons, perhaps linked to a period of low oxygen in surrounding waters during the 1970s. In the absence of lobsters as the usual top predator, extensive mussel beds have become established, and the population density of whelks has soared. Barkai and McQuaid asked themselves: "Why do rock lobsters not recolonize Marcus Island despite the high availability of food?"

In an attempt to answer their own question, they performed the obvious experiment—and made an astonishing discovery. The food has become the feeder—this time by overwhelming in number, not equaling in size (the whelks are much smaller than the lobsters). The conventional passive voice of scientific prose does not convey excitement well, but a good story easily transcends such a minor limitation. So, in Barkai and McQuaid's own words; and without any need for further commentary from me (I would only be tempted to make some arch and utterly inappropriate statement about slave revolts—Spartacus and all that):

> One thousand rock lobsters from Malgas Island were tagged and transferred to Marcus Island . . . The result was immediate. The apparently healthy rock lobsters were quickly overwhelmed by large numbers of whelks. Several hundreds were observed being attacked immediately after release and a week later no live rock lobsters could be found at Marcus Island . . . The rock lobsters escaped temporarily by swimming, but each contact with the substratum resulted in several more whelks attaching themselves until

weight of numbers prevented escape. On average each rock lobster was killed within fifteen minutes by more than three hundred *Burnupena* [whelks] that removed all the flesh in less than an hour.

Sic semper tyrannis.

· · · · ·

3. FISH AND DINOFLAGELLATES. Fish don't generally eat dinoflagellates; why should they even deign to notice such microscopic algae, floating in the plankton? But dinoflagellates certainly don't eat fish; the very notion, given the disparity in sizes, is ludicrous to the point of incomprehensibility.

Dinoflagellates do, however, *kill* fish, by indirect mechanisms long known and well studied for their immense practical significance. Under favorable conditions, dinoflagellate populations can soar to 60 million organisms per liter of water. These so-called blooms can discolor and poison the waters—"red tide" is the most familiar example—leading to massive deaths of fish and other marine organisms.

J. M. Burkholder and a group of her colleagues from North Carolina State University have studied toxic blooms associated with fish kills in estuaries of the southeastern United States. The largest event resulted in the death of nearly one million Atlantic menhaden in the estuary of the Pamlico River. The oddity of this case lies not in the killing of fish per se, a common consequence of dinoflagellate blooms. We have always regarded the deaths of fishes and other marine organisms during red tides as passive and "unintended" results of dinoflagellate toxins, or other consequences of massive algal populations during blooms. No one had supposed that dinoflagellates might actively kill fish as an evolved response for their own explicit advantage, including a potential nutritional benefit for the algal cells. And yet the dinoflagellates do seem to be killing and eating fishes in a manner suggesting active evolution for this most peculiar reversal.

The dinoflagellate lives in a dormant state, lying on the sea floor within a protective cyst. When live fish approach, the cyst breaks and releases a mobile cell that swims, grows, and secretes a powerful, water-soluble neurotoxin, killing the fish. So far, so what?—though the presence of fish does seem to induce activity by the dinoflagellate (breaking of the cyst), thus suggesting a direct link. Anatomical and behavioral evidence both suggest that dinoflagellates have actively evolved their strategy for feeding on fishes. The swimming cell, breaking out from the cyst, grows a projection, called a peduncle, from its lower surface. The cells seem to move actively toward dead or dying fishes. Flecks of tissue, sloughed off from the fish, then become attached to the peduncle and get digested. The authors describe this reversal at maximum disparity in size among my four cases:

> The lethal agent is an excreted neurotoxin. [It] induces neurotoxic signs by fish including sudden sporadic movement, disorientation, lethargy and apparent suffocation followed by death. The alga has not been observed to attack fish directly. It rapidly increases its swimming velocity to reach flecks of sloughed tissue from dying fish, however, using its peduncle to attach to and digest the tissue debris.

· · · · ·

20   4. SPONGES AND ARTHROPODS. Among invertebrates, sponges rank as the lowest of the low (the bottom rung of any evolutionary ladder), while arthropods stand highest of the high (just a little lower than the angels, that is, just before vertebrates on a linear list of rising complexity). Sponges have no discrete organs; they feed by filtering out tiny items of food from water pumped through channels in their body. Arthropods grow eyes, limbs, brains, and digestive systems; many live as active carnivores. Most arthropods wouldn't take much notice of a lowly sponge, but we can scarcely imagine how or why a sponge might subdue and ingest an arthropod.

     However, in a 1995 article, crisply titled "Carnivorous Sponges," J. Vacelet and N. Boury-Esnault of the Centre d'Oceanologie of Marseille have found a killer sponge (about as bizarre as a fish-eating dinoflagellate—but both exist). Relatives of this sponge, members of the genus *Asbestopluma*, have only been known from very deep waters (including the all-time record for sponges at more than 25,000 feet), where behavior and food preferences could not be observed. But Vacelet and Boury-Esnault found a new species in a shallow-water Mediterranean cave (less than one hundred feet), where scuba divers can watch directly.

     The deep sea is a nutritional desert, and many organisms from such habitats develop special adaptations for procuring large and rare items (while relatives from shallow waters may pursue a plethora of smaller prey). *Asbestopluma* has lost both filtering channels through the body and the specialized cells (called choanocytes) that pump the water through. So how does this deep-water sponge feed?

     The new species grows long filaments that extend out from the upper end of the body. A blanket of tiny spicules, or small skeletal projections, covers the surface of the filaments. The authors comment: "The spicule cover . . . gives the filaments a 'Velcro'-like adhesiveness"—the key to this feeding reversal at maximal anatomical distance for invertebrates. The sponge captures small crustaceans on the filaments—and they can't escape any more than a fuzz ball can detach itself from the Velcro lining of your coat pocket. The authors continue: "New, thin filaments grew over the prey, which was completely enveloped after one day and digested within a few days." The sponge, in other words, has become a carnivore.

     Four fascinating stories to give us pause about our preconceptions, particularly our dualistic taxonomies based on the domination of one category over another. The little guys sometimes turn tables and prevail—often enough, perhaps, to call the categories themselves into question.

25   I see another message in these reversals—a consequence of the reassessment that must always proceed when established orders crumble, or merely lose their claim to invariance. In our struggle to understand the history of life, we must learn where to place the boundary between contingent and unpredictable events that occur but once and the more repeatable, lawlike phenomena that may pervade life's history as generalities. (In my own view of life, the domain of contingency looms vastly larger than all Western tradition, and most psychological hope, would allow. Fortuity pervades the origin of any particular species or lineage. *Homo sapiens* is a contingent twig, not a predictable result of ineluctably rising complexity during evolution. . . .)

The domain of lawlike generality includes broad phenomena not specific to the history of particular lineages. The ecological structure of communities should provide a promising searching ground, for some principles of structural organization must transcend the particular organisms that happen to occupy a given role at any moment. I imagine, for example, that all balanced ecosystems must sustain more biomass as prey than as predators—and I would accept such statements as predictable generalities, despite my affection for contingency. I would also have been willing to embrace the invariance of other rules for sensible repetition—that single-celled creatures don't kill and eat large multicellular organisms, for example. But these four cases of reversed order give me pause.

In a famous passage from the *Origin of Species*, Charles Darwin extolled the invariance of certain ecological patterns by using observed repetition in independent colonizations to argue against a range of contingently unpredictable outcomes:

> When we look at the plants and bushes clothing an entangled bank, we are tempted to attribute their proportional numbers and kinds to what we call chance. But how false a view is this! Every one has heard that when an American forest is cut down, a very different vegetation springs up; but it has been observed that the trees now growing on the ancient Indian mounds, in the Southern United States, display the same beautiful diversity and proportion of kinds as in the surrounding virgin forests. What a struggle between the several kinds of trees must here have gone on during long centuries, each annually scattering its seeds by the thousand; what war between insect and insect—between insects, snails, and other animals with birds and beasts of prey—all striving to increase, and all feeding on each other or on the trees or their seeds and seedlings, or on the other plants which first clothed the ground and thus checked the growth of the trees! Throw up a handful of feathers, and all must fall to the ground according to definite laws; but how simple is this problem compared to the action and reaction of the innumerable plants and animals which have determined, in the course of centuries, the proportional numbers and kinds of trees now growing on the old Indian ruins!

But the same patterns do not always recur from adjacent starting points colonized by the same set of species. Even the most apparently predictable patterns of supposedly established orders may fail. Remove the lobsters from waters around one South African island, and a new equilibrium may quickly emerge—one that actively excludes lobsters by converting their former prey into a ganging posse of predators!

Thus, I sense a challenge in these four cases, a message perhaps deeper than the raw peculiarity of their phenomenology—and the resulting attack upon our dualistic and hierarchical categories. We do not yet know the rules of composition for ecosystems. We do not even know if rules exist in the usual sense. I am tempted, therefore, to close with the famous words that D'Arcy Thompson wrote to signify our ignorance of the microscopic world (*Growth and Form*, 1942 edition). We are not quite so uninformed about the rules of composition for ecosystems, but what a stark challenge and what an inspiration to go forth: "We have come to the edge of a world of which we have no experience, and where all our preconceptions must be recast."

QUESTIONS FOR ACTIVE READING

1. In your own words, define the concept of *dualism with dominance* (paragraph 3). What is Gould's opinion of this concept and the ways in which it has been used to explain the natural world?

2. How would you describe the audience Gould had in mind as he wrote this essay? Point out example of Gould's language choices, allusions to scientific or cultural concepts, and other places in the essay where you think Gould is specifically appealing to this audience. Which parts of the essay do you find most accessible and appealing, and why? Which parts are most challenging for you?

3. How is Gould's argument structured? What does Gould himself think about this method for structuring his argument?

QUESTIONS FOR THINKING CRITICALLY

1. How could you use what Gould calls "counterexamples" in biology (paragraph 4) to better develop your own perspectives and beliefs about a wide variety of issues?

2. In paragraph 15, Gould notes that "The conventional passive voice of scientific prose does not convey excitement well, but a good story easily transcends such a minor limitation." Compare Gould's sense of excitement and curiosity with Annie Dillard's recollection of her first sighting of an amoeba (p. 63). What qualities of critical thinking and thoughtful writing do these two authors share?

3. What is the "message" that Gould sees in these reversals of seemingly established orders? In an essay, define that message in your own words and describe how it either challenges or upholds your own beliefs.

❋ "The Case Against Chores"

BY JANE SMILEY (b. 1949)

Novelist and literature professor Jane Smiley has explored everything from the history of Greenland to thoroughbred horse racing in her fiction. A native of California, Smiley lived and taught for many years in Iowa. The influence of that state's proud rural culture is deeply felt in her novel *A Thousand Acres,* which won the Pulitzer Prize in 1991. Using the great Shakespearean tragedy *King Lear* as her inspiration, Smiley captured the vast sense of loss and despair felt by many Midwestern farm families during the rural economic crisis of the 1980s. Smiley's essays and book reviews have appeared in a range of periodicals. "The Case Against Chores" was originally published in *Harper's Magazine* in 1995.

I've lived in the upper Midwest for twenty-one years now, and I'm here to tell you that the pressure to put your children to work is unrelenting. So far I've squirmed out from under it, and my daughters have led a life of almost tropical idleness, much to their benefit. My son, however, may not be so lucky. His father was himself raised in Iowa and put to work at an early age, and you never know when, in spite of all my husband's best intentions, that early training might kick in.

Although "chores" are so sacred in my neck of the woods that almost no one ever discusses their purpose, I have over the years gleaned some of the reasons parents give for assigning them. I'm not impressed. Mostly the reasons have to do with developing good work habits or, in the absence of good work habits; at least habits of working. No such thing; as a free lunch any job worth doing is worth doing right, work before play, all of that. According to this reasoning, the world is full of jobs that no one wants to do. If we divide them up and get them over with, then we can go on to pastimes we like. If we do them "right," then we won't have to do them again. Lots of times, though, in a family, that *we* doesn't operate. The operative word is *you*. The practical result of almost every child-labor scheme that I've witnessed is the child doing the dirty work and the parent getting the fun: Mom cooks and Sis does the dishes; the parents plan and plant the garden, the kids weed it. To me, what this teaches the child is the lesson of alienated labor: not to love the work but to get it over with; not to feel pride in one's contribution but to feel resentment at the waste of one's time.

Another goal of chores: the child contributes to the work of maintaining the family. According to this rationale, the child comes to understand what it takes to have a family, and to feel that he or she is an important, even indispensable member of it. But come on. Would you really want to feel loved primarily because you're the one who gets the floors mopped? Wouldn't you rather feel that your family's love simply exists all around you, no matter what your contribution? And don't the parents love their children anyway, whether the children vacuum or not? Why lie about it just to get the housework done? Let's be frank about the other half of the equation too. In this day and age, it doesn't take much work at all to manage a household, at least in the middle class—maybe four hours a week to clean the house and another four to throw the laundry into the washing machine, move it to the dryer, and fold it. Is it really a good idea to set the sort of example my former neighbors used to set, of mopping the floor every two days, cleaning the toilets every week, vacuuming every day, dusting, dusting, dusting? Didn't they have anything better to do than serve their house?

Let me confess that I wasn't expected to lift a finger when I was growing up. Even when my mother had a full-time job, she cleaned up after me, as did my grandmother. Later there was a housekeeper. I would leave my room in a mess when I headed off for school and find it miraculously neat when I returned. Once in a while I vacuumed, just because I liked the pattern the Hoover made on the carpet. I did learn to run water in my cereal bowl before setting it in the sink.

5   Where I discovered work was at the stable, and, in fact, there is no housework like horsework. You've got to clean the horses' stalls, feed them, groom them, tack them up, wrap their legs, exercise them, turn them out, and catch them. You've got to clip them and shave them. You have to sweep the aisle, clean your tack and your boots, carry bales of hay and buckets of water. Minimal horsekeeping, rising just to the level of humaneness, requires many more hours than making a few beds, and horsework turned out to be a good preparation for the real work of adulthood, which is rearing children. It was a good

preparation not only because it was similar in many ways but also because my desire to do it, and to do a good job of it, grew out of my love of and interest in my horse. I can't say that cleaning out her bucket when she manured in it was an actual joy, but I knew she wasn't going to do it herself. I saw the purpose of my labor, and I wasn't alienated from it.

Probably to the surprise of some of those who knew me as a child, I have turned out to be gainfully employed. I remember when I was in seventh grade, one of my teachers said to me, strongly disapproving, "The trouble with you is you do only what you want to do!" That continues to be the trouble with me, except that over the years I have wanted to do more and more.

My husband worked hard as a child, out-Iowa-ing the Iowans, if such a thing is possible. His dad had him mixing cement with a stick when he was five, pushing wheelbarrows not long after. It's a long sad tale on the order of two miles to school and both ways uphill. The result is, he's a great worker, much better than I am, but all the while he's doing it he wishes he weren't. He thinks of it as work; he's torn between doing a good job and longing not to be doing it at all. Later, when he's out on the golf course, where he really wants to be, he feels a little guilty, knowing there's work that should have been done before he gave in and took advantage of the beautiful day.

Good work is not the work we assign children but the work they want to do, whether it's reading in bed (where would I be today if my parents had rousted me out and put me to scrubbing floors?) or cleaning their rooms or practicing the flute or making roasted potatoes with rosemary and Parmesan for the family dinner. It's good for a teenager to suddenly decide that the bathtub is so disgusting she'd better clean it herself. I admit that for the parent, this can involve years of waiting. But if she doesn't want to wait, she can always spend her time dusting.

QUESTIONS FOR ACTIVE READING

1. What experience did Smiley have that changed her beliefs about chores? At what point in her essay does she describe this experience? What would the impact of that experience be on you, as a reader, if she had described it some place else in the essay?

2. What kinds of reasons and evidence does Smiley offer to support her argument? Do you consider these reasons and evidence to be authoritative? What does her choice of reasons and evidence reveal about Smiley's intended audience?

3. How does Smiley use rhetorical questions to appeal to her readers? What is your reaction to these questions?

QUESTIONS FOR THINKING CRITICALLY

1. How does the concept of *dualism with dominance* described by Stephen Jay Gould in "Reversing Established Orders" (p. 65) apply to Smiley's description of "chores" as part of a family dynamic?

2. In paragraph 5, Smiley makes a startling analogy. What is it? Do you agree? How might student writer Eli Sharp (p. 78) respond to that analogy?

3. In what ways do Jane Smiley's and Annie Dillard's (p. 62) childhoods resemble each other? What kinds of arguments do both writers make for the benefits of encouraging curiosity and independence in children? Do you agree or disagree?

Writing Project: An Experience That Influenced a Belief

The Thinking-Writing Activities and the readings and questions in this chapter have encouraged you to become an active thinker, to examine your beliefs, and to observe how some thoughtful people have reflected on their learning experiences. As you work on this project, reread what you wrote for the activities and think about the events discussed in the readings.

The Writing Situation

Begin by considering the elements discussed in the Writing Situation section of the Thinking-Writing Model.

Purpose   Your primary purpose in writing this essay is to make clear to your readers what your belief is, narrate your experience in an interesting way, and connect the two effectively. You are not trying to convince your readers that they should adopt your belief. You are showing them what your belief is and the impact of your experience. A second purpose is to stimulate your own increased understanding of your belief, your ability to evaluate that belief, and your larger understanding of other people's beliefs.

Write an essay telling of an experience that had an important influence on a belief that you held or hold. The belief might be about yourself, about another person involved in the experience, or about the issue that the experience illustrates. The experience may have helped form your belief, changed, or strengthened it.

You should explain your belief, of course, and describe the experience, reflecting on what happened as you tell of its effects. You may want to discuss the sources of the belief (see pages 55 and 56). Follow your instructor's directions for length, format, and so forth.

Audience   When you write about your own experiences, you are an important part of the audience. This form of writing, as you have seen in Annie Dillard's essay (p. 62), acts as a catalyst for self-discovery by encouraging you to reflect on your past experiences. As you write, your guiding ideas should include these questions:

- How effectively am I communicating the reality of this experience?
- How effectively have I analyzed the significance of this experience and the impact that it had?

You will also be writing for the other readers with whom you'll share this piece of writing. Consider these questions when thinking about your audience:

- How much information about my belief should I include to help my readers to understand it and know where it came from?
- How much would my readers be likely to know about the background of the experience I am writing about? What in that background is important for them to understand?
- What details of the experience should I include to make it real for my readers? What details can I leave out?

In other words, you need to put yourself in your readers' position and view your writing through their eyes.

Subject   When you write about your own experience or create an autobiographical narrative, you are using a common and effective means of communication. Real experiences provide living examples, not abstract or hypothetical ideas. Think of how often speakers, writers, and people you know tell about experiences in order to illustrate a point. This assignment demonstrates that interaction. The belief you are writing about is probably a somewhat abstract idea; your experience is real. In a later chapter you will consider narration again and be reminded that a story illuminates an idea, but does not really prove that the idea is true.

Most of us like to learn about what someone did and what he or she thinks it means, and most of us enjoy telling of our own experiences. As you think about your many beliefs and your many experiences, try to identify a belief that will interest an audience and an experience that you can represent in sharp detail.

Writer   This Writing Project, like the others in Part One of this book, asks you to use your own experience as the basis of an essay. This makes you the authority on the subject, which should give you confidence. Your challenges are to shape your story and to connect it directly to your belief.

The Writing Process

One of this book's main goals is to help you discover your own writing process, to tap its strengths and to reduce its weaknesses. This project provides a good opportunity for you to reflect on your writing process.

Generating Ideas   Think about a suitable experience to write about. Look for an experience that had a profound effect on your belief and that may have implications for other people's lives. Once you have found your topic, ask yourself questions and make notes about your responses. Questions you might ask include these:

- What happened? Outline the major events of the experience.
- How did you respond? What were your thoughts, reactions, feelings?

- What roles did other people play? Was the location important? Recall specific details about what people did and said, and about the setting, to make your retelling vivid for your audience.
- What was the result of the experience? How did it affect your belief?
- As you reflect on it, what was the experience's value for you? How has it influenced your life?

You may also refer to the questions for generating ideas in Chapter 4.

Defining a Focus In a few sentences, summarize the main point you wish to make in your essay, given your subject, audience, and purpose. Then evaluate your focus: Is it specific enough for you to convey it clearly in an essay? Is it interesting so that your audience will find it worth reading about? Is it thoughtful so that it serves the purpose of reflection?

At this point, consider whether or not the experience you have chosen is an appropriate subject for your purpose and audience. If not, you can begin again by looking for another experience to write about.

Organizing Ideas Think about how you can order the elements of your experience. Will you start at the beginning and describe them chronologically? Or will you start at a later point in time and use a flashback to the beginning of the experience? Where will you include your observations and reflections about the experience: at the end or at various places throughout?

Drafting As you translate your ideas, notes, and early versions into coherent writing, you will need to decide how to draft in ways that will help you revise your work effectively. Because the essay you are about to write will have three distinct components—your belief, your experience, and their connections—you may want to draft each component separately and then think about connecting them.

Drafting Hints

1. Spread out all the work you did while generating ideas and drafting a focus so that you can see it while you write the sections of your draft.
2. Draft briskly. You will revise and correct later.
3. If you stop or are interrupted while drafting, be sure to save what you have written.
4. When you return to drafting, reread what you saved to resume the flow of your ideas.

Revising One of the best strategies for revision is to get an audience's reactions to your draft. Your classmates, or peers, can help you see where your draft is already successful and where it needs improvement. If your instructor allows class time for peer review, be sure to have a draft ready so that you can benefit from this activity.

Revising Strategy: Peer Response Groups   This activity works best with groups of three or four.

1. The group selects a timekeeper, who allots ten minutes to each writer. Regardless of how many response process steps have been completed, after ten minutes the group goes on to the next writer's work.

2. One person begins by reading aloud his or her draft while group members listen.

3. The writer next reads his or her writing aloud a second time. *Do not skip this step.*

4. Group members listen and write notes or comments.

5. The writer then asks each group member this question and jots down their responses: "What questions do you have about my original belief and its sources?"

6. The writer next asks each member these questions and takes notes as each answers: "What questions do you have about the experience I described? What else do you need to know about it?"

7. The writer then asks each member these questions and records their responses: "Do you understand why my belief changed as a result of this experience and what my belief is now? What could I add to make my writing clearer?"

   As soon as possible after peer review, you should revise your draft based on your peers' questions and comments. Then, if possible, put it aside for a day or two before continuing with revision. In an online classroom, you can post or email drafts of your paper and ask for written responses to the questions in Steps 5–7. Ask your instructor about additional ways to use technology for collaborative writing.

   Reread your revised draft to yourself out loud, slowly. Then think about each of the following questions. As you consider ways to improve your draft based on your answers, stop and make changes to your draft before you move on to the next question.

1. How could you improve the first paragraph? How could you get your readers' attention and make them want to read on?

2. How could you improve the order of your draft? Could you rearrange some paragraphs?

3. How could you improve the flow of your draft? Where would transitions help your audience?

4. How could you improve your sentences? Pay particular attention to sentences that are difficult to read aloud. Your audience will have trouble following them! Could you shorten hard-to-read long sentences or write them as two sentences? Where could you use parallel structure to make your sentences more graceful?

Proofreading   After you prepare a final draft, check for use of standard grammar and punctuation. Proofread carefully for omitted words and punctuation marks. Run your spell-checker program, but be aware of its limitations. Proofread again to detect the kinds of errors the computer can't catch.

Your essay should now be completed to the very best of your ability, and, of course, you will need to submit a copy to your instructor by the due date. But also try to share it with other audiences. Would members of your family enjoy reading it? Would other people who were involved in the experience want to know how it affected you? Would someone with whom you currently have a relationship understand you better by reading it?

The following essay shows how a student responded to this assignment.

Eli Sharp's Writing Process

In response to an assignment asking him to agree or disagree with a belief expressed in one of the assigned readings, Eli Sharp, a student at City College of San Francisco, chose to disagree with Jane Smiley's belief expressed in "The Case Against Chores" (p. 71) that children should not be assigned chores. The assignment also required Sharp to consult other sources and cite them according to MLA style.

To begin generating ideas, Sharp started with his own immediate emotional reaction to Smiley's essay. "The hardest part was getting out of my reactive emotional response," he wrote in response to a query from his professor. "I was trying to be in an inquiring and open-minded state, rather than just defending my own belief."

The move from personal, subjective experience to a broader outlook was supported by Sharp's reading of other sources, an eclectic mix of authors and philosophers whose own insights into childhood helped Sharp to refine his own argument. "I knew that I wanted to convince my audience, my professor and classmates, of the soundness of my belief, so I had to work through my emotional reaction and more closely examine the bases for my own belief in the value of chores," he said. As he worked, Sharp kept track of the necessary source information and was careful to ensure that everything he quoted, paraphrased, or summarized was correctly cited both in the body of the essay and on the works-cited page that is required for MLA papers.

As you read Eli Sharp's essay, note how he often refers to specific points made in "The Case Against Chores." These references both support Eli's own argument as well as help his audience—even an audience that might not be familiar with Smiley's essay—understand the larger context.

An Argument for Chores
By Eli Sharp

In her essay "The Case Against Chores," Jane Smiley argues that children are both immediately and ultimately better off it they are not required by their parents, family, or other guardians to do household chores. She succinctly sums up the conventional rationales for assigning chores and dismisses them. In her own upbringing she "wasn't expected to lift a finger," and the closest she came to cleaning up after herself was "to run water in [her] cereal bowl before setting it in the sink." All the same, she developed work habits and skills tending a stable, as, she explains, she "wasn't alienated from [the work]" (73).

Smiley seems, first of all, to assume that the reader will share in her high opinion of herself as a well-known academic and a professional writer. True, she is esteemed by her peers and enjoys an elevated social status. But are these the only qualities that chore-doling Iowans want to engender in their children? I would argue that all too often those who make a living with their minds are viewed not with awe or respect by those who do so with their hands, but with some degree of suspicion, mistrust, and the sense that somehow such people are shirking "real work."

Be this as it may, I find Smiley's argument unconvincing on many grounds. I think she's guilty of faulty inductive reasoning, or "hasty generalization," in claiming that because she turned out so well, most other children will too. And again, when, having "[. . .] over the years gleaned some of the reasons parents give for assigning [chores,]" (italics mine), she assumes her work in this regard is done (72). If she's gleaned some of the reasons and remains unimpressed, the other ones couldn't possibly be any better. Even in her title Smiley seems a bit grandiose in her assessment of her own views. It's not just "A" case against chores; it's "The" case against chores.

Perhaps Smiley most compromises the validity of her argument in my eyes with her comment about learning to run some water in her cereal bowl before setting it in the sink. Is this a chore? I hardly consider a rudiment of self-accountability, such as cleaning up after herself, to be a chore. Maybe one of those reasons for assigning tasks that she didn't glean was that children should be weaned of the idea that they can expect to be served by others, including their parents. Or is this only true of certain segments of society, those who are to learn how to serve?

Whatever Smiley's views on wider issues may be, I see the case for assigning chores to children at some stage of their development and dependence on the family as being far more sound, reasonable, and convincing than that against. For one, not all children will opt for such benevolent pastimes as stable cleaning, in the absence of assigned chores. In his short but wonderfully lucid and honest essay on his own boyhood misbehavior, Andrew O'Hagan writes, "We all took and assigned roles in cruel little dramas of our own devising. Our talk would be full of new and interesting ways to worry or harass our parents . . . ." He goes on to describe a twelve-year-old neighbor girl who claimed to grind up light bulbs and put them in her father's porridge (43). While I don't suggest that assigning chores would have any influence whatsoever on such behavior, O'Hagan's point in mentioning this questionable claim is that the idea was lauded by him and his boyhood friends. Having some chores to do can keep children from having too much time on their hands to hang around with their peers and get into trouble. "Something happened when we all got together . . .," O' Hagan writes, "We were competitive, deluded, and full of our own small powers. . . . As only dependents can be, we were full of our own independence" (40–41). Chores can help remind children of their dependence.

Smiley makes much of the insufficiency of this argument and stresses the idea that children should be loved, valued, and accepted for who they are, not what they do for the family. On the latter point, of course, I agree. However, it is the transition from dependence on the family to dependence on society, and the relative independence required, which interests me here. I suggest that some transitional stage, involving the introduction to the rules and mores of the society in which the family lives, is highly desirable. In a capitalist state society like ours, where semi-socialist institutions are required to play a subordinate role to "free enterprise," or unregulated competitive organizations, it greatly behooves a child to learn that her society does *not* value her for who she "is," but precisely for what she does, or what she's "worth" in terms of wealth, as the case may be. I don't contend that this situation owes to any specific historical cause, much less a particular political or social agenda, but that it is a normal extension of human nature, in absence of understanding and acknowledgement of a higher law. In this sense I follow Jean-Jacques Rousseau as he writes:

> Such was . . . the origin of society and law, . . . which irretrievably destroyed natural liberty, eternally fixed the law of property and inequality, converted clever usurpation into unalterable right, and, for the advantage of a few ambitious individuals, subjected all mankind to perpetual labour, slavery, and wretchedness. (79)

I believe the facts of daily life bear out this view despite the best efforts and intentions of the leaders and shapers of our society. President John F. Kennedy, in his inaugural address of January 20, 1969 (as examined by Robert Bellah in his essay on civil religion), spoke: "The same revolutionary beliefs for which our forebears fought are still at issue around the globe—the belief that the rights of man come not from the generosity of the state but from the hand of God." Nonetheless, the address concludes, "Here on earth God's work must truly be our own." Of this speech Bellah astutely observes that "It might be argued that the passages quoted reveal the essentially irrelevant role of religion in the very secular society that is America. . . . [Religion] gets only a sentimental nod . . . , before a discussion of the really serious business with which religion has nothing whatever to do" (41). The laws that govern our daily lives, in the modern world, are economic, not moral, and it is to a child's benefit to be prepared for this realization. Without entering into the question of the advisability of bringing children into such a world in the first place, I submit that the least parents can do is to *gradually* wean their child from the loving, nurturing environment of the family into the so-called "working world."

"She also taught me 'to speak the truth and shame the Devil!'" writes the poet and author Robert Graves of his mother. "Her favourite biblical exhortation went: 'My son, whatever thy hand findeth to do, do it with all thy might'" (32). This exhortation, central to many of the world's religions, sheds light on another possible advantage of chores. They give the child the opportunity to discover the simple pleasure of exertion itself.

Chores tend to be simple, manual labor. Growing up in northern Michigan, in a home built by my parents and their friends and heated entirely with wood-burning ovens, I have extensive experience with chores of this type. It really was an unusual amount of physical labor for boys (my brother and I) in the twentieth century. Felling, cutting, and splitting cordwood; shoveling masses of snow; gardening; composting; mowing; and occasionally harvesting maple sap, in addition to the usual household chores, were all on the list.

While Smiley says she took straight to stable work without the least outside obligation, there's no way I would have worked like I did without having my tasks clearly outlined for me. And, more to the point, I learned to enjoy physical labor, even in harsh conditions. The work was not oppressive, monotonous, dangerous, arbitrary, or, by a far cry, to someone else's reward and my detriment.

I was not a driven child, and I am not a driven adult. Having chores to do helped me better appreciate my leisure time. "Oh the happy, happy, never-to-be-recalled days of childhood!"writes the great novelist Lev Tolstoy. "How could one fail to love and cherish memories of such a time? Those memories refresh and elevate the soul and are a source of my best enjoyment" (52). So it is with me. The sheer physical, sensory enjoyment of the world is my abiding memory of childhood. My early childhood was virtually pure leisure, and chores were imposed on me only later in life, gradually. I often didn't want to do them beforehand, and made this very clear, but I also often enjoyed doing them once I started, and better enjoyed my meals and beverages and slept better afterward. There were more chores in winter than summer, and less daylight to do other things anyway. Still, I was never excessively tasked and spent more time playing than working, even in winter.

In view of all these advantages of assigning chores to children, all borne out in my own experience, I think the most significant is the lesson of self-accountability to be gleaned from these tasks. Children learn first-hand how much work goes into maintaining their own comfort and well-being. They may decide that such experience is unpleasant and distasteful and spend much of their adult lives seeking "better service," or expecting to be cleaned up after. But it is my opinion that they are far less likely to do so with the added experience of having been required, at some stage of their development, to take part in the daily work and maintenance of their own household.

Works Cited

Bellah, Robert N. Civil Religion in America." <u>Daedalus</u> 134 (Fall 2005): 40–55.

Graves, Robert. <u>Goodbye to All That</u>. New York: Doubleday, 1957.

O'Hagan, Andrew. "Bad Bastardness." <u>Leopard 3, Frontiers</u>. Ed. Christopher MacLehose. London: Harvill, 1994. 38–44.

Rousseau, Jean-Jacques. "On the Origin of Inequality." <u>Rousseau/Kant (13/14)</u>. Trans. G.D.H.Cole (1913). Chicago: The Great Books Foundation, 1955. 22–109.

Smiley, Jane. "The Case Against Chores." <u>Critical Thinking, Thoughtful Writing</u>. By John Chaffee. 4th Ed. Boston: Houghton, 2008. 71–73.

Tolstoy, L. N. <u>Childhood, Boyhood, Youth</u>. Baltimore: Penguin, 1972.

Alternative Writing Projects

- An Author's Change in Belief

  Explain how one of the authors of the readings in Chapter 3 changed or strengthened one or more beliefs. Be sure to present in your own words the author's original belief, what circumstances changed or strengthened it, and what it was after these circumstances. Give the title and author's name, probably at the beginning of your essay, and put quotation marks around any of the author's words that you use.

- A Friend's or Relative's Belief

  Interview a friend or relative about one of that person's most important beliefs. Prepare your questions ahead of time and write down the answers carefully. Look ahead to later chapters for some guidelines to conducting an interview. Use what your friend or relative tells you as the basis for an essay about this belief, how it developed, and what it means in the life of the person who holds it.

- A Belief That You Have Observed

  Look around your community. Can you see evidence of some belief in action? For example, is there evidence that people believe in keeping up (or showing off) their homes or gardens or cars? Is there evidence of a belief in helping one's neighbors or in keeping to oneself? Is there evidence of belief in the importance of education, political action, sports? nice clothes? Use your observation as the basis for an explanation of the belief that you have noticed and your thinking about its significance.

4

Viewing Critically, Thinking Creatively

"You must expect the unexpected, because it cannot be found by search or trial."

—Heraclitus

Critical Thinking Focus: The qualities of a creative thinker

Writing Focus: Generating original ideas

Reading Theme: The creative thinking process

Writing Project: Imagining your life lived more creatively

Creative Thinking, Critical Viewing, and Writing

Creative writing is often thought of as imaginative fiction, poetry, or drama, for which the author invents characters and situations. Creativity also plays an important role in *expository writing,* in which facts, ideas, and concepts are explored, developed, and argued.

You use creative thinking in selecting and narrowing your topic (if you are allowed to pick your own topic), in the way you generate and research ideas, in the way you organize ideas, and in the way you focus on your ideas with your thesis. You also use creative thinking to develop ideas with carefully chosen details and examples. Creative thinking helps you to develop analogies and metaphors to help your readers grasp your ideas. Finally, creative thinking allows you to write imaginative, inviting introductions that will make your readers eager to read further, and to write carefully crafted conclusions that tie in elegantly with your introductions. Of course, your critical thinking abilities are also involved in all these steps, helping you to decide which of your creative ideas to include and which to discard.

The challenge to be creative in your writing is a difficult one, but the possibilities for creativity are vast. Focusing on the following four areas for creativity in expository writing will help you further develop the creative thinking abilities you may already have. This chapter deals with the first two.

- Creativity in topic selection
- Creativity in generating ideas, researching, and drafting
- Creativity in using specific details and examples
- Creativity in writing introductions and conclusions

Creativity in Topic Selection

The topic of an essay is the subject you write about, one of the four components of the writing situation. Some topics are personal and ask you to draw on your own life experiences, others are impersonal and clearly require research, and still others are a blend of the personal and impersonal. Furthermore, some topics are fairly specific, such as, "Write about your favorite sports figure," or "Write about the effects of the war in Iraq." Others are more general: "Write about some aspect of political science." A first step is to think creatively about how to shape an assigned topic into one that interests you and that you can handle in the assigned length. A visual way to do this is to "narrow with arrows."

> My favorite sports figure → my favorite football player → my favorite quarterback → Chad Pennington
>
> Effects of the war in Iraq → different types of effects → social effects → effects on national security → effects on airports and passengers
>
> Political science → elections → recent recall in California → Schwarzenegger's victory → why he won

Notice that at any point, the arrows could take you in a different direction.

> My favorite sports figure → my favorite baseball player → my favorite shortstop → Derek Jeter
>
> Effects of the war in Iraq → different types of effects → financial effects → effects on the price of oil → long-term effects on energy consumption
>
> Political science → the 2000 presidential election → what went wrong with the process → intervention by the Supreme Court → constitutional issues raised by the intervention of the Supreme Court.

Moving from Topic to Thesis

A topic is what you are going to write about, and a thesis is what you are going to say about it. Once you have narrowed your topic, try stating it as a question.

> Why is Chad Pennington my favorite sports figure?
>
> What are the effects of the war in Iraq on energy consumption in the United States?
>
> How did Arnold Schwarzenegger manage to win the election in California?

If the answer to your question will require research, read as much as you can about the general topic area, looking for ways to modify your tentative topic question or even to change your question altogether. If you are working with a personal topic, begin making notes whether or not you have enough information to answer your question. You can broaden or narrow your topic question as you proceed.

FOUR QUALITIES OF A CRITICAL THINKER

Geneticist Barbara McClintock

Curious   People who live creatively and respond critically to their environment and experiences constantly ask questions of themselves and others. In this chapter, we will explore different categories of questions and apply them to different kinds of situations (p. 90). Biologist Barbara McClintock, whose work on genetics won a Nobel Prize in 1983, began her inquiry with a simple observation: what determined the colors of kernels of Indian corn? She spent five years of "patient, brilliant, solitary work" unraveling the puzzle. Astrophysicist Alan Lightman (p. 101) describes McClintock's love of puzzle solving as being key to the most creative work done by scientists.

Open-minded   In the autobiography McClintock prepared for the Nobel Prize Institute web site, McClintock recalled her early days in the laboratory, working with other students, as a particularly exciting time. She and her fellow students "formed a close-knit group eager to discuss all phases of genetics, including those being revealed or suggested by [their] own efforts. The group was self-sustaining in all ways. For each of [them,] this was an extraordinary period." Working collaboratively and without fear of judgment (see p. 99 for more on the "Voice of Judgment") allows for breakthroughs in creative and critical thinking.

Knowledgeable   A younger colleague at Dr. McClintock's laboratory recalled that "although McClintock had the reputation of a mystic, she always drew her conclusions from her observations—this is what she meant when she admonished [colleagues] to 'listen to the plant.'" McClintock's scientific career spanned more than sixty years, and yet throughout her long career she continued to explore and teach in her field of genetics with enthusiasm and curiosity, always aware that there was more to learn.

Creative   To think creatively involves not only the capacity to produce poetry, painting, music, and the other "creative arts," but also the ability to entertain previously unknown possibilities. In Chapter 10, we will explore the critical thinking skills necessary to analyze causation (cause and effect relationships). McClintock and other revolutionary scientists used creative as well as critical thinking to conceive of—and to prove through carefully designed experiments—the extraordinary causal relationships that explain the mystery of genetics. As the examples of Barbara McClintock, Alan Lightman, and others discussed throughout this book demonstrate, "creativity" is not limited to artists. In addition, many artists need to have a scientific and mathematical understanding of the properties of paint, film, light, and other media, as well as a deep familiarity with art history. This chapter shows how creativity enhances critical thinking as well as thoughtful writing.

Online Study Center
Barbara McClintock
Visit the Online Study Center for *Critical Thinking, Thoughtful Writing* at college.*hmco.com/pic/chaffee CTTW4e* to learn more about Barbara McClintock.

Thinking Critically About Images
Seeing and Believing

As a critical thinker and thoughtful writer, you are learning to consider many different sources of information and to test those sources against your own experience of the world. Teachers, politicians, advertisers, religious figures, and the media all use images and text to try to influence your beliefs and change your thinking. Editors of television news programs and web sites as well as newspapers and magazines are very attentive to the effect that images have when they are placed at a particular point in a publication or alongside a text. Advertisers increase the appeal of a particular product by linking attractive words and concepts to seductive images. And public health advocates create commercials, posters, and brochures that combine striking and challenging words and images to get your attention and influence your behavior.

It is important that you, as a student, a citizen, and a consumer, apply your critical thinking abilities to what you *see* as well as to what you *read*. With today's technology, it is easier than ever to integrate photographs, animation, charts and graphs, and artwork into your academic papers as well as your personal and professional writing. Learning to test the authority and credibility of visual as well as verbal sources of information will also help you to develop creative, responsible, and purposeful ways to use images in your own writing. A good way to begin is to ask questions of fact, interpretation, analysis, synthesis, evaluation, and application as you consider the accuracy and purpose of a visual image that accompanies a printed text.

In Chapter 3, you learned to think critically about your own beliefs and to understand how reasons and evidence can change based on perspective. The images in this portfolio, and the questions and activities offered here and at the Online Study Center, will help you to recognize how images in the media can sometimes present biased or incomplete information. The creators of these photos, advertisements, and web sites were keenly aware of the power these images have to influence their audience's beliefs. How likely are you to believe that something is "true" because you read about it in a newspaper, saw it on a cable news channel, or linked to it on a web site? Now, more than ever, is it "true" that a picture is worth a thousand words?

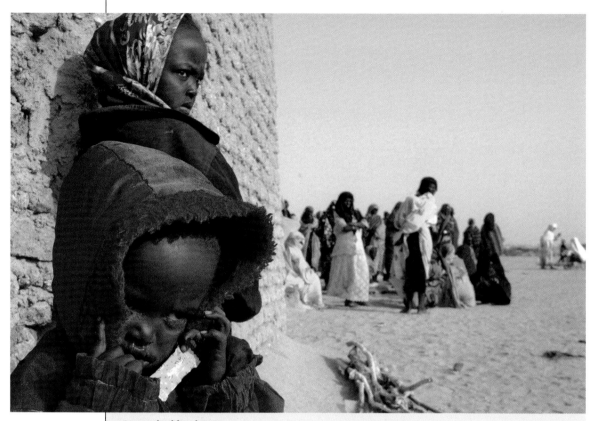

Stranded in the Desert

Civil war has torn the African nation of Sudan since the mid-twentieth century. In 2004, this Sudanese child fled to neighboring Chad, where the humanitarian group Doctors Without Borders set up the makeshift hospital where he is shown here waiting for help.

THINKING CRITICALLY ABOUT THE IMAGE

1. From what perspective is this photograph taken? What makes this perspective especially compelling? Compare this perspective (and the physical position of the photographer) with that of the image on the facing page. In what ways, and in what contexts, can visual images tell stories from the perspective of someone other than the photographer?

2. Read Sara Corbett's essay "The Lost Boys" (page 130 in Chapter 5), which is about an earlier generation of Sudanese children orphaned by civil war. Corbett uses narration and description to structure her essay. Review the Writing Project for Chapter 7 (A Narrative Showing the Effect of a Perception, page 205). Using print and online resources, create a working bibliography for a narrative essay that would provide additional context for this photograph.

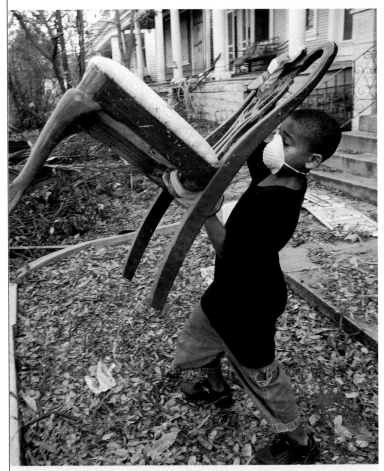

Abandoned in the Delta
A month after Hurricane Katrina devastated New Orleans, this eleven-year-old boy wears a mask to protect himself from toxins and mold as he helps retrieve belongings from his grandfather's ruined home.

THINKING CRITICALLY ABOUT THE IMAGE

1. In the aftermath of Hurricanes Katrina and Rita, many journalists and politicians debated the appropriateness of the term *refugee* to describe both those who were stranded by the hurricane and those who managed to flee but were permanently displaced. What does it mean to be a "refugee"? Chapter 6 examines the ethical use of language and the political impact of certain kinds of language. Would you apply the term *refugee* to the Sudanese child in the previous photograph? Could you also apply the term to this child? How does your understanding of the term *refugee* change according to the geographical context in which it is used?

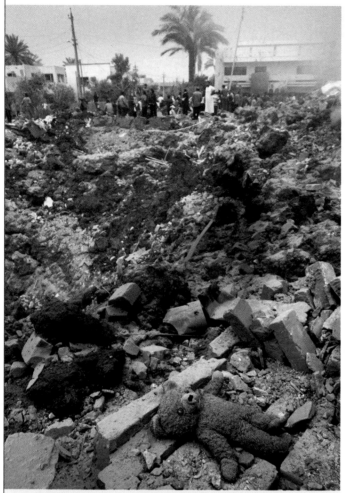

Soft Target

In April 2003, a bomb dropped from an aircraft over this Baghdad neighborhood destroyed the homes of at least twenty families as an insurgent movement took hold of Iraq.

THINKING CRITICALLY ABOUT THE IMAGE

1. Chapter 9 discusses the importance of perceptions and perspectives to critical thinking and thoughtful writing. Consider the sense of scale and proportion in this photograph. What is the relationship between the foreground and the background of this image, and what does that relationship suggest about the consequences of war?

2. Consider the importance of context to this image. How would you interpret this image if it were the consequence of a natural disaster, such as Hurricane Katrina or the devastating October 2005 earthquake in Pakistan?

Grace Under Fire

In April 2006, the Iraqi Culture Ministry sponsored an eleven-day festival of children's theater in an effort to give children "a respite from the daily bloodshed and violence" of the ongoing war and insurgency. These girls study ballet in Baghdad.

THINKING CRITICALLY ABOUT THE IMAGE

1. Three years separate this photograph from the previous image. By placing these images next to each other (or on facing pages), what kind of context might a photo-journalist or propagandist suggest—either deliberately or accidentally?

2. Chapter 10, Exploring Cause and Effect, defines and discusses causal claims and causal fallacies. In an essay, examine how either or both of the photographs on these facing pages could be used to support or expose either a causal claim or a causal fallacy about the war in Iraq.

Nine Lives and Counting
A Palestinian soldier on patrol in Beirut, Lebanon, pets a kitten in this photo from 1982.

THINKING CRITICALLY ABOUT THE IMAGE

1. Photojournalists, just like print journalists, are keen observers of detail. Chapter 7 of this book discusses objective and subjective writing. In a paragraph, describe objectively what you see in this photograph. Then, write a subjective paragraph in which you interpret this image. Why is it important to form a critical understanding of how images are selected by journalists, politicians, and others in the media?

2. How does paradox work to make this photograph especially striking?

Will You Be Mine?
In the winter of 1999, homeless men sleep on a heating grate outside of a Manhattan fur shop.

THINKING CRITICALLY ABOUT THE IMAGE

1. What are the ethical implications of photojournalism? Many images in this portfolio are of people in distress or trouble. Should photojournalists offer assistance—for example, buying food for or offering money to these homeless men—or does that compromise a journalist's objectivity?

2. Homelessness was at the forefront of the nation's political and social agenda throughout the 1980s and 1990s. What would be the thesis or claim of an opinion piece or argument that used this photograph as evidence? Compare possible claims with other students in your class. How many different ways can you find to "read" this photograph?

The Show Must Go On
The Superdome in New Orleans in the immediate aftermath of
Hurricane Katrina, and six months later during the city's fabled
celebration of Mardi Gras.

THINKING CRITICALLY ABOUT THE IMAGE

1. Chapter 10 includes a casebook of readings about Hurricane Katrina, including the
   reflections of two photojournalists who struggled to capture the impact of the disaster. In a brief essay, discuss how either or both of these photographs support the
   observations of the author of at least one of those readings.

2. What do you notice, objectively, about the composition of these two images?
   In what ways do their similarities invite reflection?

When you think that you have enough information, try answering your question in a complete sentence.

> Chad Pennington's amazing athletic ability, great leadership skills, and generous contributions to our community make him my favorite sports figure.

> The war in Iraq has a rippling effect on America's economy: the rising price of oil contributes to inflation.

> Arnold Schwarzenegger won the California recall because of the widespread dislike of Gray Davis, Schwarzenegger's prior fame and fortune, and his strategy of avoiding the political press in favor of the entertainment media.

Treat the answer to your question as a tentative thesis, but expect to modify or even discard your original question. Becoming aware of the need to make these changes is something that most writers experience, so don't become discouraged when it occurs. Instead, congratulate yourself for being willing to put in the time and effort needed for the creative process as you shape your topic.

Creativity in Generating Ideas

Books about writing sometimes speak as though generating ideas, researching, and drafting are three entirely separate stages, and the writer finishes one stage before beginning the next. This may even be true in some cases, but often writers find themselves getting new ideas while researching or beginning to draft only to realize the need for more research or brainstorming.

Here are some strategies your open and curious mind can use to develop creative ideas in your writing. Your journal, blog, or notebook is a good place to practice these strategies.

Brainstorming   *Brainstorming* is an activity in which, working individually or with a group of people, you list all the ideas you can think of related to a given topic. The goal is to produce as many ideas as possible in a specific time period. While you are engaged in this idea-generating process, it is important to relax and let your mind run free.

These guidelines should help you:

- Set a timer and keep thinking until it goes off.
- Go for quantity. You want to generate as many ideas as you can.
- Write down *all* the ideas you generate.
- Build on ideas.
- Don't criticize or discard any ideas.

Imagine, for example, that you are assigned the following topic for a research paper:

> There are many problems that students face on college campuses. Identify one such problem and then write a research paper that analyzes the causes of and possible solutions to the problem. Why does the problem occur, and what can be done to deal with it? Your paper should include relevant research findings as well as your own perspective on this problem.

Using the brainstorming strategy with a friend, you might come up with a list that includes the following student problems on your campus:

parking	classes too large
library closed too early	not enough access to computers
political tensions	plagiarism
binge drinking	use of drugs
registration too complicated	tests and papers coming in clumps
not enough social activities	some teachers just lecturing
increasing thefts	curriculum not well organized
financial aid cutbacks	

Mind Maps   *Mind maps* are visual presentations of the various ways ideas can be related to one another. For example, the Thinking-Writing Model is represented as a mind map in Figure 4.1. Mind maps are also a powerful approach for writing, helping you to generate ideas and to begin organizing them into various relationships. They are well suited to the writing process for a number of reasons. First, the organization grows naturally, reflecting the way your mind naturally makes associations and arranges information. Second, the organization can easily be revised to reflect new information and your developing understanding of how it should be organized. Third, you can express a range of relationships among the various ideas. Fourth, instead of being identified once and then forgotten, each idea remains an active part of the overall pattern, suggesting new possible relationships. Fifth, you do not have to decide initially on a beginning, subpoints, and so on; you can do this after your pattern is complete, so you save time and avoid frustration. For example, imagine that from your list of problems on campus you select "abuse of alcohol" as a paper topic. Your mind map might resemble Figure 4.1.

THINKING-
WRITING
ACTIVITY

Create a Mind Map

For this activity, you will experiment with a mind map. Your instructor will direct your choice of topic.

These guidelines should help you:

- Draw a circle in the middle of the page, and write your topic in the circle.
- Draw a few lines coming out from the circle, and label them with ideas about your topic.
- See which of your lines you could develop further. Then draw more lines from those, and label them with ideas and details about those aspects of your topic.
- Keep going until you have no more ideas about the topic, or until you see a section of your map developing into a cluster of ideas that you could write about.

FIGURE 4.1   Mind Map

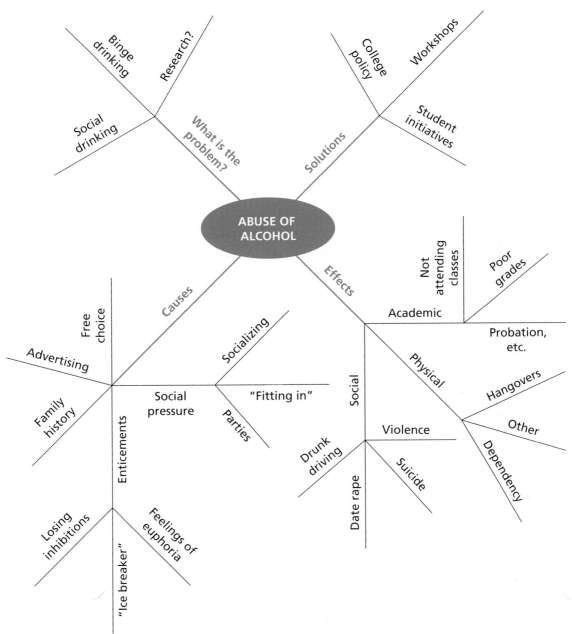

Freewriting   *Freewriting* is a sort of written brainstorming in which you write with a minimum of conscious reflection. But rather than simply list ideas, freewriters usually write in sentences. The goal is to let your ideas flow freely, without inhibition, giving your mind the opportunity to develop creative ideas in unique combinations.

These guidelines should help you:

- Set a timer and keep writing until it goes off.
- Write at a steady, comfortable pace for the entire time. If you get stuck, it is OK to write, "I am stuck. I can't think of any more ideas. I hope I get another idea," until a new idea comes to you. *Don't stop writing!*
- Don't criticize or make corrections.
- After the time limit is up, read carefully what you have written. Think about it for a few minutes. Then try the process again, starting with the most interesting ideas from your first try.

An example of freewriting about the problem of alcohol abuse might begin something like this:

Alcohol is a real problem on campus. Every party, that's all people do, is drink too much and then get silly. I think it's ok for people to drink some if they want to. They say it relaxes them and makes it easier to talk to strangers. But it's out of control, and that's a problem. There are a lot of students that drink all the time. They must be failing their classes, they sleep until noon, and they look lousy. There's got to be a better way to socialize and have fun with people besides getting bombed out of your mind. . . .

Questioning   *Asking questions* that explore a topic provides another strategy for generating ideas, just as asking questions about a topic supports critical reading. In fact, the ability to ask appropriate and penetrating questions about visual and written texts is one of the most powerful thinking and communicating tools writers possess. Asking questions enables them to go beyond the obvious, to think, read, see, and write in ways that are in-depth, complex, and articulate. Questions come in many different forms and are used for many different purposes. For instance, questions can be classified in terms of the ways people organize and interpret information. The following are six such categories of questions:

1. Fact	4. Synthesis
2. Interpretation	5. Evaluation
3. Analysis	6. Application

Thoughtful writers ask appropriate questions from all of these categories. Listed next is a description of the six categories of questions, along with sample questions from each category.

1. **Questions of Fact.** Questions of fact seek to determine the basic information of a situation: who, what, when, where, how, why. These following seek information that is relatively straightforward and objective:

Who, what, when, where, how, why?
Describe _____ .

2. **Questions of Interpretation.** Questions of interpretation seek to select and organize facts and ideas, discovering the relationships among them. Examples of such relationships include the following:

   Chronological relationships—relating things in time sequence

   Process relationships—relating aspects of growth, development, or change

   Comparison/contrast relationships—relating things in terms of their similar or different features

   Causal relationships—relating events in terms of the way some are responsible for causing others

   These questions can help you discover relationships:

   Can you retell _____ in your own words?

   What is the *main idea* of _____ ?

   What is the *time sequence* relating the following events: _____ ?

   What are the steps in the *process of growth* or *development* in _____ ?

   How would you *compare* and *contrast* the features of _____ and _____ ?

   What was/were the *cause(s)* of _____ ? What was/were the *effect(s)* of _____ ?

3. **Questions of Analysis.** Questions of analysis seek to separate an entire process or situation into its component parts and understand the relation of these parts to the whole. These questions or statements attempt to classify various elements, outline component structures, articulate various possibilities, and clarify the reasoning being presented:

   What are the *parts* or *features* of _____ ?

   Classify according to _____ .

   Outline/diagram/web _____ .

   What *evidence* can you present to support _____ ?

   What are the *possible alternatives* for _____ ?

   Explain the *reasons* you think _____ .

4. **Questions of Synthesis.** The goal of questions of synthesis is to combine ideas to form a new whole or to arrive at a conclusion, making inferences about future events, creating solutions, and designing plans of action:

   What would you *predict/infer* from _____ ?

   What ideas can you *add to* _____ ?

   How would you *create/design* a new _____ ?

What might happen if you *combined*_____ with _____?

What *solutions/decisions* would you suggest for _____?

5. **Questions of Evaluation.** The aim of evaluation questions is to help you make informed judgments and decisions by determining the relative value, truth, or reliability of things. The process of evaluation involves identifying your criteria or standards and then determining to what extent the things being evaluated meet those standards.

How would you evaluate _____ and what *standards* would you use?

Do you *agree* with _____? *Why or why not?*

How would you *decide* about _____?

What *criteria* would you use to *assess* _____?

6. **Questions of Application.** The purpose of application questions is to help you take the knowledge or concepts you have gained in one situation and apply them to other situations.

How is _____ *an example* of _____?

How would you *apply* this rule/principle to _____?

ADDITIONAL TIPS FOR GENERATING IDEAS

- When brainstorming, write down every idea, no matter how unusable it may seem at the time.
- Phone your voice mail and leave yourself a message if an idea strikes you while you're away from home.
- Talk to other people about your topic. Knowledgeable people will add information; those unfamiliar with the topic will ask useful questions.
- Ask a librarian for research suggestions.
- Note conflicting information or opinions. They are the heart of academic discussion.
- Search at Yahoo! or Google for businesses or organizations that can provide information.
- Identify and interview experts on your topic. (Be sure to acknowledge them as sources.)
- Scan television schedules, for related programs.
- Search online for sources of information.
- When drafting, don't necessarily begin with the introduction. Instead, begin with whatever section is easiest to write.

- Be willing to modify your thesis as you go along so that you don't lock yourself into a position too early.
- Avoid premature organization; draft sections on separate pages or as separate computer files. Then try arranging them in various orders.
- If you are interrupted while drafting, read what you have already written to get back into the flow.

Creative and Critical Thinking About Images

Many professional writers in a variety of contexts integrate images with their texts. From college and military recruitment brochures to advertisements to a company's annual reports, images work in both a subtle and an overt way to persuade us to do, believe, or buy something. As a creative thinker and thoughtful writer, you should begin to pay attention to the relationships between images and text in what you read. You should also think about the ways in which images can inspire, support, and reflect your own written work. (See Thinking Critically About Images on pages 1–1 to 1–8)

Images and the Writing Situation

Just as writers consider audience, subject, and purpose as they think through their writing and conduct their research, so too do creators of images (painters, cartoonists, graphic artists, photographers, and others). Whether they are recording events as they happen or reflecting imaginatively on their personal experiences, visual artists in all media are fundamentally aware that they are *communicating*—that, even without words, their images will tell a story, make an argument, show a process, or provide information.

Images and Your Audience   In your college career, you will often be asked to present information in a visual manner. Classes in the sciences and social sciences require you to present numerical data in the form of charts, graphs, and maps. In the visual arts and humanities, you may be asked to analyze a painting's message and style or to describe a film director's approach to setting a scene. Be sure to ask your instructors for each of your classes how to locate, correctly cite, and usefully include images in your own essays and research papers.

Images and Your Subject   Creative thinking teaches us that there are many different ways of experiencing and communicating information. When you use any of the idea-generation strategies discussed earlier in this chapter, try to incorporate visual as well as verbal descriptions and information. You could collect images from magazines, books, and online sources, printing them out or scanning them electronically to create a kind of visual "mind map." Or you could look online at sites such as the National Archives, *Flickr.com*, and Google Images, all of which allow you to search for images using key words related to your subject.

Online Study Center
Finding images online
Visit the Online Study Center for this book at *college.hmco.com/pic/chaffeeCTTW4e* for more information on finding images online.

Images and Your Purpose   When you have gathered images that relate to your topic, you can use questions of fact, interpretation, analysis, synthesis, evaluation, and application (pages 90–92) to help you sort through the visuals and select those that best support your purpose in writing. For example, a witty or satirical editorial cartoon about federal response to Hurricane Katrina might be appropriate for an argument essay in which you analyze the political impact of that disaster, but for a paper about the storm's long-term environmental effects, you would be better served by a map showing the loss of land or a satellite photograph showing the extent of flood damage.

Reading Images Critically

As you search for images to use in your essays, reports, and arguments, remember that the content of an image—just like the content of a text—is composed of elements that work together to convey a message. Some of these elements are similar to those you consider when evaluating a piece of writing: setting, point of view, relationships between characters, an objective or subjective perspective. Other elements are specifically visual: the use of color, the manipulations of Photoshop or other image-moderating techniques, cropping (cutting), and the arrangement of images on a page or screen. And, of course, images are frequently accompanied by text that describes and contextualizes what you are seeing; this text, called a *caption*, should also be a part of your critical interpretation of visual evidence.

In Chapter 2, we explored four different types of meaning: semantic, perceptual, syntactic, and pragmatic. Each of these four kinds of meaning can also apply to your critical "reading"—or viewing—of visual content. Let's see how each type of meaning can be used to understand how just one compelling image can convey many different layers of meaning.

Semantic Meaning (Denotation)

As we learned in Chapter 2, the denotative or *semantic meaning* of a word expresses the relationship between the word itself and an idea or feeling. When you think about the relationship between images and ideas, beginning with the denotative (or literal) meaning can help you to understand its larger purpose and argument. Photographers and artists refer to the *composition* of an image—the arrangement of elements within the frame—and that is one way to think of a picture's denotative meaning. The photograph below, for example, shows an urban scene with a boy holding a bird. The caption supplied with the photograph, however, gives us a richer level of context. You already know that a denotative or semantic reading of a word is enriched by understanding both its general properties and specific examples. Were you asked to imagine, or draw, a picture of a boy holding a bird, your image might be very different—and probably much more bucolic. The caption here, however, adds a level of specificity to the picture's semantic message. The picture might *literally* be about a boy with a bird, but its *connotative* message is far more powerful—and far less lovely.

Perceptual Meaning (Connotation)

Just as words can elicit personal and subjective feelings, so do images. You would respond quite differently to the picture if the boy, Feliciano, were smiling. Here, too, the relationship between an image and its caption is important to analyze. Remember that the images you see in the media are captured by one kind of journalist (a photographer, a cameraman) but later interpreted by reporters and editors in the newsroom. The interpretation that a journalist gives to a visual image can profoundly affect the way an audience interprets that image. Visually, the composition of this photograph conveys a definite connotative or *perceptual meaning*: the boy is sad; the background is littered and abandoned; the overall sense is of urban blight. The words in the caption accompanying the photograph reinforce this meaning: *vacant lots, slumlords, dump, addicts*. More interesting, however, is the note that the bird died "despite Feliciano's attempts to save it." What does that statement suggest about the relationship, in this case, between the

August 6, 2001. Feliciano holds up a bird that mistakenly got into some oil paint that was dumped in one of the vacant lots in the neighborhood along Broadway in Brooklyn. Local slumlords pay addicts a few dollars to dump construction debris, and much of it ends up in the nearest lot. The bird died despite Feliciano's efforts to save it.

photographer and his subject? Why are the boy and the bird so close to the front of the image (and, therefore, close to *you* as a reader) instead of the slick of dumped paint? Learning to critically examine the relationships between the words and the images in a news report can help you dig deeper into an issue's impacts—and can also help you detect bias. This relationship between images and their larger contexts can be described as syntactic meaning.

Syntactic Meaning

A word's *syntactic meaning* (see page 46 in Chapter 2) depends on its relationships with other words—relationships of content, description, and connection. The content of a photograph or image is similar to its semantic meaning—What's this all about? But once you begin to connect that content to the way it is verbally described (by a caption, in this case) as well as visually composed (what is most important or dominant in the frame; what is the emotional impact of the image; what is the relationship between the photographer and the subject?), you begin to unravel the image's syntactic meaning. A third level of syntactic meaning has to do with the connection of these ideas and their ability to make sense—to convey a larger, more meaningful idea. This photograph and its caption work together to make a profound argument about urban pollution and its littlest victims. That this image and caption work so well together to make such a clear, direct argument contributes to our understanding of the fourth type of meaning: pragmatic, or situational.

Pragmatic Meaning

This final type of meaning has to do with the context or situation of the image— who created it, who or what is in it, and the ultimate purpose of and audience for the image. Earlier we examined the relationship between the photographer and Feliciano—the facts that the boy is so close to the camera and that the photographer stuck around long enough to learn that the bird didn't survive suggest a particular engagement between journalist and subject. You'll find that many journalists and media outlets will attempt to give context and meaning to a large-scale catastrophe by focusing on the specific lives it impacts—as you'll see in several of the photos in the color section of this chapter. The photographer who took the picture on page 95, Brenda Ann Kenneally, is renowned for her work documenting troubled urban families; you can find many portfolios of her work online.

Online Study Center
Brenda Ann Kenneally
Visit the Online Study Center for *Critical Thinking, Thoughtful Writing* at *college.hmco.com/ pic/chaffeeCTTW4e* for additional information on photographer Brenda Ann Kenneally.

THINKING-
WRITING
ACTIVITY

Recalling a Creative Writing Experience

1. Write about a time when you expressed yourself creatively in writing. It may have been in an important email, a memorable poem, or a paper for a school course. Respond to the following questions as you recall the writing experience.
   - What was the writing situation that required your creativity?
   - How did you go about finding a creative idea or approach?
   - Was it successful?
   - How do you feel as you recall this experience?
2. Share your experience with the class and listen carefully to the experiences of other students. On the basis of your own writing experience and those of your peers, make some inferences or general statements about creativity.

Living Creatively

We human beings have a nearly limitless capacity to be creative; our imaginations give us the power to conceive of new possibilities and to put these innovative ideas into action. Using creative resources in this way enriches our lives and brings a special meaning to our activities. Although we might not go to the extreme of saying that the uncreative life is not worth living, it is surely preferable to live a life enriched by the joys of creativity.

Many people think that being creative is beyond them, that creativity is a mysterious gift bestowed on only a chosen few. One reason for this misconception is that people often confuse being "creative" with being "artistic"—skilled at art music, poetry, imaginative writing, drama, or dance. Although artistic people are certainly creative, there are an infinite number of ways to be creative that are *not* artistic. Being creative is a state of mind and a way of life. As the writer Eric Gill expresses it: "The artist is not a different kind of person, but each one of us is a different kind of artist."

Are you creative? Yes! Think of all the activities that you enjoy: cooking, styling a wardrobe, raising children, playing sports, rapping, dancing, repairing an engine, designing a web page. Whenever you are investing your own personal ideas, applying your own personal stamp, you are being creative. To the extent that you are expressing your unique ideas developed through inspiration and experimentation, you are being creative. Similarly, if your moves on the dance floor or the basketball court express your distinctive personality, you are being creative, as you are when you stimulate the original thinking of your children or make your friends laugh with your own brand of humor. Living life creatively means bringing your perspective and creative talents to all the areas of your life.

Becoming More Creative: Understand and Trust the Process

Although the forces that discourage you from being creative are powerful, they can nevertheless be overcome with four productive strategies:

- Understand and trust the creative process.
- Eliminate the "Voice of Judgment."
- Make creativity a priority.
- Establish a creative environment.

THINKING-
WRITING
ACTIVITY

Reflecting on Past Inhibitions to Creativity

Reflect on your own creative development and describe some of the fears and pressures that inhibit your own creativity. For example, have you ever been penalized for trying a new idea that didn't work out? Have you ever suffered the wrath of the group for daring to be different and violating the group's unspoken rules? Do you feel that your life is so filled with responsibilities and demands that you don't have time to be creative?

Discovering your creative talents requires that you understand how the creative process operates and then have confidence in the results it produces. There are no fixed procedures or formulas for generating creative ideas because creative ideas by definition go beyond established ways of thinking to the unknown and the innovative. As the ancient Greek philosopher Heraclitus once said, "You must expect the unexpected, because it cannot be found by search or trial."

Although there is no fixed path to creative ideas, there are activities you can pursue that make the birth of creative ideas possible. In this respect, generating creative ideas is similar to gardening. You need to prepare the soil; plant the seeds; ensure proper watering, light, and food; and then be patient until the ideas begin to sprout. Following are some steps for cultivating your creative garden.

Absorb yourself in the task: Creative ideas don't occur in a vacuum. They emerge after a great deal of work, study, and practice. For example, if you want to come up with creative ideas in the kitchen, you need to learn more about the art of cooking. The more knowledgeable you are, the better prepared you will be to create innovative dishes. Similarly, if you are developing a creative perspective for a college research paper, you need to immerse yourself in the subject, becoming knowledgeable about the central concepts and issues. Absorbing yourself in the task "prepares the soil" for your creative ideas.

Allow time for ideas to incubate: After absorbing yourself in the task or problem, the next stage is to stop working on it. When your conscious mind stops actively working on the task, the unconscious dimension of your mind continues working—processing, organizing, and ultimately generating innovative ideas and solutions. This process is known as *incubation* because it mirrors the process in which baby chicks gradually evolve inside the egg until the moment when they break out through the shell. In the same way, your creative mind is at work while you are going about your business until the moment of *illumination,* when the incubating idea finally erupts to the surface of your conscious mind. People report that these illuminating moments—when their mental light bulbs go on—often occur when they are engaged in activities completely unrelated to the task. For example, you may suddenly realize how to organize your research paper while you are working out at the gym.

Seize on the ideas when they emerge and follow them through: Generating creative ideas is of little use unless you recognize them when they appear and then act on them. Too often people don't pay much attention to these ideas when they occur, or they dismiss them as too impractical. Have confidence in your ideas, even if they seem a little strange. Many of the most valuable inventions in history began as improbable ideas ridiculed by the popular wisdom. For example, the idea of Velcro started with burrs covering the pants of the inventor as he walked through a field, and Post-It notes resulted from the accidental invention of an adhesive that was weaker than normal. In other words, thinking effectively means thinking creatively and thinking critically. After you use your *creative thinking* abilities to generate innovative ideas, you must employ your *critical thinking* abilities to evaluate and refine those ideas and design a practical plan for implementing them. For example, you should write down your creative idea about organizing your research paper and then begin drafting to see if it will work.

Eliminate the Voice of Judgment

The biggest threat to your creativity lies within yourself, the negative *Voice of Judgment (VOJ).* This term was coined by Michael Ray and Rochelle Myers, the authors of *Creativity in Business,* a book based on a Stanford University course. The VOJ can undermine your confidence in every area of your life, including your creative activities. For example, when you are drafting a paper, the VOJ may whisper:

> "This is a stupid idea, and no one will like it."
> "Even if I could pull this idea off, it probably won't amount to much."

These statements, and countless others like them, have the ongoing effect of making you doubt yourself and the quality of your creative thinking. As you lose confidence, you become more timid, reluctant to follow through on ideas and present them to others. After a while your cumulative insecurity will discourage you from even generating ideas in the first place, and you will end up simply conforming to established ways of thinking and the expectations of others. In so doing, you surrender an important part of yourself, the vital and dynamic creative core of your personality.

How do you eliminate this unwelcome and destructive inner voice? There are a number of effective strategies. Remember, though, that the fight, although worth the effort, will not be easy.

Become aware of the VOJ: You have probably been listening to the negative messages of the VOJ for so long that you may not even consciously be aware of it. To conquer the VOJ, you first need to recognize it when it speaks.

Restate the judgment in a more accurate or constructive way: Sometimes there is an element of truth in our self-judgments, but we may have blown the reality out of proportion. For example, if you receive a low grade on a writing assignment, your VOJ may say, "You're a failure." But you need to assess the situation accurately: "I got a low grade on this paper—I wonder what went wrong and how I can improve my performance in the future."

Get tough with the VOJ: You can't be a wimp if you hope to overcome the VOJ. Instead, you have to be strong and determined, responding as soon as the VOJ appears: "I'm throwing you out and not letting you back in!" You may feel peculiar at first, but this will soon become an automatic response when those negative judgments appear.

Create positive voices and visualizations: The best way to destroy the VOJ for good is to replace it with positive encouragement. As soon as you have stomped on, say, the judgment "You're a jerk," replace it with "No, I'm an intelligent, valuable person with many positive qualities and talents." Similarly, make extensive use of positive visualization—"see" yourself performing well on assignments, being entertaining and insightful with other people, and succeeding gloriously in your courses and activities.

Use other people for independent confirmation: The negative judgments coming from the VOJ are usually irrational, but until they are dragged out into the light of day for examination, they can be very powerful. Sharing your VOJ with people you trust is an effective strategy because they can provide an objective perspective that will reveal the irrationality and destructiveness of negative judgments.

Establish a Creative Environment

An important part of eliminating the negative voice in your mind is to establish environments in which your creative resources can flourish. This means finding or developing physical environments conducive to creative expression as well as supportive social environments. Sometimes, working with other people can be stimulating and energizing to your creative juices; at other times, you may need a private place to work without distraction. You have to find the environment(s) best suited to your own creative process; then make a special effort to do your work there.

The people in your life who form your social environment play an even more influential role in encouraging or inhibiting your creative process. When you are surrounded by people who are positive and supportive, their presence will increase your confidence and encourage you to risk expressing your creative vision. They can stimulate your creativity by providing you with fresh ideas and new perspectives. By engaging in brainstorming, they can help you generate ideas and then later can help you figure out how to refine and implement the most valuable ones.

Make Creativity a Priority

Having diminished the negative Voice of Judgment in your mind, established a creative environment, and committed yourself to trusting your creative gifts, you are now in a position to live and write more creatively. But how do you actually do this? Start small. Identify some habitual patterns in your life and break out of them. Choose new experiences whenever possible—for example, order unfamiliar items from a menu, get to know people outside your circle of friends, or deliberately choose a new type of introduction for a paper—and strive to develop fresh perspectives on aspects of your life. Resist falling back into the ruts you were in previously; remember that living things are supposed to be continually growing, changing, and evolving, *not* acting in repetitive patterns like machines.

Where Do Ideas Come From?

Creativity is the process we use to discover and develop ideas that are unusual and worthy of further elaboration. But how do we get creative ideas? Where do they come from? The following readings from the worlds of science and business may give us some clues.

"Spellbound by the Eternal Riddle, Scientists Revel in Their Captivity"

BY ALAN LIGHTMAN (b. 1948)

Alan Lightman, an astrophysicist and professor at the Massachusetts Institute of Technology, has been fascinated by the intersections of science and art since he was a small boy growing up in Tennessee. As an educator, novelist, and essayist, Lightman works to make arcane and technical concepts comprehensible, even entrancing, to a general audience. "I feel that to most people the scientific culture is like a foreign country," Lightman has said. "I take special delight when I can read a good writer from another culture, bringing me into that world. That's something I would like to do with the scientific culture." In 1996 Lightman was elected a fellow of the American Academy of Arts and Sciences and also won the 1996 American Institute of Physics Andrew Gemant Award for linking science to the humanities.

From an early age, I loved to solve puzzles. When my math teachers assigned homework, most students groaned, but I relished the job. I would save my math problems for last, right before bedtime, like bites of chocolate cake awaiting me after a long and dutiful meal of history and Latin. Then, I would devour my cake.

In geometry, I took pleasure in finding the inexorable and irrefutable relations between lines, angles and curves. In algebra, I delighted in the idea of abstraction, letting x's and y's stand for the number of nickels in a jar or the distance traveled by a train. And then solving a set of connected equations, one logical step after another. Sometimes, when the assigned problems were not challenging enough, I would make up my own problems and seek the solutions.

The biologist Barbara McClintock also enjoyed solving puzzles. In an interview with Evelyn Fox Keller, McClintock recalled that as a child she "used to love to be alone . . . just thinking about things." In high school science classes in Brooklyn, "I would solve some of the problems in ways that weren't the answers the instructor expected," she said. "It was a tremendous joy, the whole process of finding that answer, just pure joy."

Still pursuing that childlike joy in her early 40's, McClintock wondered why some kernels of Indian corn have a mixture of colors, with scattered spots of blue, red and brown. An odd puzzle, seemingly unimportant to anyone except a geneticist.

5   Realizing that the peculiar phenomenon could not be explained by the standard principles of genetic heredity, she began experiments to find an explanation. After five years of work—patient, brilliant, solitary work during which McClintock sometimes spent the fitful nights sleeping on a cot in her lab—she was led to the unorthodox conclusion that genes are not fixed links in the chain of a chromosome, but instead can change positions, rearrange themselves, and in doing so alter their function. For this revelation, she was awarded a Nobel Prize in 1983.

I believe that scientists of average abilities, like myself, and the great scientists, like McClintock, are propelled by the same forces. Why do I enjoy solving puzzles? I love the mental freedom, letting my mind roam and play. Like an athlete who gets pleasure simply from jogging around the quarter-mile track, I delight in letting my mind run. It feels good to use a machine for what it was designed to do.

I love the purity of problems with a logical solution. And the certainty, which contrasts with so much that is ambiguous and bedraggled in the world of people and society. I guiltily admit that sometimes I have closed the door on a screaming daughter, refused to listen to a dejected friend, and escaped to my little desk with its white pad of paper and lovely equations.

With most problems in mathematics and science, you are guaranteed an answer, as clean and crisp as a new $20 bill. Ever wonder how busy the traffic is on your street at different times of the day? When a scientist ponders such a question, he or she sits by the window with a pencil, paper and clock and records the number of passing cars in each minute interval throughout the day.

Even though science is constantly revising itself, constantly adapting to new information and ideas, at any moment a scientist is studying a more or less definite problem, formulated to lead to a definite answer. That answer is waiting, beckoning, challenging the scientist to find it.

10

In looking back on his early days in science, Einstein wrote that "the nothing-ness of the hopes and strivings which chases most men restlessly through life came to my consciousness with considerable vitality."

"Out yonder," he continued, "there was this huge world, which exists indepen-dently of us human beings and which stands before us like a great, eternal riddle, at least partially accessible to our inspections and thinking. The contemplation of this world beckoned like a liberation . . ."

In addition to the joy of solving riddles, there is the pleasure in craftsmanship. The pleasure in building good and useful things with one's hands. As a professional scientist, I've built only ideas, with equations, but as a child I often built various gad-gets, using resistors and capacitors, coils of wire, batteries, switches, photoelectric cells, magnets, chemicals of various kinds. With a thermostat, a light bulb and a padded cardboard box, I constructed an incubator for the cell cultures in my biology experiments.

After seeing the Boris Karloff "Frankenstein" movie, I felt compelled to build a spark-generating induction coil, requiring tedious weeks upon weeks of winding a mile's length of wire around an iron core. Every night, I asked myself the question: Could I make the thing work?

It was a personal question. And that is a paradox of science. Although the truths of science lie outside of human beings, as Einstein said, the motivations for doing science are not only human but intensely personal. Each scientist challenges him or herself at a personal level. Each scientist seeks that challenge, indeed craves that chal-lenge. Each scientist wants to feel his or her own machine revving and rumbling under the hood. Can I build this induction coil? Can I solve this equation? Can I dis-cover the organization of genes?

15

It is a curious I. It is an I that comes in the warm-ups but oddly not during the heat of the race. And there lies another paradox of science. Although some scientists do indeed have astronomical egos and launch themselves toward honors and fame, during the actual moments of scientific discovery, as in all creative discoveries, the ego magically vanishes.

Something else gets under your skin, keeps you working days and nights at the sac-rifice of your sleeping and eating and attention to your family and friends, something beyond the love of puzzle solving. And that other force is the anticipation of under-standing something about the world that no one has ever understood before you.

Einstein wrote that when he first realized that gravity was equivalent to acceleration—an idea that would underlie his new theory of gravity—it was the "happiest thought of my life." On projects of far smaller weight, I have experienced that pleasure of discovering something new. It is an exquisite sensation, a feeling of power, a rush of the blood, a sense of living forever. To be the first vessel to hold this new thing.

All of the scientists I've known have at least one more quality in common: they do what they do because they love it, and because they cannot imagine doing anything else. In a sense, this is the real reason a scientist does science. Because the scientist must. Such a compulsion is both blessing and burden. A blessing because the creative life, in any endeavor, is a gift filled with beauty and not given to everyone, a burden because the call is unrelenting and can drown out the rest of life.

This mixed blessing and burden must be why the astrophysicist Chandrasekhar continued working until his mid-80's, why a visitor to Einstein's apartment in Bern found the young physicist rocking his infant with one hand while doing mathematical calculations with the other. This mixed blessing and burden must have been the "sweet hell" that Walt Whitman referred to when he realized at a young age that he was destined to be a poet. "Never more," he wrote, "shall I escape."

QUESTIONS FOR ACTIVE READING

1. What similes and metaphors does Lightman use to try to capture the essence of what it's like to have a scientific mind, or to think scientifically? How effective is that figurative language? Could you apply any of that language to some aspect of your own life?

2. Lightman uses an implied thesis—that is, a controlling idea that isn't explicitly stated in the first paragraph. In your own words, what is Lightman's thesis?

3. In the last paragraph of his essay, Lightman borrows an oxymoron from the poet Walt Whitman. What is an oxymoron (and where is it in that paragraph)? Create an oxymoron of your own to accurately describe a personal passion.

QUESTIONS FOR THINKING CRITICALLY

1. In paragraph 15, Lightman describes the "curious I." Throughout this book, we have been examining curiosity as a key characteristic of a critical thinker and thoughtful writer. How does Lightman demonstrate his own curiosity?

2. Lightman describes two paradoxes about being a scientist (in paragraph 14, and in paragraphs 18–19). In your own words, describe those paradoxes. Do either of them apply to an area of your own life? Illustrate your own personal paradox with examples from your own experience, as Lightman does.

3. Does Lightman convince you—if you needed convincing—that scientists are just as "creative" as artists? Why, or why not?

"The 6 Myths of Creativity"

BY BILL BREEN

Bill Breen is the senior editor of *Fast Company*, a print and online magazine that has covered the business of new media and technology since the dot-com boom of the mid-1990s. A graduate of Colorado College (BA) and Trinity college, Dublin (MA), Breen studied literature in preparation for his career as a "word wrangler." Breen has written extensively on environmental issues as well as on business and technology.

Creativity

These days, there's hardly a mission statement that doesn't herald it, or a CEO who doesn't laud it. And yet despite all of the attention that business creativity has won over the past few years, maddeningly little is known about day-to-day innovation in the workplace. Where do breakthrough ideas come from? What kind of work environment allows them to flourish? What can leaders do to sustain the stimulants to creativity—and break through the barriers?

Teresa Amabile has been grappling with those questions for nearly thirty years. Amabile, who heads the Entrepreneurial Management Unit at Harvard Business School and is the only tenured professor at a top B-school to devote her entire research program to the study of creativity, is one of the country's foremost explorers of business innovation.

Eight years ago, Amabile took her research to a daring new level. Working with a team of PhDs, graduate students, and managers from various companies, she collected nearly 12,000 daily journal entries from 238 people working on creative projects in seven companies in the consumer products, high-tech, and chemical industries. She didn't tell the study participants that she was focusing on creativity. She simply asked them, in a daily email, about their work and their work environment as they experienced it that day. She then coded the emails for creativity by looking for moments when people struggled with a problem or came up with a new idea.

"The diary study was designed to look at creativity in the wild," she says. "We wanted to crawl inside people's heads and understand the features of their work environment as well as the experiences and thought processes that lead to creative breakthroughs."

Ambile and her team are still combing through the results. But this groundbreaking study is already overturning some long-held beliefs about innovation in the workplace. In an interview with *Fast Company,* she busted six cherished myths about creativity. (If you want to quash creativity in your organization, just continue to embrace them.) Here they are, in her own words.

1. Creativity Comes from Creative Types

When I give talks to managers, I often start by asking, Where in your organization do you most want creativity? Typically, they'll say R&D, marketing, and advertising. When I ask, Where do you *not* want creativity? Someone will inevitably answer, "Accounting." That always gets a laugh because of the negative connotations of creative accounting. But there's this common perception among managers that some people are creative, and most aren't. That's just not true. As a leader, you don't want to ghettoize creativity; you want everyone in your organization producing novel and useful ideas, including your financial people. Over the past couple of decades, there have been innovations in financial accounting that are extremely profound and entirely ethical, such as activity-based costing.

The fact is, almost all of the research in this field shows that anyone with normal intelligence is capable of doing some degree of creative work. Creativity depends on a number of things: experience, including knowledge and technical skills; talent; an ability to think in new ways; and the capacity to push through uncreative dry spells. Intrinsic motivation—people who are turned on by their work often work creatively—is especially critical. Over the past five years, organizations have paid more attention to creativity and innovation than at any other time in my career. But I believe most people aren't anywhere near to realizing their creative potential, in part because they're laboring in environments that impede intrinsic motivation. The anecdotal evidence suggests many companies still have a long way to go to remove the barriers to creativity.

2. Money Is a Creativity Motivator

The experimental research that has been done on creativity suggests that money isn't everything. In the diary study, we asked people, "To what extent were you motivated by rewards today?" Quite often they'd say that the question isn't relevant—that they don't think about pay on a day-to-day basis. And the handful of people who were spending a lot of time wondering about their bonuses were doing very little creative thinking.

Bonuses and pay-for-performance plans can even be problematic when people believe that every move they make is going to affect their compensation. In those situations, people tend to get risk averse. Of course, people need to feel that they're being compensated fairly. But our research shows that people put far more value on a work environment where creativity is supported, valued, and recognized. People want the opportunity to deeply engage in their work and make real progress. So it's critical for leaders to match people to projects not only on the basis of their experience but also in terms of where their interests lie. People are most creative when they care about their work and they're stretching their skills. If the challenge is far beyond their skill level, they tend to get frustrated; if it's far below their skill level, they tend to get bored. Leaders need to strike the right balance.

3. Time Pressure Fuels Creativity

In our diary study, people often thought they were most creative when they were working under severe deadline pressure. But the 12,000 aggregate days that we studied showed just the opposite: People were the least creative when they were fighting the clock. In fact, we found a kind of time-pressure hangover—when people were working under great pressure, their creativity went down not only on that day but the next two days as well. Time pressure stifles creativity because people can't deeply engage with the problem. Creativity requires an incubation period; people need time to soak in a problem and let the ideas bubble up.

In fact, it's not so much the deadline that's the problem; it's the distractions that rob people of the time to make that creative breakthrough. People can certainly be creative when they're under the gun, but only when they're able to focus on the work. They must be protected from distractions, and they must know that the work is important and that everyone is committed to it. In too many organizations, people don't understand the reason for the urgency, other than the fact that somebody somewhere needs it done today.

4. Fear Forces Breakthroughs

There's this widespread notion that fear and sadness somehow spur creativity. There's even some psychological literature suggesting that the incidence of depression is higher in creative writers and artists—the depressed geniuses who are incredibly original in their thinking. But we don't see it in the population that we studied.

We coded all 12,000 journal entries for the degree of fear, anxiety, sadness, anger, joy, and love that people were experiencing on a given day. And we found that creativity is positively associated with joy and love and negatively associated with anger, fear, and anxiety. The entries show that people are happiest when they come up with a creative idea, but they're more likely to have a breakthrough if they were happy the day before. There's a kind of virtuous cycle. When people are excited about their work, there's a better chance that they'll make a cognitive association that incubates overnight and shows up as a creative idea the next day. One day's happiness often predicts the next day's creativity.

5. Competition Beats Collaboration

There's a widespread belief, particularly in the finance and high-tech industries, that internal competition fosters innovation. In our surveys, we found that creativity takes a hit when people in a work group compete instead of collaborate. The most creative teams are those that have the confidence to share and debate ideas. But when people compete for recognition, they stop sharing information. And that's destructive because nobody in an organization has all of the information required to put all the pieces of the puzzle together.

6. A Streamlined Organization Is a Creative Organization

Maybe it's only the public-relations departments that believe downsizing and restructuring actually foster creativity. Unfortunately, I've seen too many examples of this kind of spin. One of my favorites is a 1994 letter to shareholders from a major U.S. software company: "A downsizing such as this one is always difficult for employees, but out of tough times can come strength, creativity, and teamwork."

Of course, the opposite is true: Creativity suffers greatly during a downsizing. But it's even worse than many of us realized. We studied a 6,000-person division in a global electronics company during the entire course of a 25 percent downsizing, which took an incredibly agonizing 18 months. Every single one of the stimulants to creativity in the work environment went down significantly. Anticipation of the downsizing was even worse than the downsizing itself—people's fear of the unknown led them to basically disengage from the work. More troubling was the fact that even five months after the downsizing, creativity was still down significantly.

Unfortunately, downsizing will remain a fact of life, which means that leaders need to focus on the things that get hit. Communication and collaboration decline significantly. So too does people's sense of freedom and autonomy. Leaders will have to work hard and fast to stabilize the work environment so ideas can flourish.

Taken together, these operating principles for fostering creativity in the workplace might lead you to think that I'm advocating a soft management style. Not true. I'm pushing for a smart management style. My thirty years of research and these 12,000 journal entries suggest that when people are doing work that they love and they're allowed to deeply engage in it—and when the work itself is valued and recognized—then creativity will flourish. Even in tough times.

QUESTIONS FOR ACTIVE READING

1. In your own words, describe the "6 Myths of Creativity."
2. How did Teresa Amabile, the Harvard Business School professor who studies creativity in the workplace, design her research? What kinds of information was she looking for? What seems especially surprising or interesting about her approach to research?
3. Who is the audience for Bill Breen's article? How can you tell?

QUESTIONS FOR THINKING CRITICALLY

1. Compare Alan Lightman's description of what motivates scientists ("Spellbound by the Eternal Riddle, Scientists Revel in Their Captivity," p. 101) with the qualities that motivate creativity in business. What qualities are shared? Which qualities seem to be unique to business or to science?
2. Select one of the "6 Myths of Creativity" that has special application to your own studies, work, or life. How has this myth challenged or blocked your ability to be creative? In an essay, describe the myth in your own words and devise a plan for overcoming this challenge or block and becoming more creative.
3. In your experience, which of the four strategies for becoming more creative (p. 98) is most important for innovation and success? In your response, refer to Alan Lightman's essay (p. 101) or Teresa Amabile's research.

Writing Project: Imagining Your Life Lived More Creatively

According to a French proverb, "Only he who does nothing makes a mistake." The chapter's Writing Project asks you to think creatively to imagine changes in your life. Doing this can, in fact, be very difficult. But it is important to do to avoid future regrets; often people most regret the things they did not do as they lived their lives.

> Imagine how some part of your life could be more satisfying or exciting. You will need to focus on one or more specific areas of your life, such as an important relationship, your college work, or a job that would be ideal for you. Visualize how your future will be when you creatively transform this part of your life, and think about what you must do in the present to achieve this imagined goal. Create or locate images that inspire or evoke your goal as well as how you plan to achieve it. Follow your instructor's directions for length, format, and so on.

The Writing Situation

Begin by considering the key elements of the Thinking-Writing Model.

Purpose   Your purpose is to use the strategies for thinking, living, and writing this chapter presents to create a new vision of your own life. Doing this will require you to step back from your life, to become an observer of how you have lived, or are living, or might be living, and then to create a potentially different vision.
Your essay will begin with, and include, at least one actual image.

Audience   You have an interesting and varied audience. You are your own most important audience, for who else could be more interested in the subject? Beyond yourself, you may choose to show your writing to key people in your life, especially if any of them would be affected by the changes you propose. Their reactions to early drafts could be very helpful as you revise.

Your classmates may be part of your audience if your writing is going to be shared with them. All the readers mentioned so far will be interested in what you say, and especially in the changes you propose, so include enough background information about how your life was, or is, for them to understand the impact of those changes.

Subject   Thinking and writing about our own lives can be exciting yet challenging. Often we are so busy just living our lives that we don't take time to think about how they might be different. We begin to think that whatever *is* has to be.

A potential problem is that you may believe that there is little in your life that can be changed. You are not necessarily being asked to propose major changes. What you end up writing about could be a different life or simply a richer, more fully realized version of your life now.

Writer   As the expert on your own life, you write with authority on this project. If you are the creative type, you should welcome the chance to let your imagination go! If you consider yourself unimaginative, take this opportunity to develop your creative side, using any of the strategies discussed in this chapter.

The Writing Process

The following sections guide you through the stages of the writing process. Try to be particularly conscious of how creative thinking can help you discover and connect ideas.

Generating Ideas   Review your responses to the Thinking-Writing Activities in this chapter. You will probably see a number of ideas that pertain to this project. Then, to discover more ideas and a possible focus, follow these suggestions and jot down your responses.

- Think about two or three things you do that are particularly important to you. How might they become more satisfying if you became more creative in your approach?
- Envision your life five years from now. What activities do you hope to be involved in? How could they be shaped by creative thinking? What would your ideal job situation be?
- Recall an event from the past in which you experienced a creative break-through. What was your flash of insight? Can you apply that creative insight to your current situation or future life?
- Choose a situation and brainstorm or ask questions about it.
- For a week, keep a journal about how you experience your work and work environment each day. (See "The 6 Myths of Creativity," p. 104.) What situations seem to inspire your creativity? What situations stifle your creativity?
- Collect images that suggest "creativity" to you, even if you can't quite articulate *why* they seem creative.
- Ask yourself if you have enough ideas to begin drafting your paper. If not, you may want to try again by examining another aspect of your life.

Defining a Focus   After reviewing the material you created, consider which area of your life would be most exciting to focus on. Then write a few sentences about that change. For example:

> I think that I would like to be a more creative cook. Why? How? So that my housemates and I can have more enjoyable meals when it's my turn in the kitchen; so that I can really enjoy cooking. . . . Some ways that I can do this is to take a cooking course, check some really different cookbooks out of the library—like from other countries or other regions, or vegan, or barbecue. I should spend some time with my uncle who makes such good one-dish meals, find some tasty web sites, and watch some of those cooking shows instead of surfing away.

This writer has a focus: becoming a more creative cook. She can now decide how to draft the thesis—as a simple statement or a "blueprinted" sentence that lays out the organization of the paper.

Simple statement: I want to change my life by becoming a more creative cook.

Blueprinted sentence: I plan to become a more creative cook by taking a cooking course, checking some good cookbooks out of the library, spending more time with my uncle, finding some tasty web sites, and watching some cooking shows.

If you do write a blueprinted sentence, consider whether you have listed the changes in an order that your audience can easily comprehend. Once you have established an order, use it to structure your essay.

Organizing Ideas   After you have decided on a focus, you can

- describe your current or past situation
- describe some changes you would like to make or wish you had made
- describe the improved situation
- select images that more specifically reflect your situation and/or your goal

Does this thinking suggest a method of organization? Is that organization effective, or is it too stodgy for a paper about creative thinking? How about narrating the events from a future perspective, after you have made some changes?

Map out an organizational plan that you think might work. Consult with your instructor if you are taking a creative approach to organization.

Drafting   As you translate your ideas into coherent writing, you need to draft in ways that will help you revise effectively. Because the essay you are about to write will have three distinct components—your present situation, the changes you would make, and how your life would be different—you may want to draft each component separately and then think about connecting them.

Drafting Hints

1. If you are drafting on a word processor, double or even triple space. Be sure to save your work every few minutes if your program does not do so automatically.
2. Consider drafting the three components of this essay as three separate files. You could name them "Present Situation," "Changes," and "New and Different Life." Then you can easily copy and paste them to see what organization would work best.
3. If you are drafting by hand, skip lines and write on only one side of the paper. That way you can easily rearrange them if you decide to reorganize.

Revising   One of the best revision strategies is to get an audience's reactions to your draft. Your classmates can help you see where your draft is already successful and where it needs improvement. If your instructor allows class time for peer review, have a draft ready.

Revising Strategy: Peer Response with Silent Writer   This activity, which works best with groups of three or four, introduces a different method for peer review than the one in Chapter 3. In this method, the writer is silent after reading the draft aloud twice and listens as peers respond. Follow all the steps of the directions carefully.

1. The group selects a timekeeper, who allots ten minutes to each writer. Regardless of how many steps in the response process have been completed, after ten minutes the group moves on to consider the next writer's work.
2. One person begins by reading his or her draft aloud while group members listen, giving the writer their full attention.
3. The writer then reads the draft aloud a second time. Group members listen again, this time taking notes.
4. Group members read their comments to the writer. Responses that are stated as "I" messages and are geared to helping the writer to revise work well:
   Weak response: "I like it. It sounds okay to me." (*no specific help given to writer*)

   Marginally useful: "I thought the description of your new neighborhood was entertaining." (*encouragement for the writer*)

   Useful: "Can you give me an example of the kind of task you would perform in your new job?" (*The writer learns what information the reader needs.*)

   Very useful: "I was confused when you said your aunt came into the room. I thought you said earlier that you were alone in the house." (*Again, the writers hear from someone who wasn't there when it happened, someone who needs more information.*)
5. The writer listens to questions and comments and may take notes but does *not* answer or respond aloud. The writer may ask questions after all group members have commented.
6. Continue the process until each group member has used ten minutes of response time.

As soon as possible after peer review, you should revise your draft based on your peers' questions and comments. Then, if possible, put it aside for a day or two before continuing.

Reread your revised draft out loud, slowly. Think about each of the following questions.

1. How could you improve your thesis?

2. How could you improve the order of your draft? Here you need to balance creativity against the needs of your readers. Is there a more creative way to arrange your essay without sacrificing the needs of your readers?

3. Could you provide transitions between sections of your essay to help your readers follow your ideas?

4. Is your use of language creative? Could you provide more specific adjectives and adverbs?

5. Have you given your essay an inventive title that will make your readers want to read it?

Editing and Proofreading   To prepare a final draft, edit for standard grammar and punctuation. Proofread carefully to detect omitted words and punctuation marks. Run your spell-checker program, but be aware of its limitations. Finally, ask someone you trust to proofread after you are finished.

The following essays show how two students responded to the idea of living their lives more creatively. Before writing, each of them used one of the methods on pages 98–99 for generating ideas.

Student Writing

Jessie Lange's Writing Process: Freewriting

I have to write a paper about a legend I didn't even understand. There are stairs going up a tower to a place that is a kind of nirvana, a place of happiness, but you can only reach the top if you don't believe in the legend itself. Hello? If you don't believe it, why would you spend your time climbing up? Ok, Ok, I needed to think. Usually getting outside helps me think better so I tried that up at our place in the country. I did have a great experience. I saw some deer in the mist at night. They were really hard to see and when I put up my lamp to get more light, instead of seeing them better, they almost disappeared in the light. So I turned out the light and I could see them better in the dark. I'm thinking that maybe this is like the legend. The opposite of what you would expect happens. Maybe the legend is about trying too hard. I'll try this angle and see what happens.

Discovering Creativity by Not Looking for It

By Jessie Lange

There have been numerous times when I have sat in front of a blank computer screen, a writing assignment in hand, feeling completely uninspired and uncreative. Without having even begun I think, "Now what?" There have been numerous times when I've just started filling up that screen with meaningless, dry words that really have no effect on me or anyone else. Yes, I'm getting the job done, but not the job I'd like—not my best work, not anywhere near it. One thing that I've found in my life is that in your most uncreative ruts sometimes you can't pull yourself out all on your own. You can't always, sitting in an idea-less vacuum, turn on the creativity. Sometimes you will save yourself time and produce a much more fulfilling piece of work if you take the time out to go *out* of the world of your blank screen. For me this has always meant literally getting outdoors, because somehow it always seems that I find *outside* what I've been looking for *inside*.

It was the first English assignment of my senior year of high school—an interpretation of a Buddhist legend—and I was struggling with its meaning. The legend is about a set of stairs leading to the top of the tower from where you can see the "whole horizon" and the "loveliest landscape"—a symbol of attaining nirvana. The paradox in the legend is that you can only reach the top if you do not believe in the legend itself. How would those who believe, then, ever reach the top? How can you even start the climb without making the conscious decision to do so?

Being in the country on weekends has many benefits, one of them being that I could go outside to clear my head. I lit my Williams Sonoma oil lamp and walked out into the night that offered the occasional drizzle and a strong breeze that ruffled the leaves of the tree I lay down under. I was there for an

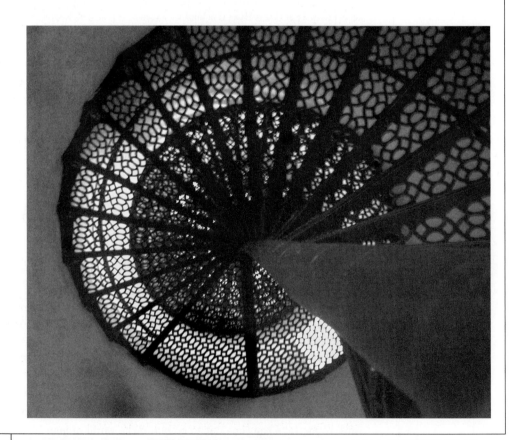

hour, feeling the drops on my face and the dampness settling into my body, before it happened. I rolled over and looked out into the field, because I sensed something the way that you can and will when you're listening with your entire body. Farther out, right before the lawn becomes high grass and eventually woods, were four white shapes moving across my line of vision. The same deer I casually glance at during the day were like ghosts grazing out there at night. Just faint, light vaporous figures against the pitch black. That moment was like seeing the "whole horizon." Those animals, moving with such grace, were unaware of my presence. For all they knew, I was another tree silently overseeing their nightly ritual. Watching these beasts—because that's what they are, wonderfully wild animals—I was witnessing a scene that could have taken place in this same spot on this same night hundreds or thousands of years before. I reached for my lantern and turned up the flame, holding it in front of me for a better view. This light, however, obstructed my vision rather than illuminating it. It was only when I put the flame aside and cupped my hands around my eyes, creating a deeper darkness, that I could really see the deer.

And then I realized that perhaps that was why only those who do not believe the legend ever climb the stairs of the tower—because when you actively search for things, like holding the light, perhaps you prevent yourself from seeing them. Had I not put my writing aside and taken that walk, I would never have found this answer, the answer I was looking for. I wrote my English essay and I also learned something about creativity in my own life. Some of your most creative moments happen when you're not looking. In the journey up the steps of the tower toward creativity, sometimes it is not those who are keenly searching for a victory of sorts, but those who are instead turning down the light, that begin the climb.

Alternative Writing Projects

1. Write an essay explaining your original, creative solution to a physical problem, one involving a piece of equipment, the use of space, overcoming some barrier, and so on. Be sure to incorporate images that illustrate the problem, the solution, or both. Here are some examples:
   - Crowd control or better seating at concerts and sporting events
   - A device that makes some activity easier or more accessible for the disabled
   - New design or redesign of highways and roads in your area
   - An imaginative new tool or transportation device

2. Write an essay explaining your original, creative solution to a social problem, such as homelessness, tensions between racial groups, or drug use among young teenagers.
3. Write an essay explaining your original, creative plan for the perfect house, the perfect party, or the perfect vacation.

5

Making Decisions and Drafting

> *The strongest principle of growth lies in human choice.*
>
> —*George Eliot*

Critical Thinking Focus: Decision making in writing and in life

Writing Focus: Making decisions about drafts

Reading Themes: Extraordinary decisions

Writing Project: Analyzing a decision to be made

A decision is a kind of commitment. You make decisions, of varying degrees of importance and impact, every day of your life. How carefully you approach that decision, how thoughtfully you evaluate your choices, and how meaningfully you follow through on your commitment to what you have decided varies with the degree of that decision's importance. For example, a knowledgeable and open-minded evaluation of your current lifestyle might lead you to decide to make a few fundamental changes—you might get more exercise, resolve to drink less on the weekends, opt for salad instead of fries. Your decision to live more healthfully might be based on the advice of your doctor and the example set by an athletic friend, but until you *commit* yourself to that decision, you're never going to succeed at lowering your cholesterol or waking up refreshed on Monday morning.

When you decide on a topic for an essay, you are also making a commitment. In the previous chapter, we looked at the process of deciding on a topic—engaging your creativity, your curiosity, your open-mindedness and your knowledge in order to *decide* on the most engaging and appropriate topic for you to write about. In this chapter, we'll examine strategies for following through on that decision, applying those same four qualities to the decision making inherent in each stage of the drafting process.

117

In addition, this chapter includes essays by and about people forced to make extraordinary decisions under the most perilous circumstances. Their insight, creativity, strength, and thoughtfulness are truly inspiring.

Decisions While Drafting

Most decisions made while drafting a piece of writing are not made in a "first this, then that" sequential order. As Chapter 1 points out, writing processes are usually recursive. Ideas are generated, drafts are made, more ideas come, revisions are necessary, more planning, maybe more drafting—back and forth until the writer says this is it. However, throughout this recursive process, writers must make decisions on subjects, audiences, purposes, and specific ideas and words.

Actually, there is a *first decision*. That is, of course, to take the step from generating ideas to drafting. Some people do this easily; others postpone it. You need to understand your own tendency here and be sure to have some strategies that get you going. Some of the strategies in Chapter 4 used to generate ideas are also useful for beginning to draft. For example,

- *Focused freewriting.* Writing freely on the selected topic can get a draft started, especially if the writer resolves to write and not stare at the screen or the blank page.
- *Listing ideas about the topic and then expressing the ideas in sentences.*
- *Deciding to write on the topic for a set amount of time,* maybe one-half hour.
- *Deciding to draft a specific section first,* usually the one you know most about.

Once you start drafting, you will face other decisions.

FOUR QUALITIES
OF A CRITICAL THINKER
Abolitionist Frederick Douglass

Curious   When curiosity becomes courageous, we are moved to question injustices in our own lives and in the lives of those around us. Such transcendent questioning becomes a passion and can lead us to take extraordinary risks in service of a larger purpose. A towering example of such passionate questioning and risk taking is Frederick Douglass. His *Narrative of the Life of Frederick Douglass, An American Slave* remains one of the most important documents in American history, laying bare the injustices of slavery while also envisioning and inspiring a revolution in civil rights.

Open-minded   A profound accomplishment of Douglass's thinking was his revelation that slavery was as demeaning to slave owners as it was to slaves themselves. A society that tolerates such injustice, he realized, is never going to be truly capable of any form of justice. As an adult, Douglass was an adviser to President Abraham Lincoln, and in later years he traveled and lectured widely to all kinds of audiences.

Knowledgeable   There may be no more stunning testament to the power of literacy and knowledge than Frederick

Decide What Your Purpose for Writing Is   Usually in college and at work, the purpose is clear. You want to complete the lab report or the English paper to fulfill the assignment as well as you can, or you want your proposal or your application to be accepted. However, if you are composing an email to go to your family list about reunion plans or a letter to the editor about a community problem, you might need to define your purpose. Do you want family members to help? Do you want the city council to act?

In your notebook or a separate file, write a sentence beginning "My purpose(s) for this (essay, email, memo) are . . ." and list them. Then write a sentence beginning "In order to fulfill my purpose, I should . . ." You are the audience for these sentences and those following the other decisions. These sentences will almost surely not be part of your draft. They will help you decide what to include.

Decide Who Your Audience Is and What Its Needs Are   As with purpose, the primary audience is often obvious in college and workplace writing—the instructor or the supervisor—but your classmates and fellow workers might be an audience, too. You often know what those audiences expect since assignments and office formats are usually explicit. If you are writing for family members or community groups, as you draft, you should think about what background information is necessary or superfluous, what tone is suitable, what level of vocabulary is appropriate, and what special needs that audience may have.

In your notebook or a separate file, write a sentence beginning "My audience is . . . Then write a sentence beginning, "My audience will expect . . . ; my audience will need to know . . . ; my audience will already know . . ."

Decide What Your Subject Is and Why It Is Interesting   As we have seen, your subject for writing can be drawn from your personal experience, or it can be a topic assigned by an instructor. If you are allowed to choose a subject, now is the time to exercise your creativity. Try the suggestions for creativity in topic selection and generating ideas presented in Chapter 3.

Douglass's life story. When he heard his first owner declare that teaching Douglass to read "would forever unfit him to be a slave," it was to Douglass "an entirely new train of thought . . . a new and special revelation." Reading and writing, the access to knowledge and the ability to communicate persuasively, would be the means to achieve freedom not only for him but also for all slaves.

Creative   As the excerpt from Douglass's *Narrative* (p. 125) demonstrates, even learning to read was an extraordinarily dangerous ambition. Just as curiosity sometimes leads to transcendent questioning, creativity can help us to negotiate especially risky or dangerous situations. Douglass, for example, first began as a small child to practice reading by befriending poor white children and bringing bread with him as he ran his errands. Later, on the run from bounty hunters, he forged documents that allowed him to travel safely to New York.

Online Study Center
Frederick Douglass
Visit the Online Study Center for *Critical Thinking, Thoughtful Writing* at *college.hmco.com/pic/ chaffee CTTW4e* to learn more about Frederick Douglass.

Decide Who You Are as a Writer   Finding your voice and taking a stand are key steps not only of the writing process but also of your intellectual development. To make a decision about what voice and tone to use in your paper, consider again your audience and purpose. Are you speaking as someone who is an expert on an issue, writing on a subject about which you have considerable personal experience? Alternatively, are you writing for an audience of experts whose conversation about a subject or issue you would like to join? As you read more widely in a variety of disciplines and attend lectures and seminars by experts in a range of fields, you will become more familiar with the different voices and vocabularies used to express ideas for specific audiences. As your knowledge increases, it will be time for you to experiment with different voices and approaches to convey that knowledge.

Decide on a Working Thesis   This is a time to be open-minded. After some drafting, you need to think again about the thesis you may have started with or think about formulating one if you have not yet done so. Reread the material in Chapter 4 about moving from a topic to a thesis statement. As you continue to draft, you will decide exactly how to state it and where to place it.

In your notebook or a separate file, write a sentence beginning "As I see it now, the thesis for this piece is . . ." Then write "Or perhaps it is better said as . . ."

Decide What Information to Use and What More You Need   Review your idea-generating activities. Look again at your tentative thesis. What information do you need to support it and to fulfill your purpose? Think about what you know; think about what you should know more about. Think about what your audience needs to know. The Critical Reading Questions of Interpretation, Analysis, and Evaluation in Chapter 2 can be helpful in this decision.

In your notebook or a separate file, write a sentence beginning "The ideas about . . . are important to my thesis." Then a sentence beginning "I need to know more about . . ." Then a sentence beginning "My audience needs to know . . ."

Decide When to Outline to Bring Order to Your Draft   Some writers make an outline or a plan before drafting; some writers outline after drafting; some writers do not outline but instead revise and redraft until they are satisfied with the organization of the piece.

A rough outline, which indicates the order of sections but is not carefully formatted, usually helps a draft get into shape. Sometimes, a draft benefits from being outlined more than once. Formal outlines, with logical patterns of letters, numbers, sentences, and phrases, can be done when a piece is close to being finished. See your handbook for formal outline specifications if you are asked to do one or if you want to be very sure about your paper's organization.

In your notebook or a separate file, outline the material in your draft, using an informal or a formal system as you find helpful.

Decide on an Introduction and a Conclusion   Although you will look carefully at these parts of your draft as you revise and refine, don't forget to work out possible beginnings and endings as you draft.

Explore as many different types of introductions and conclusions as you can if you are writing something for which there can be choices. (Some kinds of writing, such as lab reports, have expected formats that include types of beginnings and endings.)

Following are some types of beginnings:

- Background information or context
- A relevant anecdote
- A quotation or proverb that relates to the topic
- A striking statement (to be contradicted or supported)
- The problem to be addressed in the paper
- Questions connected to the content of the paper
- The who, what, where, when, how, and why of the paper's focus
- The claim, thesis, or main point
- Combinations of these types

Explore the many possibilities for endings, such as

- A summary of the paper's information
- A recommendation or call for action
- An apt quotation or proverb
- A telling anecdote
- The thesis or main point restated or stated at the end instead of the beginning
- A suggestion of the need for more discussion of the issue

A conclusion must provide a sense of closure to the piece; readers should recognize it as an ending (you should not have to write "The End"!).

Neither introductions nor conclusions should be apologetic ("I don't know much about this, but . . ."); nor should their tone differ from that of the body of the paper.

Decisions in Your Life

Throughout your life you will continue to make decisions and to deal with decisions others make that affect your life. Recalling a previous decision about your education, your relationships, your athletic activities, or any other part of your life will remind you of how important those choices are.

THINKING-
WRITING
ACTIVITY

Analyzing a Previous Decision

Think back to an important decision you made that turned out well and describe the experience as specifically as possible by reconstructing the reasoning process you used to make your decision.

- How did you *define* the decision to be made?
- What *choices* did you consider?

(Continued on next page)

- What were the various *pros and cons* of each possible choice?
- What specific plan of action did you use to implement your ideas?
- How did you review your decision to make any necessary adjustments?

Using a method to help you decide about important issues will help you make intelligent decisions and avoid poor choices.

An Organized Approach to Making Decisions

As you were reflecting on the successful decision you wrote about in the previous Thinking-Writing Activity, you probably noticed your mind working in a systematic way as you thought your way through the decision-making process. Of course, we often make important decisions with less thoughtful analysis by acting impulsively and are later forced to cope with the consequences. Our intuitions can be a useful guide to success when they are *informed intuitions*—based on lessons learned from past experience and thoughtful reflection. Naturally, there are no guarantees that careful analysis will lead to a successful result—there are often too many unknown elements and factors beyond our control. But we can certainly improve our success rate by becoming more knowledgeable about the decision-making process.

This approach consists of five steps. As you master these steps, you will be able to apply them in a natural and flexible way.

Step 1: Define the Decision and Its Goals Clearly (Audience)

This seems like an obvious step, but decision making frequently goes wrong at the starting point. For example, imagine that you are trying to decide on an academic major. In order to make an informed decision, you have to project yourself into the future, imagining the career that will be right for you. Your goals will likely include

- financial security
- personal fulfillment
- an opportunity to make use of your special talents
- employment opportunities and job security

Keeping these goals in mind as you consider various majors will give you the greatest success in discovering the field that best suits you. Your audience for this thinking exercise includes not just yourself but also anyone who can help you achieve those goals. The more specific your definition of the decision—and its goals—is, the clearer your analysis and the greater the likelihood of your success will be. Here's a strategy you can use to best define your decision:

Strategy: Write a one-page analysis describing your decision-making situation that defines your goals as clearly and specifically as possible. Write for an audience beyond yourself. Your audience might be your parents, your partner, or your career counselor.

Step 2: Consider All Possible Choices (Subject)

Successful decision makers explore all possible choices, not simply the obvious ones. In fact, the less obvious choices often turn out to be the most effective ones. For instance, one student couldn't decide whether to major in accounting or business management. While discussing his situation with his friends, he revealed that his real interest was in web site design. Although he was very talented, he considered this area only a hobby, not a possible career choice. His friends pointed out that designing web sites could prove to be his best career opportunity, but he first needed to see it as a possibility.

Strategy: List as many possible choices for your situation as you can—obvious and not obvious, practical and impractical. Ask other people for additional suggestions and keep an open mind—don't censor or prejudge any ideas. Evaluating many different possibilities will help you select a truly interesting and engaging subject.

Step 3: Gather All Relevant Information and Evaluate the Pros and Cons of Each Possible Choice (Purpose)

Each of the possible choices you identified will have certain advantages and disadvantages, so it is essential that you analyze these pros and cons in an organized fashion. This analysis will help you to define and focus your purpose. In the case of the student discussed in step 2, the career choice of accounting might on the one hand offer advantages like ready employment opportunities, the flexibility of working in many different situations and geographical locations, a moderate to high income, and job security. On the other hand, disadvantages might be that accounting does not reflect the student's deep and abiding interest, that he might become bored with it over time, and that the career might not result in the personal challenge and fulfillment that he needs.

Strategy: Using a format similar to the following, analyze the pros and cons of each of your possible choices. The "pro" list will likely help you to visualize the true purpose motivating your choice.

In many cases, you may lack sufficient information to make an informed choice. Unfortunately, this has never prevented people from plunging ahead anyway, making a decision that is more a gamble than an informed choice. But it makes much more sense to seek out the information you need in order to determine which of your choices has the best chance of success. In the case of the student, he would need certain crucial information to determine which career would be best for him: What sort of academic preparation and experience is required for the various careers? What are the prospects for employment in these areas, and how well do the positions pay? What are the day-to-day activities in each career? How happy are the people in the various careers?

Strategy: For each possible choice that you have identified, create questions regarding information you need; then obtain that information. Your purpose here is to clarify the resources you need to achieve your goal.

Step 4: Select the Choice That Seems Best Suited to the Situation

The first three steps are designed to help you analyze your decision situation: to define clearly the decision in terms of your goals, to generate possible choices, and to evaluate the pros and cons of the choices you have identified. In the fourth step, you must synthesize what you have learned, weaving together all the various threads into a conclusion that you consider your best choice. In academic writing, synthesis often evolves from the drafting process as you discern new connections among different perspectives and resources. How do you do this? There is no one simple way to identify your best choice, but the following are two useful strategies for guiding your deliberations.

Strategy: Identify and prioritize the goal(s) of your decision situation and determine which of your choices best meets these goals.

This process will probably involve reviewing and perhaps refining your definition of the decision situation. For example, for the student we have been discussing, goals included choosing a career that would (a) provide financial security, (b) provide personal fulfillment, (c) make use of special talents, and (d) offer plentiful work opportunities along with job security.

Once identified, these goals can be ranked in order of priority, which will then suggest what the best choice would be. If the student ranks goals *a* and *d* at the top of the list, a choice of accounting or business administration may make sense. However, if the student ranks goals *b* and *c* at the top, pursuing a career in graphic design and illustration may be the best selection.

Project yourself into the future, imagining as realistically as you can the consequences of each possible choice. Write your thoughts down and discuss them with your friends or colleagues.

Step 5: Implement a Plan of Action and Monitor the Results, Making Necessary Adjustments

Once you have made your best choice, you need to develop and implement a plan of action. The more specific your plan, the greater the likelihood of its success. If, for instance, the student in the example in step 2 decides to pursue a career in web site design, his plan should include reviewing the major that best meets his needs, discussing his situation with students and faculty in that department, planning what courses to take, and perhaps speaking with people working in the field. This step of the decision-making process is similar to the work of creating a research plan for writing (Chapter 14).

Strategy: Create a plan that details the steps you would take to implement your decision, along with a time line for taking these steps.

Naturally, your plan is merely a starting point. As you actually begin taking the steps in your plan, you may discover that you need to make changes and adjustments. You might find new information that suggests that your choice may be wrong. For example, as the student takes courses in HTML and design, he may realize that his interest in the field is not as serious as he once thought and that although he likes this area as a hobby, he does not want it to be his life's work. In this case, he should reconsider his other choices, perhaps adding some choices that he did not contemplate before.

Strategy: After implementing your choice, evaluate its success by identifying what is working and what is not; then make the necessary adjustments to improve the situation.

SUMMARY FOR MAKING DECISIONS IN WRITING AND IN LIFE

1. Define the decision clearly.

2. Consider all possible choices.

3. Gather all relevant information and evaluate the pros and cons of each possible choice.

4. Select the choice that seems best suited to the situation.

5. Implement a plan of action and monitor the results, making necessary adjustments.

Analyzing Decisions

The following readings illustrate decisions of tremendous, life-altering import. Frederick Douglass describes how he and fellow slaves made the momentous decision to escape to the North in 1835. Journalist Sara Corbett depicts the long and difficult journey teenage refugees from the Sudanese civil war are making toward freedom, and the often mundane but critical decisions they make as they adjust to a completely new culture and geography.

FROM **Narrative of the Life of Frederick Douglass, an American Slave**

BY FREDERICK DOUGLASS (1818–1895)

Frederick Bailey was born into slavery in 1818, his mother a field worker and his father rumored to be her white master. He spent his early childhood with his grandmother. When he was six years old, his grandmother brought him to the Lloyd Plantation, one of the oldest and largest plantations in Maryland. Frederick only saw his mother once more; she died when he was seven years old.

In 1825, Frederick was sent to live at the Baltimore home of Hugh and Sophia Auld. Sophia, a religious woman, began to teach Bailey (not yet known as Douglass) to read—until she was abruptly forbidden to continue the lessons by her husband, who believed that teaching a slave to read and write was too dangerous. Douglass quickly realized that literacy was a powerful tool for gaining his freedom.

In 1838, after laboring at various plantations and in a Baltimore shipyard, Douglass decided to flee north to New York City. Through the Underground Railroad, Douglass and his wife then moved further north to New Bedford, Massachusetts. To further protect himself from bounty hunters looking for runaway slaves, Frederick Bailey changed his name to Frederick Douglass. In 1845, he published the autobiographical *Narrative of the Life of Frederick Douglass, an American Slave,* which quickly became a bestseller.

During the Civil War, Douglass met several times with President Abraham Lincoln. After the Civil War, Douglass was perhaps the most important black advocate for equal rights and suffrage (the right to vote) in America. Douglass died in Washington, D.C., on February 20, 1895.

A t the close of the year 1834, Mr. Freeland again hired me of my master, for the year 1835. But, by this time, I began to want to live ~*upon free land*~ as well as ~*with freeland;*~ and I was no longer content, therefore, to live with him or any other slave-holder. I began, with the commencement of the year, to prepare myself for a final struggle, which should decide my fate one way or the other. My tendency was upward. I was fast approaching manhood, and year after year had passed, and I was still a slave. These thoughts roused me—I must do something. I therefore resolved that 1835 should not pass without witnessing an attempt, on my part, to secure my liberty. But I was not willing to cherish this determination alone. My fellow-slaves were dear to me. I was anxious to have them participate with me in this, my life-giving determination. I therefore, though with great prudence, commenced early to ascertain their views and feelings in regard to their condition, and to imbue their minds with thoughts of freedom. I bent myself to devising ways and means for our escape, and meanwhile strove, on all fitting occasions, to impress them with the gross fraud and inhumanity of slavery. I went first to Henry, next to John, then to the others. I found, in them all, warm hearts and noble spirits. They were ready to hear, and ready to act when a feasible plan should be proposed. This was what I wanted. I talked to them of our want of manhood, if we submitted to our enslavement without at least one noble effort to be free. We met often, and consulted frequently, and told our hopes and fears, recounted the difficulties, real and imagined, which we should be called on to meet. At times we were almost disposed to give up, and try to content ourselves with our wretched lot; at others, we were firm and unbending in our determination to go. Whenever we suggested any plan, there was shrinking—the odds were fearful. Our path was beset with the greatest obstacles; and if we succeeded in gaining the end of it, our right to be free was yet questionable—we were yet liable to be returned to bondage. We could see no spot, this side of the ocean, where we could be free. We knew nothing about Canada. Our knowledge of the north did not extend farther than New York; and to go there, and be forever harassed with the frightful liability of being returned to slavery—with the certainty of being treated tenfold worse than before—the thought was truly a horrible one, and one which it was not easy to overcome. The case sometimes stood thus: At every gate through which we were to pass, we saw a watchman—at every ferry a guard—on every bridge a sentinel—and in every wood a patrol. We were hemmed in upon every side. Here were the difficulties, real or imagined—the good to be sought, and the evil to be shunned. On the one hand, there stood slavery, a stern reality, glaring frightfully upon us,—its robes already crimsoned with the blood of millions, and even now feasting itself greedily upon our own flesh. On the other hand, away back in the dim distance, under the flickering light of the north star, behind some craggy hill or snow-covered mountain, stood a doubtful freedom—half frozen—beckoning us to come and share its hospitality. This in itself was sometimes enough to stagger us; but when we permitted ourselves to survey the road, we were frequently appalled. Upon either side we saw grim death, assuming the most horrid shapes. Now it was starvation, causing us to eat our own flesh;—now we were contending with the waves, and were drowned;—now we were overtaken, and torn to pieces by the fangs of the terrible bloodhound. We were stung by scorpions, chased by wild beasts, bitten by snakes, and finally, after having nearly reached the desired spot,—after swimming rivers, encountering wild beasts, sleeping in the woods, suffering hunger and nakedness,—we were overtaken by our pursuers, and, in our resistance, we were shot dead upon the spot! I say, this picture sometimes appalled us, and made us

> rather bear those ills we had,
> Than fly to others, that we knew not of.

In coming to a fixed determination to run away, we did more than Patrick Henry, when he resolved upon liberty or death. With us it was a doubtful liberty at most, and almost certain death if we failed. For my part, I should prefer death to hopeless bondage.

Sandy, one of our number, gave up the notion, but still encouraged us. Our company then consisted of Henry Harris, John Harris, Henry Bailey, Charles Roberts, and myself. Henry Bailey was my uncle, and belonged to my master. Charles married my aunt: he belonged to my master's father-in-law, Mr. William Hamilton.

The plan we finally concluded upon was, to get a large canoe belonging to Mr. Hamilton, and upon the Saturday night previous to Easter holidays, paddle directly up the Chesapeake Bay. On our arrival at the head of the bay, a distance of seventy or eighty miles from where we lived, it was our purpose to turn our canoe adrift, and follow the guidance of the north star till we got beyond the limits of Maryland. Our reason for taking the water route was, that we were less liable to be suspected as runaways; we hoped to be regarded as fishermen; whereas, if we should take the land route, we should be subjected to interruptions of almost every kind. Any one having a white face, and being so disposed, could stop us, and subject us to examination.

5   The week before our intended start, I wrote several protections, one for each of us. As well as I can remember, they were in the following words, to wit:–

> This is to certify that I, the undersigned, have given the bearer, my servant, full liberty to go to Baltimore, and spend the Easter holidays. Written with mine own hand, &c., 1835.
> "WILLIAM HAMILTON,
> Near St. Michael's, in Talbot county, Maryland.

We were not going to Baltimore; but, in going up the bay, we went toward Baltimore, and these protections were only intended to protect us while on the bay.

As the time drew near for our departure, our anxiety became more and more intense. It was truly a matter of life and death with us. The strength of our determination was about to be fully tested. At this time, I was very active in explaining every difficulty, removing every doubt, dispelling every fear, and inspiring all with the firmness indispensable to success in our undertaking; assuring them that half was gained the instant we made the move; we had talked long enough; we were now ready to move; if not now, we never should be; and if we did not intend to move now, we had as well fold our arms, sit down, and acknowledge ourselves fit only to be slaves. This, none of us were prepared to acknowledge. Every man stood firm; and at our last meeting, we pledged ourselves afresh, in the most solemn manner, that, at the time appointed, we would certainly start in pursuit of freedom. This was in the middle of the week, at the end of which we were to be off. We went, as usual, to our several fields of labor, but with bosoms highly agitated with thoughts of our truly hazardous undertaking. We tried to conceal our feelings as much as possible; and I think we succeeded very well.

After a painful waiting, the Saturday morning, whose night was to witness our departure, came. I hailed it with joy, bring what of sadness it might. Friday night was a sleepless one for me. I probably felt more anxious than the rest, because I was, by common consent, at the head of the whole affair. The responsibility of success or failure lay heavily upon me. The glory of the one, and the confusion of the other, were alike mine. The first two hours of that morning were such as I never experienced before, and hope never to again. Early in the morning, we went, as usual, to the field. We were spreading manure; and all at once, while thus engaged, I was overwhelmed with an indescribable feeling, in the fulness of which I turned to Sandy, who was near by, and said, "We are betrayed!" "Well," said he, "that thought has this moment struck me." We said no more. I was never more certain of any thing.

The horn was blown as usual, and we went up from the field to the house for breakfast. I went for the form, more than for want of any thing to eat that morning. Just as I got to the house, in looking out at the lane gate, I saw four white men, with two colored men. The white men were on horseback, and the colored ones were walking behind, as if tied. I watched them a few moments till they got up to our lane gate. Here they halted, and tied the colored men to the gate-post. I was not yet certain as to what the matter was. In a few moments, in rode Mr. Hamilton, with a speed betokening great excitement. He came to the door, and inquired if Master William was in. He was told he was at the barn. Mr. Hamilton, without dismounting, rode up to the barn with extraordinary speed. In a few moments, he and Mr. Freeland returned to the house. By this time, the three constables rode up, and in great haste dismounted, tied their horses, and met Master William and Mr. Hamilton returning from the barn; and after talking awhile, they all walked up to the kitchen door. There was no one in the kitchen but myself and John. Henry and Sandy were up at the barn. Mr. Freeland put his head in at the door, and called me by name, saying, there were some gentlemen at the door who wished to see me. I stepped to the door, and inquired what they wanted. They at once seized me, and, without giving me any satisfaction, tied me—lashing my hands closely together. I insisted upon knowing what the matter was. They at length said, that they had learned I had been in a "scrape," and that I was to be examined before my master; and if their information proved false, I should not be hurt.

[Douglass and his companions were caught, jailed, and released to their owners.]

QUESTIONS FOR ACTIVE READING

1. Frederick Douglass and many other nineteenth-century abolitionist writers used biblical metaphors to describe the experience of slavery and the quest for freedom. (In the next chapter, on page 165, you'll see how Martin Luther King also uses biblical imagery to describe the moral imperative for civil rights.) How effective are the religious images and allusions that Douglass makes? (Some of these allusions are quite subtle; for example, why does he specify "thirty-nine lashes" of the whip that slaves who dared attend Sabbath school risked? or his use of the word *betrayed* in paragraph 8?) What does this language suggest about Douglass's audience?

2. In this excerpt Douglass describes at least one major decision that he makes. Describe, in your own words, one such decision. What steps did he take before making a commitment to that decision? Which factors were most important to him in making that decision?

3. In academic writing, students are often discouraged from using the first person in making an argument. How would the impact of Douglass's argument be affected if he had written in the third person? When is one person's experience enough for an argument to be completely authoritative and effective?

QUESTIONS FOR THINKING CRITICALLY

1. Throughout his *Narrative,* Douglass emphasizes the power of literacy. What does literacy mean to Douglass, and why does he make an effort (even at great personal danger) to teach other slaves to become literate? Would Douglass and Malcolm X (page 147 in Chapter 6) share a common definition of *literacy?*

2. Douglass says of his "fellow-slaves": "We were linked and interlinked with each other. I loved them with a love stronger than anything I have experienced since." Given Douglass's audience for his autobiography, why does he feel it so necessary to describe the intensity of these feelings? (Remember, too, that at the time he wrote this autobiography, Douglass was married and a father.)

3. To inspire his close friends and fellow slaves at the Freeland home, Douglass "talked to them of our want of manhood, if we submitted to our enslavement without at least one noble effort to be free." What does he mean? What is a "noble effort to be free," and have you ever made such an effort? Are *you* truly "free" to make decisions about how you live your life?

"The Lost Boys"

BY SARA CORBETT

Sara Corbett received an MFA degree from the University of Iowa's highly regarded Iowa Writer's Workshop. As a journalist, she has covered subjects ranging from the reintroduction of wolves at Yellowstone to the nursing shortage to snowboarding. The author of *Venus to the Hoop: A Gold-Medal Year in Women's Basketball* (1997), for which she closely followed the 1995 Women's Olympic basketball team, Corbett covered basketball for *Conde Nast Sports for Women* magazine. Her work has also appeared in the magazines *Outside* and *Skiing Magazine*. Corbett is married to journalist Michael Paterniti.

One evening in late January, Peter Dut, twenty-one, leads his two teenage brothers through the brightly lit corridors of the Minneapolis airport, trying to mask his confusion. Two days earlier, the brothers, refugees from Africa, encountered their first light switch and their first set of stairs. An aid worker in Nairobi demonstrated the flush toilet to them—also the seat belt, the shoelace, the fork. And now they find themselves alone in Minneapolis, three bone-thin African boys confronted by a swirling river of white faces and rolling suitcases.

Finally, a traveling businessman recognizes their uncertainty. "Where are you flying to?" he asks kindly, and the eldest brother tells him in halting, bookish English. A few days earlier, they left a small mud hut in a blistering hot Kenyan refugee camp, where they had lived as orphans for nine years after walking for hundreds of miles across Sudan. They are now headed to a new home in the U.S.A. "Where?" the man asks in disbelief when Peter Dut says the city's name. "Fargo? North Dakota? You gotta be kidding me. It's too cold there. You'll never survive it!"

And then he laughs. Peter Dut has no idea why.

In the meantime, the temperature in Fargo has dropped to 15 below. The boys tell me that until now, all they have ever known about cold is what they felt grasping a bottle of frozen water. An aid worker handed it to them one day during a "cultural orientation" session at the Kakuma Refugee Camp, a place where the temperature hovers around 100 degrees.

Peter Dut and his two brothers belong to an unusual group of refugees referred to by aid organizations as the Lost Boys of Sudan, a group of roughly 10,000 boys who arrived in Kenya in 1992 seeking refuge from their country's fractious civil war. The fighting pits a northern Islamic government against rebels in the south who practice Christianity and tribal religions.

The Lost Boys were named after Peter Pan's posse of orphans. According to U.S. State Department estimates, some 17,000 boys were separated from their families and fled southern Sudan in an exodus of biblical proportions after fighting intensified in 1987. They arrived in throngs, homeless and parentless, having trekked about 1000 miles, from Sudan to Ethiopia, back to Sudan, and finally to Kenya. The majority of

5

the boys belonged to the Dinka and Nuer tribes, and most were then between the ages of eight and eighteen. (Most of the boys don't know for sure how old they are; aid workers assigned them approximate ages after they arrived in 1992.)

Along the way, the boys endured attacks from the northern army and marauding bandits as well as lions, who preyed on the slowest and weakest among them. Many died from starvation or thirst. Others drowned or were eaten by crocodiles as they tried to cross a swollen Ethiopian river. By the time the Lost Boys reached the Kakuma Refugee Camp, their numbers had been cut nearly in half.

Now, after nine years of subsisting on rationed corn mush and lentils and living largely ungoverned by adults, the Lost Boys of Sudan are coming to America. In 1999, the United Nations High Commissioner for Refugees, which handles refugee cases around the world, and the U.S. government agreed to send 3600 of the boys to the United States—since going back to Sudan was out of the question. About 500 of the Lost Boys still under the age of eighteen will be living in apartments or foster homes across the United States by the end of this year. The boys will start school at a grade level normal for their age, thanks to a tough English-language program at their refugee camp. The remaining 3100 Lost Boys will be resettled as adults. After five years, each boy will be eligible for citizenship, provided he has turned twenty-one.

Nighttime in America?

On the night that I stand waiting for Peter Dut and his brothers to land in Fargo, tendrils of snow are snaking across the tarmac. The three boys file through the gate without money or coats or luggage beyond their small backpacks. The younger brothers, Maduk, seventeen, and Riak, fifteen, appear petrified. As a social worker passes out coats, Peter Dut studies the black night through the airport window. "Excuse me," he says worriedly. "Can you tell me, please, is it now night or day?"

10   This is a stove burner. This is a can opener. This is a brush for your teeth. The new things come in a tumble. The brothers' home is a sparsely furnished two-bedroom apartment in a complex on Fargo's south side. Rent is $445 a month. It has been stocked with donations from area churches and businesses: toothpaste, bread, beans, bananas.

A caseworker empties a garbage bag full of donated clothing, which looks to have come straight from the closet of an elderly man. I know how lucky the boys are: the State Department estimates that war, famine, and disease in southern Sudan have killed more than 2 million people and displaced another 4 million. Still I cringe to think of the boys showing up for school in these clothes.

The next day, when I return to the apartment at noon, the boys have been up since five and are terribly hungry. "What about your food?" I ask, gesturing to the bread and bananas and the box of cereal sitting on the counter.

Peter grins sheepishly. I suddenly realize that the boys, in a lifetime of cooking maize and beans over a fire pit, have never opened a box. I am placed in the role of teacher. And so begins an opening spree. We open potato chips. We open a can of beans. We untwist the tie on the bagged loaf of bread. Soon the boys are seated and eating a hot meal.

Living on Leaves and Berries

The three brothers have come a long way since they fled their village in Sudan with their parents and three sisters, all of whom were later killed by Sudanese army soldiers. The Lost Boys first survived a six- to ten-week walk to Ethiopia, often subsisting on leaves and berries and the occasional boon of a warthog carcass. Some boys staved off dehydration by drinking their own urine. Many fell behind; some were devoured by lions or trampled by buffalo.

15   The Lost Boys lived for three years in Ethiopia, in UN-supported camps, before they were forced back into Sudan by a new Ethiopian government no longer sympathetic to their plight. Somehow, more than 10,000 of the boys miraculously trailed into Kenya's UN camps in the summer of 1992—as Sudanese government planes bombed the rear of their procession.

For the Lost Boys, then, a new life in America might easily seem to be the answer to every dream. But the real world has been more complicated than that. Within weeks of arriving, Riak is placed in a local junior high; Maduk starts high school classes; and Peter begins adult education classes.

Refugee Blues

Five weeks later, Riak listens quietly through a lesson on Elizabethan history at school, all but ignored by white students around him.

Nearby, at Fargo South High School, Maduk is frequently alone as well, copying passages from his geography textbook, trying not to look at the short skirts worn by many of the girls.

Peter Dut worries about money. The three brothers say they receive just $107 in food stamps each month and spend most of their $510 monthly cash assistance on rent and utilities.

20   Resettlement workers say the brothers are just undergoing the normal transition. Scott Burtsfield, who coordinates resettlement efforts in Fargo through Lutheran Social Services, says, "The first three months are always the toughest. It really does get better."

The Lost Boys can only hope so; they have few other options. A return to southern Sudan could be fatal. "There is nothing left for the Lost Boys to go home to—it's a war zone," says Mary Anne Fitzgerald, a Nairobi-based relief consultant.

Some Sudanese elders have criticized sending boys to the United States. They worry that their children will lose their African identity. One afternoon an eighteen-year-old Lost Boy translated a part of a tape an elder had sent along with many boys: "He is saying, 'Don't drink. Don't smoke. Don't kill. Go to school every day, and remember, America is not your home.'"

But if adjustment is hard, the boys also experience consoling moments. One of these came on a quiet Friday night last winter. As the boys make a dinner of rice and lentils, Peter changes into an African outfit, a finely woven green tunic with a skullcap to match, bought with precious food rations at Kakuma.

Just then the doorbell rings unexpectedly. And out of the cold tumble four Sudanese boys—all of whom have resettled as refugees over the past several years.

I watch one, an eighteen-year-old named Sunday, wrap his arms encouragingly around Peter Dut. "It's a hard life here," Sunday whispers to the older boy, "but it's a free life, too."

QUESTIONS FOR ACTIVE READING

1. Unlike Frederick Douglass, Sara Corbett writes here from an objective perspective; not having directly experienced what the "Lost Boys" have gone through, she can only report on what she observes and share what they reveal to her. How does she express the strangeness and difficulties of Peter Dut's experiences by using her own powers of observation?

2. Corbett describes episodes and circumstances that would appear to be ironic, even comic, and "stranger than fiction." However, she reports these things objectively, without judgment or editorializing. What do you, as a reader, make of the irony that Peter Dut and thousands of children like him are called "Lost Boys" by aid organizations? (To understand the irony, be sure that you know where the term *Lost Boys* comes from.) What about the contrast described in paragraph 4?

3. Despite her journalistic objectivity, Corbett does eventually appear in the first person. Where, and why? How does this change your perception of her as a writer, a journalist, a person? Do journalists have an ethical responsibility toward their subjects?

QUESTIONS FOR THINKING CRITICALLY

1. From the information about the Sudanese civil war and the Kenyan refugee camps in Corbett's article, how much choice do you think the "Lost Boys" had in determining their fates? When one of the boys, Sunday, says to Peter Dut, "It's a hard life here, but it's a free life, too," what do you think he means?

2. In what ways are Peter Dut and his brothers and friends courageous, and sources of inspiration, to each other? How did Frederick Douglass inspire courage in his own friends? What is the connection between courage and inspiration?

3. Is it ever easier to let circumstances make a decision for you? What do you think takes over when you give up control of your own destiny?

THINKING-
WRITING
ACTIVITY

Preparing for Decisions

1. Make a list of whatever important decisions in your academic or personal life you have to make now or will have to make in the near future.

2. Select one decision and apply the five-step decision-making method that begins on page 121. As you think through your decision, be sure to identify all your possible choices and to follow your thoughts wherever they lead.

There are no guarantees in life. Our decisions may or may not turn out well. Still, following an organized method for making decisions can at least assure us of having explored and evaluated many possible choices and then having selected the one that seemed to best meet our needs. In other words, we will know that we made the best decision that we could have at the time.

Writing Project: Analyzing a Decision to Be Made

This chapter includes both readings and Thinking-Writing Activities that encourage you to reflect on drafting and decision making. Be sure to reread what you wrote for those activities; you may be able to use your responses to complete this project.

Write an essay in which you analyze a decision you must make now or in the near future. Be sure to select a decision for which you already have considerable information or want to obtain more. Include all five steps of the decision-making method. After you have drafted your essay, revise it as best you can. Follow your instructor's directions for length, format, and so on.

The Writing Situation

Begin by considering the key elements in the Thinking-Writing Model on pages 7–9 in Chapter 1.

Purpose   Use this opportunity to work through an important real-life decision to obtain the best possible outcome. If others will be involved in or affected by this decision, your paper can show them your best thinking about it, making them more likely to agree with your decision. Also, in writing this paper, you can practice the creative and critical thinking involved in the five-step decision-making method. You can hone your revision skills both by carefully working through the revision questions on page 136 and by using ideas about revision from Chapter 6 as well as ideas from this chapter.

Audience   An essay about a decision implies at least two potential audiences. In describing a decision you made and the process of making that decision, you could be writing for people who are faced with similar circumstances or a closely related predicament. For example, people in communities that welcome refugees from distant lands would learn a great deal from Sara Corbett's article about the many small but important adjustments refugees must learn to make. Through describing your commitment to a decision, even at its most difficult, you can inspire people who have made a similar decision.

Subject   Decisions can be challenging to think about and difficult to make. Sometimes we haven't enough information to make an intelligent choice; sometimes we *think* we know what the right decision is yet are reluctant to actually make it. Therefore, we often tend to put off decision making for as long as possible. Keep in mind that not making a decision is, in a way, making a decision to do nothing. For this assignment, try to identify a decision that will have significant consequences. It may be what area to major in, whether to get a part-time job, whether to participate in a sport or other extracurricular activity, or whether to get a dog. The more significant the decision, the more helpful this assignment will be to you.

Writer   You approach this Writing Project as the expert on the subject since you are analyzing one of your own decisions. One challenge here is to distinguish between your own expertise about the decision-making situation and your audience's needs for enough background and information. Another challenge is to focus on the material provided earlier in this chapter because this assignment moves away from recollecting experience and asks you to apply the decision-making process to a decision you need to make soon. For example, Frederick Douglass writes with the authority of personal experience. Although Sara Corbett is not a refugee, she establishes her authority through scrupulous observation, insightful interviews, and background research.

The Writing Process

The following sections will guide you through the stages of generating, planning, drafting, and revising as you work on an essay about making a decision.

Generating Ideas   Try to be particularly conscious of both the creative and the critical thinking you do while making your decision and of the critical thinking and decision making you do as you revise.

- Is there a decision you must make in the near future? If so, this is a good opportunity for you to accomplish two things at once: writing your paper and making your decision.
- Think about how much additional information you would need to evaluate possible choices for this decision. Do you have time to locate and absorb all of it?
- Describe the decision-making situation and your goals as clearly as you can.
- Brainstorm as many possible choices as you can. Ask others involved in the decision to help.
- Eliminate choices that you know are impractical or undesirable.
- Determine what information you must find for each choice. Locate that information.
- Write each choice on a separate sheet of paper. Then divide the paper into two columns: pros and cons. Write as much as you can in each column.
- For each, freewrite for five minutes on what would happen and how you would feel if you selected that choice.
- Freewrite for five minutes on how you would know if any given choice was the right one.

Defining a Focus   Write a tentative thesis statement that clarifies your decision-making situation. You might write something like "After thinking about the situation carefully, I realize that I have only two possible choices." Or you might "blueprint" your paper by naming the possible choices: "My choices for housing next year come down to these three: living with my aunt, sharing an apartment with my friend, or looking for a live-in job situation." You may even decide to announce your decision in your thesis statement: "After carefully weighing my options, I have decided to major in business administration." Or you may find a more creative way to state your thesis.

Organizing Ideas   The five-step method for making decisions fits well with essay structure. Your description of the decision-making situation might be the beginning of an introduction, to be completed by your thesis statement. You could include your goals in the introduction or state them in a separate paragraph. Each of the potential choices, explained in as much detail as possible along with the pros and cons of that choice, could serve as a body paragraph. Your decision of the best choice and your plan for monitoring it could be the essay's conclusion.

Drafting   Begin with the easiest part to draft. Your description of the decision-making situation could begin the introduction, but consider what, if any, additional information your audience might need in order to understand the situation. The introduction can end with your tentative thesis statement.

In your conclusion or thesis statement, name the choice you have selected. You may want to explain why if you think your reason may not be obvious to your audience. Remember to explain how you will monitor the results of your decision.

Revising   One of the best revision strategies is to get an audience's reactions to your draft. Here are some questions to ask your peers about this assignment:

- What questions do you have about my decision-making situation and my goals?
- What questions do you have about the alternative choices I described? What else do you need to know about them? Can you suggest any others?
- Do you understand why I am making this decision?
- What could I add to clarify why this choice is best for me?

Armed with the information from peer review, you are now ready to begin revising by using the revision method presented on page 152 in Chapter 6. If possible, use the following directions for revising with a word processor as you work through the revision process.

Revising Strategy: Using a Computer to Revise   Use the revision method by creating a series of files, one for each time you revise using your word processor. This system will give you a complete record of your work so that you can track how each draft changes.

- Call your first draft Decision 1 and print and save it.
- Later, create a new file called Decision 2 by copying and pasting Decision 1. Then make changes to the draft as a whole, being guided by your answers

from the peer review and your answers to the Think Big questions on page 152. Print and save this draft.

- Now, consider the Think Medium questions to evaluate your individual paragraphs. Create a new file called Decision 3 by copying and pasting Decision 2. Then make whatever changes are suggested by your answers to the Think Medium questions on page 152. Print and save this draft.

- Next, consider the Think Small questions. Create a new file called Decision 4 by copying and pasting Decision 3. Then make whatever changes at the sentence level that are suggested by your answers to the Think Small questions on page 153. Print and save this draft.

- Finally, consider the Think "Picky" questions. Create a new file called Decision 5 by copying and pasting Decision 4. Then make whatever changes are suggested by your answers to the Think "Picky" questions on page 153. Run the spelling and grammar checking features of your word processing program, and use your judgment about which suggested changes to make. Print and save this draft. Decision 5 should present your very best work. It is now ready to be submitted to your instructor and any other audience you select.

You should also review "A Step-by-Step Method for Revising Any Assignment" in Chapter 6 on pages 152–153.

Editing and Proofreading   Your essay should now have been completed to the best of your ability, and, of course, you will need to submit it to your instructor by the due date. But also consider other possible audiences for this essay. Do you want to share your ideas with other people involved in your decision-making situation? Would members of your family or your close friends benefit by reading it? If your paper is about a decision that others must also make, such as selecting a major, perhaps your student newspaper would be interested in publishing it as a model of good decision making that others could emulate.

The following essays show how two students responded to this assignment.

Student Writing

Wendy Agudo's Writing Process

Wendy Agudo began to compose the following essay after a chance remark her philosophy professor made in class. Wendy had already completed the Thinking-Writing assignment on page 121, reflecting on her decision in junior high to overcome her learning disability and earn the high grades she would need to go to college and pursue a career in television journalism. The day after she completed that assignment, her philosophy professor told her class that the French philosopher Jean-Paul Sartre had said that we were "condemned to be free." Wendy began with a freewriting to sort out her feelings about how that quotation related to her own experience and then used the five steps to organized decision making (pages 122–125) to begin to plan her paper.

Jean-Paul Sartre "we are condemned to be free"—it wasn't anyone's fault, the accident. I don't blame my parents. I don't blame anyone, and they don't blame each other. It just happened. Moving to America when I was really little was probably the best thing they could have done for me. Back in Ecuador it would have been really hard for me to get the help I needed. But still I wouldn't have had to learn a new language, and mami and papa wouldn't have had to work so hard and leave me alone for so much time when I really needed them. I'm angry with Lidia because she doesn't even know how easy she has it. Lidia has always had the family support and the money and the time to do whatever she wants, but all she wants to do is sit around talking on her celly to her boy. We're at work together and we're on deadline and I'm trying to get her to shut up and pay attention and she just rolls her eyes and says something in Albanian over the phone. She has no respect but I can't be jealous, that's not right either. Does she think about where she'll be in two years? in ten years?

1. <u>Define the decision.</u> I decided not to let my brain injury get in the way of my goals.

2. <u>Consider all possible choices.</u> I didn't have a choice. Either I succeed or I fail. It's up to me.

3. <u>Gather all relevant information and evaluate the pros and cons of each choice.</u>

   - I could have stayed in the remedial class in junior high. PRO—less work. CON—where would I be today?

   - I could ignore Lidia and let her screw up. PRO—not having to confront Lidia. CON—it's my job to confront her and make sure she's learning skills. If I don't help her then I fail at some level.

   - I could let Lidia learn for herself. It worked for me. You need to take responsibility for your own life.

4. <u>Select the choice that seems best suited to the situation.</u> I can't boss Lidia around. She needs to find out for herself what the consequences of her lack of responsibility will be. Besides she won't listen to me. I can be a better example for everyone in the peer training program if I just get my own work done and set a high standard for myself.

5. <u>Implement a plan of action.</u> I owe it to my parents and to myself to succeed. I can't get jealous of Lidia or let her own decisions make my own work look bad.

Freedom

by Wendy Agudo

It's funny how some people always seem to have an excuse for everything, refusing to take responsibility for their actions. All of us have, at some point, shrugged our shoulders and made an excuse for behavior we should have regretted, or at least apologized for—being late to meet a friend, not having an assignment completed on time, not visiting an elderly relative. But making these excuses implies that we are not really in control of our own lives. When we make an excuse for our behavior, we are really saying that some other force—a train conductor, the weather, a computer, whatever—has more control over our lives than we do. To make excuses is to place limits on the extent of your personal freedom.

I see this kind of refusal to take responsibility all the time at my job. I work as a peer trainer for a small non-profit television station, teaching other young people (high school through age 25) how to use field and studio digital cameras, digital and analog video editing, and media literacy. I was fortunate enough to begin this work at the age of 18, and now at the age of 20 I consider myself very skilled and motivated. Because of my experience in a professional environment, I tend to have high expectations for my peers in this training program, who are my own age and often a little older. When they are late for a meeting, or careless with their work, or would rather go out and have fun than stay late and edit a story, I am very disappointed. I hear excuses like "I have no time because of school," or "my family this" and "my intelligence that." I could come up with many more compelling excuses myself, but yet I don't.

I believe that we all make choices in life, and that there is no reason for failure or self-pity. Many factors have contributed to my sense of responsibility, my stubbornness, and my loyalty to my family. But the most significant challenge I have faced—and that I could use as an excuse, but don't—has to do with my health.

I was born in Ecuador. When I was two years old, I accidentally fell from the second-story window of my parents' house. I landed on a pile of broken concrete and suffered brain damage, which the doctor said would be permanent. My parents could have allowed this to be a limit on my freedom, but they refused. I know I was too young to think this, but I do know that somewhere around this time I didn't allow myself to let this keep me down. As I grew I got better. It was my choice to continue and get past it.

Or maybe it was just luck.

My story doesn't have an accidentally happy ending. After I recovered from the fall there were still limitations. I was slow to walk and speak, and was dyslexic. Then, when I was four years old, my family immigrated to the United States. I was enrolled in an English-speaking public school. Between my difficulties in reading, walking, and speaking, I had to work three times as hard as anyone else just to keep up. I stuttered and had a lisp, so even when I did manage to speak English, other children teased me. Due to my dyslexia I had trouble focusing and concentrating, so I had trouble reading. Eventually I was afraid to read anything. I saw all of the other kids round me finishing with two books before I was able to get through even one. I was so discouraged that I wanted to give up.

This is another example of freedom of choice. I could have chosen to work harder, to study more, but I allowed outside circumstances—my disability—to make the choice for me. I gave up, but giving up was my own choice. It wasn't determined for me and it wasn't something I couldn't avoid. I chose to give up out of my own free will. And that choice had consequences. For many years I had very low grades and was passed from one "special" classroom to another.

At some point during junior high I realized that I wasn't going to get anywhere with such low grades. I worked harder and harder and eventually got better. I defeated the dyslexia, but it hasn't gone away. I still have dyslexia, but it doesn't control me. At least now it's something that doesn't hold me back. Eventually, I graduated from high school with honors, and I am now enrolled in college and earning "A" grades. Not bad for someone with a damaged brain!

This brings me back to the high expectations I have for other people in my peer training program. Due to the fact that I had to work so hard to develop myself, I also developed what I call high standards. I look at another peer trainer, whom I will call Lidia, as a comparison. Lidia is five months older than I am, and is also an immigrant. Her family came to the United States from Albania when she was four years old, just like me. Her parents are both doctors, and she was raised with many privileges. Although we both grew up in the same New York City neighborhood, our lives were very different. For my parents to get here from Ecuador, they had to make a dangerous and lonely journey across South America by car and on foot. We had no family in America to welcome us, and my parents had to work illegally in sweatshops for many years. But Lidia's parents joined a large family of uncles, aunts, and cousins, and her parents were able to begin practicing medicine again within a year or two of their arrival.

I have read that the environment you grow up in determines the kind of life you lead. I guess that, based on that evidence, I should have been a mother when I was still a teenager, and shouldn't have gone to college at all. But environment doesn't determine everything, and freedom to choose your own destiny isn't limited because of one or two aspects. Even in poverty, even in prison—even with a damaged brain!—you still have the freedom to choose to work hard and to make the best of your circumstances.

Lidia is always complaining at work. She takes fewer college classes than I do, and only works ten hours at the television station each week (I work 30 hours, sometimes more). Yet she is always late for meetings, loses track of equipment, and doesn't take her work assignments seriously. She assumes that everything will be easy for her, and doesn't realize that that complacency limits the choices she can make about her life. When things go wrong, she makes excuses—her car broke down, or she was out late the night before. She doesn't know how fortunate she is, and she'll never achieve as much as she could.

I believe that freedom is unlimited, and your life is determined by matters of choice. If you choose to give up, to accept less of yourself, then you will forever limit your choices and your freedom. But if you choose to continue, no matter what the obstacles, you will eventually achieve your goals. I may be disappointed in other people, but I have never been disappointed in myself. My family has sacrificed too much for me to come this far, and I will not let them down.

Student Writing

Cynthia Brown's Writing Process

Cynthia Brown's approach to this writing project exhibits those qualities of creativity, open-mindedness, knowledge, and curiosity that are the hallmarks of a critical thinker. Rather than writing about a specific decision, Cynthia reflected on a key factor—time—and how her relationship to time shaped all the major decisions she had made in her life. Cynthia drew on readings from her writing class (especially her responses to Sara Corbett's "The Lost Boys" on page 130) and notes from her philosophy class to inform her essay.

When I moved to New York, I thought I was going to go insane. As much as I loved the city, I could not bear to live here. However, I came to New York to attend college and decided it would be best to allow myself time to make this decision based on rationale as opposed to emotion. I spent the next two years carefully analyzing and weighing my options. With the passage of time, I have come to the conclusion that I cannot live the kind of life I want to live as a student if I stay in New York. I decided to transfer, upon graduation from my current college, to a small liberal arts college in the middle of nowhere. I used time to help me explore my options instead of feeling trapped within its confines. This allowed me to move through the two years with ease and come to a truly authentic decision regarding my life.

Freedom and the Constraint of Time

by Cynthia Brown

Do I believe that I am free?

The 18th-century French philosopher Baron d'Holbach says that we are drowning in a river, desperately trying to keep our heads above water, sinking, rising, sinking again, until we die. The American writer William James argued that we are free to act, to drag ourselves out of that river of circumstance any time we choose and set our own course. I believe that whatever your personal belief about the nature of your freedom, we are all captured and held by the whims of Time. Time is universal, preceding both existence and essence.

Take, for example, measurement. Everything we know about the material world, everything we experience, is measured by time. Distance, stability, stamina, progress, relationships . . . the list is endless. We run, not a mile, but ten minutes. We travel, not by miles, but by hours. We wait, not with patience but in days. To an imaginary objective observer, an angel or an alien, humans would all seem to be motivated not by internal desires or the pursuit of knowledge, but by the hands of the clock. An alien wouldn't know that you decided to stop speaking with your boyfriend because you had fallen in love with someone else; the alien would notice that the clock on your bedroom wall said 3:37 pm, and could just as easily assume that the time determined your heart's action.

People wear wristwatches, follow the sun across the sky, track the phases of the moon. New technology helps us to process time faster so we don't waste a moment of it. We have cell phones and computers so we can work faster, multitask, move several concepts and relationships through time simultaneously. We are racing time, desperate to control it, bend it to our will. Yet time is a universal law, a rule we must abide by. We might think that we are free to make decisions about our own lives, but whatever we "choose" is ultimately changed, decayed, or unraveled by the passage of time.

When we look into the heavens, we see stars and wonder just how small we are. How long would it take me to travel to the next galaxy, the next universe? Ask a physicist and she will answer you in increments of time: light years. Our imaginations can travel as far into the universe as they may please in the shortest segment time has to give us. We feel we can take a shortcut and go where we please, sometimes inventing new universes where time does not exist. We feel, briefly, ecstatically, that we have beaten time—and then we wake up, or come down, and find ourselves in a place where we are alone and helpless, desperate to come back to the places and people we know.

Suppose we were to look back at our lives and what has shaped us. Wouldn't it be nice to go back and change everything, to disappear without knowledge of our present life and be given a chance to start all over again? Alan Lightman, a renowned physicist, explores this idea in his novel *Einstein's Dreams*. Many of his stories claim that time is an endless cycle, never giving in or relenting to our wishes. Our clocks repeat themselves in a circle. We fall in and out of love, looking back at time spent in our relationships as so much wasted time, hardly daring to allow ourselves to experience the emotion itself. We are simultaneously anticipating the future and regretting the past. We move forward, waiting for time to heal our wounds.

Although we created a calendar to help us move through and keep track of time, it is an endless cycle. Day into night. Hour into hour. The refugee boy from Sudan, lost on the dark North Dakota prairie, asks a friend: "Can you tell me, please, is it now night or day?" We ask Time to be responsible, ignoring our own role in our destiny. While we are thinking of everything that has gone wrong with our lives, Time is passing through us, creating us, owning us. We are creating ourselves in Time. Are we really making our decisions based on our experience and careful analysis, or are we allowing Time to take control and be our guide?

We slip in and out of awareness of time. We wake in the morning fresh from our dreams and instinctively look at the clock. Some mornings we rise and say, "Shit, I'm late for class. My professor is going to be so mad. He wears a watch." And here, we have a choice. Do we go late, or not go at all? Both of these decisions come with consequences. We weigh them as we brush our teeth and pull a sweater over our heads. Is the decision we make truly free, or are we simply responding to the urgency of the ticking clock?

It's possible to leave the technology of clocks and cell phones behind, but just like the Lost Boys of Sudan, we are still instinctively aware of the cycles of the sun. We cannot live without sunlight; we cannot imagine the universe without darkness. Our secrets are kept in the dark, and we reveal ourselves to each other by shining a light on our deepest truths. We are determined to live in light and shadow, and from an early age we are trained to respond to the shifts from day to night and back again.

One of the earliest lessons I remember from preschool was how to tell time (tell it what? I wonder now . . .) We learned how to read the hands on a clock, and what the numbers on a digital dial meant; we were taught to "be on time," and were punished if we were late. As schoolchildren, responding to bells, we were taught to be driven by forces beyond what we can truly see—only measure (and isn't it ironic that we are not allowed to pray in schools? But that's another argument entirely). Were we learning because we were curious, eating because we were hungry, jumping up from our desks because we couldn't wait to get home? Or were we just responding, like a bunch of trained rats, to the sound of the bell?

And so we wait. We wait for time to tell us what will be and where we will end up next. Whether or not the alarm clock will let us live another day. All of our teachings and still we wait, for something as old as the universe itself, a force that will long outlast any choices or commitments or decisions we make. Time moves forward, carrying us with it whether we ask it to or not. For surely if we exist outside of this concept of time, lock ourselves in a windowless room for what we suspect are minutes, days, or years, we are certain to be driven to madness.

So when I am asked, "Are you free?"

I answer, "Well, I don't wear a wristwatch. Do you?"

Alternative Writing Projects

1. Write an essay in which you analyze a decision that must be made soon by a community or group to which you belong. Describe the circumstances leading up to this decision, and follow through the five steps of the decision-making method discussed in this chapter. When you consider alternate choices and their pros and cons, be sure to include the perspectives of several members of your community who will be affected by this decision.

2. The theme of the wandering pilgrim, or the prodigal son, is found in literature across cultures and time periods. What does it mean to "come home" after a life-changing experience? Is it more difficult to decide to run away, or to decide to come home? Think about how a tribal elder urged the Lost Boys to maintain their "African identity" in a strange new land. Have you had a comparable experience? What led you away? Why did you decide to go home? How did the experience change you?

3. Have you ever talked someone out of what you knew was a bad decision? What were the circumstances of that decision? What was your relationship to the person making the decision? What was the most effective, or surprising, argument that you made to change that person's mind?

Revising Thoughtfully, Using Language Ethically

Only where there is language is there world. **"**

—Adrienne Rich

Critical Thinking Focus: Language and power

Writing Focus: Revising language to clarify thinking

Reading Theme: Using language ethically

Writing Project: The impact of language on our lives

Every time we use language and images, we send messages about our thinking and ourselves. When we speak or write, we are not simply making sounds or writing symbols; we are conveying ideas, sharing feelings, and describing experiences. At the same time, language itself shapes and influences thinking. When language use is careless—vague, general, indistinct, imprecise, foolish, inaccurate—it leads to the same sort of thinking. The reverse is also true: clear, precise language leads to clear, precise thinking, speaking, and writing.

The careless or imprecise use of language can be more consequential than a mediocre grade or a boring essay. When you write, you assume an audience; even if your audience is "only" your teacher, you still take on the responsibility of enlightening, entertaining, and truth telling. That assumption of an audience, so fundamental to rhetoric, implies that you are writing from an *ethical* perspective. The word *ethics* comes from the Greek term *ethos*, or "character." What you say, and how you say it, reveals to your audience what kind of person you are.

To write ethically also implies that you have a *responsibility* toward your reader, your subject, and yourself. To be responsible to your reader means that you write clearly, choosing the most appropriate language, constructing a logical argument that your reader can easily follow. To be responsible to your subject requires you to be as truthful as you can, given what you know. If you are writing an

145

argument, it is your responsibility as an ethical writer to present opposing viewpoints fairly and accurately. Finally, you are responsible to your *ethos,* or how you appear in your writing. A carefully written, logically organized, interestingly illustrated essay reveals the presence of a thoughtful, interesting, curious mind.

This chapter explores the ethical implications of language—how it is used on both a personal and a social level to provoke, to haunt, to challenge, and to heal. Activities in this chapter discuss the *revision* part of the writing process, that careful reconsideration of your sources, organization, and word choice before you present your "final" paper to your audience.

THINKING-
WRITING
ACTIVITY

Language That Offends

Has your attention been drawn to the ethical or responsible use of language on your campus or in your workplace? For example, does your campus have a speech code that defines hate speech or otherwise proscribed language? Are there words you are uncomfortable using or hearing in the classroom or the office? Are you uncomfortable with that language because it offends you or because you worry about offending someone?

Recognizing Effective Use of Language

One effective way to develop your ability to use language ethically and responsibly in communicating your thoughts, feelings, and experiences is to read widely.

FOUR QUALITIES
OF A CRITICAL THINKER
Anthropologist Emory Sekaquaptewa

Curious For people and cultures that have, through colonization or warfare or natural disaster, lost their ability to retain and retell their histories, the work of anthropologists and linguists can help to salvage what would otherwise be lost forever. Dr. Emory Sekaquaptewa, an anthropologist in the Bureau of Applied Research in Anthropology of the University of Arizona and chief judge of the Hopi tribe's Appellate Court, is working with a team of linguists and Hopi elders to rediscover and retell the sixteenth-century colonial history of his people. Their curiosity about the unheard, and almost lost, Hopi perspective on Spanish colonization has led to profound new insights on the early days of the American Southwest.

Open-minded Working in archives from Arizona to Mexico, Dr. Sekaquaptewa's team unearthed centuries-old manuscripts written by Spanish soldiers led by Francisco de Coronado, who first encountered the Hopi in 1541. The researchers carefully translated and transcribed these manuscripts into English. Next, Dr. Sekaquaptewa has been translating the manuscripts from English into Hopi. These Hopi translations are then read to Hopi elders, who respond with the stories passed down for as many as twenty generations of Hopi clan culture. The biases and limits of the original Spanish perspective, for so long the "official" perspective on this part of the region's history, are

Highly regarded writers use word meanings accurately. They also often use many action verbs, concrete nouns, and vivid adjectives to communicate effectively. Another way to become a more sensitive and responsive writer is by seeking feedback from readers. In this section, you will be using all these strategies.

The following excerpt from *The Autobiography of Malcolm X* chronicles his discovery of the power of language while he was serving time in prison. Frustrated by not being able to communicate his ideas in writing, he commited himself to mastering the use of words by copying the dictionary. As you read, pay special attention to the way Malcolm X uses language to share his experiences with us. Do you find his personal quest inspiring? Why?

FROM *The Autobiography of Malcolm X*

BY MALCOLM X (1925–1965) WITH ALEX HALEY

Born as Malcolm Little in Omaha, Nebraska, the son of an activist Baptist preacher and a mother busy with her eight children, Malcolm X saw racial injustice and violence from a very young age.

Malcolm dropped out of high school after a teacher's contemptuous discouragement of his ambitions to be a lawyer and became involved in criminal activities. After a conviction for burglary in Boston, he was sentenced to prison for ten years. (In the following excerpt from his autobiography, Malcolm X describes how he used this time for reflection and intellectual growth.) Paroled in 1952, Malcolm dropped the name *Little* (which he now referred to as his "slave name") and took up the name *X* to symbolize his lost African heritage.

---

brought sharply into relief and given new context through this listening. This creative, collaborative approach to history gives indigenous peoples not only a voice but also an active role in the recovery and perpetuation of their culture.

Knowledgeable Because Hopi is a very ancient spoken language with a rich oral tradition, its survival— and the survival of the knowledge conveyed by that oral tradition—depends on the survival of the Hopi people. Dr. Sekaquaptewa's life work is to create a written record of the Hopi language and to teach Hopi people how to read and write in that language. As cultural editor of the *Hopi Dictionary*, Sekaquaptewa has worked to set individual Hopi words into larger cultural contexts.

Creative To perpetuate history and pride among young Hopi, Dr. Sekaquaptewa conducts workshops and classes for young people on a Hopi reservation in Arizona. Students translate children's books from English into Hopi to help younger people learn the language. They also learn to write creatively in Hopi about their own lives and family histories.

Online Study Center
Emory Sekaquaptewa
Visit the Online Study Center for *Critical Thinking, Thoughtful Writing* at *college.hmco.com/pic/ chaffeeCTTW4e* to learn more about Dr. Emory Sekaquaptewa.

In 1964, following a period of disappointment and disillusion with Elijah Muhammad, Malcolm X broke with the Nation of Islam, within which he had held a prominent position. Returning to the spiritual roots of his conversion to Islam, he made a hajj, or pilgrimage, to Mecca in Saudi Arabia. The sight of so many Muslims of so many different races and colors was deeply moving to Malcolm X, and upon his return to America he began working toward healing and reconciliation for all Americans of all races.

Unfortunately, the enemies he had made and the fears he had provoked did not leave Malcolm X much time to share this message; three assassins took him down as he spoke at the Audubon Ballroom in Harlem on February 15, 1965.

I became increasingly frustrated at not being able to express what I wanted to convey in letters that I wrote, especially those to Mr. Elijah Muhammad. In the street, I had been the most articulate hustler out there—I had commanded attention when I said something. But now, trying to write simple English, I not only wasn't articulate, I wasn't even functional. How would I sound writing in slang, the way I would *say* it, something such as, "Look, daddy, let me pull your coat about a cat, Elijah Muhammad—"

Many who today hear me somewhere in person, or on television, or those who read something I've said, will think I went to school far beyond the eighth grade. This impression is due entirely to my prison studies.

It had really begun back in the Charlestown Prison, when Bimbi first made me feel envy of his stock of knowledge. Bimbi had always taken charge of any conversation he was in, and I had tried to emulate him. But every book I picked up had few sentences which didn't contain anywhere from one to nearly all of the words that might as well have been in Chinese. When I just skipped those words, of course, I really ended up with little idea of what the book said. So I had come to the Norfolk Prison Colony still going through only book-reading motions. Pretty soon, I would have quit even these motions, unless I had received the motivation that I did.

I saw that the best thing I could do was get hold of a dictionary—to study, to learn some words. I was lucky enough to reason also that I should try to improve my penmanship. It was sad. I couldn't even write in a straight line. It was both ideas together that moved me to request a dictionary along with some tablets and pencils from the Norfolk Prison Colony school.

I spent two days just riffling uncertainly through the dictionary's pages. I'd never realized so many words existed! I didn't know *which* words I needed to learn. Finally, just to start some kind of action, I began copying.

In my slow, painstaking, ragged handwriting, I copied into my tablet everything printed on that first page, down to the punctuation marks.

I believe it took me a day. Then, aloud, I read back, to myself, everything I'd written on the tablet. Over and over, aloud, to myself, I read my own handwriting.

I woke up the next morning, thinking about those words—immensely proud to realize that not only had I written so much at one time, but I'd written words that

I never knew were in the world. Moreover, with a little effort, I also could remember what many of these words meant. I reviewed the words whose meaning I didn't remember. Funny thing, from the dictionary's first page right now, that "aardvark" springs to my mind. The dictionary had a picture of it, a long-tailed, long-eared, burrowing African mammal, which lives off termites caught by sticking out its tongue as an anteater does for ants.

I was so fascinated that I went on—I copied the dictionary's next page. And the same experience came when I studied that. With every succeeding page, I also learned of people and places and events from history. Actually the dictionary is like a miniature encyclopedia. Finally the dictionary's A section had filled a whole tablet—and I went on into the B's. That was the way I started copying what eventually became the entire dictionary. It went a lot faster after so much practice helped me to pick up handwriting speed. Between what I wrote in my tablet, and writing letters, during the rest of my time in prison I would guess I wrote a million words.

I suppose it was inevitable that as my word-base broadened, I could for the first time pick up a book and read and now begin to understand what the book was saying. Anyone who has read a great deal can imagine the new world that opened. Let me tell you something: from then until I left the prison, in every free moment I had, if I was not reading in the library, I was reading on my bunk. You couldn't have gotten me out of books with a wedge. Between Mr. Muhammad's teachings, my correspondence, my visitors—usually Ella and Reginald—and my reading of books, months passed without my even thinking about being imprisoned. In fact, up to then, I never had been so truly free in my life.

The Norfolk Prison Colony's library was in the school building. A variety of classes was taught there by instructors who came from such places as Harvard and Boston universities. The weekly debates between inmate teams were also held in the school building. You would be astonished to know how worked up convict debaters and audiences would get over subjects like "Should Babies Be Fed Milk?"

Available on the prison library's shelves were books on just about every general subject. Much of the big private collection that Parkhurst had willed to the prison was still in crates and boxes in the back of the library—thousands of old books. Some of them looked ancient: covers faded, old-time parchment-looking binding. Parkhurst, I've mentioned, seemed to have been principally interested in history and religion. He had the money and the special interest to have a lot of books that you wouldn't have in general circulation. Any college library would have been lucky to get that collection.

As you can imagine, especially in a prison where there was heavy emphasis on rehabilitation, an inmate was smiled upon if he demonstrated an unusually intense interest in books. There was a sizable number of well-read inmates, especially the popular debaters. Some were said by many to be practically walking encyclopedias. They were almost celebrities. No university would ask any student to devour literature as I did when this new world opened to me, of being able to read and *understand*.

I read more in my room than in the library itself. An inmate who was known to read a lot could check out more than the permitted maximum number of books. I preferred reading in the total isolation of my own room.

15   When I had progressed to really serious reading, every night at about ten (P.M.) I would be outraged with the "lights out." It always seemed to catch me right in the middle of something engrossing.

Fortunately, right outside my door was a corridor light that cast a glow into my room. The glow was enough to read by, once my eyes adjusted to it. So when "lights out" came, I would sit on the floor where I could continue reading in that glow.

At one-hour intervals the night guards paced past every room. Each time I heard the approaching footsteps, I jumped into bed and feigned sleep. And as soon as the guard passed, I got back out of bed onto the floor area of that light-glow, where I would read for another fifty-eight minutes—until the guard approached again. That went on until three or four every morning. Three or four hours of sleep a night was enough for me. Often in the years in the streets I had slept less than that.

QUESTIONS FOR ACTIVE READING

1. How does Malcolm X organize this excerpt from his autobiography? Why is this method of organization particularly effective? Create a simile to describe this organization strategy (for example, "it's like a light going on," or "it's like a tree putting out leaves after a long winter").

2. For whom is Malcolm X writing, and what is his purpose? (In fact, if you read closely, you might detect more than one assumed audience, and many layers of purpose.) What language does he use and what images does he create to appeal to a specific audience?

3. Malcolm X uses contrast throughout this excerpt—especially the contrast between what his audience might *expect,* and what actually *occurs.* These contrasts are occasionally humorous, and often moving. Find three examples of these contrasts in this excerpt, and explain what makes them effective.

QUESTIONS FOR THINKING CRITICALLY

1. Malcolm X states that, although he was an articulate "street hustler," this ability was of little help in expressing his ideas in writing. Explain the differences between expressing your ideas orally and in writing, including the advantages and disadvantages of each form of language expression.

2. Malcolm X envied one of the other inmates, Bimbi, because his stock of knowledge enabled him to take charge of any conversation he was in. Explain why knowledge—and our ability to use it—leads to power in our dealings with others. Describe a situation from your own experience in which having expert knowledge about a subject enabled you, through writing, to influence the thinking of other people.

3. About pursuing his mastery of language and exploring books, Malcolm X states, "Up to then, I never had been so truly free in my life." Explain what you think he means by this statement. Then describe a time in your life when you felt "truly free."

Making Decisions When Revising Drafts

Revision is the key to producing your best possible work. It is very rare for a first draft to represent the most effective writing of which a person is capable. Most accomplished writers expect their work to undergo a number of revisions based on their own re-evaluation and on feedback from others. The difference between outstanding and mediocre writing often depends on revision.

Many of the concepts in the five-step decision-making approach discussed in Chapter 5 can be applied to revising your drafts.

- You *define the decision and your goals* by identifying what in a draft needs to be revised and what should be left as it is.
- You *consider possible choices* for improving a draft, especially with major components such as composing and placing the thesis statement, presenting evidence, and arranging material in sequences, sections, or paragraphs. You also often have various choices among words and sentence patterns when you work at the editing level of revision.
- You *gather relevant information* and *evaluate the pros and cons* of the different choices in order to select the one that best meets the needs of the writing situation. Sometimes you may want to write down the different possibilities; in other instances, you may just try them out in your mind.
- After *implementing* your choices by revising a draft, you *evaluate* your writing by *reading it again,* slowly and completely, to be sure that the whole piece is as good as you can make it.

Collaborating with classmates or other trusted readers in all these decisions will usually be very helpful. Other readers can see your drafts more objectively and can help you "re-see" and revise them.

Specific Decisions to Make at Several Levels

The following suggestions should help you revise your drafts.

Read your entire draft slowly and carefully. You may find, as many writers do, that reading out loud helps you to identify parts that don't "sound" right. Also, ask someone whose judgment you trust to read the draft and help you to decide what improvement is needed. If your class allows peer review either in person or online, be prepared for this opportunity by having a draft ready.

The next step is to determine at what level should you begin to make changes. Revision means much more than correcting grammar, punctuation, and spelling. In fact, those corrections are often made separately, as editing and proofreading, to distinguish them from larger aspects of revision.

A helpful way to decide where to begin revising is to move through the following hierarchy of questions about your draft. If you find yourself answering any of the questions in a manner that suggests ways to improve your writing, stop and try to make the changes or additions to your draft before you move on to the next level. There is no point in worrying about punctuation if your draft lacks focus or good examples.

However, remember that revision, like all steps of the writing process, is recursive. You may detect content, organization, or wording problems while you are checking punctuation; you may fix a typo while you're rewording the thesis statement. The following hierarchy emphasizes the importance of looking first at major concerns, but you should be prepared to move around among the levels of revision as you make your decisions about a draft.

A STEP-BY-STEP METHOD FOR REVISING ANY ASSIGNMENT

The following method can be used both for revising your own papers and for reviewing your classmates' papers. It can be applied to any assignment. For easy reference as you move through the assignments in this book and those for other courses, an edited version of this method is reprinted on the inside back cover of this text. Refer to this method as you reach the Revising section of each Writing Project in the following chapters.

1. **Think big.** Look at the draft as a whole.

   ❑ Does it fulfill the assignment's purpose in terms of topic and length?
   ❑ Does it have a clear focus?
   ❑ What parts of the draft, if any, do not relate to its focus?
   ❑ How could the draft be reorganized to make it more logical for your audience?
   ❑ What evidence could be added to help to accomplish your purpose?
   ❑ How could the flow between paragraphs be made smoother?
   ❑ Is your point of view about your subject consistent throughout?

   Develop alternatives based on the answers to these questions, decide which alternatives will improve your draft, and then make changes to your draft before proceeding to the next level of revision.

2. **Think medium.** Look at the draft paragraph by paragraph. First consider the *introduction*.

   ❑ How could you rewrite your lead to make your audience more interested in continuing to read? (See the suggestions for being creative with introductions in Chapter 5.)
   ❑ Can you make the tone of the introduction match the tone of the rest of the draft?
   ❑ How could you more effectively indicate your purpose for writing?

Then look at each of your *body paragraphs*.

- ❏ Does each support the thesis or claim?
- ❏ Does each present relevant, specific evidence about the subject not presented elsewhere?
- ❏ Which, if any, body paragraphs should be combined or eliminated?
- ❏ Have you chosen or created useful and interesting visuals?
- ❏ Which body paragraphs use topic sentences effectively? Which don't?
- ❏ Where could you use transitions to improve the flow within or between body paragraphs?

Now look at your *conclusion*. This is your last opportunity to accomplish your purpose with your intended audience.

- ❏ How could you make your conclusion more effective? (See the suggestions for being creative with conclusions in Chapter 5.)
- ❏ Does the tone of the conclusion match your overall tone?

Again, develop alternatives and make changes to your draft before proceeding to the next level.

3. **Think small.** Look at your draft sentence by sentence.

- ❏ Which sentences are difficult to understand? How could you reword them?
- ❏ Which, if any, sentences are so long that your audience could get lost in them?
- ❏ Where are there short, choppy sentences that can be combined?
- ❏ Which sentences seem vague? How could you clarify them?
- ❏ Which, if any, sentences have errors in standard English grammar or usage? How could you correct them?

Make necessary changes to your draft before proceeding to the next level.

4. **Think "picky."** Look at your draft as the fussiest critic might.

- ❏ Which words are not clear or not quite right for your meaning? What words could you use instead?
- ❏ Are any words spelled incorrectly? (Run the spell-checker program on your computer, but don't rely on it alone.)
- ❏ Are the pages numbered consecutively?
- ❏ Does the physical appearance of your draft meet the assignment's requirements for format?
- ❏ Is there anything else you can do to improve your draft?

THINKING-
WRITING
ACTIVITY

Using the Revision Method

Apply each step of the revision method to an essay you have written for this course (your instructor will advise you about which one to select). Although this process may initially seem time-consuming and rather mechanical, you will soon begin to integrate these ideas in a more natural and flexible way. As you become more experienced as a writer, the revision method will eventually become an integral part of your writing process.

Beyond considering your own earlier experiences, you can deepen your understanding of revision by reading the following selection by an expert writer.

"The Maker's Eye: Revising Your Own Manuscripts"

By Donald M. Murray (b. 1924)

Known as both a professional journalist and a brilliant teacher, Donald M. Murray won the Pulitzer Prize for his editorials in the *Boston Herald* in 1954. Since then, he has taught writing at the University of New Hampshire and Boston University and is now a columnist for *The Boston Globe*. He has acted as a writing coach for several national newspapers and written poetry for many journals. Now in retirement, he published his memoir, *My Twice-Lived Life,* in 2001.

Murray has also authored several books on the craft of writing and teaching writing, including *Learning by Teaching, Expecting the Unexpected, and Crafting a Life in Essay, Story, Poem.* His work has been highly influential in the way writing is taught. In this selection, he describes his own revision process, one that has served him well.

When students complete a first draft, they consider the job of writing done—and their teachers too often agree. When professional writers complete a first draft, they usually feel that they are at the start of the writing process. When a draft is completed, the job of writing can begin.

That difference in attitude is the difference between amateur and professional, inexperience and experience, journeyman and craftsman. Peter F. Drucker, the prolific business writer, calls his first draft "the zero draft"—after that he can start counting. Most writers share the feeling that the first draft, and all of those which follow, are opportunities to discover what they have to say and how best they can say it.

To produce a progression of drafts, each of which says more and says it more clearly, the writer has to develop a special kind of reading skill. In school we are taught to decode what appears on the page as finished writing. Writers, however, face a different category of possibility and responsibility when they read their own drafts. To them the words on the page are never finished. Each can be changed and rearranged, can set off a chain reaction of confusion or clarified meaning. This is a different kind of reading, which is possibly more difficult and certainly more exciting.

Writers must learn to be their own best enemy. They must accept the criticism of others and be suspicious of it; they must accept the praise of others and be even more suspicious of it. Writers cannot depend on others. They must detach themselves from their own pages so that they can apply both their caring and their craft to their own work.

5 Such detachment is not easy. Science fiction writer Ray Bradbury supposedly puts each manuscript away for a year to the day and then rereads it as a stranger. Not many writers have the discipline or the time to do this. We must read when our judgment may be at its worst, when we are close to the euphoric moment of creation.

Then the writer, counsels novelist Nancy Hale, "should be critical of everything that seems to him most delightful in his style. He should excise what he most admires, because he wouldn't thus admire it if he weren't . . . in a sense protecting it from criticism." John Ciardi, the poet, adds, "The last act of writing must be to become one's own reader. It is, I suppose, a schizophrenic process, to begin passionately and to end critically, to begin hot and to end cold; and, more important, to be passion-hot and critic-cold at the same time."

Most people think that the principal problem is that writers are too proud of what they have written. Actually, a greater problem for most professional writers is one shared by the majority of students. They are overly critical, think everything is dreadful, tear up page after page, never complete a draft, see the task as hopeless.

The writer must learn to read critically but constructively, to cut what is bad, to reveal what is good. Eleanor Estes, the children's book author, explains: "The writer must survey his work critically, coolly, as though he were a stranger to it. He must be willing to prune, expertly and hard-heartedly. At the end of each revision, a manuscript may look . . . worked over, torn apart, pinned together, added to, deleted from, words changed and words changed back. Yet the book must maintain its original freshness and spontaneity."

Most readers underestimate the amount of rewriting it usually takes to produce spontaneous reading. This is a great disadvantage to the student writer, who sees only a finished product and never watches the craftsman who takes the necessary steps back, studies the work carefully, returns to the task, steps back, returns, steps back, again and again. Anthony Burgess, one of the most prolific writers in the English-speaking world, admits, "I might revise a page twenty times." Roald Dahl, the popular children's writer, states, "By the time I'm nearing the end of a story, the first part will have been reread and altered and corrected at least 150 times. . . . Good writing is essentially rewriting. I am positive of this."

10 Rewriting isn't virtuous. It isn't something that ought to be done. It is simply something that most writers find they have to do to discover what they have to say and how to say it. It is a condition of the writer's life.

There are, however, a few writers who do little formal rewriting, primarily because they have the capacity and experience to create and review a large number of invisible drafts in their minds before they approach the page. And some writers slowly produce finished pages, performing all the tasks of revision simultaneously, page by page, rather than draft by draft. But it is still possible to see the sequence followed by most writers most of the time in rereading their own work.

Most writers scan their drafts first, reading as quickly as possible to catch the larger problems of subject and form, then move in closer and closer as they read and write, reread and rewrite.

The first thing writers look for in their drafts is *information.* They know that a good piece of writing is built from specific, accurate, and interesting information. The writer must have an abundance of information from which to construct a readable piece of writing.

Next, writers look for meaning in the information. The specifics must build a pattern of significance. Each piece of specific information must carry the reader toward meaning.

Writers reading their own drafts are aware of *audience.* They put themselves in the reader's situation and make sure that they deliver information which a reader wants to know or needs to know in a manner which is easily digested. Writers try to be sure that they anticipate and answer the questions a critical reader will ask when reading the piece of writing.

Writers make sure that the *form* is appropriate to the subject and the audience. Form, or genre, is the vehicle which carries meaning to the reader, but form cannot be selected until the writer has adequate information to discover its significance and an audience which needs or wants that meaning.

Once writers are sure the form is appropriate, they must then look at the *structure,* the order of what they have written. Good writing is built on a solid framework of logic, argument, narrative, or motivation which runs through the entire piece of writing and holds it together. This is the time when many writers find it most effective to outline as a way of visualizing the hidden spine by which the piece of writing is supported.

The element on which writers may spend a majority of their time is *development.* Each section of a piece of writing must be adequately developed. It must give readers enough information so that they are satisfied. How much information is enough? That's as difficult as asking how much garlic belongs in a salad. It must be done to taste, but most beginning writers underdevelop, underestimating the reader's hunger for information.

As writers solve development problems, they often have to consider questions of *dimension.* There must be a pleasing and effective proportion among all the parts of the piece of writing. There is a continual process of subtracting and adding to keep the piece of writing in balance.

Finally, writers have to listen to their own voices. *Voice* is the force which drives a piece of writing forward. It is an expression of the writer's authority and concern.

It is what is between the words on the page, what glues the piece of writing together. A good piece of writing is always marked by a consistent, individual voice.

As writers read and reread, write and rewrite, they move closer and closer to the page until they are doing line-by-line editing. Writers read their own pages with infinite care. Each sentence, each line, each clause, each phrase, each word, each mark of punctuation, each section of white space between the type has to contribute to the clarification of meaning.

Slowly the writer moves from word to word, looking through language to see the subject. As a word is changed, cut, or added, as a construction is rearranged, all the words used before that moment and all those that follow that moment must be considered and reconsidered.

Writers often read aloud at this stage of the editing process, muttering or whispering to themselves, calling on the ear's experience with language. Does this sound right—or that? Writers edit, shifting back and forth from eye to page to ear to page. I find I must do this careful editing in short runs, no more than fifteen or twenty minutes at a stretch, or I become too kind with myself. I begin to see what I hope is on the page, not what actually is on the page.

This sounds tedious if you haven't done it, but actually it is fun. Making something right is immensely satisfying, for writers begin to learn what they are writing about by writing. Language leads them to meaning, and there is the joy of discovery, of understanding, of making meaning clear as the writer employs the technical skills of language.

25   Words have double meanings, even triple and quadruple meanings. Each word has its own potential for connotation and denotation. And when writers rub one word against the other, they are often rewarded with a sudden insight, an unexpected clarification.

The maker's eye moves back and forth from word to phrase to sentence to paragraph to sentence to phrase to word. The maker's eye sees the need for variety and balance, for a firmer structure, for a more appropriate form. It peers into the interior of the paragraph, looking for coherence, unity, and emphasis, which make meaning clear.

I learned something about this process when my first bifocals were prescribed. I had ordered a large section of the reading portion of the glass because of my work, but even so, I could not contain my eyes within this new limit of vision. And I still find myself taking off my glasses and bending my nose towards the page, for my eyes unconsciously flick back and forth across the page, back to another page, forward to still another, as I try to see each evolving line in relation to every other line.

When does this process end? Most writers agree with the great Russian writer Tolstoy, who said, "I scarcely ever reread my published writings, if by chance I come across a page, it always strikes me: all this must be rewritten; this is how I should have written it."

The maker's eye is never satisfied, for each word has the potential to ignite new meaning. This article has been twice written all the way through the writing process, and it was published four years ago. Now it is to be republished in a book. The editors make a few small suggestions, and then I read it with my maker's eye. Now it has been re-edited, re-vised, re-read, re-re-edited, for each piece of writing to the writer is full of potential and alternatives.

30   A piece of writing is never finished. It is delivered to a deadline, torn out of the typewriter on demand, sent off with a sense of accomplishment and shame and pride and frustration. If only there were a couple more days, time for just another run at it, perhaps then . . .

QUESTIONS FOR ACTIVE READING

1. Murray identifies elements for writers to examine when critically reading their drafts: information, audience, form, structure, development, dimension, and voice. Reread any essay you have written for this course, paying attention to each of these elements. How would you revise the essay further to better express your meaning?

2. Reread that same essay aloud to yourself and see if your "ear's experience with language" suggests any additional changes.

3. Murray quotes several authors in his essay, identifying each with a short phrase. Does that additional information influence how you read that quote and "listen" to its speaker? In what way?

QUESTIONS FOR THINKING CRITICALLY

1. Murray begins by contrasting the "student" and the "professional" writer. How do you, as a member of his audience, feel about your place in this comparison?

2. Compare the kind of writing that Murray is discussing to the writing that Malcolm X describes. How might Malcolm X interpret Murray's idea that "the words on the page are never finished"?

3. How does Murray establish his authority as a writer? Are you satisfied that he is someone whose advice you should follow? Why or why not?

Donald Murray discusses (paragraph 15) the importance of *audience* to writers and the revision process. It's evident from the last paragraph of his essay, however, that he is describing a revision process that is paper-based. Today's writers—students and professionals alike—are far more likely to perform almost every step of the writing process on the computer. You are also probably very comfortable with going online, chatting with friends, looking up information, downloading music, and watching video *while* you are writing—and all at the same computer!

Just as you have access to an infinitely larger range of information and resources than scholars did even in the late twentieth century, your potential audience is likely to be not just local but also global. In the following article, journalist Mary Blume describes the impact of globalization on language. If you are to use language ethically and responsibly, you will need to learn to *listen*—to be attentive to the ways in which people from very different backgrounds and perspectives make efforts to communicate, to negotiate, and to share information.

"If You Can't Master English, Try Globish"

BY MARY BLUME

Essayist and reporter Mary Blume has lived in Paris since 1960 and covered the Paris beat for the *International Herald Tribune* for more than thirty years. Her books include *A French Affair: The Paris Beat 1965–1998* (1999) and *Cote d'Azur: Inventing the French Riviera* (1994). The *International Herald Tribune,* owned by the *New York Times,* is an English-language daily newspaper published internationally, with special focus on global affairs.

It happens all the time: during an airport delay the man to the left, a Korean perhaps, starts talking to the man opposite, who might be Colombian, and soon they are chatting away in what seems to be English. But the native English speaker sitting between them cannot understand a word.

They don't know it, but the Korean and the Colombian are speaking Globish, the latest addition to the 6,800 languages that are said to be spoken across the world. Not that its inventor, Jean-Paul Nerrière, considers it a proper language.

"It is not a language; it is a tool," he says. "A language is the vehicle of a culture. Globish doesn't want to be that at all. It is a means of communication."

Nerrière doesn't see Globish in the same light as utopian efforts such as Kosmos, Volapuk, Novial or staunch Esperanto. Nor should it be confused with barbaric Algol (for Algorithmic language). It is a sort of English lite: a means of simplifying the language and giving it rules so it can be understood by all.

5   "The language spoken worldwide, by 88 percent of mankind, is not exactly English," Nerrière says. "I don't think people who think this gives them an edge are right because it's not useful if they cannot be understood by English speakers." His primer, Parlez Globish, is an attempt to codify worldspeak and since its publication by Eyrolles in Paris last year, he says, his Web site www.jpn-globish.com has had almost 36,000 hits.

A retired IBM marketing executive, Nerrière speaks excellent English but switches to Globish if he is not getting through. "I look at their faces. Lack of understanding is very easy to decipher."

The main principles of Globish are a vocabulary of only 1,500 words in English (the OED lists 615,000), gestures and repetition. Grammar will be dealt with in the next volume, "Découvrez le Globish," due next month.

The Web site also includes song lyrics because Nerrière reckons this is an excellent way to learn words, even if they are not on the Globish 1,500. "Strangers in the Night" is one choice, but what is the student to do when Sinatra goes "scoobie-doobie-do"?

"Doesn't matter," Nerrière replies buoyantly. "I saw 'A Chorus Line' three or four times on Broadway and I know all the songs by heart. I never understood the line 'If Troy Donahue can be a movie star, you can be a movie star,' but I managed to reproduce it well enough in a way [that] it could be understood."

10   The point, he says, is to reach the threshold of understanding. But neither threshold nor understanding is on the 1,500-word list. "In Globish it would be the target, the goal, the objective. I use three words to reach the point where you would be understood everywhere."

The list goes from *able* to *zero*. *Niece* and *nephew*, for example, are not included, "but you can replace them with *the children of my brother*," Nerrière says. He feels he erred in putting in both *beauty* and *beautiful* and in including *much* and *many* but not *lot*.

"*Much* is for ideas; *many* is for things you can count. *A lot* works for both cases; the others require a little more understanding."

The seeds for Globish came about in the 1980s when Nerrière was working for IBM in Paris with colleagues of about forty nationalities. At a meeting where they were to be addressed by two Americans whose flight had been delayed, they started exchanging shoptalk in what Nerrière calls "une certaine forme d'anglais perverti." Then the Americans arrived and beyond their opening phrases, "Call me Jim," "Call me Bill," no one understood a word. And Jim and Bill, needless to say, did not understand perverted English.

One might say that, except for Jim and Bill of course, everyone was speaking Globish though they didn't know it. "They all, like me, spoke low-quality English, not really Globish. One might have a vocabulary of 2,000 words, another of 1,200 and not the same words. One of the things of interest in Globish is that with 1,500 words you can express everything. People all over the world will speak with the same limited vocabulary."

15   With many corporations imposing English as the lingua franca wherever their base, Nerrière sees a great future for Globish, which he has trademarked. Learning it by computer and practicing it by free-access telephone will make things even easier. And there is a new law in France that gives employees the right to twenty hours per year of instruction in a given subject.

"The idea is to increase their employability by teaching them skills unrelated to their present employment. For me, the odds of someone asking for a course in macramé are very small and the odds of asking for a course in Maltese are also small. Why not Globish? If it could be of use in this small grocery shop where I work, maybe it will help me in the big hotel where I hope to be."

There is an other advantage, he argues. "At twenty hours a year you need twenty-four years to learn English with no result whatsoever since it would be spread too thin for the learner to remember what had been said two weeks earlier. With Globish you not only have free telephone access via the Internet, but you could get cheap lessons in places like India, where people speak good English and wages are low."

Nerrière reckons that with 182 hours plus learning "Strangers in the Night," the student should be able to communicate in Globish. It is not a pretty language—full of redundancies and lumpy constructions—but Nerrière repeats that it is nothing but a tool when proper English is not understood. It is not the language of Hamlet, Faulkner or Virginia Woolf," he explains.

But the worst thing for the French about this international language is that it isn't French. Nerrière argues rather subtly that if people learned Globish, the French language would remain unsullied because franglais would die out.

20   "It would end this crazy French terror about English and francophonie. The French say you are killing the French language, and I say, no, we are saving it from being killed by English."

There is one possible hiccup in this scheme. The fluent Globish speaker will not be understood by native English speakers. No problem: Nerrière already is preparing a Globish version in English in addition to the Italian and Spanish editions, which will be out shortly. So he is not only protecting French from invasion, but he is getting Americans to become, so to speak, bilingual.

"Absolutely!" Nerrière says triumphantly. "This is the way to get Americans to learn another language."

QUESTIONS FOR ACTIVE READING

1. Given what you know about the *International Herald Tribune*, what can you assume about the audience for this article? Why would the subject of this article be interesting and relevant to that audience?

2. How does Jean-Paul Nerrière define *language*? How does he define *Globish*? What is the distinction between these two definitions, in Nerrière's view?

3. Do you think that Nerrière's plan to "get Americans to learn another language" could be successful? Consider your own experience learning (or not learning) another language in school as you form your response.

QUESTIONS FOR THINKING CRITICALLY

1. What is the purpose of Globish? At the library, locate George Orwell's essay "Politics and the English Language" or his novel *1984*. How might Orwell interpret the purpose and necessity of Globish?

2. The Writing Project in Chapter 8 (page 254) asks you to define a concept that is important to your life right now. Following the steps of this Writing Project, write an essay in which you define the concept of *language* within the context of your own academic, professional, or personal goals.

3. In paragraph 14, Nerrière suggests that Globish allows people to express all kinds of ideas while using a very limited vocabulary. What is the most recent new concept, term, or phrase that you have added to your vocabulary? In a brief narrative essay, describe how you first encountered this addition to your vocabulary and how knowing this term impacts some aspects of your life.

Using Language Ethically

Language reflects thinking, and thinking is shaped by language. Language not only provides multiple ways of expressing the same ideas, thoughts, and feelings but also helps to structure those thoughts. In turn, patterns of thinking breathe life into language.

The relationship between thinking and language is *interactive;* both processes are continually influencing each other in many ways. The interactive qualities of language also extend to its communicative purpose. We use language to persuade, to entertain, to inform, and to delight; yet we also know that language can be used to conceal the truth, to foment hatred, to create terror. As a critical thinker, it is your ethical responsibility to continually evaluate the quality and reliability of what you communicate to others through text, visuals, and speech. Malcolm X recognized, at a personal level, how powerful language can be; later in this chapter, Daniel Pipes explains how language, used for unethical purposes, can cause tremendous damage.

FIGURE 6.1   Clear Language and Clear Thinking

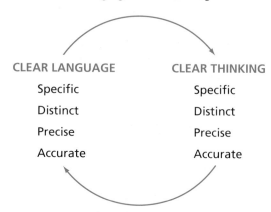

CLEAR LANGUAGE

Specific

Distinct

Precise

Accurate

CLEAR THINKING

Specific

Distinct

Precise

Accurate

When language use is sloppy—vague, general, indistinct, imprecise, foolish, inaccurate, and so on—it leads to the same sort of thinking. And the reverse is also true. Clear and precise language leads to clear and precise thinking, as shown in Figure 6.1. The opposite of clear, effective language is language that fails to help the reader picture or understand what the writer means because it is vague or ambiguous.

Improving Vague Language

Although our ability to name and identify gives us the power to describe the world in a precise way, we often tend to describe it in words that are imprecise and general. Such nonspecific words are termed *vague* words. Consider the following sentences:

- I had a *nice* time yesterday.
- That is an *interesting* book.
- She is an *old* person.

In each of these cases, the italicized word does not provide a precise description of the thought, feeling, or experience that the writer or speaker is trying to communicate. Vagueness occurs whenever a word is used to represent an area of experience without clearly defining it. A *vague word* is one that lacks a clear and distinct meaning.

Although the vagueness of general measurement terms can lead to confusion, other forms of vagueness are more widespread and often more problematic. Terms such as *good* and *enjoyable,* for example, are imprecise and unclear. Vagueness of this sort permeates every level of human discourse, undermines clear thinking, and is extremely difficult to combat. To use language clearly and precisely, you must develop an understanding of the way language functions and commit yourself to breaking the entrenched habit of using vague expression.

THINKING-
WRITING
ACTIVITY

Vague Language

Most words of general measurement—short, tall, big, small, heavy, light, and so on—are vague. The exact meanings of these words depend on the specific situation in which they are used and on the particular perspective of the person using them. For example, give specific definitions for the following italicized words by filling in the blanks. Then compare your responses with those of your classmates. Can you account for the differences in meaning?

1. A *middle-aged* person is one who is _____ years old.

2. A *tall* person is one who is over _____ feet _____ inches tall.

3. It's *cold* when the temperature is _____ degrees.

4. A person is *wealthy* when he or she is worth _____ dollars.

Vagueness is always a matter of degree. In fact, you can think of your descriptive/informative use of language as falling somewhere on a scale between extreme generality and extreme specificity. The following statements move from the general to the specific.

General

↓

She is really smart.

She does well in school.

She gets straight As.

She earned an A+ in physics.

Specific

Although different situations require various degrees of specificity, you should work to become increasingly more precise in your use of language.

When you are revising your own work, try to recognize and improve vague language, remembering your obligation to your audience to be as clear as possible. Be on the lookout for vague words such as *nice, good, fine, interesting, well, special, bad, really, very, old, young, situation,* and so on. Resist the temptation to improve vague words by putting *very* or *really* in front of them. Instead, if you have written, "The dessert was good," ask yourself, "How or why was it good?" Then substitute your answer for the vague word: "The dessert was full of fresh, plump strawberries flavored with orange juice and bits of mint." Now your audience can enjoy it with you!

Using Figurative Language

Thus far in this section, we have been concerned with saying and writing exactly what we mean as precisely as possible. However, there is another way to use language to express thinking: to say something we do not literally mean. Of course, there are some writing situations for which figurative language is inappropriate. When in doubt, check with your instructor. But when we do use figurative language effectively, our readers or listeners understand that we are not speaking literally but rather that we are speaking figuratively, using a figure of speech. Here we will focus on two figures of speech that may already be familiar: *simile* and *metaphor*.

Both simile and metaphor are based on a special kind of comparative thinking called an analogy, which is a limited comparison of two essentially unlike things for the purpose of illuminating or enriching our understanding. Analogies differ from the more common comparisons that examine the similarities and differences of two items in the same general category, such as two items on a menu or two methods of learning a language. Similes and metaphors focus on unexpected likenesses between items from different categories. Thus, when we compare a baby's skin to velvet, we may be calling attention to the skin's color or softness, but we are not suggesting that it makes a nice jacket or can be dyed different colors.

Consider the following example:

> Life's but a walking shadow, a poor player
> That struts and frets his hour upon the stage,
> And then is heard no more . . .
>
> —*Shakespeare, Macbeth*

In this famous metaphor, Shakespeare is comparing two things that at first seem to have nothing in common: life and an actor. Yet a closer look reveals that even though they are dissimilar in many ways, they share some undeniable similarities.

It is simple to distinguish similes from metaphors. Similes are explicitly stated comparisons that include the words *as, like,* or *than.* For example, "To the goalie, Mia Hamm's shot appeared as a photon of light." On the other hand, metaphors are implicitly stated comparisons, usually using some part of the verb *to be,* and do not include the words *as, like,* or *than.* Thus, it would be a metaphor to say, "To the goalie, Mia Hamm's shot was a photon of light."

When should you use figurative language in your writing? Extensive reading will help you develop a feel for opportunities, but here are four suggestions:

- **When you are having trouble finding the right words.** Powerful or complex emotions can make you speechless or make you say things like "Words cannot express what I feel." For example, if you are trying to describe your feelings of love for someone, you might write, "As breathtaking as the first rose in spring, this is the first great love of my life," or "Like the fragile yet supple petals of the rose, my feelings are tender and sensitive."

- **When you want to express a profound thought in a strikingly original way.** For example, you want to express an idea about the meaning of life, which the simple word *life* does not convey. Shakespeare wrote, "(Life) is a tale/ Told by an idiot, full of sound and fury,/ Signifying nothing." Forrest Gump said, "Life is like a box of chocolates." You might write, "Life is a football game," or "Life is an earthquake."

- **When you want to add an extra dimension to a description.** Alan Lightman recalls that he "would save [his] math problems for last, right before bedtime, like bites of chocolate cake awaiting [him] after a long and dutiful meal of history and Latin." You might write, "The spilled flour settled all over the apartment like a soft snow."
- **When you want to amuse your audience.** The great pool hustler Minnesota Fats wrote, "A pool player in a tuxedo is like a hotdog with whipped cream on it." By putting together two things that don't go together, like hotdogs and whipped cream, Minnesota Fats made his audience smile. You might write, "My twin brothers get along like ice cream and sauerkraut."

THINKING-
WRITING
ACTIVITY

Creating Similes and Metaphors

1. Use your creative thinking skills to create a simile for a subject of your own choosing, noting at least two points of comparison.

2. Now use your creative thinking skills to create a metaphor (implied analogy) for a subject of your own choosing, noting at least two points of comparison.

3. Create a metaphor for life that represents your feelings and explain the points of similarity.

Figurative language that has become cliché is not effective. "He runs like a deer" and "I slept like a baby" were wonderful similes the first time they were used, but they have become old and tired: clichés. Use your creative thinking skills to write original, striking figures of speech.

Very skillful speakers and writers are able to weave similes and metaphors together into a striking tapestry. As you read the following selection by Martin Luther King Jr., notice how he uses figurative language effectively while being clear and precise about both the problem and the solution.

"I Have a Dream"

By Martin Luther King Jr. (1929–1968)

The son of an influential Baptist minister, Martin Luther King Jr. began his involvement with the civil rights movement in 1955, when as a Baptist minister in Montgomery, Alabama, he led the Montgomery bus boycott after Rosa Parks, an African-American woman, heroically refused to give up her seat at the front of a public bus.

Greatly influenced by the nonviolent resistance of Mohandas K. Ghandi, King advocated an approach to protesting injustice that continues to resonate in progressive movements worldwide. Through education and outreach, marches, silent sit-ins at segregated lunch counters, and other acts of nonviolent resistance, King and his followers consistently met acts of barbarism with gestures of peace. He was awarded the Nobel Peace Prize in 1964.

And yet the violence he so peacefully—but forcefully—resisted eventually claimed him (as it did Ghandi). Dr. King was assassinated while standing on the balcony of the Lorraine Motel in Memphis, Tennessee, on April 4, 1968.

The speech that follows was delivered during the great March on Washington in 1963. That peaceful march and demonstration for human rights remains one of the most indelible images of twentieth-century American culture.

Five score years ago, a great American, in whose symbolic shadow we stand, signed the Emancipation Proclamation. This momentous decree came as a great beacon light of hope to millions of Negro slaves who had been seared in the flames of withering injustice. It came as a joyous daybreak to end the long night of captivity.

But one hundred years later, we must face the tragic fact that the Negro is still not free. One hundred years later, the life of the Negro is still sadly crippled by the manacles of segregation and the chains of discrimination. One hundred years later, the Negro lives on a lonely island of poverty in the midst of a vast ocean of material prosperity. One hundred years later, the Negro is still languishing in the corners of American society and finds himself an exile in his own land. So we have come here today to dramatize an appalling condition.

In a sense we have come to our nation's capital to cash a check. When the architects in our republic wrote the magnificent words of the Constitution and the Declaration of Independence, they were signing a promissory note to which every American was to fall heir. This note was a promise that all men would be guaranteed the unalienable rights of life, liberty, and the pursuit of happiness.

It is obvious today that America has defaulted on this promissory note insofar as her citizens of color are concerned. Instead of honoring this sacred obligation, America has given the Negro people a bad check; a check which has come back marked "insufficient funds." But we refuse to believe that the bank of justice is bankrupt. We refuse to believe that there are insufficient funds in the great vaults of opportunity of this nation. So we have come to cash this check—a check that will give us upon demand the riches of freedom and the security of justice. We have also come to this hallowed spot to remind America of the fierce urgency of *now*. This is no time to engage in the luxury of cooling off or to take the tranquilizing drugs of gradualism. *Now* is the time to make real the promises of Democracy. *Now* is the time to rise from the dark and desolate valley of segregation to the sunlit path of racial justice. *Now* is the time to open the doors of opportunity to all of God's children. *Now* is the time to lift our nation from the quicksands of racial injustice to the solid rock of brotherhood.

5   It would be fatal for the nation to overlook the urgency of the moment and to underestimate the determination of the Negro. This sweltering summer of the Negro's legitimate discontent will not pass until there is an invigorating autumn of freedom and equality. 1963 is not an end, but a beginning. Those who hope that the Negro needed to blow off steam and will now be content will have a rude awakening if the nation

returns to business as usual. There will be neither rest nor tranquillity in America until the Negro is granted his citizenship rights. The whirlwinds of revolt will continue to shake the foundations of our nation until the bright day of justice emerges.

But there is something that I must say to my people who stand on the warm threshold which leads into the palace of justice. In the process of gaining our rightful place we must not be guilty of wrongful deeds. Let us not seek to satisfy our thirst for freedom by drinking from the cup of bitterness and hatred. We must forever conduct our struggle on the high plane of dignity and discipline. We must not allow our creative protest to degenerate into physical violence. Again and again we must rise to the majestic heights of meeting physical force with soul force. The marvelous new militancy which has engulfed the Negro community must not lead us to a distrust of all white people, for many of our white brothers, as evidenced by their presence here today, have come to realize that their destiny is tied up with our destiny and their freedom is inextricably bound to our freedom. We cannot walk alone.

And as we walk, we must make the pledge that we shall march ahead. We cannot turn back. There are those who are asking the devotees of civil rights, "When will you be satisfied?" We can never be satisfied as long as the Negro is the victim of the unspeakable horrors of police brutality. We can never be satisfied as long as our bodies, heavy with the fatigue of travel, cannot gain lodging in the motels of the highways and the hotels of the cities. We cannot be satisfied as long as the Negro's basic mobility is from a smaller ghetto to a larger one. We can never be satisfied as long as a Negro in Mississippi cannot vote and a Negro in New York believes he has nothing for which to vote. No, no, we are not satisfied, and we will not be satisfied until justice rolls down like waters and righteousness like a mighty stream.

I am not unmindful that some of you have come here out of great trials and tribulations. Some of you have come fresh from narrow jail cells. Some of you have come from areas where your quest for freedom left you battered by the storms of persecution and staggered by the winds of police brutality. You have been the veterans of creative suffering. Continue to work with the faith that unearned suffering is redemptive.

Go back to Mississippi, go back to Alabama, go back to South Carolina, go back to Georgia, go back to Louisiana, go back to the slums and ghettos of our northern cities, knowing that somehow this situation can and will be changed. Let us not wallow in the valley of despair.

10   I say to you today, my friends, that in spite of the difficulties and frustrations of the moment I still have a dream. It is a dream deeply rooted in the American dream.

I have a dream that one day this nation will rise up and live out the true meaning of its creed: "We hold these truths to be self-evident; that all men are created equal."

I have a dream that one day on the red hills of Georgia the sons of former slaves and the sons of former slaveowners will be able to sit down together at the table of brotherhood.

I have a dream that one day even the state of Mississippi, a desert state sweltering with the heat of injustice and oppression, will be transformed into an oasis of freedom and justice.

I have a dream that my four little children will one day live in a nation where they will not be judged by the color of their skin but by the content of their character.

15

I have a dream today.

I have a dream that one day the state of Alabama, whose governor's lips are presently dripping with the words of interposition and nullification, will be transformed into a situation where little black boys and black girls will be able to join hands with little white boys and white girls and walk together as sisters and brothers.

I have a dream today.

I have a dream that one day every valley shall be exalted, every hill and mountain shall be made low, the rough places will be made plain, and the crooked places will be made straight, and the glory of the Lord shall be revealed, and all flesh shall see it together.

This is our hope. This is the faith with which I return to the South. With this faith we will be able to hew out of the mountain of despair a stone of hope. With this faith we will be able to transform the jangling discords of our nation into a beautiful symphony of brotherhood. With this faith we will be able to work together, to pray together, to struggle together, to go to jail together, to stand up for freedom together, knowing that we will be free one day.

20

This will be the day when all of God's children will be able to sing with new meaning:

My country, 'tis of thee, Sweet land of liberty, Of thee I sing: Land where my fathers died, Land of the pilgrims' pride, From every mountain-side Let freedom ring.

And if America is to be a great nation, this must become true. So let freedom ring from the prodigious hilltops of New Hampshire. Let freedom ring from the mighty mountains of New York. Let freedom ring from the heightening Alleghenies of Pennsylvania!

Let freedom ring from the snowcapped Rockies of Colorado!

Let freedom ring from the curvaceous peaks of California!

25

But not only that; let freedom ring from Stone Mountain of Georgia!

Let freedom ring from Lookout Mountain of Tennessee!

Let freedom ring from every hill and molehill of Mississippi. From every mountainside, let freedom ring.

When we let freedom ring, when we let it ring from every village and every hamlet, from every state and every city, we will be able to speed up that day when all of God's children, black men and white men, Jews and Gentiles, Protestants and Catholics, will be able to join hands and sing in the words of the old Negro spiritual, "Free at last! free at last! thank God almighty, we are free at last!"

QUESTIONS FOR ACTIVE READING

1. Of the rich metaphors King uses, which two or three do you find most effective or striking? Why?

2. This text is at once a speech and a sermon. Locate a recording of King's delivery of this great sermon, and listen to his delivery. How does King's voice, his emphasis on particular phrases, his call-and-response engagement with his audience, change the way you silently "read" the printed text?

3. The cadences and the figurative language of "I Have a Dream" are profoundly influenced by King's lifelong immersion in the African-American Baptist church. Are those rhythms and biblical allusions familiar to you? Do you need to understand those allusions in order to fully appreciate the ethical and moral implications of his call to action?

QUESTIONS FOR THINKING CRITICALLY

1. King exhorts the marchers to "continue to work with the faith that unearned suffering is redemptive." In the same year as the March on Washington, Malcolm X delivered a speech in Detroit in which he noted that "there is nothing in our book, the Koran, that teaches us to suffer peacefully. Our religion teaches us to be intelligent. Be peaceful, be courteous, obey the law, respect everyone; but if someone puts his hands on you, send him to the cemetery." Can these two views be reconciled? How do you think injustice should best be fought?

2. Do you have faith in individual people, or in society as a whole, to address and correct a specific injustice? Describe an injustice that you have witnessed, and evaluate how either individuals or a community has responded to that injustice.

3. King dreams of a nation where people are judged by the "content of their character"— their *ethic*. What is the content of your own character? How do you measure up to your own ethical ideals?

Using Language to Influence

Because of the intimate relationship between language and thinking, people naturally use language to influence the thinking of others. One of the reasons Dr. King's speech was so influential was that he invoked the cadences and the vocabulary of the Bible. President Bill Clinton used the same strategy when he promised Americans "a new covenant" between the government and the people. Later, George W. Bush became president after promoting an agenda of "compassionate conservatism." Conversely, the term *weapons of mass destruction* was so terrifying that many people believe it was one of the reasons that Congress voted to support the war in Iraq.

Manufacturers and advertising professionals choose language just as carefully to influence buying decisions. Americans are told that the Energizer bunny "keeps going and going." We are invited to "Join the Pepsi generation" and challenged to stop eating chips: "I bet you can't eat just one." And we are told over and over, "It's Miller time."

Whatever your political positions or buying habits, there are people who make a profession of using language to influence others' thinking. They are interested in influencing—and sometimes in controlling—your thoughts, feelings, and behavior.

To avoid being unconsciously manipulated by these efforts, you need to be aware of how language functions. This knowledge will help you to distinguish actual arguments, information, and reasons from techniques of persuasion that others use to get you to accept their views without thinking critically. Three types of language often used to promote the uncritical acceptance of views are euphemistic language, clichés, and emotive language.

Euphemistic Language

The term *euphemism* is derived from a Greek word meaning "to speak with good words." Using a euphemism involves substituting a pleasanter, less objectionable expression for a blunt or more direct one. For example, an entire collection of euphemisms exists to disguise the unpleasantness of death: *passed away, went to her reward, departed this life,* and *blew out the candle.*

Why do people use euphemisms? Probably to help smooth out the "rough edges" of life, to make the unbearable bearable and the offensive inoffensive. Sometimes people use them to make their occupations sound more dignified (a garbage collector, for instance, might be called a "sanitation engineer"). Sometimes euphemisms can be humorous, as are the following "New Euphemisms for Bad Stuff at School."

Course failure	Unrequested course reregistration
Incomplete course grade	An unrequited educational encounter
Suspension	Mandatory discontinued attendance
Absence	A non-school learning experience

Euphemisms can become dangerous, though, when they are used to evade or to create misperceptions of serious issues. An alcoholic may describe herself as a "social drinker," thus denying her problem and need for help. A politician may indicate that one of his statements was "somewhat at variance with the truth"—meaning that he lied. Another example would be to describe rotting slums as "substandard housing," making deplorable conditions appear reasonable and the need for action less urgent. In the following brief essay, foreign, policy analyst Daniel Pipes argues against the use of euphemistic language to describe acts of terrorism.

"Beslan Atrocity: They're Terrorists— Not Activists"

BY DANIEL PIPES (b. 1949)

Policy analyst Daniel Pipes is frequently consulted by media, industry, universities, and governments worldwide for his expert opinions and analysis of ongoing developments in the Middle East.

He is the director of the Middle East Forum, a think tank that provides analysis about radical Islam to business, academic, and government entities. He was director of the Foreign Policy Research Institute from 1986 to 1993, and has been a board member of the United States Institute of Peace. The following article was written after Islamic terrorists took over a school in Beslan, Russia, in 2004, a siege that led to the deaths of four hundred people. Most of the dead were children, their teachers, and their parents, who had been celebrating the first day of the school year.

"**I** know it when I see it" was the famous response by a U.S. Supreme Court justice to the vexed problem of defining pornography. Terrorism may be no less difficult to define, but the wanton killing of schoolchildren, of mourners at a funeral, or workers at their desks in skyscrapers surely fits the know-it-when-I-see-it definition.

The press, however, generally shies away from the word *terrorist*, preferring euphemisms. Take the assault that led to the deaths of some four hundred people, many of them children, in Beslan, Russia, on September 3. Journalists have delved deep into their thesauruses, finding at least twenty euphemisms for terrorists:

Assailants—*National Public Radio*

Attackers—the *Economist*

Bombers—the *Guardian*

Captors—the *Associated Press*

Commandos—*Agence France-Presse* refers to the terrorists both as "members du commando" and "commando"

Criminals—the *Times* (London)

Extremists—*United Press International*

Fighters—the *Washington Post*

Group—the *Autralian*

Guerrillas—in a *New York Post* editorial

Gunmen—*Reuters*

Hostage-takers—the *Los Angeles Times*

Insurgents—in a *New York Times* headline

Kidnappers—the *Observer* (London)

Militants—the *Chicago Tribune*

Perpetrators—the *New York Times*

Radicals—the *BBC*

Rebels—in a *Sydney Morning Herald* headline

Separatists—the *Christian Science Monitor*

And my favorite:

Activists—the *Pakistan Times*

The origins of this unwillingness to name terrorists seems to lie in the Arab-Israeli conflict, prompted by an odd combination of sympathy in the press for the Palestinian Arabs and intimidation by them. The sympathy is well known; the intimidation less so. Reuters' Nidal al-Mughrabi made the latter explicit in advice for fellow reporters in Gaza to avoid trouble on the web site www.newssafety.com, where one tip reads: "Never use the word *terrorist* or *terrorism* in describing Palestinian gunmen and militants; people consider them heroes of the conflict."

The reluctance to call terrorists by their rightful name can reach absurd lengths of inaccuracy and apologetics. For example, National Public Radio's *Morning Edition* announced on April 1, 2004, that "Israeli troops have arrested twelve men they say were wanted militants." But CAMERA, the Committee for Accuracy in Middle East Reporting in America, pointed out the inaccuracy and NPR issued an on-air correction on April 26: "Israeli military officials were quoted as saying they had arrested twelve men who were 'wanted militants.' But the actual phrase used by the Israeli military was 'wanted terrorists.'"

5   (At least NPR corrected itself. When the *Los Angeles Times* made the same error, writing that "Israel staged a series of raids in the West Bank that the army described as hunts for wanted Palestinian militants," its editors refused CAMERA's request for a correction on the grounds that its change in terminology did not occur in a direct quotation.)

Metro, a Dutch paper, ran a picture on May 3, 2004, of two gloved hands belonging to a person taking fingerprints off a dead terrorist. The caption read: "An Israeli police officer takes fingerprints of a dead Palestinian. He is one of the victims (*slachtoffers*) who fell in the Gaza strip yesterday." One of the victims!

Euphemistic usage then spread from the Arab-Israeli conflict to other theaters. As terrorism picked up in Saudi Arabia such press outlets as *The Times (London)* and the Associated Press began routinely using *militants* in reference to Saudi terrorists. Reuters uses it with reference to Kashmir and Algeria.

Thus has *militants* become the press's default term for terrorists.

These self-imposed language limitations sometimes cause journalists to tie themselves into knots. In reporting the murder of one of its own cameraman, the BBC, which normally avoids the word *terrorist,* found itself using that term. In another instance, the search engine on the BBC web site includes the word *terrorist* but the page linked to [it] has had that word expurgated.

10   Politically correct news organizations undermine their credibility with such subterfuges. How can one trust what one reads, hears, or sees when the self-evident fact of terrorism is being semi-denied?

Worse, the multiple euphemisms for *terrorist* obstruct a clear understanding of the violent threats confronting the civilized world. It is bad enough that only one of five articles discussing the Beslan atrocity mentions its Islamist origins; worse is the miasma of words that insulates the public from the evil of terrorism.

QUESTIONS FOR ACTIVE READING

1. How are the terms listed by Daniel Pipes euphemistic? That is, why are these terms (in Pipes's opinion) less accurate, or less objectionable, than the term *terrorist?*

2. What does the word *wanton* (paragraph 1) mean, and what are the connotations of its use by Pipes to describe the actions of terrorists?

3. To what does Pipes attribute the use of euphemisms to describe terrorist actions?

4. What other euphemisms can you identify that are used to describe current events?

Questions for Thinking Critically

1. The conservative Fox News network uses the term *homicide bombers*, as opposed to the more commonly used *suicide bombers*, to describe people who blow themselves up when they set off bombs meant to kill others as well. What is the difference between these two terms? Which terms, in your opinion, is more accurate? In an extended definition essay (see page 252 in Chapter 8), explain your thinking.

2. Go online to find more information about the attacks on the Beslan school. Which of the terms listed by Pipes did you find in the articles and analysis you consulted? Which term, based on your interpretations of the events, seems most accurate?

3. Working with a small group, look up each of the terms listed by Pipes in a good dictionary and in a thesaurus. In what ways are the derivations and usages of these terms similar, and in what ways are they different? Which words are considered to be synonyms for each other? Create a spectrum (see page 175) ranging from "most objectionable" to "least objectionable" and place each term at a point on that spectrum that reflects your research.

THINKING- WRITING ACTIVITY 	**Thinking Critically About Euphemisms** Select an important social problem such as drug use, crime, poverty, juvenile delinquency, support for wars in other countries, racism, or unethical or illegal behavior in government. List several euphemisms commonly used to describe the problem; then explain how these euphemisms can lead to dangerous misperceptions and serious consequences.

Clichés

Clichés function in a similar way to *euphemisms* in that they tend to dilute meaning and avoid the complexities of an issue. A cliché is an overused phrase, usually employing figurative language, and so often repeated that the phrase becomes an automatic pattern. For example, if someone says "Sly as a . . .," what word comes next? Or "Sharp as a . . ."? On page 165, in the discussion of figurative language, the point was made that clichés usually start off as fresh wordings. People like the way the phrase sounds and repeat it over and over, year after year. After a while, the phrase loses its freshness and also its clear reference to what is being discussed.

What does it really mean to be "drunk as a skunk"? First of all, skunks do not imbibe alcohol. But, more important, this cliché is not helpful to a discussion of intoxication. The issue may be a drinker's health or safety—or the safety of those around that person. What does it really mean to say that someone is "sly as a fox"? The issue may be manipulative behavior that can cause serious problems, not just wily strategies.

In addition, the use of clichés indicates lazy thinking. Imagine how clever it must have seemed the first time someone said in a meeting that the group should "think outside the box." Yet a person who uses that phrase now is not being clever, just repeating a tired phrase, and will probably be considered inarticulate. Clichés may not create serious problems in casual conversation, but they do cloud meaning and should not be used in your academic writing.

THINKING-
WRITING
ACTIVITY

Cliché and Proverb

Different societies and different time periods give rise to different clichés.

1. Write down two or three phrases that you consider to be clichés. Try to recall where you have read or heard them. Share this writing with classmates to see if they know these phrases and if they think that they are clichés.

   Proverbs and famous quotations are also often repeated, but they function differently from clichés because they tend to encourage thinking.

2. Write down a proverb or a famous quotation that you know, and write a few sentences about how it stimulates your thinking.

3. Select a cliché and write a few sentences about how it does not help you think clearly about an issue to which it could apply.

Emotive Language

What is your immediate reaction to each of the following words?

tyrant	*peaceful*	*disgusting*	*God*	*filthy*
mouthwatering	*bloodthirsty*	*freedom*	*jihad*	

Most of these words probably arouse strong feelings in you. In fact, this ability to evoke feelings accounts for the extraordinary power of language.

Certain words (like those just listed) are used to stand for the emotive areas of your experience. These emotive words symbolize the whole range of human feelings from powerful emotions ("I detest you!") to the subtlest of feelings.

Emotive language often plays a double role: it not only symbolizes and expresses our feelings but also arouses or *evokes* feelings in others. When you tell someone, "You're my best friend," you usually are not simply expressing your feelings for the person; you also hope to inspire that person to have similar feelings for you. Even when communicating factual information, we make use of the emotive influence of language to interest other people in what we are saying. For example, go to the Online Study Center for *Critical Thinking, Thoughtful Writing* and compare the *New York Times* account of the events of 9/11 with the *People's Daily* account. Which account do you find more emotive? Which seems more objective? Which do you find more engaging? Why?

Although an emotive word may be an accurate description of feelings, it is not the same as a factual statement because it is true only for the speaker—not for others. For instance, even though you may feel that a movie is "tasteless" and "repulsive," someone else may find it "exciting" and "hilarious." By describing your feelings about the movie, you are giving your personal evaluation, which often may differ from the personal evaluations of others (it is not unusual to see conflicting reviews of the same movie). A factual statement, on the other hand, is a statement with which rational people will agree, providing that suitable evidence to verify it is available (for example, the fact that mass transit uses less energy than automobiles). When emotive words are used in larger groups (such as sentences, paragraphs, compositions, poems, plays, or novels), they become even more powerful. Martin Luther King Jr., speech "I Have a Dream" (p. 165) is a dramatic example of the force of effective emotive language.

One way to think about the meaning and power of emotive words is to see them on a scale or continuum, from mild to strong. For example:

overweight   fat   obese

The thinker Bertrand Russell used this continuum to illustrate how we perceive the same trait in various people:

- I am *firm.*
- You are *stubborn.*
- He/she is *pigheaded.*

We usually tend to perceive ourselves favorably ("I am firm"). I am speaking to you face to face, so I view you only somewhat less favorably ("You are stubborn"). But since a third person is not present, I can use stronger emotive language ("He/she is pigheaded"). Try this technique with two other emotive words:

1. I am . . .   You are . . .   He/she is . . .

2. I am . . .   You are . . .   He/she is . . .

Emotive words usually signal that a personal opinion or evaluation, rather than a fact, is being stated. Speakers occasionally do identify their opinions as opinions, using phrases like "In my opinion" or "I feel that." Often, however, speakers do not identify their opinions as such because they want you to treat their judgments as facts. In these cases, the combination of the informative use and the emotive use of language can be misleading and even dangerous.

A final point to consider about emotive language is that it can be used in a reverse way, as we have seen in the section on euphemism. George Orwell gives examples of this in his classic essay "Politics and the English Language." He points out that such usages deliberately drain the emotion from terms in order to lessen the shock of the information being conveyed. "Defenseless villages are bombarded from the air, the inhabitants driven out into the country-side, the cattle machine-gunned, the huts set on fire with incendiary bullets: this is called *pacification.*"

THINKING-
WRITING
ACTIVITY

Evaluating Emotive Language

Identify examples of emotive language in the following passages and explain how the writer is using that language to influence people's thoughts and feelings.

We need another and a wiser and perhaps a more mystical concept of animals. Remote from universal nature, and living by complicated artifice, man in civilization surveys the creature through the glass of his knowledge and sees thereby a feather magnified and the whole image in distortion. We patronize them for their incompleteness, for their tragic fate of having taken form so far below ourselves. And therein we err, and greatly err. For the animal shall not be measured by man. In a world older and more complete than ours they move finished and complete, gifted with senses that you have lost or never attained, living by voices you shall never hear.

—Henry Beston, *The Outermost House*

Every criminal, every gambler, every thug, every libertine, every girl ruiner, every home wrecker, every wife beater, every dope peddler, every moonshiner, every crooked politician, every pagan Papist priest, every shyster lawyer, every white slaver, every brothel madam, every Rome-controlled newspaper, every black spider—is fighting the Klan. Think it over. Which side are you on?

—From a Ku Klux Klan circular

Writing Project: The Impact of Language on Our Lives

This chapter explores the essential role of language in developing sophisticated thinking abilities. The goal of clear, effective thinking and communication is accomplished through the joint efforts of thought and language. Learning to use the appropriate language style, which depends on the social context in which you are operating, requires both critical judgment and flexible expertise with various language forms. Critically evaluating the pervasive attempts of advertisers and others to bypass your critical faculties and influence your thinking involves insight into the way language and thought create and express meaning. We will be examining these relationships between language and thought further in upcoming chapters.

The following Writing Project provides an opportunity for you to apply what you have learned in this chapter to your own writing.

Write a paper in which you discuss some specific aspect of your experience with language. Analyze some way or ways in which words have affected you.

You could write about a favorite poem or song lyric, about how the language of a religious ceremony or political statement influenced you, or about advertisements that made you desire or reject a product. You might tell of the impact of statements made by your parents, grandparents, teachers, or friends. You could recount one event or several situations, positive or negative effects. Whenever possible, connect your experience to concepts explained in this chapter. Follow your instructor's directions for topic limitations, length, format, and so on.

The guidelines you need to consider are those involved in writing any paper that connects your personal experience with a complex issue.

1. Present your experience vividly and use specific details.
2. Clearly state your point or thesis about the effect(s) the experience had on you. Think about the best place in your paper to do this.
3. Be explicit about the connections you see between your experience and the concepts about language that they illustrate. You may want to quote from the chapter. If you do, cite material as directed by your instructor.
4. Consider using some of the language techniques explored in this chapter (such as figurative language).

The Writing Situation

Begin by considering the key elements in the Thinking-Writing Model on pages 7–9 in Chapter 1.

Purpose   One purpose you have here is to connect abstract ideas about language with real-life experiences so that you and your readers can understand the concepts better. As with any writing project, another major purpose is to make your points clear and convincing to your audience.

Audience   As always, consider who could benefit from reading your paper. Perhaps your ideas would appeal to a larger audience, in which case you could submit your writing for publication, possibly in the "My Turn" column in *Newsweek*, the opinion pages of your campus newspaper, or some other publication or web site.

Subject   Because language is such a large subject, one involving fairly simple as well as very complex ideas, writing about a real-life experience can clarify—and test—the ideas you choose to write about.

Writer   Because this project draws on your own experience, you are in a position of authority. However, the project asks you to focus on an aspect of your experience that you might not have thought about before, and it requires an analytical approach rather than a narrative one, even though you may decide to tell of an event. Therefore, you will need a sort of double consciousness as a writer: you first want to recall your experience as directly as you can, but then you will have to distance yourself as you analyze the effect of language on the experience.

The Writing Process

The following sections will guide you through the stages of generating, planning, drafting, and revising as you work on this writing assignment.

Generating Ideas

1. Think of times when something you heard, read, or even said had an impact on you. Did someone use harsh language that upset you or comforting language that soothed you? Did you say something funny, helpful, embarrassing, or astute? Has a particular phrase ever made you want to do or try something? Why?
2. Do you find any common denominator among several experiences, or does one experience stand out and ask to be told as a single story?
3. Have your significant language experiences involved spoken words more often than written ones?
4. Have any of your experiences involved more than one language or more than one dialect or level of usage?

Defining a Focus   What do you want your audience to understand about the way the experience has affected you? If you are going to recount several experiences, is it important to make that clear in your thesis? Draft a thesis statement that makes a point about your experience(s).

Share your tentative thesis with classmates. Do they consider your idea worthwhile? Next, list things you might say to develop your thesis. How do your peers respond?

Organizing Ideas   The organization of this paper will depend on whether you are discussing one or more experiences. However you approach it, you will need to consider what arrangement will best help your audience understand the effects of your experience. If you are using specific concepts from the chapter, you will have to think about how and where to present them so that their relevance is clear. Using a mind map or a web may help you organize your ideas. Here is one possible format:

First experience	Second experience	*Why the two experiences are related*
Circumstances	Circumstances	_____
What was said	What was said	_____
How it affected you	How it affected you	_____

Drafting   Start with the part that will be easiest to write. Look at your freewriting, your possible thesis statement, and your list or map of ideas. Now, work those early-stage writings into a coherent draft. Remember that shaping ideas is your biggest concern at this stage. Trust yourself to speak about your own experiences and to explain what they mean to you.

After you have drafted enough material, give attention to paragraphs. Where does your material cluster into divisions? Which paragraphs need topic sentences? Where in the paragraphs should topic sentences be placed?

Draft an opening paragraph and a conclusion. What connections exist between them? Will they create an effective beginning and a good ending for your essay?

Revising   Begin your revision by referring to "A Step-by-Step Method for Revising Any Assignment," on page 152. Each author included in this chapter offers guidelines and inspiration for revising and clarifying your writing. What would Donald Murray draw your attention to? Are your word choices as specific, insightful, and sharp-eyed as Malcolm X's engagement with a dictionary would provide?

The following essay shows how one student responded to this assignment. While revising, she applied concepts about language she had learned in this chapter. Her essay is followed by a poem by Roberto Obregon.

Student Writing

Jessie Lange's Writing Process

Student Jessie Lange decided to write about an experience she had with her younger brother. She took the advice given, to start with the part that would be easiest to write. She began to describe her experience, which would become the third paragraph of her essay below, this way:

> After my first four months of college, I returned home for the winter break. After all this, I returned home to be more affected by one word uttered by my younger brother than I had been by my classes.

Then Jessie thought about the precise language used in the readings in this chapter, and she realized that her readers would not know what "all this" meant and her readers also would not know how much younger her brother was. So she revised in this way:

> After my first four months of college, I returned home for the winter break. After four months of reading inspirational writers, attending the lectures of powerful speakers, learning about language itself in my linguistics course, speaking French, and having discussions with intelligent professors who are at the top of their field, I returned home to be more affected by one word uttered by my twelve-year-old brother than I had been by any of the speaking and listening I'd engaged in first semester.

Jessie continued this process as she drafted and revised, and finally produced this essay.

The Power of Language

By Jessie Lange

Language is indeed one of the most powerful things we possess. It is how we communicate our ideas, how we put our abstract feelings for others into words, and it is what we use to describe and evaluate our human experience. Being a "good speaker" in public is something we value highly as we do effective communication in our personal lives. One of the most incredible things about language is the power that just a phrase or even a single word can have. In fact, just a few words often have more of an impact than long speeches and rambling sentences. How does it happen that a small combination of letters can have such a tremendous effect on us?

In the play *Kiss of the Spider Woman* by Manuel Puig, one of the characters, Molina, comments on the power of language. Molina, a gentle soul and an expert storyteller, is desperately in love with the man with whom he is sharing a prison cell. "How does it happen that sometimes someone says something and wins someone else over forever?" he wonders. If only he knew, he could win the love of his cell-mate, Valentin. What Molina is acknowledging is that it doesn't take an infinite number of words to say something powerful. It can be a phrase or even a single word that has the most profound impact on others. In this case, it is the "one thing" uttered that causes another to fall in love with you. In the everyday, there are particular words and phrases that stay with us, that we roll over in our minds, repeating them to ourselves again and again. There are certain words that have such an impact that they stay with us eternally longer than the time it took to utter them. I recently had a personal experience with the effects of this.

After my first four months of college, I returned home for the winter break. After four months of reading inspirational writers, attending the lectures of powerful speakers, learning about language itself in my linguistics course, speaking French, and having discussions with intelligent professors who are at the top of their field, I returned home to be more affected by one word uttered by my twelve-year-old brother than I had been by any of the speaking or listening I'd engaged in first semester. My brother and I have always been extremely close. We do not have the "sibling rivalry" I so often hear about from others. And so being apart had been a struggle. The fact that we had been apart so long and the impending separation just a few weeks away were probably much of the reason his words had such an effect on me. We were saying goodnight one night and my brother who, in many ways, is a miniature me, was holding my hand. I'd just finished assuring him that he was the "bomb" and he was smiling at me. Somewhere out of his slim twelve-year-old frame a thought emerged in the form of speech: "I wish I could take you with me," he said. "Where?" I asked, thoroughly confused. His smile broadened. "Everywhere," he said matter-of-factly. Such a simple word but, to me, so profoundly meaningful, causing a complete overflow of emotion. I had visions of never letting go of his hand. Of bringing him to college with me, of going to school with him, of bringing him all through my life and never missing a day or a second of his getting older. Just one word: *Everywhere*.

If I've learned anything about language, it's that the cliché "quality, not quantity" definitely applies. It took one utterance from my brother to almost bring me to tears. With one word, I could imagine myself holding his fingers in mine wherever I went, wherever we went.

Alternative Writing Projects

1. Write an essay about the most current uses of doublespeak. Be sure to have a focus, a main point that your examples support.

2. Write an essay about how names define or don't define who we are. You might look at Louise Erdrich's essay "The Names of Women" (page 236 in Chapter 8) for help. If you decide to include any of her material, talk to your instructor about how to do so.

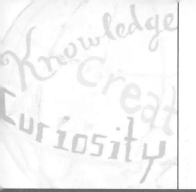

PART 2

Thinking and Writing to Shape Our World

All of us actively shape, as well as discover, the world of our experience in which we live. Our world does not exist as a finished product waiting for us to perceive it, think about it, and describe it with words and pictures. Instead, we are active participants in composing our world—selecting, organizing, and interpreting sensations into a coherent whole. Many times, our shaping of this world will reflect basic thinking patterns that we rely on constantly whenever we think, act, speak, or write.

Part Two explores four basic ways of relating and organizing: relationships in space and time, relationships of comparison, relationships of cause, and relationships of classification and definition. The Writing Projects at the end of each chapter ask you to integrate ideas from other sources into your essays as you explore these relationships and the thinking/organizing patterns that develop from them.

7

Exploring Perceptions

Writing to Describe and Narrate

> " ...a thing is not seen because it is visible, but conversely, visible because it is seen... "
>
> —Plato

The way we make sense of the world is through thinking, but our first experiences of the world come to us through our senses: sight, hearing, smell, touch, and taste. These senses are our bridges to the world, making us aware of what occurs outside us. The process of becoming aware of the world through our senses is known as *perceiving.*

This chapter and Chapter 11 will explore the way the perceiving process operates and how it relates to the ability to think, read, and write effectively. In particular, these chapters examine the way each of us shapes personal experience by actively selecting from, organizing, and interpreting the information provided by our senses. In a way, we each view the world through a pair of individual "contact lenses" that reflect our past experiences and our unique personalities. As critical thinkers, we want to become aware of the nature of our own lenses in order to offset any bias or distortion they may be causing. We also want to become aware of the lenses of others so that we can better understand why they view things the way that they do.

Developing insight into the nature of people's lenses—our own and others'—is essential to becoming an effective writer. When we write, it's helpful to understand our own point of view, to be aware of our own biases. That doesn't mean that we should strive to be completely "objective." In fact, such absolute objectivity is not possible because we can never completely remove our personal lenses. However, understanding our lenses helps us achieve our goals as writers. For example, if we want to present our ideas objectively, then we can work to compensate for our inherent bias. On the other hand, if our intention is to persuade others, we may choose to enhance and strengthen our point of view.

Analogously, we need to understand our audience's lenses if we are to communicate our thoughts and feelings effectively through our writing. This involves appreciating their point of view and understanding their biases. We can then use this knowledge to craft our writing, shape our language, and utilize the appropriate terminology and logic.

Once again, we can see the essential union of writing and thinking, communicating and knowing. This chapter will provide you with a foundation for understanding how you develop your beliefs and knowledge about the world and how you can communicate your ideas through clear, expressive, and compelling writing. Let's begin by exploring our main source of information—the perceiving process. Some of the most basic patterns of thinking and of presenting ideas draw directly on perceptions. This chapter will focus on three such patterns: description, process, and narrative.

Thinking Critically About Perceptions

Becoming Aware of Your Own Perceptions

At almost every waking moment of life, our senses are being bombarded by a tremendous number of stimuli: images to see, noises to hear, odors to smell, textures to feel, and flavors to taste. Experiencing all such sensations at once could create what the nineteenth-century American philosopher William James called "a bloomin' buzzin' confusion." Yet to us, the world usually seems much more orderly and understandable. Why is this so?

In the first place, our sense equipment can receive sensations only within certain limited ranges. For example, there are many sounds and smells that animals can detect but we cannot; animals' sense organs have broader ranges in these areas than ours do. A second reason we can handle sensory bombardment is that from the stimulation available, we select only a small amount on which to focus our attention. To demonstrate this, complete the following Thinking-Writing Activity.

This simple exercise demonstrates that for every sensation on which you focus, there are countless others that you are simply ignoring. If you were aware of everything that was happening at every moment, you would be completely overwhelmed. By selecting particular sensations, you are able to make sense of your world in a

FIGURE 7.1   Recognizing a Pattern

relatively orderly way. That is, you are *perceiving,* a process by which you actively select, organize, and interpret what is experienced by the senses.

It is tempting to think that our senses simply record what is happening out in the world, as if we were human camcorders. We are not, however, passive receivers of information, containers into which sense experience is poured. Instead, we are active participants who are always trying to understand the sensations we are encountering. As we perceive the world, our experiences are the result of combining the sensations we receive with our understanding of these sensations. For instance, examine the collection of markings in Figure 7.1. What do you see? If all you see is a collection of black spots, try turning the illustration sideways; you will probably perceive a familiar animal.

From this example you can grasp how, when you perceive the world, you are doing more than simply recording what your senses experience; instead, you are actively making sense of these sensations. The collection of green spots suddenly became the figure of an animal because your mind was able to actively organize the spots into a pattern you recognized. Or think about times when you looked up at white, billowy clouds and saw different figures and designs. The figures you were perceiving were not actually in the clouds but were the result of your giving meaningful form to shapes you were experiencing.

The same is true for virtually everything we experience. Our perceptions of the world result from combining information provided by our senses with the way we actively make sense of this information. And since making sense of information is

FOUR QUALITIES
OF A CRITICAL THINKER
Neurologist Oliver Sacks

Curious   Neurology—the study of the human brain—may be the last great medical frontier. Scientists like Dr. Oliver Sacks who explore and write about neurology must not only work with the latest technological advances and clinical treatments but also be open to discussions about ethics, compassion, creativity, and even poetry. Born in 1933 to two London physicians, Sacks recounts in his 2001 memoir, *Uncle Tungsten: Memories of a Chemical Boyhood,* that his uncle's light factory inspired an early fascination with the periodic table and with chemistry.

Open-minded   As a 2002 article in *Wired* Magazine puts it, Sacks's greatest revolution is in the way in which

medical cases are described. Traditionally, the doctor in case descriptions is the "hero," diagnosing and struggling to cure a disease. For Sacks, however, his great interest is in how people with incurable neurological conditions themselves struggle to adapt to a suddenly challenging world. And, indeed, as a clinician, he has treated an astonishing range of people from all backgrounds; in the 1960s, he was even a consulting physician for the Hell's Angels in California. Among the extraordinary people he has treated and described is autistic animal scientist Dr. Temple Grandin (an essay by Grandin appears on page 191), whose profile appears in his 1995 book *An Anthropologist on Mars.*

THINKING-
WRITING
ACTIVITY

What Do You Sense Right Now?

Respond to the following questions in writing, using a spontaneous, free-flowing style. Record your sensations as you experience them rather than first taking time to reflect and deliberate.

1. What can you *see?* (for example, the shape of the letters on the page, the design of the clothing on your arm)

2. What can you *hear?* (for example, the hum of the air circulator, the rustling of a page)

3. What can you *feel?* (for example, the pressure of the clothes against your skin, the texture of the page on your fingers)

4. What can you *smell?* (for example, the perfume someone is wearing, the odor of stale cigarette smoke)

5. What can you *taste?* (for example, the aftertastes of your last meal)

Compare your responses with those of your classmates. Did they perceive sensations different from the ones you perceived? If so, how do you explain these differences?

what we are doing when we are thinking, perceiving the world involves using our minds in an active way. Of course, we are usually not aware that we are using our minds to interpret sensations we are experiencing. We simply see the animal or the figures in the clouds as if they were really there.

Knowledgeable   Although Sacks is best known for his 1985 book *The Man Who Mistook His Wife for a Hat*, a collection of essays written for a general audience about individuals suffering from very rare neurological diseases, he continues to work as a clinician, teacher, and researcher. His greatest clinical discovery, the use of the drug L-Dopa to cure elderly patients who were literally "frozen" in their bodies because of a bout of the infectious disease encephalitis in their youth, is described in his 1973 book *Awakenings*.

and countless essays that humanize complex medical conditions for a general audience, Sacks was awarded the Lewis Thomas Prize, which "recognizes the scientist as poet," in 2002 by Rockefeller University.

Creative   Dr. Sacks's work has inspired numerous playwrights, poets, composers, and artists. His book *Awakenings* was adapted for the stage by Nobel Prize–winning playwright Harold Pinter and was subsequently made into a movie starring Robin Williams. The author of nine books

Online Study Center
Oliver Sacks
Visit the Online Study Center for *Critical Thinking, Thoughtful Writing* at *college.hmco.com/pic/ chaffeeCTTW4e* to learn more about Oliver Sacks.

Actively Selecting, Organizing, and Interpreting Sensations

When we actively perceive the sensations we are experiencing, we are usually engaged in three distinct activities:

- *Selecting* certain sensations to pay attention to
- *Organizing* these sensations into a design or pattern
- *Interpreting* what this design or pattern means

In the case of Figure 7.1, you were able to perceive an animal because you selected certain markings to concentrate on, organized these markings into a pattern, and interpreted this pattern as representing a dog.

Of course, when we perceive, the three operations of selecting, organizing, and interpreting are usually performed quickly, automatically, and often simultaneously. Also, because they are so rapid and automatic, we are not normally aware of performing these operations.

Take a few moments to explore more examples that illustrate how you actively select, organize, and interpret your perceptions of the world. Carefully examine Figure 7.2. Do you see both the young woman and the old woman? If you do, try switching back and forth between the two images. As you do so, notice how for each image, you are doing the following things:

FIGURE 7.2   Young Woman/Old Woman

- *Selecting* certain lines, shapes, and shadings on which to focus your attention
- *Organizing* these lines, shapes, and shadings into different patterns
- *Interpreting* these patterns as representing things you can recognize—a hat, a nose, a chin

So far, we have been exploring how the mind actively participates in the ways we perceive the world. By combining the sensations we are receiving with the way our minds select, organize, and interpret these sensations, we perceive a world that is stable and familiar. Thus, each of us develops a perspective on the world, one that usually makes sense to us.

The process of perceiving takes place on various levels. At the most basic level, *perceiving* refers to the selection, organization, and interpretation of sensations: for example, being able to perceive various objects such as a basketball. However, we also perceive larger patterns of meaning at more complex levels, as in watching the action of a group of people engaged in a basketball game. Although these are different situations, both engage us in the process of perceiving.

Noting Differences in People's Perceptions

As we have noted, we are not usually aware of our active participation in perceiving the world. We normally assume that what we are perceiving is what is actually taking place. Only when we find that our perception of an event differs from others' perceptions of it are we forced to examine the manner in which we are selecting, organizing, and interpreting the event. Many artists and photographers believe that what an individual viewer sees in a picture mirrors something within the viewer himself.

In most cases, people in a group will have a variety of perceptions about what is taking place in the photograph below. Some will see the twins simply as identical, dressed up for a family event. Others will focus on differences, especially in the eyes, smile, and posture. In each case, the perception depends on how the viewer is actively using his or her mind to organize and interpret what is taking place.

THINKING-
WRITING
ACTIVITY

Comparing Your Perceptions with Others'

Carefully examine this photograph of twins and then explore your reactions. What do you think is happening in this picture? Explain by answering the following questions.

1. Describe as specifically as possible what you perceive as taking place in the picture.

2. Describe what you think will take place next.

3. Identify which details of the picture inform your perceptions.

4. Compare your perceptions with those of your classmates. List several perceptions that differ from yours.

Writing Thoughtfully About Perceptions

Although the verb *describe* can be used to mean the giving of any detailed account, it more precisely indicates the reporting of sensory impressions: what you see, hear, feel, smell, or taste—your perceptions. Look back at the questions on page 187 to note how your five senses responded; also, reflect on what you have been reading about selecting, organizing, and interpreting sensations. This material should help you understand the two types of descriptions that you will be writing about in the Thinking-Writing Activity on page 195, descriptions that you might also write in other college courses or in work situations.

Writing Objectively and Subjectively

Descriptions can be broadly divided into two categories: *objective,* involving as little judgment as possible, or *subjective,* involving whatever personal judgment is appropriate to a writer's purpose.

Objective descriptions are often expected in scientific, medical, engineering, and law enforcement writing. The purpose of an objective description is to help the audience sense an object or situation as it is. Later, judgments and implications can be drawn from objective descriptions, but the cleanest possible rendering is needed as a starting point. Of course, the selection and presentation of *any* ideas or information involve conscious and unconscious judgments. However, when objectivity is the purpose, you should try to perceive with as little bias as you can and to describe in language that is as neutral as possible.

In other writing situations, descriptions are intended to be more subjective. Then the explicit purpose is to shape the audience's opinion of the object under scrutiny. Subjective descriptions occur in literary texts of all kinds: stories, poems, personal essays, and biographies; in argumentative pieces; and in personal writing such as letters to friends and journal entries. Think of how a novelist describes characters or settings; think of how an attorney might reword the police report's objective description of a victim in order to influence a jury; think of how you would describe your new special person to a close friend! You may want to use the first person (*I*) when writing a subjective description to help your audience realize that this description is how you see it. When writing a subjective description, you will be selecting details purposefully and using language that creates the effect that you want your audience to experience.

Objective Language	Subjective Language
A German shepherd	A vicious, snarling dog
A lake at night	A shimmering mirror of moonlight
Drove at 85 mph	Recklessly tore down the road
A six-foot five-inch man	A towering man
Quit my job	Told them to take their job and shove it
Filed for divorce	Got revenge on the lowlife
Won the election	Stole victory from the real winner

Contrasting Objective And Subjective Writing

The reading that follows has, as its subject, the abilities of animals to perceive and "feel." However, the reading is both "objective" and "subjective," as the author—who is autistic—writes about her own processes of thinking and feeling.

"Animal Feelings"

BY TEMPLE GRANDIN (b. 1947)
FROM *Animals in Translation: Using the Mysteries of Autism to Decode Animal Behavior*

Dr. Temple Grandin, a professor of animal science at Colorado State University, is renowned for her work on developing humane facilities for both the care and the slaughter of livestock. As an autistic person, she has written extensively on the ways in which autists perceive the world and the similarities between her own perceptions and those of animals. Her work was first brought to wide attention by neurologist and author Oliver Sacks in his book *An Anthropologist on Mars,* the title of which is Grandin's phase for describing how she feels around "neurotypical" people. Grandin's books include *Thinking in Pictures: And Other Reports from My Life with Autism* (1996) and *Animals in Translation: Using the Mysteries of Autism to Decode Animal Behavior* (2005), from which the following selection is excerpted.

Animals Aren't Ambivalent

Mammals and birds have the same feelings people do. Researchers are just now discovering that lizards and snakes probably share most of these emotions with us, too. Just to give a couple of examples: the skink lizard in Australia is monogamous, and rattlesnake mamas here in the United States protect their young from predators the same way a mammal would. The fact that some snake mothers take care of their babies came as a big surprise, since researchers have always believed snakes weren't social at all and that mothers abandoned their babies after birth. We still don't know much about the social lives of snakes, but at least now we know that they *have* a social life.

We know animals and humans share the same core feelings partly because we know quite a bit how our core emotions are created by the brain, and there's no question animals share that biology with us. Their emotional biology is so close to ours that most of the research on the neurology of emotions—or *affective neuroscience*—is done with animals. When it comes to the basics of life, like getting eaten by a tiger or protecting the young, animals feel the same way we do.

The main difference between animal emotions and human emotions is that animals don't have *mixed emotions* the way normal people do. Animals aren't ambivalent; they don't have *love-hate* relationships with each other or with people. That's one of the reasons humans love animals so much; animals are loyal. If an animal loves you he loves you no matter what. He doesn't care what you look like or how much money you make.

This is another connection between autism and animals: autistic people have mostly simple emotions, too. That's why normal people describe us as *innocent.* An autistic person's feelings are direct and open, just like animal feelings. We don't hide our feelings, and we aren't ambivalent. I can't even imagine what it would be like to have feelings of love and hate for the same person.

5

Some people will probably think this is an insulting thing to say about autistic people, but one thing I appreciate about being autistic is that I don't have to deal with all the emotional craziness my students do. I had one fantastic student who flunked out of school because she broke up with her boyfriend. There's so much psychodrama in normal people's lives. Animals never have psychodrama.

Children don't, either, Emotionally, children are more like animals and autistic people, because children's frontal lobes are still growing and don't mature until sometime in early adulthood. I mentioned earlier that the frontal lobes are one big association cortex, tying everything together, including emotions like love and hate that would probably be better off staying separate. That's another reason why a dog can be like a person's child: children's emotions are straightforward and loyal like a dog's. A seven-year-old boy or girl will race through the house to greet Dad when he comes from work the same way a dog will. I think animals, children, and autistic people have simpler emotions because their brains have less ability to make connections, so their emotions stay more separate and compartmentalized.

Of course, no one knows why an autistic *grown-up* has trouble making connections, since our frontal lobes are normal-sized. All we know right now is that researchers find "decreased connectivity among cortical regions and between the cortex and subcortex." The way I visualize it is that a normal brain is like a big corporate office building with telephones, faxes, e-mail, messengers, people walking around and talking—a big corporation has zillions of ways for messages to get from one place to another. The autistic brain is like the same big corporate office building where the only way for anyone to talk to anyone else is by fax. There's no telephone, no e-mail, no messengers, and no people walking around talking to each other. Just faxes. So a lot less stuff is getting through as a consequence, and everything starts to break down. Some messages get through okay; other messages get distorted when the fax misprints or the paper jams; other messages don't get through at all.

The point is that even though autistic people have a normal-sized neocortex including normal-sized frontal lobes, our brains *function* as if our frontal lobes were either much smaller or not fully developed. Our brains function more like a child's brain or an animal's brain, but for different reasons.

When the different parts of the brain are relatively separate from each other and don't communicate well, you end up with simple, clear emotions due to compartmentalization. A child can be furious at his mom or dad one second, then completely forget about it the next, because being mad and being happy are separate states. A child hops from one to the other depending on the situation.

10

You see the exact same thing with animals. Strong emotions in animals are usually like a sudden thunderstorm. They blow in and then blow back out. Two dogs who live together in the same house can be snarling one second, then go back to being best friends the next. Normal people need a lot more time to get over an angry emotion, and even when a normal adult does get over a bad emotion, he's made a lasting connection between the angry emotion and the person or situation that made him angry. When a normal person gets furiously angry with a person he loves, his brain hooks up *anger* and *love* and remembers it. Thanks to his highly developed frontal lobes, which connect everything up with everything else, his brain learns to have mixed emotions about that person or situation.

Another big difference between animals and people is that animals probably don't have the complex emotions people do, like shame, guilt, embarrassment, greed, or wanting bad things to happen to people who are more successful than you. There are different schools of thought about simple and complex emotions, but the definition I use is brain-based. Simple emotions are the primary emotions such as fear and rage that come from the reptilian and the mammalian brains. Complex emotions, or secondary emotions, also come from the reptilian and the mammalian brains, but they light up the neocortex as well. The secondary emotions build on the primary emotions and involve more thought and interpretation. For instance, shame, guilt, and embarrassment probably all come out of the same primary emotion of *separation distress,* which I'll talk about shortly. Your culture and upbringing teach you when to feel shame versus when to feel embarrassment or guilt, but all three start out in the brain as the pain of being isolated.

I don't want to give the impression that animals *never* have more than one feeling at the same time. Later on I'll talk about the fact that cows often feel curious and afraid at the same time. (Jaak Panksepp, author of *Affective Neuroscience*, classifies curiosity as a core emotion.) Biologically it's possible for more than one basic emotional system to be activated in an animal's brain at the same time, so technically an animal is capable of experiencing a mixed emotion.

But in real life one emotion usually ends up completely replacing the other, and some of the core emotions probably do "turn off" others. For instance, brain research shows that play and rage are incompatible emotions, which anyone who has ever watched two dogs play fighting can tell you. Once in a while a play fight will turn into a real fight, and when that happens the two dogs don't show the slightest sign (friendly tail wags, toothy smiles) that they're experiencing happy play feelings along with angry fight feelings. Once a play fight has turned real, *all* of the dog's body language and vocal communication is angry.

No Freud for Dogs

Another huge difference between animals and people: I don't think animals have the defense mechanisms Sigmund Freud described in humans. Projection, displacement, repression, denial—I don't think we see these things in animals. Defense mechanisms defend against anxiety, and all defense mechanisms depend on repression in some way. Using repression, you push whatever it is you're afraid of down into your unconscious mind and focus your conscious mind on a stand-in. Or, in the case of the higher, more mature defense mechanisms, like humor, altruism, or intellectualization, you use humor, empathy, and thought to push away the "real" emotion, which is fear.

The reason I believe animals don't have Freudian defense mechanisms is that animals and autistic people don't seem to have repression. Or, if they do, they have it only to a weak degree. I don't think I have any of Freud's defense mechanisms, and I'm always amazed when normal people do. One of the things that blows my mind about normal human beings is denial. When I see a packing plant getting into a bad situation,

I'll say, "That's not going to work," and everyone will immediately think I'm being really negative. But I'm not. It would be obvious to anyone outside the situation that what they're doing isn't going to work, but people inside the bad situation can't see it because their defense mechanisms protect them from seeing it until they're ready. That's denial, and I can't understand it at all. I can't even imagine what it's like.

15   That's because I don't have an unconscious. Normal people can push bad things out of their conscious minds into their unconscious minds, but I can't. Normal people can't always *keep* the bad stuff locked up, of course, but at least they have more freedom from it than I do. That's why I can't watch any violent movies with rape or torture scenes. The pictures stay in my conscious mind. Once they're there, I can't get rid of them. The only way I can block a bad image is by thinking about something else, but the bad image still pops back up in my mind, like a pop-up ad on the Internet. The way I think about it is that a normal brain has a built-in pop-up zapper, but my brain doesn't. To get rid of the pop-up image I have to consciously click on another screen.

I don't know *why* my brain doesn't have an unconscious, but I think it's connected to the fact that pictures are my "native language," not words. Lots of studies show that the language parts of your brain block your memory for images. Language doesn't *erase* your image memories; the images are still there, inside your head. But language keeps the images from becoming conscious. Psychologists call this *verbal overshadowing,* and I'll talk about it more in my chapter on animal thinking. For the time being, let's just say that while I don't know why I don't seem to have an unconscious, I think my problems with language have a lot to do with it. Language isn't a natural ability for me, so maybe the language parts of my brain don't have the same power to overshadow the pictures.

I know it's a leap to go from saying that I don't have an unconscious to saying I don't have defense mechanisms, but based on my personal experience I think it's true. No one has ever tried to test animals for defense mechanisms, but animals act as if they don't have them, either. You never see an animal act as if a dangerous situation is safe. You might see a dog act like he's not afraid when he is, but that's not the same thing. The dog knows there's danger and is using a standard dog strategy to avoid provoking the threatening dog any further.

A friend of mine has two dogs, one a gentle female collie and the other a macho golden retriever. (You might not have thought a golden retriever could be macho, but this one is.) When my friend walks the collie *alone* past the two ferocious-acting German shepherds down the street, the collie looks straight ahead and acts as if she's deaf and blind. She does this because staring is a provocation. She's averting her eyes to avoid challenging them.

The reason we can say the collie is only pretending not to be afraid of the other dogs when she's alone, instead of not feeling fear because she'd repressed it, is that she stops orienting to motion. All animals orient to movement. It's automatic. Since no dog can be oblivious to two German shepherds who are charging straight toward her, the collie has to consciously override her most basic orienting response. She has to *actively* ignore the other dogs.

QUESTIONS FOR ACTIVE READING

1. Note which paragraphs of the excerpt from "Animal Feelings" are subjective and which paragraphs are objective. How does the subject of each paragraph influence whether or not the author, Temple Grandin, chooses the subjective or objective voice?
2. Grandin uses comparison and contrast effectively in this reading. What are the subjects and concepts that she compares and contrasts? What kind of evidence does she use to illustrate these comparisons?
3. What is the difference between "simple" and "complex" emotions?

QUESTION FOR THINKING CRITICALLY

1. Temple Grandin objectively considers and analyzes her own processes of perception in order to better understand the lives of animals. In a descriptive essay, analyze the ways in which you perceive a certain emotion or "feeling." What circumstances cause you to feel that emotion? Has your response to those circumstances changed as you have matured? Describe one or two key influences on how you perceive a specific circumstance and tell how you have learned an emotional response.
2. In an objective essay, describe the behavior of an animal or a group of animals (wild or domestic) with which you are familiar. Before you begin, look up the term *personifica-tion*. In your essay, be particularly aware of moments when you personify the behavior that you are objectively observing and describing. How do audience and circumstance influence whether or not a writer might use personification to describe behavior? What does personification suggest about the limits of human perceptions?
3. Go online for more information about Temple Grandin and about autism. How do Grandin's history and writing challenge your perceptions of people with autism?

THINKING-WRITING ACTIVITY	*Creating Objective and Subjective Descriptions* Write two separate paragraphs in which you describe the same person or object in two different ways. Make one paragraph as objective as possible; make the other primarily subjective in order to create a particular impression for your readers. Each paragraph should have about six to eight sentences. Which of these paragraphs will have a strong topic sentence? Why? Which may not have a topic sentence or may have one that makes no claim? Why?

Chronological Relationships

Chronological forms of writing organize events or ideas in a time sequence. The focus in chronological writing is on using description to illustrate growth, development, or change—from a person's life story to the steps in creating a favorite dish. The *chronological pattern* organizes a topic into a series of events in the time sequence in which they occurred. Many chronologies are narratives or stories. For example, Scott Russell Sanders uses chronology to describe how carpentry skills are passed, in his family, from father to son. The process mode of thinking organizes an activity into a series of steps necessary for reaching a certain end. Here the focus is on describing aspects of growth, development, or change, as you might do when explaining how to prepare a favorite dish or perform a new dance.

Narratives

Perhaps the oldest and most universal form of chronological expression is the *narrative,* a story about real or fictional experiences. Many people who study communication believe that narrative is the starting point for other patterns of presentation because we often process our perceptions in storylike ways.

Every human culture has used narratives to pass on values and traditions from one generation to the next, as exemplified by such enduring works as the *Odyssey,* the Bible, and the Koran. One of America's great storytellers, Mark Twain, once said that a good story has to accomplish something and arrive somewhere. In other words, if a story is to be effective in engaging the interest of the audience, it has to have a purpose. The purpose may be to provide more information on a subject, to illustrate an idea, to lead the audience to a particular way of thinking, or to entertain. An effective narrative does not merely record the complex, random, and often unrelated events of life. Instead, it has focus, an ordered structure, and a meaningful point of view.

Writing About Processes

A second type of time-ordered thinking pattern is the *process relationship,* which describes events or experiences in terms of their development. From birth, we are involved with processes in every facet of life. They can be classified in various ways: *natural* (such as growing physically), *mechanical* (such as assembling a bicycle), *physical* (such as learning a sport), *mental* (such as developing a way of thinking), and *creative* (such as writing a poem).

Writing about a process involves two basic tasks. The first is to divide the process being analyzed into parts or stages. The second is to explain the movement of the process through these parts or stages from beginning to end. The stages identified should be separate and distinct and should involve no repetition or significant omissions.

Processes are explained for two purposes. One is to give instructions on how to do something, such as build a wall or set up a computer. Instructions will often use the pronoun *you* and imperative or command verb forms. This is an excellent example of grammar, meaning, and purpose working together; the Lowe's web site instructions clearly illustrate this kind of process writing. The other purpose of process writing, as demonstrated by Scott Russell Sanders, is to describe a process but not necessarily teach someone to do it.

In your academic reading, you'll notice both kinds of process writing. For example, a biology textbook will explain the process of photosynthesis—something that your professor might expect you to understand, but certainly not to do yourself! (If you could, you'd be green.) On the other hand, when your biology professor gives you instructions for dissecting a frog, those instructions describe a process that you are expected to do.

Examples of Process Writing

Read the following two examples of process writing. What is the purpose of each? How can you tell? What are some words in each that indicate sequence?

Jacketing was a sleight-of-hand I watched with wonder each time, and I have discovered that my father was admired among sheepmen up and down the valley for his skill at it: He was just pretty catty at that, the way he could get that ewe to take on a new lamb every time. Put simply, jacketing was a ruse played on a ewe whose lamb had died. A substitute lamb quickly would be singled out, most likely from a set of twins. Sizing up the tottering newcomer, Dad would skin the dead lamb, and into the tiny pelt carefully snip four leg holes and a head hole. Then the stand-in lamb would have the skin fitted onto it like a snug jacket on a poodle. The next step of disguise was to cut out the dead lamb's liver and smear it several times across the jacket of pelt. In its borrowed and bedaubed skin, the new baby lamb then was presented to the ewe. She would sniff the baby impostor endlessly, distrustful but pulled by the blood-smell of her own. When in a few days she made up her dim sheep's mind to accept the lamb, Dad snipped away the jacket and recited his victory: Mother him like hell now, don't ye? See what a hellava dandy lamb I got for ye, old sister? Who says I couldn't jacket day onto night if I wanted to, now-I-ask-ye?
—Ivan Doig, *This House of Sky*

If you are inexperienced in relaxation techniques, begin by sitting in a comfortable chair with your feet on the floor and your hands resting easily in your lap. Close your eyes and breathe evenly, deeply, and gently. As you exhale each breath let your body become more relaxed. Starting with one hand direct your attention to one part of your body at a time. Close your fist and tighten the muscles of your forearm. Feel the sensation of tension in your muscles. Relax your hand and let your forearm and hand become completely limp. Direct all your attention to the sensation of relaxation as you continue to let all tension leave your hand and arm. Continue this practice once or several times each day, relaxing your other hand and arm, your legs, back, abdomen, chest, neck, face, and scalp. When you have this mastered and can relax completely, turn your thoughts to scenes of natural tranquillity from your past. Stay with your inner self as long as you wish, whether thinking of nothing or visualizing only the loveliest of images. Often you will become completely unaware of your surroundings. When you open your eyes you will find yourself refreshed in mind and body.
—Laurence J. Peter, *The Peter Prescription*

THINKING-
WRITING
ACTIVITY

Writing Process Descriptions

Write two substantive paragraphs about two processes that you understand very well. In one, give instructions to a specific audience who would benefit from learning how to perform this activity. In the other, explain a process—but do not give instructions.

In the following essay, surgeon and writer Atul Gawande uses the description of a technical medical procedure to describe the ways in which young surgical residents become experienced, confident practitioners of their art.

"The Learning Curve"

BY ATUL GAWANDE (b. 1965)

Atul Gawande received his MD from Harvard Medical School and an MPH from the Harvard School of Public Health. He is a doctor at a Boston hospital and a staff writer for *The New Yorker*, contributing essays on public health issues as well as specific cases and experiences from his own practice. A collection of these essays, *Complications: A Surgeon's Notes on an Imperfect Science*, was published in 2002.

The patient needed a central line. "Here's your chance," S., the chief resident, said. I had never done one before. "Get set up and then page me when you're ready to start."

It was my fourth week in surgical training. The pockets of my short white coat bulged with patient printouts, laminated cards with instructions for doing CPR and reading EKGs and using the dictation system, two surgical handbooks, a stethoscope, wound-dressing supplies, meal tickets, a penlight, scissors, and about a dollar in loose change. As I headed up the stairs to the patient's floor, I rattled.

This will be good, I tried to tell myself: my first real procedure. The patient—fiftyish, stout, taciturn—was recovering from abdominal surgery he'd had about a week earlier. His bowel function hadn't yet returned, and he was unable to eat. I explained to him that he needed intravenous nutrition and that this required a "special line" that would go into his chest. I said that I would put the line in him while he was in his bed, and that it would involve my numbing a spot on his chest with a local anesthetic, and then threading the line in. I did not say that the line was eight inches long and would go into his vena cava, the main blood vessel to his heart. Nor did I say how tricky the procedure could be. There were "slight risks" involved, I said, such as bleeding and lung collapse; in experienced hands, complications of this sort occur in fewer than one case in a hundred.

But, of course, mine were not experienced hands. And the disasters I knew about weighed on my mind: the woman who had died within minutes from massive bleeding when a resident lacerated her vena cava; the man whose chest had to be opened because a resident lost hold of a wire inside the line, which then floated down to the patient's heart; the man who had a cardiac arrest when the procedure put him into ventricular fibrillation. I said nothing of such things, naturally, when I asked the patient's permission to do his line. He said, "OK."

I had seen S. do two central lines; one was the day before, and I'd attended to every step. I watched how she set out her instruments and laid her patient down and put a rolled towel between his shoulder blades to make his chest arch out. I watched how she swabbed his chest with antiseptic, injected lidocaine, which is a local anesthetic, and then, in full sterile garb, punctured his chest near his clavicle with a fat three-inch needle on a syringe. The patient hadn't even flinched. She told me how to avoid hitting the lung ("Go in at a steep angle," she'd said. "Stay *right* under the clavicle"), and how to find the subclavian vein, a branch to the vena cava lying atop the lung near its apex ("Go in at a steep angle. Stay *right* under the clavicle"). She pushed the needle in almost all the way. She drew back on the syringe. And she was in. You knew because the syringe filled with maroon blood. ("If it's bright red, you've hit an artery," she said. "That's not good.") Once you have the tip of this needle poking in the vein, you somehow have to widen the hold in the vein wall, fit the catheter in, and snake it in the right direction—down to the heart, rather than up to the brain—all without tearing through vessels, lung, or anything else.

To do this, S. explained, you start by getting a guide wire in place. She pulled the syringe off, leaving the needle in. Blood flowed out. She picked up a two-foot-long twenty-gauge wire that looked like the steel D string of an electric guitar, and passed nearly its full length through the needle's bore, into the vein, and onward toward the vena cava. "Never force it in," she warned, "and never, ever let go of it." A string of rapid heartbeats fired off on the cardiac monitor, and she quickly pulled the wire back an inch. It had poked into the heart, causing momentary fibrillation. "Guess we're in the right place," she said to me quietly. Then to the patient: "You're doing great. Only a few minutes now." She pulled the needle out over the wire and replaced it with a bullet of thick, stiff plastic, which she pushed in tight to widen the vein opening. She then removed this dilator and threaded the central line—a spaghetti-thick, flexible yellow plastic tube—over the wire until it was all the way in. Now she could remove the wire. She flushed the line with a heparin solution and sutured it to the patient's chest. And that was it.

Today, it was my turn to try. First, I had to gather supplies—a central-line kit, gloves, gown, cap, mask, lidocaine—which took me forever. When I finally had the stuff together, I stopped for a minute outside the patient's door, trying to recall the steps. They remained frustratingly hazy. But I couldn't put it off any longer. I had a page-long list of other things to get done: Mrs. A needed to be discharged; Mr. B needed an abdominal ultrasound arranged; Mrs. C needed her skin staples removed. And every fifteen minutes or so I was getting paged with more tasks: Mr. X was nauseated and needed to be seen; Miss Y's family was here and needed "someone" to talk to them; Mr. Z needed a laxative. I took a deep breath, put on my best don't-worry-I-know-what-I'm-doing look, and went in.

I placed the supplies on a bedside table, untied the patient's gown, and laid him down flat on the mattress, with his chest bare and his arms at his sides. I flipped on a fluorescent overhead light and raised his bed to my height. I paged S. I put on my gown and gloves and, on a sterile tray, laid out the central line, the guide wire, and other materials from the kit. I drew up five cc's of lidocaine in a syringe, soaked two sponge sticks in the yellow-brown Betadine, and opened up the suture packaging.

S. arrived. "What's his platelet count?"

10   My stomach knotted. I hadn't checked. That was bad: too low and he could have a serious bleed from the procedure. She went to check a computer. The count was acceptable.

Chastened, I started swabbing his chest with the sponge sticks. "Got the shoulder roll underneath him?" S. asked. Well, no, I had forgotten that, too. The patient gave me a look. S., saying nothing, got a towel, rolled it up, and slipped it under his back for me. I finished applying the antiseptic and then draped him so that only his right upper chest was exposed. He squirmed a bit beneath the drapes. S. now inspected my tray. I girded myself.

"Where's the extra syringe for flushing the line when it's in?" Damn. She went out and got it.

I felt for my landmarks. *Here?* I asked with my eyes, not wanting to undermine the patient's confidence any further. She nodded. I numbed the spot with lidocaine. ("You'll feel a stick and a burn now, sir.") Next, I took the three-inch needle in hand and poked it through the skin. I advanced it slowly and uncertainly, a few millimeters at a time. This is a big goddamn needle, I kept thinking. I couldn't believe I was sticking it into someone's chest. I concentrated on maintaining a steep angle of entry, but kept spearing his clavicle instead of slipping beneath it.

"Ow!" he shouted.

15   "Sorry," I said. S. signaled with a kind of surfing hand gesture to go underneath the clavicle. This time, it went in. I drew back on the syringe. Nothing. She pointed deeper. I went in deeper. Nothing. I withdrew the needle, flushed out some bits of tissue clogging it, and tried again.

"*Ow!*"

Too steep again. I found my way underneath the clavicle once more. I drew the syringe back. Still nothing. He's too obese, I thought. S. slipped on gloves and a gown. "How about I have a look?" she said. I handed her the needle and stepped aside. She plunged the needle in, drew back on the syringe, and, just like that, she was in. "We'll be done shortly," she told the patient.

She let me continue with the next steps, which I bumbled through. I didn't realize how long and floppy the guide wire was until I pulled the coil out of its plastic sleeve, and, putting one end of it into the patient, I very nearly contaminated the other. I forgot about the dilating step until she reminded me. Then, when I put in the dilator, I didn't push quite hard enough, and it was really S. who pushed it all the way in. Finally, we got the line in, flushed it, and sutured it in place.

Outside the room, S. said that I could be less tentative the next time, but that I shouldn't worry too much about how things had gone. "You'll get it," she said. "It just takes practice." I wasn't so sure. The procedure remained wholly mysterious to me. And I could not get over the idea of jabbing a needle into someone's chest so deeply and so blindly. I awaited the X-ray afterward with trepidation. But it came back fine: I had not injured the lung and the line was in the right place.

My second try at placing a central IV line went no better than the first. The patient was in intensive care, mortally ill, on a ventilator, and needed the line so that powerful cardiac drugs could be delivered directly to her heart. She was also heavily sedated, and for this I was grateful. She'd be oblivious of my fumbling.

My preparation was better this time. I got the towel roll in place and the syringes of heparin on the tray. I checked her lab results, which were fine. I also made a point of draping more widely, so that if I flopped the guide wire around by mistake again, it wouldn't hit anything unsterile.

For all that, the procedure was a bust. I stabbed the needle in too shallow and then too deep. Frustration overcame tentativeness and I tried one angle after another. Nothing worked. Then, for one brief moment, I got a flash of blood in the syringe, indicating that I was in the vein. I anchored the needle with one hand and went to pull the syringe off with the other. But the syringe was jammed on too tightly so that when I pulled it free I dislodged the needle from the vein. The patient began bleeding into her chest wall. I held pressure the best I could for a solid five minutes, but still her chest turned black and blue around the site. The hematoma made it impossible to put a line through there anymore. I wanted to give up. But she needed a line and the resident supervising me—a second-year this time—was determined that I succeed. After an X-ray showed that I had not injured her lung, he had me try on the other side, with a whole new kit. I missed again, and he took over. It took him several minutes and two or three sticks to find the vein himself, and that made me feel better. Maybe she was an unusually tough case.

When I failed with a third patient a few days later, though, the doubts really set in. Again, it was stick, stick, stick, and nothing. I stepped aside. The resident watching me got it on the next try.

•　　•　　•　　•　　•

Surgeons, as a group, adhere to a curious egalitarianism. They believe in practice, not talent. People often assume that you have to have great hands to become a surgeon, but it's not true. When I interviewed to get into surgery programs, no one made me sew or take a dexterity test or checked to see if my hands were steady. You do not even need all ten fingers to be accepted. To be sure, talent helps. Professors say that every two or three years they'll see someone truly gifted come through a program— someone who picks up complex manual skills unusually quickly, sees tissue planes before others do, anticipates trouble before it happens. Nonetheless, attending surgeons say that what's most important to them is finding people who are conscientious, industrious, and boneheaded enough to keep at practicing this one difficult thing day and night for years on end. As a former residency director put it to me, given a choice between a PhD who had cloned a gene and a sculptor, he'd pick the PhD every time. Sure, he said, he'd bet on the sculptor's being more physically talented; but he'd bet on the PhD's being less "flaky." And in the end that matters more. Skill, surgeons believe, can be taught; tenacity cannot. It's an odd approach to recruitment, but it continues all the way up the ranks, even in top surgery departments. They start with minions with no experience in surgery, spend years training them, and then take most of their faculty from these homegrown ranks.

25   And it works. There have now been many studies of elite performers— concert violinists, chess grand masters, professional ice skaters, mathematicians, and so forth—and the biggest difference researchers find between them and lesser performers is the amount of deliberate practice they've accumulated. Indeed, the most important talent may be the talent for practice itself. K. Anders Ericsson, a cognitive psychologist and an expert on performance, notes that the most important role that innate factors play may be in a person's *willingness* to engage in sustained training. He has found, for example, that top performers dislike practicing just as much as others do. (That's why, for example, athletes and musicians usually quit practicing when they retire.) But, more than others, they have the will to keep at it anyway.

·   ·   ·   ·   ·

I wasn't sure I did. What good was it, I wondered, to keep doing central lines when I wasn't coming close to hitting them? If I had a clear idea of what I was doing wrong, then maybe I'd have something to focus on. But I didn't. Everyone, of course, had suggestions. Go in with the bevel of the needle up. No, go in with the bevel down. Put a bend in the middle of the needle. No, curve the needle. For a while, I tried to avoid doing another line. Soon enough, however, a new case arose.

The circumstances were miserable. It was late in the day, and I'd had to work through the previous night. The patient weighed more than three hundred pounds. He couldn't tolerate lying flat because the weight of his chest and abdomen made it hard for him to breathe. Yet he had a badly infected wound, needed intravenous antibiotics, and no one could find veins in his arms for a peripheral IV. I had little hope of succeeding. But a resident does what he is told, and I was told to try the line.

I went to his room. He looked scared and said he didn't think he'd last more than a minute on his back. But he said he understood the situation and was willing to make his best effort. He and I decided that he'd be left sitting propped up in bed until the last possible minute. We'd see how far we got after that.

I went through my preparations: checking his blood counts from the lab, putting out the kit, placing the towel roll, and so on. I swabbed and draped his chest while he was still sitting up. S., the chief resident, was watching me this time, and when everything was ready I had her tip him back, an oxygen mask on his face. His flesh rolled up his chest like a wave. I couldn't find his clavicle with my fingertips to line up the right point of entry. And already he was looking short of breath, his face red. I gave S. a "Do you want to take over?" look. Keep going, she signaled. I made a rough guess about where the right spot was, numbed it with lidocaine, and pushed the big needle in. For a second, I thought it wouldn't be long enough to reach through, but then I felt the tip slip underneath his clavicle. I pushed a little deeper and drew back on the syringe.

30 Unbelievably, it filled with blood. I was in. I concentrated on anchoring the needle firmly in place, not moving it a millimeter as I pulled the syringe off and threaded the guide wire in. The wire fed in smoothly. The patient was struggling hard for air now. We sat him up and let him catch his breath. And then, laying him down one more time, I got the entry dilated and slid the central line in. "Nice job" was all S. said, and then she left.

I still have no idea what I did differently that day. But from then on my lines went in. That's the funny thing about practice. For days and days, you make out only the fragments of what to do. And then one day you've got the thing whole. Conscious learning becomes unconscious knowledge, and you cannot say precisely how.

·   ·   ·   ·   ·

I have now put in more than a hundred central lines. I am by no means infallible. Certainly, I have had my fair share of complications. I punctured a patient's lung, for example—the right lung of a chief of surgery from another hospital, no less— and, given the odds, I'm sure such things will happen again. I still have the occasional case that should go easily but doesn't, no matter what I do. (We have a term for this. "How'd it go?" a colleague asks. "It was a total flog," I reply. I don't have to say anything more.)

But other times everything unfolds effortlessly. You take the needle. You stick the chest. You feel the needle travel—a distinct glide through the fat, a slight catch in the dense muscle, then the subtle pop through the vein wall—and you're in. At such moments, it is more than easy; it is beautiful.

·   ·   ·   ·   ·

It is 2 P.M. I am in the intensive-care unit. A nurse tells me Mr. G.'s central line has clotted off. Mr. G. has been in the hospital for more than a month now. He is in his late sixties, from South Boston, emaciated, exhausted, holding on by a thread—or a line, to be precise. He has several holes in his small bowel, and the bilious contents leak out onto his skin through two small reddened openings in the concavity of his abdomen. His only chance is to be fed by vein and wait for these fistulae to heal. He needs a new central line.

35 I could do it, I suppose. I am the experienced one now. But experience brings a new role: I am expected to teach the procedure instead. "See one, do one, teach one," the saying goes, and it is only half in jest.

There is a junior resident on the service. She has done only one or two lines before. I tell her about Mr. G. I ask her if she is free to do a new line. She misinterprets this as a question. She says she still has patients to see and a case coming up later. Could I do the line? I tell her no. She is unable to hide a grimace. She is burdened, as I was burdened, and perhaps frightened, as I was frightened.

She begins to focus when I make her talk through the steps—a kind of dry run, I figure. She hits nearly all the steps, but forgets about checking the labs and about Mr. G.'s nasty allergy to heparin, which is in the flush for the line. I make sure she registers this, then tell her to get set up and page me.

I am still adjusting to this role. It is painful enough taking responsibility for one's own failures. Being handmaiden to another's is something else entirely. It occurs to me that I could have broken open a kit and had her do an actual dry run. Then again, maybe I can't. The kits must cost a couple of hundred dollars each. I'll have to find out for next time.

Half an hour later, I get the page. The patient is draped. The resident is in her gown and gloves. She tells me that she has saline to flush the line with and that his labs are fine.

40

"Have you got the towel roll?" I ask.

She forgot the towel roll. I roll up a towel and slip it beneath Mr. G.'s back. I ask him if he's all right. He nods. After all he's been through, there is only resignation in his eyes.

The junior resident picks out a spot for the stick. The patient is hauntingly thin. I see every rib and fear that the resident will puncture his lung. She injects the numbing medication. Then she puts the big needle in, and the angle looks all wrong. I motion for her to reposition. This only makes her more uncertain. She pushes in deeper and I know she does not have it. She draws back on the syringe: no blood. She takes out the needle and tries again. And again the angle looks wrong. This time, Mr. G. feels the jab and jerks up in pain. I hold his arm. She gives him more numbing medication. It is all I can do not to take over. But she cannot learn without doing, I tell myself. I decide to let her have one more try.

QUESTIONS FOR ACTIVE READING

1. Why does Gawande conclude this essay as he does? How do you, as a reader, respond?

2. Obviously, Gawande is not writing for an audience who are about to perform the insertion of a large intravenous tube into the main blood vessel of the heart. Yet he gives a significant amount of detail as he describes the process of doing so. Each time he describes the insertion of such a tube, or "central line," his perceptions of the procedure change. What are the differences in Gawande's perceptions of each incident? What is Gawande's purpose for each description?

3. How does Gawande use chronology to organize his essay? Why is this a particularly effective organizational choice, given his subject and purpose?

QUESTIONS FOR THINKING CRITICALLY

1. Gawande describes a kind of apprenticeship, a way in which knowledge and skills are passed along from one surgeon to another through example and practice.

Is apprenticeship always the best way to learn, or teach, a particular skill or body of knowledge?

2. "Skill, surgeons believe, can be taught; tenacity cannot." Do you agree, or disagree? Describe a time in your life when being *tenacious* helped you to overcome an obstacle, to master a skill, or to solve a problem.

3. Why does Gawande describe the experience in paragraph 33 as "beautiful"? What, exactly, is "beautiful" about it? Have you experienced that same kind of "beauty" in accomplishing something difficult?

Writing Project: A Narrative Showing the Effect of a Perception

The readings and Thinking-Writing activities in this chapter encourage you to become more aware of your perceptions, to use description to convey those perceptions, and to choose the appropriate organizing structure (chronology, narrative, and/or process) for writing about those perceptions.

Write a narrative essay describing the influence another person's perceptions had on your understanding of yourself, on a skill or body of knowledge you are learning, or on a significant decision you have made (or are in the process of making). When were you first made aware of this issue, conflict, idea, or skill? How did this other person (or persons) make their perceptions known to you? Were you initially in conflict with that other person, or have you always been in agreement? If there have been points of conflict in your relationship, did you learn and grow from them? How have your own perceptions grown and changed since knowing this other person (or persons)?

As part of your preparation for writing your essay, find a magazine or newspaper article dealing with the perception and quote from it at least once in your essay. Document the quoted material according to your instructor's directions. If an academic documentation format such as that of the Modern Language Association (MLA) or American Psychological Association (APA) is required, be sure that your entry conforms exactly to the models in a writing handbook.

The Writing Situation

Begin by considering the key elements in the Thinking-Writing Model on pages 7–9 in Chapter 1.

Purpose   You have a variety of purposes here. You have the opportunity to recall and relate a significant experience. You also can think about an issue that concerns

The following principles for writing narratives are not fixed rules; you may have good reasons for not following some of them. In general, though, they should help you to write an effective essay.

1. Identify the relevant issue fully so that the narrative has a meaningful context.

2. State your thesis well; place it effectively in your paper.

3. Use description to introduce your readers to the people involved and to let them visualize the place. Consider whether subjective or objective description, or a combination of the two, will best serve your purpose.

4. Tell the story as fully as seems appropriate for your intended audience, without either rambling excessively or leaving out important details or events.

5. Be sure to begin and end effectively. The conclusion is likely to be especially important in this essay since you may want to reiterate your main point there.

you and learn more about it by finding the required article. In addition, you will be improving your ability to connect what you read with your own ideas, something you must do regularly as a college student. Most important, you can inform your classmates, your instructor, and your other readers about an issue that concerns you or skill that interests you and about the impact of another person's perception of that same issue.

Audience   As always, you are a member of your own audience and perhaps the person who will enjoy the narrative most since it is connected with your life. Your classmates will be a good audience, both to learn from your narrative and to share your experience. In addition, they are valuable as peer reviewers of your draft, reacting as intelligent readers who are also immersed in the assignment. Of course, anyone else who has had a similar experience would also benefit from reading your essay. Perhaps your campus newspaper would be interested. Finally, your instructor remains the audience who will judge how well you have planned, drafted, and revised. As a writing teacher, he or she cares about a clear focus, logical organization, specific details, and correctness. Keep these aspects in mind as you revise, edit, and proofread.

Subject   Although you and your readers are probably concerned about many perceptual issues, both you and they may need to be reminded of how an issue and a person's perceptions of it can affect someone else.

Writer   You are in a dual position here. You are, of course, the expert on your own story. This is both an advantage and a disadvantage: no one can argue with you about your story, but you still need to remember that your audience was not there. You must provide them with sufficient background and description to make them feel as if they did share your experience, but you don't want to overwhelm them with details. Therefore, you will need to be selective as you decide what to include and what to omit. Also, remember that you are not the expert on the article from which you plan to quote, so do think carefully about what it says and where to use it in your own work.

The Writing Process

The following sections will guide you through the stages of generating, planning, drafting, and revising as you work on a descriptive and illustrative narrative.

Generating Ideas

1. You may immediately recall a meaningful experience that you want to narrate. If not, think about past events that were worrisome, frightening, amusing, or exciting and then think again about the context of the event.

2. You may be deeply involved in dealing with others' perceptions of issues because of who you are, where you live, or which organizations you support. If so, you should have no problem identifying a concern you want to address. If not, look around, talk with friends and family members, read newspapers and magazines, and watch the news.

3. Think locally. Look at issues in your community or those connected with your college or job. Then try to recall any experiences in which another person's perceptions had an impact on you.

Defining a Focus Draft a thesis statement that connects your experience with the perception you plan to write about. You may want to emphasize the directness of the connection, or you may need to show that what is not obvious is indeed related. Perhaps you may wish to emphasize a time element: "I didn't understand at the time, but now I see that . . ." or "I knew at that moment that . . ." You may want to focus on the impact this perception has had on your life.

Organizing Ideas You could tell the story first and then connect it with the perceptual stereotype. Or you might make statements about the perception regularly throughout the narration as different events illustrate various aspects of the situation. In either case, your use of chronological order will help your audience follow the events of your story. Therefore, unless you see some serious reason not to do so, give background information first and then guide your audience through the time sequence of the events. You need to consider what arrangements will best help your audience see their connection to the issue. Be sure to select and place carefully the material quoted from your source and to incorporate it smoothly into your writing by introducing and commenting on it.

    If you are using process writing in your essay, determine if the process itself can provide the organizational structure for the entire essay. Otherwise, be sure that each step of the process is clearly explained within each relevant paragraph.

Drafting   Begin with the easiest part to write, possibly the experience itself. Tell it fully; then plan to increase its effectiveness by including sharp details and a tight sequence of events at the revision stage. The paragraphs within the narrative may or may not have topic sentences. This is one of the differences between narration and exposition. Since your purpose is to connect the experience with others' perceptions, you may want to have topic sentences for the paragraphs that do that.

After you have drafted the narrative, draft the paragraphs that state the thesis and make the connection between the experience and the issue. Then establish and write any necessary transitions.

Revising, Editing, and Proofreading   Use the step-by-step method on pages 152–154 in Chapter 6 to revise your essay and prepare a final draft.

The following essay demonstrates how a student writer used a combination of description, process writing, and chronological ordering to illustrate how the perceptions of other people influenced his own decision.

Student Writing

Joshua Chaffee's Writing Process

Living so close to "Ground Zero," the site where the World Trade Center used to stand in New York City, Joshua Chaffee had an overwhelming number of perceptions, emotions, and experiences to sort through as he contemplated this essay. This experience was to define both his perceptions of his community and how he understood himself. Joshua knew he wanted to draw upon his experience as he approached this essay, but he also knew that he had to be careful with his organization and his descriptions. Often, when writing about something so overwhelming—and something experienced, even at a distance, by so many people—it becomes difficult to stay focused on your audience and your purpose. Joshua brought in the perceptions of other people to balance his own feelings. Here is an excerpt from Joshua's rough outline for this essay.

1. How did New Yorkers respond to 9/11?—keep it personal and specific; what did I personally witness? (Probably keep my emotions out of it—stick to what I perceived, not how I "felt"—that's too subjective and probably overwhelming. . . .)

2. Connect those perceptions to why I want to be a journalist. Can I talk to or find an article by another New York journalist who covered 9/11?—need to make a logical connection between 9/11 and why I want to be a journalist . . .

3. Incorporate as assignment for the "Feature Writing" course—how writing about New York (the La Frieda interview? the profile I did of Alan Kaufman and his pickle shop?) can give a voice to all New Yorkers, and connect that to my response to 9/11.

4. Conclusion?—maybe connect whatever I choose from "Feature Writing" to the behavior I witnessed on 9/11? A larger observation about why I love New York and want to stay here and do something for New Yorkers. . . .

We're All at Ground Zero

By Joshua Chaffee

From my bedroom window, I can see the six-story remainder of the World Trade Center's steel siding, forked in the ground, shooting up towards its former resting place in the New York City skyline. The site is lit through the entire night with an otherworldly glow, and men are working there, at "Ground Zero," when I go to sleep and when I wake up.

Outside my house, hundreds of people gather to cheer and offer their gratitude towards the workers. Each night I have joined them. At one point, a truck stops beside the crowd and a fireman inside exclaims, "We've just contacted two Port Authority Police Officers on the second floor and we're digging them out right now!" What follows is an eruption of yelling and cheering far greater than I have ever heard.

In an interview I did with former *New York Times* columnist turned novelist Anna Quindlen, she told me, "September 11th was a time that made me proud of the journalism profession. Journalists provided a huge public service to people because they created an instant sense of community. It was a time when I seriously considered writing columns again." After 9/11, Anna Quindlen re-affirmed her passion for journalism, while I discovered mine for the first time. It hit me on a Monday in late October of 2001.

About a month into the journalism course I was taking junior year, I found myself wedged in between Pat and Lisa La Frieda, scribbling madly onto a notepad because the air coolers in the meat locker were too loud for me to use my tape recorder. Outside the sun had yet to come up and, only weeks after September 11th, the air still smelled of ash. Inside, Pat La Frieda wore the same long, bloodstained white jacket and black knit cap characteristic of Italian-American butchers generations ago, when his grandparents owned La Frieda Meats. As he spoke to me, men hoisted sides of beef onto their shoulders while others sprayed the floor tiles with hoses to flush the blood into drains. The smell of cold, fresh meat permeated every corner of the long white room, a smell Pat relished as he slowly strolled past the lockers.

La Frieda Meats is located in Greenwich Village, one block east of the Hudson River and across the street from a controversial empty lot where an 18-story, luxury high-rise is planned to go up. The high-rise would be eight stories taller than any building near it, thus casting a long six-block shadow over the neighborhood. Pat had a lot to say on the topic. One question and he took off like a racehorse: "People have got to welcome advancement. You can't live in the past, saying how the Village used to be. Look, when my grandparents owned this meat packing business, they delivered the meat by horse drawn wagons every morning. Where would I be if I still used horses today!"

However, on the other side of me, his sister Lisa had a different point of view. Lisa is a large woman with heavy dark makeup. She jumped in, cutting off Pat, "Yeah, but you know what'll happen when they put in a luxury building? All the tenants will start screaming about my trucks coming in at four in the morning. And paying that much for an apartment, they probably got the right to complain." Sandwiched between Pat and Lisa, I tried to keep up with their words, which were barely audible above the meat coolers. I couldn't hold back a smile, though. Walking around a meat packing warehouse at six in the morning before school and talking to Pat and Lisa—I would rather be here than anywhere else, including my bed.

That Monday night I wrote about Pat and Lisa La Frieda, piecing their ideas into my article on the effects of the anticipated luxury high-rise. Hours later, I found myself still at my computer with a bowl of Chex Mix, writing and thinking about the interviews that morning. I understood what I had felt when I was standing in that frigid warehouse. I had realized my passion, and knew exactly what I wanted to be doing in the future. As a journalist, I have the opportunity to go out and have a half-hour conversation with some of the most interesting people—people I might otherwise never speak to. Then I come home and write about them; I give Pat and Lisa La Frieda a voice that they might never have used before—a voice that can be heard by hundreds of people.

The city is too big to know everyone's story. Most people don't know Alan Kaufman, the owner of the only remaining fresh pickle shop in the Lower East Side; or Joe Oliva, the 16-year security guard at Night Court, where every criminal arrested in Manhattan comes to be arraigned; or Chef José, the chef at a private Manhattan school, who was the head chef at United Airlines for most of his life. But, by opening up the worlds of everyone around us, journalists can unite a community.

This, I believe, is what Anna Quindlen meant by journalists creating "an instant sense of community," and this is what attracts me to the profession. Immediately after September 11, we all felt alone and frightened. But journalists showed us that everyone else was experiencing the same feelings, and that together we could help each other to understand and move on from what happened. When we are alone, our surroundings can seem overwhelming and unfriendly. But, through the telling of people's stories and the revealing of the true fabric of the city, New York can begin to feel as intimate as your family, and as small as a Village. All around the city people have come together. The city has united in a community of shared pain, devoted to its country and to each other. Everyone felt his or her hearts come down with those towers, but as we start to rebuild, we have each other for support.

Alternative Writing Projects

1. Ask someone with an interesting profession for permission to observe her or him at work. Keep careful notes, and if allowed, take audio and video recordings of that person at work. Write up an objective report of your findings. What were your perceptions of that kind of work before you began making your observations? How did your perceptions change? Next, draw up a list of questions for your subject based on your observations. Finally, write an objective profile of a day in the life of that particular kind of worker, using his or her own subjective comments as illustrations and evidence.

2. Create a podcast walking tour of a part of your campus or your community. Your audience will only be able to rely on your ability to verbally evoke particular sights, smells, and circumstances, so your descriptions must be especially rich and accurate. Then exchange podcasts with another student and offer each other constructive criticism on the quality of each other's language and the accuracy of each other's descriptions.

Exploring Concepts

Writing to Classify and Define

8

> " *Our life is what our thoughts make it.* "
>
> —*Marcus Aurelius*

Critical Thinking Focus: The conceptualizing process

Writing Focus: Defining and applying concepts

Reading Theme: Gender issues

Writing Project: Defining an important concept

Internet, beauty, hip-hop culture, channel surfing, truth, bungee jumping, attitude, and thinking are only a few examples of concepts in a world filled with them. As you speak and write, you refer to concepts you have formed. Your academic study involves learning new concepts as well, and success in college and in your career requires understanding the conceptualizing process.

When you read textbooks or listen to lectures and take notes, you have to grasp key concepts and follow them as they are developed and supported. Many courses require you to apply the key concepts you have learned to new sets of circumstances. When you write essays, conduct research, or participate in group projects, you are expected to focus on certain concepts, develop and present a thesis (itself a concept), and support it with relevant evidence.

Your academic writing will often require the definition of terms or concepts. Chapter 6 discussed the fact that words are complex carriers of meaning—with meanings varying from person to person. This chapter will explore further implications of this complexity as it pertains to your writing.

The Writing Project in the chapter asks you to write a full definition of a concept that is important to your life. As you write this essay, you will see that definition usually involves using all the patterns of thinking that Chapter 7 discussed.

Definition is a very important thinking and writing pattern. When you write an essay that defines a concept, that concept is the subject of your essay. A clear idea of your audience will help you determine the kind of illustrations you will need to provide as well as the complexity of the language with which you describe those illustrations. Finally, the purpose of your essay (to demonstrate to your teacher that you have understood a concept, to introduce a complex concept to an audience unfamiliar with the subject, to explore how a concept has changed over time, and so on) will determine the rhetorical strategies you will use. The analytical activity of classification, which underlies defining, is essential to good thinking. Definition and classification rely on comparative relationships in order to establish categories by means of similarities and in order to distinguish among concepts within categories by identifying differences. Definitions usually include descriptions and sometimes employ causal, chronological, or process analyses to make distinctions or to show the development of a concept. Understanding the thinking patterns that you have already worked with and being able to use them effectively can ease the difficult task of defining concepts.

To help you define significant concepts, this chapter will explain the conceptualizing process, present readings that involve definitions, and give you opportunities to define some terms that are significant in various aspects of your life.

What Are Concepts?

Concepts are general ideas that you use to organize your experience and, in so doing, bring order to your life. In the same way that words are the vocabulary of language, concepts are the vocabulary of thought. As organizers of your experience, concepts work in conjunction with language to identify, describe, distinguish, and relate all the various aspects of your world.

Developing expertise in the conceptualizing process improves your ability to form, apply, and relate concepts. This complex conceptualizing process is going on all the time in your mind, enabling you to think in a distinctly human way. When you form opinions or make judgments, you are applying and relating concepts.

How do you use concepts to organize and make sense of experience? Think back to the first day of the semester. For most students, this is a time to evaluate their courses by trying to determine which concepts apply.

- Will this course be interesting? useful? challenging?
- Is the instructor stimulating? demanding? understanding?
- Are the other students friendly? intelligent? conscientious?

Each of these descriptive words or phrases represents a concept you are attempting to apply so that you can understand what is occurring at the moment and also anticipate what will occur. As the course progresses, you gather more information from experiences in class. This information may support your initial concepts, or it may conflict with them. If it supports them, you tend to maintain them ("Yes, I can see that this is going to be a difficult course"). When the information you receive conflicts with your initial concepts, you tend to find new concepts to explain the situation ("No, I can see that I was wrong—this course isn't going to be as difficult as I first thought"). A diagram of this process might look something like the one in Figure 8.1 on page 216.

Throughout this thinking process you are making evaluations that establish classifications of kinds or types: What *kind* of course—difficult? easy? What *kind* of teacher? What *kind* of reading? What *kind* of student am I in relation to this course? And you are consciously or unconsciously using definitions that you have formulated: When I say "difficult course," I mean one that . . . When I say "demanding teacher," I mean one who . . . And so on.

FOUR QUALITIES
OF A CRITICAL THINKER
Psychologist Steven Pinker

Curious   Of all the concepts we will explore in this chapter, there may be none so fascinating—or fundamental—as *language*. Without language, we would lose our abilities to communicate, to remember, to create, even to think. Although marine biologists argue convincingly that whale songs are a kind of speech, and many studies have demonstrated that the great apes can be taught basic sign language, it is only humans who have the extraordinary ability to assign words and sounds to *ideas*, not just to things. It is language that allows us to be curious, to imagine, to propose and to define. In recent years cognitive psychologists and neuroscientists have begun to illuminate this most basic human ability. Dr. Steven Pinker, a psychologist of language at Harvard University, has proposed that the human ability to not only *use* language but to think in terms of concepts and abstractions is wired into our very genes. This theory has profound social and political as well as psychological connotations for how we understand the concept of *language*.

Open-Minded   The idea that language and other human behaviors might be biologically inherent rather than solely shaped by the environment is politically charged, and Pinker has come under attack by scientists opposed to the idea of *sociobiology*, that is, the idea that

human behavior is determined as much by our genes as by our nurturing. In his book *The Blank Slate: The Modern Denial of Human Nature* (2002), Pinker sought to create a more open-minded and rational dialogue between scientists and activists who argue for the "blank slate" theory of human development (the idea, with roots in eighteenth-century western European philosophy, that humans are born with perfectly empty, clear minds—"blank slates"—that are shaped and nurtured by their environment). Scientists and others who support this theory of human development accuse sociobiologists of deliberately or inadvertently supporting racist or sexist ideas, such as the notion that men are "inherently" better at math and mechanics than women, or that women are "naturally" more emotional than men. Pinker argues carefully but passionately against the politicization of science, urging his fellow researchers (and the general public, which votes on related issues such as stem cell research and early childhood education) to be attentive to what the scientific evidence is revealing to us every day about the makeup of the human genome and the wiring of the human brain.

Knowledgeable   Pinker and other linguists such as Noam Chomsky have sought to prove that the human brain

Changing Your Concepts

Identify an initial concept you had about an event in your life (a new job, attending college, getting married, and so on). After identifying your initial concept, describe the experiences that led you to change or modify the concept; then explain the new concept you formed to explain the situation. Your essay should include the following elements and use these rhetorical strategies:

- The initial concept (definition)
- New information provided by additional experiences (narration and description)
- The new concept formed to explain the situation (definition)

has evolved to recognize fundamental linguistic structures from a very early age, and pediatric neuroscience has demonstrated that small children everywhere in the world have an extraordinary ability to learn languages from birth up until the age of about 10. Grammar, these linguists argue, is a kind of "deep structure" that all humans are born with; although a child's environment can certainly assist in developing language abilities, magnetic resonance imaging (MRIs) of the brain actually show activity within the anatomy of the brain itself as it thinks, speaks, remembers, and visualizes. He argues that what apes and whales do is *not* "language," even though it may serve as some sort of communication. Pinker derives his knowledge from years of research with children, closely documenting their acquisition of language. As a psychologist, he also draws on his knowledge of different diseases of the brain that affect specific kinds of language-based abilities.

Creative   Scientists who challenge the status quo—from Galileo to Darwin to Pinker—need to demonstrate complete mastery of their field's knowledge in order to support their provocative arguments and theories. Yet the courage, the impetus, to ask the kinds of questions that lead to scientific revolutions are rooted in creativity. Like language itself, creativity is a concept unique to human beings. No other species imagines alternatives to the realities they already

know; no other species is so tragically aware of its inevitable end. Yet Pinker's hypotheses about sociobiology and the language instinct raise profound, and profoundly disturbing, questions about those human achievements we are most likely to conceptualize as *creative*: art, music, dance, or poetry, for example. If there is a language gene, is there then also a music gene? For all of the millennia of artists and poets who have attributed their talents to divine inspiration or a personal muse, could it be that they were simply genetically wired—predisposed—to be creative, and that they may have had no choice in the matter? As Pinker and other scientists lay bare the inner workings of the brain, what are the possible social and ethical impacts on what we as a society value about our humanity?

Online Study Center
Steven Pinker
Visit the Online Study Center for *Critical Thinking, Thoughtful Writing* at *college.hmco.com/pic/ chaffeeCTTW4e* to learn more about Steven Pinker

FIGURE 8.1   Experience Leads to Action

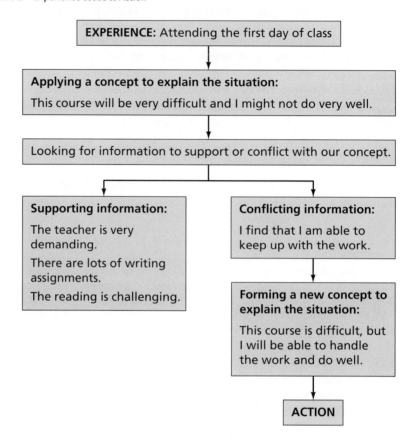

The Importance of Concepts

Learning to understand and write about concepts will help you in every area of your life: academic, career, and personal. In college study, each academic discipline or subject uses many different concepts to organize experience, give explanations, and solve problems. Here is a sampling of college-level concepts: *entropy, subtext, Gemeinschaft, cell, metaphysics, relativity, parallel processing, prehistory, unconscious, aesthetic, minor key, interface, health, quantum mechanics, schizophrenia*. To make sense of how disciplines function, you need to understand what the concepts of that discipline mean, how to define them, how to apply them, and how they relate to other concepts.

Although each academic discipline has its own unique and specific concepts, some concepts change their definition according to the disciplinary "lens" used to interpret it. In the following passage from *Colour: Art & Science*, physiologist Trevor Lamb describes how the concept of *color* is understood by different academic disciplines.

Although the idea of "colour" may seem a simple concept, it conjures up very different ideas for each of us. To the physicist, colour is determined by the wavelength of light. To the physiologist and psychologist, our perception of colour involves neural responses in the eye and the brain, and is subject to the limitations of our nervous system. To the naturalist, colour is not only a thing of beauty but also a determinant of survival in nature. To the social historian and linguist, our understanding and interpretation of colour are inextricably linked to our own culture. To the art historian, the development of colour in painting can be traced both in artistic and technological terms. And for the painter, colour provides a means of expressing feelings and the intangible, making possible the creation of a work of art. . . . In the field of colour, the arts and the sciences now travel in unison, and together they provide a rich and comprehensive understanding of the subject.

You will regularly present your understanding of definitions, of applications, and of relationships among concepts in your written work. You will also learn the methods of investigation, patterns of thought, and forms of reasoning that various disciplines use to form larger conceptual theories and methods. Successful completion of writing, research, and presentation assignments in your college courses will depend on your understanding of the key concepts that form the core of each discipline.

Regardless of their specific knowledge content, all careers require conceptual abilities, whether you are trying to apply a legal principle, develop a promotional theme, or devise a new computer program. Similarly, expertise in forming and applying concepts helps you to make sense of your personal life, understand others, and make informed decisions. The Greek philosopher Aristotle said that the intelligent person is a "master of concepts."

The Structure of Concepts

Concepts, in addition to being general ideas that you use to identify and organize your experience, are useful for distinguishing and connecting one thing to another. Concepts allow you to organize your world into patterns that make sense to you.

In their role of organizers of experience, concepts act to group aspects of your experience on the basis of their similarity. Consider the object that you usually write with: a notebook computer. The concept *notebook computer* represents an instrument that you use for writing. Now look around the classroom at other instruments people are using to write. You use the concept *notebook computer* to identify these as well, even though they may look quite different from yours. Thus, the concept *notebook computer* not only helps you to make distinctions in your experience by indicating how notebook computers differ from handhelds, cell phones, or desktops; it also helps you to determine which items are similar enough to all be called notebook computers. When you put items into a group with a single description—such as *notebook computers*—you are focusing on their similarities:

- They use internal hard drives.
- They are used for writing, research, communication, and entertainment.
- Each is portable.

Being able to see and name the similarities among certain things in your experience is the way you form concepts and is crucial for making sense of your world. If you were not able to do this, everything in the world would appear to be different, with its own individual name.

The Process of Classifying

The process by which you group things on the basis of their similarities is known as *classifying*. Classifying is a natural human activity that goes on all the time. In most cases, however, you are not conscious of classifying something in a particular sort of way; you do so automatically. The process of classifying is one of the main ways that you order, organize, and make sense of your world. Because no two things or experiences are exactly alike, your ability to classify things into various groups is what enables you to recognize things in your experience. When you perceive a notebook computer, you recognize it as a *kind* of object you have seen before. Even though you may not have seen this particular notebook computer, you recognize that it belongs to a category of things that is familiar.

The best way to understand the structure of concepts is to visualize them by means of a model. Examine Figure 8.2. The *sign* is the word or symbol used to name or designate the concept; for example, the word *triangle* is a sign. The *referents* represent all the various examples of the concept; the three-sided figure we are using as our model is an example of the concept *triangle*. The *properties* of the concept are the features that all things named by the word or sign share in common; all examples of the concept *triangle* share the characteristics of being a polygon and having three sides. These are the properties that we refer to when we define concepts; thus, "A triangle is a three-sided polygon."

Let's take another example. Suppose you wanted to explore the structure of the concept *automobile*. The sign that names the concept is the word *automobile* or the symbol 🚗 . Referents of the concept include the 2004 MINI Cooper currently

FIGURE 8.2   Model of a Concept

FIGURE 8.3   Model of Concept *Automobile*

PROPERTIES
(Qualities that all examples of
the concept share in common)

PROPERTIES
Wheels, chassis, engine,
seats for passengers

CONCEPT

SIGN
(Word/symbol that
names the concept)

REFERENTS
(Examples of
the concept)

SIGN
"Automobile"
🚗

REFERENTS
2006 Toyota Prius
2004 MINI Cooper

residing in the garage as well as the 2006 Toyota Prius parked in front of the house. The properties that all things named by the sign *automobile* include are wheels, a chassis, an engine, seats, and so on. Figure 8.3 shows a conceptual model of the concept *automobile*.

THINKING-
WRITING
ACTIVITY

Diagramming Concepts

Using the model we have developed, diagram the structure of three of the following concepts as well as those of two concepts of your own choice: *dance, success, student, religion, music, friend.*

Forming Concepts

You form—and apply—concepts to organize your experience, make sense of what is happening, and anticipate what may happen in the future. You form concepts by the interactive processes of *generalizing* (focusing on the common properties shared by a group of things) and *interpreting* (finding examples of the concept). The common properties form the necessary requirements that must be met in order for you to be able to apply the concept to your experience. If you examine the diagrams of concepts in the last section, you can see that the process of forming concepts involves moving back and forth between the referents (examples) of the concept and the properties (common features) shared by all examples of the concept. Let's further explore the way this interactive process of forming concepts operates.

Consider the following conversation between two people trying to form and clarify the concept *philosophy*.

A: What is your idea of what philosophy *means*?
B: Well, I think philosophy involves expressing important beliefs that you have—like discussing the meaning of life, assuming that there is a meaning.
A: Is explaining my belief about who's going to win the Super Bowl engaging in philosophy? After all, this is a belief that is very important to me—I've got a lot of money riding on the outcome!
B: I don't think so. A philosophical belief is usually a belief about something that is important to everyone—like what standards we should use to guide our moral choices.
A: What about the message that was in my fortune cookie last night: "Eat, drink, and be merry, for tomorrow we diet!"? This is certainly a belief that most people can relate to, especially during a holiday season! Is this philosophy?

B: I think that's what my grandmother used to call "foolosophy"! Philosophical beliefs are usually deeply felt views to which we have given a great deal of thought—not something plucked out of a cookie.

A: What about my belief in the golden rule "Do unto others as you would have them do unto you" because "What goes around comes around"? Doesn't that have the qualities that you mentioned?

B: Now you've got it!

As we review this dialogue, we can see that forming the concept *philosophy* works hand in hand with applying the concept to different examples. When two or more things work together in this way, we say that they *interact*. In this case, there are two parts of this interactive process.

We form concepts by generalizing, by focusing on the similar features among different things. In the previous dialogue, the things about which generalizations are being made are types of beliefs—beliefs about the meaning of life or about standards we use to guide our moral choices. By focusing on the similar features of these beliefs, the dialogue's two participants develop a list of properties philosophical beliefs share, including (1) beliefs dealing with important issues in life about which everyone is concerned and (2) beliefs reflecting deeply felt views—views to which people have given much thought. These common properties act as the requirements a viewpoint must meet to be considered a philosophical belief.

We apply concepts by interpreting, by looking for different examples of a concept and seeing if they meet the requirements of the concept we are developing. In the preceding dialogue, one participant attempts to apply the concept of *philosophy* to the following examples:

a belief about the outcome of the Super Bowl

a fortune cookie message: "Eat, drink, and be merry, for tomorrow we diet."

Each of these proposed examples suggests the development of new requirements for the concept to help clarify how the concept can be applied. Applying a concept to different possible examples thus becomes the way we develop and gradually sharpen our idea of it.

Even when a proposed example turns out not to be a valid one, the process of questioning often clarifies our understanding of that concept. For instance, although the proposed example of a belief about the outcome of the Super Bowl turned out not to be an example of the concept *philosophy*, examining it helped to clarify the concept and suggest other examples.

The process of developing concepts involves a constant back-and-forth movement between generalizing and interpreting. As the back-and-forth movement progresses, we gradually develop a list of specific requirements for an example of the concept; at the same time, we gain a clearer sense of how the concept is defined. We are also developing a collection of examples that embody the qualities of the concept and demonstrate situations in which the concept applies. This interactive process is illustrated in Figure 8.4.

FIGURE 8.4   Movement from General Concept to Well-Defined Concept

THINKING-
WRITING
ACTIVITY

Forming a Concept

Select a type of music with which you are familiar and write a dialogue similar to the one just examined. In the course of the dialogue, be sure to include the following:

1. Examples from which you are generalizing (such as specific bands)
2. General properties shared by various types of this music (e.g., "Jazz is a uniquely American form of music which uses complex rhythms and improvisation.")
3. Examples to which you are trying to apply the developing concept (such as the music of Marian McPartland, Miles Davis, or Thelonius Monk)

Forming concepts involves performing the operations of generalizing and interpreting together for two reasons.

1. You cannot form a concept unless you know how it might apply. If you have absolutely no idea what *jazz* or *philosophy* might exemplify, you cannot begin to form the concept, even in vague or general terms.
2. You cannot gather examples of the concept unless you know what they might be examples of. Until you begin to develop some idea of what the concepts *jazz* or *philosophy* might be (based on certain similarities among various things), you won't know where to look for examples of the concept (or how to evaluate them).

This interactive process is the way that you usually form all concepts, particularly the complicated ones. In college, much of your education is focused on carefully forming and exploring key concepts such as *democracy, dynamic equilibrium*, and *personality*.

Applying Concepts

Making sense of our experience means finding the right concept to explain what is going on. To determine whether the concept we have selected fits a situation, we have to determine whether the requirements that form the concept are being met.

To figure out which concept applies to the situation, we must do the following:

1. Be aware of the properties that form the boundaries of the concept.

2. Determine whether the experience meets those requirements, for only if it does can we apply the concept to it.

If we have the requirements of the concept clearly in mind, we can proceed to figure out which of these requirements are met by the experience. This is how we apply concepts, which is one of the most important ways we have for figuring out what is taking place in our experience.

Determining the Requirements of a Concept

In determining the requirements of a concept, we ask ourselves: *Would something still be an example of this concept if that thing did not meet this requirement?* If the answer to this question is *no*—that something would not be an example of this concept if it did not meet this requirement—we can say the requirement is a necessary part of the concept.

Consider the concept *dog*. Which of the following descriptions are requirements that must be met by an example of this concept?

1. Is an animal

2. Normally has four legs and a tail

3. Bites the mail carrier

It is clear that descriptions 1 and 2 are requirements that must be met to apply the concept *dog* because if we apply our test question—"Would something be an example of this concept if that thing did not meet this requirement?"—we can say that the thing would not be an example of the concept *dog* if it did not fit the first two descriptions: if it was not an animal and did not normally have four legs and a tail.

This does not seem to be the case, however, with description 3. If we ask ourselves the same test question, we can see that the thing might still be an example of the concept *dog* even if it did not bite the mail carrier. Even though some dogs do in fact bite mail carriers, this is not a requirement for being a dog.

Of course, there may be other things that meet these requirements but are not dogs. For example, a cat is an animal (description 1) that normally has four legs and a tail (description 2). What this means is that the requirements of a concept tell us only what attributes something must have to be an example of the concept. As a result, we often have to identify additional requirements that will define the concept more sharply. These requirements determine when the concept can be applied and indicate those things that qualify as examples of it. When we are able to identify all the requirements of the concept, we say these requirements are both necessary and sufficient for applying the concept.

Analyzing Complex Concepts

Although dealing with concepts like *dog* and *cat* may seem simple, matters become somewhat confusing when you start analyzing the more complex concepts you will encounter in your academic study. For example, consider the concepts of *masculinity* and *femininity*, two of the more emotionally charged and politically contentious concepts in our culture. There are many different perspectives on what these concepts mean, what they should mean, or whether we should be using them at all. See if you can identify properties and examples of these two concepts by completing the following Thinking-Writing Activity.

THINKING-
WRITING
ACTIVITY

Exploring the Concepts of Masculine and Feminine

Identify what you consider the essential properties (specific requirements that must be met to apply the concept) for each of these concepts as well as examples of people or behavior that illustrates these properties. For example, you might identify physical risk taking as a property of the concept *masculinity* and identify Russell Crowe as a person who illustrates this quality. Or you might identify intuition as a property of the concept *femininity*, illustrating this with the behavior "knowing without the conscious use of rational processes."

General Properties   *Specific Examples*

FEMININITY

1. _____   1. _____

2. _____   2. _____

3. _____   3. _____

MASCULINITY

1. _____   1. _____

2. _____   2. _____

3. _____   3. _____

Compare your list with those of your classmates. What similarities and differences do you notice? What factors might account for these similarities and differences? Look back at your responses after you have read the following selections.

A Casebook on Gender and Sexuality

It would seem to be the easiest characteristic to define, the most basic classification into which we can sort human beings: Are you a man or a woman? Is your behavior feminine or masculine? And yet the dazzling variety of human responses, preferences, fears, and favors blurs these apparently simple distinctions into a never-ending source of pleasure and conflict. Not surprisingly, the similarities and differences between men and women have inspired poets and storytellers as well as provoked the interests of social scientists and essayists. In the following casebook, writers across genres and perspectives attempt to define and classify the concepts of gender and sexuality.

"Choosing Clothes, but Not Husbands"

BY JOSEPH BERGER

Journalist Joseph Berger immigrated to New York City from Russia as a small boy just after the Second World War. He began his professional career as an English teacher at a Bronx, New York, public school and joined the staff of the *New York Post* as a reporter in 1971. He has covered religion, education, and science for the *Post* and *New York Newsday* and since 1985 for the *New York Times*, where "Choosing Clothes, but Not Husbands" first appeared in November 2004. In his 2001 memoir, *Displaced Persons: Growing Up American after the Holocaust*, Berger eloquently explored the tensions of a family caught between historical events, lost cultures, and missed opportunities. His insight and experience are evident in this article about female Afghan immigrants in New York City who are balancing tradition and possibility in their own lives.

By all appearances, Ashrat Khwajazadah and Naheed Mawjzada are thoroughly modern American women.

Long-haired and dark-eyed, they spurn the headscarves and modest outfits customarily worn by Afghan women, preferring hip-hugging slacks. Both of them are in their early twenties and both of them have taken a route still somewhat controversial among Afghans in Flushing, Queens—going to college to pursue professions. Ms. Khwajazadah studied speech pathology at Queens College and Ms. Mawjzada majors in political science at Adelphi University. Both also defy the ideal of a reticent Afghan womanhood, with Ms. Mawjzada speaking up forcefully when men talk politics at the dinner table.

But there are incongruities. Both of them, by design, have never dated. Like most young women in their Afghan enclave in Flushing, they are waiting for their parents to pick their spouses.

"It's been drilled into your head since you were a little girl: 'Don't talk with guys, don't ruin your reputation, everyone will gossip about you,'" said Ms. Khwajazadah, a high-spirited woman who came here as a two-year-old with her refugee parents. Nevertheless, she added, "I'm happy with my decision."

"I'm very close with my family and that helps me because they want to do what's best for me," she said.

In testing how far they can go in forsaking tradition, these women illustrate the delicate balance younger Afghans, particularly women, have had to strike as they grow up in a comparatively freewheeling society with parents—often uneducated and unable to speak English—who have held tight to their Afghan conventions.

To be sure, the Afghans' transition is an old immigrant story—one that could be told about the Irish, Italians and Jews of the nineteenth century or the newer groups that have seasoned New York City's stew. Those newcomers too looked on with anger or resignation as their children gradually (and their grandchildren more cavalierly) adopted the prevailing culture.

But the Afghan version has its own endemic twists, community advocates say. Older Afghans, particularly women, often have had no schooling whatsoever. Even today, some families insist that girls, whose non-Afghan friends roam freely, return home immediately after school. It is not uncommon for girls to be engaged as young as thirteen and be married by sixteen.

The Afghan story in New York has garnered more than the usual curiosity because Afghanistan has drawn so much attention on the world stage, first in the military response to September 11 and now as the fragile government of President Hamid Karzai tries to establish democracy, including expansion of women's rights.

There are 5,446 Afghans in New York City and over 9,100 in the metropolitan area, according to the 2000 census. A large proportion came here with grants of asylum after treacherous odysseys to escape either the Soviet occupation of 1979 or Taliban rule that began in 1996.

Manizha Naderi, the twenty-eight-year-old director of Women for Afghan Women, which offers counseling and instructional programs, remembers how at four years old she crossed the desert into Pakistan on a single motorcycle that also carried her parents, her two-year-old brother, nine-month-old sister and the driver.

The two largest enclaves of Afghans are in Flushing—north of Queens College and in the largely Chinese and Korean area north of Northern Boulevard. Flushing has four Afghan mosques, a half-dozen kabob houses and the Kouchi Market, which besides native spices and breads carries Afghan mandolins (rababs) and billiards-like board games (karams).

New Yorkers commonly encounter Afghan men in the fried chicken restaurants they own and in the ubiquitous sidewalk coffee carts of Midtown. But women are more out of sight. A quarter of Afghan women have never been to school and only half have completed high school, according to a study by Andrew A. Beveridge, a sociology professor at Queens College, and Kaisa Hagen, a student there. Only one quarter work outside the home, compared with 60 percent for other New York women.

Ms. Naderi said that "Afghanistan has a very patriarchal culture and women don't have rights," and those views migrate here.

15   "Men have corrupted views of Islam and actually believe women are second-class citizens and are there to take care of them," she said. "They don't let them go to school or to work."

Afghans from the capital, Kabul, are less bound by tradition than those from the villages, and those who fled the Soviets are more conservative than those who fled the Taliban. Some Afghan Muslims who have been here for decades are so acculturated they put up Christmas trees, but in general Afghans here are trying to sustain crucial remnants of their culture.

For more than a few families even the notion of educating their daughters beyond high school is regarded as daring, Ms. Naderi said. But more leaders are encouraging it. Mohammed Sherzad, the imam of Masjid Hazrat-I-Abubakr Sadiq, on Union Street in north Flushing (there is a similarly named mosque nearby from which Imam Sherzad was ousted) looks favorably upon women who postpone having children until they finish college.

"A good woman is one who is educated, both for her children and her society," he said.

Dr. Tahira Homayun, a gynecologist whose husband is an economic adviser to President Karzai, said some Afghan girls have more successful school careers than their brothers because struggling families often press boys to work.

20   Ms. Naderi said that as a result of the community's lingering patriarchal structures, violence toward wives is much more common than the community admits.

"There's a saying that the food your husband feeds you doesn't come for free," she said. "And men actually think they have a right under the Koran to beat their wives."

But no characteristic seems more ironclad than the convention of having parents arrange their children's marriages.

"Afghan people can't meet each other prior to getting engaged," said a sixty-five-year-old mother of six who was taking English classes given by Women for Afghan Women. She asked that her name not be used because seeing her name in print made her uncomfortable. "It's an embarrassment for the family."

Much of that stigma derives from the treasured principle of family honor. If a daughter chooses to find her own spouse, her father's stature will be diminished, the family name tainted by gossip, and her sisters may find it harder to marry.

25   "The girl is a trophy piece," said Ms. Mawjzada, the daughter of a coffee vendor who in addition to studying at Adelphi works in customer service at Geico insurance. "If the girl has a good reputation, the family has a good reputation."

Parents are more willing to close their eyes to a teenage Don Juan, and marriage customs for a man are also more lenient. Bashir Rahim, a twenty-nine-year-old computer technician, says if he meets a girl that interests him at a family gathering, he might ask her for her address, then send his parents to her home to start a conversation about marriage.

Girls learn by trial and error how far they can stretch tradition, but defying the code outright exacts a steep price. Ms. Naderi was married at sixteen to a man she chose on her own. Her mother and grandmother did not speak to her for ten years.

"My mother still tells me she can't look at people because they know her daughter married in this way," she said.

Masuda Sultan, a twenty-six-year-old Flushing woman who is doing graduate work in public administration at the Kennedy School of Government at Harvard, was not even sixteen when her father, the owner of a fried chicken restaurant in Harlem, contrived with an acquaintance to have her married to a doctor twice her age. She got to see her future husband three times before the wedding.

30

"I actually thought it could work," she recalled. "When your actions are limited and you're from a certain world and you're young and you respect your family, you go along with their wishes even if you have extreme doubts."

Key issues like how far she could go in school were left murky. But when it became clear after the wedding that Ms. Sultan wanted to put off having children until she finished college, the tensions became irreconcilable. Ms. Sultan lapsed into what she called a deep depression, and after three years she and her husband agreed to divorce, a rare and humiliating event in the Afghan community and one that often attaches blame to the woman. Ms. Sultan, who moved back with her parents into the same room she had shared with her sister, recalled that female friends found it so difficult to believe that she could leave her husband for the reasons she did that they asked if he beat or betrayed her.

"The core issue was really a different philosophy of what it means to be Afghan and what it means to be American," she said. "Ultimately I was being treated as a child and my role was set and I was told what I could and couldn't do."

QUESTIONS FOR ACTIVE READING

1. How does the author, Joseph Berger, use comparison and contrast to suggest conflict? What concepts does he compare and contrast?

2. What kinds of evidence, illustration, and authority does the author cite in order to give substance to his thesis?

3. Why would the subject of this article be of interest to readers of the *New York Times*? What other kinds of readers or audiences does this subject appeal to, and why?

QUESTIONS FOR THINKING CRITICALLY

1. How do the young Afghan women portrayed in this article negotiate the different concepts of femininity and women's social roles held by their traditional families and their new American communities?

2. How are certain concepts—such as *reputation*, *gossip*, and *honor*—used by the writer of this article and by the people he interviews? How does each concept and the impact of the word *used to express it* change according to its cultural context? (See Chapter 6 for more on the impact of language choices.)

3. What kinds of decision-making strategies do the young Afghan immigrants in this article use in order to appease their families while also fulfilling their own ambitions? Review Decisions In Your Life (in Chapter 5) and describe how applying these decision-making steps did, or could have, assisted these women in their decisions.

"The Inheritance of Tools"

by Scott Russell Sanders (b. 1945)

A native of Ohio, Scott Russell Sanders writes fiction, science fiction, biography, and personal essays. His essay collections include *Writing from the Center* (1995) and *Hunting for Hope* (1998). These essays, which often focus on life in the Midwest, deal with the daily problems of living and with the relationships and values passed on between generations. In the following essay he uses an overall narrative frame, the story of the day he heard the news that his father had died, to enclose a number of other, smaller, narratives. His narratives are made stronger by the detailed description he uses. Note especially his description of his own pain and his family's reaction to it in the hours immediately following the phone call from his mother.

At just about the hour when my father died, soon after dawn one February morning when ice coated the windows like cataracts, I banged my thumb with a hammer. Naturally I swore at the hammer, the reckless thing, and in the moment of swearing I thought of what my father would say: "If you'd try hitting the nail it would go in a whole lot faster. Don't you know your thumb's not as hard as that hammer?" We both were doing carpentry that day, but far apart. He was building cupboards at my brother's place in Oklahoma; I was at home in Indiana, putting up a wall in the basement to make a bedroom for my daughter. By the time my mother called with news of his death—the long distance wires whittling her voice until it seemed too thin to bear the weight of what she had to say—my thumb was swollen. A week or so later a white scar in the shape of a crescent moon began to show above the cuticle and month by month it rose across the pink sky of my thumbnail. It took the better part of a year for the scar to disappear, and every time I noticed it I thought of my father.

The hammer had belonged to him, and to his father before him. The three of us have used it to build houses and barns and chicken coops, to upholster chairs and crack walnuts, to make doll furniture and bookshelves and jewelry boxes. The head is scratched and pockmarked, like an old plowshare that has been working rocky fields, and it gives off the sort of dull sheen you see on fast creek water in the shade. It is a finishing hammer, about the weight of a bread loaf, too light, really, for framing walls, too heavy for cabinet work, with a curved claw for pulling nails, a rounded head for pounding, a fluted neck for looks, and a hickory handle for strength.

The present handle is my third one, bought from a lumberyard in Tennessee, down the road from where my brother and I were helping my father build his retirement house. I broke the previous one by trying to pull sixteen-penny nails out of floor joists—a foolish thing to do with a finishing hammer, as my father pointed out. "You ever hear of a crowbar?" he said. No telling how many handles he and my grandfather had gone through before me. My grandfather used to cut down hickory trees on his farm, saw them into slabs, cure the planks in his hayloft, and carve handles with a drawknife. The grain in hickory is crooked and knotty, and therefore tough, hard to split, like the grain in the two men who owned this hammer before me.

After proposing marriage to a neighbor girl, my grandfather used this hammer to build a house for his bride on a stretch of river bottom in northern Mississippi. The lumber for the place, like the hickory for the handle, was cut on his own land. By the day of the wedding he had not quite finished the house, and so right after the ceremony he took his wife home and put her to work. My grandmother had worn her Sunday dress for the wedding, with a fringe of lace tacked on around the hem in honor of the occasion. She removed this lace and folded it away before going out to help my grandfather nail siding on the house. "There she was in her good dress," he told me some fifty-odd years after that wedding day, "holding up them long pieces of clapboard while I hammered, and together we got the place covered up before dark." As the family grew to four, six, eight, and eventually thirteen, my grandfather used this hammer to enlarge his house room by room, like a chambered nautilus expanding its shell.

5 By and by the hammer was passed along to my father. One day he was up on the roof of our pony barn nailing shingles with it, when I stepped out the kitchen door to call him for supper. Before I could yell, something about the sight of him straddling the spine of that roof and swinging the hammer caught my eye and made me hold my tongue. I was five or six years old, and the world's commonplaces were still news to me. He would pull a nail from the pouch at his waist, bring the hammer down, and a moment later the *thunk* of the blow would reach my ears. And that is what had stopped me in my tracks and stilled my tongue, that momentary gap between seeing and hearing the blow. Instead of yelling from the kitchen door, I ran to the barn and climbed two rungs up the ladder—as far as I was allowed to go—and spoke quietly to my father. On our walk to the house he explained that sound takes time to make its way through air. Suddenly the world seemed larger, the air more dense, if sound could be held back like any ordinary traveler.

By the time I started using this hammer, at about the age when I discovered the speed of sound, it already contained houses and mysteries for me. The smooth handle was one my grandfather had made. In those days I needed both hands to swing it. My father would start a nail in a scrap of wood, and I would pound away until I bent it over.

"Looks like you got ahold of some of those rubber nails," he would tell me. "Here, let me see if I can find you some stiff ones." And he would rummage in a drawer until he came up with a fistful of more cooperative nails. "Look at the head," he would tell me. "Don't look at your hands, don't look at the hammer. Just look at the head of that nail and pretty soon you'll learn to hit it square."

Pretty soon I did learn. While he worked in the garage cutting dovetail joints for a drawer or skinning a deer or tuning an engine, I would hammer nails. I made innocent blocks of wood look like porcupines. He did not talk much in the midst of his tools, but he kept up a nearly ceaseless humming, slipping in and out of a dozen tunes in an afternoon, often running back over the same stretch of melody again and again, as if searching for a way out. When the humming did cease, I knew he was faced with a task requiring great delicacy or concentration, and I took care not to distract him.

He kept scraps of wood in a cardboard box—the ends of two-by-fours, slabs of shelving and plywood, odd pieces of molding—and everything in it was fair game. I nailed scraps together to fashion what I called boats or houses, but the results usually bore only faint resemblance to the visions I carried in my head. I would hold up these constructions to show my father, and he would turn them over in his hands admiringly, speculating about what they might be. My cobbled-together guitars might have been alien spaceships, my barns might have been models of Aztec temples, each wooden contraption might have been anything but what I had set out to make.

10   Now and again I would feel the need to have a chunk of wood shaped or short-ened before I riddled it with nails, and I would clamp it in a vise and scrape at it with a handsaw. My father would let me lacerate the board until my arm gave out, and then he would wrap his hand around mine and help me finish the cut, showing me how to use my thumb to guide the blade, how to pull back on the saw to keep it from bind-ing, how to let my shoulder do the work.

"Don't force it," he would say, "just drag it easy and give the teeth a chance to bite."

As the saw teeth bit down, the wood released its smell, each kind with its own fra-grance, oak or walnut or cherry or pine—usually pine because it was the softest, eas-iest for a child to work. No matter how weathered and gray the board, no matter how warped and cracked, inside there was this smell waiting, as of something freshly baked. I gathered every smidgen of sawdust and stored it away in coffee cans, which I kept in a drawer of the workbench. When I did not feel like hammering nails, I would dump my sawdust on the concrete floor of the garage and landscape it into highways and farms and towns, running miniature cars and trucks along miniature roads. Looming as huge as a colossus, my father worked over and around me, now and again bending down to inspect my work, careful not to trample my creations. It was a landscape that smelled dizzyingly of wood. Even after a bath my skin would carry the smell, and so would my father's hair, when he lifted me for a bedtime hug.

•   •   •   •   •

I tell these things not only from memory but also from recent observation, because my own son now turns blocks of wood into nailed porcupines, dumps cans full of saw-dust at my feet and sculpts highways on the floor. He learns how to swing a hammer from the elbow instead of the wrist, how to lay his thumb beside the blade to guide a saw, how to tap a chisel with a wooden mallet, how to mark a hole with an awl before starting a drill bit. My daughter did the same before him, and even now, on the brink of teenage aloofness, she will occasionally drag out my box of wood scraps and car-penter something. So I have seen my apprenticeship to wood and tools reenacted in each of my children, as my father saw his own apprenticeship renewed in me.

The saw I use belonged to him, as did my level and both of my squares, and all four tools had belonged to his father. The blade of the saw is the bluish color of gun barrels, and the maple handle, dark from the sweat of hands, is inscribed with curving leaf designs. The level is a shaft of walnut two feet long, edged with brass and pierced by three round windows in which air bubbles float in oil-filled tubes of glass. The middle window serves for testing if a surface is horizontal, the others for testing if a surface is plumb or vertical. My grandfather used to carry this level on the gun rack behind the seat in his pickup, and when I rode with him I would turn around to watch the bubbles dance. The larger of the two squares is called a framing square, a flat steel elbow, so beat up and tarnished you can barely make out the rows of numbers that show how to figure the cuts on rafters. The smaller one is called a try square, for marking right angles, with a blued steel blade for the shank and a brass-faced block of cherry for the head.

15   I was taught early on that a saw is not to be used apart from a square: "If you're going to cut a piece of wood," my father insisted, "you owe it to the tree to cut it straight."

Long before studying geometry, I learned there is a mystical virtue in right angles. There is an unspoken morality in seeking the level and the plumb. A house will stand, a table will bear weight, the sides of a box will hold together, only if the joints are square and the members upright. When the bubble is lined up between two marks etched in the glass tube of a level, you have aligned yourself with the forces that hold the universe together. When you miter the corners of a picture frame each angle must be exactly forty-five degrees, as they are in the perfect triangles of Pythagoras, not a degree more or less. Otherwise the frame will hang crookedly, as if ashamed of itself and of its maker. No matter if the joints you are cutting do not show. Even if you are butting two pieces of wood together inside a cabinet, where no one except a wrecking crew will ever see them, you must take pains to ensure that the ends are square and the studs are plumb.

I took pains over the wall I was building on the day my father died. Not long after that wall was finished—paneled with tongue-and-groove boards of yellow pine, the nail holes filled with putty and the wood all stained and sealed—I came close to wrecking it one afternoon when my daughter ran howling up the stairs to announce that her gerbils had escaped from their cage and were hiding in my brand new wall. She could hear them scratching and squeaking behind her bed. Impossible! I said. How on earth could they get inside my drum-tight wall? Through the heating vent, she answered. I went downstairs, pressed my ear to the honey-colored wood, and heard the *scritch scritch* of tiny feet.

"What can we do?" my daughter wailed. "They'll starve to death, they'll die of thirst, they'll suffocate."

"Hold on," I soothed. "I'll think of something."

20   While I thought and she fretted, the radio on her bedside table delivered us the headlines: Several thousand people had died in a city in India from a poisonous cloud that had leaked overnight from a chemical plant. A nuclear-powered submarine had been launched. Rioting continued in South Africa. An airplane had been hijacked in the Mediterranean. Authorities calculated that several thousand homeless people slept on the streets within sight of the Washington Monument. I felt my usual helplessness

in the face of all these calamities. But here was my daughter, weeping because her gerbils were holed up in a wall. This calamity I could handle.

"Don't worry," I told her. "We'll set food and water by the heating vent and lure them out. And if that doesn't do the trick, I'll tear the wall apart until we find them."

She stopped crying and gazed at me. "You'd really tear it apart? Just for my gerbils? The *wall?*" Astonishment slowed her down only for a second, however, before she ran to the workbench and began tugging at drawers, saying, "Let's see, what'll we need? Crowbar. Hammer. Chisels. I hope we don't have to use them—but just in case."

We didn't need the wrecking tools. I never had to assault my handsome wall, because the gerbils eventually came out to nibble at a dish of popcorn. But for several hours I studied the tongue-and-groove skin I had nailed up on the day of my father's death, considering where to begin prying. There were no gaps in that wall, no crooked joints.

I had botched a great many pieces of wood before I mastered the right angle with a saw, botched even more before I learned to miter a joint. The knowledge of these things resides in my hands and eyes and the webwork of muscles, not in the tools. There are machines for sale—powered miter boxes and radial-arm saws, for instance—that will enable any casual soul to cut proper angles in boards. The skill is invested in the gadget instead of the person who uses it, and this is what distinguishes a machine from a tool. If I had to earn my keep by making furniture or building houses, I suppose I would buy powered saws and pneumatic nailers; the need for speed would drive me to it. But since I carpenter only for my own pleasure or to help neighbors or to remake the house around the ears of my family, I stick with hand tools. Most of the ones I own were given to me by my father, who also taught me how to wield them. The tools in my workbench are a double inheritance, for each hammer and level and saw is wrapped in a cloud of knowing.

25   All of these tools are a pleasure to look at and to hold. Merchants would never paste NEW NEW NEW! signs on them in stores. Their designs are old because they work, because they serve their purpose well. Like folk songs and aphorisms and the grainy bits of language, these tools have been pared down to essentials. I look at my claw hammer, the distillation of a hundred generations of carpenters, and consider that it holds up well beside those other classics—Greek vases, Gregorian chants, *Don Quixote,* barbed fish hooks, candles, spoons. Knowledge of hammering stretches back to the earliest humans who squatted beside fires, chipping flints. Anthropologists have a lovely name for those unworked rocks that served as the earliest hammers. "Dawn stones," they are called. Their only qualification for the work, aside from hardness, is that they fit the hand. Our ancestors used them for grinding corn, tapping awls, smashing bones. From dawn stones to this claw hammer is a great leap in time, but no great distance in design or imagination.

·   ·   ·   ·   ·

On that iced-over February morning when I smashed my thumb with the hammer, I was down in the basement framing the wall that my daughter's gerbils would later hide in. I was thinking of my father, as I always did whenever I built anything, thinking how he would have gone about the work, hearing in memory what he would have said about the wisdom of hitting the nail instead of my thumb. I had the studs and plates nailed together all square and trim, and was lifting the wall into place when the phone rang upstairs. My wife answered, and in a moment she came to the basement door and called down softly to me. The stillness in her voice made me drop the framed wall and hurry upstairs. She told me my father was dead. Then I heard the details over the phone from my mother. Building a set of cupboards for my brother in Oklahoma, he had knocked off work early the previous afternoon because of cramps in his stomach. Early this morning, on his way into the kitchen of my brother's trailer, maybe going for a glass of water, so early that no one else was awake, he slumped down on the linoleum and his heart quit.

For several hours I paced around inside my house, upstairs and down, in and out of every room, looking for the right door to open and knowing there was no such door. My wife and children followed me and wrapped me in arms and backed away again, circling and staring as if I were on fire. Where was the door, the door, the door? I kept wondering. My smashed thumb turned purple and throbbed, making me furious. I wanted to cut it off and rush outside and scrape away at the snow and hack a hole in the frozen earth and bury the shameful thing.

I went down into the basement, opened a drawer in my workbench, and stared at the ranks of chisels and knives. Oiled and sharp, as my father would have kept them, they gleamed at me like teeth. I took up a clasp knife, pried out the longest blade, and tested the edge on the hair of my forearm. A tuft came away cleanly, and I saw my father testing the sharpness of tools on his own skin, the blades of axes and knives and gouges and hoes, saw the red hair shaved off in patches from his arms and the backs of his hands. "That will cut bear," he would say. He never cut a bear with his blades, now my blades, but he cut deer, dirt, wood. I closed the knife and put it away. Then I took up the hammer and went back to work on my daughter's wall, snugging the bottom plate against a chalk line on the floor, shimming the top plate against the joists overhead, plumbing the studs with my level, making sure before I drove the first nail that every line was square and true.

QUESTIONS FOR ACTIVE READING

1. Examine the details Sanders gives (paragraphs 17 and 26–28, especially) about building a wall to divide a room. Can you clearly visualize what Sanders is doing at each step? Is each concept clearly defined? Why, at the end of the essay, does Sanders feel the need to describe so clearly each step in the process?

2. How does Sanders use chronological order in this essay? What objects, images, or ideas connect the different periods of time that he describes?

3. What is a "dawn stone"? Why does Sanders describe it in this essay, and what does it represent to him?

QUESTIONS FOR THINKING CRITICALLY

1. In paragraphs 16–23, Sanders describes an ethical obligation in carpentry. What, in your own words, is that obligation? How does Sanders relate that obligation to larger problems in the world? Is carpentry, for Sanders, a metaphor for some greater lesson or world-view? (The very last words of the essay should provide a clue; there might also, of course, be more than one metaphor.)

2. Sanders describes a kind of "apprenticeship" that has been passed down in his family for generations. In Sanders's view, is that apprenticeship especially "masculine" or "feminine"? Is there a skill, or a kind of knowledge, that has been passed down in your family? How was that knowledge or skill imparted to you? How do you intend to pass it along to your own children?

3. What do you make of Sanders's description of his grief, and his early attempt to come to terms with that grief, in paragraphs 27 and 28? Is there anything particularly "Masculine" about that grief?

"My Papa's Waltz"

BY THEODORE ROETHKE (1908–1963)
FROM *The Collected Poems of Theodore Roethke*

The theme of fathers lost and found, fatherhood as conflicted and yearned for, permeates the work of Theodore Roethke. His German father, grandfather, and uncles owned and operated greenhouses in Saginaw, Michigan; the image of the greenhouse as a fragile shelter, a transparent place of life even in the most brutal of climates, gives a poignant force to several poems in his second volume of verse, *The Lost Son and Other Poems* (1948). The death of Roethke's father from cancer in 1923 shaped his adolescence and may have contributed to the severe bouts of depression that periodically shook him for the rest of his life. In an autobiographical essay, Roethke observed that "I believe that the spiritual man must go back in order to go forward"; this regression into the personal as well as poetic past in order to develop his own voice and persona shaped his poetic project.

Roethke held several university teaching appointments and was widely published during his life. He was awarded the Guggenheim Fellowship (1950), *Poetry* magazine's Levinson Prize (1951), and major grants from the Ford Foundation and the National Institute of Arts and Letters in 1952. His posthumously published and final book, *The Far Field* (1964), received the National Book Award.

The whiskey on your breath
Could make a small boy dizzy;

But I hung on like death:
Such waltzing was not easy.

We romped until the pans
Slid from the kitchen shelf;
My mother's countenance
Could not unfrown itself.

The hand that held my wrist
Was battered on one knuckle;
At every step you missed
My right ear scraped a buckle.

You beat time on my head
With a palm caked hard by dirt,
Then waltzed me off to bed
Still clinging to your shirt.

QUESTIONS FOR ACTIVE READING

1. Although poets often use figurative language in richly imaginative ways, there is just one simile in this poem. Where is that simile, and what does it reveal about the relationship between the father and the son?

2. Reading the poem out loud (to yourself, or to each other in the classroom), what do you notice about its rhyming and its rhythm? Do these patterns remind you of other kinds of poems, rhymes, or songs? In what way?

3. Is the narrator of the poem a small boy, or an adult writing from the perspective of a small boy? How can you tell?

QUESTIONS FOR THINKING CRITICALLY

1. Fatherhood, and the loss of or search for a father figure, is an overarching theme of Roethke's work. Based on this poem, how would you define Roethke's concept of fatherhood (not the specific father described here)?

2. In what ways do the father and the mother in this poem evoke the "masculine" and "feminine" qualities?

3. Compare and contrast the ways in which Roethke and (in a later reading) Carol Tavris describe how men express love and caring. Of these authors, whose perspective do you think is most accurate? Are you basing your assessment on your own personal experience and relationships, or on more abstract classifications of behavior?

"The Names of Women"

BY LOUISE ERDRICH (b. 1954)
FROM *The Blue Jay's Dance*

A member of the Turtle Mountain band of the Chippewa nation of Native Americans, writer Louise Erdrich (born in 1954) explores the fragmented, sorrowful, and ongoing conflict between Native Americans and the larger American culture in her novels, poetry, and essays. Raised in a family of seven children, and the mother of six children herself, Erdrich finds within the entanglements of family all of the story and metaphor necessary to tell larger truths about the ways in which men and women, Native American and "American," and adults and children relate to and conflict with one another. Her first novel, *Love Medicine* (1984), won the National Book Critics Circle Award, and her subsequent novels *The Beet Queen* (1986) and *Tracks* (1988) were also bestsellers. Her recent novel, *The Last Report on the Miracles at Little No Horse* (2001), was a finalist for the National Book Award. In an interview with the online magazine *Salon*, Erdrich described how having grown up in a household of storytellers influences her writing: "My mother read, my father told them to me. Lots of stories. That's the way they are. They're always making stories out of things—'This happened today and he is connected to so and so.' It's a small town thing." Erdrich lives in Minneapolis and runs a small independent bookstore.

Ikwe is the word for woman in the language of the Anishinabe, my mother's people, whose descendants, mixed with and married to French trappers and farmers, are the Michifs of the Turtle Mountain reservation in North Dakota. Every Anishinabe *Ikwe*, every mixed-blood descendant like me, who can trace her way back a generation or two, is the daughter of a mystery. The history of the woodland Anishinabe—decimated by disease, fighting Plains Indian tribes to the west and squeezed by European settlers to the east—is much like most other Native American stories, a confusion of loss, a tale of absences, of a culture that was blown apart and changed so radically in such a short time that only the names survive,

And yet, those names.

The names of the first women whose existence is recorded on the rolls of the Turtle Mountain Reservation, in 1982, reveal as much as we can ever recapture of their personalities, complex natures, and relationships. These names tell stories, or half stories, if only we listen closely.

There once were women named *Standing Strong, Fish Bones, Different Thunder*. There once was a girl called *Yellow Straps*. Imagine what it was like to pick berries with *Sky Coming Down*, to walk through a storm with *Lightning Proof*. Surely, she was struck and lived, but what about the person next to her? People always avoided *Steps Over Truth*, when they wanted a straight answer, and *I Hear*, when they wanted to keep a secret. *Glittering* put coal on her face and watched for enemies at night. The woman named *Standing Across* could see things moving far across the lake. The old ladies gossiped about *Playing Around*, but no one dared say anything to her face. *Ice was good at gambling. Shining One Side* loved to sit and talk to *Opposite the Sky*. They both knew *Sounding Feather, Exhausted Wind*, and *Green Cloud*, daughter of *Seeing Iron. Center of the Sky* was a widow. *Rabbit, Prairie Chicken*, and *Daylight* were all little girls. *She Tramp* could make great distance in a day of walking. *Cross Lightning* had a powerful smile. When *Setting Wind* and *Gentle Woman Standing* sang together the whole tribe listened. *Stop the Day* got her name when at her shout the afternoon went still. *Log* was strong, *Cloud Touching Bottom* weak and consumptive. *Mirage* married *Wind*. Everyone loved *Musical Cloud*, but children hid from *Dressed in Stone. Lying Down Grass* had such a gentle voice and touch, but no one dared to cross *She Black of Heart*.

5   We can imagine something of these women from their names. Anishinabe historian Basil Johnston notes that "such was the mystique and force of a name that it was considered presumptuous and unbecoming, even vain, for a person to utter his own name. It was the custom for a third person, if present, to utter the name of the person to be identified. Seldom, if ever, did either husband or wife speak the name of the other in public."

Shortly after the first tribal roll, the practice of renaming became an ecclesiastical exercise, and, as a result, most women in the next two generations bear the names of saints particularly beloved by the French. *She Knows the Bear* became Marie. *Sloping Cloud* was christened Jeanne. *Taking Care of the Day* and *Yellow Day Woman* turned into Catherines. Identities are altogether lost. The daughters of my own ancestors, *Kwayzancheewin—Acts Like a Boy* and *Striped Earth Woman*—go unrecorded, and no hint or reflection of their individual natures comes to light through the scatter-shot records of those times, although they must have been genetically tough in order to survive: there were epidemics of typhoid, flu, measles and other diseases that winnowed the tribe each winter. They had to have grown up sensible, hard-working, undeviating in their attention to their tasks. They had to have been lucky. And if very lucky, they acquired carts.

·   ·   ·   ·   ·

It is no small thing that both of my great-grandmothers were known as women with carts.

The first was Elise Eliza McCloud, the great-granddaughter of *Striped Earth Woman*. The buggy she owned was somewhat grander than a cart. In her photograph, Elise Eliza gazes straight ahead, intent, elevated in her pride. Perhaps she and her daughter Justine, both wearing reshaped felt fedoras, were on their way to the train that would take them from Rugby, North Dakota, to Grand Forks, and back again. Back and forth across the upper tier of the plains, they peddled their hand-worked tourist items—dangling moccasin brooches and little beaded hats, or, in the summer, the wild berries, plums, and nuts that they had gathered from the wooded hills. Of Elise Eliza's industry there remains in the family only an intricately beaded pair of buffalo horns and a piece of real furniture, a "high-boy," an object once regarded with some awe, a prize she won for selling the most merchandise from a manufacturer's catalogue.

The owner of the other cart, Virginia Grandbois, died when I was nine years old: she was a fearsome and fascinating presence, an old woman seated like an icon behind the door of my grandparents' house. Forty years before I was born, she was photographed on her way to fetch drinking water at the reservation well. In the picture she is seated high, the reins in her fingers connected to a couple of shaggy fetlocked draft ponies. The barrel she will fill stands behind her. She wears a man's sweater and an expression of vast self-pleasure. She might have been saying *Kaygoh*, a warning, to calm the horses. She might have been speaking to whomever it was who held the camera, still a novel luxury.

Virginia Grandbois was known to smell of flowers. In spite of the potato picking, water hauling, field and housework, she found the time and will to dust her face with pale powder, in order to look more French. She was the great-great-granddaughter of the daughter of the principal leader of the *A-waus-e*, the Bullhead clan, a woman whose real name was never recorded but who, on marrying a Frenchman, was "recreated" as Madame Cadotte. It was Madame Cadotte who acted as a liaison between her Ojibway relatives and her husband so that, even when French influence waned in the region, Jean-Baptiste Cadotte stayed on as the only trader of importance, the last governor of the fort at Sault St. Marie.

By the time I knew Virginia Grandbois, however, her mind had darkened, and her body deepened, shrunk, turned to bones and leather. She did not live in the present or in any known time at all. Periodically, she would awaken from dim and unknown dreams to find herself seated behind the door in her daughter's house. She then cried out for her cart and her horses. When they did not materialize, Virginia Grandbois rose with great energy and purpose. Then she walked towards her house, taking the straightest line.

That house, long sold and gone, lay over one hundred miles due east and still Virginia Grandbois charged ahead, no matter what lay in her path—fences, sloughs, woods, the yards of other families. She wanted home, to get home, to be home. She wanted her own place back, the place she had made, not her daughter's, not anyone else's. Hers. There was no substitute, no kindness, no reality that would change her mind. She had to be tied to the chair, and the chair to the wall, and still there was no reasoning with Virginia Grandbois. Her entire life, her hard-won personality, boiled down in the end to one stubborn, fixed, desperate idea.

•   •   •   •   •

I started with the same idea—this urge to get home, even if I must walk straight across the world. Only, for me, the urge to walk is the urge to write. Like my great-grandmother's house, there is no home for me to get to. A mixed-blood, raised in the Sugarbeet Capital, educated on the Eastern seaboard, married in a tiny New England village, living now on a ridge directly across from the Swan Range in the Rocky Mountains, my home is a collection of homes, of wells in which the quiet of experience shales away into sweet bedrock.

Elise Eliza pieced the quilt my mother slept under, a patchwork of shirts, pants, other worn-out scraps, bordered with small rinsed and pressed Bull Durham sacks. As if in another time and place, although it is only the dim barrel of a four-year-old's memory, I see myself lying wrapped under smoky quilts and dank green army blankets in the house in which my mother was born. In the fragrance of tobacco, some smoked in home-rolled cigarettes, some offered to the Manitous whose presence still was honored, I dream myself home. Beneath the rafters, shadowed with bunches of plants and torn calendars, in the nest of a sagging bed, I listen to mice rustle and the scratch of an owl's claws as it paces the shingles.

Elise Eliza's daughter-in-law, my grandmother Mary LeFavor, kept that house of hand-hewed and stacked beams, mudded between. She managed to shore it up and keep it standing by stuffing every new crack with disposable diapers. Having used and reused cloth to diaper her own children, my grandmother washed and hung to dry the paper and plastic diapers that her granddaughters bought for her great-grandchildren. When their plastic-paper shredded, she gathered them carefully together and one day, on a summer visit, I woke early to find her tamping the rolled stuff carefully into the cracked walls of that old house.

•   •   •   •   •

It is autumn in the Plains, and in the little sloughs ducks land, and mudhens, whose flesh always tastes greasy and charred. Snow is coming soon, and after its first fall there will be a short, false warmth that brings out the sweet-sour odor of highbush cranberries. As a descendant of the women who skinned buffalo and tanned and smoked the hides, of women who pounded berries with the dried meat to make winter food, who made tea from willow bark and rosehips, who gathered snakeroot, I am affected by the change of seasons. Here is a time when plants consolidate their tonic and drop seed, when animals store energy and grow thick fur. As for me, I start keeping longer hours, writing more, working harder, though I am obviously not a creature of a traditional Anishinabe culture. I was not raised speaking the old language, or adhering to the cycle of religious ceremonies that govern the Anishinabe spiritual relationship to the land and the moral order within human configurations. As the wedding of many backgrounds, I am free to do what simply feels right.

My mother knits, sews, cans, dries food and preserves it. She knows how to gather tea, berries, snare rabbits, milk cows, and churn butter. She can grow squash and melons from seeds she gathered the fall before. She is, as were the women who came before me, a repository of all of the homey virtues, and I am the first in a long line who has not saved the autumn's harvest in birch bark *makuks* and skin bags and in a cellar dry and cold with dust. I am the first who scratches the ground for pleasure, not survival, and grows flowers instead of potatoes. I record rather than practice the arts that filled the hands and days of my mother and her mother, and all the mothers going back into the shadows, when women wore names that told us who they were.

Questions for Active Reading

1. Erdrich describes a culture, the Anishinabe nation of Native Americans, for whom names and naming carried a "mystique." What is the connection, in this essay, between defining and naming a person?

2. Study Erdrich's description of her great-grandmother Virginia Grandbois. How does Erdrich use classification—or, more specifically, the impossibility of classification—to describe this woman who seems to "not live in the present or in any known time at all"? In how many ways is this elderly woman neither here nor there, neither completely Ojibwe nor French, neither at home nor away? What does Virginia Grandbois's story suggest about the fate of Native Americans?

3. In many traditional cultures men and women have more than one "name"—a name they were given at birth, another (often secret) name given at adolescence or initiation, a public name that links them to some adventure or characteristic (as in "The Names of Women"). How many different names are you known by? To what extent do you believe your name defines your character?

Questions for Thinking Critically

1. What are the "homey virtues" that Erdrich lovingly describes in paragraph 17, and what is Erdrich's own attitude toward those "virtues"?

2. What does the list of names in paragraph 4 suggest about the place of women in the traditional Anishinabe culture?

3. A "tribal roll" (paragraph 6) is a listing registered with the Bureau of Indian Affairs of all the members of a specific Native American *tribe* (or *nation*, which has come to be a more widely accepted term than *tribe*). What, according to Erdrich, was lost in the transcription of Anishinabe women's names onto official government documents? What other factors caused the changing, blurring, or loss of these women's identities and their stories?

"Men and Their Hidden Feelings"

by Richard Cohen

Richard Cohen has been a columnist for the *Washington Post* since 1976. Born in New York City, he graduated from New York University and began his career as a journalist in New York. He joined *The Washington Post* in 1968 after attending the Columbia University Graduate School of Journalism, and after doing, as he puts it, "some postgraduate work" at Fort Dix, New Jersey, and Fort Leonard Wood, Missouri. At the *Post* he covered all sorts of stories—night police, city hall, education, state government, and national politics. His reporting has carried him into perilous situations in the Middle East and Africa, and Ground Zero immediately after the September 11 attacks. Cohen's graceful writing and engagement with topics of intimate interest as well as global import have earned him a devoted readership.

My friends have no friends. They are men. They think they have friends, and if you ask them whether they have friends they will say yes, but they don't really. They think, for instance, that I'm their friend, but I'm not. It's OK. They're not my friends either.

The reason for that is that we are all men—and men, I have come to believe, cannot or will not have real friends. They have something else—companions, buddies, pals, chums, someone to drink with and someone to wench with and someone to lunch with, but no one when it comes to saying how they feel—especially how they hurt.

Women know this. They talk about it among themselves. I heard one woman describe men as the true Third World people—still not yet emerged. To women, this inability of men to say what they feel is a source of amazement and then anguish and then, finally, betrayal. Women will tell you all the time that they don't know the men they live with. They talk of long silences and drifting off and of keeping feelings hidden and never letting on that they are troubled or bothered or whatever.

If it's any comfort to women, they should know that it's nothing personal. Men treat other men the same way.

For instance, I know men who have suffered brutal professional setbacks and never mentioned it to their friends. I know of a guy who never told his best friend that his own son had a rare childhood disease. And I know others who never have sex with their wives, but talk to their friends as though they're living in the Playboy Mansion, either pretending otherwise or saying nothing.

This is something men learn early. It is something I learned from my father, who taught me, the way fathers teach sons, to keep my emotions to myself. I watched him and learned from him. One day we went to the baseball game, cheered and ate and drank, and the next day he was taken to the hospital with yet another ulcer attack. He had several of them. My mother said he worried a lot, but I saw none of this.

Legend has it that men talk a lot about sex. They don't. They talk about it only in the sense that it is treated like sports. They joke about it and rate women from 1 to 10. But they almost never talk about it in a way that matters—the quality of it. They almost never talk in real terms, in terms other than a cartoon, in terms that apply to them and the woman or women with whom they have a relationship.

Women do talk that way. Women talk about fulfillment, and they admit—maybe complain is the better word—to nonexistent sex lives. No man would admit to having virtually no sex life, yet there are plenty who do.

When I was a kid, I believed that it was men who had real friendships and women who did not. This seemed to be the universal belief, and boys would talk about this. We wondered about girls, about what made them so catty that they could not have friendships, and we really thought we were lucky to be men and have real friends.

5

10   We thought our friendships would last forever; we talked about them in some sort of Three Musketeer fashion—all for one and one for all. If one of us needed help, all of us would come running. We are still good friends, some of us, anyway, and I still feel that I will fight for them, but I don't think I could confide in them. No—not that.

Sometimes I think that men are walking relics—outmoded and outdated, programmed for some other age. We have all the essential qualities for survival in the wild and for success in battle, but we run like hell from talking about our feelings. We are, as the poet said in a different context, truly a thing of wonder.

Some women say that they have always had this ability to confide in one another—to talk freely. Others say that this is something relatively new—yet another benefit of the women's movement. I don't know. All I know is that they have it, and most men don't, and even the men who do—the ones who can talk about how they feel—talk to women. Have we been raised to think of feelings and sentiment as feminine? Can a man talk intimately with another man and not wonder about his masculinity? I don't know. I do know it sometimes makes the other men feel uncomfortable.

I know this is a subject that concerns me, and yet I find myself bottling it all up—keeping it all in. I've been on automatic pilot for years now.

It would be nice to break out of it. It would be nice to join the rest of the human race, connect with others in a way that makes sense, in a way that's meaningful—in a way that's more than a dirty joke and a slap on the back. I wonder whether it can be done.

15   If it can, it will happen because women will insist on it, because they themselves have shown the way, come out of the closet as women, talked about it, organized, defined an agenda, set their goals and admitted that as women—just as women—they have problems in common. So do men. It's time to talk about them.

QUESTIONS FOR ACTIVE READING

1. According to Cohen, what are the properties of men's relationships? Why does he think that these properties do not fit a definition of *friendship*?

2. What fundamental distinction does Cohen make between men and women? That is, how does he *classify* men and women? Do you agree with his classification? Why, or why not?

3. Examine the kind of evidence that Cohen offers in paragraph 5 to support his thesis. Would his argument be stronger if he had talked about, or named, *specific* men? What are the risks of generalizing about human behavior?

QUESTIONS FOR THINKING CRITICALLY

1. How do you think those men who might have considered themselves to be Cohen's "friends" felt after reading this column (which appeared in the *Washington Post*)? What are the risks that journalists—or any writers, really—take when they use material from their personal lives in their work?

2. Richard Cohen makes broad generalizations about categories of people. What are the inherent risks of making an argument based on very broad classifications or categories (such as "all men" or "all women")? How does Cohen successfully—or unsuccessfully—address those risks?

3. What are these "feelings" that Cohen describes? Is he arguing that men don't *have* feelings, or just that men don't *discuss* feelings? Do you think it's as important to discuss feelings as to have them? To what extent is your response to that question based on your upbringing? On your current peer group or profession?

"How Friendship Was 'Feminized'"

BY CAROL TAVRIS (b. 1944)

Social psychologist Carol Tavris earned her Ph.D. from the University of Michigan. She has long been interested in exploring human relationships and conveying and explaining the results of her observations to a wider audience. For many years, Tavris was the editor of the influential magazine *Psychology Today,* and her articles on human behavior have appeared in magazines as diverse as *The New York Times, Discover, Science Digest, Human Nature, New York, Vogue,* and *Harper's.* She is also the author of widely adopted college-level psychology textbooks and teaches in the department of psychology at UCLA. Among her books for a general audience are *Anger: The Misunderstood Emotion* (1989) and *Mismeasure of Women: Why Women Are Not the Better Sex, the Inferior Sex, or the Opposite Sex* (1993), which won the American Association for Applied and Preventive Psychology's Distinguished Media Contribution Award. In a review published in *The Chronicle of Higher Education* of books about women and anger, Tavris noted that "of course, gender differences are eternally fascinating, a source of amusement, anger, and exasperation; trying to understand one's own and the "other sex" is America's second-favorite indoor sport. (And it's part of the job description if you're female.)" Tavris is a Fellow of the American Psychological Association. She lives in Los Angeles, California.

Once upon a time and not so very long ago, everyone thought that men had the great and true-blue friendships. The cultural references stretched through time and art. Damon and Pythias, Hamlet and Horatio, Butch Cassidy and the Sundance Kid. The Lone Ranger never rode off with anyone but Tonto, and Laurel never once abandoned Hardy in whatever fine mess he got them into.

Male friendships were said to grow from the deep roots of shared experience and faithful camaraderie, whereas women's friendships were portrayed as shallow, trivial and competitive, like Scarlett O'Hara's with her sisters. Women, it was commonly claimed, would sell each other out for the right guy, and even for a good time with the wrong one.

Some social scientists told us that this difference was hard wired, a result of our evolutionary history. In the early 1970's, for example, the anthropologist Lionel Tiger argued in "Men in Groups" that "male bonding" originated in prehistoric male hunting groups and was carried on today in equivalent pack-like activities: sports, politics, business and war.

Apparently, women's evolutionary task of rummaging around in the garden to gather the odd yam or kumquat was a solo effort, so females do not bond in the same way. Women prattle on about their feelings, went the stereotype, but men act.

5   My, how times have changed. Today, we are deluged in the wave of best-selling books that celebrate female friendships—"Girlfriends," "Sisters," "Mothers and Daughters" and its clever clone, "Daughters and Mothers." The success of this genre is partly because the book market is so oriented to female readers these days.

But it is also a likely result of two trends that began in the 1970's and 1980's: Female scholars began to dispel the men-are-better stereotype in all domains and women became the majority of psychotherapists. The result was a positive reassessment of the qualities associated with women, including a "feminizing" of definitions of intimacy and friendship.

Accordingly, female friendships are now celebrated as the deep and abiding ones, based as they are on shared feelings and confidences. Male friendships are scorned as superficial, based as they are on shared interests in, say, the Mets and Michelle Pfeiffer.

In our psychologized culture, "intimacy" is defined as what many women like to do with their friends: talk, express feelings and disclose worries. Psychologists, most of whom are good talkers, validate this definition as the true measure of intimacy. For example, in a study of "intimacy maturity" in marriage, published in the *Journal of Personality and Social Psychology,* researchers equated "most mature" with "most verbally expressive." As a woman, I naturally think this is a perfectly sensible equation, but I also know it is an incomplete one. To label people mature or immature, you also have to know how they actually behave toward others.

What about all the men and women who support their families, put the wishes of other family members ahead of their own or act in moral and considerate ways when conflicts arise? They are surely mature, even if they are inarticulate or do not express their feelings easily. Indeed, what about all the men and women who define intimacy in terms of deeds rather than words: sharing activities, helping one another or enjoying companionable silence? Too bad for them. That's a "male" definition, and out of favor in these talky times.

10   Years ago, my husband had to have some worrisome medical tests, and the night before he was to go to the hospital we went to dinner with one of his best friends who was visiting from England. I watched, fascinated, as male stoicism combined with English reserve produced a decidedly unfemale-like encounter. They laughed, they told stories, they argued about movies, they reminisced. Neither mentioned the hospital, their worries or their affection for each other. They didn't need to.

It is true that women's style of intimacy has many benefits. A large body of research in health psychology and social psychology finds that women's greater willingness to talk about feelings improves their mental and physical health and makes it easier to ask for help.

But as psychologists like Susan Nolen-Hoeksema of Stanford University have shown, women's fondness for ruminating about feelings can also prolong depression, anxiety and anger. And it can keep women stuck in bad jobs or relationships, instead of getting out of them or doing what is necessary to make them better.

Books and movies that validate women's friendships are overdue, and welcome as long as they don't simply invert the stereotype. Playing the women-are-better game is fun, but it blinds us to the universal need for intimacy and the many forms that friendship takes. Maybe men could learn a thing or two about friendship from women. But who is to say that women couldn't learn a thing or two from them in exchange?

QUESTIONS FOR ACTIVE READING

1. What perspectives does Tavris present that are different from those of Richard Cohen? What ideas in her essay are similar to those in his?

2. In your own words, paraphrase both Cohen's and Tavris's definitions of *friendship*. Then, write your own definition of *friendship*, in which you explicitly agree or disagree with the ideas of Cohen and/or Tavris.

3. How does Tavris suggest classifying people as either "mature" or "immature"? Why does she make this distinction? What other characteristics would you say define someone (male or female) as "mature" or "immature"?

QUESTIONS FOR THINKING CRITICALLY

1. What is Tavris's larger point in the final paragraph of her essay? Is she the only author in this casebook to suggest a resolution, or at least a compromise? How does she use examples and illustrations to support this conclusion?

2. To a certain extent, both Tavris's and Cohen's views on the expression of feelings are culturally determined—they are both writing from a modern, middle-class, educated American perspective. In what ways does American popular culture support either Tavris's or Cohen's view of the expression of "feelings" by men and women? For example, think about the explosion of "confessional" television talk shows—why do such shows attract such large audiences, even though practically no one in the audience is personally acquainted with the "guests" and really has no reason to care about their "feelings"?

3. Do you look for the same qualities in a friend as you do in a romantic partner? What are the similarities and the differences, for you, in these two categories of relationships?

"Girl"

BY JAMAICA KINCAID (b. 1949)
FROM *At the Bottom of the River*

Born on the Caribbean island of Antigua and named Elaine Potter Richardson by her parents, Jamaica Kincaid left home for America at the age of sixteen to work as an au pair in the wealthy New York City suburbs of Westchester. She moved to New York City to study photography and then spent a year at Franconia College in New Hampshire. In 1973, facing her family's disapproval over her published writing, she changed her first name to Jamaica, to evoke her Caribbean heritage, and her last name to Kincaid, simply because she liked the sound of it. Her articles in such magazines as *Ingenue* led, eventually, to a staff writing position at *The New Yorker*, where she wrote on a wide range of subjects (including gardening, her great passion). Her first novel, *A Small Place* (1988), delves into the painful legacy of colonization in the Caribbean, a theme that recurs throughout her fiction. She has also explored the impact of colonialism's legacy at the more intimate level of family, in such novels as *Lucy* (1990), *The Autobiography of My Mother* (1996), and *My Brother* (1997).

Wash the white clothes on Monday and put them on the stone heap; wash the color clothes on Tuesday and put them on the clothesline to dry; don't walk barehead in the hot sun; cook pumpkin fritters in very hot sweet oil; soak your little cloths right after you take them off; when buying cotton to make yourself a nice blouse, be sure that it doesn't have gum on it, because that way it won't hold up well after a wash; soak salt fish overnight before you cook it; is it true that you sing benna in Sunday school?; always eat your food in such a way that it won't turn someone else's stomach; on Sundays try to walk like a lady and not like the slut you are so bent on becoming; don't sing benna in Sunday school; you mustn't speak to wharf-rat boys, not even to give directions; don't eat fruits on the street—flies will follow you; *but I don't sing benna on Sundays at all and never in Sunday school*; this is how to sew on a button; this is how to make a buttonhole for the button you have just sewed on; this is how to hem a dress when you see the hem coming down and so to prevent yourself from looking like the slut I know you are so bent on becoming; this is how you iron your father's khaki shirt so that it doesn't have a crease; this is how you iron your father's khaki pants so they don't have a crease; this is how you grow okra—far from the house, because okra tree harbors red ants; when you are growing dasheen, make sure it gets plenty of water or else it makes your throat itch when you are eating it; this is how you sweep a corner; this is how you sweep a whole house; this is how you sweep a yard; this is how you smile to someone you don't like too much; this is how you smile to someone you don't like at all; this is how you smile to someone you like completely; this is how you set a table for tea; this is how you set a table for dinner; this is how you set a table for dinner with an important guest; this is how you set a table for lunch; this is how you set a table for breakfast; this is how to behave in the presence of men who don't know you very well, and this way they won't recognize immediately the slut I have warned you against becoming; be sure to wash every day, even if it is with your own spit; don't squat down to play marbles—you are not a boy, you know; don't pick people's flowers—you might catch something; don't throw stones at blackbirds, because it might not be a blackbird at all; this is how to make a bread pudding; this is how to make doukona; this is how to make pepper pot; this is how to make a good medicine for a cold; this is how to make a good medicine to throw away a child before it even becomes a child; this is how to catch a fish; this is how to throw back a fish you don't like, and that way something bad won't fall on you; this is how to bully a man; this is how a man bullies you; this is how to love a man, and if this doesn't work there are other ways, and if they don't work don't feel too bad about giving up; this is how to spit up in the air if you feel like it, and this is how to move quick so that it doesn't fall on you; this is how to make ends meet; always squeeze bread to make sure it's fresh; *but what if the baker won't let me feel the bread?;* you mean to say that after all you are really going to be the kind of woman who the baker won't let near the bread?

QUESTIONS FOR ACTIVE READING

1. Who is speaking in this monologue, and who is being spoken to? How can you tell?
2. What are the properties of correct behavior for a "girl," according to this speaker, and what are the consequences of defying that behavior?
3. There's a phrase that's repeated three times in this monologue. What is that sentence? Why is it repeated, and how does it foreshadow the very last lines of this monologue?

QUESTIONS FOR THINKING CRITICALLY

1. When you were growing up, who told you how to behave? Did anyone ever tell you (either explicitly, or by implication) that there were correct ways to behave like a "lady" or a "gentleman"? Were these household rules, or just friendly guidelines? Is there anything that the speaker of this monologue says that reminds you of something you were told when you were a child?
2. What kind of future does the speaker of this monologue foresee for the listener? Is there anything surprising in the advice given?
3. Did you find anything comic in this monologue? If so, what made you laugh, and why?

Using Concepts to Classify

When you apply a concept to an object, idea, or experience, you are in effect classifying it by placing it in a group of things that are defined by the properties or requirements of the concept. In fact, the same things can often be classified in many different ways. For example, if someone handed you a tomato and asked, "Which category does this tomato belong in, fruit or vegetable?" how would you respond?

The fact is that a tomato can be classified as both a fruit and a vegetable because its botanical definition does not seem consistent with its uses as a food.

Let's consider another example. Imagine that you are walking on undeveloped land with some other people when you come across an area of soggy ground with long grass and rotting trees. One person in your group surveys the parcel and announces, "That's a smelly marsh. All it does is breed mosquitoes. It ought to be covered with landfill and built on so that we can use it productively." Another member of your group disagrees with the classification "smelly marsh," stating, "This is a wetland of great ecological value. There are many plants and animals that need this area and other areas like it to survive. Wetland areas also help to prevent the rivers from flooding, by absorbing excess water during heavy rains." Which person is right? Should the wet area be classified as a "smelly marsh" or as a "valuable wetland"? Actually, the wet area can be classified both ways. The classification that you select depends on your needs and your interests.

These examples illustrate how the way you classify reflects and influences the way you see the world, the way you think about the world, and the way you behave in the world. You classify many of the things in your experience differently than others do because of your individual needs, interests, and values. For instance,

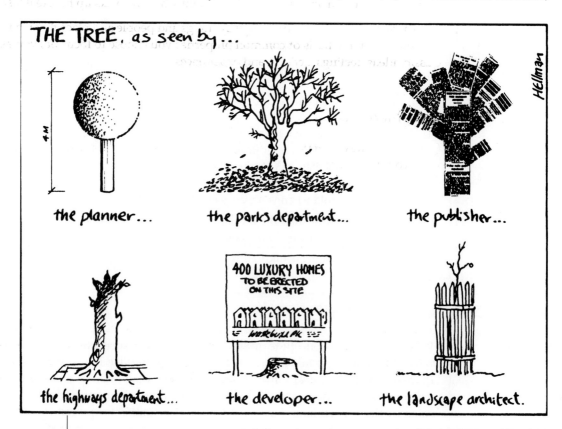

THE TREE, as seen by...

the planner...   the parks department...   the publisher...

the highways department...   the developer...   the landscape architect.

smoking marijuana might be classified by some as "use of a dangerous drug" and by others as a "harmless good time." Some view SUVs as "gas guzzlers"; others see the same cars as "safer, more comfortable vehicles." Some people categorize body piercing as "perverse abuse" while others think of it as "creative self-expression." The way you classify aspects of your experience reflects the kind of individual you are and the way you think and feel about the world.

Classifying People and Their Actions

You also place people in various categories. The specific categories you select depend on who you are and how you see the world. Similarly, each of us is placed in a variety of classifications by other people. Here, for instance, are some of the categories in which certain people have placed one of this book's authors:

Classification	People Who Classify Him
First-born son	His parents
Taxpayer	Internal Revenue Service
Tickler	His children
Bagel with cream cheese	Restaurant where he picks up his breakfast

Not only do you continually classify things and people and place them in various groups on the basis of common properties you choose to focus on; you also classify ideas, feelings, actions, and experiences.

THINKING-
WRITING
ACTIVITY

Classification and Your Self

List some of the different ways that you can be classified and identify the people who would classify you that way.

_____   _____

_____   _____

_____   _____

Writing and Classifying

The intellectual act of classifying is an essential part of writing in three ways.

First, writings themselves are classified into many different forms. You know this already, of course. Novels, poems, essays, news stories, blogs, emails, lab reports—the list is almost endless. And each of these forms of writing has subclassifications: science fiction, political blogs, romance novels, and so forth. Different classifications of writing, or _genres_, have different purposes and styles.

Classification and Ethics

Each of these following classifications represents a separate legal concept, one with its own properties and referents (examples). Of course, even when you clearly understand what the concept means, the complexity of the circumstances often makes it difficult to determine which concept applies.

Classification	Circumstance	Example
1. Manslaughter	Killing someone accidentally	Driving while intoxicated
2. Self-defense	_____	_____
3. Premeditated murder	_____	_____
4. Mercy killing	_____	_____
5. Diminished capacity	_____	_____

Court cases raise complex and disturbing issues. During a trial, trying first to identify the appropriate concept of the crime and then to determine which of the related concepts—*guilty* or *not guilty*—also applies is a challenging process. This is also true of many of life's other complex situations: you must work hard at identifying appropriate concepts to apply to the circumstances you are trying to make sense of, then be prepared to change or modify these concepts on the basis of new information or better insights. Explain, for instance, why the killing of another person might be classified in different ways, depending on the circumstances.

You are aware of this as a reader. As a college writer, you must become more aware of using styles and formats appropriate to the kind of writing that you are doing for your classes.

Second, almost any piece of writing is organized by classifying material into sections, chapters, or paragraphs in which the content is sorted and arranged in logical ways. Usually, writers put similar material together so that readers can think about related items that have been assembled for their easy comprehension. You—and other writers—do this when you revise drafts to create good paragraphs that each focus on one idea. You do this when you are sorting your research notes into topics (or categories) in order to organize a paper, report, or presentation.

Third, much writing concentrates on presenting *kinds, categories, types,* or *classifications* of concepts. Readings in this chapter discuss different classifications of masculinity and feminity. This book itself is divided into different categories of approaches to thinking and writing.

THINKING-
WRITING
ACTIVITY

Identifying Classifications

1. Think of any reading selection in this book that you recall as being well organized. Turn to it and see how the writer classified or sorted the material into logical arrangements. Note the classifications of information. Perhaps topic sentences of paragraphs will show you what the writer has done.

2. Share your observations with classmates. See if they agree.

3. How did analyzing this piece of writing provide ideas about organizing your own work?

Defining Concepts

When you define a concept, you usually identify the necessary properties or requirements that determine when the concept can be applied. In fact, the word *definition* is derived from a Latin word meaning "boundary." A definition provides the boundaries of whatever territory in your experience can be described by the concept.

Definitions also use examples of the concept being defined. Consider the following:

Oxymoron	A rhetorical figure in which incongruous or contradictory terms are combined as in *a deafening silence* and *a mournful optimist.* —*The American Heritage Dictionary of the English Language*
An edible	Good to eat and wholesome to digest, as a worm to a toad, a toad to a snake, a snake to a pig, a pig to a man, and a man to a worm. —Ambrose Bierce
Facts, theories	Facts and theories are different things, not rungs in a hierarchy of increasing certainty. Facts are the world's data. Theories are structures of ideas that explain and interpret facts. Facts do not go away when scientists debate rival theories to explain them. Einstein's theory of gravitation replaced Newton's, but apples did not suspend themselves in mid-air pending the outcome. —Stephen Jay Gould

Contrast these definitions with the one illustrated in the following passage from Charles Dickens's *Hard Times:*

"Bitzer," said Thomas Gradgrind. "Your definition of a horse." "Quadruped. Graminivorous. Forty teeth, namely twenty-four grinders, four eye teeth, and twelve incisive. Sheds coat in the spring; in marshy countries sheds hoofs, too. Hoofs hard, but requiring to be shod with iron. Age known by marks in mouth." That (and much more) Bitzer. "Now girl number twenty," said Mr. Gradgrind, "you know what a horse is."

Although Bitzer has certainly done an admirable job of listing some of the necessary properties or requirements of the concept *horse*, it is unlikely that "girl number twenty" has any better idea of what a horse is than she had before since Bitzer's definition relies exclusively on a technical listing of the properties characterizing the concept *horse* without giving any examples that might illustrate the concept more completely. Definitions like this which rely exclusively on a technical description of the concept's properties are not very helpful unless you already know what the concept means. A more concrete way of communicating the concept *horse* would be to point out various animals that qualify as horses and other animals that do not. You could also explain why they do not. (For example, "That can't be a horse because it has two humps and its legs are far too long.")

Although examples do not take the place of a clearly understood definition, they are often very useful in clarifying, supplementing, and expanding such a definition. If someone asked you, "What is a horse?" and you replied by giving examples of different kinds of horses (thoroughbred racing horses, plow horses for farming, quarter horses for cowhands, circus horses), you certainly would be communicating a good portion of the meaning of *horse*. Giving examples of a concept complements and clarifies the necessary requirements for the correct use of that concept.

Giving an effective definition of a concept requires

- Identifying the general qualities of the concept, which determine when it can be correctly applied
- Classifying it, which means identifying its category, type, or "family"
- Using appropriate examples that embody its general qualities
- Differentiating it from other items in its classification

The process of providing definitions of concepts is basically the same process that you use to develop concepts.

Writing Thoughtfully to Define Concepts

Writing a full definition, often called an *extended definition*, is among the most important and most difficult of writing activities. Defining terms is a necessary part of college-level writing and speaking. For productive discussions about complex issues, all involved must agree on the meanings of significant terms, so clear definitions are often required. Difficulties arise because significant terms related to complex issues are usually abstract concepts, with possibilities of different definitions for different people. For example, the common political terms *conservative* and *liberal* often have varied meanings, even to people who identify themselves as one or the other.

No one has much trouble agreeing on definitions of physical objects. A table, a tree, a television set—not many arguments arise about what these objects are. But like *liberal* and *conservative*, concepts such as *religion, love, democracy, femininity*, and *masculinity* can be defined in different ways. If people discussing ideas like these do not establish definitions, their discussions will not be productive. Worse, these discussions sometimes lead to disagreements, arguments, and even wars. The readings and Thinking-Writing Activities in this chapter have been selected and planned to demonstrate the importance of definitions.

Notice how with both simple objects and complex concepts, defining is somewhat easier as long as a single word is being examined. As soon as modifying and classifying ideas are added, defining becomes more challenging and more significant to critical thinking. A *beautiful* table, a *good* tree to plant in a *small* yard, the *best* computer to buy for *your family room*—now these objects call for fuller definitions. The *kind* of democracy that can work in a country with a *history of despotism*, the *kind* of love that a *parent* might have for an *adult child*—these are the types of concepts that people must define in order to present arguments, to make decisions, to solve problems. These are the kinds of terms that you might want to define in the Writing Project in this chapter because they are the kinds that involve judgments; they are important to our lives because they influence our actions.

Clear, satisfying definitions can be as extended as book chapters, articles, or entire books; however, a definition often will be developed in a paragraph or two as a vital part of a paper or report. In the Writing Project for this chapter, you will write an essay that defines; you will see the need for using a variety of thinking/organizing patterns as you develop it. The guidelines for writing definitions are not fixed rules; there may be times when you would have good reasons for varying or adapting some of them. Try to use them, though, unless you have good reason not to.

GUIDELINES FOR WRITING DEFINITIONS OF CONCEPTS	1. Establish the need for a definition. Why is it needed? Do people disagree on the meaning of the concept? Are there multiple meanings? Are earlier definitions no longer satisfactory? Is this a new concept or new terminology? 2. Choose carefully the word or words in which you state the concept. Definitions provide precision, so you need to be sure that you have presented the concept in the words that are most indicative. 3. Incorporate two kinds of dictionary definitions: the short one that gives meaning, as in a regular college dictionary, and a longer one giving the history of the word's usage, which can be found in the *Oxford English Dictionary*. Word origins and past meanings can often illuminate the meaning that you want to present. 4. Be sure that you identify the category into which the concept fits. 5. Show comparative thinking. Point out similar concepts, but then make clear how your concept is distinct. Think of analogies that can illuminate the meaning of the concept.

6. Provide specific examples to show what the concept means. Illustrative anecdotes are often effective.

7. Include the meaning of the concept in the thesis statement. Give careful thought to where you state the thesis.

8. Throughout your definition, emphasize that you are establishing the meaning you believe the concept has within the context that you have identified.

9. Address the foregoing principles in separate paragraphs or sections of the definition. Provide each paragraph with a clear topic sentence whenever appropriate.

10. Document any sources that you use. Introduce source material into your definition, explain and comment on it, and cite it correctly.

Writing Project: Defining an Important Concept

This chapter has included readings, questions, and Thinking-Writing Activities that encourage you to define concepts that affect your life. Be sure to reread what you wrote for the activities; you may be able to use some of that material in completing this project.

Write an essay in which you define a concept that is important to your life now or to your future life. Include explanations of why this concept is significant for you and why it needs defining or redefining. You may want to think of a concept that is expressed in a phrase rather than in a single word. Include material from two sources in addition to any dictionaries that you consult. Integrate your sources into your essay and document them as your instructor advises. After you have drafted your essay, revise it to the best of your ability. Follow your instructor's directions for topic limits, length, format, and so on.

Begin by considering the key elements in the Thinking-Writing Model in Chapter 1 on pages 7–9.

The Writing Situation

Purpose   You have several purposes here. You want to think about and formulate a definition that will be significant as you continue your college studies, decide on your profession, or enter a new phase in your personal life. Indeed, all of us need to be able to define the complex terms that are foundations for our thinking, our decisions, and our actions in life. In addition, you can improve your ability to present a full definition in order to clarify your own thinking and to increase your audience's understanding.

Audience   You have a multilevel audience. *You* are an important audience, for in facing the challenge of defining a complex concept, you can think more clearly about some aspect of your life. Your classmates can learn from your definition and also can be a valuable audience in peer reviews of a draft, reacting as intelligent readers who are not as knowledgeable as you about the concept that pertains to your life. In addition, you should think about and identify people outside your class who might enjoy or profit from reading your definition. If you are writing about a concept that impacts people in your community or on your campus, your paper can both share information and urge action.

Subject   All of us need to be able to define abstract, complex terms that are foundations for our thinking, our decisions, and our actions in life. College courses, family life, spiritual concerns, and romantic relationships all involve concepts that need to be well defined. Clear definitions help us understand what we mean when we speak and write, understand what others mean when they communicate with us, and—most important—avoid confusion and conflict. For this assignment, try to identify an important concept that is central to how you see yourself and your future. Concepts like *creative expression, enlightened free choice, authentic person, fulfillment, achieving potential, meaningful empathy, social responsibility, critical thinker,* and (of course) *thoughtful writer* are all examples with broad implications in a person's life.

Writer   This project provides you with the opportunity to participate in the "conversation of ideas" that is the lifeblood of thoughtful, reflective people in a society. By defining a complex concept, you are explaining how the concept you have selected has personal meaning for you. You are also suggesting to others—your audience—how they might think about your analysis of the concept. The definition you propose may help them understand something in their experience more clearly, or it may provide an added meaning they have not previously considered. The outside sources integrated into your analysis ensure that your definition is grounded in a common understanding that goes beyond your own experience.

The Writing Process

The following sections will guide you through the recursive stages of generating, planning, drafting, and revising as you work on an essay in which you define a significant concept. Try to be particularly conscious of both the critical thinking you do as you articulate your definition and the critical thinking and decision making you do as you revise.

Generating Ideas

- Refer back to the responses you wrote for the Thinking-Writing Activities for the readings on gender issues. These concepts are important in many people's lives, so perhaps you will write about one of them—or perhaps what you read and wrote will lead you to another concept to define.

- Think about the activities or concerns that are central to your life. Some of these are probably rather serious, as are the subjects discussed in this chapter, but some parts are surely more lighthearted, like sports you play or watch, television comedies, thriller movies, or parties.

- Next, think of concepts inherent in some of your activities, such as a satisfying relationship or what it means to be a good athlete, college student, or practitioner of your religion.

- Now, list the properties of two or three concepts that you have identified. Include specific examples. How should each example be classified?

- Think about why any of these concepts need to be defined or redefined. Do people agree on the meaning? Have you formulated a meaning that is more precise and accurate?

- Share your lists and thinking with classmates and, if you can, with people involved in the area in which the concept is important.

- Use as many thinking patterns as you can to discover ideas about your concept. What is it different from? similar to? analogous to? Describe it; think about what causes it; think about what effects it has.

- Look up the concept's key words in a good college-level dictionary and also in the *Oxford English Dictionary*. Ask your instructor or one of your college librarians to explain the *OED* to you. See if you can use any of your concept's word history in your definition.

- Freewrite for at least five minutes about why the concept is important to your life, why it needs to be defined, and what information needs to be in your definition.

Defining a Focus

- Look at your freewriting and lists to see what main idea you are moving toward in your definition. Write this idea in any way that you can.

- Now draft a thesis statement that gives the key ideas in your definition. Recently a student defining *freedom of religion* had this as her thesis sentence: "To me, freedom of religion means more than simply being able to practice our religions as we believe that we should; it also means that we must understand and respect other people's religions." Another student, working on a definition of today's *superwoman*, wrote, "The main properties of a superwoman are being capable, tenacious, and independent."

- Be sure that your thesis statement emphasizes the meaning of the concept that you are defining.

Organizing Ideas   Essays emphasizing definition are not easy to organize because there are so many approaches to a clear definition of a complex concept. Because the thesis—the essence of the definition—needs to be placed in a context and explained in a number of ways, the question of where to state the thesis is especially crucial. This is the kind of essay in which it might come at the end. When you state the thesis at the end, you need to lead up to it or preview it throughout the essay. However, you will want to think of stating the thesis provisionally near the beginning and referring to it elsewhere in the paper as you establish your definition.

Identify the approaches that you have used in your generative writing and early drafts. Where have you used contrast, comparison, analogy, narration, and so on? The material developed by each of these approaches is likely to form a paragraph. The definitions that you have found in your dictionary and in the *OED* will need a paragraph or two to connect them with the definition that you are developing. As always, give careful thought to paragraphing. Try your drafted paragraphs in different orders to discover which will best help your readers understand your definition.

Because it is important that your readers understand the need for a definition, explaining that need is an effective way to begin. Explaining the significance of this concept in your life might be part of the beginning or conclusion.

Drafting   Be sure to identify source material as you include it in your draft. See the Appendix for further guidelines on citing source material

Begin with the easiest paragraph to draft. Explaining the concept's significance in your life is likely to be easy since you are writing about your thoughts and feelings; showing the need for a definition should not be difficult because you are writing about one of your convictions. As you draft, be sure that each paragraph contains real-life examples that pertain to the meaning of the concept—unless for some good reason a specific paragraph does not need examples.

After you draft your paragraphs, make every effort to write topic sentences that focus on how the material in each paragraph helps to establish the meaning of your concept.

As you draft the conclusion, be sure that it provides a satisfying ending with some reference to the thesis and emphasis on the meaning of the concept.

Revising, Editing, and Proofreading   Use the step-by-step method on pages 152–154 in Chapter 6 to revise and polish your essay.

The following two essays use definition and classification to define concepts. The first essay explores the meaning of the term *freedom*; the second investigates the concept of *masculinity*.

Student Writing

Nawang Doma Sherpa's Writing Process

An immigrant from the Himalayan nation of Nepal, student Nawang Doma Sherpa's perspective on *freedom* is informed both by the extraordinary choices and challenges she has made in her life as well as by her strong Buddhist faith. In her essay, she examines the concept of *freedom* through the lenses of both her immigrant experience and her faith, describing how achieving a sense of *freedom* has allowed her to define herself and her life. To generate ideas for her essay, she returned to her journal notes on the Thinking-Writing activity "Defining a Concept."

General qualities of religion: I know what I believe, but everyone has their own very private reasons for what they believe in—it seems like everyone in my class has a different religion, but their faith—why they believe, or how they believe is the same. I think we're all looking for reasons for our lives. Why are we here?

Classification? What kind of human activity is it?: It's a mysterious activity. There has always been religion just as there have been dreams. In Nepal our religion, Buddhism, determined so much—from how our days were structured to how we treated our parents and our neighbors. Here it seems like everyone has a different religion, or no religion at all. American society sometimes seems very religious—there's lots of talk about God and religion in politics for example—but it's not like the kind of everyday practice and discipline that I grew up with

What is my definition of religion?: For me Buddhism is what I practice as well as what I believe. I live my life as a Buddhist, and it helps me to make rational choices about my life. Being free and contributing to make this world a better and more peaceful place is the only aim of Buddhism.

Freedom for Enlightenment

by Nawang Doma Sherpa

Human freedom is dependent upon two qualities: our relationships with others, and our need to believe in a higher purpose for our lives. All the different roles that each of us play in this world—child, student, peer, parent, and countless other relations—are intricate and interwoven with each other. In addition to the roles we each play, the mysterious phenomenon of religion both brings people together (as families and as entire societies) and drives them apart. In my own life, I have struggled with determining my freedom both in relationship to my family's traditions and expectations, and to my Buddhist faith.

I define myself on the basis of my achievements and flaws. In other words, I am who I am because of what I have done in my past—not because of the high goals and beautiful dreams I have set for my future. Both my own experience and the teachings of Buddhism have shown me that the future is both unpredictable and unknowable, but the past and present are reality and fact. The philosopher Jean-Paul Sartre noted that "man is nothing else but what he makes of himself," and I have come to share this view. We are free to determine our own fates, but we are not always fully aware of the responsibilities that come with this freedom. For me, religion and family duties helped me to acknowledge both my freedom and my responsibilities. However, it has not always been easy to accept these things.

I was born in Nepal into a middle class Sherpa family. They allowed me to pursue an education by attending a private girl's school for nine years and then a co-education school for another two years. After I graduated, I decided on my own to come to the United States. I moved to New York City, applied to college, and I now work to support myself and pay my tuition. This was a very unusual decision for a young girl from a traditional Nepalese family to make. Even though I am grown up, I still miss the love and care of my parents, especially the comfort of my mother's embrace and our home. My parents wanted me to stay in Nepal after I graduated, because it is traditional for girls of my social class to get married after they complete high school. But I made the decision to leave, to travel halfway around the world and live on very little money, entirely of my own free will. But if you ask me if I plan to spend the rest of my life away from Nepal, my family, and my home, I would not be able to answer you. I can only say that I will continue to make decisions based on my experience and my faith.

I practiced Buddhism, like most people in Nepal, and I feel free as a Buddhist. I could change my religion if I wanted to, because Buddhism encourages people to determine their own best choices for themselves rather than adhere strictly to one "perfect" or "correct" God. For me, Buddhism is rational. Ancestors have passed along the teaching of Buddha from generation to generation, and the core of that teaching is that we can free ourselves by understanding our inner self. The "eight-fold path" that all Buddhists follow determines how we relate to ourselves and to each other: right speech, understanding, good deeds, determination, effort, awareness, thinking, and living. By understanding and accepting responsibility for our actions and beliefs, we achieve freedom. This makes us more responsible for who we are because by following this eight-fold path we will never hurt others and we will never fail in creating our image. Being free and contributing to make this world a better and more peaceful place is the only aim of Buddhism.

Freedom is possible, but with it comes responsibility. Freedom allows us to be conscious and aware, to explore and create new options and make choices that define us in the future. To deny your freedom is to deny responsibility for the choices that you make. I exercised free choice, and at the same time achieved freedom from my society's conservative expectations, by choosing to pursue a college education in America rather than getting married and staying in Nepal. But I have to accept the responsibility for this decision: my family misses me terribly, and I sometimes find it very difficult to balance work and school and to support myself financially. I am fortunate to have both the support of my family and the strength of my religion as I move forward into my future.

Jorden Carlsen's Writing Process

In response to an assignment asking him to develop an extended definition of an abstract concept related to the course readings, Jorden Carlsen, a student at City College of San Francisco, chose to explore the concept of *masculinity*.

Actually, I was stuck at first on choosing a topic. But masculinity is an interesting concept to me because its meaning is kind of vague; people aren't sure exactly what it means. So I thought it was open enough that I could come up with my own conclusions about it. What I wanted to do was to get the audience, my classmates and teacher, to agree that masculinity can be a positive ideal, and I didn't want to lose them along the way. I didn't want to make my essay too complex or outlandish.

To get started, I sat down and began writing ideas about masculinity on a piece of paper, just a list. From that, I could decide which direction to take. Then I began to do research. I used Google to find newspaper and magazine articles. I read about ten articles, and then I went back to my list to see which ideas I could support. Then I highlighted the parts of the articles I wanted to use to support these ideas.

I got rid of some of the ideas on my list and added some new ones. While I was doing this, I was able to write some sentences that I thought sounded good. These later became either topic sentences or supports in the body paragraphs of my essay.

Doing the research helped me get going. I could see that I could combine some of the ideas on my list to go together to form paragraphs. From there, I did an outline.

Deciding what ideas to use at the beginning was the hardest part. I began with what had attracted me to the topic, that the concept isn't exactly clear.

In the body, I decided to deal with some negative ideas about masculinity first and then move on to more positive ones and my own personal ideas. As I wrote, I actually convinced myself even more that my thesis was correct, that the concept of masculinity can be a positive tool for men. So my conclusion came right out of that. I was sold on the idea.

Masculinity Makes a Good Man

by Jorden Carlsen

Nowadays it is difficult to pin down exactly what characteristics make someone a "real" man, and when most of us say a "real man," we mean a masculine man. We know that such a man should be physically strong and not run away at the sight of a spider, but what else has come to mean a man is masculine? To some being masculine means that a man is never able to show any sign or weakness, and to others it means that all a man need do is be a good provider. I think there is more to it than that. I think that masculinity should be an ideal for men to live up to. It shouldn't limit a man's emotion or make him afraid to be seen as weak. Instead, the ideal of masculinity should be something that can encourage men to live up to their full potential in life. It should be something that makes men want to be good providers, stay in good physical shape, and be generally reliable. Masculinity can and should be used as a tool to help men make the most of themselves.

For some people the idea of *masculinity* has become self-defeating. For them it has become synonymous with experiencing uncomfortable social pressures, denying their emotions, having unsavory world-views, or having a fear of showing any kind of weakness. Sara B. Kimmel explains one view of this present situation in her article "Measuring Masculine Body Ideal Distress: Development of a Measure." This article is mainly concerned with many men's dissatisfaction with their bodies and the stress this dissatisfaction causes them. Kimmel notes that "boys and men are comparing themselves to increasingly unattainable masculine body images and are thus increasingly likely to evaluate their body image negatively." For these men, wanting to have a body that they see as masculine has made them unhappy with the body they have. As bad as it may sound, I think slight dissatisfaction can be a good thing for people who are out of shape in that it can encourage them to exercise or eat right, but like many things, can go too far and do more harm than good by, for example, leading to steroid use or eating disorders.

Kimmel also mentions an instrument called "The Conformity to Masculinity Norms Inventory," which has been used to assess conformity to masculine norms in the dominant culture in U.S. society. I found something among the topics included in their survey disturbing. Two of the factors that were included in the "Masculinity Norms" were "Power over

Women" and "Disdain for Homosexuals." Why is it [that] people see these things as masculine? I certainly cannot tell you. I believe that a man should respect people, not control or show disdain for them. Doing so can only display a man's insecurities and other shortcomings that take away from the depth of character that makes a real man.

Another drawback to masculinity is that some believe that a real man should not show his emotion, or even worse, not have any. Is this another example of something taken too far? I think it is possible that this belief could have its origins in men's need to do what needs to be done. It has served men best in the past to be able to put their emotions aside and deal with the task at hand, but when there is no task that needs to be done, men don't need to hide their emotions. Yet in his essay titled "Complexion," Richard Rodriguez wrote, "More important than any of this was the fact that a man never verbally revealed his emotions" (516). Through his writing Rodriguez is able to show his range of emotion, which displays his personal strength to face adversity and shows that being emotional can be a part of being a "real" man.

Having a weakness doesn't make a man less masculine; it makes him human. But for some reason it has become construed that for a man to be masculine, he cannot have any weakness. This had led to many kinds of negative consequences for men the world over. I believe this a direct link to male violence. Many men now think that if anyone in any way, no matter how small, threatens to expose a weakness on their part, this person must be violently attacked in order to demonstrate that they are not weak. This has led to all kinds of despicable behavior from verbal attacks to gang warfare. These men don't see the irony that this behavior is covering up the bigger weakness of their own insecurity. Being vulnerable doesn't make men less masculine; it is how they handle the situation and themselves that makes them who they are.

What I believe to be basic to the view of what a man is supposed to be is his ability to provide. The pinnacle of manhood is his role of the hunter-gatherer. When a man can feed and clothe himself and his family, he is on the forefront of manliness. One of the main ideas in an article titled "Man-of-Action Heroes: The Pursuit of Heroic Masculinity in Every-day Consumption," written by Douglas B. Holt, professor of Marketing at the University of Oxford, and Craig J. Thompson, professor of Marketing at the University of Wisconsin, is that one of the main ideals of masculinity in America is that of a man who is a provider, what they call in the article "Breadwinner Masculinity" (427). These are the men who throughout history have been there for their families, clans, or villages, and have been able to keep everyone alive by bringing home the bacon. It may not always be glorious, but putting dinner on the table is often much more important to a culture's well-being than fighting on the battlefield. This is why men who work hard are seen as masculine. Advances in technology are taking working men farther and farther from hunting game and gathering crops, but that doesn't make them any less masculine. A man who spends eight hours a day doing quality control at the computer factory is putting dinner on the table just as much as an iron worker, and they both deserve the title of *masculine breadwinner*.

Take a moment to picture in your mind a masculine man. Chances have it that the man you saw wasn't extremely overweight or had arms that wouldn't stretch a rubber band put around his biceps. When most of us think of a masculine man, we tend to think of one who has an amount of physical prowess. This is mostly likely because strong men are more likely to be better protectors and better suited for the kind of physical labor that in the past kept our predecessors fed. This ideal can be good to encourage a man to stay healthy and in good shape. I know this from personal experience. When my running shoes have a fine layer of dust and I no longer recognize any of the people who work behind the counter at the gym, I know that I'm not living up to part of my potential. A man doesn't have to be an Olympic bodybuilder to have a masculine body. I see it more as a matter of physical ability. I don't do aerobic exercise because I think I'm fat. What gets my running shoes on is my personal drive to have physical stamina in case of the event I may need it, or want it. The physical side of masculinity is something that all men can tap into as encouragement to keep their body physically able, no matter their body type.

Much of what people perceive about masculinity is strength, but I think most people miss the most important strength of all: strength of character. This comes in many forms, from that of reliability to that of integrity. It's what I think about when I think about how a good man should behave. Real men do not take candy from children. They are the defenders of what is right and the ones who are willing to face risk for others. This is where the depth of masculinity lies. A man who is not a provider or [possessor] of any physical prowess will suddenly take on an air of masculinity when he stands up for what is right. Rodriguez wrote in his essay, "To be formal is to be steady. A man of responsibility, a good provider. Someone formal is also constant. A person to be relied upon in adversity" (515). This is from the part of the essay where he is describing one of the three F's, the concept of what it is to be a man. Living up to the masculine ideal of character isn't always the easiest form of masculinity, but it is the most fulfilling.

Masculinity can be a good ideal for a man to live up to. It also can be taken too far or interpreted in a bad way that takes away from a man's character or leads him to unhealthy behavior, but if viewed correctly, and in the right context, it can be a guide for all men to help them live up to their potential. It can give them drive in life to do things that they may not have otherwise seen or had the motivation to do. *Masculinity* is just a concept, but it is one that has the power to lead a man to be more than he is, and that makes it powerful.

Works Cited

Holt, Douglas B., and Craig J. Thompson. "Man-of-Action Heroes: The Pursuit of Heroic Masculinity in Everyday Consumption." <u>Journal of Consumer Research</u> Sept. 2004: 425–439.

Kimmel, Sara B. "Measuring Masculine Body Ideal Distress: Development of a Measure." <u>International Journal of Men's Health</u> Spring 2004. 18 April 2005 <http://www.findarticles.com/p/articles/mi_m0PAU/is_1_3/ai_n6191073/print>.

Rodriguez, Richard. "Complexion." <u>Great Writing</u>. Ed. Harvey S. Weiner and Nora Eisenberg. 3rd ed. San Francisco: McGraw, 2002: 513–516.

Alternative Writing Projects

Compare and contrast how a distinctive concept (such as *masculinity* or *femininity*) is understood by two different cultures or social groups. Joseph Berger's essay (page 224 in Chapter 8) is an example of such an essay. You may draw upon your personal experience as part of your evidence to support your definition of a concept, and you might consider interviewing someone from a different culture or social group to compare the person's first-hand experiences with your own.

9

Exploring Perspectives and Relationships

Writing to Compare and Evaluate

> *Nothing that God ever made is the same thing to more than one person.*
>
> —*Zora Neale Hurston*

Chapter 7 introduced the concept of *perceptions* and showed how writers use their perceptions when they describe, narrate, and explain processes. As critical thinkers, active readers, and thoughtful writers, however, we need to go beyond simply recognizing that people have different perceptions. We have to think carefully about perceptions. In addition, we need to see how *perceptions*—messages from the senses—are connected to *perspectives*—points of view that develop from and also influence perceptions.

This chapter emphasizes critical evaluation and comparison of perceptions and perspectives. It will help you think about the differing points of view that people bring to what they say and write. Perspectives often conflict with one another, so you then must try to determine which one makes the most sense. You need to be able to analyze the differences and similarities that you find.

Because so many life situations and college assignments involve comparing and contrasting perspectives in an organized way, this chapter presents strategies for using comparative analysis in thinking and writing. The Writing Project asks you to analyze different perspectives on one event or issue.

Perceptions and Perspectives

Perspectives, or points of view, are what people express when they speak and write and also the vantage points from which they perceive events or issues. So a complex interaction exists between perceptions and perspectives. People's perspectives are formed by beliefs, interests, needs, age, gender, nationality, ethnicity, health, education—the multiple factors of life. These factors of perspective influence perceptions; at the same time, perceptions continuously influence perspectives.

To understand how various people can be exposed to the same stimuli or events and yet have different perceptions, it helps to imagine that each of us views the world through personal "contact lenses," an analogy from the previous

FOUR QUALITIES
OF A CRITICAL THINKER
Internet Entrepreneur Jimmy Wales

Curious   In this chapter you will learn about responsible curiosity. When exploring an area of interest, a compelling research question, or an important political issue, it is your responsibility as a critical thinker and an engaged citizen to learn about different perspectives, and to ensure that those perspectives are both accurate and fair. As you have probably been cautioned by your teachers and your friends, the Internet is an extraordinary source of an infinite array of perspectives and perceptions, but a significant percentage of that information ranges from the slightly biased to the completely wrong. The various projects of Wikimedia, a group of collaborative online resources founded by Internet entrepreneur Jimmy Wales, demonstrate how the collective input of responsible critical thinkers can create sources of information that are accurate, fair, and presented from a global array of perspectives and experiences. In your research, you will find various Wikimedia resources to be an invaluable starting point for your work.

Open-minded   Wikipedia, a collaborative encyclopedia that was the first Wikimedia project, is written and edited entirely by volunteer contributors. There are now Wikipedia sites in more than sixty languages, and entries have been written in more than one-hundred languages. In an interview, Wales pointed out that this diversity of perspective—bringing in marginalized cultures, voices, and languages to share their expertise with the world—is one of the greatest strengths of Wikimedia projects. "The Wikipedia for a lot of people harkens back to what we all thought the Internet was for in the first place," he observes. "When most people first started the Internet, they thought, oh, this is fantastic, people can communicate from all over the world and build knowledge and share information." Entirely nonprofit and volunteer-driven, Wikipedia is the ultimate expression of open-mindedness. Through a series of open-source, open-access chat rooms and other paths of communication, each Wikipedia entry is communally checked for accuracy, fairness, and the quality of its citations and illustrations. Until Wikipedia, print encyclopedias—for all their pretenses of objectivity—could only present one unified voice, one point of view, that was nearly impossible to amend or update once in print. With Wikipedia, both access to and control of information passes to a global community who use the technology to collaborate, learn, and grow.

FIGURE 9.1 Differing Perceptions of an Event

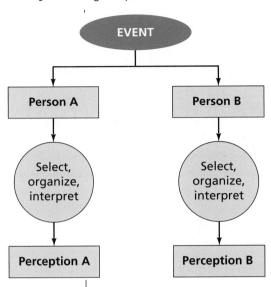

chapter. (You might think of the factors that go into forming perspectives as the prescription for the lenses!)

We aren't usually aware that we are wearing these lenses. Instead, without our realizing it, our lenses act as filters that select and shape what we perceive.

To understand how people perceive the world, we have to understand their individual lenses, which influence how they actively select, organize, and interpret the events in their experience. A diagram of the process might look like Figure 9.1. A more comic demonstration of the different "lenses" we all wear provides the punchline of the *Dilbert* cartoon on the next page.

Knowledgeable   Wiki resources grow organically through collaboration and community. The various projects of Wikimedia itself are built by tens of millions of mostly anonymous users in collaboration with one another, sharing and checking their created knowledge together. Users compare specific entries with their own knowledge, perspectives, and perceptions, and amend or add to each entry based on their own experience and information. As a fully volunteer project, Wikipedia depends on the ability and integrity of each contributor. For example, Wikipedia contributors have created "active improvement teams" that have implemented policies to check all entries for bias, to screen for spam, and to set and adhere to encyclopedia standards.

Creative   The software that structures all Wikimedia projects can be easily and freely adapted by anyone who wishes to create a communally edited web site. You may, at some point in your academic career, be asked to create or participate in a wiki as a classroom project. The Wikimedia organization itself has branched out from Wikipedia to create wiki learning centers, online textbooks, dictionaries, a collection of quotations (in more than thirty languages), an archive of public-domain books and other

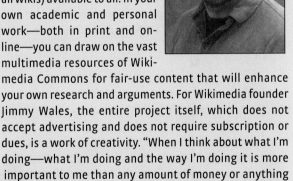

texts, and even Wikispecies, a taxonomy database created by and for scientists but (as with all wikis) available to all. In your own academic and personal work—both in print and online—you can draw on the vast multimedia resources of Wikimedia Commons for fair-use content that will enhance your own research and arguments. For Wikimedia founder Jimmy Wales, the entire project itself, which does not accept advertising and does not require subscription or dues, is a work of creativity. "When I think about what I'm doing—what I'm doing and the way I'm doing it is more important to me than any amount of money or anything like that because it's my artistic work," he has said. How does this insight change the way you might define "creativity" or "creative" work?

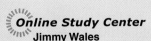

Online Study Center
Jimmy Wales
Visit the Online Study Center for *Critical Thinking, Thoughtful Writing* at *college.hmco.com/pic/ chaffee CTTW4e* to learn more about Jimmy Wales

Differing Perspectives

Examine the following pairs of statements. In each pair, two people are being exposed to the same basic stimulus or event, yet the perception of one differs greatly from that of the other. Explain how the various perceptions might have developed.

1. a. That chili was much too spicy to eat.

  Explanation: _____

  b. That chili needed more hot peppers and chili powder to spice it up a little.

  Explanation: _____

2. a. People who wear lots of makeup and jewelry are very sophisticated.

  Explanation: _____

  b. People who wear lots of makeup and jewelry are ostentatious and overdressed.

  Explanation: _____

3. a. The music young people enjoy listening to is a highly creative cultural expression.

  Explanation: _____

  b. The music young people enjoy listening to is obnoxious noise.

  Explanation: _____

4. a. I really enjoy how stimulating and intellectually challenging this English class is.

  Explanation: _____

  b. This English class is too much work. All the teacher wants to do is make us think, think, think. It makes my head hurt.

  Explanation: _____

Effective critical thinkers are aware of the lenses that they—and others—are wearing. People unaware of the nature of their own lenses can often mistake their own perceptions for objective truth, not having examined either the facts or others' perceptions of a given issue.

In the cartoon "The Investigation," each witness is giving what he or she (or it!) believes is an accurate description of the man in the center, and all are unaware that their descriptions are being influenced by who they are and the way that they perceive things.

Selecting Perceptions: Why Do We Notice the Things We Notice?

We tend to select perceptions about subjects that have been called to our attention. For instance, at the age of three, one author's child suddenly became aware of beards. On entering a subway car, she would ask in a penetrating voice, "Any beards here?" and proceed to count them out loud. In so doing, she naturally focused her parents' attention—as well as that of other passengers—on beards.

THE INVESTIGATION

Another aspect of our perceiving lenses is our tendency to notice what we need, desire, or otherwise find interesting. When we go shopping, we focus on whatever items we are looking for. Walking down the street, we tend to notice certain kinds of people or events while completely ignoring others. Even while watching a movie or reading a book, we tend to concentrate on and remember the elements most meaningful to us. Another person can perform *exactly* the same actions—shop at the same store, walk down the same street, read the same book, or go to the same movie—and yet notice and remember entirely different things.

Although we tend to focus on what is familiar, normally we are not aware of doing so. In fact, we often take for granted what is familiar to us—the taste of chili or eggs, the street that we live on, our family or friends—and normally don't think about how we perceive it. When something happens that makes the familiar seem strange and unfamiliar, though, we do become aware of our perceptions and start to evaluate them.

To sum up, we actively select our perceptions on the basis of

- What has been called to our attention
- What our needs or interests are
- What our moods or feelings are
- What seems familiar or unfamiliar
- What our backgrounds are

The way in which we select perceptions is a paramount factor in shaping the lenses through which we view the world, and it influences our writing to a great extent. Our writing is based on the points we choose to make, the details we select to include. Even when different people are writing about the same subject, the results are often very different because their lenses and their perspectives lead them to make different selections.

Organizing Perceptions

Not only do you actively select certain perceptions; you also actively organize them into meaningful relationships and patterns. Carefully examine Figure 7.2 in Chapter 7 on page 188. Do you see both the young woman and the old woman? If you do, try switching your perspective back and forth between the two images. As you do so, notice how for each image, you are doing the following things:

- *Selecting* certain lines, shapes, and shadings on which to focus your attention
- *Organizing* these lines, shapes, and shadings into different patterns
- *Interpreting* these patterns as representing things you can recognize—a hat, a nose, a chin

We naturally try to order and organize what we are experiencing into patterns and relationships that make sense to us. When we succeed in doing so, the completed whole means more than the sum of the individual parts. We are continually organizing the world in this way during virtually every waking moment. We do not live in a world of isolated sounds, patches of color, random odors, and individual textures. Instead, we live in a world of objects and people, language and music—a world in which all these individual stimuli are woven together. We are able to perceive this world of complex experiences because we can organize the individual stimuli we are receiving into relationships that have meaning for us.

This organizing process is integral to the writing process. When you write an essay, compose a letter, or create a story, you are actively organizing the ideas you selected to include into various relationships. Instead of simply stringing together words, you are developing a coherent structure through which to communicate thoughts and feelings.

Interpreting Perceptions

Besides selecting and organizing perceptions, we also actively interpret what we perceive: we are figuring out what something means. One of the elements that influences interpretations is the *context*, or overall situation, within which the perception is occurring. For example, imagine that you see a man running down the street. Your interpretation of his action will depend on the specific context. For example, is there a bus waiting at the corner? Is a police officer running behind him? Is the man wearing a jogging suit?

We are continually trying to interpret what we perceive, whether it is a design, someone else's behavior, or a social situation. As in the example of someone running down the street, many perceptions can be interpreted in more than one way. When a situation has more than one possible interpretation, it is ambiguous. The more ambiguous a situation is, the greater its possible meanings or interpretations.

Casebook: Perception and Perspective on Reporting Katrina

Journalists, law enforcement officers, social scientists, and medical workers are among the professions who must rely on their ability to quickly and accurately sort through a barrage of perceptions, sometimes under extreme conditions. In August 2005, Hurricanes Katrina and Rita devastated millions of square miles of the United States Gulf Coast, hitting New Orleans and the Mississippi coast with particular force. Although the impact of a major hurricane on New Orleans had been predicted, scientifically modeled, and prepared for; although federal and state government officials as well as meteorologists tracked the storm for days before it hit and assured the public that they were prepared, the storm's aftermath overwhelmed the abilities and sensibilities of even the most seasoned journalists, aid workers, and others.

In the following three essays, a journalist, a pair of social scientists, and a New Orleans–based reporter take a critical and sobering look at how the panic of the moment led to the perpetuation of frightening rumors and the evocation of vicious racial stereotypes as journalists and government officials alike struggled to reconcile their perceptions of what was actually happening with their expectations based on (optimistic, as it turned out) models and predictions.

"They Shoot Helicopters, Don't They?"

HOW JOURNALISTS SPREAD RUMORS DURING KATRINA

BY MATT WELCH

Journalist Matt Welch is the assistant opinion editor for the *Los Angeles Times*. He writes and publishes frequently, both in the mainstream press and at his blog (mattwelch.com), on politics, culture, and social issues. For much of the 1990s, he lived and worked in central Europe, where he cofounded the region's first post-communist English-language newspaper. For three years Welch was an editor at *Reason,* a libertarian-leaning social and political journal, where "They Shoot Helicopters, Don't They?" first appeared in December 2005.

On September 1, 72 hours after Hurricane Katrina ripped through New Orleans, the Associated Press news wire flashed a nightmare of a story: "Katrina Evacuation Halted Amid Gunfire . . . Shots Are Fired at Military Helicopter."

The article flew across the globe via at least 150 news outlets, from India to Turkey to Spain. Within 24 hours commentators on every major American television news network had helped turn the helicopter sniper image into the disaster's enduring symbol of dysfunctional urbanites too depraved to be saved.

Golfer Tiger Woods spoke for many of us on September 2 when he remarked, during a tournament in Boston, that "it's just unbelievable . . . how people are behaving, with the shootings and now the gang rapes and the gang violence and shooting at helicopters who are trying to help out and rescue people."

Like many early horror stories about ultra-violent New Orleans natives, whether in their home city or in far-flung temporary shelters, the AP article turned out to be false. Evacuation from the city of New Orleans was never "halted," according to officials from the Coast Guard, the Federal Emergency Management Agency (FEMA), and the Louisiana National Guard. The only helicopter airlifts stopped were those by a single private company, Acadian Ambulance, from a single location: the Superdome. And Acadian officials, who had one of the only functional communications systems in all of New Orleans during those first days, were taking every opportunity to lobby for a massive military response.

5   More important, there has been no official confirmation that a single military helicopter over New Orleans—let alone a National Guard Chinook in the pre-dawn hours of September 1—was fired upon. "I was at the Superdome for eight days, and I don't remember hearing anything about a helicopter getting shot at," says Maj. Ed Bush, public affairs officer for the Louisiana Air National Guard. With hundreds of Guard troops always on duty inside and outside the Superdome before, during, and after Hurricane Katrina, if there had been gunfire, "we would have heard it," Bush maintains. "The instant reaction over the radio would have been overwhelming."

The Air Force, to which the Air National Guard reports, also has zero record of helicopter sniping. "We investigated one incident and it turned out to have been shooting on the ground, not at the helicopter," Air Force Maj. Mike Young told the *New York Times* on September 29.

Aside from the local National Guard, the other government agency with scores of helicopters over New Orleans was the U.S. Coast Guard, which rescued more than 33,000 people. "Coast Guard helicopters," says spokeswoman Jolie Shifflet, "were not fired on during Hurricane Katrina rescue operations."

How about the Civil Air Patrol (CAP), the all-volunteer, Air Force–assisting network of around 58,000 private Cessna pilots, 68 of whom flew a total of 833 aid missions after the hurricane? "To my knowledge," says CAP Public Affairs Manager Jim Tynan, "none of our pilots on any Katrina-related mission were taking ground fire."

That doesn't mean that people weren't shooting at helicopters. As Lt. Comdr. Tim Tobiasz, the Coast Guard's operations officer for New Orleans airspace, told me, "It's tough to hear in a helicopter. You have two turbine engines. . . . I don't know if you could hear a gunshot below." And the Bureau of Alcohol, Tobacco, and Firearms arrested a 21-year-old man in the Algiers neighborhood of New Orleans on September 6 for firing a handgun out his window while helicopters flew nearby.

10 But the basic premise of the article that introduced the New Orleans helicopter sniper to a global audience was dead wrong, just like so many other widely disseminated Katrina nightmares. No seven-year-old rape victim with a slit throat was ever found, even though the atrocity was reported in scores of newspapers. The Convention Center freezer was not stacked with 30 or 40 dead bodies, nor was the Superdome a live-in morgue. (An estimated 10 people died inside the two buildings combined, and only one was slain, according to the best data from National Guard officials at press time.)

Tales of rapes, carjackings, and gang violence by Katrina refugees quickly circulated in such evacuee centers as Baton Rouge, Houston, and Leesville, Louisiana—and were almost as quickly debunked.

From a journalistic point of view, the root causes of the bogus reports were largely the same: The communication breakdown without and especially within New Orleans created an information vacuum in which wild oral rumor thrived. Reporters failed to exercise enough skepticism in passing along secondhand testimony from victims (who often just parroted what they picked up from the rumor mill), and they were far too eager to broadcast as fact apocalyptic statements from government officials—such as Mayor Ray Nagin's prediction of 10,000 Katrina-related deaths (there were [fewer] than 900 in New Orleans at press time) and Police Superintendent Edwin Compass' reference on *The Oprah Winfrey Show* to "little babies getting raped"—without factoring in discounts for incompetence and ulterior motives.

Just about every local official and emergency responder with access to the media in those first heartbreaking days basically screamed, and understandably so, for federal assistance. With their citizens stranded, desperate, and even dying; with their own response a shambles; and with their families and employees in mortal jeopardy, they had ample temptation to exaggerate the wretchedness of local conditions and ample fatigue to let some whoppers fly.

"I think that's exactly what it was," says Maj. Bush. "But the problem is they were doing it on the radio, and then the people in the dome would hear it."

15 The information vacuum in the Superdome was especially dangerous. Cell phones didn't work, the arena's public address system wouldn't run on generator power, and the law enforcement on hand was reduced to talking to the 20,000 evacuees using bullhorns and a lot of legwork. "A lot of them had AM radios, and they would listen to news reports that talked about the dead bodies at the Superdome, and the murders in the bathrooms of the Superdome, and the babies being raped at the Superdome," Bush says, "and it would create terrible panic. I would have to try and convince them that no, it wasn't happening."

The reports of rampant lawlessness, especially the persistent urban legend of shooting at helicopters, definitely delayed some emergency and law enforcement responses. Reports abounded, from places like Andover, Massachusetts, of localities refusing to send their firefighters because of "people shooting at helicopters." The National Guard refused to approach the Convention Center until September 2, 100 hours after the hurricane, because "we waited until we had enough force in place to do an overwhelming force," Lt. Gen. H. Steven Blum told reporters on September 3.

"One of my good friends, Col. Jacques Thibodeaux, led that security effort," Bush says. "They said, 'Jacques, you gotta get down here and sweep this thing.' He said he was braced for anything. And he encountered nothing—other than a whole lot of people clapping and cheering and so glad that they were here."

At the same time, it is plausible that the exaggerations helped make the outside response quicker than it otherwise would have been, potentially saving lives. As with many details of this natural and manmade disaster, we may never know.

But in the meantime, truth became a casualty, news organizations that were patting their own backs in early September were publishing protracted mea culpas by the end of the month, and the reputation of a great American city has been, at least to some degree, unfairly tarnished.

20

"New Orleanians have been kind of cheated because now everybody thinks that they just turned to animals and that there was complete lawlessness and utter abandon," says Maj. Bush. "And that wasn't the case. . . . There's a whole bunch of stuff out there that never happened at the dome, as I think America's beginning to find out, slowly."

QUESTIONS FOR ACTIVE READING

1. To what factors does Matt Welch attribute the wild, and ultimately false, rumors of chaos that circulated in the media immediately after Hurricane Katrina?

2. How does Welch, as a reporter, use the process described in Figure 9.1, "Differing Perceptions of an Event"?

3. How does Welch, as a journalist, work to select, organize, and interpret information? What kinds of evidence and illustrations does he use?

QUESTIONS FOR THINKING CRITICALLY

1. What do the kinds of rumors and stories (ultimately proven to be false) suggest about the perceptions journalists had about the people of New Orleans? How did those perceptions influence, or distort, their ability to report the news?

2. What can journalists do, even in a time of crisis, to be sure that they are reporting objectively? Is it possible to be truly objective "in the heat of the moment"?

3. How many of the stories that Welch ultimately disproves did you hear reported in the days immediately after Hurricane Katrina? How did those stories influence your perception of the behavior of both the victims and the officials who were supposed to be helping?

FROM "Myth-Making in New Orleans"

BY BRIAN THEVENOT

The following analytical essay, by a reporter for the New Orleans *Times-Picayune,* examines the ethical impact of journalists who find themselves both objective reporters and subjective witnesses, even victims. The excerpts from the article reprinted here focus on Thevenot's direct experience and perceptions at the height of the disaster, followed by a reflection on how journalists can keep their ability to be critical, objective thinkers even in the face of overwhelming circumstances. The middle section of this article, not reprinted here, describes how Thevenot briefly became a much-quoted "authority" in other mainstream media outlets. To read the complete article, go to *http://www.ajr.org/Article.asp?id=3998*. Under the direction of David Meeks, the paper's city editor, the *Times-Picayune* won the Pulitzer Prize in 2006 in two categories: for breaking news and for public service.

As I walked briskly through the dimly lit area inside the food service entrance of New Orleans' Ernest N. Morial Convention Center, the thought of pulling back the sheets covering the four stinking, decomposing corpses in front of me seemed wrong, even perverse. Before I'd even thought to ask, one of the two soldiers who escorted me, Arkansas National Guardsman Mikel Brooks, nixed the prospect of looking inside the freezer he and another soldier said contained "30 or 40" bodies.

"I ain't got the stomach for it, even after what I saw in Iraq," he said.

I didn't push it. Now I wish I had, as gruesome as that may seem. The soldiers might have branded me a morbid fiend and run me the hell out of there, but my story in the September 6 edition of the *Times-Picayune* would have been right, or at least included a line saying I'd been denied the opportunity to lay eyes on the freezer.

Instead, I quoted Brooks and another soldier, by name, about the freezer's allegedly grim inventory, including the statement that it contained a "7-year-old with her throat cut." Neither the mass of bodies nor the allegedly expired child would ever be found. As I later reported, an internal review by Arkansas Guard Lt. Col. John Edwards found that Brooks and others who repeated the freezer story had heard it in the food line at Harrah's Casino, a law enforcement and military staging area a block away. Edwards told me no soldier had actually seen bodies in a freezer.

5 I retell this story not to deflect blame—factual errors under my byline are mine alone—but as an example of how one of hundreds of myths got reported in the early days of Hurricane Katrina's aftermath. I corrected the freezer report—along with a slew of other rumors and myths transmitted by the media—in a September 26 *Times-Picayune* story coauthored by my colleague Gordon Russell. In that piece, we sought to separate fact from fiction on the narrow issue of reported violence at the Louisiana Superdome and the Convention Center.

We hadn't anticipated the massive shockwave of self-correction that story would send through the international media. The examination of myths of violence—and their confirmation by New Orleans Mayor C. Ray Nagin and then-Police Superintendent Eddie Compass—became the story for days on end, a moment of mass-scale media introspection that ultimately resulted in a healthy revision of history's first draft.

The *Los Angeles Times*, the *New York Times* and the *Washington Post* followed up with similar, well-researched efforts debunking myths and coming to essentially the same conclusion we had: While anarchy indeed reigned in the city, and subhuman conditions in the Dome and the Convention Center shocked the nation's conscience, many if not most of the alarmist reports of violence were false, or at least could not be verified. Dozens of other newspapers and television outlets joined in, offering news and opinion pieces, many doggedly questioning what they and others had earlier reported.

Our myth-debunking story put me in the eye of the debate's swirling storm. National television outlets praised our work, quoted it frequently and sought me out for interviews as their latest instant expert. A few bloggers had the opposite reaction, hanging me in virtual effigy as a symbol of the failings of the dreaded "MSM"—the mainstream media, that evil monolith—and concocting conspiracy theories to explain the media's errant early reports. Questions of race and class pervaded the debate in all media: Did the reporting of violence stem from journalists' willingness to believe the worst about poor African Americans? What role did the refugees themselves, along with local black public officials—both of whom served as sources for many of the false stories—play in creating the myths?

The *New York Times* tempered its assessment of false reports, writing "some, though not all, of the most alarming stories that coursed through the city appear to be little more than figments of frightened imaginations." But the *Times*' piece differed in scope from ours, assessing reports of crime citywide instead of only at the Dome and the Convention Center. The *Times* also reported on property crimes such as widespread looting—definitely not a myth, I can confirm as an eyewitness—as part of the paper's exhaustive review. We concentrated exclusively on violent crime.

10   Jim Dwyer, one of the lead reporters on the *Times*' story, says he came to Louisiana for two weeks specifically to ascertain the truth of early wild reports of crime. As we did at the *Picayune*, Dwyer says he had taken an interest when the tenor of some reports, many unattributed, relayed nightmarish scenes that seemed to defy common sense.

"I just thought that some of the reports were so garish, so untraceable and always seemed to stop short of having actual witnesses to the atrocities . . . . like a galloping mythical nightmare had taken control," Dwyer told me.

The paper also dispatched stringers to shelters in Houston and Austin, Dwyer says, where they found no shortage of secondhand or thirdhand accounts of rape and murder—but none that seemed credible enough to discount Dwyer's original thesis. "Nobody could say they saw rapes and murders. It was always three or four steps removed, like 'my sister's uncle's cousin'" had seen the violence, he says.

Dwyer also reviewed his own paper's reporting, but found that, while the *Times* had reported unconfirmed accounts of treachery, as did many others, its reporters had generally couched them with the caveat that they couldn't be confirmed.

"I read all of it. We certainly reported stuff that Compass said, that Nagin said, but with pretty clear markers that it couldn't be verified," he says. "Also, the reports hadn't taken over our coverage in as powerful a way [as they did in some other media]. The atrocities didn't become the story. The paper kept its eye on the perilous conditions the people were in."

By the time the *Times-Picayune*'s story ran—followed quickly by the *L.A. Times*' and the *New York Times*' pieces—nearly a month after the storm, there was no shortage of reports to second-guess. Many were attributed to refugees, cops and soldiers and even top public officials. Others appeared with weak attribution or none at all. Consider one example, this unattributed September 1 exchange on Fox News Channel between host John Gibson and correspondent David Lee Miller, live from New Orleans:

Gibson: "These are pictures of the cops arriving on the scene, armed and ready to take on the armed thugs . . . Thugs shooting at rescue crews."

Miller: "Hi, John, as you so rightly point out, there are so many murders taking place. There are rapes, other violent crimes taking place in New Orleans."

Kicking it up a notch and taking it worldwide, the normally staid *Financial Times* of London offered this September 5 description of the Convention Center, attributed to unnamed refugees: "Girls and boys were raped in the dark and had their throats cut and bodies were stuffed in the kitchens while looters and madmen exchanged fire with weapons they had looted."

The story went on to quote some flood victims by name: "Geraldine Lavy said her son protected four Australian tourists from rapists in the convention centre. 'Can you imagine? Four white women on their own?'" A man named Larry Martin told the *Times* that looters and gunmen "were shooting at buses, the rapes, the murders, the sodomy." The piece also reported, with no attribution, the apocryphal tale that "several hundred corpses are reported to have been gathered by locals in one school alone" in St. Bernard Parish, the badly flooded community just east of the city.

That one struck me as familiar: The *Picayune*'s small team of reporters in New Orleans—most of the staff had been forced to evacuate to Baton Rouge after our headquarters nearly flooded—heard a similar report of up to 300 bodies piled at Marion Abramson High School in Eastern New Orleans. We dispatched two reporters to the school in a delivery truck, which got stuck while driving through high water. The reporters then canoed to the school, went inside—and found no bodies, and had nothing to write for their trouble.

·   ·   ·   ·   ·

As New Orleanians, playing a key role in correcting the international image of our own citizens gave us a deep satisfaction. Mostly poor, overwhelmingly African American, flood victims in the two shelters had been, in the most egregious cases, portrayed as beasts, raping and killing one another and even shooting at rescue workers trying to save them.

As journalists, reporting myths and later correcting them offer vital lessons on ramping up skepticism in initial reporting from chaotic environments—even if the sources are authoritative ones. We have three basic tools to use here, one during the reporting, the other during publishing, the third during any needed correction of initial reports.

The first is the persistent questioning of sources—about their sources: How do you know that? Did you see it? Who told you this? Are you 100 percent sure this happened? Who else can confirm it?

The second, wisely suggested in a column by former *Washington Post* Ombudsman Michael Getler, is careful and frequent qualification: "There is a journalistic device that is informative, accurate and protective, but that too often doesn't get used. It is a simple sentence that says: This account could not be independently verified."

25 The second time I wrote about the bodies in the freezer, as part of a narrative piece I penned for [*American Journalism Review*], I added just such a qualification. . . . At the time, a few days after I'd been to the Convention Center, I still had no higher-level confirmation of a body count—because no official count had been taken. So I added a sentence saying the presence and number of bodies at the center was "still unconfirmed amid a swirl of urban myths churned up by the storm."

The revision came as a result of a conversation with an editor in which I initially recommended cutting the mention of 40 bodies altogether unless I could confirm it independently before deadline. We compromised, adding the qualifier and strict attribution of the number to the guardsmen.

The third tool, which lately has been on display by many, though not all, media outlets, is an attitude that embraces the correcting of major news stories as news itself, not something to be buried in a corrections box.

"I think you treat it as a separate story, and it should have A1 prominence," says Hub Brown, an associate professor of broadcast journalism at the S. I. Newhouse School of Public Communications at Syracuse University. "Of course, print journalists are so much more meticulous at correcting their mistakes . . . . Why not have a segment in the newscast that says, 'We've reported this through the past day, and it turned out to be wrong?'"

That sort of record correction would be a lot less painful—indeed, not painful at all—if journalists' initial dispatches contained detailed attribution, especially for high-temperature reports out of disaster zones. With stories like Katrina, in which rock-solid information in many cases proved so elusive, that should extend even to the point of publishing exactly how official sources came to know the information in question. David Carr, a media columnist for the *New York Times*, was one of the first to question some of the early Katrina reporting in a September 19 column headlined "More Horrible Than Truth: News Reports."

30 While Carr, in his column and in an interview, asserted that the media should shoulder their share of the blame, he was stunned at the degree to which public officials solidified the myths. "In New Orleans, that's what set this apart" from other examples of misinformation reported by the media, he says. "I was actually prepared a week before and had a column set to go, but then I realized the top police official and the top elected official were confirming these rumors. So how could I go after reporters on the ground receiving confirmation that this happened?"

Carr revised the column to address public officials' roles. Many have given Nagin and Compass a pass, saying they probably repeated exaggerations by mistake in a desperate attempt to get help for a truly desperate situation. Carr, however, suggests they were driven in part by political motives.

"Usually the first reaction of officials in crisis is to obfuscate and tamp down the rumors," he says. "Nagin and Compass stood there with a can of gasoline . . . . In part what they were trying to do was explain that they had a mess on their hands—and that the feds had dropped the ball—by communicating an atmosphere of chaos that rendered their inability understandable."

In the worst of the storm reporting, tales of violence, rapes, murders and other mayhem were simply stated as fact with no attribution at all.

I am among those who committed this sin. In [a] previous A . . . piece, although I attributed the account of bodies in the freezer and added that it could not be confirmed, I got loose with the attribution at another point in the story, describing the Convention Center as "a nightly scene of murders, rapes and regular stampedes."

35   What I later confirmed is that occasional gunfire, stampedes and terror did indeed plague the Convention Center. But only one death could be called a suspected homicide, a body with a gunshot wound, according to Kristen Meyer, spokeswoman for the state Department of Health and Hospitals. Meyer also confirmed that four bodies were retrieved from just inside the food service entrance, the same place I witnessed the four bodies lying under sheets. Widespread reports of rapes could not be confirmed.

Only one of those bodies has since been identified by name by her family, that of 79-year-old Clementine Eleby, who was not the gunshot victim, Meyer says.

While the media should learn lessons from Katrina, appropriate caution can't lead to paralysis. Backing off aggressive reporting of scenes where "official" information and sources, in some cases, literally don't exist isn't an option. The many early Katrina stories marred by exaggerations or errors still stand out as a point of pride for the media. The quick reaction to the storm by reporters put accounts—most of them true and confirmed—of dire suffering in the faces of the public and authorities, prompting them to take action that saved lives.

• • • • •

As the debate about misreported Katrina violence rolled through blogs and more mainstream outlets, a conventional wisdom emerged: White middle-class reporters only believed and reported atrocities because they were predisposed to accept the worst about poor, black flood victims.

The race and class dynamics here are far more complicated. Many of the worst stories were attributed to poor, black flood victims themselves, along with African American public officials.

40   Brown, the Syracuse professor and an African American who teaches about diversity in the media, says that's no surprise. Black people are sometimes unconsciously biased against black people, too. "The fact that racism exists in the country doesn't mean everybody of one race feels one way, and everybody of another race feels the other," he says. "Sometimes victims of racism believe the worst about themselves. That's part of what makes it so harmful."

[Keith] Woods, [dean of faculty at the Poynter Institute,] an African American who has been writing and teaching about reporting on racial issues for years, doesn't buy the charge that the reports were driven largely by racial bias. It's not necessarily a gigantic leap in logic, he says, to believe that New Orleanians would murder one another in desperate times—they murder one another with regularity during normal times.

"I spent most of my life in the city of New Orleans, and when I left, it was the murder capital of the country," Woods says. "If you were to tell me a bunch of people murdered each other in the Dome and Convention Center, why wouldn't I believe it? . . . Race played a role, but it's an indecipherable role. It's useless trying to spend a lot of time trying to figure it out because you have to climb into the psyche of the people who were there."

You also have to deal in hypothetical comparisons. What would the media have reported if the Dome had been packed with white people?

The reality of being white in New Orleans and most of America, of course, substantially increases the likelihood of being middle class, and thus substantially decreases the likelihood of being anywhere near a shelter of any kind during a disaster of Katrina proportions.

45   I'll offer another hypothetical comparison that takes class out of the issue and leaves only race: If Katrina had hit a poor, white trailer-park town in, say, the Florida Panhandle, and white refugees and white public officials had offered the media tales of rape and murder, would any of us have doubted their "eyewitness" or "official" accounts?

There's no simple answer. White trailer-park towns don't typically include a Dome that might end up packed with about 30,000 people, with no power, no working toilets and scant medical care.

While the role of race can't be definitively measured, I have little doubt that, consciously or unconsciously, some white reporters and probably a smaller number of black ones found it more plausible that babies had been raped and children knifed in a black crowd than they would [have been] in a theoretical white one.

But I don't think race was the overriding factor.

I'm more inclined to go with an expanded version of Aaron Brown's gossip-line theory: that stories that may have started with some basis in fact got exaggerated and distorted as they were passed orally—often the only mode of communication—through extraordinarily frustrated and stressed multitudes of people, including refugees, cops, soldiers, public officials and, ultimately, the press.

50   The confusion was created by a titanic clash of communications systems. Stone-age storytelling got amplified by space-age technology.

A person might have seen a man passed out from dehydration in the Superdome, for instance, and assumed he was dead, then assumed there must be more dead. In the retelling, it becomes, "There's bodies in the Dome." Retold a few more times by stressed and frightened people—all the way up to the mayor—and it became, "There's so many bodies in the Dome you can't count them."

Then the media arrived, with satellite phones and modems, BlackBerrys, television trucks with the ability to broadcast worldwide and the technology to post on the Internet in an instant—and most of them not realizing that normal rules of sourcing no longer ensured accuracy.

The gossip line then circled the globe, as officials, hurricane victims, and rescue and security personnel began to confirm nightmarish scenarios, sincerely believing what they were saying and wanting desperately to get the word out—and get help on the way.

I can assure you that Mikel Brooks and his fellow guardsman sincerely believed what they told me. They talked to me out of disgust at the horrors, real and imagined. They did not "lie," which implies intent. They were consumed with a more important job at the time than nailing down every report they heard and believed: giving food and water to the living to keep them from joining the dead. It was my job to make sure what they said was true.

Ultimately, I followed up and did that job, as did many others. What Woods finds curious about the media-bashing on the Katrina story is that critics don't credit the media for doing the research to prove their early reports wrong.

"Don't forget, the journalists kept reporting—the reason you know that things were reported badly is because the journalists told you."

QUESTIONS FOR ACTIVE READING

1. Why does Thevenot write, here, in the first person? How common is it to read or hear a news story recounted in the first person? What does Thevenot wish to convey about his perceptions and his perspective?

2. How does Thevenot use chronology to organize his essay? Why is it especially important that his argument follows a chronological structure?

3. Thevenot notes the usefulness of this journalistic device: "This account could not be independently verified." Why, in the opinion of Thevenot and other journalists he interviewed for this essay, is that device especially useful? Why was it not often enough used in the reporting on Hurricane Katrina? How might new media technologies make it either *more* difficult or *less* difficult to independently verify an account?

QUESTIONS FOR THINKING CRITICALLY

1. In the third paragraph, Thevenot describes an especially difficult ethical dilemma that he and many reporters faced in the days immediately after Hurricane Katrina. What was that ethical dilemma? What are the ethical limits of news media reporting, and how should those limits be determined and enforced?

2. What was the process by which "myths" were created about conditions in New Orleans? Who does Thevenot hold responsible for that myth-making?

3. Like Matt Welch (page 271), Thevenot finds that flawed or stereotyped perceptions about race and class fueled the myths and interfered with the discovery and reporting of the truth. In an essay, compare and contrast the views of Welch and Thevenot on this subject.

"Finding and Framing Katrina: The Social Construction of Disaster"

BY RUSSELL R. DYNES AND HAVIDÁN RODRIGUEZ

Russell R. Dynes and Havidán Rodriguez both work at the Disaster Research Center at the University of Delaware, Newark. Both social scientists conducted field research after hurricanes in the southern United States and in the Caribbean. The Disaster Research Center has also studied the impact of the 9/11 terrorist attacks, the 2004 Asian earthquake and tsunami, and many other natural and human-caused disasters since its founding in 1963. More information about the Disaster Research Center is at *http://www.udel.edu/DRC/.* In the following essay, Dynes and Rodriguez study the ways in which "meaning" was constructed in the aftermath of Hurricanes Katrina and Rita. Analyzing hundreds of hours of continuous coverage, the two scientists found that a few very specific "framing themes" set the tone for the coverage and provided instant perceptions, some deeply flawed, that nevertheless created the "first draft of history." The work of Dynes and Rodriguez complements the firsthand accounts of citizens and citizen-journalists like Matt Welch and Brian Thevenot.

For the past several weeks, the major programmatic themes and news headlines generated by the media, but particularly television, have centered on hurricanes, specifically Hurricane Katrina, and more recently, Hurricane Rita. These themes have provided graphic glimpses of the human toll and suffering that such disaster events can have; but in drawing these pictures, television stations have also conveyed irrational and exaggerated information (many times based on rumors or incorrect information based on unverified data) focusing on both human loss and physical destruction. The aftermath of such hurricanes is bad enough without such promotion.

All disasters are not equal. Just as disasters are a quantitative leap over routine community emergencies, it is hard to compare Katrina to any other recent U.S. hurricane. The Galveston hurricane might be the closest parallel, but not many commentators could go beyond superficial comparisons. Also, Galveston was in 1900 and was not covered by TV. Thus, the images of desolation and destruction as a consequence of this storm did not reach the international community with the speed and intensity of Hurricane Katrina.

Katrina impacted an extensive geographical area of the United States. The combined impact of high winds, rain, storm surge distressed levees, and flooding created conditions that affected and disrupted the lives of hundreds of communities and millions of people. Further, there [were] a significant loss of life, extensive or total destruction of property, [and] disruption of lifeline services, and the sources of livelihood (including employments) were significantly impacted, if not totally lost. Help from nearby communities was difficult to come by since they were in similar circumstances. The scope of the impact made dormant political divisions important. Katrina crossed state lines, parish boundaries, ideological positions, and activists' concerns. It also separated extended families, and disrupted, if not severed, community, government, and industrial activities and functions. These effects were exacerbated by a lack of an adequate and coordinated response at the local, state, and federal level.

Framing Katrina

Katrina was the first hurricane to hit the United States to the accompaniment of continuous (24/7) TV coverage. Certainly, Andrew (1992) had considerable TV coverage, but that was before competitive twenty-four hour cable coverage. In social science terms, television constructed the frame of meaning to which audiences and decision-makers came to understand Katrina. For some along the coast, personal experience with Katrina might have helped. If you were on Dauphin Island or in Moss Point, Biloxi, Bay St. Louis, north or south of Highway 10, in Kenner or in a bar on Bourbon Street, the storm was slightly different. However, for most of us, the reality of the storm came through TV networks. Even for "victims" who lost electrical power, if it came back, the coffee pot and the TV were the first appliances back on so that one's own experiences would be understood and confirmed in the context of the information provided by the media.

5   Of course, TV had considerable advantages in framing the storm, but it also framed distortions that we will touch on later. The advantage of TV as an informational source is its visual imagery, usually backed by musical effects. People believe what they see, especially when it is considered "live." When the season started, it was not clear whether Katrina would be a one-night special or the beginning of a new prime-time series. However, Katrina, like any new series, had a lengthy and colorful promotion, called weather reports. After the long prelude, monitoring the wind speed and its direction, the impact of Katrina was slowly revealed. Generating facts about the consequences of the disaster's impact in many different locations takes time. Consequently, factual information about the impact was much less in terms of "air time," than on the available time that TV has to program. Given the disparity of time and few facts, TV tends to draw on common cultural assumptions (including myths) about what will happen. These assumptions include extensive damage, death and injury, concern for children, the ill and the elderly, forecasting mental health trauma, the absence of authority, extensive looting and the incompetence of government and the inevitability of social disorder; in essence, a state of chaos and anarchy. These assumptions and others framed the details of what came to be known as Katrina.

With new technology, including split screen, individual segments can be magnified; feeds can also be combined from several states within one screen. Programming formats to retain viewer attention suggest that the most dramatic stories in the last segment will be elaborated on in the next. Reporters also have the independence to create their own stories (Wenger and Quarantelli, 1989) and dispersed film crews have latitude to find their own stories, [to] ask their own questions and to develop their own special vocabularies, such as being surrounded by "toxic soup," missed by snipers or unable to find FEMA representatives. When one network had a "hot" story, other networks soon appeared on the same scene.

Over time, however, New Orleans became the feature presentation, and the rest of Louisiana and Mississippi became very minor themes. Certainly, because of the breaks in the levees and the flooding, the helicopter rescues, film clips of looting, [and] angry crowds at the Superdome and the Convention Center, it was vivid TV drama and suspense. Many viewers would have fond recollections of New Orleans and also TV personnel could find some high dry ground there. So New Orleans became the center of operations for the media regarding Katrina. Its mayor and police superintendent were available for interviews, but New Orleans was presented as a disorganized city on the brink of collapse, less from the storm than from its residents. On September 2, *The Army Times* (newspaper) reported that "combat operations are now underway on the streets. . . . This place is going to look like little Somalia . . . . We're going to go out and take the city back." "This will be a combat operation to get this city under control," was the lead comment by the commander of Louisiana National Guard's Joint Task Force. Several weeks after the storm, the story of Katrina can now be better told.

Framing Themes

Certain programmatic themes emerged in the TV coverage, identified here as finding damage, finding death, finding help, finding authority and finding the bad guys.

Finding Damage. Certainly, TV excels in presenting damage. Often, however, it is difficult to place that damage either in a particular geographical location or within a meaningful social context. In certain ways, that lack of context can enhance concern, as well as sympathy. It allows viewers to use their own imaginations projecting the meaning of such losses for those people who live in the area, or to the home owners of what is now not salvageable. Electronic technology can enhance the images and provide views from all angles. The levee system and the canals in New Orleans provided outlines of the destruction of neighborhoods.

10

Finding Death. From the very beginning of the hurricane impact, and with the onset of flooding in New Orleans, there were predictions of the death toll. The Mayor of New Orleans predicted the figure at 10,000 and there were repeated statements that FEMA had ordered 25,000 body bags. Several days into the flood, there was repeated visual evidence of bodies in the flooded area and continuous allegations that such conditions pose serious health risks. However, the Pan American Health Organizations have reviewed the research of the epidemiological risks of dead bodies in disaster situations and concluded that dead bodies seldom constitute health risks and suggest that the anxiety which leads to the inept removal of bodies often destroys information necessary for identification (PAHO, 2004). In such cases, family members are unnecessarily exposed to a second episode of unresolved grief.

As of October 15th, the death toll in Louisiana was declared to be 972 and in Mississippi 221. In Louisiana, the search for bodies was recently declared complete, but the state has released only 61 bodies and made the names of only 32 victims public (*New York Times*, Oct. 5, Al). This raises the question [of] whether predictions regarding the total death toll in the early response period have any value. Although Katrina has one of the highest death rates in U.S. hurricane history, it is still significantly lower (10%) than the projected number publicized. This raises questions about why these projections were released and reemphasized by the local government. Perhaps it was to speed up efforts to provide assistance and disaster relief aid from the state and federal level. This can also reflect the inherent difficulties and problems with estimating the death toll immediately following disaster impact. It is noteworthy that in past disaster events initial death estimates could be quite low, particularly in impact-isolated areas of developing countries. This was certainly the case with the 2004 Indian Ocean tsunami when initial estimates suggested several thousand dead and now the actual figure comes closer to 300,000.

Finding Help. In the immediate post-impact period, reporters often asked those they were interviewing whether they had received any type of help or aid, often inquiring directly if FEMA had been there. In every disaster, the first to help (the "first" responders) are actually neighbors, family members and other community members. Most persons (including reporters) do not think of such usual assistance as help; rather "help" is someone they do not know. Also, more recently, the term "first responders" has come into vocabulary to describe police, fire, and EMS personnel. Perhaps that terminology has created the expectation for "victims" to anticipate that a first responder would be at their house "quickly." Nevertheless, "true" first responders are also community members who have been impacted by the same events, but who are characterized by altruistic behavior in their response to these disaster events.

In addition, TV coverage early in the response period revealed tremendous confusion about the role of FEMA, both on the part of TV reporters and those they interviewed; this problem was exacerbated given the inadequate response and performance of the FEMA and DHS bureaucracy in the initial stages of the response process. There was also an initial tendency to describe FEMA as the organizational location for a national 911 phone number; if hurricane victims called, someone would allegedly respond to their needs and provide the necessary assistance. This misunderstanding regarding the role of FEMA in assisting state and local governments among state and local officials, as well as by victims, added to the perception of the lack of help.

The perception of the absence of help in the face of overwhelming need combined with bureaucratic niggling can persuade members of a national TV audience of the need to volunteer, to come to the disaster locale to help remedy that lack of help. At times, they can fill a need. On the other hand, at considerable personal expense in time and money, volunteers may arrive days later to find they are not needed or that they are not welcomed by government personnel at the scene. Just as victims might need helpers, helpers also need victims. Frustrated helpers are often prime candidates for TV interviewers, accusing government bureaucrats of preventing their involvement while emphasizing their skills and their sacrifice as well as their conviction that they are needed.

15

Certainly, there may be a lack of knowledge by victims about the help that is available within a community and the location where information might be obtained. It is also possible that some victims will have much higher expectations about the nature and/or scope of help that will be available. Many will discover that the type of homeowner's insurance on which they have paid for years will not cover their losses as they had long expected, nor will a reimbursement be quickly forthcoming. The long-run problem of "finding help" will be a topic of conversation in town councils, state legislatures, in Congress, and in the media for years to come.

Finding Authority. First of all, let us admit that the issue of authority in disasters is complex. Part of the complexity centers on the relationship among political jurisdictions and the understanding that current political officials have of that relationship. This is further complicated by the fact that U.S. political system officials come and go after elections, but disasters do not happen on that schedule. In fact, for most political officials, every disaster is their first in office. Historically, in the United States, responsibility for dealing with disaster response is located at the local level. If the demands are too great for the local community, the responsibility to assist the "locals" is assumed to involve the state. Again, if state resources are not sufficient, the federal government is expected to provide additional resources. There are certain events (e.g., a terrorist attack) which are not respectful of local or state boundaries and in those cases, federal assistance can be predicted to be necessary. In those cases, federal resources and personnel are often pre-positioned. As such, this creates the expectation that resources will be made immediately available to be used by local and state officials.

With the long lead time to Katrina, some TV reporters were already on location interviewing local officials who usually expressed their expectation that FEMA would be immediately available. The same conversations were repeated in other localities, but the director of FEMA, also appearing in the media, seemed equivocal about assuming total responsibility; that ambivalence, in time, led to his replacement and eventually his resignation. Appearing before a congressional committee after his resignation, Michael Brown asserted that one of the problems with the response to Hurricane Katrina was that local officials in Louisiana were dysfunctional, thus trying to shift the blame away from the federal government, and in this case, FEMA.

In addition to the problems of legal authority among different levels of political units, the notion of authority has been complicated by the adoption of a "command and control" vocabulary by some emergency management organizations. In a disaster with diffuse impact such as Katrina, the notion of having command and control is self-delusional. However, in the reorganization of FEMA and its inclusion in the new Department of Homeland Security, a standardized organizational system identified as the "Incident Command System" was administratively decreed as normative for disasters in the United States. There are elements of that notion which have considerable utility. For example, the notion of a command post as a location for coordinating the activities of the multiple organizations that will become involved in a disaster response makes sense. However, the idea that this is the location of someone who is commanding those organizations in their activities and is in control of the incident is out of touch with the reality and the events that are taking place.

The media's constant question as to "Who's in Charge?" seems to be based on what might be called the "Oz Theory of Authority," with apologies to Max Weber.

The Oz theory is that behind some curtain, there is a wizard. It is the media's responsibility to pull back that curtain to reveal the wizard commander. Perhaps the best advice is that if the question is answered by persons identifying themselves as being in command, the person being interviewed does not understand the complexity of the response. A response to a disaster such as Katrina is complicated and involves coordination and extensive communication, a complex task accomplished by many different groups and individuals. The decision-making necessary is decentralized and usually made at levels much lower in the status hierarchy implied by the command and control model. In other words, there is no curtain and no wizard, simply a very complicated mosaic of individuals and organizations with skills, resources, energy, the capacity to improvise, and the knowledge of the impacted community. Merging their knowledge and energy in a coordinated effort is the real wizardry.

20   **Finding the Bad Guys**. Probably the most dramatic "evidence" of social chaos assumed to be created by Katrina was centered on New Orleans. The city was heavily populated by poor African Americans who lived in areas that were the first ones flooded. They were directed to go to the Superdome, where assistance would be available. The photographic opportunity to show "mobs" of residents located together provided the backdrop for repetitive stories of looting, rape, murder, sniping and roving gangs preying on tourists. Such stories introduced the next time segment with an implication that it would continue as the major programmatic theme. Such rumors were also promulgated by the New Orleans police department and other local officials; they were even presented as facts by local officials on *The Oprah Winfrey Show*. There were stories of piles of bodies in the Superdome and outside the Convention Center, where bodies were stored in basement freezers. One of the consequences of these stories was the diversion of security forces to follow up on such reports when they were needed for other duties. Also, as the climate of fear increased, some EMS personnel refused assignments, citing their own apprehension.

While it is common for rumors of looting and all kinds of anti-social behavior to emerge in most major disasters, the volume and persistence of such rumors on TV in Katrina was unparalleled. The staff of writers from the *Times-Picayune* provided a major critique of those stories in the September 26th issue. Among their stories, they quoted the Orleans Parish district attorney pointing out that there were only four murders in New Orleans in the week following Katrina, making it a "typical" week in that city, which expected 200 homicides throughout the year.

When the Louisiana National Guard at the Superdome turned over the dead to federal authorities, that representative arrived with an 18-wheel refrigerated truck since there were reports of 200 bodies there. The actual total was six; of these, four died of natural causes, one from a drug overdose and another had apparently committed suicide. While four other bodies were found in the streets near the Dome, presumably no one had been killed inside as had been previously reported. There were more reports that 30 to 40 bodies were stored in the Convention Center freezers in its basement. Four bodies were recovered; one appeared to have been slain. Prior to this discovery, there had been reports of corpses piled inside the building.

In reference to reports of rapes during the six days that the Superdome was used as a shelter, the head of the N.O.P.D. sex crime unit said that he and his officers lived inside the Dome and ran down every rumor of rape and atrocity. In the end, they made two arrests for attempted sexual assault and concluded the other incidents rumored had not happened, although it is important to note that rape is generally underreported in nondisaster times.

In reference to claims of looting, similar observations can lead to quite different conclusions. Is the person sifting through debris a friend or relative, or a looter? Is the person pushing a grocery cart full of clothes someone flooded out of his home trying to save what few possessions he had left, or is it filled with looted materials? Are claims of looting at times used to inflate future insurance settlements? Again, rumors of looting are common in other disasters, but valid cases are rare. Some valid cases of looting can involve security forces brought in to protect against looting.

25   It does seem to someone who has studied disaster behavior over a long period that the rumors of anti-social behavior were particularly virulent in New Orleans. Certainly, media coverage facilitated that impression. On the other hand, New Orleans has always had a reputation as the place for "hedonistic behavior," particularly among some religious observers, in part because of its repute for Mardi Gras. Perhaps, for many TV viewers, it was a short step from the Big Easy to the Big Mess, thus lending public credibility to the stories disseminated through the media.

Fractured Frames

There were many frames [that] were briefly mentioned on TV, but never became a focal point of stories. While there was preoccupation with death, there was less concern for the possibilities for suffering. Asking victims who have lost family members or their entire possessions "How They Feel?" evokes sound bites which are neither cathartic nor reflective. They may evoke the initiation of a longer period of suffering the consequences of being a victim. But that longer period will be of little interest in future programming. Loss of jobs, economic security, and familiar neighbors, along with possible relocation and the initiation of a journey into the unknown are seldom captured in a short response. And the transition from being a victim to being a survivor will not be newsworthy to prime time audiences, nor will the rediscovery of racism and poverty, which flooded the screens. Much of the flood damage seen was difficult to differentiate from the dilapidation of sub-standard housing. The loss of fragile resources was more hurtful for those who had little to lose. The lack of resources also created the inability to evacuate easily and efficiently. Also, many of the medical problems experienced by evacuees had little to do with the hurricane itself, but were the result of the quality and availability (or lack thereof) of health care services prior to the hurricane.

There were other views that were difficult to visualize. One could not see the historic depletion of wetlands along the Gulf Coast, which for centuries had cushioned the effects on coastal areas. Nor could one easily see the quality of building codes and their previous enforcement, or the abundance of manufactured homes in certain coastal areas. It is also noteworthy that there has been a significant move-ment of the U.S. population toward high-risk coastal areas. Population density in coastal (high-risk) regions continues to increase, sometimes at a higher rate than the non-coastal populations. Currently, coastal counties constitute about 17 percent of the land mass (excluding Alaska) in the U.S., but 53 percent of the U.S. population (153 million people) live in these areas. Also, coastal population increased by 28% from 1980 to 2003, and ten of the fifteen cities with the highest population counts are in coastal counties. Such population movement results in more building in desirable coastal areas. Further, in some coastal areas, gambling has become a major economic sector. When Camille hit Biloxi in 1969, there were no casinos to be blown across the highway.

Hurricane Katrina was an event of catastrophic proportions, resulting in an exten-sive loss of life, property and human suffering; problems that were greatly compounded by significant deficiencies in governmental preparedness and response at all levels. Nevertheless, now that the waters have receded, we have come to realize that the images of chaos and anarchy portrayed by the mass media were primarily based on rumors and inaccurate assumptions. Some of these were supported by official statements by elected officials. This view of the drama of disasters is assumed to be another version of "reality TV." Now, a month after Hurricane Katrina, less attention is given to the hundreds of thousands of displaced, uprooted from their communities, and their loss of economic livelihood. The efforts for reconstruction are not likely to appear in prime time any time soon.

QUESTIONS FOR ACTIVE READING

1. In your own words, describe each "framing theme" that Dynes and Rodriguez iden-tified in media coverage following Hurricanes Katrina and Rita. Would Matt Welch (page 271) and Brian Thevenot (page 275) agree with those framing themes?

2. What other structuring devices (narration, description, and so forth) do Dynes and Rodriguez use to organize their argument? Point out especially useful or interesting instances of these strategies.

3. In your own words, describe the "Oz Theory of Authority." Do you agree with the authors (and with Welch and Thevenot) that this is an accurate explanation for some of what occurred as a result of Hurricanes Katrina and Rita? Can you think of any other natural or human-made disaster situations that exposed the "Oz Theory of Authority" in operation?

QUESTIONS FOR THINKING CRITICALLY

1. In a research paper, examine more deeply the impact of one of the "fractured frames" described in the last paragraphs of this essay. Consult at least one first-person source (quoted in another story, or from a blog) and at least one more objective scientific or journalistic source.

2. Paragraph 24 describes how different perceptions, influenced by biases about class or race, can make what looks like a "looter" to one person appear simply to be a flooded-out homeowner rescuing his few possessions to another. Think back to this chapter's earlier discussion of selecting, organizing, and interpreting perceptions. In what ways do Dynes and Rodriguez find people mistakenly selecting, organizing, and interpreting perceptions? In your own opinion, what can the media or the government do, in future disasters, to help create and broadcast accurate and fair perceptions?

3. Does the media have an obligation to correct erroneous reporting, even if those mistakes were not made deliberately or maliciously? Who should be responsible for correcting errors in news reports? Do we, as consumers of the news media, also have a responsibility to double-check what we hear, compare different accounts, and listen for corrections? Why, or why not?

THINKING-
WRITING
ACTIVITY

Five Accounts of the Assassination of Malcolm X, 1965

Let's examine a situation in which a number of different people had differing perceptions about an event they were describing. Chapter 6 of this book contains a passage by Malcolm X (pages 147–150) written when he was just beginning his life's work. A few years later, this work came to a tragic end with his assassination at a meeting in Harlem. As you read through the various accounts, pay particular attention to the perceptions each presents. After reading the accounts, analyze some of the differences in these perceptions by writing answers to the questions that follow.

1. What details of the events has each writer selected to focus on?

2. How has each writer organized the selected details? Remember that most newspapers give what they consider the most important information first.

3. How does each writer depict Malcolm X, his followers, the gunmen, and the significance of the assassination?

The New York Times (February 22, 1965)

Malcolm X, the 39-year-old leader of a militant Black Nationalist movement, was shot to death yesterday afternoon at a rally of his followers in a ballroom in Washington Heights. The bearded Negro extremist had said only a few words of greeting when a fusillade rang out. The bullets knocked him over backwards.

A 22-year-old Negro, Thomas Hagan, was charged with the killing. The police rescued him from the ballroom crowd after he had been shot and beaten.

Pandemonium broke out among the 400 Negroes in the Audubon Ballroom at 160th Street and Broadway. As men, women and children ducked under tables and flattened themselves on the floor, more shots were fired. The police said seven bullets struck Malcolm. Three other Negroes were shot. Witnesses reported that as many as 30 shots had been fired. About two hours later the police said the shooting had apparently been a result of a feud between followers of Malcolm and members of the extremist group he broke with last year, the Black Muslims. . . .

Life (March 5, 1965)

His life oozing out through a half dozen or more gunshot wounds in his chest, Malcolm X, once the shrillest voice of black supremacy, lay dying on the stage of a Manhattan auditorium. Moments before, he had stepped up to the lectern and 400 of the faithful had settled down expectantly to hear the sort of speech for which he was famous—flaying the hated white man. Then a scuffle broke out in the hall and Malcolm's bodyguards bolted from his side to break it up—only to discover that they had been faked out. At least two men with pistols rose from the audience and pumped bullets into the speaker, while a third cut loose at close range with both barrels of a sawed-off shotgun. In the confusion the pistol man got away. The shotgunner lunged through the crowd and out the door, but not before the guards came to their wits and shot him in the leg. Outside he was swiftly over-taken by other supporters of Malcolm and very likely would have been stomped to death if the police hadn't saved him. Most shocking of all to the residents of Harlem was the fact that Malcolm had been killed not by "whitey" but by mem-bers of his own race.

The New York Post (February 22, 1965)

They came early to the Audubon Ballroom, perhaps drawn by the expectation that Malcolm X would name the men who firebombed his home last Sunday. . . . I sat at the left in the 12th row and, as we waited, the man next to me spoke of Malcolm and his followers: "Malcolm is our only hope. You can depend on him to tell it like it is and to give Whitey hell."

There was a prolonged ovation as Malcolm walked to the rostrum. Malcolm looked up and said "A salaam aleikum (Peace be unto you)" and the audience replied "We aleikum salaam (And unto you, peace)."

Bespectacled and dapper in a dark suit, sandy hair glinting in the light, Malcolm said: "Brothers and sisters . . ." He was interrupted by two men in the center of the ballroom, who rose and, arguing with each other, moved forward. Then there was a scuffle at the back of the room. I heard Malcolm X say his last words: "Now, brothers, break it up," he said softly. "Be cool, be calm."

Then all hell broke loose. There was a muffled sound of shots and Malcolm, blood on his face and chest, fell limply back over the chairs behind him. The two men who had approached him ran to the exit on my side of the room, shooting wildly behind them as they ran. I heard people screaming, "Don't let them kill him." "Kill those bastards." At an exit I saw some of Malcolm's men beating with all their strength on two men. I saw a half dozen of Malcolm's followers bending over his inert body on the stage. Their clothes stained with their leader's blood.

Four policemen took the stretcher and carried Malcolm through the crowd and some of the women came out of their shock and one said: "I hope he doesn't die, but I don't think he's going to make it."

Associated Press (February 22, 1965)

A week after being bombed out of his Queens home, Black Nationalist leader Malcolm X was shot to death shortly after 3 (P.M.) yesterday at a Washington Heights rally of 400 of his devoted followers. Early today, police brass ordered a homicide charge placed against a 22-year-old man they rescued from a savage beating by Malcolm X supporters after the shooting. The suspect, Thomas Hagan, had been shot in the left leg by one of Malcolm's bodyguards as, police said, Hagan and another assassin fled when pandemonium erupted. Two other men were wounded in the wild burst of firing from at least three weapons. The firearms were a .38, a .45 automatic and a sawed-off shotgun. Hagan allegedly shot Malcolm X with the shotgun, a double-barrelled sawed-off weapon on which the stock also had been shortened, possibly to facilitate concealment. Cops charged Reuben Frances, of 871 E. 179th St., Bronx, with felonious assault in the shooting of Hagan, and with Sullivan Law violation—possession of the .45. Police recovered the shotgun and the .45.

The Amsterdam News (February 27, 1965)

"We interrupt this program to bring you a special newscast . . .," the announcer said as the Sunday afternoon movie on the TV set was halted temporarily. "Malcolm X was shot four times while addressing a crowd at the Audubon Ballroom on 166th Street." "Oh no!" That was my first reaction to the shocking event that followed one week after the slender, articulate leader of the Afro-American Unity was routed from his East Elmhurst home by a bomb explosion. Minutes later we alighted from a cab at the corner of Broadway and 166th St. just a short 15 blocks from where I live on Broadway. About 200 men and women, neatly dressed, were milling around, some with expressions of awe and disbelief. Others were in small clusters talking loudly and with deep emotion in their voices. Mostly they were screaming for vengeance. One woman, small, dressed in a light gray coat and her eyes flaming with indignation, argued with a cop at the St. Nicholas corner of the block. "This is not the end of it. What they were going to do to the Statue of Liberty will be small in comparison. We black people are tired of being shoved around." Standing across the street near the memorial park one of Malcolm's close associates commented: "It's a shame." Later he added that "if it's war they want, they'll get it." He would not say whether Elijah Muhammed's followers had anything to do with the assassination. About 3:30 P.M. Malcolm X's wife, Betty, was escorted by three men and a woman from the Columbia Presbyterian Hospital. Tears streamed down her face. She was screaming, "They killed him!" Malcolm X had no last words. . . . The bombing and burning of the No. 7 Mosque early Tuesday morning was the first blow by those who are seeking revenge for the cold-blooded murder of a man who at 39 might have grown to the stature of respectable leadership.

Changes in Perceptions and Perspectives

Just as journalists, scientists, and disaster officials change their perspectives after gaining increased knowledge, your ways of viewing the world will develop and change through the experiences you have, the knowledge you acquire, and your reflections on your experiences and knowledge. As you think critically about perceptions, you will learn more about how you make sense of the world. This understanding may strengthen your perceptions, or it may change them.

Obtaining More Accurate Perceptions: Adjusting the Lenses

So far, we have emphasized the great extent to which, by selecting, organizing, and interpreting, we directly affect our perceptions. We have suggested that each of us views the world through his or her own unique lenses, that no two of us perceive the world in exactly the same way. In addition, the sources on which we rely for the most up-to-date and ostensibly most accurate, objective information are themselves compromised by different and conflicting perceptions and perspectives as they try to negotiate enormous amounts of changing information.

Because we actively participate in selecting, organizing, and interpreting the sensations we experience, our perceptions are often incomplete, inaccurate, or subjective. To complicate the situation further, our own limitations in perceiving are not the only factors that can cause us problems. Other people often purposefully create perceptions and misperceptions. An advertiser who wants to sell a product may try to create the impression that our lives will be changed if we use it. Or a person who wants to discredit someone else may spread untrue rumors about her.

Develop Awareness

The only way to correct the mistakes, distortions, and incompleteness of our perceptions is to become aware of the ordinarily unconscious process by which we perceive and make sense of the world. By doing so, we will be able to think critically about what is going on and to correct our mistakes and distortions. In other words, we can use our critical thinking abilities to create a clearer and more informed idea of what is taking place. As the readings on the aftermath of Hurricane Katrina have shown, we cannot rely on the validity of our perceptions alone. If we remain unaware of how our process of perceiving operates and of our active role in it, we will be unable to control it. We will be convinced that the way we see the world is the way the world is, even when our perceptions are mistaken, distorted, or incomplete.

Besides asking questions, we have to become aware of the personal perspectives that we bring to our perceptions. Each of us brings to every situation a whole collection of expectations, interests, fears, and hopes that can influence what we are perceiving.

Consider the following situations:

- You and your family have been advised to evacuate in the path of a forthcoming hurricane, but you remember from the experiences of people in New Orleans and Houston that to flee could leave your property vulnerable to looting or could result in a very long, hot, uncomfortable road trip that might not in the end have been necessary. How do you balance the recommendations of current authority with recent past experience?
- Your teacher asks you to evaluate the performance of a colleague who is giving a report to the group. You don't like this other student because he acts as if he's superior to everyone else in the group. How do you evaluate his report?
- You are asked to estimate the size of an audience attending an event that your organization has sponsored. How many people are there?

In each of these cases, your perceptions might be influenced by whatever hopes, fears, or prejudices you brought to the situation, causing your observations to be distorted or inaccurate. Although you usually cannot eliminate the personal feelings that influence your perceptions, you can become aware of these feelings and try to control them.

Get Input from Others

The first step in critically examining your perceptions is to be willing to ask questions about them. As long as you believe that the way you see things is the only way to see them, you will not be able to recognize when your perceptions are distorted or inaccurate.

For instance, if you believe that your interpretation of the twins shown in the photo in the Thinking-Writing Activity on page 189 is the only correct one, you will probably not consider other interpretations. But if you are willing to entertain other possible interpretations, you will open the way to more fully developing your perception of what is taking place.

As noted in Chapter 7, critical thinkers strive to see things from different perspectives. One of the best ways to do so is by communicating with others. This means exchanging and critically examining ideas in an open and organized way. Engaging in dialogue is one of the main ways to check your perceptions—by asking others what their perceptions are and comparing and contrasting them with yours.

This is exactly what you did when you discussed the various possible interpretations of the twins in the photo. By comparing your perceptions with those of your classmates, you developed a more complete sense of how differently events can be viewed as well as an appreciation of the reasons supporting the different perspectives.

Find Evidence

Also, you should try to discover independent proof or evidence regarding your perceptions. You can evaluate the accuracy of your perceptions when evidence is available in the form of records, photographs, videotapes, or the results of experiments. What independent forms of evidence could verify your perceptions about the twins?

Keep an Open Mind

Thinking critically about perceptions means trying to avoid developing impulsive or superficial ones that you are unwilling to change. As explained in Chapter 3, a critical thinker is *thoughtful* in approaching the world and open to modifying his or her views in light of new information or better insights. Consider the following perceptions:

- Women are very emotional.
- Politicians are corrupt.
- All Muslims are potential terrorists.
- People who are good athletes are usually poor students.
- The government doesn't care about poor people.

These types of general perceptions are known as *stereotypes* because they express a belief about an entire group of people without recognizing the individual differences among members of the group.

For instance, it is probably accurate to say that there are some politicians who are corrupt, but this is not the same as saying that all, or even most, politicians are corrupt. Stereotypes affect our perceptions of the world because they encourage us to form inaccurate and superficial ideas about a whole group of people ("Teenagers are reckless drivers"). When we meet someone who falls into this group, we automatically perceive that person as possessing a stereotyped quality ("This person is a teenager, so he is a reckless driver"). Even if we find that the person does not fit our stereotyped perception ("This teenager is not a reckless driver"), this sort of superficial and thoughtless labeling does not encourage us to change our perceptions of the group as a whole. Instead, it encourages us to overlook the conflicting information in favor of our stereotyped perceptions ("All teenagers are reckless drivers—except this one"). In contrast, when we are perceiving in a thoughtful fashion, we try to see what a person is like as an individual instead of trying to fit him or her into a pre-existing category.

Sometimes stereotypes are so built into a culture that it is difficult for a person to be aware of them until they are brought to his or her attention. The perspective, or view of the world, that the culture presents may not even acknowledge the possibility of other perspectives, so it can be very difficult for an individual to become aware of them and then to "switch lenses" to try to see a situation from those viewpoints.

True critical thinkers can and do switch lenses, and in their writing they help others to do so as well. The following two readings present varying perspectives on Native Americans. One was written by a famous eighteenth-century American; the other was written in the early twentieth century by a member of the Sioux nation. As you read these accounts, think about what factors probably contributed to the writers' perspectives.

"Remarks Concerning the Savages of North America"

BY BENJAMIN FRANKLIN (1706–1790)

Perhaps no other figure so captures the American imagination—or the America as once imagined—as Benjamin Franklin. Born into a family of Boston soapmakers, Franklin became a printer's apprentice to his brother, James, at the age of twelve. As brothers tend to do, Benjamin and James quarreled repeatedly; in 1723, Benjamin ran away to Philadelphia. After several difficult years of hard work, Franklin was established enough in his own printing business to marry Deborah Read in 1730. He began publishing and contributing to a newspaper, the *Pennsylvania Gazette,* and in 1733 he started publishing Poor Richard's Almanack.

Franklin used his prominent position as a businessman and journalist to undertake civic initiatives that are still cornerstones of American communities. Franklin helped to establish the first free lending library, the first public hospital, and the first organized firefighting company in America. Politically, Franklin was elected to the Second Continental Congress in 1775 and helped to draft the Declaration of Independence. In 1776, Franklin was appointed the ambassador to the Court of Louis XVI for the American colonies. Franklin died at the age of eighty-four, back home in Philadelphia. His funeral was attended by 20,000 people.

In the following essay, excerpted from a longer work published in 1784, Franklin uses the term savages ironically. His admiration and respect for Native Americans is rooted in the diplomatic relationships he established with the Iroquois Nation in the 1760s. When, in 1763, a vigilante army of white settlers massacred a settlement of Conestoga Iroquois—including women and children—Franklin responded by mustering an army of Quakers and other citizens, including Governor Penn himself. The action probably saved more than one hundred Conestoga lives.

S avages we call them, because their Manners differ from ours, which we think the Perfection of Civility; they think the same of theirs.

Perhaps, if we could examine the Manners of different Nations with Impartiality, we should find no People so rude, as to be without any Rules of Politeness; nor any so polite, as not to have some Remains of Rudeness.

The Indian Men, when young, are Hunters and Warriors; when old, Counsellors; for all their Government is by Counsel of the Sages; there is no Force, there are no Prisons, no Officers to compel Obedience, or inflict Punishment. Hence they generally study Oratory, the best Speaker having the most Influence. The Indian Women till the Ground, dress the Food, nurse and bring up the Children, and preserve and hand down to Posterity the Memory of public Transactions. These Employments of Men and Women are accounted natural and honourable. Having few artificial Wants, they have abundance of Leisure for Improvement by Conversation. Our laborious Manner of Life, compared with theirs, they esteem slavish and base; and the Learning, on which we value ourselves, they regard as frivolous and useless. An Instance of this occurred at the Treaty of Lancaster, in Pennsylvania, *anno* 1744, between the Government of Virginia and the Six Nations. After the principal Business was settled, the Commissioners from Virginia acquainted the Indians by a Speech, that there was at Williamsburg a College, with a Fund for Educating Indian youth; and that, if the Six Nations would send down half a dozen of their young Lads to that College, the Government would take care that they should be well provided for, and instructed in all the Learning of the White People. It is one of the Indian Rules of Politeness not to answer a public Proposition the same day that it is made; they think it would be treating it as a light matter, and that they show it Respect by taking time to consider it, as of a Matter important. They therefore deferr'd their Answer till the Day following; when their Speaker began, by expressing their deep Sense of the kindness of the Virginia Government, in making them that Offer; "for we know," says he, "that you highly esteem the kind of Learning taught in those Colleges, and that the Maintenance of our young Men, while with you, would be very expensive to you. We are convinc'd, therefore, that you mean to do us Good by your Proposal; and we thank you heartily. But you, who are wise, must know that different Nations have different Conceptions of things; and you will therefore not take it amiss, if our Ideas of this kind of Education happen not to be the same with yours. We have had some Experience of it; Several of our young People were formerly brought up at the Colleges of the Northern Provinces; they were instructed in all your Sciences; but, when they came back to us, they were bad Runners, ignorant of every means of living in the Woods, unable to bear either Cold or Hunger, knew neither how to build a Cabin, take a Deer, or kill an Enemy, spoke our Language imperfectly, were therefore neither fit for Hunters, Warriors, nor Counsellors; they were totally good for nothing. We are however not the less oblig'd by your kind Offer, tho' we decline accepting it; and, to show our grateful Sense of it, if the Gentlemen of Virginia will send us a Dozen of their Sons, we will take great Care of their Education, instruct them in all we know, and make *Men* of them."

Having frequent Occasions to hold public Councils, they have acquired great Order and Decency in conducting them. The old Men sit in the foremost Ranks, the Warriors in the next, and the Women and Children in the hindmost. The Business of the Women is to take exact Notice of what passes, imprint it in their Memories (for they have no Writing), and communicate it to their Children. They are the Records of the Council, and they preserve Traditions of the Stipulations in Treaties 100 Years back; which, when we compare with our Writings, we always find exact. He that would speak, rises. The rest observe a profound Silence. When he has finish'd and sits down, they leave him 5 to 6 Minutes to recollect, that, if he has omitted anything he intended to say, or has anything to add, he may rise again and deliver it. To interrupt another, even in common Conversation, is reckon'd highly indecent. How different this is from the conduct of a polite British House of Commons, where scarce a day passes without some Confusion, that makes the Speaker hoarse in calling *to Order;* and how different from the Mode of Conversation in many polite Companies of Europe, where, if you do not deliver your Sentence with great Rapidity, you are cut off in the middle of it by the Impatient Loquacity of those you converse with, and never suffer'd to finish it!

5   The Politeness of these Savages in Conversation is indeed carried to Excess, since it does not permit them to contradict or deny the Truth of what is asserted in their Presence. By this means they indeed avoid Disputes; but then it becomes difficult to know their Minds, or what Impression you make upon them. The Missionaries who have attempted to convert them to Christianity, all complain of this as one of the great Difficulties of their Mission. The Indians hear with Patience the Truths of the Gospel explain'd to them, and give their usual Tokens of Assent and Approbation; you would think they were convinc'd. No such matter. It is mere Civility.

A Swedish Minister, having assembled the chiefs of the Susquehanah Indians, made a Sermon to them, acquainting them with the principal historical Facts on which our Religion is founded; such as the Fall of our first Parents by eating an Apple, the coming of Christ to repair the Mischief, his Miracles and Suffering, &c. When he had finished, an Indian Orator stood up to thank him. "What you have told us," says he, "is all very good. It is indeed bad to eat Apples. It is better to make them all into Cyder. We are much oblig'd by your kindness in coming so far, to tell us these Things which you have heard from your Mothers. In return, I will tell you some of those we had heard from ours. In the Beginning, our Fathers had only the Flesh of Animals to subsist on; and if their Hunting was unsuccessful, they were starving. Two of our young Hunters, having kill'd a Deer, made a Fire in the Woods to broil some Part of it. When they were about to satisfy their Hunger, they beheld a beautiful young Woman descend from the Clouds, and seat herself on that Hill, which you see yonder among the blue Mountains. They said to each other, it is a Spirit that has smelt our broiling Venison, and wishes to eat of it; let us offer some to her. They presented her with the Tongue; she was pleas'd with the Taste of it, and said, 'Your kindness shall be rewarded; come to this Place after thirteen Moons, and you shall find something that will be of great Benefit in nourishing you and your Children to the latest Generations.' They did so, and, to their Surprise, found Plants they had never seen before; but which, from that ancient time, have been constantly cultivated among us, to our great Advantage. Where her right Hand had touched the Ground, they found Maize; where her left hand had touch'd it, they found Kidney-Beans; and where her Backside had sat on it, they found Tobacco." The good Missionary, disgusted with this idle Tale, said, "What I delivered to you were sacred Truths; but what you tell me is mere Fable, Fiction, and Falshood." The Indian, offended, reply'd, "My brother, it seems your Friends have not done you Justice in your Education; they have not well instructed you in the Rules of common Civility. You saw that we, who understand and practise those Rules, believ'd all your stories; why do you refuse to believe ours?"

When any of them come into our Towns, our People are apt to crowd round them, gaze upon them, and incommode them, where they desire to be private; this they esteem great Rudeness, and the Effect of the Want of Instruction in the Rules of Civility and good Manners. "We have," say they, "as much Curiosity as you, and when you come into our Towns, we wish for Opportunities of looking at you; but for this purpose we hide ourselves behind Bushes, where you are to pass, and never intrude ourselves into your Company."

Their Manner of entering one another's village has likewise its Rules. It is reckon'd uncivil in travelling Strangers to enter a Village abruptly, without giving Notice of their Approach. Therefore, as soon as they arrive within hearing, they stop and hollow, remaining there till invited to enter. Two old Men usually come out to them, and lead them in. There is in every Village a vacant Dwelling, called *the Strangers' House*. Here they are plac'd, while the old Men go round from Hut to Hut, acquainting the Inhabitants, that Strangers are arriv'd, who are probably hungry and weary; and every one sends them what he can spare of Victuals, and Skins to repose on. When the Strangers are refresh'd, Pipes and Tobacco are brought; and then, but not before, Conversation begins, with Enquiries who they are, whither bound, what News, &c.; and it usually ends with offers of Service, if the Strangers have occasion of Guides, or any Necessaries for continuing their Journey; and nothing is exacted for the Entertainment.

The same Hospitality, esteem'd among them as a principal Virtue, is practis'd by private Persons; of which Conrad Weiser, our Interpreter, gave me the following Instance. He had been naturaliz'd among the Six Nations, and spoke well the Mohock Language. In going thro' the Indian Country, to carry a Message from our Governor to the Council at Onondaga, he call'd at the Habitation of Canassatego, an old Acquaintance, who embrac'd him, spread Furs for him to sit on, plac'd before him some boil'd Beans and Venison, and mix'd some Rum and Water for his Drink. When he was well refresh'd, and had lit his Pipe, Canassatego began to converse with him; ask'd how he had far'd the many Years since they had seen each other; whence he then came; what occasion'd the Journey, &c. Conrad answered all his Questions; and when the Discourse began to flag, the Indian, to continue it, said, "Conrad, you have lived long among the white People, and know something of their Customs; I have been sometimes at Albany, and have observed, that once in Seven Days they shut up their Shops, and assemble all in the great House; tell me what it is for? What do they do there?" "They meet there," says Conrad, "to hear and learn *good Things*." "I do not doubt," says the Indian, "that they tell you so; they have told me the same; but I doubt the Truth of what they say, and I will tell you my Reasons. I went lately to Albany to sell my Skins and buy Blankets, Knives, Powder, Rum, &c. You know I us'd generally to deal with Hans Hanson; but I was a little inclin'd this time to try some other Merchant. However, I call'd first upon Hans, and asked him what he would give for Beaver. He said he could not give any more than four Shillings a Pound; 'but,' says he, 'I cannot talk on Business now; this is the Day when we meet together to learn *Good Things*, and I am going to the Meeting.' So I thought to myself, 'Since we cannot do any Business to-day, I may as well go to the meeting too,' and I went with him. There stood up a Man in Black, and began to talk to the People very angrily. I did not understand what he said; but, perceiving that he look'd much at me and at Hanson, I imagin'd he was angry at seeing me there; so I went out, sat down near the House, struck Fire, and lit my Pipe, waiting till the Meeting should break up. I thought too, that the Man had mention'd something of Beaver, and I suspected it might be the Subject of their Meeting. So, when they came out, I accosted my Merchant. 'Well, Hans,' says I, 'I hope you have agreed to give more than four Shillings a Pound.' 'No,' says he, 'I cannot give so much; I cannot give more than three shillings and sixpence.' I then spoke to several other Dealers, but they all sung the same song,—Three and sixpence,—Three and sixpence. This made it clear to me, that my Suspicion was right; and, that whatever they pretended of meeting to learn *good Things*, the real purpose was to consult how to cheat Indians in the Price of Beaver. Consider but little, Conrad, and you must be of my Opinion. If they met so often to learn *good Things*, they would certainly have learnt some before this time. But they are still ignorant. You know our Practice. If a white Man, in travelling thro' our Country, enters one of our Cabins, we all treat him as I treat you; we dry him if he is wet, we warm him if he is cold, we give him Meat and Drink, that he may allay his Thirst and Hunger; and we spread soft Furs for him to rest and sleep on; we demand nothing in return. But, if I go into a white Man's House at Albany, and ask for Victuals and Drink, they say, 'Where is your Money?' and if I have none, they say, 'Get out, you Indian Dog.' You see they have not yet learned those little *Good Things*, that we need no Meetings to be instructed in, because our Mothers taught them to us when we were Children; and therefore it is impossible their Meetings should be, as they say, for any such purpose, or have any such Effect; they are only to contrive *the Cheating of Indians in the Price of Beaver*."

QUESTIONS FOR ACTIVE READING

1. What is Franklin's definition of *savage*? This term has long since ceased to be appropriate when used to refer to indigenous peoples; do you think that Franklin, writing two hundred years ago, was also aware of how inappropriate this term could be? Explain your answer with reference to Franklin's own examples and argument.

2. What two ideals is Franklin comparing in this essay? How does he use comparison to structure this essay?

3. Franklin was widely known for his wit, of which there is a sly example in paragraph 6. Identify the joke. Why does Franklin include it? Is he simply being sarcastic, or is he making a much larger and subtler comparison of perspectives?

QUESTIONS FOR THINKING CRITICALLY

1. What does Franklin mean when he says, "Perhaps, if we could examine the Manners of different Nations with Impartiality, we should find no People so rude, as to be without any Rules of Politeness; nor any so polite, as not to have some Remains of Rudeness"?

2. What does the Iroquois speaker mean when he says, "If the Gentlemen of Virginia will send us a Dozen of their Sons, we will take great Care of their Education, instruct them in all we know, and make *Men* of them"?

3. In paragraph 9, Franklin recounts the experience of the Iroquois elder Canassatego when he went to a "great House" to "hear and learn *good Things*." Why does Franklin use Canassatego's exact language, rather than explaining or translating his perspective for his English-speaking colonial audience? What is the tremendous irony that Canassatego's perspective gives to the concept of "*good Things*"?

FROM *The School Days of an Indian Girl*

BY ZITKALA-SA (GERTRUDE SIMMONS BONNIN) (1876–1938)

A member of the Yankton Sioux nation, Zitkala-Sa was born on the Pine Ridge Reservation in South Dakota and raised in a traditional tipi on the Missouri River. At the end of the nineteenth and beginning of the twentieth centuries, many surviving Native American nations were forced from their traditional lands onto "reservations," lands managed by the American government. Children on these reservations were forced to sacrifice their native languages, cultures, and traditions, often sent away from their families to religious or secular boarding schools. In the following autobiographical essay, Zitkala-Sa recounts her time spent at a Quaker boarding school for Native American children in Wabash, Indiana. The experience left her feeling divided between identities and cultures, a division that galvanized her into pursuing further education and devoting her life to justice for Native Americans. She graduated from Earlham College with plans to become a teacher, and her musical talents brought her to the Boston Conservatory. In 1900, she went to Paris with the Carlisle Indian Industrial School (CIIS) as violin soloist for the Paris Exposition. But the loss and destruction of her own culture haunted her, and led to her first book, the 1901 collection *Old Indian Legends*.

Zitkala-Sa became increasingly active politically, along with her husband, Ray Bonnin of the Sioux nation. She worked to increase voter participation by Native Americans, and in 1930, she formed the National Council of American Indians, where she served as president until her death in 1938.

The Cutting of My Long Hair

The first day in the land of apples was a bitter-cold one; for the snow still covered the ground, and the trees were bare. A large bell rang for breakfast, its loud metallic voice crashing through the belfry overhead and into our sensitive ears. The annoying clatter of shoes on bare floors gave us no peace. The constant clash of harsh noises, with an undercurrent of many voices murmuring an unknown tongue, made a bedlam within which I was securely tied. And though my spirit tore itself in struggling for its lost freedom, all was useless.

A paleface woman, with white hair, came up after us. We were placed in a line of girls who were marching into the dining room. These were Indian girls, in stiff shoes and closely clinging dresses. The small girls wore sleeved aprons and shingled hair. As I walked noiselessly in my soft moccasins, I felt like sinking to the floor, for my blanket had been stripped from my shoulders. I looked hard at the Indian girls, who seemed not to care that they were even more immodestly dressed than I, in their tightly fitting clothes. While we marched in, the boys entered at an opposite door. I watched for the three young braves who came in our party. I spied them in the rear ranks, looking as uncomfortable as I felt.

A small bell was tapped, and each of the pupils drew a chair from under the table. Supposing this act meant they were to be seated, I pulled out mine and at once slipped into it from one side. But when I turned my head, I saw that I was the only one seated, and all the rest at our table remained standing. Just as I began to rise, looking shyly around to see how chairs were to be used, a second bell was sounded. All were seated at last, and I had to crawl back into my chair again. I heard a man's voice at one end of the hall, and I looked around to see him. But all the others hung their heads over their plates. As I glanced at the long chain of tables, I caught the eyes of a paleface woman upon me. Immediately I dropped my eyes, wondering why I was so keenly watched by the strange woman. The man ceased his mutterings, and then a third bell was tapped. Every one picked up his knife and fork and began eating. I began crying instead, for by this time I was afraid to venture anything more.

But this eating by formula was not the hardest trial in that first day. Late in the morning, my friend Judewin gave me a terrible warning. Judewin knew a few words of English, and she had overheard the paleface woman talk about cutting our long, heavy hair. Our mothers had taught us that only unskilled warriors who were captured had their hair shingled by the enemy. Among our people, short hair was worn by mourners, and shingled hair by cowards!

5   We discussed our fate some moments, and when Judewin said, "We have to submit, because they are strong," I rebelled.

"No, I will not submit! I will struggle first!" I answered.

I watched my chance, and when no one noticed I disappeared. I crept up the stairs as quietly as I could in my squeaking shoes,—my moccasins had been exchanged for shoes. Along the hall I passed, without knowing whither I was going. Turning aside to an open door, I found a large room with three white beds in it. The windows were covered with dark green curtains, which made the room very dim. Thankful that no one was there, I directed my steps toward the corner farthest from the door. On my hands and knees I crawled under the bed, and cuddled myself in the dark corner.

From my hiding place I peered out, shuddering with fear whenever I heard footsteps near by. Though in the hall loud voices were calling my name, and I knew that even Judewin was searching for me, I did not open my mouth to answer. Then the steps were quickened and the voices became excited. The sounds came nearer and nearer. Women and girls entered the room. I held my breath, and watched them open closet doors and peep behind large trunks. Some one threw up the curtains, and the room was filled with sudden light. What caused them to stoop and look under the bed I do not know. I remember being dragged out, though I resisted by kicking and scratching wildly. In spite of myself, I was carried downstairs and tied fast in a chair.

I cried aloud, shaking my head all the while until I felt the cold blades of the scissors against my neck, and heard them gnaw off one of my thick braids. Then I lost my spirit. Since the day I was taken from my mother I had suffered extreme indignities. People had stared at me. I had been tossed about in the air like a wooden puppet. And now my long hair was shingled like a coward's! In my anguish I moaned for my mother, but no one came to comfort me. Not a soul reasoned quietly with me, as my own mother used to do; for now I was only one of many little animals driven by a herder.

The Snow Episode

A short time after our arrival we three Dakotas were playing in the snowdrifts. We were all still deaf to the English language, excepting Judewin, who always heard such puzzling things. One morning we learned through her ears that we were forbidden to fall lengthwise in the snow, as we had been doing, to see our own impressions. However, before many hours we had forgotten the order, and were having great sport in the snow, when a shrill voice called us. Looking up, we saw an imperative hand beckoning us into the house. We shook the snow off ourselves, and started toward the woman as slowly as we dared.

Judewin said: "Now the paleface is angry with us. She is going to punish us for falling into the snow. If she looks straight into your eyes and talks loudly, you must wait until she stops. Then, after a tiny pause, say, 'No.'" The rest of the way we practiced upon the little word "no."

As it happened, Thowin was summoned to judgment first. The door shut behind her with a click.

Judewin and I stood silently listening at the keyhole. The paleface woman talked in very severe tones. Her words fell from her lips like crackling embers, and her inflection ran up like the small end of a switch. I understood her voice better than the things she was saying. I was certain we had made her very impatient with us. Judewin heard enough of the words to realize all too late that she had taught us the wrong reply.

"Oh, poor Thowin!" she gasped, as she put both hands over her ears.

Just then I heard Thowin's tremulous answer, "No."

With an angry exclamation, the woman gave her a hard spanking. Then she stopped to say something. Judewin said it was this: "Are you going to obey my word the next time?"

Thowin answered again with the only word at her command, "No."

This time the woman meant her blows to smart, for the poor frightened girl shrieked at the top of her voice. In the midst of the whipping the blows ceased abruptly, and the woman asked another question: "Are you going to fall in the snow again?"

Thowin gave her bad password another trial. We heard her say feebly, "No! No!"

With this the woman hid away her half-worn slipper, and led the child out, stroking her black shorn head. Perhaps it occurred to her that brute force is not the solution for such a problem. She did nothing to Judewin nor to me. She only returned to us our unhappy comrade, and left us alone in the room.

During the first two or three seasons misunderstandings as ridiculous as this one of the snow episode frequently took place, bringing unjustifiable frights and punishments into our little lives.

Within a year I was able to express myself somewhat in broken English. As soon as I comprehended a part of what was said and done, a mischievous spirit of revenge possessed me. One day I was called in from my play for some misconduct. I had disregarded a rule which seemed to me very needlessly binding. I was sent into the kitchen to mash the turnips for dinner. It was noon, and steaming dishes were hastily carried into the dining room. I hated turnips, and their odor which came from the brown jar was offensive to me. With fire in my heart, I took the wooden tool that the paleface woman held out to me. I stood upon a step, and, grasping the handle with both hands, I bent in hot rage over the turnips. I worked my vengeance upon them. All were so busily occupied that no one noticed me. I saw that the turnips were in a pulp, and that further beating could not improve them; but the order was, "Mash these turnips," and mash them I would! I renewed my energy; and as I sent the masher into the bottom of the jar, I felt a satisfying sensation that the weight of my body had gone into it.

Just here a paleface woman came up to my table. As she looked into the jar she shoved my hands roughly aside. I stood fearless and angry. She placed her red hands upon the rim of the jar. Then she gave one lift and a stride away from the table. But lo! the pulpy contents fell through the crumbled bottom to the floor! She spared me no scolding phrases that I had earned. I did not heed them. I felt triumphant in my revenge, though deep within me I was a wee bit sorry to have broken the jar.

As I sat eating my dinner, and saw that no turnips were served, I whooped in my heart for having once asserted the rebellion within me.

•   •   •   •   •

Four Strange Summers

25   After my first three years of school, I roamed again in the Western country through four strange summers.

During this time I seemed to hang in the heart of chaos, beyond the touch or voice of human aid. My brother, being almost ten years my senior, did not quite understand my feelings. My mother had never gone inside of a schoolhouse, and so she was not capable of comforting her daughter who could read and write. Even nature seemed to have no place for me. I was neither a wee girl nor a tall one; neither a wild Indian nor a tame one. This deplorable situation was the effect of my brief course in the East, and the unsatisfactory "teenth" in a girl's years.

It was under these trying conditions that, one bright afternoon, as I sat restless and unhappy in my brother's cabin, I caught the sound of the spirited step of my brother's pony on the road which passed by our dwelling. Soon I heard the wheels of a light buckboard, and Dawee's familiar "Ho!" to his pony. He alighted upon the bare ground in front of our house. Tying his pony to one of the projecting corner logs of the low-roofed cottage, he stepped upon the wooden doorstep.

I met him there with a hurried greeting, and as I passed by, he looked a quiet "What?" into my eyes.

When he began talking with my mother, I slipped the rope from the pony's bridle. Seizing the reins and bracing my feet against the dashboard, I wheeled around in an instant. The pony was ever ready to try his speed. Looking backward, I saw Dawee waving his hand to me. I turned with the curve in the road and disappeared. I followed the winding road which crawled upward between the bases of little hillocks. Deep water-worn ditches ran parallel on either side. A strong wind blew against my cheeks and fluttered my sleeves. The pony reached the top of the highest hill, and began an even race on the level lands. There was nothing moving within that great circular horizon of the Dakota prairies save the tall grasses, over which the wind blew and rolled off in long, shadowy waves.

Within this vast wigwam of blue and green I rode reckless and insignificant. It satisfied my small consciousness to see the white foam fly from the pony's mouth.

Suddenly, out of the earth a coyote came forth at a swinging trot that was taking the cunning thief toward the hills and the village beyond. Upon the moment's impulse, I gave him a long chase and a wholesome fright. As I turned away to go back to the village, the wolf sank down upon his haunches for rest, for it was a hot summer day; and as I drove slowly homeward, I saw his sharp nose still pointed at me, until I vanished below the margin of the hilltops.

In a little while I came in sight of my mother's house. Dawee stood in the yard, laughing at an old warrior who was pointing his forefinger, and again waving his whole hand, toward the hills. With his blanket drawn over one shoulder, he talked and motioned excitedly. Dawee turned the old man by the shoulder and pointed me out to him.

"Oh han!" (Oh yes) the warrior muttered, and went his way. He had climbed the top of his favorite barren hill to survey the surrounding prairies, when he spied my chase after the coyote. His keen eyes recognized the pony and driver. At once uneasy for my safety, he had come running to my mother's cabin to give her warning. I did not appreciate his kindly interest, for there was an unrest gnawing at my heart.

As soon as he went away, I asked Dawee about something else.

"No, my baby sister, I cannot take you with me to the party to-night," he replied. Though I was not far from fifteen, and I felt that before long I should enjoy all the privileges of my tall cousin, Dawee persisted in calling me his baby sister.

That moonlight night, I cried in my mother's presence when I heard the jolly young people pass by our cottage. They were no more young braves in blankets and eagle plumes, nor Indian maids with prettily painted cheeks. They had gone three years to school in the East, and had become civilized. The young men wore the white man's coat and trousers, with bright neckties. The girls wore tight muslin dresses, with ribbons at neck and waist. At these gatherings they talked English. I could speak English almost as well as my brother, but I was not properly dressed to be taken along. I had no hat, no ribbons, and no close-fitting gown. Since my return from school I had thrown away my shoes, and wore again the soft moccasins.

While Dawee was busily preparing to go I controlled my tears. But when I heard him bounding away on his pony, I buried my face in my arms and cried hot tears.

My mother was troubled by my unhappiness. Coming to my side, she offered me the only printed matter we had in our home. It was an Indian Bible, given her some years ago by a missionary. She tried to console me. "Here, my child, are the white man's papers. Read a little from them," she said most piously.

I took it from her hand, for her sake; but my enraged spirit felt more like burning the book, which afforded me no help, and was a perfect delusion to my mother. I did not read it, but laid it unopened on the floor, where I sat on my feet. The dim yellow light of the braided muslin burning in a small vessel of oil flickered and sizzled in the awful silent storm which followed my rejection of the Bible.

40

Now my wrath against the fates consumed my tears before they reached my eyes. I sat stony, with a bowed head. My mother threw a shawl over her head and shoulders, and stepped out into the night.

After an uncertain solitude, I was suddenly aroused by a loud cry piercing the night. It was my mother's voice wailing among the barren hills which held the bones of buried warriors. She called aloud for her brothers' spirits to support her in her helpless misery. My fingers grew icy cold, as I realized that my unrestrained tears had betrayed my suffering to her, and she was grieving for me.

Before she returned, though I knew she was on her way, for she had ceased her weeping, I extinguished the light, and leaned my head on the window sill.

Many schemes of running away from my surroundings hovered about in my mind. A few more moons of such a turmoil drove me away to the Eastern school. I rode on the white man's iron steed, thinking it would bring me back to my mother in a few winters, when I should be grown tall, and there would be congenial friends awaiting me.

Incurring My Mother's Displeasure

In the second journey to the East I had not come without some precautions. I had a secret interview with one of our best medicine men, and when I left his wigwam I carried securely in my sleeve a tiny bunch of magic roots. This possession assured me of friends wherever I should go. So absolutely did I believe in its charms that I wore it through all the school routine for more than a year. Then, before I lost my faith in the dead roots, I lost the little buckskin bag containing all my good luck.

45

At the close of this second term of three years I was the proud owner of my first diploma. The following autumn I ventured upon a college career against my mother's will.

I had written for her approval, but in her reply I found no encouragement. She called my notice to her neighbors' children, who had completed their education in three years. They had returned to their homes, and were then talking English with the frontier settlers. Her few words hinted that I had better give up my slow attempt to learn the white man's ways, and be content to roam over the prairies and find my living upon wild roots. I silenced her by deliberate disobedience.

Thus, homeless and heavy-hearted, I began anew my life among strangers.

As I hid myself in my little room in the college dormitory, away from the scornful and yet curious eyes of the students, I pined for sympathy. Often I wept in secret, wishing I had gone West, to be nourished by my mother's love, instead of remaining among a cold race whose hearts were frozen hard with prejudice.

During the fall and winter seasons I scarcely had a real friend, though by that time several of my classmates were courteous to me at a safe distance.

My mother had not yet forgiven my rudeness to her, and I had no moment for letter-writing. By daylight and lamplight, I spun with reeds and thistles, until my hands were tired from their weaving, the magic design which promised me the white man's respect.

At length, in the spring term, I entered an oratorical contest among the various classes. As the day of competition approached, it did not seem possible that the event was so near at hand, but it came. In the chapel the classes assembled together, with their invited guests. The high platform was carpeted, and gayly festooned with college colors. A bright white light illumined the room, and outlined clearly the great polished beams that arched the domed ceiling. The assembled crowds filled the air with pulsating murmurs. When the hour for speaking arrived all were hushed. But on the wall the old clock which pointed out the trying moment ticked calmly on.

One after another I saw and heard the orators. Still, I could not realize that they longed for the favorable decision of the judges as much as I did. Each contestant received a loud burst of applause, and some were cheered heartily. Too soon my turn came, and I paused a moment behind the curtains for a deep breath. After my concluding words, I heard the same applause that the others had called out.

Upon my retreating steps, I was astounded to receive from my fellow students a large bouquet of roses tied with flowing ribbons. With the lovely flowers I fled from the stage. This friendly token was a rebuke to me for the hard feelings I had borne them.

Later, the decision of the judges awarded me the first place. Then there was a mad uproar in the hall, where my classmates sang and shouted my name at the top of their lungs; and the disappointed students howled and brayed in fearfully dissonant tin trumpets. In this excitement, happy students rushed forward to offer their congratulations. And I could not conceal a smile when they wished to escort me in a procession to the students' parlor, where all were going to calm themselves. Thanking them for the kind spirit which prompted them to make such a proposition, I walked alone with the night to my own little room.

A few weeks afterward, I appeared as the college representative in another contest. This time the competition was among orators from different colleges in our state. It was held at the state capital, in one of the largest opera houses.

Here again was a strong prejudice against my people. In the evening, as the great audience filled the house, the student bodies began warring among themselves. Fortunately, I was spared witnessing any of the noisy wrangling before the contest began. The slurs against the Indian that stained the lips of our opponents were already burning like a dry fever within my breast.

But after the orations were delivered a deeper burn awaited me. There, before that vast ocean of eyes, some college rowdies threw out a large white flag, with a drawing of a most forlorn Indian girl on it. Under this they had printed in bold black letters words that ridiculed the college which was represented by a "squaw." Such worse than barbarian rudeness embittered me. While we waited for the verdict of the judges, I gleamed fiercely upon the throngs of palefaces. My teeth were hard set, as I saw the white flag still floating insolently in the air.

Then anxiously we watched the man carry toward the stage the envelope containing the final decision.

There were two prizes given, that night, and one of them was mine!

60   The evil spirit laughed within me when the white flag dropped out of sight, and the hands which furled it hung limp in defeat.

Leaving the crowd as quickly as possible, I was soon in my room. The rest of the night I sat in an armchair and gazed into the crackling fire. I laughed no more in triumph when thus alone. The little taste of victory did not satisfy a hunger in my heart. In my mind I saw my mother far away on the Western plains, and she was holding a charge against me.

QUESTIONS FOR ACTIVE READING

1. Zitkala-Sa uses a strikingly apt metaphor in paragraph 9. What is that metaphor? How many different layers of meaning does it have here?

2. Zitkala-Sa recounts her experiences through the perspective of a child. What are the advantages to this perspective in telling her story? What are the disadvantages?

3. In what ways do the Bible or representations of Christianity figure in this narrative?

QUESTIONS FOR THINKING CRITICALLY

1. Compare Zitkala-Sa's experience with the missionary school to the conversation between an Iroquois elder and a group of Virginia politicians who offered to educate six young Iroquois men at a Williamsburg, Virginia, college (the college, William and Mary, is today one of the oldest continuing institutions of higher learning in America). In what ways does Zitkala-Sa's experience reflect the observations of the Iroquois elders, both in terms of the perils of assimilation as well as the rifts created between family members?

2. What is the "evil spirit" that Zitkala-Sa refers to in paragraph 60?

3. Did your education—and think broadly here of "education," not just of "school"—involve the taming or controlling of some part of your spirit or personality? What did you give up, and why? What did that loss teach you, if anything?

Writing Thoughtfully About Perspectives

Comparison and Contrast

Whenever we place two or more perspectives, or two or more other things, together and examine them for similarities and differences, we are engaging in the powerful thinking pattern called *comparison and contrast*. To be precise, when we *compare*, we are focusing on likenesses or areas of agreement; when we *contrast*, we are focusing on differences or areas of disagreement. Generally, the items examined are from the same category. We will discuss writing about items from the same category in the next section, Thinking in Comparisons. Sometimes, in order to make a point or to explain something, we may compare items from different categories. We will discuss these unusual comparisons in the Analogy section (pages 315–317).

Thinking in Comparisons

We use comparison and contrast informally in our daily lives when we make decisions such as what food to buy or which TV programs to watch. When we use comparison and contrast in a formal way by following certain established principles, we are using it to think critically to arrive at a significant conclusion. That is, we use it not only to list areas of similarity or difference but also to help achieve a clearer understanding or new insight. When we use comparison and contrast to examine different perspectives, we do so in order to understand each perspective, to see if one is superior to another, to see if we ourselves have yet another perspective, and so on.

The principles for using comparison and contrast to think critically are straightforward.

1. *Compare or contrast two or more things that have something essential in common (that is, items from the same category).* Thus, it makes sense to compare two accounts of the same event or two essays on affirmative action.

2. *Establish important bases or points for comparison and contrast.* In everyday situations, it is fairly easy to determine which points are important. In deciding between two cars, the important points may be price, model, and safety features; exterior color or exact trunk capacity may be lesser concerns. But when you are working with written texts, finding points for comparison and contrast and deciding which of them are important require careful thought. When comparing or contrasting two accounts of the same event, important points might include the actual presence of the writers at the event or the writers' reliance on the accounts of others, the language the writers use to describe the participants or actions, and which details the writers have included or omitted. The writer's gender or the length of an account might or might not be significant.

3. *Develop or locate relevant, specific evidence for each point.* Opinions valued by critical thinkers are those supported by evidence. In everyday situations, evidence usually means facts: the prices of two different cars, the presence or absence of air bags, and so on. With written texts, the evidence comes from the texts themselves, in the form of either accurate paraphrases or direct quotations.

4. *Determine the significance of the comparison and contrast: What can be learned from it?* What should be done as a result? In everyday situations, this significance is often a determination: one car is superior to another and is therefore the one to purchase. When you are working with written texts, the significance may be that the texts disagree on important points; therefore, you may decide that one is more persuasive than the other.

GUIDELINES
FOR USING
COMPARISONS
IN WRITING

When you are ready to present the results of your critical thinking in writing for others to read and consider, you need to present your thinking in such a way that readers will be able to follow it and, hopefully, agree with your conclusion. Therefore, for writing, you should also follow these principles:

1. *Early and accurately, introduce the things to be compared and contrasted.* When you work with written texts, this means identifying what the texts are (personal essays, poems, newspaper accounts, excerpts from books, and so on) and naming the titles and authors, probably in the introductory paragraph.

2. *Develop a thesis which states that you will examine likenesses and differences.* Because you will be discussing two or more things and introducing points about each, the audience will be confronting a difficult reading task. A clear statement of what is to come can offer them a framework to follow.

3. *Organize the comparison or contrast in the way that will be easiest for the audience to follow.* There are three ways to organize a comparison and contrast: block, point-by-point, or a careful combination of the two.

   - *Block* means that after the introduction, you first present all the material about the first subject; then, you present all the material about the second. The selection by Russell R. Dynes and Havidán Rodriguez on pages 282–289 uses block organization.
   - *Point-by-point* means that for each key point or basis of comparison, you first give information about one of the things being compared and contrasted, then give information about the other. In this way, you can move back and forth between the two things being compared and contrasted. The selection by Benjamin Franklin on pages 296–300 uses point-by-point organization.
   - You can also use a *combination* of these two patterns when there are some items of similarity or difference that you can present in blocks, followed by points that you may want to address separately. Topic sentences and transitions are very important in a combination method!

4. *Bring up the same bases or points of comparison or contrast for each subject, and in the same order.* An incomplete comparison results when, for instance, the language used in one text is addressed but the language used in another is not discussed. If an important detail appears in one text but not in the other, it is reasonable to simply tell the audience this: "No mention is made of a doctor in this account."

5. *Assist the audience by using words, phrases, or sentences that show relationships and shifts.* Logical connections that exist in your mind may not necessarily be apparent to your audience, but you can point them out by using appropriate expressions.

Comparison words and phrases	Contrast words and phrases
Same	Different, differ from, difference
Similar, similarly	In contrast
Like, alike	Unlike
Reminds me of	On the other hand
Resembles	Conversely
Shows connections with	
Both	Is separate from

6. *State the significance of your comparison and contrast at the place in the essay where it will be most effective.* Sometimes writers use the significance as the opening lead, sometimes they incorporate it into the thesis statement, and sometimes they save it for the conclusion. In deciding where to place it, ask yourself where it will have the greatest impact on your audience.

"A Natural Disaster, and a Human Tragedy"

by Ted Steinberg

Ted Steinberg is a professor of history and law at Case Western University, with a particular interest in the history of American environmental law and policy. His book *Acts of God: The Unnatural History of Natural Disaster in America* (Oxford, 2000) was a nominee for a Pulitzer Prize. He has also written about the legal implications of American environmental policy for the *New York Times* and the *Los Angeles Times*, among numerous other newspapers and magazines. "A Natural Disaster, and a Human Tragedy" was published in the September 23, 2005, edition of *The Chronicle of Higher Education*, a leading newspaper and journal about academic life.

Is Hurricane Katrina "our tsunami," as the mayor of Biloxi, Miss., A. J. Holloway, has said? Does it make sense to compare today's disaster to a catastrophe that killed upward of 200,000 impoverished people, injured roughly half a million, displaced millions more, and was felt across a huge geographic span that included Sumatra, Thailand, India, Sri Lanka, and eastern Africa?

In searching for meaning in the current calamity, we can learn something about the root causes of such disasters by pinpointing the proper historical analogy.

Although it is no doubt an overstatement to compare Katrina to the 2004 tsunami, the two have some things in common. Both demonstrated the vulnerability of the poor in the face of natural calamity: Consider Katrina's victims who suffered through the aftermath at the Superdome and convention center. That was a man-made disaster that clearly could have been averted if the federal government, specifically the Federal Emergency Management Agency, had quickly marshaled the political will and resources to evacuate those without access to cars, instead of promoting on its Web site a faith-based charity that was clearly no match for the problem.

Likewise, both disasters demonstrated the tragic consequences of reckless coastal development. In Asia, industrial fish farms, tourist resorts, and refineries combined over the last generation to destroy huge stretches of coastal mangrove forest. The forest helps stabilize the land, and offers a form of natural protection that can soften the blow of a tsunami. Bangladesh experienced many fewer deaths in the disaster because of the conservation of its coastal mangroves than did Indonesia, where two-thirds of the forest has been destroyed.

5   In New Orleans, meanwhile, the dredging of channels to accommodate petrochemical companies has compromised huge amounts of marshland. Such changes, combined with the erosion of the area's barrier islands, and the Bush administration's policy of opening up more wetlands to development, weakened the natural frontline defense against a hurricane storm surge and left the city more vulnerable to death and destruction.

Both disasters also show the problems with neoliberal imperatives, based in a theory of political economy that idealizes the free market and chips away at the public sector at home, while worshiping at the altar of free trade and investment abroad. Foreign capital, whether in the form of tourism or the cash-cropping of fish, played a role in opening the coast around the Indian Ocean to the destructive force of the tsunami. In the aftermath of the disaster, the World Bank is leading the effort to expand the reach of those very same enterprises at the expense of the poor. The poor suffered the most in the calamity, and they are now experiencing the brutalizing effects of what the activist journalist Naomi Klein has rightly termed "disaster capitalism," as foreign corporations seek to profit from the reconstruction while the residents of the fishing villages that formerly occupied the area are being forced to relocate. In June 2005 Oxfam found that because the flow of aid has tended to go to business people and landowners, many of the poor have been made even poorer by the disaster.

What form the postdisaster rebuilding of the Gulf region will take remains to be seen. But this much is clear: Those poor people who had to suffer through the stench, the heat, and the overflowing toilets were victims of a way of thinking that goes back 25 years. Neoliberalism is a philosophy that has been shared by Republicans and Democrats alike (which is, by the way, why I'm not entirely convinced by those who argue that this kind of mistreatment would not have happened under a Kerry administration), and it was the root cause behind the failed evacuation. It is an ethos that deludes its adherents into thinking that "a thousand points of light" are better at solving America's problems than the federal government. It is a worldview that would rather put its faith in volunteer efforts than pony up the money and resources to safely evacuate the roughly 120,000 people in New Orleans who, we knew in advance, had no access to cars.

When it comes to hurricane evacuation, American officials ought to take a page out of Fidel Castro's handbook. The American news media never miss an opportunity to poke fun at the Communists. I would not want to defend all of Castro's policies, but whatever their faults, the Communists in Cuba have figured out how to use government resources to organize an efficient civil-defense system for protecting their people—staging exercises to practice evacuation, providing shelters in advance with medical personnel, and even bringing in trucks before a storm so people can save their material possessions. It hardly needs mentioning that being alive is one of the prerequisites for enjoying the freedom that Americans value so much.

So there is a great deal that the tsunami and the present hurricane have in common. But a much better historical comparison exists closer to home, one that highlights the irresponsible decision making and denial on the part of government officials that, combined with profit-driven land development, largely explains why the poor pay with their lives in such disasters. I have in mind the 1928 hurricane that took the lives of at least 1,836 people in Florida, the vast majority of them poor migrant workers who drowned as the waters of Lake Okeechobee rose up over a dike and pounded them to death.

10

That disaster is comparable to what is happening in the wake of Hurricane Katrina not just because the victims in both cases are overwhelmingly poor and African American. They compare because, in both cases, there were clear signs, in advance, that they were disasters waiting to happen—literally unnatural disasters.

In the case of the 1928 Florida hurricane, the warning was telegraphed several years in advance. Earlier in the century state authorities had overseen a massive drainage project that reclaimed land around the shores of Lake Okeechobee and turned it into valuable agricultural enterprises. Yet living around the lake had its price. In 1922 heavy rains caused the water to rise more than four feet and flooded Clewiston and Moore Haven, towns along the lake's southern shore that housed the black laborers who worked the rich agricultural land nearby.

In 1924 storms again raised the lake level, causing more flooding. Then, in the summer of 1926, heavy rains raised the level of the lake yet again, leading a journalist named Howard Sharp to beg state officials to take steps to lower the water: "The lake is truly at a level so high as to make a perilous situation in the event of a storm," he wrote in the *Tampa Tribune*.

The Everglades Drainage District, headed by some of the highest officials in the state, including Gov. John W. Martin and Attorney General J. B. Johnson, took no action to lower the water. By September 1 the level of Lake Okeechobee exceeded 18 feet. The levees around the lake were built to only 21 feet, and anyone even remotely familiar with the area knew that a stiff wind could cause the lake to rise as much as three feet. The mathematics of fatality and destruction were painfully obvious. Yet the drainage commissioners, beholden to wealthy agricultural and commercial interests—who wanted the lake water high to help with irrigating crops and navigation—refused to act.

Nobody listened, and on September 18, 1926, a Category 4 storm ripped across Florida and caused the waters of Lake Okeechobee to wash over a dike and kill at least 150 people (though 300 seems more likely) in Moore Haven, which had an entire population of only 1,200 at the time.

15   After the disaster, the attorney general explained: "The storm caused the loss and damage. . . . It is not humanly possible to guard against the unknown and against the forces of nature when loosed." Interpreting the event as a "natural" disaster masked the calamity's man-made causes and scarcely moved anyone to action to help ward off a future catastrophe, which, it turned out, was just around the corner.

On September 16, 1928, a powerful storm, with a barometric low of 27.43 inches—even lower than that recorded in 1926—swept ashore near Palm Beach. After the notorious 1900 Galveston hurricane (which left at least 8,000 dead), it was the deadliest storm in twentieth-century American history. Most of those who died were black migrant workers, virtually all of whom drowned in the towns along the southern shore of Lake Okeechobee, as the howling winds sent a wall of water crashing over the dikes in a grim repetition of what had happened two years before.

Sightseers, brimming with morbid curiosity, filed into the region to see the mounds of swollen, rotting corpses firsthand. According to one report, "the visitor would stare for moments entranced, then invariably turn aside to vomit." Bodies were still being found more than a month after the disaster, when searching ceased for lack of funds.

Again, Sharp seemed remarkably prescient, writing a week before the storm that those who advocated a high water level in Lake Okeechobee were taking "a terrible responsibility on themselves." And again, a member of the Everglades drainage commission—this time Ernest Amos, the state comptroller—called the disaster an "act of God," in what is surely one of history's more irresponsible outbursts of denial.

After Hurricane Katrina swept through New Orleans, President Bush, sounding much like state officials in Florida in the 1920s, said: "I don't think anybody antici-pated the breach of the levees." Seeing the calamity as primarily the work of unfore-seen and unpredictable forces, however, amounts to a form of moral hand-washing.

20   In fact, multiple warnings had gone out. FEMA has known about the potential for large loss of life in New Orleans, probably for a generation. Ten years ago *Weath-erwise* magazine called New Orleans "the Death Valley of the Gulf Coast" because the city is surrounded by water and not particularly well served by major roadways. In 2000, in talking about the general decline in death rates from natural disasters in the twentieth century, I called attention in my book *Acts of God* to New Orleans and wrote: "Think twice before assuming that high death tolls are a thing of the past." Mark Fischetti, a contributing editor to *Scientific American*, made the same prediction in an excellent report in the magazine in 2001. The journalists John McQuaid and Mark Schleifstein reported extensively in 2002 on the potential for calamity in the *Times-Picayune*. And as recently as May 2005, Max Mayfield, the director of the National Hurricane Center, was quoted as saying, "I can't emphasize enough how concerned I am with southeast Louisiana because of its unique characteristics, its complex levee system."

Is the current disaster the American tsunami? No, it's the Hurricane Katrina calamity. But the same blind faith in the free market and private enterprise, coupled with the brutal downsizing of the public sector, and a very explicit pattern of denial in the face of impending natural calamity, help explain why America's most vulnerable saw their lives washed out to sea.

QUESTIONS FOR ACTIVE READING

1. Identify Ted Steinberg's thesis. How soon in his essay does he name those things which he will compare and contrast? What is the connection between those identifications and his thesis statement?
2. Does Steinberg use a block organization or a point-by-point organization for his essay?
3. Circle the words, phrases, and sentences Steinberg uses that signal relationships among those things he is comparing and contrasting.

QUESTIONS FOR THINKING CRITICALLY

1. From paragraph 6 on, Steinberg's argument becomes explicitly economic. How does he define *neoliberal imperatives,* and to what does he contrast such an economic system? Have other resources that you have consulted about the impact of Hurricanes Katrina and Rita discussed the economic backgrounds?
2. In this chapter we have examined the need to develop and appreciate multiple perspectives as critical thinkers. How many fields of expertise—different academic and/or professional perspectives—does Steinberg draw upon to write his essay? As a class, make a list of all the different areas of expertise that writers in this chapter rely upon or quote in order to gain different perspectives on the aftermath of Hurricanes Katrina and Rita. In your own life as a worker, a student, and a citizen, how can you work to become better informed without necessarily becoming an "expert" yourself?
3. In the second paragraph of his essay, Steinberg argues for the need to find a "proper historical analogy" for understanding both the aftermath of Katrina and the devastation caused by the Asian tsunami of 2004. In your own words, describe this analogy. (The next section of this chapter will explore analogy more fully as a strategy for critical thinking.)

Analogy

We noted earlier that comparative relationships involve examining the similarities and differences of two items in the same general category, such as two perspectives, two items on a menu, or two methods of birth control. There is another kind of comparison, however, one that does not focus on things in the same category. Such comparisons are known as *analogies,* and their goal is to clarify or illuminate a concept from one category by saying that in some ways, it resembles a concept from a very different category.

The purpose of an analogy is not the same as the purpose of the comparison we have been discussing. We noted that the goal of comparing similar things is often to make a choice and that the process of comparing can provide us with information on which we can base an intelligent decision. The main goal of analogies, however, is not to choose or decide; it is to illuminate our understanding. Identifying similarities between very different things can often stimulate us to see these things in a new light or from a different perspective.

We often create and use analogies to put a point across. Used appropriately, an analogy can help to illustrate what we are trying to communicate. This device is particularly useful when we have difficulty finding the right words to represent our experiences. Similes and metaphors, two figures of speech based on analogy that help us to "say things for which we have not words," are discussed on pages 163–165 in Chapter 6.

In addition to communicating experiences that resist simple characterization, analogies are useful when a writer is explaining a complicated concept. For instance, we might compare the eye to a camera lens or compare the body's immune system to the National Guard (corpuscles are called to active duty and rush to the scene of danger when undesirable elements threaten the well-being of the organism).

Analogies are often used to describe shape or size. They help our readers to visualize size if we describe an object as "about the size of a dollar bill" or a piece of property as "roughly the size of two football fields."

Analogies enliven discourse by evoking images that illuminate the points of comparison. Consider the following analogies and explain the points of comparison.

"Laws are like cobwebs, which may catch small flies, but let wasps and hornets break through."—Jonathan Swift

"Like as the waves make towards the pebbled shore, so do our minutes hasten to their end."—William Shakespeare

"Some books are to be tasted, others to be swallowed, and some few to be chewed and digested."—Francis Bacon

"He has all the qualities of a dog, except its devotion."—Gore Vidal

In addition to *simple analogies* like the preceding ones that are designed to make one or two penetrating points, *extended analogies* have a more ambitious purpose. They attempt to illuminate a more complex subject by identifying a number of points of comparison. For example, we might seek to explain the theory of causal determinism by drawing an analogy between the universe and a watch or by analogizing the chemical interaction of molecules to a choreographed dance.

A word of caution about using analogies is in order here. Since they are based on items from different categories and have only limited points of similarity, be very careful when writing or reading arguments based on analogies. The failed U.S. military policy in Vietnam was partially based on the "domino theory," which held that since the countries in Southeast Asia had common borders, if one country became Communist, the other countries would also "fall" to Communism, just as a row of dominoes would all fall if one were knocked down. However, the countries were separate entities, places with people, history, cultures, and policies of their own. They were not small game pieces like dominoes, so the theory proved false. Analogies do have value for describing and explaining, but by their very nature, they have limited value in an argument.

Writing Project: Comparing Perspectives on an Issue or Event

This chapter has included both readings and Thinking-Writing Activities that encourage you to reflect on the nature of perception and on comparing and contrasting different perspectives. Be sure to reread what you wrote for those activities; you may be able to use the material when completing this project.

Write an essay comparing and contrasting two or more written texts that present different perspectives on the same event or issue. Your primary purpose is to present some significant insights about the perspectives and the texts. Follow your instructor's directions for choosing texts and for the paper's length and format.

Begin by considering the key elements in the Thinking-Writing Model in Chapter 1 on pages 7–9.

The Writing Situation

Purpose   Along with presenting significant insights about the texts and their subject, you will better understand how to use the thinking patterns of comparison and contrast. Also, you will think more about the implications of different perspectives presented in various accounts. And, since comparative papers invite logical organization, your planning abilities should improve. Finally, you will be sharing your insights about the texts with your audience.

Audience   One audience for this paper would be anyone interested in the subject discussed in your choice of texts. This audience might be outside of your college since most events or issues that are written about have community, national, or international significance. If you can, identify such an audience and see if you can share your paper with them by publishing it in a newspaper or newsletter or by otherwise distributing it. If the texts pertain to history, sociology, psychology, or some other academic subject, perhaps people studying those subjects would want to read your essay.

You should consider whether or not your audience has read the texts that you are analyzing. If they have, you will not need to include much summary of content or explanation of context. If your readers have not read the texts, you will have to include a brief summary and perhaps an explanation of why the texts were written.

To communicate with your audience, you will need to include enough evidence from the texts to demonstrate your points. You should not merely *tell* your audience that a likeness or difference exists; you must *show* them the evidence so they can see it for themselves.

Subject   If your instructor specifies which texts you should compare and contrast, consider why he or she may have chosen them. A question to ask yourself is what those texts have in common. If your instructor has left the choice to you, remember that you must use texts that have something essential in common. It helps a great deal to pick texts that genuinely interest you, either because of their subject matter or because of their style. Or you may decide to select an issue or event that interests you and use your research skills to locate texts about the topic. In that case, it may be necessary to provide paraphrases or summaries of the texts for your audience.

Writer   This project asks you to bring your critical reading and thinking skills to other writers' works and to analyze their perspectives. Your position of authority and your comfort level may depend on how much you know about the subject. However, neither your personal opinions nor your experiences are the focus of this project. You must be as objective as possible as you write and as thoughtful as possible as you establish the significance of your analysis.

The Writing Process

The following sections will guide you through the stages of generating, planning, drafting, and revising as you work on your essay. Try to be particularly conscious of applying the principles discussed in this chapter and of the critical thinking you do when you revise.

Generating Ideas   Once you have decided which texts you will use, reread each of them several times. Likenesses and differences may not be immediately apparent, nor may any significance strike you at the start. Doing some preliminary writing may help.

- Make a list of the ideas in each text.
- Make a list of what you notice about each text. Are you struck by the opening the choice of words, the author's bias or objectivity, the presence or absence of specific details, or any other elements or characteristics?
- After you have made these lists, begin to look for bases or points of likeness or difference. Doing this requires abstract thinking on your part, but patience will yield results.

- Collaboration can be productive. Talk with others about the texts.
- Read the student papers at the end of this chapter. They may help you to see what needs to be done.
- Carefully read any other models your instructor provides.
- Try freewriting for five minutes on what the texts have in common, then for five minutes on how they differ.
- Once you have established some bases for comparison or contrast, go back to the texts themselves and look for passages you could quote to illustrate your points.
- If you own the publication(s) in which the texts appear, use a highlighting pen to mark areas you may wish to quote. If you don't own them, copy the quotations or make photocopies to highlight.
- Now begin to think about significance. What are you beginning to observe about the texts? What are you beginning to feel about them?
- Try freewriting for five minutes on any or all of these questions:

  Does one text do a better job than the other? If so, in what way or ways?

  Do you agree with either or both texts? If not, what *is* your perspective?

  Have the texts caused you to re-evaluate or change your own ideas or perspectives?

  Do the texts have different styles or vocabularies?

Defining a Focus   Write a thesis statement that will clearly inform your audience that you are going to explore similarities, differences, or both. You might decide to write something like "After studying both of these accounts carefully, I saw two distinct differences." Or you might decide to name the areas of likeness or difference: "The authors are similar in their recognition of the need for more education and their determination in pursuing that education." You may even decide to announce the personal significance of your comparisons in your thesis statement: "Seeing the biased way in which one of the texts presented this event made me wary of accepting any printed reports at face value."

Organizing Ideas   This assignment fits well with what you have already learned about essay structure but requires you to move a few steps beyond what you have accomplished previously. Your description of the issue or event and of the texts that describe it can give you an introduction that will end with your thesis statement. The actual discussion of likenesses and/or differences will take place in the body paragraphs, and the significance of your analysis can be introduced or expanded upon in the conclusion. The major decision you will have to make is whether to use block or point-by-point organization or some combination of the two.

Drafting   Begin with the easiest paragraph to draft. If you are using point-by-point, remember to begin each body paragraph with a topic sentence indicating that this point will be discussed for both (or all) texts: for example, "Both accounts agree on the cause of the contamination." Then provide the audience with as much information as is needed to help them see what you mean. Use the quotations you highlighted to support your points and let the audience see that the texts really do say very similar—or very different—things. You will, of course, have to decide on the most logical order for the body paragraphs: which point to present first, which second, and so on.

Generally, readers have an easier time following point-by-point organization, but some writing situations call for block. Fortunately, word processors make it easy to move material around, so try it both ways to see which will be easier for your audience.

In your conclusion, name or expand upon the significance of your analysis, but be careful not to make too broad a statement. Consideration of two or three texts does not prove, for instance, that all texts are racist or sexist, but discovering racism or sexism in some texts should encourage you and your readers to be aware that these perspectives may be present in others.

Revising, Editing, and Proofreading   Use the Step-by-Step method in Chapter 6 on pages 152–154 to revise and polish your essay.

Student Writing

Jennifer Wade's Writing Process

Student Jennifer Wade felt an immediate and powerful personal connection to this chapter's readings by Benjamin Franklin and Zitkala-Sa. Sorting out her personal perspective and comparing it to the "official" or "objective" accounts she had obtained from family and archival history was a particular challenge for Jennifer and led to a very compelling essay in which she explores the ambivalence she feels as she tries to reconcile her European and her Cherokee ancestry. Many forms of academic and professional writing do not (by convention or by common agreement) allow for the use of the personal voice. In Jennifer's case, however, as with the readings by Matt Welch and Brian Thevenot, a personal perspective lends her essay a particular authority.

Where Did All of the Cherokees Go?

by Jennifer Wade

Almost twenty-five years ago on Tuesday, December 2, 1980, around one o'clock in the morning, my mother gave birth to me in an Indian hospital. Shortly after my birth I received an identification card from the United States Department of the

Interior Affairs Tahlequah Agency. My identification card states that 5/64 of the red blood flowing through my veins is Cherokee Indian blood. I have oftentimes wondered why the government issues identification cards to the chosen few who are a part of something that has become almost nonexistent. What happened in order for the American government to go to great extremes to acknowledge such small traces of a certain descent? My identification card tells me who I am, yet I do not feel like a Cherokee Indian. Nor do I look like one.

According to the web site of the U.S. Department of the Interior, which includes the Bureau of Indian Affairs, the Cherokee nation adopted a new Constitution in 1975 that "establishes a Cherokee Register for the inclusion of any Cherokee for membership purposes in the Cherokee Nation." It was through this agreement that I was enrolled as a member of the Nation at my birth. My father gave me the Cherokee blood and shortly thereafter left me with my mother. She resented my father and everything about him, including my Cherokee heritage. I grew up being a part of something exclusive, and yet I never experienced the culture. As generations pass, the Cherokee Indians will become extinct. After twenty-five years I decided it was time for me to meet my ancestors. I wanted to know where I came from and what had happened to them.

As my research began, I found that I shared many of the beliefs and values my ancestors did. According to Professor Theda Perdue, the Cherokees believed Earth was created by something powerful. They believed the rock sky where everyone lived became overcrowded, and so a water beetle created an island and sent the Cherokee down to inhabit the new land (The Cherokee 13). It is as though God sent his people back to live as a mortal again. The Cherokees too had their own Adam and Eve, but they called them Kana'ti and Selu. From this man and woman came all others (13). Although the Cherokees speak an alien language and look like weatherbeaten scavengers, their beliefs are similar to others'. Through this discovery, I have found that all ethnicities have a universal code of conduct.

Unfortunately, there are those who choose to ignore the universal code of conduct when interacting with other ethnicities. Frank W. Porter III, director of the Chelsea House foundation for American Indian Studies, make this point clear: "The Europeans believed they had 'discovered' a New World," but their religious bigotry, cultural bias, and materialistic world-view kept them from appreciating and understanding the people who lived in it (7). These narcissistic views all but destroyed a strong nation of people. All that remain are a few American citizens with meaningless identification cards reminding us of what we once were, or could have been.

Comedian Chris Rock points out, in his stand-up routine *Bigger, Blacker, and Better*, "You ain't never gonna find a family of American Indians chillin' out in Red Lobster." You will not because they do not exist anymore. Somewhere in Oklahoma you may find people with long, straight, jet black hair and dark brown eyes who probably have an identification card, but they, like me, are only a glimpse of what the Cherokee Indians once were.

In a sense the Cherokee Indians caused their own demise. Had they had the mentality of their counterparts, the outcome may have been different. The Cherokees were generous and willing to compromise with the Europeans who were invading their homeland. Perdue explains that the Cherokees were "incredibly adaptable" (39). If they had chosen to live like the Europeans, could they have survived and lived peacefully together? In the book *Voices From the Trail of Tears*, Vicki Rozema reports of an article written in 1828 by Elias Boudinot in which a chief from a Cherokee tribe explains how generous the Cherokees had been as he sits in the house of General Knox looking out his window at what once was free land where his people hunted and lived: "They [the white people] asked only to let them tie it [a great canoe] to a tree—we consented. They then said some of their people were sick, and they asked [to] put them under the shade of the trees," (4) and so the Cherokees consented. They kept consenting until everything they had was gone. Soon they were fighting to the death for the clothes on their back. Never before had the Cherokees encountered such an enemy. It was not enough for the Europeans to be satisfied with food and shelter; they wanted everything.

I am left with feeling guilt because I think like the European does. One is not enough; I want two. As the Cherokee nation died, so too did its teachings; *do unto others as they would do unto you* is a philosophy I was taught at an early age. The Cherokees understood this philosophy and applied it accordingly. The Europeans applied this philosophy as they saw fit. In most cases they had to receive in order to get. This is the "you scratch my back and I will scratch yours" mentality.

But despite my ambivalence, many others of Cherokee heritage are taking the initiative to keep our culture's heritage and traditions alive. Museums across the Carolinas (where the Cherokee nation originated) and Oklahoma (where I was born) commemorate both the livelihoods of the Cherokee peoples and the tragedies of the Trail of Tears. An effort to create a written language to preserve the rich Cherokee oral traditions of storytelling, genealogy, and folk wisdom is being perpetuated by the Internet.

It can be peculiar how the nature of human interaction can work. I am a descendant of European and Cherokee heritage because of events beyond any one person's control. Hundreds of years ago a big boat bumped into a peaceful nation of

	a	e	i	o	u	v [ə]
	D a	**R** e	**T** i	Ꮼ o	Ꮕ u	i v
	Ꮝ ga Ꮙ ka	**Ᏺ** ge	**Ᏹ** gi	**A** go	**J** gu	**E** gv
	Ꮀ ha	**Ᏸ** he	**Ꮟ** hi	**Ꮂ** ho	**�** hu	**Ꮣ** hv
	W la	**Ꮈ** le	**P** li	**G** lo	**M** lu	**Ꮑ** lv
	Ꮉ ma	**Ꮋ** me	**H** mi	**Ꮎ** mo	**Ᏼ** mu	
	Ꮎ na Ꮏ hna **G** nah	**Ꮄ** ne	**h** ni	**Z** no	**Ꮔ** nu	**Ꮕ** nv
	Ꮚ qua	**Ꮗ** que	**Ꮘ** qui	**Ꮖ** quo	**Ꮜ** quu	**Ꮝ** quv
	Ꮝ s **Ꮢ** sa	**Ꮞ** se	**b** si	**Ꮠ** so	**Ꮡ** su	**R** sv
	Ꮣ da **W** ta	**Ꮥ** de **Ꮦ** te	**Ꮧ** di **Ꮨ** ti	**V** do	**S** du	**Ꮫ** dv
	Ꮬ dla **Ꮭ** tla	**L** tle	**C** tli	**Ꮴ** tlo	**Ꮵ** tlu	**P** tlv
	G tsa	**Ꮴ** tse	**Ir** tsi	**K** tso	**d** tsu	**Ꮯ** tsv
	G wa	**Ꮾ** we	**Ꮻ** wi	**Ꮼ** wo	**Ꮽ** wu	**6** wv
	Ꮿ ya	**ꮴ** ye	**Ꮈ** yi	** fi** yo	**G** yu	**B** yv

Fig. 9.1   Cherokee Syllabary

tribal people who were too generous in their offers. Today it is known as the United States of America. We are one of the strongest and largest nations in the world because of ruthless generals who wanted it all. Our history teaches us that George Washington and Benjamin Franklin liberated us from an unruly king and brought us a new world full of opportunity and prosperity. Although all of these statements are true, they do not tell us what it cost the world. From the very moment the first Europeans set foot on what they thought was India, the world lost a great nation of philosophical people. We are left with identification cards that remind us of the remnants of Cherokee blood pumping through the hearts of a select few.

Works Cited

Leone, Bruno, and Brenda Stalcup, eds. <u>Native American Rights</u>. San Diego: Green Haven Press, 1998.

Mooney, Thomas. <u>Exploring Your Cherokee Ancestry</u>. Cherokee National Historic Society, 1990.

Perdue, Theda. <u>The Cherokees</u>. New York: Chelsea House, 1989.

Rozena, Vicki. <u>Voices From the Trail of Tears</u>. Winston: John F. Blair, Publisher, 2003.

United States. Dept. of the Interior. <u>Indian Ancestry—Cherokee Indian Ancestry</u>. 10 Oct. 2003. 3 Nov. 2005 <http://www.doi.gov/cheeroke.html>.

"Cherokee syllabary." Wikipedia. 30 October 2005 <http://en.wikipedia.org/wiki/Image: Cherokee_Syllabary.png>.

Alternative Writing Project: Comparing Two Reviews

Find a recent review of a movie that you have seen or of a restaurant at which you have eaten. Compare the review with your experience. Do you agree with the reviewer? Identify specific examples of points you agree with and explain why. Do you disagree with the reviewer? Identify specific examples of these, too. Write an essay presenting your analysis of the review as it relates to your experience with the movie or at the restaurant.

Exploring Cause and Effect

Writing to Speculate

> *The present contains nothing more than the past, and what is found in the effect was already in the cause.*
>
> —Henri Bergson

Critical Thinking Focus: Causal reasoning

Writing Focus: Presenting causal reasoning

Reading Theme: Longevity and society

Writing Project: Exploring causes of a recent event

Previous chapters have examined thinking and writing patterns that help us make sense of the world. As we explore our world, we humans tend to ask why things are as they are: Why do some marriages endure for years and others end in divorce? Why does a coastal area of the country have relatively calm summers for several years, then experience a record-breaking hurricane? Why do certain political ideas take hold during particular periods of history?

When we contemplate such questions, we are asking about (1) *causes*, factors that contribute to events and bring them about, and (2) *effects*, events that result directly or indirectly from causes or from other events. Much thinking about causes and effects occurs in an impromptu way. For example, about a divorce, we might guess, "I think the marriage failed because of financial problems." Though that might in fact be one reason, other factors are probably also involved. Determining causes is complicated because

- An event may have more than one cause
- An event may have various types of causes
- Determining causes with certainty is often impossible

When we think about causal relationships in an organized way, ever conscious of the difficulty and uncertainty of the task, we are using a critical thinking process called *causal analysis*.

The Writing Project in this chapter asks you to find information about some causes of a recent event and then to write a paper in which you present this information. The chapter should help you to write effectively about causal relationships.

Kinds of Causal Relationships

Causal patterns of thinking involve relating events in terms of the influence or effect they have on one another. The following statements are all examples of causal statements.

- Since I was the last to leave, I turned off the lights.
- Taking plenty of vitamin C really cured that terrible cold I had.
- I accidentally toasted my hand along with the marshmallows by getting too near the campfire.

In these statements, the words *since, turned off, cured,* and *getting too near* all point to the fact that something has caused something else to take place.

FOUR QUALITIES OF A CRITICAL THINKER

Environmental Lawyer Robert F. Kennedy

Curious   When seeking a topic for a cause-and-effect essay or research project, you will find yourself most motivated by something that has a direct impact on you. Certainly this was the case in the 1960s for fishermen on New York State's great Hudson River, who noticed that the vast numbers and variety of fish on which their families had subsisted for generations— sturgeon, shad, trout, blue crab, eel, even shrimp—had dramatically declined in both quality and quantity. At the same time, the river was becoming fouled with industrial pollution. In this case, curiosity about the connection between the decline of the fish population and the rise of industrial pollution led to a search for answers that has, in the last decades, resulted in one of America's most inspiring and successful environmental rehabilitation projects—the cleanup of the Hudson River, and the regulations of all industries that operate on or near bodies of water.

Open-minded   The organization that resulted from these early meetings is now called Riverkeepers, and is both

led and represented by Robert F. Kennedy (son of the slain senator Robert Kennedy and nephew of John F. Kennedy). With his commitment to the environment as well as his profound understandings of economics and commerce, Kennedy has forged an alliance between industry and environmentalists that, working together, has resulted in a Hudson River ecosystem that might be more thriving now than at any point in the previous 150 years. Kennedy, a lawyer, recognizes that carefully supported arguments and persuasive negotiations between environmental activists, fishermen and sporting groups, local governments, and industry results in solutions that are broadly supported and easier to implement.

Knowledgeable   At that 1966 meeting of the concerned citizens who were to form the core of Riverkeepers, a fisherman and ex-Marine pointed out two little-known laws that he had independently researched: the Rivers and Harbors Act of 1888 and the Refuse Act of 1889. Both of these laws

WORDS THAT INDICATE CAUSE AND EFFECT	*Cause*	*Effect*
	because	because of
	reason(s), for this reason (these reasons)	as a result, result, resulted in
	affect, effect (verb)	consequently, consequence
	bring about	therefore
	a factor in	since
	cure, infect	thus
	lead, lead to	accordingly
	produce (verb)	happens whenever
	encourage, encouragement	follows from, follows that
	discourage	ensues
	influence	
	solve	

What additional cause and effect words can you think of?

not only forbade pollution of American waterways, but promised financial rewards for anyone who reported such pollution. This fisherman wasn't a lawyer, but he took the initiative to educate himself in the finer points of American environmental law. On the basis of these two acts, Riverkeepers successfully sued several Hudson River-area industrial companies, using the proceeds of the suits to strengthen their organization and support education and research into the waterway's diverse ecosystem. Today, searchable electronic databases of legal cases and precedents make citizen activists even more powerful. In addition, Kennedy, a professor of environmental law at Pace University, involves (with special permission from the courts) second- and third-year law students to participate in the trial of cases against Hudson River polluters. In this way, future environmental lawyers gain valuable experience.

Creative Among the more inventive and welcoming programs established by Riverkeepers is a community outreach program that addresses the spiritual nature of environmental action. Although faith and politics are a volatile mixture in much of American culture, Riverkeepers has found a truly creative energy in an otherwise contentious conversation. For the last several years, Riverkeepers has held a series of conversations meant to unite a coalition of faith-based groups and programs around the idea that protecting the Hudson River from polluters is as much a spiritual duty as it is an environmental necessity. Working together to unite many voices and traditions, this coalition has created a "living document" entitled *A Statement of Shared Values and Committed Action* that is meant to be shared with gatherings and congregations of any faith tradition.

Online Study Center
Robert F. Kennedy
Visit the Online Study Center for *Critical Thinking, Thoughtful Writing* at *college.hmco.com/pic/ chaffee CTTW4e* to learn more about Robert F. Kennedy.

You are probably realizing that you make causal statements all the time and that you are constantly thinking in terms of causal relationships. In fact, the goal of much of your thinking is to figure out why something happened or how something came about. One advantage of causal analysis is that it enables you to make reasonable predictions because you are able to clarify the causal relationships involved and make predictions based on your understanding.

The purpose of much of your academic writing will be causal analysis, either to demonstrate that you fully understand the factors contributing to a specific situation or result (for example, why a certain genetic mutation leads to Type I diabetes in humans) or the effects of particular behaviors (for example, why a combination of poor eating habits and lack of exercise can bring on Type II diabetes in susceptible adolescents and adults). Your audience may at first be your professor, but it's clear that this kind of thinking and the writing it produces will be useful in the workplace and the community as well. Thinking carefully and skeptically about causes and effects is excellent training for your further research, and it will help you to solve complex problems and make well-informed decisions.

Causal Chain

Although you may think of causes and effects in isolation—A caused B—in reality, causes and effects rarely appear by themselves. There is not just one cause of a resulting effect; there is a whole string of causes, as illustrated by the structures in Figure 10.1. These interrelated causes form more complex patterns, including three that we will examine next: *causal chains, contributory causes*, and *interactive causes*. Consider the following scenario:

FIGURE 10.1   Causal Chain

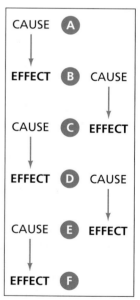

Your paper on the topic "life span and poverty" is due on Monday morning. You have reserved the whole weekend to work on it and are just getting started when the phone rings. A favorite childhood friend is in town and wants to stay with you for the weekend. You say *yes*. By Sunday night, you've had a great weekend but have made little progress on your paper. You brew a pot of coffee and get started. At 3:00 A.M. you are too exhausted to continue. Deciding to get a few hours' sleep, you set the alarm clock for 6:00 A.M., giving yourself plenty of time to finish up. When you wake up, it's nine o'clock; the alarm failed to go off. Your class starts in forty minutes. You have no chance of getting the paper done on time. On your way to class, you mentally review the causes of this disaster. No longer concerned about life after death, you are very worried about your own longevity after this class!

- What causes in this situation are responsible for your paper's being late?
- What do you think is the single most important cause?
- What do you think your instructor will identify as the most important cause? Why?

A *causal chain*, as illustrated by the preceding example, is a situation in which one thing leads to another, which then leads to another, and so on over a period of time. In writing about causal chains, your narrative would use chronological ordering (see page 195 in Chapter 7). There is not just one cause of the resulting effect. Which event or circumstance in the chain is the "tipping point," the most important contributing factor to the effect? Your answer will depend on your perspective on the situation. You might see the cause of the unfinished paper as a defective alarm clock. Your instructor, though, might see the cause of the problem as overall lack of planning.

**THINKING-
WRITING
ACTIVITY**

Creating a Causal Chain

1. Create a scenario in which you make a series of decisions that culminate in a significant conclusion. For example, your decision to take a course outside of your major might lead to a conversation with the professor, which leads you to explore a career option that you had not previously considered, and so on. The scenario might be based on an actual experience in your life or one created through your imagination.

2. Review the scenario you have just created. Explain how the "real" cause of the final effect could vary, depending on your perspective on the situation.

Contributory Causes

In addition to operating in causal chains over a period of time, causes can also work simultaneously to produce an effect. This results in a situation in which a number of different *contributory causes* bring something about. Instead of working in isolation, each cause contributes to bringing about the final effect. When this situation occurs, each cause serves to support and reinforce the action of the other causes, a condition illustrated in Figure 10.2.

Consider the following situation:

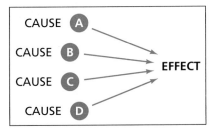

FIGURE 10.2   Contributory Causes

It is the end of the term, and you have been working incredibly hard at school—writing papers, preparing for exams, finishing up course projects. You haven't been getting enough sleep, and you haven't been eating regular, well-balanced meals. To make matters worse, you have been under intense pressure in your personal life, having serious arguments with the person you have been dating, and this situation is constantly on your mind. It is the middle of the flu season, and many people you know have been sick with various respiratory infections. Walking home one evening, you get soaked by an unexpected downpour. By the time you get home, you are shivering. You soon find yourself in bed with a thermometer in your mouth—you are sick!

What was the "cause" of your illness? In this situation, you can see that evidently, a combination of factors led to your physical breakdown: low resistance, getting wet and chilled, being exposed to various germs and viruses, physical exhaustion, lack of proper eating, and so on. Taken by itself, no one factor might have been enough to cause your illness. Together, they all contributed to the final outcome. The readings on longevity later in this chapter demonstrate the complexity of interrelated causes.

Creating a Contributory-Cause Scenario

Create a similar scenario, detailing the contributory causes that led to your asking someone for a date, choosing a major, losing or winning a game, or another effect.

Interactive Causes

Causes rarely operate in isolation but instead often influence (and are influenced by) other factors. Imagine that you are scheduled to give a PowerPoint presentation to a large group of people. As your moment at the podium approaches, you become anxious, which results in a dry mouth and throat, making your voice sound more like a croak. The prospect of sounding like a bullfrog increases your anxiety, which in turn dries your mouth and constricts your throat further, reducing your croak to something much worse—silence.

Different factors can relate to each other through reciprocal influences that flow back and forth from one to the other. Understanding this type of *interactive causal relationship* helps you to organize and make sense of your experiences. For instance, to comprehend social relationships (families, teams, groups of friends), you consider the complex ways in which each individual influences—and is influenced by—all the other members of the group. Student Daniel Eggers explored the complex interactive causal relationships that continue to affect poverty in the African-American community decades after Dr. Martin Luther King Jr.'s "I Have A Dream" speech (page 165 in Chapter 6). Understanding biological systems and other systems is similar to understanding social systems. To comprehend and explain how an organ such as the heart, liver, or brain functions, you have to describe its complex, interactive relationships with all the other parts of the biological system. Figure 10.3 illustrates these dynamic causal relationships.

FIGURE 10.3   Interactive Causes

THINKING-
WRITING
ACTIVITY

Identifying Causal Patterns

Read the following passages that illustrate causal patterns of thinking. For each passage, identify the kind of causal relationship (chain, contributory, or interactive). Draw a chart or figure that illustrates this relationship, and explain how the causes are related to one another.

1. Nothing posed a more serious threat to the bald eagle's survival than a modern chemical compound called DDT. Around 1940, a retired Canadian banker named Charles L. Broley began keeping track of eagles nesting in Florida. Each breeding season, he climbed into more than 50 nests, counted the eaglets and put metal bands on their legs. In the late 1940s, a sudden drop-off in the number of young produced led him to conclude that 80 percent of his birds were sterile. Broley blamed DDT. Scientists later discovered that DDE, a breakdown product of DDT, causes not sterility, but a fatal thinning of eggshell among birds of prey. Applied on cropland all over the United States, the pesticide was running off into waterways where it concentrated in fish. The bald eagles ate the fish and the DDT impaired their ability to reproduce. They were not alone, of course. Ospreys and pelicans suffered similar setbacks.—Jim Doherty, "The Bald Eagle and DDT"

2. It is popularly accepted that Hitler was the major cause of World War II, but the ultimate causes go much deeper than one personality. First, there were long-standing German grievances against reparations levied on the nation following its defeat in World War I. Second, there were severe economic strains that caused resentment among the German people. Third, there were French and English

THINKING-
WRITING
ACTIVITY

reluctance to work out a sound disarmament policy and American noninvolvement in the matter. Finally, there was the European fear that communism was a much greater danger than National Socialism. These factors contributed to the outbreak of World War II.—Gilbert Muller, *The American College Handbook*

3. You crunch and chew your way through vast quantities of snacks and confectioneries and relieve your thirst with multicolored, flavored soft drinks, with and without calories, for two basic reasons. The first is simple; the food tastes good, and you enjoy the sensation of eating it. Second, you associate these foods, often without being aware of it, with the highly pleasurable experiences depicted in the advertisements used to promote their sale. Current television advertisements demonstrate this point: people turn from grumpiness to euphoria after crunching a corn chip. Others water ski into the sunset with their loved ones while drinking a popular soft drink. People entertain on the patio with friends, cook over campfires without mosquitoes, or go to carnivals with granddad munching away at the latest candy or snack food. The people portrayed in these scenarios are all healthy, vigorous, and good looking; one wonders how popular the food they convince you to eat would be if they would crunch or drink away while complaining about low back pain or clogged sinuses.—Judith Wurtman, *Eating Your Way Through Life*

Ways of Testing Causes

Necessary Condition and Sufficient Condition

In addition to the three patterns of causality we have just examined, we need to consider necessary and sufficient conditions. A *necessary condition* is a factor that is required to bring about a certain result: for example, an intact light bulb is required for a lamp's illumination. However, by itself, an intact light bulb is not sufficient to provide illumination: you also need electricity, which is another necessary condition.

A *sufficient condition* is a factor that of itself is always sufficient for bringing about a certain result. For example, a pinch on the arm is a sufficient cause for discomfort. Of course, even with a sufficient condition, there may be an additional necessary condition, or several necessary conditions, for a result to occur. Having healthy nerves in the arm and being conscious are two necessary conditions for someone's feeling a sensation when pinched on the arm.

Immediate Cause and Remote Cause

Yet another way to think critically about causes is to classify them by how close in time the cause is to its result. Something that happens just before an event that it causes is called an *immediate cause*. A factor that also helped to bring about this same

THINKING-
WRITING
ACTIVITY

Seeing Causal Relationships

1. Study the photograph of young people at a bar and see how many causal relationships are being suggested. What are your perceptions of why they are there and why some of them have the expressions that they do? See what perceptions your classmates have and notice how they differ.

2. Carefully examine the Budweiser ad in the background. What do you think are the causal relationships among advertisements for alcoholic drinks, these young peoples' apparent moods, and the drinking behaviors of college students you know.

3. What are the causes of your attitudes toward drinking alcohol? Have your attitudes changed since attending college? If you wish, share your analysis of your perspectives with your classmates.

event but that occurred further back in time is called a *remote cause*. For example, a last-minute touchdown could be the immediate cause of a football championship, but wise trades made for key players before the season began might be remote causes.

Identifying Causal Fallacies

Because causality plays such a dominant role in the way we make sense of the world, it is not surprising that people make many mistakes and many errors in judgment in trying to determine causal relationships. These mistakes and errors can lead to unsound arguments, or *fallacies*. The following are some of the most common fallacies associated with causality.

- Questionable cause
- Misidentification of the cause
- *Post hoc ergo propter hoc*
- Slippery slope

Questionable Cause

The fallacy of *questionable cause* occurs when someone presents a causal relationship for which no real evidence exists. Superstitious beliefs such as "If you break a mirror, you will have seven years of bad luck" usually fall into this category. Some people feel that astrology, a system of beliefs tying one's personality and fortunes in life to the position of the planets at the moment of birth, also falls into this category.

Consider the following passage from the *Confessions* of philosopher St. Augustine (C.E. 354–386). Does it seem to support the causal assertions of astrology or deny them? Why?

> Firminus had heard from his father that when his mother had been pregnant with him, a slave belonging to a friend of his father's was also about to bear. It happened that since the two women had their babies at the same instant, the men were forced to cast exactly the same horoscope for each newborn child down to the last detail, one for his son, the other for the little slave. Yet Firminus, born to wealth in his parents' house, had one of the more illustrious careers in life whereas the slave had no alleviation of his life's burden.

Other examples of this fallacy include beliefs such as

- Lottery numbers that occur in dreams are more likely to be winners than random choices.
- Spending money is the best way to solve most problems.
- Movies that have the highest box-office numbers are of the best quality and most deserving of awards.

Misidentification of the Cause

In causal situations we are not always certain about what is causing what—in other words, about what is the cause and what is the effect. For example, in the following pairs of items, which is the cause, and which is the effect? Why?

- Headaches and tension
- Failure in school and personal problems
- Shyness and lack of confidence
- Substance abuse and emotional difficulties

Sometimes a third factor is responsible for two effects that we are examining. Headaches and tension may both be the result of a third element—such as some new medication a person is taking. When we fail to recognize the third element, we commit the fallacy of *ignoring a common cause*. There also exists the fallacy of *assuming a common cause*—such as assuming that a person's sore toe and earache both stem from the same cause.

Post Hoc Ergo Propter Hoc

The translation of the Latin phrase *post hoc ergo propter hoc* is "After that, therefore because of that." It refers to situations in which, because two things occur closely together in time, we assume that one has caused the other. Suppose your team wins the game each time you wear your favorite shirt; you just may be tempted to conclude that the one event (wearing your favorite shirt) has some influence on the other event (winning the game). As a result, you may continue to wear this shirt "for good luck." It is easy to see how this sort of mistaken thinking can lead to all sorts of superstitious beliefs. Consider the following causal conclusion arrived at by Mark Twain's fictional character Huckleberry Finn in the following passage. How would you analyze his conclusion?

> I've always reckoned that looking at the new moon over your left shoulder is one of the carelessest and foolishest things a body can do. Old Hank Bunker done it once, and bragged about it; and in less than two years he got drunk and fell off a shot tower and spread himself out so that he was just a kind of layer. . . . But anyway, it all came of looking at the moon that way, like a fool.

Can you identify any of your own superstitious beliefs or practices that may have resulted from *post hoc* thinking?

Slippery Slope

The causal fallacy of *slippery slope* is illustrated in the following advice:

> Don't miss that first deadline, because if you do, it won't be long before you're missing all your deadlines. This will spread to the rest of your life, as you will be late for every appointment. This terminal procrastination will ruin your career, and friends and relatives will abandon you. You will end up a lonely failure who is unable to ever do anything on time.

> Slippery slope thinking asserts that one undesirable action will inevitably lead to a worse action, which will necessarily lead to still a worse one, all the way down the "slippery slope" to some terrible disaster at the bottom. Although this progression may indeed occur, there certainly is no causal guarantee that it will. Create slippery slope scenarios for one of the following warnings:

- If you get behind on one credit card payment . . .
- If you fail that first test . . .
- If you eat that first potato chip . . .

SUMMARY:
CAUSAL
FALLACIES

Questionable Cause: Presenting a causal relationship for which no real evidence exists

Misidentification of Cause: Uncertainty about what is the cause and what is the effect: ignoring a common cause, assuming a false common cause

Post Hoc Ego Propter Hoc: Assuming a causal relationship between situations occurring closely together in time

Slippery Slope: Asserting that one undesirable action will lead to a worse action, which will lead to still a worse one—down, down the slippery slope

THINKING-
WRITING
ACTIVITY

Diagnosing Causal Fallacies

Review the four causal fallacies just described; then identify and explain the errors of reasoning illustrated in the following examples.

1. The person who won the lottery says she dreamed the winning numbers. I'm going to start writing down the numbers that I dream about.
2. Yesterday I forgot to take my vitamins, and I immediately got sick. That mistake won't occur again!
3. I'm warning you: if you miss a class, it won't be long before you flunk out of school and ruin your future.
4. I always take the first seat in the bus. Today I took another seat, and the bus broke down.
5. I think the reason I'm not doing well in school is that I simply don't have enough time to study, and my classes aren't interesting, either.

Detecting Causal Claims

Sometimes people use causal reasoning because they want us to see cause-and-effect relationships that they believe exist. When they do this, we say they are making *causal claims*. Consider the following examples.

1. Politicians assure us that a vote for them will result in better schools and lower taxes.
2. Advertisers tell us that using a detergent will leave our wash "cleaner than clean, whiter than white."

3. Doctors tell us that eating a balanced diet will result in a longer life.

4. Educators tell us that a college degree is worth an average of $830,000 additional income over an individual's lifetime.

5. Utility companies inform us that using nuclear energy will result in less pollution.

In each of these examples, certain causal claims are being made about how the world operates in an effort to persuade us to adopt a certain point of view. As critical thinkers, it is our responsibility to evaluate these various causal claims to determine whether they are valid or questionable.

THINKING-
WRITING
ACTIVITY

Evaluating Causal Claims

Explain how you might go about evaluating the causal claims previously listed.

- *Example:* Electing politicians and claims about getting better schools and lower taxes.

- *Evaluation:* Speak to teachers and principals about school needs. Understand what a politician in a specific office can and cannot do about education. Learn about budgets for school systems. Remember your own school experiences and think about why they were good or bad. Learn about taxes and schools in your area.

Exploring Cause and Effect: Human Longevity and Social Impact

The United States and other developed nations are witnessing an unprecedented boom in the number of people living far into their eighth, ninth, and even tenth decades of life. We seem to hear increasing amounts of—and increasingly conflicting—advice from our doctors, the pharmaceutical industry, and others about the *causes* of healthy longevity. And older people themselves brim with simple wisdom about living a long, healthy, and happy life. At the same time, economists and researchers are raising the alarm about the *effects* of having a rapidly aging population. The economic burden of an increasingly aged and frequently infirm population on its younger citizens is evident each election cycle as the challenges to Social Security, Medicare, and other benefits are debated. And, of course, the problems of poor health for older people around the world who lack access to adequate health care and support networks require careful and compassionate attention to the causal relationships between age and health. The first essay that follows explores the most recent scientific and anecdotal thinking behind the *causes* of human longevity. In the second essay, an economist and a medical doctor analyze the *effects* of an aging population on a society unprepared to care for its elders.

"How to Live to Be 100"

BY RICHARD CORLISS (b. 1944) AND MICHAEL D. LEMONICK (b. 1953)

The cover article in *Time* Magazine's August 30, 2004, issue was part of a package of features about how some people live physically healthy and mentally robust lives up to, and even beyond, their one hundredth birthdays. Combining anecdote (stories based on personal observation and experience) with objective scientific research, the authors are careful to present both interactive and contributory causes to extreme old age. Richard Corliss has been with *Time* since 1980. A senior writer for the magazine, Corliss is also a distinguished movie critic. Michael D. Lemonick is a senior science writer and editor at *Time*.

Margaret Dell is 96, but you'd need to check the birth date on her driver's license to believe it. Sporting a baseball cap with a Harley-Davidson logo on it, she is the designated driver for her seventysomething friends who no longer feel comfortable behind the wheel. Last winter a snowfall threatened to keep her from her appointed automotive rounds. She took a shovel and cleared a path to her car. Driving keeps Dell young. That and knitting. She constantly knits. She makes baby booties and caps and blankets for friends and family whenever a baby arrives—the newborn getting an early blessing from the ageless. And every month, she donates several blankets to a charity for unwed mothers. Driving, knitting . . . and tennis. She plays two or three times a week. She has a much younger doubles partner who "covers the court. I'm a little afraid to run too much because of the circulation in my legs," she explains.

When she was in her 80s, she played in a doubles tournament that required that the ages of both partners add up to at least 100. Her partner was in his early 20s; they won the tournament.

A lifetime nonsmoker and nondrinker, Dell lives alone in a two-story house in Bethesda, MD, her bedroom on the second floor. "I could stay on the first floor, but I try to make myself walk up those stairs and keep going that way." She buys her own groceries; don't even ask if you can shop for her. At home she likes a chicken or turkey sandwich for lunch. If she eats at the country club after tennis, she usually finishes only half and saves the rest for dinner. (The doggie bag is the senior citizen's medical-supply kit.)

Driving, tennis, knitting . . . and eating chocolates. She keeps them in a drawer by her easy chair. "I am very bad about those Hershey Kisses," she confesses. "And I love those little Dove ice cream things. I take one before I go to bed." That's the only medication Dell will take without a fight. She's no fan of doctors. Some years back, she took a fall, and her doctor prescribed an MRI. "I just refused to go," she says. "They were having a party. It was my 90th birthday." And the party girl left his office. Fortunately, nothing was broken. But Dell knew that.

5   More than what she knows, it's how she glows that impresses people. "She has a light in her eyes that is very alive, alert and interested," says Carole Dell. "It radiates

over her whole face. Her face is kind of timeless. It's deeply lined, but she's actually beautiful." Spoken like a proud daughter-in-law with 96 reasons to be proud. Ninety-six and counting.

How does science explain someone like Margaret Dell? How can a woman closing in on the start of her second century be so robustly, almost defiantly, healthy, while men and women decades younger are languishing feebly in nursing homes, plagued with failing bodies and failing minds and wishing they hadn't been so unlucky as to live so long?

For most of human history, a long and healthy life has been shrugged off as a gift from the gods—or maybe the undeserved reward for a lifetime of plain cussedness. But to gerontologists, the vagaries of aging have become the focus of intense scientific research.

Scientists are as obsessed with the question of why the superold survive and thrive as Ponce de Leon was to find the Fountain of Youth. They want to understand why the Japanese islands of Okinawa are home to the world's largest population of centenarians, with almost 600 of its 1.3 million inhabitants living into their second century—many of them active and looking decades younger than their actual years. Like weekend visitors on the summer ferry to Martha's Vineyard, scientists and sociologists clog the boats to Sardinia and Nova Scotia, Canada, to see why those craggy locales harbor outsize clusters of the superold. (Gerontologists are not so beguiled by the Russian Caucasus, where exaggerated longevity claims sparked a series of Dannon yogurt commercials 30 years ago.)

As well as studying these populations intensively to unlock their secrets, scientists have also taken a hard look at the very old in the U.S., most notably in the New England Centenarian Study, led by Dr. Thomas Perls, a geriatrician at Boston University, and in a major study under way at the National Institute on Aging. While the very old are happy to offer homespun explanations for their longevity— "I never took a drink"; "I drank a shot of whiskey every day"—experts are trying to unravel and understand the biological factors that allow some people to reach 100 while others drop off in their 70s or 80s. Researchers are particularly interested in determining which factors allow up to 30 percent of those who reach 100 to do so in sufficient mental and physical health: a whopping 90 percent of centenarians, according to Perls, remain functionally independent up to age 92. "It's not 'the older you get, the sicker you get,' but 'the older you get, the healthier you've been,'" he says. "The advantage of living to 100 is not so much how you are at 100 but how you got there."

It's pretty obvious even to nonscientists that how you get there depends partly on the genes you are born with and partly on lifestyle—what and how much you eat, where you live and what types of stress and trauma you experience. How much depends on each factor, though, was unknown until Swedish scientists tackled the problem in 1998. They did it by looking at the only set of people who share genes but not lifestyle: identical twins who were separated at birth and reared apart. If genes were most important, you would expect the twins to die at about the same age. In fact, they don't, and the average difference convinced the scientists that only about

20 percent to 30 percent of how long we live is genetically determined. The dominant factor is lifestyle.

"You could have Mercedes-Benz genes," says Dr. Bradley Willcox, of the Pacific Health Research Institute in Honolulu, "but if you never change the oil, you are not going to last as long as a Ford Escort that you take good care of. Those who have healthier genes and live healthier lives—those guys really survive for a long *time*."

Studies of Seventh-Day Adventists in Utah support this finding. Those unusually clean-living Americans are genetically diverse, but they avoid alcohol, caffeine and tobacco—and they tend to live an average of eight years longer than their countrymen. All of this is good news, with a Surgeon General's warning attached: you can't change your genes, but you can change what you eat and how much you exercise. "The lesson is pretty clear from my point of view in terms of what the average person should be doing," says Perls. "I strongly believe that with some changes in health-related behavior, each of us can earn the right to have at least 25 years beyond the age of 60—years of healthy life at good function. The disappointing news is that it requires work and willpower."

At least that's true for many Americans, whose fat- and calorie-packed diets and largely exercise-free lives are a prescription for heart disease and plenty of other ills. For Okinawans, by contrast, the traditional way of life seems tailor-made for living forever—one day at a *time*.

Each day, Seiryu Toguchi, 103, of Motobu, Okinawa, wakes at 6 A.M., in the house in which he was born, and opens the shutters. "It's a sign to my neighbors," he says, "that I am still alive." He does stretching exercises along with a radio broadcast, then eats breakfast: whole-grain rice and miso soup with vegetables. He puts in two hours of picking weeds in his 1,000-sq.-ft. field, whose crops are goya—a variety of bitter gourd—a reddish-purple sweet potato called imo, and okra. A fellow has to make a living, so Toguchi buys rice and meat with the profits from his produce.

15   Since his wife Kame's death seven years ago, at 93, he has done all the housework himself. He rejected his children's suggestion to come live with them because, he explains, "I enjoy my freedom." Although his doctors insist Toguchi is in excellent health, the farmer takes no chances. "If he feels that something is wrong," says his daughter Sumiko Sakihara, 74, "even in the middle of the night, he calls a taxi and goes to the hospital." But he doesn't want the other villagers to worry, so, she says, "he writes a note explaining where he is and tapes it to the shutters."

At 12:30 Toguchi eats lunch: goya stir-fry with egg and tofu. He naps for an hour or so, then spends two more hours in his field. After dinner he plays traditional songs—a favorite is "Spring When I Was 19"—on the three-stringed sanshin and makes an entry in his diary, as he has every night for the past decade. "This way," he says, "I won't forget my Chinese characters. It's fun. It keeps my mind sharp." For a nightcap he may have a sip of the wine he makes from aloe, garlic and turmeric. And as he drifts off, he says, "My head is filled with all the things I want to do tomorrow."

Scientists working for the U.S. National Institutes of Health and Japan's Ministry of Health have been following oldsters like Toguchi since 1976 in the Okinawa Centenarian Study (OCS) and they've learned that he's typical. Elderly Okinawans tend to get plenty of physical and mental exercise. Their diets, moreover, are exemplary: low in fat and salt, and high in fruits and vegetables packed with fiber and antioxidant substances that protect against cancer, heart disease and stroke. They consume more soy than any other population on earth: 60–120 g a day, compared to 30–50 g for the average Japanese, 10 for Chinese and virtually 0 g for the average American. Soy is rich in flavonoids—antioxidants strongly linked to low rates of cancer. This may be one of many reasons why the annual death rate from cancer in Okinawa is far below the U.S. rate.

But it's not just what Okinawans eat; it's how much. They practice a dietary philosophy known as hara hachi bu—literally, eight parts out of 10 full. Translation: they eat only to the point at which they are about 80 percent sated. That makes for a daily intake of no more than 1,800 calories, compared to the more than 2,500 that the average American man scarfs down. And as scientists have learned from lab animals, the simple act of calorie restriction can have significant effects on longevity.

Aging Okinawans also have a much lower incidence of dementia—Alzheimer's or other forms of senility—than their U.S. and European counterparts do. Part of that may also owe to diet; it's high in vitamin E, which seems to protect the brain. But perhaps just as important is a sense of belonging and purpose that provides a strong foundation for staying mentally alert well into old age. Okinawans maintain a sense of community, ensuring that every member, from youngest to oldest, is paid proper respect and feels equally valued. Elderly women, for example, are considered the sacred keepers of a family's bond with the ancestors, maintaining the family altars and responsible for organizing festivals to honor them. OCS data show that elderly Okinawans express a high level of satisfaction with life, something that is not as true in Western societies, where rates of suicide and depression are high among the elderly.

20   Need convincing evidence that our modern lifestyle can shorten lives? Look what happens when Okinawans move permanently off the island. They pick up the diet and cultural behaviors of their adopted country—and within a generation, their lifespans decrease and their rates of cancer and heart attack zoom. Even on the island, young males are following the seductive, virulent American style and renouncing imo for hamburgers. "Okinawan male life expectancy used to be No. 1 in Japan," says Dr. Makoto Suzuki, leader of the study of Okinawan elders. "It started to decline 10 years ago and hit 26th out of 47 prefectures in the 2000 census. I expect it to decline even further in the next census."

Oldsters in Sardinia, another wellspring of longevity, have many similarities to their Okinawan counterparts—except that the Sardinian ratio of centenarians is about equal for men and women (in most societies, 100-plus females outnumber males by 3 or 4 to 1). They maintain very active lives and powerful social networks; extended family and friends are available to share troubles and take some of the emotional burden out of life. Says researcher Gianni Pes, part of a team from Sardinia's University of Sassari, which is studying the group: "The 100-year-olds are less depressed than average 60-year-olds."

That makes perfect sense to Leonard Poon, director of the University of Georgia Gerontology Center. Since 1988 he has studied American centenarians—he calls them "expert survivors"—and compared them to people in their 80s ("master survivors") and to relative youngsters in their 60s. Poon found that out of 16 personality traits, the experts exhibited four coping mechanisms. First, he says, "centenarians are more dominant. They want to have their way," and they are not easily pushed around. Many are characterized by "suspiciousness. They do not take information on the superficial level" but will question an issue and think it through. They tend to be practical rather than idealistic. And in their approach to life, they are likely to be more relaxed. In other words, they are strong but not inflexible characters.

Poon also determined that people whose age reaches three figures tend to have a high level of cognition, demonstrating skill in everyday problem solving and learning. That's another reason exercise is important: to keep plenty of blood flowing to the brain as well as to stay in shape. Many of his subjects aren't rich; some of them have homes with mud floors. But they make good out of making do. "Many have their own gardens," he notes. "They can their own vegetables. They're living down to earth."

Like the Okinawans, Sardinians and Nova Scotians, the U.S. centenarians enjoy a strong social-support system. Few Americans live in a village anymore, but having outlived family and friends of the same age, the superold find new helpers and confidants among people younger by a generation or more. It might be someone to help with groceries or car trips or simply a sympathetic voice on the other end of the line. Maintaining a connection with the world, with younger people, keeps their outlook youthful.

25   With so much evidence that lifestyle is the key to healthy aging, it might be tempting to ignore the role of genes altogether. That would be a mistake. Brothers of centenarians are 17 times as likely to live to 100 as are people without 100-year-olds in the family, while sisters of centenarians are 8.5 times as likely to live into their second century. Given statistics like that, says Winifred Rossi, director of the National Institute on Aging's study on exceptional survival, "we are interested in looking for some kind of genetic component to longevity." Her approach is to look at family members, especially the children, of centenarians. Says Perls, who does similar research: "Kids of centenarians who are in their 70s and early 80s are very much following in the footsteps of their parents, with a 60 percent reduced risk of heart disease, stroke and diabetes. They are the model for successful aging and a great group to study."

Indeed, despite what the Swedish and Adventist studies suggest, there's evidence that in some families, at least, genes exert pretty powerful effects on life-span. The centenarians registered in the New England Centenarian Study, for example, showed no consistent patterns in diet, exercise or healthy habits that could explain their extended years. About 20 percent had smoked at some point in their lives, and some had eating habits that should have made them obese or unhealthy but somehow did not. At least 10 percent to 15 percent had a history of heart disease, stroke or diabetes for more than 20 years. Something in that group's genes was protecting them from succumbing to diseases that had felled the average American decades earlier. "These people still get to 100," says Perls. "They seem to have a functional reserve or adaptive capacity that allows them to get disease but not necessarily suffer from it. The key seems to be resilience."

Some of that resilience may be linked to human leukocyte antigen (HLA) genes, a group clustered on chromosome 6 that affects vulnerability to such autoimmune diseases as lupus, rheumatoid arthritis and multiple sclerosis. Centenarians living in Okinawa, for example, have variants of HLA that tend to protect against those diseases. Perls has found a region on chromosome 4 that centenarians and their siblings and children in the U.S. seem to have in common and that sets them apart from shorter-lived individuals. The finding has not yet been replicated by other groups, but Perls expects to publish a paper in the next month detailing his results.

What exactly that stretch of DNA does remains to be discovered, but it may be a key not just to long life but also to the resilience found among U.S. centenarian-study participants, with their 20 percent smoking rate and imperfect eating habits. That group may be especially genetically blessed, and researchers are eager to tap its secrets.

We certainly need them. For as medical science adds years to our collective lives, we chip away at them by doing things—stewing at our desk jobs, eating fatty processed foods, blowing a gasket in a freeway traffic jam, exercising no more than our fingers at the computer—that centenarians can't imagine. Most of them were born into an America as remote from today's metaphorically as the craggy villages of Sardinia, Okinawa and Nova Scotia are geographically. In the early 1900s people walked miles to work not by choice but out of necessity; cars were still a luxury. People tilled the fields because their farmer parents needed cheap help. People ate what they grew because it was there. Most labor was manual then, and most nutrients were natural. Preserved food was what Aunt Maud sealed in a jar. Tobacco and alcohol were available, but most of today's centenarians didn't indulge to excess.

They trigger our awe and our nostalgia as representatives of a flinty, hardscrabble culture that hardly exists today. They lived out a parable of man at one with nature. They used their bodies as they were designed and programmed over the millennia: for walking, for working, for being fed from the earth's natural bounty. It makes one wonder whether the next generation of oldsters will last quite as long. They will need not just the luck of the genetic draw but also the strength to renounce the lure of fast-food days and couch-potato nights that add yards of butt lard and shorten life-spans by years.

Will Americans in the supersize age resolve to go medieval on their own bodies? It would help, if they want to live to 100. As Poon says of his research pools, "I don't have any fat centenarians." And if research really does extend life by a vigorous couple of decades, the new millions of centenarians will need a support system that spreads beyond family and friends to include a hugely expensive Social Security and Medicare apparatus. The coming gerontocracy won't come cheap.

But that's for the future. Any child of today who hopes to live into the twenty-second century without the aid of medical miracles should look to the past, and consider the lessons today's centenarians took from the nineteenth century. There's a poetry of common sense in their scheme for immortality. Eat sensibly. Keep walking. Keep knitting. If you can't keep friends, make new ones. Plan so much invigorating work that there's just no *time* to die. And no regret when you do.

QUESTIONS FOR ACTIVE READING

1. With reference to Figures 10.1, 10.2, and 10.3, create a diagram that illustrates the various causes that contribute to extreme longevity in the United States and elsewhere in the world. (This is a kind of summary—try this note-taking strategy to help you work through and understand a complex reading.)

2. The authors ask two key questions in paragraph 6. How do those questions suggest the purpose and strategy of their causal argument?

3. Of all the causes suggested for living a very long yet healthy life discussed in this article, which could be classified as contributory causes? Which are interactive causes? Can you identify any causal fallacies in the beliefs and observations of the people quoted and described in the article?

QUESTIONS FOR THINKING CRITICALLY

1. Which of the longevity-promoting behaviors and lifestyle choices described in this article would you be willing to adopt? If you were to make certain lifestyle changes (such as not drinking alcohol, exercising more strenuously, or restricting your calorie intake), what would be the short-term effects? Would it be worth making these sacrifices to achieve the potential long-term effects?

2. Do the authors make any implied or overt value judgments about modern, Western lifestyles as compared with more traditional lifestyles? In a source-based essay, compare and contrast one aspect of your lifestyle today with the way someone your age would have lived fifty or hundred years ago. (For example, would you have already been married and a parent at your age? Would you have succumbed to a childhood disease or infection?) Review Chapter 9 for more information about thinking through comparisons and evaluations.

3. How important, in your experience, is a positive and optimistic outlook on your quality of life? On the other hand, is it more realistic and useful to be cautious or even pessimistic? When you consider the possibility of living to be one hundred, to what degree is your enthusiasm (or lack thereof) for the idea tempered by optimism or pessimism?

Writing Thoughtfully About Causal Relationships

Clearly, because of the complexity of determining cause and effect, writing a causal analysis requires special care. Causal analyses range all the way from rigorous scientific studies that can establish causes with some degree of certainty to theorizing about events in our personal lives. The causal analysis assignments you will encounter in college are likely to be of two types: those for which you conduct some kind of study to determine causality and then report your results, and those for which you research what others have said about the causes of an event and report their findings.

For the first type, you are likely to be given a format, such as for a lab report or an experimental design. It will be important for you to follow directions as you plan and conduct your study, and important for you to observe the conventions of the discipline in which you are writing as you prepare your report. Models are extremely helpful, so study them carefully if your professor provides them. If not, ask a librarian for guidance.

The second type, in which you report what others have said about the causes of an event, can be structured as an essay. Daniel Eggers's thoughtful analysis on page 349 is an example of such an essay. If you consult other sources of information, you must properly cite and document those sources (see Appendix).

PRINCIPLES FOR ANALYZING CAUSES

1. Be cautious. Causal relationships are difficult to prove. You may have to use wording such as *possible cause* or *may have affected*.

2. Name and describe the event or issue and people's reactions to it in your introduction.

3. In your thesis statement, indicate that you will be analyzing the causes of this event or issue or that you will be reporting what others have said about its causes.

4. Discuss each cause in a separate section (at least one body paragraph for each cause).

5. Amplify how or why each cause brought about the event or makes the issue important or controversial. Simply naming the cause is not enough.

6. Whenever possible, focus on immediate rather than remote causes. See page 332 to review these terms.

7. Use the labels in this chapter (contributory, causal chain, interactive, sufficient, and so on) to identify causal relationships if they are suitable for the style of your paper.

8. Represent accurately any sources that you use and document them honestly and correctly.

9. Avoid logical fallacies such as *post hoc ergo propter hoc*. See pages 333–336 to review these fallacies.

10. In your conclusion, name the causes and discuss the level of certainty for each of them. You may, of course, wish to do more than this in your conclusion.

Writing Project: Exploring Some Causes of a Recent Event

This chapter has included both readings and Thinking-Writing Activities that encourage you to think about causal relationships in your own life and in the environment. Be sure to reread what you wrote for those activities; you may be able to use some of the material when completing this project.

Write an essay in which you report and discuss some of the causes of a specific local or national event that occurred within the last three years. You might want to choose an event that had an environmental impact, or, depending on your interests or your instructor's assignment, you might want to write about something else that has affected the lives of many people (such as recent Supreme Court decisions or a current international crisis). Include material from two to four sources, being certain to cite and document those sources accurately.

After you have drafted your essay, revise it to the best of your ability. Follow your instructor's directions for topic choices, length, format, documentation style, and so on.

Begin by considering the key elements in the Thinking-Writing Model in Chapter 1 on pages 7–9.

The Writing Situation

Purpose   You have a variety of purposes here. You can satisfy your own curiosity about why an event occurred and explain the causes to others. You can improve your ability to think critically about causal relationships. You can hone your revision skills by working through the revision questions that follow.

Audience   You have a range of readers within your audience. *You* are an important audience, for in researching and analyzing causes, you can become a better thinker and possibly a more concerned citizen. Your classmates can be a valuable audience for review of a draft, reacting as intelligent readers who are not as knowledgeable as you about the causes of this event. Others interested in the event may find your essay enlightening. Finally, your instructor remains the audience who will judge how well you have planned, drafted, and revised. As a writing teacher, he or she cares about a clear focus, logical organization, specific details and examples, accurate documentation of sources, and correctness. Your classmates and your instructor will be interested in how you have applied this chapter's ideas.

Subject   You should reflect on the event or issue in terms of its causes and effects on the community. For example, if you decide to write about an event such as Hurricane Katrina that had a disproportionate effect on the poor, consider that all of us need to be concerned about both positive and negative environmental changes. Not only our future, but our children's and their children's futures depend on our careful stewardship of the earth. At the same time, there are competing economic and political pressures that can act against a strict conservationist view. By researching and analyzing a specific event, we can add to our own knowledge and that of our audience, thereby preparing all for responsible future action.

Writer   You will be using sources for this essay, but your paper should be written in your own voice and include your own observations and experiences. You will report and document the published writers' words and ideas and comment upon them as you think appropriate. If you find disagreement among your sources, don't discard any of them: the lack of agreement gives you a variety of views to report and consider.

The Writing Process

The following sections will guide you through the stages of generating, planning, drafting, and revising as you work on your essay. Try to be particularly conscious of both the critical thinking you find in your sources and the critical thinking you do as you examine them.

Generating Ideas

- Within your instructor's parameters for the assignment, begin by finding an event that interests you. If one comes to mind immediately, you can begin to research it. If not, begin by brainstorming a list of all the local and national events you can remember from the last few years.
- After you have selected an event, use your college library and the Internet. Consult Chapter 14 and your handbook about locating sources. Search for full texts of articles from reputable publications. Check titles for words like *causes, factors, results in, reasons,* or *underlie.*
- Locate or print the sources that you identify and read them, using the strategies for active and critical reading discussed in Chapter 2. First, check to see that they do indeed discuss the causes of the event, not just the event itself. Then see what causes they identify and how they label them (contributory, interactive, and so on). If they do not label them, try to do that yourself. Also, look for language that indicates the source's level of certainty about these causes ("has been definitely identified as a cause," or "may be partially responsible").
- Highlight sections of the source that you will include (if you own the source or have photocopied it). If you are required to do so, make note cards based on the marked sections.
- Think about how much information you have. Do you need more? If so, continue researching, reading, and marking until you have enough to answer the question "Why did this event take place?"

Defining a Focus   Write a thesis statement that will make clear to your audience that you are going to analyze *why* the event occurred or why the issue is critical. Here are two possible ways to frame this type of thesis.

The first is simply to report what your sources say and whether or not they are in agreement.

A second type of thesis requires you to take a position on the causal relationships involved. For example, you could write, "Having consulted four sources dealing with the causes of this event, I agree with three of them but reject a theory proposed in the fourth."

Organizing Ideas   If you made note cards, read through them two or three times. Then spread them all out on a table or desk so that you can see them all at once. Begin to group them into stacks: one to describe the event and one for each cause mentioned. Ideally, doing this will help you to integrate material from your different sources into various parts of your essay. You may decide not to use a few note cards; this often happens and indicates that you have done a good job of finding sufficient information. If you discover that you don't have enough information, you can do more research.

If you didn't make note cards, spread your marked sources out and try to plan how you will use information from each.

Review the principles for writing an essay of causal analysis on page 345 of this chapter. In addition, you will need to determine the order of your body paragraphs. For a causal chain, you will probably want chronological order. For contributory causes, you may want to use climactic (least to most important) order. For interactive causes, you may want to try different orders until you discover which will make the interaction of the causes easiest for your audience to understand.

Drafting   Draft one section from each stack of note cards. A highly specific description of the event could become the introduction. Quotations from eyewitnesses or participants in the event can help to interest your audience. The introduction can conclude with the tentative thesis statement you have written.

Begin each body paragraph with a topic sentence that names the possible or verifiable cause being discussed. Then provide the audience with as much information as necessary to help them understand how that cause actually could or did bring about the event.

Be sure to note the author, URL, and title and page of any information from any source you use. Do not trust yourself to add documentation as you revise your paper. It's easy to lose track and therefore to plagiarize accidentally.

In your conclusion, you can summarize the causes and discuss the level of certainty, or uncertainty, about them. If you found considerable disagreement among your sources, you can comment on that. If research is still ongoing about the causes, you can say so. You can, of course, do more than this in your conclusion, depending on your content.

On a separate page, draft a Works Cited list, using the format specified by your instructor.

Revising, Editing, and Proofreading   Use the step-by-step method in Chapter 6 on pages 152–154 to revise and polish your essay.

The following essay shows how two students responded to this assignment.

Student Writing | # Daniel Eggers's Writing Process

In response to an assignment asking him to update and add to an argument put forth in one of the assigned readings, Daniel Eggers, a student at City College of San Francisco, chose to consider whether or not the dream proposed by Dr. Martin Luther King Jr. had been achieved. When his research showed that it had not, he began to look for causes.

One of the most important decisions that I made in writing this essay was how to plan my approach. Since the validity of my arguments would be gauged through the supporting data, the majority of my effort went into locating appropriate sources, on which the framework of my essay would then be established. That is why I chose to produce a malleable thesis to begin with—so that I could later reshape it to allow the supporting sources to fit together nicely.

Although the majority of my effort went into locating sources, I still needed to produce a thesis and establish a framework to tie all of the sources together by creating supporting arguments for my thesis. My research suggested that there were many possible causes for racial inequality that were interrelated. Since the economy plays such an important role in American society, the first cause, to which all of the arguments could relate, was the involvement of African Americans in the economy. In the first paragraph I listed the origins of poverty for so many African Americans. These include the loss of low-skilled jobs, leading to deeper levels of poverty, which increases the development of ghettos and thus further isolates the African-American population. The causal chain could have gone in many different directions, but it was the material in my supporting sources that helped me to see the progression of causes.

Luckily, some of the sources I chose discussed recent events, such as the 2000 Presidential election and Hurricane Katrina, so writing comments about these sources came somewhat naturally. This is where I think the greatest advantage in writing this essay lay, with engaging a subject that ignited my curiosity, fascination, and interest.

Was It Only a Dream?

by Daniel Eggers

In the fall of 1963, on the one-hundredth anniversary of the Emancipation Proclamation, Martin Luther King Jr. stood before nearly two-hundred and fifty-thousand people in Washington, D.C., to present his famous speech, "I Have a Dream." This speech was a momentous event for the civil rights movement, and even today we are still able to hear King's voice saying the words: "I have a dream that one day this nation will rise up and live out the true meaning of its creed: 'We hold these truths to be self-evident; that all men are created equal'" (531). Through King's speech we are able to partake in his vision of a future where racial inequalities no longer exist. Many people, despite the giant steps taken by the civil rights movement, feel that racial equality will never be achieved. I, myself, having researched the events of the civil rights movement, as well as recent events concerning race, feel that, though one day we may see King's dream come true, we still have a long way to go before racial equality will become a reality.

Now, over forty years after King's speech, many African Americans are still an underprivileged group, especially because of their position in the economy. Michael Hughes and Carolyn J. Kroehler reported in *Sociology: the Core* that in 2001, "for every dollar in wealth owned by a white household, the average African American household owns [only] sixteen cents" (183–184). This considerable economic inequality places limitations on the lifestyles of many African Americans by barring their access to decent housing, good education, adequate healthcare, and nutritious foods. Though the problem of African American poverty is clearly shown through statistics, the origins of the problem are not easily defined. Hughes and Kroehler state that due to the vanishing number of low-skilled jobs in the last decade, "poor urban African Americans find themselves relegated to all-black neighborhoods where they are socially isolated from mainstream American life" (233). These all-black neighborhoods, or what some would refer to as ghettos, are symbols of economic inequality in America. King refers to these all-black neighborhoods in his speech as a source of discontent for the devotees of civil rights: "We will not be satisfied as long as the Negro's basic mobility is from a smaller ghetto to a larger one" (530).

Most who can recognize African American poverty as a sizable fracture in our society can reasonably argue that it must be granted the attention it deserves in order to be repaired. However, the problem of African American poverty seldom receives attention in mainstream America. The media largely ignores gradually developing social and economic problems and places the spotlight on immediate high-profile events. Such was the case with Hurricane Katrina, whose aftermath, given ample media coverage by all the major networks, revealed some desperate levels of African American poverty, as well as incompetence and neglect of city, state, and federal governments to provide relief to the victims. An article in the *Wall Street Journal* by Shelby Steele discusses the aftermath of Hurricane Katrina with its connection to racial issues. Steele states, in light of Katrina's aftermath, "Here was a poverty with an element of surrender in it that seemed to confirm the worst charges against [African Americans]: that [they] are inferior, that nothing really helps [them], that the modern world is beyond [their] reach" (20). The extensive media coverage given to Katrina, though horrifying and depressing, gave the American people an unforgettable example of extreme African American poverty stemming from the injustice of racial inequality.

Because the scales of economic distribution tilt disproportionately away from African Americans, the country has not obtained racial equality, but what steps can be taken to correct this inequity? Providing access to a good education seems to be one viable solution, and today there are numerous community colleges and vocational schools at which a person can acquire the necessary skills to earn a decent living. However, poverty looms like a cloud over many African Americans' prospects for acquiring an education. This is especially true because of the steady rise in the costs of tuition, housing, and transportation.

In addition to financial obstacles, some African American students are now facing a reversal of affirmative action when being considered for admission to higher education. One case occurred in Florida in 1999 with Governor Jeb Bush's abolishment of affirmative action in university admissions. K. Chandler reported in the *Westside Gazette* that due to this revocation of racial background being considered in the state universities' admissions process, the number of African American incoming freshmen to Florida universities dropped from a high of 17.6 percent in 1999 to 15.8 percent in 2004. A similar case is given by James T. Patterson in his book, *Brown v. Board of Education*, in which a 1996 Court of Appeals ruling required the University of Texas Law School to stop enforcing its affirmative action guidelines for admission. This decision resulted in African American enrollment there dropping from thirty-one to four in the following year (2006). Numbers like these illustrate the importance of affirmative action laws in maintaining equal opportunities in education for African Americans, and their reversal is a huge step backwards in the battle for racial equality.

There are many more holes in the system to explore when analyzing the racial inequalities within America. Consider the disenfranchisement of some African American voters during the 2000 presidential election in Florida. Bob Drogin reported in a *Los Angeles Times* article that in Gadsden County, a poor rural county of Florida predominantly occupied by African Americans, "one in eight voters' [. . .] ballots were rejected as invalid." This article contrasts the wealthier and predominantly white county of Leon, where only two in one thousand ballots were rejected, which causes questions to arise about the fairness of the voting process. Clearly these discrepancies resulted from issues concerning class and racial inequality. Drogan reported that Leon County could afford to purchase more effective ballot processing machines for each of its districts, which would notify a voter if a ballot was not filled out correctly, while in Gadsden County, because of the lack of funds to purchase ballot processing machines, the ballots had to be taken to a main election office to be processed.

These technicalities are significant because, had the 179,855 ballots—noted by Drogan—that went uncounted in Florida been processed, we could possibly have seen a different outcome in the election, especially since George W. Bush defeated Al Gore by a mere 537 votes. The disenfranchisement of some African Americans during this election is also significant because it shows just how far away they are from gaining the equal voting rights to which they are entitled under the Fifteenth Amendment.

What history shows is that as long as a minority group is fighting to gain equal rights, there will be a group who will do what it can to halt its progress. Such was the circumstance involving the *Brown v. Board of Education* case of 1954. James T. Patterson noted that in response to the ruling, which outlawed segregation in public schools, white supremacist groups mobilized to resist desegregation. For example, Bryant Bowles, who founded the National Association for the Advancement of White People, organized protests and ordered white students to boycott a high school in Delaware. It was not only through boycotts and protests that Bowles tried to slow the civil rights movement, but also through threats of violence toward people who supported that school's desegregation (74–75).

Today the methods of supremacists are less direct and more covert, using economic, political, and psychological oppression to maintain racial inequality. The previously mentioned examples of Katrina and the disenfranchisement of African Americans in the Florida 2000 election would suffice as modern methods of oppression, but every now and then a supremacist will slip in an ounce of truth concerning his/her opinion about race. Bob Herbert wrote a column in the *New York Times* that discusses some cruel words said on the radio by the former secretary of education in the Reagan cabinet, Bill Bennett: "I do know that it's true that if you wanted to reduce crime, you could—if that were your sole purpose—you could abort every black baby in this country, and your crime rate would go down." Bennett went on to say, "That would be an impossible, ridiculous, and morally reprehensible thing to do, but your crime rate would go down." Bennett's statement makes clear that racism, so prevalent throughout American history, still exists today.

African Americans have a problematic disposition within our culture. It's sort of a double standard where they are expected to fit in and be functioning cogs within the machine of American society, yet they are not truly accepted and are often treated as outsiders. W. E. B. DuBois describes this condition best in *The Souls of*

Black Folk by saying, "One ever feels his two-ness,—an American, a Negro; two souls, two thoughts, two unreconciled strivings; two warring ideals in one dark body, whose dogged strength alone keeps it from being torn asunder" (38). But despite this disposition, along with the obstacles of oppression that were placed here as soon as the first enslaved Africans were brought to these shores, change will always be a constant, so the possibility for a future of justice and racial equality for African Americans may one day come to pass. However, the nation is still quite a distance from achieving this goal, but as long as we can recognize how far the civil rights movement has come and become aware of what must be done to push the movement forward, then the dream that millions of Americans from all racial groups share with Martin Luther King Jr. will never remain only a dream.

Works Cited

Chandler, K. "Black Enrollment in Florida Colleges Plummets as Percentage of Hispanics Surges." <u>Western Gazette</u>. 18 August 2005. 14 November 2005 <http://proquest.umi.com/pdqweb?did=904005401&sid=1&clientId=65274&RQT=309&Vname=PDQ>.

Drogin, Bob. "2 Florida Counties Show Election Day's Inequities." <u>Los Angeles Times</u>. 12 Mar. 2001. 16 November 2005 <http://www.latimes.com/>.

Du Bois, W. E. B. <u>The Souls of Black Folk</u>. Massachusetts: Bedford Books, 1997.

Herbert, Bob. "Impossible, Ridiculous, Repugnant." <u>New York Times</u>. 6 Oct. 2005. 16 November 2005 <http://www.nytimes.com/>.

Hughes, Michael, and Carolyn J. Kroehler. <u>Sociology: the Core</u>. 7th ed. New York: McGraw, 2005.

King, Jr., Martin Luther. "I Have a Dream." <u>Great Writing: A Reader for Writers</u>. 3rd ed. Ed. Harvey S. Wiener. New York: McGraw. 2002. 529–532.

Patterson, James T. <u>Brown v. Board of Education: A Civil Rights Milestone and Its Troubled Legacy</u>. New York: Oxford UP, 2001.

Steele, Shelby. "Witness: Blacks, Whites, and the Politics of Shame in America." 26 October 2005. <u>Wall Street Journal</u>. 14 November 2005, <http://online.wsj.com/public/us?mod=OHP20M017>.

Alternative Writing Project: Utopias and Dystopias

In their article "How to Live to Be 100" (p. 338) authors Richard Corliss and Michael D. Lemonick suggest many lifestyle changes that, along with favorable genes, might help the average person to live to be at least 100 years old. In an essay, suggest ways in which a society made up of people who lived well past the century mark would be either a utopia or a dystopia. (Be sure to look up both words; your essay should define the term in your own words and within the context of your own argument.) How joyful would a society be, for example, if everyone practiced the physical discipline and appetite control some scientists suggest? What would be the benefits and challenges to a society where the population continually increased because people were living longer? Your essay could be quite imaginative, but even the most compelling science-fiction or fantasy is based on some semblance of probability—so be sure to complement your suppositions with some research.

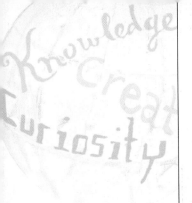

PART 3
Thinking and Writing to Explore Issues and Take Positions

As you have become more confident in your thinking and writing abilities, you may also have developed more respect for the thinking and writing of others. You have probably observed how academic work and even democracy itself depend on understanding sources of beliefs and various perspectives. You have been learning how to evaluate information and how to express your own perspectives clearly.

Part One of this book helped you focus on yourself as a thinker and a writer, and you wrote from your experiences and observations. Part Two asked you to explore important thinking patterns and to incorporate some ideas from others into your writing. Here in Part Three assignments will lead to the presentation of your ideas and those from sources in well-reasoned writing.

The Writing Projects at the end of each chapter in Part Three ask you to integrate material from several sources into your written work. As you do so, you will learn effective, responsible ways of introducing, commenting on, and documenting ideas from others. You will consider the principles that underlie research and citation, and you will use appropriate formats for academic writing.

11

Believing and Knowing

Writing to Analyze

> A belief is not merely an idea the mind possesses, it is an idea that possesses the mind.
>
> —Robert Bolton

Writers write about what they believe, and their purposes often include explaining their beliefs and persuading others to adopt them. Yet what exactly are beliefs, and how are they constructed? When should they be kept, when should they be modified, and when should they be discarded? What are the differences between believing and knowing, and how do writers handle these differences? How do writers present beliefs they hold with varying degrees of certainty?

In this information age, we are flooded with data, stories, and pictures from television, radio, newspapers, magazines, books, and computers. Thus, critical thinkers and thoughtful writers face a continuing challenge to evaluate information they receive and to redefine their beliefs accordingly.

Chapter 3 examined the sources of beliefs, especially those related to personal life. This chapter continues that discussion by further examining the structure of beliefs, by presenting guidelines for evaluating beliefs, and by drawing distinctions between believing and knowing and between knowledge and truth. This chapter presents some of the ways in which beliefs take shape and some of the ways in which they are presented. The concepts of *interpretation, evaluation, conclusion, prediction, report, inference,* and *judgment* will provide a vocabulary to help you think about your beliefs and those of others.

The Writing Project at the end of the chapter asks you to analyze some influences on your beliefs about a social or an academic issue.

Ways of Forming Beliefs

Throughout our lives, we form beliefs about the world around us to explain why things happen as they do, to predict how things will happen, and to govern the choices we make. For example, consider the following statements and answer "Yes," "No," or "Not sure" to each.

1. Human beings need to eat in order to stay alive.

2. Smoking marijuana is a harmful activity.

3. Every human life is valuable.

4. Developing your mind is as important as taking care of your body.

5. People should care about other people, not just about themselves.

Your responses to these statements reflect certain beliefs you have, beliefs not all people share.

What exactly are beliefs? *Beliefs* represent an interpretation, evaluation, conclusion, or prediction that a person believes to be true. You may not have considered these different representations of beliefs before, but, if you think about it, you might see that most of your beliefs fit into one of these categories. Sometimes it might be important as you consider a belief to see which type it is. For example, *interpretation* suggests that other explanations are possible, and *prediction* makes clear that an event has not yet happened. Such understandings help when thinking critically about your beliefs.

The statement "I believe that the U.S. Constitution's guarantee of 'the right of the people to keep and bear arms' does not prohibit all governmental regulation of firearms" represents an interpretation of the Second Amendment. To say, "I believe that watching daytime talk shows is unhealthy because they focus almost exclusively on the seamy side of human life" expresses an *evaluation* of daytime talk shows. The statement "I believe that one of the main reasons two out of three people in the world go to bed hungry each night is that industrially advanced nations like the United States have not done a satisfactory job of sharing their resources" expresses a *conclusion* about the problem of world hunger. To say, "I believe that if drastic environmental measures are not undertaken to slow the global warming trend, the polar icecaps will melt and the earth will be flooded" is to make a *prediction* about events that will occur in the future.

Besides expressing an interpretation, evaluation, conclusion, or prediction about the world, a belief also expresses an *endorsement* of its accuracy—an indication that the belief is held to be true by the writer or speaker. This endorsement is a necessary dimension of a belief. For example, the statement "Astrological predictions are meaningless because there is no persuasive evidence that the position of the planets has any effect on human affairs" expresses a belief even though it doesn't specifically include the words *I believe*.

In addition, it is necessary to recognize that beliefs are not static—at least not if we apply a critical approach. We continually form and re-form our beliefs throughout much of our lives. This process often follows the following sequence:

1. We *form* beliefs in order to explain what is taking place. (These initial beliefs are often based on our past experiences.)

2. We *test* these beliefs by acting on the basis of them.

FOUR QUALITIES
OF A CRITICAL THINKER
Habitat for Humanity Founder Millard Fuller

Curious   Sometimes it is a life-changing experience that shakes our beliefs about ourselves and the world, renewing our curiosity by completely changing the way we see our lives and the lives of others. For Habitat for Humanity founder Millard Fuller, that experience was profoundly religious. A successful businessman, Fuller and his wife decided to give away nearly everything they owned and to devote their lives to serving the poor. Although the Fullers experienced this conversion within a Christian context, these same core values of abandoning the pursuit of material riches in order to contribute to the well-being of the less fortunate are universal ethical and spiritual principles. In the early 1970s the Fullers and their family moved to Africa, where they developed a system for building houses that drew on the resources of local communities. Realizing that this system could assist poor people in America, the Fullers moved back to the United States in 1976 and founded Habitat for Humanity.

Open-minded   Two readings in this chapter ("Homeless in Prescott, Arizona" and "For Katrina Evacuee, Getting Help Is a Full-Time Job") challenge conventional beliefs about the

causes of homelessness and the reasons why people may become homeless. Habitat for Humanity, for example, challenges the biased view that people who live in poverty have somehow chosen that "lifestyle," or are not willing to work to improve their living conditions. The fundamental premise of Habitat for Humanity is to involve people and communities in the building of their own homes. Mortgages for these homes are provided at no interest, in keeping with the Fuller's spiritual beliefs. The mortgage payments made by families who own Habitat for Humanity houses go towards the building of other houses and communities. This approach towards empowering the poor and building communities earned Fuller the Presidential Medal of Freedom in 1996. Former President Jimmy Carter, who has worked with Habitat for Humanity since 1984, has said that "Habitat has successfully removed the stigma of charity by substituting it with a sense of partnership. The people who will live in the homes work side by side with the volunteers, so they feel very much that they are on an equal level."

Knowledgeable   In recent years, Habitat for Humanity University has increased the mission of the original

3. We *revise* (or "re-form") these beliefs if our actions do not achieve our goals.

4. We *retest* these revised beliefs by again using them as a basis for action.

As we actively participate in this ongoing process of forming and re-forming beliefs, we are using our critical thinking abilities to identify and critically examine our beliefs by, in effect, asking the following questions.

- How effectively do these beliefs explain what is taking place?
- To what extent are the beliefs consistent with other beliefs about the world?
- How effectively do the beliefs help us to predict what will happen in the future?
- To what extent are these beliefs supported by sound reasons and compelling evidence derived from reliable sources?

This process of critical exploration enables us to develop more understanding of various situations and to exert more control over them.

organization by providing online education to, in the words of its mission statement, "provide learning opportunities, facilitate knowledge-sharing and actively assist in leadership development to end poverty housing throughout the world." Online education allows for people in remote and underserved communities to benefit from the collective knowledge of Habitat for Humanity, offering courses in everything from sustainability and empowerment to basic construction techniques and financial management. The multimedia courses are free of charge, as Habitat for Humanity envisions them being used by a wide range of community-based nonprofit organizations, including college service-learning and other student groups. If you have participated in a community service project, how did you evaluate and share what you learned from that experience?

Creative   As the organization has grown internationally, Habitat for Humanity has created new ways for people to support their mission. Its Global Village program attracts volunteers who travel all over the world to help build Habitat for Humanity houses and provide support for Habitat communities. In addition, like all organizations that exist to help people in times of crisis, Habitat for Humanity has had to sustain its flexibility and creativity in order to quickly address

urgent issues, such as the Asian tsunami of 2004 and the devastation wrought by hurricanes Katrina and Rita on the Gulf Coast in 2005. Habitat for Humanity has also developed creative partnerships with for-profit groups in order to build affordable housing and develop communities in increasingly expensive housing markets. For example, in Austin, Texas, Habitat for Humanity partnered with a for-profit developer and other community groups to build houses in a diverse community called Heritage Village, where Habitat for Humanity-subsidized houses exist alongside traditionally-financed homes.

Online Study Center
Millard Fuller
Visit the Online Study Center for *Critical Thinking, Thoughtful Writing* at *college.hmco.com/pic/ chaffeeCTTW4e* to learn more about Millard Fuller.

THINKING-
WRITING
ACTIVITY

Identifying Beliefs

Describe beliefs you have that fall in each of these categories (interpretation, evaluation, conclusion, prediction) and then explain the reason(s) you have for endorsing the beliefs.

1. **Interpretation** (an explanation or analysis of the meaning or significance of something)

   My interpretation is that . . .

   Supporting reason(s):

2. **Evaluation** (a judgment of the value or quality of something, based on certain standards)

   My evaluation is that . . .

   Supporting reason(s):

3. **Conclusion** (a decision made or an opinion formed after consideration of the relevant facts or evidence)

   My conclusion is that . . .

   Supporting reason(s):

4. **Prediction** (a statement about what will happen in the future)

   My prediction is that . . .

   Supporting reason(s):

Beliefs Based on Personal Experience

The introductory discussion of beliefs in Chapter 3 identified four sources of beliefs: people of authority, recorded references, observed evidence, and personal experience. The last two involve direct experience. Yet how we interpret and understand direct experience—what conclusions we draw from what we perceive—depends to some extent on what we already believe. In offering evidence to support their beliefs, people generally choose those perceptions and experiences that fit with their previous beliefs; contradictory experiences may be ignored or downplayed.

In the following pair of readings, two writers offer differing beliefs about the situation of the homeless in the United States, based on their perceptions of direct experience. B. C. chooses to live as a homeless person in "Homeless in Prescott, Arizona" while Katrina evacuee Donna Fenton does all she can to try to escape from her homelessness, as related in Nicholas Confessore's article "For Katrina Evacuee, Getting Help Is a Full-Time Job."

Before you begin to read, write down two or three of your beliefs about homelessness and the homeless. After you have read both pieces, write a few sentences about how your beliefs were affected by your reading these articles. If possible, share your statements with your classmates.

"Homeless in Prescott, Arizona"

BY B. C.

This narrative was one of thousands of stories submitted to National Public Radio's National Story Project. In 1999, novelist Paul Auster asked listeners to NPR's *Weekend All Things Considered* program to submit brief stories about some incident or anecdote "that revealed the mysterious and unknowable forces at work in our lives.... In other words, true stories that sounded like fiction." For more than a year, Auster read selected stories on the radio program. In 2001, he collected and published 179 of the stories in *I Thought My Father Was God: And Other True Tales From NPR's National Story Project.*

Last spring I made a major life change, and I wasn't suffering from a midlife crisis. At fifty-seven I'm way beyond that. I decided I could not wait eight more years to retire, and I could not be a legal secretary for eight more years. I quit my job; sold my house, furnishings, and car; gave my cat to my neighbor; and moved to Prescott, Arizona, a community of thirty thousand, nestled in the Bradshaw Mountains with a fine library, community college, and a beautiful town square. I invested the proceeds from selling everything and I now receive $315 a month in interest income. That is what I live off of.

I am anonymous. I am not on any government programs. I do not receive any kind of welfare, not even food stamps. I do not eat at the Salvation Army. I do not take handouts. I am not dependent on anyone.

My base is downtown Prescott, where everything I need is within a radius of a mile and a half—easy walking. To go farther afield, I take a bus that makes a circuit of the city each hour and costs three dollars for a day pass. I have a post-office box—cost, forty dollars a year. The library is connected to the Internet, and I have an e-mail address. My storage space costs twenty-seven dollars a month, and I have access to it twenty-four hours a day. I store my clothes, cosmetic and hygiene supplies, a few kitchen items, and paperwork there. I rent a secluded corner of a backyard a block from my storage area for twenty-five dollars a month. This is my bedroom, complete with arctic tent, sleeping bag, mattress, and lantern. I wear a sturdy pack with a water bottle, flashlight, and Walkman, toiletries and rain gear.

Yavapai College has an Olympic-size pool and a women's locker room. I take college classes and have access to these facilities; cost, thirty-five dollars a month. I go there every morning to perform my "toilet" and shower. I go to the Laundromat with a small load of clothes whenever I need to; cost, fifteen dollars a month. Looking presentable is the most important aspect of my new lifestyle. When I go to the library, no one can guess I'm homeless. The library is my living room. I sit in a comfortable chair and read. I listen to beautiful music through the stereo system. I communicate with my daughter via e-mail and type letters on the word processor. I stay dry when it's wet outside. Unfortunately, the library does not have a television, but I've found a student lounge at the college that does. Most of the time I can watch *The News Hour, Masterpiece Theater*, and *Mystery*. To further satisfy my cultural needs, I attend dress rehearsals at the local amateur theater company, free of charge.

5   Eating inexpensively and nutritiously is my biggest challenge. My budget allows me to spend two hundred dollars a month for food. I have a Coleman burner and an old-fashioned percolator. I go to my storage space every morning and make coffee, pour it into my thermos, load my backpack, go to the park, and find a sunny spot to enjoy my coffee and listen to *Morning Edition* on my Walkman. The park is my back-yard. It's a beautiful place to hang out when the weather is clement. I can lie on the grass and read and nap. The mature trees provide welcome shade when it's warm.

My new lifestyle has been comfortable and enjoyable so far because the weather in Prescott during the spring, summer, and fall has been delightful, though it did snow Easter weekend. But I was prepared. I have a parka, boots, and gloves, all warm and waterproof.

Back to eating. The Jack in the Box has four items that cost one dollar—Breakfast Jack, Jumbo Jack, a chicken sandwich, and two beef tacos. After I enjoy my coffee in the park, I have a Breakfast Jack. There's a nutrition program at the adult center where I can eat a hearty lunch for two dollars. For dinner, back to the Jack in the Box. I buy fresh fruit and veggies at Albertson's. Once in a while I go to the Pizza Hut—all you can eat for $4.49. When I return to my storage space in the evening, I make popcorn on my Coleman burner. I only drink water and coffee; other beverages are too expensive.

I've discovered another way to have a different eating experience and to combine it with a cultural evening. There's an art gallery downtown, and the openings of the new shows are announced in the newspaper. Two weeks ago I put on my dress and panty hose, went to the opening, enjoyed eating the snacks, and admired the paintings.

I've let my hair grow long, and I tie it back in a ponytail like I did in grade school. I no longer color it. I like the gray. I do not shave my legs or underarms and do not polish my fingernails [or] wear mascara, foundation, blush, or lipstick. The natural look costs nothing.

10   I love going to college. This fall, I'm taking ceramics, chorale, and cultural anthropology—for enrichment, not for credit. I love reading all the books I want to but never had enough time for. I also have time to do absolutely nothing.

Of course there are negatives. I miss my friends from back home. Claudette, who works at the library, befriended me. She was a feature writer for the local newspaper and is adept at getting information from people. Eventually, I told her who I was and how I live. She never pressures me to live differently, and I know she's there for me if I need her.

I also miss Simon my cat. I keep hoping that a cat will come my way, particularly before winter sets in. It would be nice to sleep and snuggle with a furry body.

I hope I can survive the winter. I've been told that Prescott can have lots of snow and long stretches of freezing temperatures. I don't know what I'll do if I get sick. I'm generally an optimist, but I do worry. Pray for me.

"For Katrina Evacuee, Getting Help Is a Full-Time Job"

BY NICHOLAS CONFESSORE (b. 1975)

The following article was published in the New York Times *in March 2006, almost six months after Hurricane Katrina devastated the Gulf Coast. Before joining the Metropolitan Desk as a reporter at the* Times, *Nick Confessore was a senior correspondent for* American Prospect *and an editor of the* Washington Monthly.

Donna Fenton no longer consults the scrap of paper in her pocketbook when she needs the phone number for the Red Cross, or New York City's welfare office, or the Federal Emergency Management Agency.

"I know them all by heart," said Ms. Fenton, 37, who left Biloxi, MS, after Hurricane Katrina destroyed her home there. "I call them every day. That's my job."

She starts in the morning, calling from the rooms she and her family share at a Ramada hotel near La Guardia Airport, or from the hotel's basement conference room. She knows what numbers will lead to someone helpful and the ones that will plunge her into a thicket of indifference or incomprehension. She keeps going for hours, sometimes until 3 o'clock the next morning.

The days and nights can blur together, a fog of dial tones, beige wallpaper and overly cheerful automated voices. "Everything they asked for, I sent in," she said. "I sent it in the second time, and then I sent it in a third time."

5 What she wants, she says, is enough money to move into a new apartment in New York so she can begin anew the life that Katrina ripped apart. "It wasn't like we had any luxuries," she said. "But we were scraping by."

About 20 families left homeless by Katrina still live at the Ramada, and, all things considered, Ms. Fenton is among the more fortunate evacuees. Because she went to high school in New York, the city is not wholly foreign to her. She has found a job that pays about as well as the one she held managing two restaurants in Biloxi. Her husband, Matt, has found part-time work at an auto body shop.

Ms. Fenton is polite, organized and determined.

But more than five months after arriving in Queens with a change of clothes and a tapped-out bank account, moving on has been much harder than she thought it would be. Many obstacles she has encountered are familiar to other Katrina evacuees living in New York as they sort out their next moves and deadlines approach, after which the federal government will no longer pay for hotel rooms.

Some obstacles are more rare.

10 Ms. Fenton, who has lupus, collapsed at a Manhattan welcome center last September after filling out paperwork from half a dozen agencies and charities. Doctors found that days of irregular sleep and roadside food had worsened her condition, producing an enlarged heart and an irregular heartbeat.

"In the South," she said, "we eat a lot of vegetables. That's impossible to do in a hotel or on the road." She spent four days in the hospital.

A Red Cross worker placed Ms. Fenton, her husband, and four of her five children—Akreem, 16; Ashley, 14; LaTanya, 10; and Danielle, 9—at the Ramada, and gave her a debit card with a $1,565 limit. The children were placed in public school, but debit-card money quickly dwindled. "That doesn't go far for six people," she said.

So Ms. Fenton began working the phones. A $2,358 check for rent assistance from FEMA arrived in October. But a second check, for what the agency calls "immediate needs," never materialized. She also got no response from the Small Business Administration to a loan application she filed almost as soon as she arrived in the city. The FEMA check was soon used up—on clothes, food, and transportation, and for her family, as well as for her oldest son, William, 21, and his fiancee, Amanda McGee, who also live at the hotel.

Twice, Ms. Fenton said, she found apartments, but was afraid to sign leases because she was not sure FEMA's promised rental assistance would arrive.

15 Filling paperwork was a constant headache. Faxes to and from agencies seemed to disappear regularly. "It was like Russian roulette," she said.

FEMA granted her an extension to stay at the hotel, she said, but then forgot to issue an authorization code for the second of the two rooms her family occupied. That meant more time pleading on the phone.

A FEMA spokeswoman, Nicole Andrews, acknowledged last week that the process could be "pretty tough for anyone who has been traumatized like these people have."

There were bright spots. A recreation center in Brooklyn offered free memberships to the Ramada evacuees. At Christmas, a nearby church gave $100 gift cards to the families.

But Ms. Fenton's health was a continuing problem. In October, a hotel maid found her unconscious in her room. More hospital stays followed, six in all, as she battled to control her lupus. Then, in February, her appendix burst, resulting in a two-week hospital stay.

20 Her son William was told by doctors that he had post-traumatic stress syndrome stemming from the hurricane. More recently, her daughter LaTanya disappeared from the hotel and was found wandering the streets nearby. "She was saying that she didn't want to go back to the hotel," Ms. Fenton said.

Two weeks ago, an unlicensed driver slammed into their car, destroying the family's main means of transportation. Her husband has borrowed cars from colleagues at work to take the younger children to school.

A new apartment, however, has remained elusive, and with it a normal life. With all the time she spends on the phone, she said, she cannot start the job waiting for her at a Brooklyn check-cashing business.

In January, a real estate agent helped line up a new apartment in Bushwick, Brooklyn. But without another rental assistance check, Ms. Fenton was afraid to move, despite the apartment building owner's encouragement.

"I know I can't live there for free," she said. "I don't want to get us there and then stick this lady with not being able to pay the rent." She recently learned that the second rent check had been lost in the mail, and a replacement could not be issued until it was found.

25

"From what I'm hearing, it's a long process," said Ms. Fenton, still hopeful of moving to the Bushwick apartment.

She pulled on her coat. She needed to go to Manhattan to pick out furniture for the possible new apartment from a Salvation Army warehouse. It was her second trip there: the first time, the table and chairs she had ordered arrived with the legs broken.

"That's the most agitating part," she said. "Everything is done over and over. All of this has been done before."

QUESTIONS FOR ACTIVE READING

1. Identify passages in "Homeless in Prescott, Arizona" and "For Katrina Evacuee, Getting Help Is a Full-Time Job" that express interpretations, evaluations, conclusions, and predictions.

2. What differences can you find between the *New York Times*'s expository presentation and B. C.'s narrative approach? What do you see as the strengths of each approach? To what extent are the purposes of each text similar, even though their writing situations are very different?

3. Compare and contrast B. C.'s beliefs about negotiating homelessness with the beliefs of Donna Fenton. What does each woman believe about who is responsible for helping the homeless? What accounts for the difference in their perceptions?

QUESTIONS FOR THINKING CRITICALLY

1. Are any of your beliefs about homelessness based on direct experience? If so, whose experiences are closer to yours: B. C.'s or Donna Fenton's? Write a first-person narrative like "Homeless in Prescott, Arizona" that describes your experience for an audience otherwise unfamiliar with homelessness.

2. Does the term *homeless* accurately describe the way B. C. has chosen to live? Which woman—Donna Fenton or B. C.—seems to most closely reflect stereotypes about homelessness in America?

3. How did your beliefs affect your response to each reading?

Beliefs Based on Indirect Experience

No matter how much we have experienced in our lives, the fact is, of course, that no one person's direct experiences are enough to establish an adequate set of accurate beliefs. We all depend on the experience of others to provide us with beliefs and also to serve as foundations for those beliefs. For example, does Antarctica exist? How do we know? Have we ever been there and seen it with our own eyes? Probably not;

nevertheless, we believe in the existence of Antarctica and its ice and penguins. Of all the beliefs each of us has, few are actually based on our direct personal experience. Instead, other people have in some way or form communicated to us virtually all these beliefs and the evidence for them. As we reach beyond our personal experiences to form and revise our beliefs, we find that information is provided by two sources: people of authority and recorded references.

As we have seen in the essays discussing homelessness by B. C. and about Donna Fenton, the beliefs of others cannot be accepted without question. Each of us views the world through individual lenses that shape and influence the way we select and present information. Comparing different sources helps to make these lenses explicit and highlights the different interests and purposes involved. In fact, examining sources may lead us to recognize that there are a variety of competing viewpoints, some fairly similar, some quite contradictory. In critically reviewing the beliefs of others, it is essential for us to pursue the same goals of accuracy and completeness that we set when examining beliefs based on personal experience. As a result, we focus on the reasons or evidence that support the information others are presenting.

THINKING-
WRITING
ACTIVITY

The Origin of a Belief

Select one of the beliefs that you identified in the Thinking-Writing Activity at the beginning of this chapter. What indirect sources helped shape it: your family, friends, teachers, religious leaders, television, the Internet? What direct personal experiences or observations have had an impact on it? Note specifically how some of these influences shaped your belief.

Evaluating Sources and Information

When we depend on information that others provide, we need to ask key questions. The most crucial part of determining the reliability of a source's information is determining the reliability of the source itself.

How Reliable Is the Source?

We know that some sources—such as advertising—can be very unreliable whereas other sources, such as *Consumer Reports* magazine (which does not accept advertising), are generally considered reliable. Sometimes, however, the reliability of a source of information is not immediately clear. In those cases, we have to use a variety of standards or criteria to evaluate a source's reliability, whether the source is written or audible.

Special care should be taken when evaluating information from web sites. See Guidelines for Evaluating the Reliability of a Web Site in Chapter 14 on pages 512–513.

What Are the Source's Purposes and Interests?

Evaluating information means thinking critically about the perceiving lenses through which the source of the information views the situation. Is this source presenting an argument or giving information? Are you looking at a report, an inference, or a judgment (see pages 373–374). In other words, what is the rhetorical purpose of the piece? How is the purpose reflected in the selection of details and in wording and tone?

You also need to think about the piece's audience. Who is the intended audience? Is it friendly, neutral, or hostile? Is it informed or new to the subject? Writers or speakers can focus on specific audiences without being dishonorable, but sometimes they can emphasize one point of view or tap emotions in manipulative ways. Can you detect any slanting, or does this source's material seem balanced?

How Knowledgeable or Experienced Is the Source?

When seeking information from indirect sources, we want to locate people of authority or recorded references that can offer a special understanding of a subject. When a car begins making strange noises, we search for someone who knows cars. When we want to learn more about a social issue such as homelessness, we turn to articles and books written by people who have studied the problem.

In seeking information from sources, it is important to distinguish between nonexpert sources and expert sources who have training, education, and experience in a particular area. Also, any expert source's credentials should be up-to-date. A book about careers in the computer industry published twenty years ago is not likely to be reliable.

Sports and entertainment figures often endorse products in television commercials, but their testimony is not very convincing if those products have nothing to do with sports or entertainment (and if these "experts" have been paid large sums of money and told exactly what to say). Finally, we should not accept expert opinion without question or critical examination, even if the experts meet all of our criteria.

Was the Source Able to Make Accurate Observations?

You may have heard of law-enforcement training courses where actors stage simulated crimes before an unsuspecting class. Students in the class are then quickly informed that the situation has been staged to test their powers of observation and asked to record what happened in as much detail as they can remember. Invariably many witnesses are quite mistaken about much of what they remember while others can recall many fine details exactly. The same is true in any kind of eyewitness account: some people have quite sharp memories while others may "remember" many imagined details. In addition, a person's vantage point as a witness may color the reliability of the testimony. The amount of light, obstructions to vision, and other matters can make his or her perceptions less than wholly reliable.

The reliability of an indirect source also depends on the personal viewpoints and beliefs the source brings to a situation. These feelings, expectations, and interests often influence what a witness perceives without his or her full awareness of the process. For example, a group that sponsored an antiwar rally at a political convention might claim a crowd of more than five thousand while politicians issue a report estimating rally attendance at about two thousand. We have seen that two different writers can draw very different conclusions after spending time working in a homeless shelter. What further questions could be asked, and how might additional sources be located to evaluate the reliability of such differing sources?

How Reputable Is the Source?

When evaluating the reliability of sources, it is useful to consider how accurate and reliable their information has been in the past. If someone has consistently given sound information over a period of time, we gradually develop confidence in the accuracy of that person's reports. Police officers and news media reporters must continually evaluate the reliability of information sources. Of course, this works the other way as well. When people consistently give inaccurate or incomplete information, others lose confidence in their reliability. Nevertheless, few people provide information that is either completely reliable or completely unreliable. You probably realize that your own reliability tends to vary, depending on the situation, the type of information you are providing, and the person to whom you are giving it. Thus, in trying to evaluate information offered by others, you have to explore the following factors before arriving at a provisional conclusion, which you may have to revise later in light of additional information.

How Valuable Is Information from This Source?

Of course, you also need to assess the credibility of the information itself by asking these questions: What are the main ideas being presented? What evidence is provided? Does the information seem accurate? Is it up-to-date? Does anything seem false? Does anything seem to have been left out?

THINKING-
WRITING
ACTIVITY

Evaluating a Source of a Belief

Select one of the beliefs that you discussed in the Thinking-Writing Activity on page 360 that is based on sources such as people of authority or recorded references. Now, based on the criteria just discussed, evaluate the reliability of one source of your belief.

Believing and Knowing

Developing beliefs that are as accurate as possible is important to us as critical thinkers because the more accurate our beliefs are, the better we are able to understand the world around us and to make predictions about the future. As the preceding discussion has suggested, however, the accuracy of the beliefs we form can vary tremendously.

We use the word *knowing* to distinguish beliefs supported by strong reasons or evidence (such as the belief that life exists on earth) from beliefs for which there is less support (such as the belief that life exists on other planets) or from beliefs disproved by reasons or evidence to the contrary. This saying expresses another way to understand the difference between believing and knowing:

"You can believe what is not so, but you cannot know what is not so."

In the following essay, an astrophysicist considers a question that would seem to have an obvious answer. In doing so, he analyzes the difference between believing and knowing.

"Is the Earth Round or Flat?"

BY ALAN LIGHTMAN (b. 1948)

Alan Lightman, a professor at the Massachusetts Institute of Technology, is a physicist as well as a writer of fiction and nonfiction. His 1993 novel *Einstein's Dreams* has inspired plays and musical compositions and was a runner-up for the 1994 PEN New England/Boston Globe Winship Award. In 1996, Lightman was elected a fellow of the American Academy of Arts and Sciences and also won the 1996 American Institute of Physics Andrew Gemant Award for linking science to the humanities.

I propose that there are few of you who have personally verified that the Earth is round. The suggestive globe in the den or the Apollo photographs don't count. These are secondhand pieces of evidence that might be thrown out entirely in court. When you think about it, most of you simply believe what you hear. Round or flat, whatever. It's not a life-or-death matter, unless you happen to live near the edge.

A few years ago I suddenly realized, to my dismay, that I didn't know with certainty if the Earth were round or flat. I have scientific colleagues, geodesists they are called, whose sole business is determining the detailed shape of the Earth by fitting mathematical formulae to someone else's measurements of the precise locations of test stations on the Earth's surface. And I don't think those people really know either.

Aristotle is the first person in recorded history to have given proof that the Earth is round. He used several different arguments, most likely because he wanted to convince others as well as himself. A lot of people believed everything Aristotle said for 19 centuries.

His first proof was that the shadow of the Earth during a lunar eclipse is always curved, a segment of a circle. If the Earth were any shape but spherical, the shadow it casts, in some orientations, would not be circular. (That the normal phases of the moon are crescent-shaped reveals the moon is round.) I find this argument wonderfully appealing. It is simple and direct. What's more, an inquisitive and untrusting person can knock off the experiment alone, without special equipment. From any given spot on the Earth, a lunar eclipse can be seen about once a year. You simply have to look up on the right night and carefully observe what's happening. I've never done it.

Aristotle's second proof was that stars rise and set sooner for people in the East than in the West. If the Earth were flat from east to west, stars would rise as soon for Occidentals as for Orientals. With a little scribbling on a piece of paper, you can see that these observations imply a round Earth, regardless of whether it is the Earth that spins around or the stars that revolve around the Earth. Finally, northbound travelers observe previously invisible stars appearing above the northern horizon, showing the Earth is curved from north to south. Of course, you do have to accept the reports of a number of friends in different places or be willing to do some traveling. Aristotle's last argument was purely theoretical and even philosophical. If the Earth had been formed from smaller pieces at some time in the past (or *could* have been so formed), its pieces would fall toward a common center, thus making a sphere. Furthermore, a sphere is clearly the most perfect solid shape. Interestingly, Aristotle placed as much emphasis on this last argument as on the first two. Those days, before the modern "scientific method," observational check wasn't required for investigating reality. Assuming for the moment that the Earth is round, the first person who measured its circumference accurately was another Greek, Eratosthenes (276–195 B.C.). Eratosthenes noted that on the first day of summer, sunlight struck the bottom of a vertical well in Syene, Egypt, indicating the sun was directly overhead. At the same time in Alexandria, 5,000 stadia distant, the sun made an angle with the vertical equal to 1/50 of a circle. (A stadium equaled about a tenth of a mile.) Since the sun is so far away, its rays arrive almost in parallel. If you draw a circle with two radii extending from the center outward through the perimeter (where they become local verticals), you'll see that a sun ray coming in parallel to one of the radii (at Syene) makes an angle with the other (at Alexandria) equal to the angle between the two radii. Therefore, Eratosthenes concluded that the full circumference of the Earth is $50 \times 5,000$ stadia, or about 25,000 miles. This calculation is within one percent of the best modern value.

For at least 600 years educated people have believed the Earth is round. At nearly any medieval university, the quadrivium was standard fare, consisting of arithmetic, geometry, music, and astronomy. The astronomy portion was based on the *Tractatus de Sphaera,* a popular textbook first published at Ferrara, Italy, in 1472 and written by a 13th century, Oxford-educated astronomer and mathematician, Johannes de Sacrobosco. The *Sphaera* proves its astronomical assertions, in part, by a set of diagrams with movable parts, a graphical demonstration of Aristotle's second method of proof. The round Earth, being the obvious center of the universe, provides a fixed pivot for the assembly. The cutout figures of the sun, the moon, and the stars revolve about the Earth.

By the year 1500, 24 editions of the *Sphaera* had appeared. There is no question that many people *believed* the Earth was round. I wonder how many *knew* this. You would think that Columbus and Magellan might have wanted to ascertain the facts for themselves before waving good-bye. To protect my honor as a scientist, someone who is supposed to take nothing for granted, I set out with my wife on a sailing voyage in the Greek islands. I reasoned that at sea I would be able to calmly observe landmasses disappear over the curve of the Earth and thus convince myself, firsthand, that the Earth is round.

Greece seemed a particularly satisfying place to conduct my experiment. I could sense those great ancient thinkers looking on approvingly, and the layout of the place is perfect. Hydra rises about 2,000 feet above sea level. If the Earth has a radius of 4,000 miles, as they say, then Hydra should sink down to the horizon at a distance of about 50 miles, somewhat less than the distance you were to sail from Hydra to Kea. The theory was sound and comfortable. At the very least, I thought, you would have a pleasant vacation.

As it turned out, that was all you got. Every single day was hazy. Islands faded from view at a distance of only eight miles, when the land was still a couple of degrees above the horizon. I learned how much water vapor was in the air but nothing about the curvature of the Earth.

10

I suspect that there are quite a few items you take on faith, even important things, even things you could verify without much trouble. Is the gas you exhale the same as the gas you inhale? (Do you indeed burn oxygen in your metabolism, as they say?) What is your blood made of? (Does it indeed have red and white "cells"?) These questions could be answered with a balloon, a candle, and a microscope.

When you finally do the experiment, you relish the knowledge. At one time or another, you have all learned something for yourselves, from the ground floor up, taking no one's word for it. There is a special satisfaction and joy in being able to tell somebody something you have pieced together from scratch, something you really know. I think that exhilaration is a big reason why people do science.

Someday soon, I'm going to catch the Earth's shadow in a lunar eclipse, or go to sea in clear air, and find out for sure if the Earth is round or flat. Actually, the Earth is reported to flatten at the poles, because it rotates. But that's another story.

QUESTIONS FOR ACTIVE READING

1. Using an active reading technique from Chapter 2, read the first and the last paragraphs of this article. Now that you have read the entire article, would you say that technique gave you a good preview?

2. Why is it important to know that Lightman is a scientist? Would an artist or a social worker write about this subject in this way?

3. Where is Lightman using a lighthearted tone? Identify some phrases that show this. Where is he serious? Identify some phrases that show this. What is the effect of these tones?

Questions for Thinking Critically

1. Is it practical for a person to actually conduct a scientific experiment in order to "know" something? Do you think that Lightman is really proposing this? What is he implying?

2. Give one conclusive "proof" for the roundness of the earth that the author identifies and explain why it seems a valid proof.

3. In the next-to-last paragraph, Lightman writes about "a special satisfaction and joy in being able to tell somebody something you have pieced together from scratch. . . . I think that exhilaration is a big reason why people do science." Have you experienced satisfaction, joy, and exhilaration after completing a scientific experiment? Have you experienced such emotions after completing some other kind of project? Do you think that satisfaction, joy, and exhilaration are important emotions to experience in one's work?

Thinking-Writing Activity

Weighing Your Beliefs and Knowledge

Look again at the beliefs you have written about for previous activities. Could you say about any of them "I know this" rather than merely "I believe this"? Why? Write answers to these questions.

Knowledge and Truth

Authorities often disagree about the true nature of a given situation or the best course of action. It is common, for example, for doctors to disagree about a diagnosis, for economists to differ on the state of the economy, or for psychiatrists to disagree on whether a convicted felon is a menace to society or a victim of social forces.

What do we do when experts disagree? As critical thinkers, we must analyze and evaluate all the available information, develop our own well-reasoned beliefs, and recognize when we lack sufficient information to arrive at well-reasoned beliefs. We must realize, too, that such beliefs may evolve over time as we obtain more information or improve our insight.

Although there are compelling reasons to view knowledge and truth as evolving, some people resist doing so. Either they take refuge in a belief in the absolute, unchanging nature of knowledge and truth as presented by the appropriate authorities, or they conclude that there is no such thing as knowledge or truth and that trying to seek either is futile.

Understanding Relativism

In this latter view of the world, known as *relativism*, all beliefs are considered "relative" to the person or context in which they arise. For the relativist, all opinions are equal in validity to all others; no one is ever in a position to say with confidence that one view is right and another one wrong. Although a relativistic view is appropriate in some areas of experience—for example, in matters of taste such as fashion—in many other areas it is not. Knowledge, in the form of well-supported beliefs, does exist. Some beliefs are better than others, not because an authority has proclaimed them so but because they can be analyzed in terms of the criteria discussed earlier in this chapter.

Understanding Falsifiable Beliefs

Another important criterion for evaluating certain beliefs is that the beliefs be *falsifiable*. This means that it is possible to state conditions—tests—under which the beliefs could be disproved and that the beliefs then pass those tests. For example, if you believe that you can create ice cubes by placing water-filled trays in a freezer, you can conduct an experiment to determine whether your belief is accurate. If no ice cubes form after you put the trays in the freezer, your theory is disproved. If, however, you believe that your destiny is related to the positions of the planets and stars (as astrologers do), it is not clear how you can conduct an experiment to determine whether your belief is accurate. Since a belief that is not falsifiable can never be proved, such a belief is questionable.

The Media and Truth

We are all aware in a general way that the media can shape our beliefs by the information they provide and the interpretations they give to that information. We may not be aware, however, of some of the subtle ways in which this is done or of the profound influences that result. As you read the following essays, consider how your beliefs might be shaped by the sources that these writers discuss.

The following article originally appeared in *Newsweek*. It reports on studies conducted by a University of Pennsylvania professor, concerning the influence of television on people's beliefs.

Ways of Presenting Beliefs

When you write, you are presenting your beliefs. No matter what its form—letters, research papers, blog, business documents, even stories and poems—your written expression states what you believe. When you write, you present your beliefs in three ways: reports, inferences, and judgments. Your choice of words establishes which of the three you are using:

- *Report:* My bus was late today.
- *Inference:* My bus will probably be late tomorrow.
- *Judgment:* The bus system is unreliable.

Now try to identify which of the three is being used in these statements:

1. Each modern nuclear warhead has over one hundred times the explosive power of the bomb dropped on Hiroshima.

2. With all the billions of planets in the universe, the odds are that there are other forms of life in the cosmos.

3. In the long run, the energy needs of the world will best be met by solar energy technology rather than nuclear energy or fossil fuels.

As you examine these various statements, you can see that they provide readers with different types of information. For example, the first statement in each list reports aspects of the world that can be verified—that is, checked for accuracy. Appropriate investigation can determine whether the bus was actually late today and whether modern nuclear warheads really have the power attributed to them. When you describe the world in ways that can be verified through investigation, you are *reporting factual information.*

Looking at the second statement in each list, you can see that each provides a different sort of information than the first one does. These statements cannot be verified. There is no way to investigate and determine with certainty whether the bus will indeed be late tomorrow or whether there is life on other planets. Although these conclusions may be based on facts, they go beyond them. When you describe the world in ways based on factual information yet go beyond it to make statements about what is not currently known, you are *inferring* conclusions about the world.

Finally, as you examine the third statement in each list, it is apparent that these statements differ from both factual reports and inferences. In each the speaker is applying certain standards (criteria) to deem the bus service as unreliable and solar energy as more promising than nuclear energy or fossil fuels. You are *judging* when you describe the world in ways that evaluate it on the basis of certain criteria.

You continually use these ways of describing and organizing your world—reporting, inferring, and judging—to make sense of your experience. In most instances, you are not aware that you are actually performing these activities, nor are you usually aware of the differences among them. Yet these three activities work together to help you see the world as a complete picture.

Identifying Reports, Inferences, and Judgments

1. Write three statements that you believe—one as a report, one as an inference, and one as a judgment.

2. Locate a short article from a newspaper, magazine, or online news service and identify the reports, inferences, and judgments it contains.

3. Share your statements and your findings with classmates.

Reporting Factual Information

Statements written as reports express the most accurate beliefs you have about the world. Factual beliefs have earned this distinction because they are verifiable, usually by using one or more of your senses. For example, consider the following factual statement: "That young woman is wearing a brown hat in the rain." This statement about an event in the world is considered factual because you can verify it immediately with sensual experience—what you can (in principle or in theory) see, hear, touch, taste, or smell. It is important to say *in principle* or *in theory* because often you do not use all of your senses to check out what you are experiencing. Look again at the factual statement: you would normally be satisfied to see this event without insisting on touching the hat or giving the person a physical examination. If necessary, however, you could perform these additional actions.

You use the same reasoning when you believe other people's factual statements that you are not in a position to check immediately. For instance:

- The Great Wall of China is more than fifteen hundred miles long.
- There are large mountains and craters on the moon.
- Your skin is covered with germs.

You consider these factual statements because even though you cannot verify them with your senses at the moment, you could in principle or in theory do so *if* you were flown to China, *if* you were rocketed to the moon, or *if* you were to examine your skin with a powerful microscope. The process of verifying factual statements involves identifying the sources of information on which they are based and evaluating the reliability of these sources.

You communicate factual information to others by means of reports. A *report* is a description of something that has been experienced, then communicated in as accurate and complete a way as possible. Through reports you share your sensory experiences with other people, and this sharing enables you to learn much more about the world than you would if you were confined to knowing only what you experience.

Because factual reports play such an important role in the exchange and accumulation of information about the world, it is important that they be as accurate and complete as possible. This brings us to a problem. We have already seen in previous chapters that our perceptions and observations often are not accurate or complete. This means that sometimes when we think we are making true factual reports, they actually are inaccurate or incomplete. For instance, consider our earlier factual statement: "That young woman is wearing a brown hat in the rain." Here are questions you could ask concerning the accuracy of the statement:

- Is the woman actually young, or does she merely look young?
- Is the person actually a woman, or a man disguised as a woman?
- Is that really a hat the woman is wearing, or is it something else (such as a helmet or a paper bag)?

Of course, there are methods you could use to answer these questions. Can you describe some of them?

Besides difficulties with observations, the "facts" that you see in the world actually depend on more *general beliefs* that you have about how the world operates. Consider this question: "Why did the man's body fall from the top of the building to the sidewalk?" Having had some general science courses, you might respond, "The body was simply obeying the law of gravity" and consider that a factual statement. But how did people account for this sort of event before Newton formulated the law of gravity? Some popular responses might have included the following:

- Things always fall down, not up.
- The spirit in the body wanted to join with the spirit of the earth.

In the past, when people made statements like these—such as "Humans can't fly"— they thought they were stating facts. Increased knowledge and understanding have since shown these "factual beliefs" to be inaccurate, so they have been replaced by "better" beliefs. These better beliefs explain the world in a way that is more accurate and predictable. Will many of the beliefs now considered to be factually accurate also be replaced by more precise and predictable beliefs? If history is any indication, this will most certainly happen. Newton's formulations have already been replaced by Einstein's, based on the latter's theory of relativity. Einstein's have been refined and modified as well and may someday also be replaced.

THINKING-
WRITING
ACTIVITY

Evaluating Factual Information

1. Locate and carefully read, watch, or listen to a report that deals with a major social issue.
2. Identify the main idea and key points of the article.
3. Describe the factual statements used to support the main idea.
4. Evaluate the accuracy of the factual information.
5. Evaluate the reliability of the sources of the factual information.

Inferring from Evidence or Premises

Imagine yourself in the following situations.

1. It is 2:00 A.M. and your roommate comes crashing into the room. He staggers to his bed and falls across it, dropping (and breaking) a nearly empty whiskey bottle. Startled, you gasp, "What's the matter?" With alcohol fumes blasting from his mouth, he mumbles: "I jus' wanna hadda widdel drink!" What do you conclude?

2. Your roommate has just learned that she passed a math exam for which she had done absolutely no studying. Humming the refrain "I did it my way," she comes dancing over to you with a huge grin on her face and says, "Let me buy you dinner to celebrate!" What do you conclude about how she is feeling?

3. It is midnight and the library is about to close. As you head for the door, you spy your roommate shuffling along in an awkward waddle. His coat bulges out in front as if he's pregnant. When you ask, "What's going on?" he gives you a glare and hisses, "Shhh!" Just before he reaches the door, a pile of books slides from under his coat and crashes to the floor. What do you conclude?

In these examples, it would be reasonable to make the following conclusions.

1. Your roommate is drunk.

2. Your roommate is happy.

3. Your roommate is stealing library books.

Although these conclusions are reasonable, they are not factual reports; they are inferences. You have not directly experienced your roommate's "drunkenness," "happiness," or "stealing." Instead, you have inferred it on the basis of your roommate's behavior and the circumstances. What clues in these situations might lead to these conclusions? One way of understanding the inferential nature of these views is to ask yourself the following questions.

1. Have you ever pretended to be drunk when you weren't? Could other people tell?

2. Have you ever pretended to be happy when you weren't? Could other people tell?

3. Have you ever been accused of stealing something when you were perfectly innocent? How did this happen?

From these examples you can see that whereas factual beliefs can in principle be verified by direct observation, *inferential beliefs* go beyond what can be directly observed. For instance, in the previous examples, your observation of some of your roommate's actions led you to infer things that you were not observing directly— "He's drunk," "She's happy," "He's stealing books."

Making such simple inferences is something you do all the time. It is so automatic that usually you are not even aware that you are going beyond your immediate observations or that you may be having trouble distinguishing between what you *observe* and what you *infer*. Making such inferences enables you to see the world as a complete picture, to fill in the blanks and to supplement the fragmentary sensations being presented to your senses. Presenting your inferences along with your beliefs in writing paints a complete picture for your readers.

Your writing may also include *predictions* of what will occur in the near future. Predictions and expectations are also inferences because you attempt to determine what is currently unknown from what is already known.

It is possible that your inferences may be wrong; in fact, they frequently are. You may infer that the woman sitting next to you is wearing two earrings and then discover that she has only one. You may expect the class to end at noon but find that the teacher lets you out early—or late. In the last section, we concluded that not even factual beliefs are ever absolutely certain. Comparatively speaking, inferential beliefs are much more uncertain than factual beliefs, so it is important to distinguish between the two.

The distinction between what is observed and what is inferred is given particular attention in courtroom settings, where defense lawyers usually want witnesses to describe only what they observed—not what they inferred as they observed. When a witness includes an inference such as "I saw him steal it," the lawyer may object that the statement represents a "conclusion of the witness" and move to have the observation struck from the record. For example, imagine that you are a defense attorney listening to the following testimony. At what points would you object by saying, "This is a conclusion of the witness"?

> I saw Harvey running down the street, right after he knocked the old lady down. He had her purse in his hand and was trying to escape as fast as he could. He was really scared. I wasn't surprised because Harvey has always taken advantage of others. It's not the first time that he's stolen, either; I can tell you that. Just last summer he robbed the poor box at St. Anthony's. He was bragging about it for weeks.

Finally, keep in mind that even though in *theory* facts and inferences can be distinguished, in *practice* it is almost impossible to communicate with others in speech or writing by sticking only to factual observations. A reasonable approach is to state your inference along with the observable evidence on which the inference is based (e.g., John seemed happy because . . .). Our language has an entire collection of terms (*seems, appears, is likely,* and so on) that signal when we are making an inference and not expressing an observable fact. Thoughtful writers use these words carefully and deliberately.

Many of the predictions that you make are inferences based on your past experiences and information that you presently have. Even when there appear to be sound reasons supporting them, these inferences are often wrong due to incomplete information or unanticipated events. The fact that even people whom society considers "experts" regularly make inaccurate predictions should encourage you to exercise caution when presenting your beliefs as inferences. Here are some examples:

> "So many centuries after the Creation, it is unlikely that anyone could find hitherto unknown lands of any value."—The Advisory Committee to King Ferdinand and Queen Isabella of Spain, before Columbus's voyage in 1492.

"What will the soldiers and sailors, what will the common people say to 'George Washington, President of the United States'? They will despise him to all eternity."—John Adams, 1789

"What use could the company make of an electrical toy?"—Western Union's rejection of the telephone in 1878

"The actual building of roads devoted to motor cars is not for the near future in spite of many rumors to that effect."—a 1902 article in *Harper's Weekly*

"You ain't goin' nowhere, son. You ought to go back to driving a truck."—Jim Denny, Grand Ole Opry manager, firing Elvis Presley after one performance, 1954.

THINKING-
WRITING
ACTIVITY

Factual and Inferential Beliefs

Examine the following list of statements, noting which are *factual beliefs* (based on observations) and which are *inferential beliefs* (conclusions that go beyond observations). For each factual statement, describe how you might go about verifying the information. For each inferential statement, describe a factual observation on which the inference could be based. (*Note:* Some statements may contain both factual beliefs and inferential beliefs.)

- When my leg starts to ache, that means snow is on the way.
- The grass is wet—it must have rained last night.
- I think that it's pretty clear from the length of the skid marks that the accident was caused by that person's driving too fast.
- Fifty men lost their lives in the construction of the Queensboro Bridge.
- Nancy said she wasn't feeling well yesterday—I'll bet that she's out sick today.

Now consider the following situations. What inferences might you be inclined to make on the basis of what you are observing? How could you investigate the accuracy of an inference?

- A student in your class is consistently late for class.
- You see a friend driving a new car.
- An instructor asks the same student to stay after class several times.
- You don't receive any birthday cards.

So far, we have been exploring relatively simple inferences. Many of the inferences people make, however, are much more complicated. In fact, much of our knowledge of the world rests on our ability to make complicated inferences in a systematic and logical way. However, just because an inference is more complicated does not mean that it is more accurate; in fact, the opposite is often the case. One of the masters of inference is the legendary Sherlock Holmes. In the following passage, Holmes makes an astonishing number of inferences upon meeting Dr. Watson. Study Holmes's conclusions carefully. Are they reasonable? Can you explain how he reaches them?

> "You appeared to be surprised when I told you, on our first meeting, that you had come from Afghanistan."
>
> "You were told, no doubt."
>
> "Nothing of the sort. I knew you came from Afghanistan. From long habit the train of thoughts ran so swiftly through my mind that I arrived at the conclusion without being conscious of intermediate steps. There were such steps, however. The train of reasoning ran, 'Here is a gentleman of a medical type, but with the air of a military man. Clearly an army doctor, then. He is just come from the tropics, for his face is dark, and that is not the natural tint of his skin, for his wrists are fair. He has undergone hardship and sickness, as his haggard face says clearly. His left arm has been injured. He holds it in a stiff and unnatural manner. Where in the tropics could an English army doctor have seen much hardship and got his arm wounded? Clearly in Afghanistan.' The whole train of thought did not occupy a second. I then remarked that you came from Afghanistan, and you were astonished."

—Sir Arthur Conan Doyle, *A Study in Scarlet*

THINKING-
WRITING
ACTIVITY

Analyzing an Incorrect Inference

Describe an experience in which you made an incorrect inference. For example, it might have been a situation in which you mistakenly accused someone, an accident based on a miscalculation, a poor decision based on an inaccurate prediction, or some other event. Analyze that experience by answering the following questions.

1. What was (were) your mistaken inference(s)?

2. What was the factual evidence on which you based your inference(s)?

3. Looking back, what could you have done to avoid making the erroneous inference(s)?

The following essay illustrates the ongoing process by which natural scientists use inferences to discover factual information and to construct theories explaining the information.

"Evolution as Fact and Theory"

BY STEPHEN JAY GOULD (1941–2002)

Stephen Jay Gould started his academic career as a professor of geology at Harvard University but expanded his interests into evolutionary biology. He was curator of invertebrate paleontology at Harvard's Museum of Comparative Zoology and a writer with a gift for translating complex scientific theories into informed, but witty, prose that nonscientists can understand and enjoy. His essays appeared in magazines such as *Natural History* and *Discover* and were collected in the books *Ever Since Darwin, The Panda's Thumb,* and *The Flamingo's Smile.* This essay illustrates the ongoing process by which natural scientists use inferences to discover factual information and to construct theories explaining that information.

K irtley Mather, who died last year at age 89, was a pillar of both science and the Christian religion in America and one of my dearest friends. The difference of half a century in our ages evaporated before our common interests. The most curious thing we shared was a battle we each fought at the same age. For Kirtley had gone to Tennessee with Clarence Darrow to testify for evolution at the Scopes trial of 1925. When I think that we are enmeshed again in the same struggle for one of the best documented, most compelling and exciting concepts in all of science, I don't know whether to laugh or cry.

According to idealized principles of scientific discourse, the arousal of dormant issues should reflect fresh data that give renewed life to abandoned notions. Those outside the current debate may therefore be excused for suspecting that creationists have come up with something new, or that evolutionists have generated some serious internal trouble. But nothing has changed; the creationists have not a single new fact or argument. Darrow and Bryan were at least more entertaining than we lesser antagonists today. The rise of creationism is politics, pure and simple; it represents one issue (and by no means the major concern) of the resurgent evangelical right. Arguments that seemed kooky just a decade ago have re-entered the mainstream.

Creationism Is Not Science

The basic attack of the creationists falls apart on two general counts before we even reach the supposed factual details of their complaints against evolution. First, they play upon a vernacular misunderstanding of the word "theory" to convey the false impression that we evolutionists are covering up the rotten core of our edifice. Second, they misuse a popular philosophy of science to argue that they are behaving scientifically in attacking evolution. Yet the same philosophy demonstrates that their own belief is not science, and that "scientific creationism" is therefore meaningless and self-contradictory, a superb example of what Orwell called "newspeak."

In the American vernacular, "theory" often means "imperfect fact"—part of a hierarchy of confidence running downhill from fact to theory to hypothesis to guess. Thus the power of the creationist argument: evolution is "only" a theory, and intense debate now rages about many aspects of the theory. If evolution is less than a fact, and scientists can't even make up their minds about the theory, then what confidence can we have in it? Indeed, President Reagan echoed this argument before an evangelical group in Dallas when he said (in what I devoutly hope was campaign rhetoric): "Well, it is a theory. It is a scientific theory only, and it has in recent years been challenged in the world of science—that is, not believed in the scientific community to be as infallible as it once was."

5   Well, evolution *is* a theory. It is also a fact. And facts and theories are different things, not rungs in a hierarchy of increasing certainty. Facts are the world's data. Theories are structures of ideas that explain and interpret facts. Facts do not go away when scientists debate rival theories to explain them. Einstein's theory of gravitation replaced Newton's, but apples did not suspend themselves in mid-air pending the outcome. And human beings evolved from apelike ancestors whether they did so by Darwin's proposed mechanism or by some other, yet to be discovered.

Moreover, "fact" does not mean "absolute certainty." The final proofs of logic and mathematics flow deductively from stated premises and achieve certainty only because they are *not* about the empirical world. Evolutionists make no claim for perpetual truth, though creationists often do (and then attack us for a style of argument that they themselves favor). In science, "fact" can only mean "confirmed to such a degree that it would be perverse to withhold provisional assent." I suppose that apples might start to rise tomorrow, but possibility does not merit equal time in physics classrooms.

Evolutionists have been clear about this distinction between fact and theory from the very beginning, if only because we have always acknowledged how far we are from completely understanding the mechanisms (theory) by which evolution (fact) occurred. Darwin continually emphasized the difference between his two great and separate accomplishments: establishing the fact of evolution, and proposing a theory—natural selection—to explain the mechanism of evolution. He wrote in *The Descent of Man:* "I had two distinct objects in view; firstly, to show that species had not been separately created, and secondly, that natural selection had been the chief agent of change. . . . Hence if I have erred in . . . having exaggerated its [natural selection's] power . . . I have at least, as I hope, done good service in aiding to overthrow the dogma of separate creations."

Thus Darwin acknowledged the provisional nature of natural selection while affirming the fact of evolution. The fruitful theoretical debate that Darwin initiated has never ceased. From the 1940s through the 1960s, Darwin's own theory of natural selection did achieve a temporary hegemony that it never enjoyed in his lifetime. But renewed debate characterizes our decade, and while no biologist questions the importance of natural selection, many now doubt its ubiquity. In particular, many evolutionists argue that substantial amounts of genetic change may not be subject to natural selection and may spread through populations at random. Others are challenging Darwin's linking of natural selection with gradual, imperceptible change through all intermediary degrees; they are arguing that most evolutionary events may occur far more rapidly than Darwin envisioned.

Scientists regard debates on fundamental issues of theory as a sign of intellectual health and a source of excitement. Science is—and how else can I say it?—most fun when it plays with interesting ideas, examines their implications, and recognizes that old information may be explained in surprisingly new ways. Evolutionary theory is now enjoying this uncommon vigor. Yet amidst all this turmoil no biologist has been led to doubt the fact that evolution occurred; we are debating *how* it happened. We are all trying to explain the same thing: the tree of evolutionary descent linking all organisms by ties of genealogy. Creationists pervert and caricature this debate by conveniently neglecting the common conviction that underlies it, and by falsely suggesting that we now doubt the very phenomenon we are struggling to understand.

Using another invalid argument, creationists claim that "the dogma of separate creations," as Darwin characterized it a century ago, is a scientific theory meriting equal time with evolution in high school biology curricula. But a prevailing viewpoint among philosophers of science belies this creationist argument. Philosopher Karl Popper has argued for decades that the primary criterion of science is the falsifiability of its theories. We can never prove absolutely, but we can falsify. A set of ideas that cannot, in principle, be falsified is not science.

The entire creationist argument involves little more than a rhetorical attempt to falsify evolution by presenting supposed contradictions among its supporters. Their brand of creationism, they claim, is "scientific" because it follows the Popperian model in trying to demolish evolution. Yet Popper's argument must apply in both directions. One does not become a scientist by the simple act of trying to falsify another scientific system; one has to present an alternative system that also meets Popper's criterion—it too must be falsifiable in principle.

"Scientific creationism" is a self-contradictory, nonsense phrase precisely because it cannot be falsified. I can envision observations and experiments that would disprove any evolutionary theory I know, but I cannot imagine what potential data could lead creationists to abandon their beliefs. Unbeatable systems are dogma, not science. Lest I seem harsh or rhetorical, I quote creationism's leading intellectual, Duane Gish, Ph.D., from his recent (1978) book *Evolution? The Fossils Say No!* "By creation we mean the bringing into being by a supernatural Creator of the basic kinds of plants and animals by the process of sudden, or fiat, creation. We do not know how the Creator created, what processes He used, *for He used processes which are not now operating anywhere in the natural universe* [Gish's italics]. This is why we refer to creation as special creation. We cannot discover by scientific investigations anything about the creative processes used by the Creator." Pray tell, Dr. Gish, in the light of your last sentence, what then is "scientific" creationism?

The Fact of Evolution

Our confidence that evolution occurred centers upon three general arguments. First, we have abundant, direct, observational evidence of evolution in action, from both the field and the laboratory. It ranges from countless experiments on change in nearly everything about fruit flies subjected to artificial selection in the laboratory to the famous British moths that turned black when industrial soot darkened the trees upon which they rest. (The moths gain protection from sharp-sighted bird predators by blending into the background.) Creationists do not deny these observations; how could they? Creationists have tightened their act. They now argue that God only created "basic kinds," and allowed for limited evolutionary meandering within them. Thus toy poodles and Great Danes come from the dog kind and moths can change color, but nature cannot convert a dog to a cat or a monkey to a man.

The second and third arguments for evolution—the case for major changes—do not involve direct observation of evolution in action. They rest upon inference, but are no less secure for that reason. Major evolutionary change requires too much time for direct observation on the scale of recorded human history. All historical sciences rest upon inference, and evolution is no different from geology, cosmology, or human history in this respect. In principle, we cannot observe processes that operated in the past. We must infer them from results that still survive: living and fossil organisms for evolution, documents and artifacts for human history, strata and topography for geology.

15   The second argument—that the imperfection of nature reveals evolution—strikes many people as ironic, for they feel that evolution should be most elegantly displayed in the nearly perfect adaptation expressed by some organisms—the camber of a gull's wing, or butterflies that cannot be seen in ground litter because they mimic leaves so precisely. But perfection could be imposed by a wise creator or evolved by natural selection. Perfection covers the tracks of past history. And past history—the evidence of descent—is our mark of evolution.

Evolution lies exposed in the *imperfections* that record a history of descent. Why should a rat run, a bat fly, or porpoise swim, and I type this essay with structures built of the same bones unless we all inherited them from a common ancestor? An engineer, starting from scratch, could design better limbs in each case. Why should all the large native mammals of Australia be marsupials, unless they descended from a common ancestor isolated on this island continent? Marsupials are not "better," or ideally suited for Australia; many have been wiped out by placental mammals imported by man from other continents. This principle of imperfection extends to all historical sciences. When we recognize the etymology of September, October, November, and December (seventh, eighth, ninth, and tenth, from the Latin), we know that two additional items (January and February) must have been added to an original calendar of ten months.

The third argument is more direct: transitions are often found in the fossil record. Preserved transitions are not common—and should not be, according to our understanding of evolution . . .—but they are not entirely wanting, as creationists often claim. The lower jaw of reptiles contains several bones, that of mammals only one. The nonmammalian jawbones are reduced, step by step, in mammalian ancestors until they become tiny nubbins located at the back of the jaw. The "hammer" and the "anvil" bones of the mammalian ear are descendants of these nubbins. How could such a transition be accomplished?, the creationists ask. Surely a bone is either entirely in the jaw or in the ear. Yet paleontologists have discovered two transitional lineages of therapsids (the so-called mammal-like reptiles) with a double jaw joint—one composed of the old quadrate and articular bones (soon to become the hammer and anvil), the other of the squamosal and dentary bones (as in modern mammals). For that matter, what better transitional form could we desire than the oldest human, *Australopithecus afarensis*, with its apelike palate, its human upright stance, and a cranial capacity larger than any ape's of the same body size but a full 1,000 cubic centimeters below ours? If God made each of the half dozen human species discovered in ancient rocks, why did he create an unbroken temporal sequence of progressively more modern features—increasing cranial capacity, reduced face and teeth, larger body size? Did he create a mimic evolution and test our faith thereby?

Conclusion

I am both angry at and amused by the creationists; but mostly I am deeply sad. Sad for many reasons. Sad because so many people who respond to creationist appeals are troubled for the right reason, but venting their anger at the wrong target. It is true that scientists have often been dogmatic and elitist. It is true that we have often allowed the white-coated, advertising image to represent us—"Scientists say that Brand X cures bunions ten times faster than . . ." We have not fought it adequately because we derive benefits from appearing as a new priesthood. It is also true that faceless bureaucratic state power intrudes more and more into our lives and removes choices that should belong to individuals and communities. I can understand that requiring that evolution be taught in the schools might be seen as one more insult on all these grounds. But the culprit is not, and cannot be, evolution or any other fact of the natural world. Identify and fight your legitimate enemies by all means, but we are not among them.

I am sad because the practical result of this brouhaha will not be expanded coverage to include creationism (that would also make me sad), but the reduction or excision of evolution from high school curricula. Evolution is one of the half dozen "great ideas" developed by science. It speaks to the profound issues of genealogy that fascinate all of us—the "roots" phenomenon writ large. Where did we come from? Where did life arise? How did it develop? How are organisms related? It forces us to think, ponder, and wonder. Shall we deprive millions of this knowledge and once again teach biology as a set of dull and unconnected facts, without the thread that weaves diverse material into a supple unity?

20   But most of all I am saddened by a trend I am just beginning to discern among my colleagues. I sense that some now wish to mute the healthy debate about theory that has brought new life to evolutionary biology. It provides grist for creationist mills, they say, even if only by distortion. Perhaps we should lie low and rally around the flag of strict Darwinism, at least for the moment—a kind of old-time religion on our part.

But we should borrow another metaphor and recognize that we too have to tread a straight and narrow path, surrounded by roads to perdition. For if we ever begin to suppress our search to understand nature, to quench our own intellectual excitement in a misguided effort to present a united front where it does not and should not exist, then we are truly lost.

QUESTIONS FOR ACTIVE READING

1. Gould defines *facts* as the "world's data" and refers to observing an apple fall from the tree as Isaac Newton is alleged to have done. Identify some of the facts Gould presents as evidence to support the theory of evolution.

2. Gould defines *theories* as "structures of ideas that explain and interpret facts," such as Newton's theory of gravitation, which was introduced to explain facts like falling

apples. In addition to facts, Gould states, the theory of evolution is supported by reasonable inferences. Identify some inferences that he cites as evidence.

3. Gould begins this essay with allusions to the Scopes trial of 1925, Darrow, and Bryan. He seems to assume that his readers will know what he is talking about. If you know about this event, how does this reference set the scene for his 1981 essay? If you don't know about it, was your understanding reduced?

QUESTIONS FOR THINKING CRITICALLY

1. What does Gould say about creationism? Find specific statements. Is Gould presenting reports, inferences, or judgments about this concept?

2. Gould calls Kirtley Mather a "pillar of both science and the Christian religion in America." Do you know people who are both scientific and spiritual? What do those people say about these two approaches to the world?

3. How can the qualities of a critical reader and thinker be useful in considering the issues involved in discussions of evolution and creationism? In other words, how can being curious, open-minded, knowledgeable, and creative help here?

The comic strip below was probably intended to be funny, but it reflects what Gould says about theories as "structures of ideas that explain and interpret facts." Historical facts are interpreted differently at different times; theories about history change. School textbooks about United States history of fifty years ago usually focused on the Founding Fathers, pioneers moving westward, and military actions. Books published now usually include material on Native Americans, women, slaves, and daily life. You might want to discuss this change with your grandparents or older friends.

Judging by Applying Criteria

Identify and write a description of a friend, a course you have taken, or the college you attend. Be sure your descriptions are specific and include what you think about the friend, the course, and the college.

1. _____ is a friend I have. He/she is . . .

2. _____ is a course I have taken. It was . . .

3. _____ is the college I attend. It is . . .

Now review your writing. Does it include factual descriptions? Note any facts that can be verified. Your writing may also contain inferences based on factual information. Can you identify any? In addition, your writing may include judgments about the person, the course, and the school—descriptions that express your evaluation based on certain criteria. Facts and inferences help you figure out what is actually happening (or will happen); the purpose of judgments is to express your evaluation about what is happening (or will happen). For example:

- My new car has broken down three times in the first six months. (Factual report)
- My new car will probably continue to have difficulties. (Inference)
- My new car is a lemon. (Judgment)

When you label your new car a "lemon," you are making a judgment based on certain criteria. For instance, a lemon is usually a newly purchased item—often an automobile—with which you have repeated problems. For another example of judging, consider the following statements:

- Carla always does her work thoroughly and completes it on time. (Factual report)
- Carla will probably continue to do her work in this fashion. (Inference)
- Carla is a very responsible person. (Judgment)

By judging Carla to be responsible, you are evaluating her on the basis of the criteria or standards that you believe indicate a responsible person. One such criterion is completing assigned work on time. Can you identify additional criteria for judging someone as being responsible?

Review your previous description of a friend, a course, or your college. Can you identify any judgments in your description? For each judgment you have listed, identify the criteria on which you based the judgment.

Many of our disagreements with others focus on differences in judgments. To write thoughtfully, you need to approach such differences intelligently by following these guidelines:

- Make explicit the criteria or standards used as a basis for the judgment.
- Try to establish the reasons that justify these criteria.

For instance, if you write "Professor Andrews is an excellent teacher," you are basing your judgment on certain criteria of teaching excellence. Once these standards are made explicit, they can be discussed to see whether they make sense and what justifies them. Of course, your idea of what makes an excellent teacher may be different from someone else's, so you can test your conclusion by comparing your criteria with those of your classmates. When disagreements occur, use these two steps for resolution.

In short, not all judgments are equally good or equally poor. The credibility of a judgment depends on the criteria used to make the judgment and on the evidence or reasons that support these criteria. For example, there may be legitimate disagreements about judgments on the following points:

- Who was the greatest United States president?
- Which movie deserves the Oscar this year?
- Which is the best baseball team this year?

However, in these and countless other cases, the quality of judgments depends on presenting the criteria used for the competing judgments and then demonstrating that your candidate best meets the agreed-upon criteria by providing supporting evidence and reasons. With this approach, you can often engage in intelligent discussion and establish which judgments are best supported by the evidence.

THINKING-
WRITING
ACTIVITY

Analyzing Judgments

Review the following two passages, which illustrate various judgments. For each passage, do the following:

1. Identify the evaluative criteria on which the judgments are based.
2. Describe the reasons or evidence the author uses to support the criteria.
3. Explain whether you agree or disagree with the judgments and give your rationale.

One widely held misconception concerning pizza should be laid to rest. Although it may be characterized as fast food, pizza is not junk food. Especially when it is made with fresh ingredients, pizza fulfills our basic nutritional requirements. The crust provides carbohydrates; from the cheese and meat or fish comes protein; and the tomatoes, herbs, onions, and garlic supply vitamins and minerals.—Louis Philip Salamone, "Pizza: Fast Food, Not Junk Food"

Let us return to the question of food. Responsible agronomists report that before the end of the year millions of people if unaided might starve to death. Half a billion deaths by starvation is not an uncommon estimate. Even though the United States has done more than any other nation to feed the hungry, our relative affluence makes us morally vulnerable in the eyes of other nations and in our own eyes. Garrett Hardin, who has argued for a "lifeboat" ethic of survival (if you take all the passengers aboard, everybody drowns), admits that the decision not to feed all the hungry requires of us "a very hard psychological adjustment." Indeed it would. It has been estimated that the 3.5 million tons of fertilizer spread on American golf courses and lawns could provide up to 30 million tons of food in overseas agricultural production. The nightmarish thought intrudes itself. If we as a nation allow people to starve while we could, through some sacrifice, make more food available to them, what hope can any person have for the future of international relations? If we cannot agree on this most basic of values—feed the hungry—what hopes for the future can we entertain?—James R. Kelly, "The Limits of Reason"

Distinguishing Among Reports, Inferences, and Judgments

Although the activities of reporting, inferring, and judging tend to be woven together in your experiences and in your writing, it is important to be able to distinguish these activities. Each plays a different role in helping you make sense of the world for yourself and for your audience, and you should be careful not to confuse these roles. For instance, although writers may appear to be reporting factual information, they may actually be expressing personal evaluations, which are not factual. Consider the statement "Los Angeles is a smog-ridden city drowning in automobiles." Although seeming to be reporting factual information, the writer really is expressing his or her personal judgment. Of course, writers can identify their judgments with such phrases as "in my opinion," "my evaluation is," and so forth.

Sometimes, however, writers do not identify their judgments. In some cases they do not do so because the context within which they are writing (such as a newspaper editorial) makes it clear that the information is judgment rather than fact. In other cases, however, they want their judgments to be treated as factual information. Confusing the activities of reporting, inferring, and judging, whether accidental or deliberate, can be misleading and even dangerous.

Confusing factual information with judgments can be personally damaging as well. For example, there is a big difference between these two statements:

- I failed my exam today. (Factual report)
- I am a failure. (Judgment)

Stating the fact "I failed my exam today" describes your situation in a concrete way, enabling you to evaluate (judge) it as a problem you can hope to solve through reflection and hard work. If, however, the situation causes you to make the judgment "I am a failure," this sort of general evaluation will not encourage you to explore solutions to the problem or improve your situation.

Finally, another main reason for distinguishing among the activities of reporting, inferring, and judging concerns the accuracy of statements. We noted, for instance, that factual statements tend to be reasonably accurate because they are by nature verifiable whereas inferences are usually much less certain. As a result, it is crucial to be aware of whether you are presenting a belief as a report, an inference, or a judgment. If you write the superintendent of your apartment building a note saying, "My thermostat is broken," an inference on your part based on the fact that you feel uncomfortably hot, you will feel foolish if you later discover that you have a fever and that the thermostat is functioning well.

Presenting Beliefs in Your Writing

Understanding and evaluating beliefs pertains in three particular ways to your college papers as well as to the writing you will do in other settings. First, as you are better able to distinguish among reports, inferences, and judgments, you will be able to present different types of beliefs more accurately. Although you may not often use the term *report*, *inference*, or *judgment*, you will word your beliefs in precise ways that indicate the level of speculation behind your statements.

Second, a strong relationship exists between the thesis of a paper and your beliefs about the topic. The thesis, most of all, expresses what you believe is the main point of your paper. As you work to clarify your thesis statement, you also clarify your beliefs about the issue you are addressing. And when you state the thesis clearly in your paper, you are making your beliefs clear to your readers.

Third, as a college writer and quite possibly as a working professional, you will regularly use source material in your papers. The techniques for evaluating beliefs will help you evaluate sources of information. Then, as you present in your researched writing what others have said, you can comment on their beliefs as you integrate the material into your papers. (See Chapter 14 on research.)

Writing Project: Analyzing Influences on Your Beliefs About a Social or Academic Issue

This chapter has included both readings and Thinking-Writing Activities that encourage you to think about the sources of your beliefs. Be sure to reread what you wrote for the activities as you may be able to use some of your work in completing this project.

Write an essay in which you consider some influences on the development of your beliefs about a social issue or an idea related to an academic field. As much as possible, apply the concepts discussed in this chapter.

As a college student, you receive much of your information about social or academic issues from print and electronic sources. Therefore, you should analyze at least two media sources such as newspaper, magazine, or journal articles; material from a web site; a film or a DVD; a book or book chapter. In addition, think about what your teachers and other people have told you and perhaps, about personal experiences.

Begin by considering the key elements of the Thinking-Writing Model in Chapter 1 on pages 7–9.

The Writing Situation

Purpose   Your primary purpose here is to further your own development as a capable college student. You will be exploring some of the ways in which you come to accept concepts. In addition, you will be sharing your insights with your audience, which always provides another purpose: to write an effective paper.

On a technical level, you are required to take different kinds of information and pull them together. Such *synthesis* is the central purpose of many kinds of academic and professional writing. Most research papers, case studies, field reports, project summaries, product proposals, and business plans use information that must be analyzed and synthesized.

You also have an intellectual purpose. You will look closely at your own ways of defining what you believe and what you consider true as well as what you do not believe and what you consider false.

Audience   As usual, your classmates are a good audience for this paper, both in draft and finished versions, since they are doing the same assignment and will want to see how you handle it. In addition, people interested in the social issue or academic field will naturally be potential readers. If you are taking a class pertaining to your subject, you could share your paper with those students. If you are writing about a social issue relevant to your community, you could share your work in a newsletter or on a web site.

Of course, your instructor remains the audience who will judge how well you have articulated your beliefs, how you have selected the influences on your beliefs, how you have handled the sources, and how you have planned, drafted, revised, and edited your essay.

Subject   Examining the sources of beliefs and evaluating evidence are among the most challenging of activities. If you are just beginning to learn about the issue on which you are writing, you may not have enough background to be very inquisitive or judgmental. However, you should be aware of criteria that any thoughtful student can detect: specific support for a claim, whether information is current, appropriateness of examples and authorities, and responsible attribution. Also, you have some understanding of reports, inferences, predictions, and judgments to apply to your analysis.

Writer   For this Writing Project, you should be as open as possible to new ways of thinking about your beliefs. After such critical analysis, some writers find that their beliefs have been strengthened; others may realize that some of their beliefs were based on unreliable information and need to be re-evaluated.

As with the Writing Projects in Part One, you are in a position of authority here when you are writing about your own reactions and realizations. At the same time, since you are writing about a social issue or an academic field instead of about your personal life, you are a writer who is dealing with other people's beliefs in addition to your own. After writing the paper, you may want to consider whether you are a more accepting or more skeptical person.

The Writing Process

The following sections will guide you through the stages of planning, drafting, and revising your essay analyzing the sources of your beliefs.

Generating Ideas

- Identify some ideas in the Thinking-Writing Activities that you may be able to use. Then write informally about them.
- Think about teachers, books, films, articles, the Internet, and other sources of information in your field that have provided you with information that you believe. Why have they had this effect?
- Think about any sources that you are reluctant to trust or believe. Why have they had this effect?
- What concepts in this field do you believe most firmly?
- Are there some that you question?
- Freewrite for five minutes about your ideas for this project.
- Look at the list of questions for exploring topics in Chapter 4. Which of them can help you generate ideas for this project?

Defining a Focus

- The Writing Project itself provides a wide-angle focus, but you must sharpen it in order to produce an understandable paper.
- Notice if your issue or idea has several components. For example, the issue of high-stakes testing in public schools raises questions about the kind of tests used, the effects on students' passing to the next grade, the effects on school funding or ratings, and the effects on curriculum. You may want to focus only on one aspect. Perhaps your beliefs about evolution in biology or parallel processing in computer science are really beliefs about several components of the general idea.
- Write down your belief to be sure that you can state it well. If you haven't decided on one belief, write several. Are they interpretations, evaluations, conclusions, or predictions in your statement? Do these terms help you find a focus?
- Consider your level of belief. Are you strongly convinced that your belief is plausible? Do you have questions about it? Why?
- Focus on differences. Does a popular press, television, or web site account differ from what a book says or what a professor has taught you?
- Draft a thesis statement that gives direction to the essay.
- Create a map, web, or rough outline so that you can see how ideas might cluster or separate. See Chapter 4 for idea-generation strategies.

Organizing Ideas   If you created a map or rough outline while you were looking for a focus, review it and try to be more specific about how to arrange the ideas for your paper.

- Have you drafted a tentative thesis that states your belief, one that says something about the sources of the belief, or one that includes both? What kind would be most effective?

- If you have several sources for your belief, does each one deserve at least a paragraph?
- If your beliefs have changed, have you discussed this matter in an effective place?
- If you are contrasting two differing perspectives, have you structured the contrast logically?
- If you are presenting similar perspectives, have you structured the comparison logically?
- Have you planned a conclusion? Does it refer to the influences on your beliefs?
- Remember that you may modify your plan or outline as you draft.

Drafting

- Begin with the part easiest to draft. Is it writing about your instructors or dealing with your print or electronic sources?
- Perhaps you should then shift to a part that is hard to draft and at least make some notes or write questions.
- Draft a new outline or map, if necessary, as you rethink what you want to say. Look at the preliminary thesis statement that you drafted. Do you need to rework it now, or should you wait until you have drafted more?
- Shape the paragraphs that will make up the body of your essay. Draft clear topic sentences; think about where the topic sentence should be placed in each paragraph.
- Draft an opening paragraph and a concluding paragraph, understanding that you may want to revise them substantially later.

Revising, Editing, and Proofreading   Use the Step-by-Step method in Chapter 6 on pages 152–154 to revise your essay and prepare a final draft.

Student Writing

Jessie Lange's Writing Process

The following essay was written for a criminal justice course. Jessie's professor asked students to demonstrate how media treatments of a current criminal justice issue helped to shape the beliefs they hold about that issue. For students in a criminal justice course, who might someday be dealing with offenders or victims of a particular kind of crime, the ability to distinguish between personal beliefs and objective evidence (and to make a distinction between how they might personally feel about an issue and what the law says about that issue) is of critical importance. But Jessie realized that as a concerned citizen, it was also her responsibility to be informed about criminal justice issues that might impact her as a woman, a voter, and a future parent. Jessie used the Thinking-Writing Activity entitled Evaluating Factual Information on page 376 to discuss her two key sources.

Dealing with Sex Offenders

By Jessie Lange

In the past few years we have heard much about Megan's Law, which states that people should be made aware of charged sex offenders in their community. While I wholeheartedly believe that people, for the protection of themselves and their children, have the right to know, there is another twist on the issue I hadn't thought about until I heard a story recently on *60 Minutes*. The story involved Stephanie's Law—a new law in place in some states under which sex offenders are kept *after* they have served their time to go through a therapy program in an attempt to "cure" them. The question that this provoked in me was not whether the state should have the right to hold sexual criminals beyond their sentence, but whether they can be cured at all. If not, should they ever be released back into a world where they are likely to do more damage, destroy more lives?

A recent *New York Times* article described a rehabilitation program in Texas whereby prisoners are immersed in religion—taking classes, having discussions, and owning up to their "sins." Interestingly, while there are 79 men convicted of "robbery, drug possession, and murder" participating, those convicted of sexual crimes are not accepted into the program. This is partly because they are "looked down on by other prisoners" and partly because, according to criminologists, "sexual criminals are the most difficult to rehabilitate."

In fact, there is a question as to whether this rehabilitation is even possible. Sexual criminals in particular seem to be under the influence of urges which are out of their control. The *60 Minutes* report said that, while many may have good intentions in being treated through therapy and returning to society, it may be out of their hands. They may say they understand their wrongs, they may feel cured, but if they are released it seems impossible for even the offenders to know if they will be able to control their impulses. If there is such a question, do they deserve a chance at freedom when it means potentially committing another crime?

There is no question in my mind that, while many sex offenders do not repent for what they have done and have no real interest in being cured, there are also many for whom their crimes are almost out of their hands—as disgusting to them as to anyone else. The *New York Times* ran an article entitled "Sex Offender Agrees to Be Castrated." In Illinois, a convicted child sex offender is having himself castrated "in an effort to win a lighter sentence." The offender, in fact, "volunteered to be castrated even before he was convicted" previously of an attack on a young girl. It seems as though the man is making an attempt to control his urges but, according to the article, "experts disagree on whether castration helps" in controlling these urges.

Both the *New York Times* and *60 Minutes* have good reputations as reliable media sources. I read this paper and watch this show regularly. (I'm pleased that my parents introduced me to them.) I think that these reports are as reliable as the popular press can be. If I decide to do research on this subject and write a substantial paper, I will have to use criminal justice and sociology journals and try to interview one or two experts, as well.

I have not had any personal experience with sex offenders, but I have read and heard enough to know that their crimes destroy not only the lives of victims but also the lives of families and friends of the victims and that their crimes can so haunt victims that these fears are never resolved. In addition, victims of sexual crimes may grow up to inflict these crimes on others, continuing the cycle. In my opinion, the damage done by sex offenders and the risk of untreatable urges to commit these crimes, a risk illustrated by the high percentage of repeat offenders, is too great to justify their release. At least not until there is a proven "cure," a sure-fire way to *know* that they are treatable, have been treated, and will not continue to make victims of others.

Through the media, I have come to understand that many may be operating on urges not within their control, but this does not justify their release. At some point the blame has to fall on the individual. If they were to learn that their rehabilitation was an impossibility, I think that those who are truly disgusted by their crimes might even agree that they are too dangerous to be returned to a society where they have already done so much damage.

Works Cited

Niebuhr, Gustav. "Using Religion to Reform Criminals." <u>New York Times</u> 18 Jan. 1998, late ed.: A16.

"Sex Offender Agrees To Be Castrated." <u>New York Times</u> 18 Jan. 1998: A6.

<u>60 Minutes</u>. WCBS, New York. 24 June 1997.

Alternative Writing Project: Evolving Beliefs in an Academic Field

Locate a college or high school science, history, or literature textbook from forty or fifty years ago. Compare several specific points made in the decades-old book with points made in one of your textbooks in the same field.

In order to establish a context for what you observe, ask your instructor or a librarian to guide you to sources that discuss changes in theories in the field that your material is about. For example, in history, you could examine material about multicultural or gender-based approaches; in literature, material about "the canon"; in science, material about a specific discovery in genetics or physics.

Write an essay presenting the differences and similarities that you have found and comment on what beliefs they seem to reflect. Follow your instructor's directions for topic limitation, length, format, and citation methods.

12

Solving Problems

Writing to Propose Solutions

> " *Whatever creativity is, it is in part a solution to a problem.* "
>
> —*Brian Aldiss*

Critical Thinking Focus: The problem-solving model

Writing Focus: Applying the problem-solving model

Reading Theme: Solving a social problem

Writing Project: Proposing a solution to a problem

Problem solving is one of the most powerful of human thinking patterns, and writing is the main system we use to analyze challenging problems and propose solutions. On a personal level, you have probably written an email about a problem in your life. You may have been trying to sustain a romantic relationship with someone while geographically separated, helping a friend resolve a personal crisis, or writing to family members to coordinate a holiday reunion. To address civic problems, you and your neighbors may have written letters to newspapers or petitioned your local government. Writing memos, reports, and proposals to solve problems is an integral part of most careers, from finance to filmmaking.

Although proposing solutions is a common form of writing, it is challenging. In order to compose an insightful solution, you need to do the following:

- *Define the problem clearly.* Your audience needs to understand that there *is* a problem and know exactly what it is.
- *Analyze the problem systematically.* Complex problems are often a confusing tangle of needs, ideas, frustrations, goals, and pieces of information. You need to disentangle the issues so that your audience can understand the core of the problem and what alternatives are possible.
- *Propose a well-reasoned solution.* After presenting a lucid analysis of the problem, along with feasible alternatives, you need to reach a conclusion that you support with

thoughtful reasoning and solid evidence. As part of your proposed solution, you should explain why other alternative solutions are less desirable than yours. You should also address anticipated objections to your solution and explain how these difficulties can be overcome.

You will notice that the problem-solving method is similar to the decision-making method discussed in Chapter 5. However, this chapter presents the process in more detail; the focus is on problems instead of on decisions, and you will be considering social as well as personal issues. The chapter readings address societal problems. Finally, the Writing Project involves analyzing a social or personal problem that needs a solution.

Problems in Personal and Civic Life

Throughout your life, you will continually be solving problems. As a student, for example, you deal with a steady stream of academic assignments—quizzes, exams, research projects, essays, papers, and audiovisual presentations. In order to

FOUR QUALITIES
OF A CRITICAL THINKER
Economist Muhammad Yunus

Curious   Muhammad Yunus (b. 1940), a Bangladeshi professor of economics, was struck by a visit he made in the mid-1970s to an impoverished village. He spoke to a local woman who was trying to make and sell bamboo stools, but found it almost impossible to profit from her hard work because she frequently had to borrow money, at exorbitant interest rates, to purchase the raw bamboo. Yunus, who was awarded the 2006 Nobel Peace Prize for his work with the Bangladesh-based Grameen Bank, could have walked away from the woman. Instead, a combination of human compassion and intellectual curiosity inspired him to lend the woman money himself, and then follow through to see the impact of such a small, interest-free loan on one woman's economic productivity. The great innovation of Yunus' Grameen Bank, which he founded himself based on that experience, is the practice of "micro-credit," or the granting of very small loans to specific individuals who wish to start a small business. No collateral is required for these loans, and their small size allows borrowers to repay them quickly and without fear of reprisal. Although there is a separate Nobel Prize for economics, the Nobel Foundation recognized through this award that there is a connection between peace and economic prosperity.

Open-minded   The Grameen Bank and the practice of micro-credit is a significant challenge to the often repressive social and economic conditions in which women in the Third World live. Micro-credit is an especially powerful way to help women in the developing world achieve economic independence as well as greater political and social status by allowing them to solve their own problems. More than 90 percent of the Grameen Bank's clients are women, and more than 98 percent of the loans are repaid—a far more successful rate of repayment than any banking system in any First-World country. As these solve these academic problems effectively—how to do well on an exam, for example—you need to define the problem (what areas will the exam cover, and what will its format be?), identify and evaluate various alternatives (what are possible study approaches?), and then combine all these factors to reach a solution (what will your study plan and schedule be?). Relatively simple problems like preparing for an exam do not require a systematic or complex analysis. You can solve them with effort and concentration. However, the difficult and complicated problems in your personal life, such as choosing a college major or ending a relationship, may be a different story. Because these are such crucial situations, you will need to solve such problems in the best possible way by using all your creative and critical thinking skills.

The problems that exist in society also need the very best thinking of all citizens. The fear of terrorism is far too real, parents feel stressed about their children's safety, drugs and alcohol continue to destroy lives, and both racism and sexism create conflicts. These problems may seem overwhelming, and it is true that you cannot control them in the same way that you can control your own life situations. Still, by thinking creatively and critically about such issues, and by gathering information,

societies recognize that their future prosperity depends as much on women as on men—and as women accumulate the resources they need to send themselves and their daughters to school—opportunities for social justice are created, and societies both strengthened and reformed.

Knowledgeable   Yunus' initial ideas for micro-credit were met with tremendous skepticism by both academic economists and the banking community. The idea of extending loans to the very poor—and especially to very poor women—seemed to be a direct contradiction of current economic theory. In his autobiography, Yunus describes how his work with the Grameen Bank has taught him that "our knowledge base about people and their interactions is still very inadequate." The most sophisticated and theoretical approaches to economics, he suggests, cannot alone provide the knowledge and information needed to solve real-world problems. An understanding of how economics impacts *individual people*, Yunus argues, needs to be considered as a foundation of economic knowledge as well.

Creative   "Poverty in the world is an artificial creation," Yunus has stated. This challenging, innovative way of thinking about poverty is a profound example of how creative thinking can solve even the most intractable problems. Yunus, like all truly creative problem-solvers, arrived at a solution after reimagining the problem. In his autobiography, Yunus writes: "My experience working in the Grameen Bank has given me faith; an unshakable faith in the creativity of human beings. It leads me to believe that humans are not born to suffer the misery of hunger and poverty."

Online Study Center
Muhammad Yunus
Visit the Online Study Center for *Critical Thinking, Thoughtful Writing* at *college.hmco.com/pic/ chaffee CTTW4e* to learn more about Muhammad Yunus

you can at least develop your own views about contending with them. Then you will be in a position to act on such problems and to vote for candidates whose positions are similar to yours.

Basics of the Problem-Solving Method

Consider the following personal problem:

> My best friend is addicted to drugs, but he won't admit it. Jack always liked to drink, but I never thought too much about it. After all, a lot of people like to drink socially, get relaxed, and have a good time. But over the last few years, he's started using other drugs as well as alcohol, and it's ruining his life. He's stopped taking classes at college and will soon lose his job if he doesn't change. Last week I told him that I was really worried about him, but he told me that he has no drug problem and that in any case it really isn't any of my business. I don't know what to do. I've known Jack since we were in elementary school together, and he's a wonderful person. It's as if he's in the grip of some terrible force and I'm powerless to help him.

In working through this problem, the writer of this description could only think of one possible course of action to try. But if he or she chose instead to approach the problem as a critical thinker, the writer would have to think carefully and systematically through several possibilities in order to reach a solution.

In order to think effectively in situations like this, we usually ask ourselves a series of questions. These are the questions to ask in a five-step problem-solving method:

1. What is the *problem*?

2. What are the *alternatives*?

3. What are the *advantages* and/or *disadvantages* of each alternative?

4. What is the *solution*?

5. How well is the solution *working*?

Put yourself in the position of the student whose friend seems to be addicted to drugs and alcohol and apply the questions to that problem.

1. What Is the Problem?

There are a variety of ways to define the problem. For instance, you might define it simply as "Jack has a drug dependency." You might view the problem as "Jack has a drug dependency, but he won't admit it." You might even define the problem as "Jack has a drug dependency, but he won't admit it—and I want to help him solve this problem." Notice that each redefinition of the problem results in a more *specific* definition, which in turn helps you better understand the essence of the problem and your responsibility with respect to it.

2. What Are the Alternatives?

In dealing with this problem, you can consider a wide variety of possible actions before selecting the best ones. Identify some of the alternatives.

> (Example): Speak to my friend in a candid and forceful way to convince him that he has a serious drug dependency.

3. What Are the Advantages and Disadvantages of Each Alternative?

Evaluate the strengths and weaknesses of each alternative you have identified so that you can weigh your choices and determine the best course of action.

> Speak to my friend in a candid and forceful way to convince him that he has a serious problem.
>
> *Advantage:* He may respond to my direct emotional appeal, acknowledge that he has a problem, and seek help.
>
> *Disadvantage:* He may react angrily, further alienating me from him and making it more difficult for me to have any influence on him.

4. What Is the Solution?

After evaluating the various alternatives, select the one you think would be most effective for solving the problem and describe the sequence of steps you would take to act on that alternative.

5. How Well Is the Solution Working?

The final step in the process comes after you have begun to implement your choice of action. You review the solution and decide whether it is working well. If it is not, you must modify your solution or perhaps try an alternate solution you disregarded earlier. In this situation, trying to figure out the best way to help your friend recognize addiction and seek treatment leads to a series of decisions. This is what the critical thinking process is all about—trying to make sense of what is going on in the world and acting appropriately in response. When we solve problems effectively, our thinking process exhibits a coherent organization, following the general approach just outlined.

This problem-solving method lends itself to the organization of an essay or argument. For your writing to be truly effective in describing a problem and proposing a solution, you will need to consider additional rhetorical issues.

Audience   When writing about Jack's situation, the evidence you draw on and the voice in which you write will have to do with your immediate audience. If you are writing directly to Jack, you will want to be as candid, caring, and explicit as possible. You might want to describe, in a letter to Jack, a particularly difficult or embarrassing moment when his addition interfered with your relationship. On the other hand, if you are writing to Jack's family to urge members to intervene, you will want to be less personal about Jack's effects on your own life and instead describe the effect of his behavior on his grades and his job performance.

Purpose   When describing a personal problem and exploring possible solutions, your purpose depends not only on your immediate audience but also on the outcome you desire. For example, if you were to write directly to Jack in this situation, your purpose might be either to urge him to seek help to preserve your relationship—or to inform him that you have reached the limits of your tolerance, and you are ending your friendship although you still wish him well. Your purpose will, obviously, influence your choice of language as well as the structure of your writing.

If we can understand the way the mind operates when we are thinking effectively, we can apply this understanding to improve our thinking in new, challenging situations. In the remainder of this chapter, we will explore a more sophisticated version of this problem-solving approach and apply it to a variety of complex, difficult problems.

THINKING-
WRITING
ACTIVITY

Analyzing a Problem Solved Previously

1. Write a description of a problem in your personal life that you have recently solved.

2. Explain how you went about solving the problem. What were the steps, strategies, and approaches you used to understand the problem and to make an informed decision about a possible solution?

3. Analyze your thinking process by applying the five-step problem-solving method we have been exploring.

4. Share your problem with classmates and have them try to analyze and solve it. Then explain the solution you arrived at.

The Problem-Solving Method in Detail

Imagine yourself in the following situation. What would be your next move, and what are your reasons for deciding on it?

You are about to begin your second year of college, following a very successful first year. Until now, you have financed your education through a combination of savings, financial aid, and a part-time job (sixteen hours a week) at a local store. However, you just received a letter from your college saying that your financial aid package has been reduced by half due to budgetary problems. The letter concludes, "We hope this aid reduction will not prove to be too great an inconvenience." From your perspective, the loss of aid isn't an inconvenience—it's a disaster! Your budget last year was already tight, and with your job, you barely had enough time to study, participate in a few college activities, and have a modest (but essential) social life. To make matters worse, your mother has been ill, reducing her income and creating financial problems at home. You're panicking—what in the world are you going to do?

As noted earlier, at first a difficult problem often seems like a confused tangle of information, feelings, alternatives, opinions, considerations, and risks. The problem just described is a complicated situation that does not seem to have a single simple solution. Without applying a systematic approach, your thoughts might wander through the tangle of issues in this manner:

I want to stay in school, . . . but I'm not going to have enough money. . . . I could work more hours at my job, . . . but I might not have enough time to study and get top grades . . . and if all I'm doing is working and studying, what about my social life? . . . and what about Mom and the kids? They will need my help. . . . I could drop out of school for a while, . . . but if I don't stay in school, what kind of future do we have?

Very often, when faced with difficult problems like this one, you simply may not know where to begin to try to solve them. Every issue is connected to many others. Frustrated by not knowing where to take the first step, you may give up trying to understand the problem. Or you may behave in one of the following ways:

1. Act impulsively without thought or consideration ("I'll just quit school").

2. Follow someone else's advice without seriously evaluating the suggestion ("Tell me what I should do—I'm tired of thinking about this").

3. Do nothing as you wait for events to make the decision for you ("I'll just wait and see what happens").

None of these approaches is likely to succeed in the long run, and each can gradually reduce your confidence in dealing with complex problems. An alternative to these reactions is to *think critically* about the problem, analyzing it with an organized approach based on the following five-step method.

DETAILED METHOD FOR SOLVING PROBLEMS

Step 1: What is the problem?

   a. What do I know about the situation?

   b. What results am I seeking in this situation?

   c. How can I define the problem?

(Continued)

Step 2: What are the alternatives?

    a. What are the boundaries of the problem situation?

    b. What alternatives are possible within these boundaries?

Step 3: What are the advantages and disadvantages of each alternative?

    a. What are the advantages?

    b. What are the disadvantages?

    c. What additional information do I need in order to evaluate this alternative?

Step 4: What is the solution?

    a. Which alternative(s) will I pursue?

    b. What steps can I take to act on this/these alternative(s)?

Step 5: How well is the solution working?

    a. What is my evaluation?

    b. What adjustments are necessary?

Even when we are using an organized method for working through difficult problems and arriving at thoughtful conclusions, our minds may not always work in a logical, step-by-step fashion. Effective problem solvers typically pass through all the steps we will be examining, but not always in sequence.

Instead, the best problem solvers take a flexible approach to the process, one in which they utilize a repertoire of problem-solving strategies as needed. Sometimes, exploring the various alternatives helps them to go back and redefine the original problem. Similarly, seeking to implement the solution can often suggest a new alternative or alternatives that combine the best points of previous ones. This recursive approach is shown in Figure 12.1.

The key point is that although the problem-solving steps are presented in a logical sequence here, you need not follow them in a mechanical and unimaginative fashion. At the same time, in learning a problem-solving method like this, it is generally not wise to omit steps because each one deals with an important aspect of the problem. As you become more proficient in using the method, you will find that you can apply its concepts and strategies to problem solving in an increasingly flexible and natural fashion, just as learning the basics of an activity like driving a car gradually results in a more integrated performance of the skills involved.

Before You Begin: Accepting the Problem

To solve a problem, you must first be willing to *accept* the problem by acknowledging that it exists and committing yourself to trying to solve it. Sometimes you may have difficulty recognizing a problem unless it is pointed out to you. At other times,

FIGURE 12.1   A Flexible Approach to Problem Solving

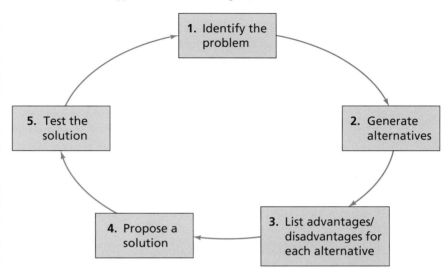

you may actively resist acknowledging a problem, even when it is pointed out to you. The person who confidently states, "I don't really have any problems," sometimes has very serious problems—but is simply unwilling to acknowledge them.

However, mere acknowledgment is not enough to solve a problem, and indeed it would make for a very brief and unsatisfying essay. Once you have identified a problem, you must commit yourself to solving it. Successful problem solvers are highly motivated and willing to persevere through the many challenges and frustrations of the problem-solving process. How do you find this motivation and commitment? There are not simple answers, but the following strategies may help:

- *List the benefits.* Making a detailed list of the benefits you will derive from successfully dealing with the problem is a good place to begin. Such a process helps you clarify why you might want to tackle the problem, motivates you to get started, and serves as a source of encouragement when you encounter difficulties or lose momentum.

- *Formalize your acceptance.* You can formalize your acceptance of a problem by "going on record," either by preparing a signed declaration or by signing a "contract" with someone else. This formal commitment can serve as an explicit statement of original intentions to which you can refer if your resolve weakens.

- *Accept responsibility for your life.* Former U.S. Attorney General Robert F. Kennedy, who was assassinated in 1968, once said, "Some people see things as they are, and ask, 'Why?' I see things as they could be, and ask, 'Why not?'" You have the potential to control the direction of your own life, but to do so, you must accept your freedom to choose and the responsibility that goes with it.

- *Create a "worst case" scenario.* Some problems persist because people are able to ignore their possible implications. When you create a worst-case scenario, you

remind yourself, as graphically as possible, of the potentially disastrous consequences of your actions. For example, looking at vivid color photographs and
research conclusions can remind a person that excessive smoking, drinking, or
eating can lead to myriad health problems and social and psychological
difficulties as well as death.

- *Identify the constraints.* If you are having trouble accepting a problem, it is
usually because something is holding you back. For example, you might be
concerned about the amount of time and effort involved, you might be reluctant to confront the underlying issues the problem represents, you might be
worried about finding out unpleasant things about yourself or others, or you
might be inhibited by other problems in your life, such as a tendency to pro-
crastinate. Whatever the constraints, using this strategy involves identifying
and describing all the factors that are preventing you from confronting the
problem and then addressing them one at a time.

Step 1: What Is the Problem?

The problem-solving process begins by determining exactly what the central issues
of the problem are. Otherwise, your chances of solving it are considerably reduced.
You may even spend time trying to solve the wrong problem. For instance, consider
the different formulations of the following problems. How might they lead a person
in different directions when trying to solve it?

"School is boring" versus "I am bored in accounting class."

"I'm unlovable" versus "I was just turned down for a date."

In each of these cases, a very general conclusion (first formulation) has been replaced
by a more specific characterization of the problem (second formulation).

General conclusions ("I'm a failure") do not suggest productive ways of resolv-
ing the difficulties. They are too absolute, too all-encompassing. On the other hand,
more specific descriptions of the problem situation ("I just failed an exam") do permit you to attack problems with useful strategies. In short, the way you define a
problem determines not only how you will go about solving it but also whether you
feel that the problem can be solved at all. Correct identification of a problem is
essential if you are going to be able to successfully analyze it and reach an appropriate conclusion. Incorrectly identifying the problem can lead to pursuing an
unproductive, even destructive, course of action.

This process of identifying the problem and arriving at a specific characterization
of it can help you to articulate a clear thesis (for an essay or research project) or claim
(for an argument).

Consider the problem of the college student whose financial aid package was cut
(pages 402–403) and analyze it using this problem-solving method. Ask:

1. What do I know about the situation?

2. What is my purpose for writing about the problem?

3. What results am I aiming for in this situation (what is my purpose?)?

4. How can I define the problem?

Step 1A: What do I know about the situation? Solving a problem begins with determining what you *know* to be the case and what you *think* may be the case. To explore the problem successfully, you need to have a clear idea of the details of your beginning circumstances. You can identify and organize what you know about the problem situation by posing key questions. By asking—and trying to answer—questions of fact, you are establishing a sound foundation for exploring your problem as well as developing an interesting, arguable thesis or claim. Imagine that you are the student described earlier who is facing a reduction in financial aid. Answer the following questions of fact—who? what? where? when? how? why?—about your problem.

- *Who* are the people involved in this situation?
  Who will benefit from my solving this problem?
  Who can help me solve this problem?
- *What* are the various parts or dimensions of the problem?
  What are my strengths and resources for solving this problem?
- *When* did the problem begin?
  When should the problem be resolved?
- *How* did the problem arise or develop?
- *Why* is solving this problem important to me?
  Why is this problem difficult to solve?
- Additional questions: _____

Step 1B: What results am I aiming for in this situation? The second part of answering the question "What is the problem?" consists of identifying the specific results or objectives you are trying to achieve. Your purpose for writing about this problem is to solve it. If you are able to achieve your specific results or objectives, you will have satisfied your purpose for writing. Whereas the first part of step 1 oriented you in terms of the history of the problem and the current situation, this part encourages you to look to the future. To identify results, you need to ask yourself the question "What are the objectives that, once achieved, will solve this problem?" For instance, one of the results or objectives in the sample problem might be having enough money to pay for college. Describe additional results you might be trying to achieve in this situation.

1. Having enough money to pay for college.

2. _____

3. _____

4. _____

Step 1C: How can I define the problem? After exploring what you know about the problem and the results you want to achieve, you need to conclude step 1 by defining the problem as clearly and specifically as possible. This is a crucial task in the problem-solving process because this definition will determine the direction of your analysis. Chapter 8 illustrates the thinking processes for successful definition.

Often, identifying the central issue of a problem is a complex process. For example, the statement "My problem is relating to other people" suggests a complicated situation with many interacting variables that resists simple definition. In fact, you may not even begin to develop a clear definition of the problem until you engage in the process of trying to solve it. Or you might begin by believing that your problem is, say, not having the ability to succeed but end by concluding that the problem is really a fear of success.

As you will see, the same insights also apply to social problems. For example, the problem of high school dropouts might initially be defined in terms of problems in the school system whereas later formulations might identify drug use or social pressure as the core of the problem.

Although there are no simple formulas for defining challenging problems, you can try several strategies to identify the central issue most effectively:

- *View the problem from different perspectives.* As you saw in Chapters 3, 7, and 8, perspective taking is a key ingredient of thinking critically; it can also help you to zero in on many problems. When you describe how various individuals might view a given problem—such as the high school dropout rate—the essential ingredients of the problems begin to emerge. In the student financial-aid problem, how would you describe the student's perspective? the college's perspective? the student's family's perspective?

- *Identify component problems.* Larger problems are often made up of component problems. To define a larger problem, it is often necessary to identify and describe the subproblems that comprise it. A student's poor school performance, for example, might result from a number of factors like ineffective study habits, inefficient time management, and preoccupation with a personal problem. Defining, and dealing effectively with, a larger problem means defining and dealing with the subproblems first. Can you identify two possible subproblems in the financial aid problem?

- *State the problem clearly and specifically.* A third defining strategy is to state the problem as clearly and specifically as possible as you examine your objectives for solving it. Stating this sort of precise description of the problem is an important step toward solving it. If you state the problem in very general terms, you won't have a clear idea of how best to proceed in dealing with it. However, if you can describe it in specific terms, your description will begin to suggest actions you can take to solve the problem. Examine the differences between the statements of the following problem:

General: "My problem is money."

More specific: "My problem is needing to budget my money so that I won't always run out of it near the end of the month."

Most specific: "My problem is my need to develop the habits and discipline to budget my money so that I won't always run out of it near the end of the month."

Review your analysis of the student's financial aid problem; then state the problem in writing as clearly and specifically as you can.

Step 2: What Are the Alternatives?

Once you have clearly and specifically identified a problem, your next move is to examine each possible action that might help you to solve it. Before you list the alternatives, however, it makes sense to explore the situation's boundaries to determine which actions are possible and which are not.

Step 2A: What are the boundaries of the problem situation? Boundaries are limits that you simply cannot change. They are part of the problem, and they must be accepted and dealt with. At the same time, you must be careful not to identify as boundaries circumstances that *can* be changed. For instance, again imagining yourself as the student with the financial aid problem, you might assume that your problem must be solved in your current location, without realizing that transferring to a less expensive college could be one of your options. Identify additional boundaries that might be part of this sample situation and list some of the questions you should answer about these boundaries.

Step 2B: What alternatives are possible within these boundaries? After you have established a general notion of the boundaries of the problem situation, you can proceed to identify the possible courses of action that can occur within them. Of course, identifying all the possible alternatives is not always easy; in fact, that may be part of your problem. Often we cannot see a way out of a problem because our thinking is set in certain ruts, fixed in certain perspectives. We may be blind to other approaches, either because we reject them without seriously considering them ("That will never work!") or because they simply do not occur to us. You can use several strategies to overcome these obstacles:

- *Discuss the problem with other people.* Discussing possible alternatives with others uses a number of the aspects of critical thinking we explored in Chapter 1. Other people can often suggest alternatives we haven't thought of since they are outside the situation and thus have a more objective perspective, and since they naturally view the world differently than we do because of their past experiences and their personalities. In addition, discussions are often creative experiences that generate ideas participants would not have come up with on their own.

- *Brainstorm ideas.* Group brainstorming builds on the strengths of working with other people to generate ideas and solve problems. In a typical brainstorming session, either in person or online, a group of people work together to propose as many ideas as possible in a specific time period. As ideas are produced, they are not judged or evaluated, as this tends to inhibit the free flow of ideas and discourage people from making suggestions. Evaluation is deferred until a later stage. People are encouraged to build on the ideas of others since the most creative ideas are often generated through the constructive interplay of various minds.

- *Change your location.* Your perspectives on a problem are often tied to the circumstances in which the problem exists. For example, a problem you may be having in school is connected with your daily experiences and your habitual reactions to them. Sometimes you need a fresh perspective, which you can gain by getting away from the problem situation so that you can view it more clearly in a different light. Perhaps spending a day or two out of town will help, or even taking a long walk in a different neighborhood.

Using these strategies, as well as your own reflections, identify as many alternatives to help solve the financial aid problem that you can think of.

1. Attend school part-time

2. _____

3. _____

4. _____

Step 3: What Are the Advantages and Disadvantages of Each Alternative?

Once you have identified the alternatives, your next step is to evaluate them. Each possible course of action offers certain advantages in the sense that if you were to select that alternative, there would be some positive results. At the same time, each possible course of action probably also has disadvantages in the sense that if you were to select that alternative, you may incur a cost or risk some negative results. Determine how helpful each course of action would or would not be in solving the problem.

Step 3A: What are the advantages of each alternative? The alternative we listed in step 2 for the sample problem ("Attend college part-time") might include the following advantages.

Alternative	*Advantages*
Attend college part-time	1. Doing this would remove some of the immediate time and money pressures I am experiencing while still allowing me to prepare for the future.
	2. I would have more time to focus on the courses that I would be taking and to work additional hours.

Identify the advantages of each of the alternatives that you listed in step 2. Be sure that your responses are thoughtful and specific. For example, how many additional hours could you work? How much additional income would doing that generate?

Step 3B: What are the disadvantages of each alternative? The alternative we listed in step 2 for the sample problem might include the following disadvantages.

Alternative	*Disadvantages*
Attend college part-time	1. It would take me much longer to complete my schooling, thus delaying my progress toward my goals.
	2. I might lose motivation and drop out before completing school because the process would be taking so long.
	3. Being a part-time student might threaten my eligibility for financial aid.

Now identify the disadvantages of each of the alternatives that you listed for step 2. Make sure that your responses are thoughtful and specific. For example, how much longer would it take you to get your degree?

Step 3C: What additional information do I need to evaluate each alternative? The next part of step 3 consists of determining what you must know (information needed) to best evaluate and compare the alternatives. For each alternative there are questions that you must answer in order to establish which alternatives make sense and which do not. In addition, you need to figure out the most reliable sources for this information.

The information—and the sources of it—that must be located for the first alternative in the sample problem might include the following.

Information Needed

1. How long will it take me to complete my degree?
2. How long can I continue in school without losing interest and dropping out?
3. Will I threaten my eligibility for financial aid if I become a part-time student?

   Sources: Myself, other part-time students, school counselors, financial aid office

Identify the information needed and the sources of this information for each of the alternatives that you identified on pages 409–410. Be sure that your responses are thoughtful and specific.

Step 4: What Is the Solution?

The purpose of steps 1 through 3 is to analyze your problem in a systematic and detailed fashion. After breaking down the problem in this way, your final step is to decide on a thoughtful course of action based on your increased understanding. Even though conducting this sort of analysis does not guarantee finding a specific solution to the problem, it should deepen your understanding of exactly what the problem is. And in locating and evaluating the alternatives, it should give you some very good ideas about the general direction in which you should move and the immediate steps you should take.

Step 4A: Which alternative(s) will I pursue? There is no simple formula to tell you which alternatives to select. As you work through the different courses of action that are possible, you may find that you can immediately rule some out. In the sample problem, for example, you may know with certainty that you do not want to attend college part-time (alternative 1) because you will forfeit your remaining financial aid. However, it may not be as simple to select which of the other alternatives you wish to pursue. How do you decide?

The decisions we make usually depend on what we believe is most important to us. These beliefs are known as *values*. Our values are the starting points of our actions and strongly influence our decisions. For example, if we value staying alive (as most of us do), we will make many decisions each day that express this value—eating proper meals, not walking in front of moving traffic, and so on.

Our values help us set priorities in life—that is, decide what aspects of our lives are most important to us. We might decide that for the present, going to school is more important than having an active social life. In this case, going to school has higher priority than having an active social life. Unfortunately, our values are not always consistent with each other—we may have to choose either going to school or having an active social life. Both activities may be important to us; they are simply not compatible with each other. Very often the *conflicts* between our values constitute the problem. Let's examine some strategies for selecting alternatives that might help to solve the sample problem.

- *Evaluate and compare alternatives.* Although each alternative may have certain advantages and disadvantages, not all advantages are equally desirable or potentially effective. For example, giving up college entirely would certainly solve some aspects of the sample problem, but its obvious disadvantages would rule out this solution for most people. Thus, it makes sense to try to evaluate and rank the various alternatives on the basis of how effective they are likely to be and how they match up with your value system. A good place to begin is at the "Results" stage, step 1B. Examine each of your alternatives and evaluate how well it will contribute to achieving the results you are aiming for in the situation. You may want to rank the alternatives or develop your own rating system to assess their relative effectiveness.

  After evaluating the alternatives in terms of their anticipated *effectiveness*, the next step is to evaluate them in terms of their *desirability* relative to your needs, interests, and value system. Again, you can use either a ranking or a rating system to assess their relative desirability. After completing these two separate evaluations, you can select whatever alternatives seem most appropriate. Review the alternatives you identified in the sample problem; then rank or rate them according to their potential effectiveness and desirability.

- *Synthesize a new alternative.* After reviewing and evaluating the alternatives you have generated, you may develop a new alternative that combines the best qualities of several options while avoiding the disadvantages some of them would have if implemented exclusively. In the sample problem, you might combine attending college part-time during the academic year with attending school during summer session so that progress toward your degree wouldn't be impeded. Examine the alternatives you identified and develop a new option that combines the best elements of several of them.

- *Try out each alternative—in your imagination.* Focus on each alternative and try to imagine, as concretely as possible, what it would be like if you actually selected it. Visualize what impact your choice would have on your problem and what the implications would be for your life as a whole. By trying out the alternative in your imagination, you can sometimes avoid unpleasant results or unexpected consequences. As a variation of this strategy, you can sometimes test alternatives on a very limited basis in a practice situation. Suppose you are trying to overcome your fear of speaking out in groups. You can practice various speaking techniques with your friends or family until you find an approach that works for you.

Step 4B: What steps can I take to act on the alternative(s) chosen? Once you have decided on an alternative to pursue, your next move is to plan what steps to take in acting on it. Planning the specific steps you will take is extremely important. Although thinking carefully about your problem is necessary, it is not enough if you hope to solve the problem. You have to take action. In the sample problem, for example, imagine that one of the alternatives you have selected is "find additional sources of income that will enable me to work part-time and attend school full-time." The specific steps you would take might include these:

- Contact the financial aid office to learn what other forms of monetary aid are available and how to apply for them.
- Contact some local banks to find out what sort of student loans they offer.
- Look for a higher-paying job to earn more money without working additional hours.
- Discuss your problem with students in similar circumstances in order to generate new ideas.

Identify the steps you would have to take to pursue the alternative(s) you identified on pages 409–410.

Plans, of course, do not implement themselves. Once you know what actions are needed, you have to make a commitment to taking the necessary steps. This is where many people stumble in the problem-solving process; they remain paralyzed by inertia or fear. Having a clear sense of purpose—and an audience who will be directly affected by your decisions—will help keep you motivated. To overcome such blocks and inhibitions, you sometimes need to re-examine your original acceptance of the problem, perhaps making use of some of the strategies you explored on pages 405–406. Once you get started, the rewards of actively attacking your problem are often enough incentive to keep you focused and motivated.

Step 5: How Well Is the Solution Working?

As you work toward reaching a reasonable and informed conclusion, be wary of falling into the trap of thinking that there is only one "right" solution and that if you don't figure out what it is and implement it, all is lost. You should remind yourself that any analysis of problem situations, no matter how careful and systematic, is ultimately limited. You simply cannot anticipate or predict everything that will happen in the future. Consequently, every decision you make is provisional in the sense that your ongoing experience will inform you whether it is working out or needs to be modified.

Step 5A: What is my evaluation? In many cases the relative effectiveness of your efforts will be apparent. In other cases you will find it helpful to pursue a more systematic evaluation along the lines suggested in the following strategies.

- *Compare the results with the goals.* The essence of evaluation is comparing the results of your efforts with your initial goals. For example, the goals of the sample problem are embodied in the results you specified on pages 409–410. Compare the anticipated results of the alternative(s) you selected. To what extent will your choice(s) meet these goals? Are any goals not likely to be met by your alternative(s)? If so, which ones? Could they be addressed by other alternatives? Asking these questions and others will help you to assess the success of your efforts and will provide a foundation for future decisions.

- *Get other perspectives.* As you have seen throughout the problem-solving process, getting the opinions of others is a productive strategy at virtually every stage, and this is certainly true of evaluation. It is not always easy to accept the evaluations of others, but keeping an open mind about outside opinions is a very valuable attitude to cultivate because it will stimulate and guide you to produce your best efforts.

    To receive specific, practical feedback, you need to ask specific, practical questions that will elicit such information. General questions ("What do you think of this?") typically receive overly general, unhelpful answers ("It sounds okay to me"). Be focused when soliciting feedback and remember that you do have the right to ask people for *constructive* comments—that is, to provide suggestions for improvement rather than just to tell you what they think is wrong. For example, you could say, "What do you know about me that you think will help me maintain my motivation to stay in school—even if it takes two years longer than I had planned?" Or you can ask, "Do you have any ideas about how I can cut my expenses by 10 percent each month?"

Step 5B: What adjustments are necessary? As a result of your review, you may discover that the alternative you selected is not feasible or is not producing satisfactory results. Even when things initially appear to be working reasonably well, an active thinker continues to ask questions such as "What might I have overlooked?" and "How could I have done this differently?" Of course, asking—and trying to answer—questions like this is even more essential if solutions are hard to come by (as they usually are in real-world problems) and if you are to retain the flexibility and optimism you will need to tackle a new option.

"As soon as one problem is solved, another rears its ugly head."

THINKING-
WRITING
ACTIVITY

Analyzing a Problem in Your Life

This Thinking-Writing Activity provides you with the opportunity to apply the problem-solving method to an important *un*solved problem in your own life. First, select from your own life a problem that you are currently grappling with and have not been able to solve. Next, strengthen your acceptance of the problem by using several strategies described on pages 405–406. Finally, work your way through each of the problem-solving steps outlined on pages 403–404. Write out responses to the questions in each step, and be sure to discuss your problem with other class members to generate fresh perspectives and unusual alternatives that might not have occurred to you. Your ultimate goal is to decide on a provisional solution to your problem and establish a plan of action that will help you move in the right direction.

Solving Social Problems

The problems we have analyzed up to this point are "personal" problems in the sense that they represent individual challenges we encounter as we live our lives. Problems are not only of a personal nature, however. We also face problems as members of a community, the larger society, and the world.

As with personal problems, we need to approach these kinds of problems in an organized and thoughtful way in order to explore the issues, develop a clear understanding, and decide on an informed plan of action. For example, racism and prejudice seem to be on the rise at many college campuses. There has been an increase of overt racist incidents at colleges and universities during the past several years, which is particularly disturbing given the lofty egalitarian ideals of higher education. Experts from different fields have offered a variety of explanations to account for this behavior.

Making sense of this kind of complex, challenging situation is not a simple process. The famous newspaperman H. L. Mencken once said, "To every complex question there is a simple answer—and it's wrong!" In this chapter we have seen that complex problems do not have simple solutions, whether they are personal problems or larger social problems like racial prejudice or world hunger. We have also learned that by working through these complex problems thoughtfully and systematically, we can achieve a deeper understanding of their many interacting elements as well as develop and implement strategies for solving them.

A thoughtful problem solver employs all the critical thinking abilities we have examined in this book. And although we might agree with Mencken's evaluation of simple answers to complex questions, we would expand upon it: "To many complex questions there are complex answers—and these are well worth pursuing."

The following reading selections deal with the problem of campus racism and hate crime. The information that they present provides a framework for thoughtful analysis and productive solutions. The first article, from the *Baltimore Sun*, describes a campus reaction to a blatant display of racism at a 2006 Halloween party. "Young Hate" examines the insidious problem of intolerance on college campuses while "When Is It Rape?" explores the issues related to the problem of "date rape."

THINKING-
WRITING
ACTIVITY

Analyzing a Social Problem

Work with one or more of the following articles. After reading the article(s) carefully, identify and analyze the problem being discussed by using the problem-solving method explained in this chapter.

"Hopkins Targets Campus Racism"

BY SUMATHI REDDY

This article describes one university's reaction to a shocking incident of racial provocation by fraternity members who thought their actions were merely funny. The incident occurred despite a significant effort by the campus over the past several years to educate all students and staff in tolerance and diversity. Reporter Sumathi Reddy is a graduate of Barnard College/Columbia University. She began her career in journalism at New York's *Newsday* and moved to the *Baltimore Sun* in 2004. In 2006, she was awarded a prestigious International Reporting Fellowship, sponsored by the Johns Hopkins University School of Advanced International Studies.

Johns Hopkins University students and faculty members will have more diversity training, and the history of racism will be incorporated into the campus curriculum and workshops, Hopkins President William R. Brody announced yesterday, responding to an outcry over a racially offensive fraternity party.

In a letter to students and members of the faculty and staff, Brody outlined several other steps, including the creation of a university-wide commission to make recommendations to ensure that new equality guidelines are followed. Also, he said, the administration will work for better communication with multicultural groups.

In the letter, Brody said that racism "is still an issue in our university community."

"We have made progress," he wrote, pointing to the formation 10 years ago of the Diversity Leadership Council. "But no one ever believed, even before last weekend's events, that we had done all we should. We all knew that we still had lots of work to do toward making Johns Hopkins the diverse, tolerant, respectful and welcoming community we want it to be."

5   The announcement followed a Sigma Chi fraternity party Saturday night that was advertised as "Halloween in the Hood." The party included a skeleton pirate dangling from a noose, which students called a symbol of a lynching.

The party's invitation, which was posted on the Facebook web site, described Baltimore as "the HIV pit" and encouraged attendees to wear "regional clothing from our locale" such as "bling bling ice ice, grills" and "hoochie hoops."

The party ignited a debate on campus about racial tension and discrimination, and the Black Student Union led a protest Monday demanding steps, some of which were addressed in the announcement yesterday. Other demands include a cultural center, more faculty members of color and a department of African-American studies.

The local chapter of the National Association for the Advancement of Colored People will support the Black Student Union's efforts at a [scheduled] rally. . .

"From the statement that we heard from a variety of students on campus, there . . . has been for a while a climate and atmosphere of racial insensitivity, prejudice and tension," said Marvin "Doc" Cheatham, president of the NAACP's Baltimore chapter.

"We will, of course, allow the students to take whatever action they deem appropriate to address their concerns, but there is a larger picture and a systemic problem that we must address as an organization representative of the entire Baltimore City community."

Senior Christina Chapman, president of the Black Student Union, said the organization will deliver a formal list of demands today.

"I'm happy that these things are being mentioned," she said of Brody's letter. "But I won't be truly satisfied until I really see a change, until I see a lot more faculty of color, until I see a department that grants PhDs in Africana studies, until we see some sort of multicultural space."

Black Student Union members have charged that the invitations to the fraternity party reflected students' condescension toward Baltimore and its residents.

The university's coordinator of Greek life had warned the fraternity to withdraw the "racist and offensive" invitation, but it remained in an altered, yet offensive form.

When Black Student Union members sent 10 members to the party at the fraternity's house in the 200 block of E. 33rd St., they took pictures of the skeleton pirate and students in costumes they called offensive. They showed the pictures to campus security, which shut down the party early Sunday morning.

On Monday, Black Student Union members held a protest, after which university officials announced that Sigma Chi had been suspended pending an investigation.

A day later [the] fraternity's international headquarters announced that the student author of the party invitation had been expelled from the fraternity and that it also is conducting an investigation.

Fraternity members have declined to comment, though three members apologized at a public forum Monday during which more than 100 students came to air their concerns before a panel of the university's top administrators.

Paula Berger, Hopkins's dean of undergraduate education, said the university's investigation will take at least several more days before a decision is made on whether to convene a hearing panel.

She said members of the fraternity and the Black Student Union have met and reported constructive meetings.

"I think there's a much better understanding, and clearly the students want to work to address issues which extend far beyond any one frat and, frankly, any one multicultural group," Berger said.

Of the student goal of an African-American studies department, Berger said any such discussions will evolve from the university's interdisciplinary Center for Africana Studies program. The university appointed its first full-time director this year.

She said the university will continue to make recruiting faculty members of color a top priority. Administrators say that progress on that front has been inadequate.

The university's undergraduate faculty includes six tenured black members and two on the tenure track.

25

"One of the difficulties is everybody is after the same set of people," Berger said, referring to peer institutions." But we're not content with where we are on that."

"We've not been blind to these issues. I think we have to grow . . . but I don't think we're fundamentally flawed in some fatal way. We've got work to do, and we intend to do it."

Chapman said minority students have not been satisfied with the pace of progress at the university.

"We're looking for a lot more," she said. "Promises are great but I feel we really just need change. We really need to feel like people are truly listening for the sake of listening and not listening for the sake of trying to maintain a good name for the university."

QUESTIONS FOR ACTIVE READING

1. In what ways are different members of the Johns Hopkins University community applying the detailed method for solving problems to their specific situation?

2. In your own words, state the *general* problem described by this article, and then list the specific *characterizations* of that problem. Is the prominence given to one of those characterizations in this article really the most important in the larger context of the general problem? Be prepared to show how the structure of this newspaper article demonstrates the relative importance of these specific characterizations.

3. Are there any voices missing from this article? If you were this newspaper's editor, whose voices and perspectives would you recommend including, and why?

QUESTIONS FOR THINKING CRITICALLY

1. The detailed problem-solving method described in this chapter emphasizes the need for additional perspectives and constructive conversations when addressing complex social problems. How are those strategies being applied to the situation at Johns Hopkins University?

2. What thinking and communicating strategies did the fraternity ignore when planning for its offensive Halloween party? What might members have assumed about their audience and purpose? In what ways can something like a party or another casual social event reflect rhetorical and critical thinking principles—or lack thereof?

3. Compare the incidents and issues described in this article with those discussed in David Shenk's "Young Hate" (page 420). Nearly twenty years separate the incidents described in these two articles. Have there been any positive changes in the way the different communities described in these articles anticipate or respond to these issues? In your opinion, why or why not?

"Young Hate"

by David Shenk (b. 1966)

David Shenk, a graduate of Brown University, is an award-winning author of four books and a contributor to numerous magazines, including *National Geographic, The New Yorker, Harper's, The New Republic, Wired, Technology Review,* and *The American Scholar.* His book *The Forgetting,* which is about Alzheimer's disease, won first prize in the British Medical Association's Popular Medical Book Awards and was the basis for a PBS film in January 2004. Shenk's other books are *The End of Patience,* about the current Information Age; *Data Smog,* also about information and technology; and *Skeleton Key: A Dictionary for Deadheads.* Shenk lives in Brooklyn.

"Young Hate" was first published in 1989 in *Career Vision,* a magazine distributed on college campuses.

Death to gays. Here is the relevant sequence of events: On Monday night Jerry Mattioli leads a candlelight vigil for lesbian and gay rights. *Gays are trash.* On Tuesday his name is in the school paper and he can hear whispers and feel more, colder stares than usual. On Wednesday morning a walking bridge in the middle of the Michigan State campus is found to be covered with violent epithets warning campus homosexuals to *be afraid, very afraid,* promising to *abolish faggots from existence,* and including messages specifically directed at Mattioli. Beginning Friday morning fifteen of the perpetrators, all known to Mattioli by name and face, are rounded up and quietly disciplined by the university. *Go home faggots.* On Friday afternoon Mattioli is asked by university officials to leave campus for the weekend, for his own safety. He does, and a few hours later receives a phone call from a friend who tells him that his dormitory room has been torched. MSU's second annual "Cross-Cultural Week" is over.

"Everything was ruined," Mattioli says. "What wasn't burned was ruined by smoke and heat and by the water. On Saturday I sat with the fire investigator all day, and we went through the room, literally ash by ash. . . . The answering machine had melted. The receiver of the telephone on the wall had stretched to about three feet long. That's how intense the heat was."

"Good news!" says Peter Jennings. A recent *Washington Post*–ABC News poll shows that integration is up and racial tension is down in America, as compared with eight years ago. Of course, in any trend there are fluctuations, exceptions. At the University of Massachusetts at Amherst, an estimated two thousand whites chase twenty blacks in a clash after a 1986 World Series game, race riots break out in Miami in 1988 and in Virginia Beach in 1989; and on college campuses across the country, our nation's young elite experience an entire decade's aberration from the poll's findings: incidents of ethnic, religious, and gender-related harassment surge throughout the eighties.

What is the best way to deal with people espousing racist views? How can we best encourage such people to develop more open-minded ideas?

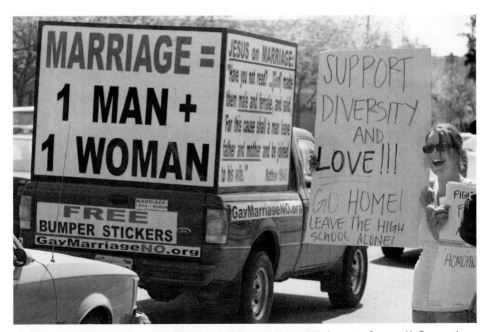

Have you ever participated in a public demonstration or rally? How did being part of a crowd influence the way you communicated? For example, did you take part in spontaneous discussions, or prepare a banner, or participate in chants? Would your thinking about an issue be influenced by that kind of communication from the opposing side?

Greatest hits include Randy Bowman, a black student at the University of Texas, having to respectfully decline a request by two young men wearing Ronald Reagan masks and wielding a pistol to exit his eighth-floor dorm room through the window; homemade T-shirts, *Thank God for AIDS* and *Aryan by the Grace of God,* among others, worn proudly on campus; Jewish student centers shot at, stoned, and defaced at Memphis State, University of Kansas, Rutgers (*Six million, why not*), and elsewhere; the black chairperson of United Minorities Council at U Penn getting a dose of hi-tech hate via answering machine: *We're going to lynch you, nigger shit. We are going to lynch you.*

5   The big picture is less graphic, but just as dreadful: reports of campus harassment have increased as much as 400 percent since 1985. Dropout rates for black students in predominantly white colleges are as much as five times higher than white dropout rates at the same schools and black dropout rates at black schools. The Anti-Defamation League reports a sixfold increase in anti-Semitic episodes on campuses between 1985 and 1988. Meanwhile, Howard J. Ehrlich of the National Institute Against Prejudice and Violence reminds us that "up to 80 percent of harassed students don't report the harassment." Clearly, the barrage of news reports reveals only the tip of a thoroughly sour iceberg.

Colleges have responded to incidents of intolerance—and the subsequent demands of minority rights groups—with the mandatory ethnic culture classes and restrictions on verbal harassment. But what price tranquility? Libertarian and conservative student groups, faculty, and political advisors lash out over limitations on free speech and the improper embrace of liberal political agendas. "Progressive academic administrations," writes University of Pennsylvania professor Alan Charles Kors in the *Wall Street Journal*, "are determined to enlighten their morally benighted students and protect the community from political sin."

Kors and kind bristle at the language of compromise being attached to official university policy. The preamble to the University of Michigan's new policy on discriminatory behavior reads, in part, "Because there is tension between freedom of speech, the right of individuals to be free from injury caused by discrimination, and the University's duty to protect the educational process . . . it may be necessary to have varying standards depending on the locus of regulated conduct." The policy tried to "strike a balance" by applying different sets of restrictions to academic centers, open areas, and living quarters, but in so doing, hit a wall. Before the policy could go into effect, it was struck down in a Michigan court as being too vague. At least a dozen schools in the process of formulating their own policies scurried in retreat as buoyant free-speech advocates went on the offensive. Tufts University president Jean Mayer voluntarily dismissed his school's "Freedom of Speech versus Freedom from Harassment" policy after a particularly inventive demonstration by late-night protesters who used chalk, tape, and poster board to divide the campus into designated free speech, limited speech, and non-free speech zones. "We're not working for a right to offensive speech," says admitted chalker Andrew Zappia, co-editor of the conservative campus paper, *The Primary Source*. "This is about protecting free speech, in general, and allowing the community to set its own standards about what is appropriate. . . .

"The purpose of the Tufts policy was to prosecute people for what the university described as 'gray area'—meaning unintentional—harassment." Zappia gives a hypothetical example: "I'm a Catholic living in a dorm, and I put up a poster in my room [consistent with my faith] saying that homosexuality is bad. If I have a gay roommate or one who doesn't agree with me, he could have me prosecuted, not because I hung it there to offend him, but because it's gray area harassment.... The policy was well intended, but it was dangerously vague. They used words like *stigmatizing, offensive, harassing*—words that are very difficult to define."

Detroit lawyer Walter B. Connolly, Jr., disagrees. He insists that it's quite proper for schools to act to protect the victims of discrimination as long as the restrictions stay out of the classroom. "Defamation, child pornography, fighting words, inappropriate comments on the radio—there are all sorts of areas where the First Amendment isn't the preeminent burning omnipotence in the sky.... Whenever you have competing interests of a federal statute [and] the Constitution, you end up balancing."

10   If you want to see a liberal who follows this issue flinch, whisper into his or her ear the name Shelby Steele. Liberals don't like Steele, an (African American) English professor at California's San Jose State; they try to dismiss him as having no professional experience in the study of racial discrimination. But he's heavily into the subject, and his analyses are both lucid and disturbing. Steele doesn't favor restrictions on speech, largely because they don't deal with what he sees as the problem. "You don't gain very much by trying to legislate the problem away, curtailing everyone's rights in the process," he says. In a forum in which almost everyone roars against a shadowy, usually nameless contingent of racist thugs, Steele deviates, choosing instead to accuse the accusers. He blames not the racists, but the weak-kneed liberal administrators and power-hungry victims' advocates for the mess on campuses today.

"Racial tension on campus is the result more of racial equality than inequality," says Steele. "On campuses today, as throughout society, blacks enjoy equality under the law—a profound social advancement.... What has emerged in recent years ... in a sense as a result of progress ... is *a politics of difference*, a troubling, volatile politics in which each group justifies itself, its sense of worth and its pursuit of power, through difference alone." On nearly every campus, says Steele, groups representing blacks, Hispanics, Asians, gays, women, Jews, and any combinations therein solicit special resources. Asked for—often demanded, in intense demonstrations—are funds for African-American (Hispanic . . .) cultural centers, separate (face it, segregated) housing, ethnic studies programs, and even individual academic incentives—at Penn State, minority students are given $275 per semester if they earn a C average, twice that if they do better than 2.75.

These entitlements, however, do not just appear *deus ex machina*. Part two of Steele's thesis addresses what he calls the "capitulation" of campus presidents. To avoid feelings of guilt stemming from past discrimination against minority groups, Steele says, "[campus administrators have] tended to go along with whatever blacks put on the table, rather than work with them to assess their real needs.... Administrators would never give white students a theme house where they could be 'more comfortable with people of their own kind,' yet more and more universities are doing this for black students." Steele sees white frustration as the inevitable result.

"White students are not invited to the negotiating table from which they see blacks and others walk away with concessions," he says. "The presumption is that they do not deserve to be there, because they are white. So they can only be defensive, and the less mature among them will be aggressive."

Course, some folks see it another way. The students fighting for minority rights aren't wicked political corrupters, but champions of a cause far too long suppressed by the white male hegemony. Responsive administrators are engaged not in capitulation, but in progress. And one shouldn't look for the cause of this mess on any campus, because he doesn't live on one. His address used to be the White House, but then he moved to 666 St. Cloud Road. Ronald Reagan, come on down.

Dr. Manning Marble, University of Colorado: "The shattering assault against the economic, social, and political status of the black American community as a whole [is symbolized by] the Reagan Administration in the 1980s. The Civil Rights Commission was gutted; affirmative action became a 'dead letter'; social welfare, health care, employment training, and educational loans were all severely reduced. This had a disproportionately more negative impact upon black youth."

The "perception is already widespread that the society at large is more permissive toward discriminatory attitudes and behaviors, and less committed to equal opportunity and affirmative action," concluded a 1988 conference at Northern Illinois University. John Wiener, writing in *The Nation*, attacks long-standing institutions of bigotry, asserting, for example, that "racism is endemic to the fraternity subculture," and praises the efforts of some schools to double the number of minority faculty and increase minority fellowships. On behalf of progressives across the land, Wiener writes off Shelby Steele as someone who is content to "blame the victim."

So the machine has melted, the phone has stretched to where it is useless. This is how intense the heat is. Liberals, who largely control the administration, faculty, and students' rights groups of leading academic institutions, have, with virtually no intensive intellectual debate, inculcated schools with their answers to the problem of bigotry. Conservatives, with a long history of insensitivity to minority concerns, have been all but shut out of the debate, and now want back in. Their intensive pursuit of the true nature of bigotry and the proper response to it—working to assess the "real needs" of campuses rather than simply bowing to pressure—deserves to be embraced by all concerned parties, and probably would have been by now but for two small items: (a) Reagan, their fearless leader, clearly *was* insensitive to ethnic/feminist concerns (even Steele agrees with this); and (b) some of the more coherent conservative pundits *still* show a blatant apathy to the problems of bigotry in this country. This has been sufficient ammunition for liberals who are continually looking for an excuse to keep conservatives out of the dialogue. So now we have clashes rather than debates: on how much one can say, on how much one should have to hear. Two negatives: one side wants to crack down on expression, the other on awareness. The machine has melted, and it's going to take some consensus to build a new one. Intellectual provincialism will have to end before young hate ever will.

A Month in the Life of Campus Bigotry

April 1 Vandals spray-paint "Jewhaters will pay" and other slogans on the office walls of *The Michigan Daily* (University of Michigan) in response to editorials condemning Israel for policies regarding the Palestinians. Pro-Israeli and pro-Palestinian shanties defaced; one is burned.

U of M: Fliers circulated over the weekend announce "White Pride Month."

Southern Connecticut State University reportedly suspends five fraternity officers after racial brawl.

April 2 Several gay men of the University of Connecticut are taunted by two students, who yell "faggot" at them.

April 3 The University of Michigan faculty meet to discuss a proposal to require students to take a course on ethnicity and racism.

April 4 Students at the University of California at Santa Barbara suspend hunger strike after university agrees to negotiate on demands for minority faculty hiring and the changed status of certain required courses.

April 5 The NCAA releases results of survey on black student athletes, reporting that 51 percent of black football and basketball players at predominantly white schools express feelings of being different; 51 percent report feelings of racial isolation; 33 percent report having experienced at least six incidents of individual racial discrimination.

The *New York Times* prints three op-ed pieces by students on the subject of racial tension on campus.

Charges filed against a former student of Penn State for racial harassment of a black woman.

April 6 University of Michigan: Hundreds of law students wear arm bands, boycott classes to protest lack of women and minority professors.

Michigan State University announces broad plan for increasing the number of minority students, faculty, and staff; the appointment of a senior advisor for minority affairs; and the expansion of multicultural conferences. "It's not our responsibility just to mirror society or respond to mandates," President John DiBioggio tells reporters, "but to set the tone."

April 7 Wayne State University (Detroit, Michigan) student newspaper runs retraction of cartoon considered offensive following protest earlier in the week.

Controversy develops at the State University of New York at Stony Brook, where a white woman charges a popular black basketball player with rape. Player denies charges. Charges are dismissed. Protests of racial and sexual assault commence.

April 12 Twelve-day sit-in begins at Wayne State University (Michigan) over conditions for black students on campus.

April 14 Racial brawl at Arizona State.

April 20 Demonstrations at several universities across the country (Harvard, Duke, Wayne State, Wooster College, Penn State, and so on) for improvements in black student life.

Separate escort service for blacks started at Penn State out of distrust of the regular service.

April 21 200-student sit-in ends at Arizona State University when administrators agree to all thirteen demands.

April 24 Proposed tuition increase at City Universities of New York turns into racial controversy.

April 25 After eighteen months in office, Robert Collin, Florida Atlantic University's first black dean, reveals he has filed a federal discrimination complaint against the school.

Two leaders of Columbia University's Gay and Lesbian Alliance receive death threat. "Dear Jeff, I will kill you butt fucking faggots. Death to COLA!"

April 26 A black Smith College (Massachusetts) student finds note slipped under door,". . . African monkey do you want some bananas? Go back to the jungle. . . ."

"I don't think we should have to constantly relive our ancestors' mistakes," a white student at the University of North Carolina at Greensboro tells a reporter. "I didn't oppress anybody. Blacks are now equal. You don't see any racial problems anymore."

White Student Union is reported to have been formed at Temple University in Philadelphia, "City of Brotherly Love."

April 28 Note found in Brown University (Rhode Island) dorm. "Once upon a time, Brown was a place where a white man could go to class without having to look at little black faces, or little yellow faces or little brown faces, except when he went to take his meals. Things have been going downhill since the kitchen help moved into the classroom. Keep white supremecy [sic] alive!!! Join the Brown chapter of the KKK today." Note is part of series that began in the middle of the month with "Die Homos." University officials beef up security, hold forum.

April 29 Controversy reported over proposed ban on verbal harassment at Arizona State.

April 30 Anti-apartheid shanty at University of Maryland, Baltimore County, is defaced. Signs read "Apartheid now," and "Trump Plaza."

University of California at Berkeley: Resolution is passed requiring an ethnic studies course for all students.

University of Connecticut: Code is revised to provide specific penalties for acts of racial intolerance.

QUESTIONS FOR ACTIVE READING

1. What is your reaction to Shenk's opening phrase, "*Death to gays*"? Why do you think that he began his article this way?

2. What evidence does Shenk offer for his claim: "So now we have clashes rather than debates: on how much one can say, on how much one should have to hear. Two negatives: one side wants to crack down on expression, the other on awareness." Who are the "sides" to which he refers? What are their positions, according to Shenk?

3. How do you react to Shenk's list of items in "A Month in the Life of Campus Bigotry"? How does this list function as a conclusion to the Article?

QUESTIONS FOR THINKING CRITICALLY

1. Has your own campus experienced incidents of bigotry directed at people because of their race, sexual orientation, religion, or some other quality? If so, describe one such incident and analyze its probable causes. If your campus has not seen "young hate," explain why.

2. Have you ever been the victim of prejudice or discrimination? If so, describe your experience and explain how the incident made you feel about yourself and the people victimizing you.

3. Using the problem-solving method in this chapter, analyze the problem of bigotry on college campuses—yours or others. Develop some practical solutions for dealing with this troubling issue.

"When Is It Rape?"

BY NANCY GIBBS

Nancy Gibbs is an editor-at large for *Time* magazine. She has written nearly one hundred stories and also was a major contributor to the issue commemorating September 11. She won the Luce Award and the Society of Professional Journalists' Sigma Delta Chi Magazine Writing Award. Gibbs, who holds degrees from Yale and Oxford Universities, has taught journalism at Princeton. She joined *Time* in 1985.

Be careful of strangers and hurry home, says a mother to her daughter, knowing that the world is a frightful place but not wishing to swaddle a child in fear. Girls grow up scarred by caution and enter adulthood eager to shake free of their parents' worst nightmares. They still know to be wary of strangers. What they don't know is whether they have more to fear from their friends.

Most women who get raped are raped by people they already know—like the boy in biology class, or the guy in the office down the hall, or their friend's brother. The familiarity is enough to make them let down their guard, sometimes even enough to make them wonder afterward whether they were "really raped." What people think of as "real rape"—the assault by a monstrous stranger in the shadows—accounts for only one out of five attacks.

So the phrase "acquaintance rape" was coined to describe the rest, all the cases of forced sex between people who already knew each other, however casually. But that was too clinical for headline writers, and so the popular term is the narrower "date rape," which suggests an ugly ending to a raucous night on the town.

These are not idle distinctions. Behind the search for labels is the central mythology about rape; that rapists are always strangers, and victims are women who ask for it. The mythology is hard to dispel because the crime is so rarely exposed. The experts guess—that's all they can do under the circumstances—that while one in four women will be raped in her lifetime, less than 10 percent will report the assault, and less than 5 percent of the rapists will go to jail.

5   Women charge that date rape is the hidden crime; men complain it is hard to prevent a crime they can't define. Women say it isn't taken seriously; men say it is a concept invented by women who like to tease but not take the consequences. Women say the date-rape debate is the first time the nation has talked frankly about sex; men say it is women's unconscious reaction to the excesses of the sexual revolution. Meanwhile, men and women argue among themselves about the "gray area" that surrounds the whole murky arena of sexual relations, and there is no consensus in sight.

In court, on campus, in conversation, the issue turns on the elasticity of the word *rape*, one of the few words in the language with the power to summon a shared image of a horrible crime.

At one extreme are those who argue that for the word to retain its impact, it must be strictly defined as forced sexual intercourse: a gang of thugs jumping a jogger in Central Park, a psychopath preying on old women in a housing complex, a man with an ice pick in a side street. To stretch the definition of the word risks stripping away its power. In this view, if it happened on a date, it wasn't rape. A romantic encounter is a context in which sex *could* occur, and so what omniscient judge will decide whether there was genuine mutual consent?

Others are willing to concede that date rape sometimes occurs, that sometimes a man goes too far on a date without a woman's consent. But this infraction, they say, is not as ghastly a crime as street rape, and it should not be taken as seriously. The New York *Post*, alarmed by the Willy Smith case, wrote in a recent editorial, "if the sexual encounter, *forced or not*, has been preceded by a series of consensual activities—drinking, a trip to the man's home, a walk on a deserted beach at three in the morning—the charge that's leveled against the alleged offender should, it seems to us, be different than the one filed against, say, the youths who raped and beat the jogger."

This attitude sparks rage among women who carry scars received at the hands of men they knew. It makes no difference if the victim shared a drink or a moonlit walk or even a passionate kiss, they protest, if the encounter ended with her being thrown to the ground and forcibly violated. Date rape is not about a misunderstanding, they say. It is not a communications problem. It is not about a woman's having regrets in the morning for a decision she made the night before. It is not about a "decision" at all.

Rape is rape, and any form of forced sex—even between neighbors, coworkers, class-mates and casual friends—is a crime.

10   A more extreme form of that view comes from activists who see rape as a metaphor, its definition swelling to cover any kind of oppression of women. Rape, seen in this light, can occur not only on a date but also in a marriage, not only by violent assault but also by psychological pressure. A Swarthmore College training pamphlet once explained that acquaintance rape "spans a spectrum of incidents and behaviors, ranging from crimes legally defined as rape to verbal harassment and inappropriate innuendo." No wonder, then, that the battles become so heated. When innuendo qualifies as rape, the definitions have become so slippery that the entire subject sinks into a political swamp. The only way to capture the hard reality is to tell the story.

A 32-year-old woman was on business in Tampa last year for the Florida supreme court. Stranded at the courthouse, she accepted a lift from a lawyer involved in her project. As they chatted on the ride home, she recalls, "he was saying all the right things, so I started to trust him." She agreed to have dinner, and afterward, at her hotel door, he convinced her to let him come in to talk. "I went through the whole thing about being old-fashioned," she says. "I was a virgin until I was twenty-one. So I told him talk was all we were going to do."

But as they sat on the couch, she found herself falling asleep. "By now, I'm comfortable with him, and I put my head on his shoulder. He's not tried anything all evening, after all." Which is when the rape came. "I woke up to find him on top of me, forcing himself on me. I didn't scream or run. All I could think about was my business contacts and what if they saw me run out of my room screaming rape.

"I thought it was my fault. I felt so filthy, I washed myself over and over in hot water. Did he rape me? I kept asking myself. I didn't consent. But who's gonna believe me? I had a man in my hotel room after midnight." More than a year later, she still can't tell the story without a visible struggle to maintain her composure. Police referred the case to the state attorney's office in Tampa, but without more evidence it decided not to prosecute. Although her attacker has admitted that he heard her say no, maintains the woman, "he says he didn't know that I meant no. He didn't feel he'd raped me, and he wanted to see me again."

Her story is typical in many ways. The victim herself may not be sure right away that she has been raped, that she had said no and been physically forced into having sex anyway. And the rapist commonly hears but does not heed the protest. "A date rapist will follow through no matter what the woman wants because his agenda is to get laid," says Claire Walsh, a Florida-based consultant on sexual assaults. "First comes the dinner, then a dance, then a drink, then the coercion begins." Gentle persuasion gives way to physical intimidation with alcohol as the ubiquitous lubricant. "When that fails, force is used," she says. "Real men don't take no for an answer."

15   The Palm Beach case serves to remind women that if they go ahead and press charges, they can expect to go on trial along with their attacker, if not in a courtroom then in the court of public opinion. The *New York Times* caused an uproar on its own staff not only for publishing the victim's name but also for laying out in

detail her background, her high-school grades, her driving record, along with an unattributed quote from a school official about her "little wild streak." A freshman at Carleton College in Minnesota, who says she was repeatedly raped for four hours by a fellow student, claims that she was asked at an administrative hearing if she performed oral sex on dates. In 1989 a man charged with raping at knife point a woman he knew was acquitted in Florida because his victim had been wearing lace shorts and no underwear.

From a purely legal point of view, if she wants to put her attacker in jail, the survivor had better be beaten as well as raped, since bruises become a badge of credibility. She had better have reported the crime right away, before taking the hours-long shower that she craves, before burning her clothes, before curling up with the blinds down. And she would do well to be a woman of shining character. Otherwise the strict constructionist definitions of rape will prevail in court. "Juries don't have a great deal of sympathy for the victim if she's a willing participant up to the nonconsensual sexual intercourse," says Norman Kinne, a prosecutor in Dallas. "They feel that many times the victim has placed herself in the situation." Absent eyewitnesses or broken bones, a case comes down to her word against his, and the mythology of rape rarely lends her the benefit of the doubt.

She should also hope for an all-male jury, preferably composed of fathers with daughters. Prosecutors have found that women tend to be harsh judges of one another—perhaps because to find a defendant guilty is to entertain two grim realities: that anyone might be a rapist, and that every woman could find herself a victim. It may be easier to believe, the experts muse, that at some level the victim asked for it. "But just because a woman makes a bad judgment, does that give the guy a moral right to rape her?" asks Dean Kilpatrick, director of the Crime Victim Research and Treatment Center at the Medical University of South Carolina. "The bottom line is, Why does a woman's having a drink give a man the right to rape her?"

Last week the Supreme Court waded into the debate with a 7-to-2 ruling that protects victims from being harassed on the witness stand with questions about their sexual history. The Justices, in their first decision on "rape shield laws," said an accused rapist could not present evidence about a previous sexual relationship with the victim unless he notified the court ahead of time. In her decision, Justice Sandra Day O'Connor wrote that "rape victims deserve heightened protection against surprise, harassment, and unnecessary invasions of privacy."

That was welcome news to prosecutors who understand the reluctance of victims to come forward. But there are other impediments to justice as well. An internal investigation of the Oakland police department found that officers ignored a quarter of all reports of sexual assaults or attempts, though 90 percent actually warranted investigation. Departments are getting better at educating officers in handling rape cases, but the courts remain behind. A New York City task force on women in the courts charged that judges and lawyers were routinely less inclined to believe a woman's testimony than a man's.

20   The present debate over degrees of rape is nothing new; all through history, rapes have been divided between those that mattered and those that did not. For the first few

thousand years, the only rape that was punished was the defiling of a virgin, and that was viewed as a property crime. A girl's virtue was a marketable asset, and so a rapist was often ordered to pay the victim's father the equivalent of her price on the marriage market. In early Babylonian and Hebrew societies, a married woman who was raped suffered the same fate as an adulteress—death by stoning or drowning. Under William the Conqueror, the penalty for raping a virgin was castration and loss of both eyes— unless the violated woman agreed to marry her attacker, as she was often pressured to do. "Stealing an heiress" became a perfectly conventional means of taking—literally—a wife.

It may be easier to prove a rape case now, but not much. Until the 1960s it was virtually impossible without an eyewitness; judges were often required to instruct jurors that "rape is a charge easily made and hard to defend against; so examine the testimony of this witness with caution." But sometimes a rape was taken very seriously, particularly if it involved a black man attacking a white woman—a crime for which black men were often executed or lynched.

Susan Estrich, author of *Real Rape*, considers herself a lucky victim. This is not just because she survived an attack 17 years ago by a stranger with an ice pick, one day before her graduation from Wellesley. It's because police, and her friends, believed her. "The first thing the Boston police asked was whether it was a black guy," recalls Estrich, now a University of Southern California law professor. When she said yes and gave the details of the attack, their reaction was, "So you were really raped." It was an instructive lesson, she says, in understanding how racism and sexism are factored into perceptions of the crime.

A new twist in society's perception came in 1975, when Susan Brownmiller published her book *Against Our Will: Men, Women and Rape*. In it she attacked the concept that rape was a sex crime, arguing instead that it was a crime of violence and power over women. Throughout history, she wrote, rape has played a critical function. "It is nothing more or less than a conscious process of intimidation, by which *all men* keep *all women* in a state of fear."

Out of this contention was born a set of arguments that have become politically correct wisdom on campus and in academic circles. This view holds that rape is a symbol of women's vulnerability to male institutions and attitudes. "It's sociopolitical," insists Gina Rayfield, a New Jersey psychologist. "In our culture men hold the power, politically, economically. They're socialized not to see women as equals."

25   This line of reasoning has led some women, especially radicalized victims, to justify flinging around the term *rape* as a political weapon, referring to everything from violent sexual assaults to inappropriate innuendoes. Ginny, a college senior who was really raped when she was sixteen, suggests that false accusations of rape can serve a useful purpose. "Penetration is not the only form of violation," she explains. In her view, *rape* is a subjective term, one that women must use to draw attention to other, nonviolent, even nonsexual forms of oppression. "If a woman did falsely accuse a man of rape, she may have had reasons to," Ginny says. "Maybe she wasn't raped, but he clearly violated her in some way."

Catherine Comins, assistant dean of student life at Vassar, also sees some value in this loose use of "rape." She says angry victims of various forms of sexual intimidation cry rape to regain their sense of power. "To use the word carefully would be to be careful for the sake of the violator, and the survivors don't care a hoot about him." Comins argues that men who are unjustly accused can sometimes gain from the experience. "They have a lot of pain, but it is not a pain that I would necessarily have spared them. I think it ideally initiates a process of self-exploration. 'How do I see women?' 'If I didn't violate her, could I have?' 'Do I have the potential to do to her what they say I did?' Those are good questions."

Taken to extremes, there is an ugly element of vengeance at work here. Rape is an abuse of power. But so are false accusations of rape, and to suggest that men whose reputations are destroyed might benefit because it will make them more sensitive is an attitude that is sure to backfire on women who are seeking justice for all victims. On campuses where the issue is most inflamed, male students are outraged that their names can be scrawled on a bathroom-wall list of rapists and they have no chance to tell their side of the story.

"Rape is what you read about in the New York *Post* about seventeen little boys raping a jogger in Central Park," says a male freshman at a liberal-arts college, who learned that he had been branded a rapist after a one-night stand with a friend. He acknowledges that they were both very drunk when she started kissing him at a party and ended up back in his room. Even through his haze, he had some qualms about sleeping with her: "I'm fighting against my hormonal instincts, and my moral instincts are saying, 'This is my friend and if I were sober, I wouldn't be doing this.'" But he went ahead anyway. "When you're drunk, and there are all sorts of ambiguity, and the woman says 'Please, please' and then she says no sometime later, even in the middle of the act, there still may very well be some kind of violation, but it's not the same thing. It's not rape. If you don't hear her say no, if she doesn't say it, if she's playing around with you—oh, I could get squashed for saying it—there is an element of say no, mean yes."

The morning after their encounter, he recalls, both students woke up hung over and eager to put the memory behind them. Only months later did he learn that she had told a friend that he had torn her clothing and raped her. At this point in the story, the accused man starts using the language of rape. "I felt violated," he says, "I felt like she was taking advantage of me when she was very drunk. I never heard her say 'No!,' 'Stop!,' anything." He is angry and hurt at the charges, worried that they will get around, shatter his reputation and force him to leave the small campus.

30   So here, of course, is the heart of the debate. If rape is sex without consent, how exactly should consent be defined and communicated, when and by whom? Those who view rape through a political lens tend to place all responsibility on men to make sure that their partners are consenting at every point of a sexual encounter. At the extreme, sexual relations come to resemble major surgery, requiring a signed consent form. Clinical psychologist Mary P. Koss of the University of Arizona in Tucson, who is a leading scholar on the issue, puts it rather bluntly: "It's the man's penis that is doing the raping, and ultimately he's responsible for where he puts it."

Historically, of course, this has never been the case, and there are some who argue that it shouldn't be—that women too must take responsibility for their behavior, and that the whole realm of intimate encounters defies regulation from on high. Anthropologist Lionel Tiger has little patience for trendy sexual politics that make no reference to biology. Since the dawn of time, he argues, men and women have always gone to bed with different goals. In the effort to keep one's genes in the gene pool, "it is to the male advantage to fertilize as many females as possible, as quickly as possible and as efficiently as possible." For the female, however, who looks at the large investment she will have to make in the offspring, the opposite is true. Her concern is to "select" who "will provide the best set-up for their offspring." So, in general, "the pressure is on the male to be aggressive and on the female to be coy."

No one defends the use of physical force, but when the coercion involved is purely psychological, it becomes hard to assign blame after the fact. Journalist Stephanie Gutmann is an ardent foe of what she calls the date-rape dogmatists. "How can you make sex completely politically correct and completely safe?" she asks. "What a horribly bland, unerotic thing that would be! Sex is, by nature, a risky endeavor, emotionally. And desire is a violent emotion. These people in the date-rape movement have erected so many rules and regulations that I don't know how people can have erotic or desire-driven sex."

Nonsense, retorts Cornell professor Andrea Parrot, co-author of *Acquaintance Rape: The Hidden Crime*. Seduction should not be about lies, manipulation, game playing or coercion of any kind, she says. "Too bad that people think that the only way you can have passion and excitement and sex is if there are miscommunications, and one person is forced to do something he or she doesn't want to do." The very pleasures of sexual encounters should lie in the fact of mutual comfort and consent: "You can hang from the ceiling, you can use fruit, you can go crazy and have really wonderful sensual erotic sex, if both parties are consenting."

It would be easy to accuse feminists of being too quick to classify sex as rape, but feminists are to be found on all sides of the debate, and many protest the idea that all the onus is on the man. It demeans women to suggest that they are so vulnerable to coercion or emotional manipulation that they must always be escorted by the strong arm of the law. "You can't solve society's ills by making everything a crime," says Albuquerque attorney Nancy Hollander. "That comes out of the sense of overprotection of women, and in the long run that is going to be harmful to us."

35   What is lost in the ideological debate over date rape is the fact that men and women, especially when they are young, and drunk, and aroused, are not very good at communicating. "In many cases," says Estrich, "the man thought it was sex, and the woman thought it was rape, and they are both telling the truth." The man may envision a celluloid seduction, in which he is being commanding, she is being coy. A woman may experience the same event as a degrading violation of her will. That some men do not believe a woman's protests is scarcely surprising in a society so drenched with messages that women have rape fantasies and a desire to be overpowered.

By the time they reach college, men and women are loaded with cultural baggage, drawn from movies, television, music videos and "bodice ripper" romance novels. Over the years they have watched Rhett sweep Scarlett up the stairs in *Gone With the Wind;* or Errol Flynn, who was charged twice with statutory rape, overpower a protesting heroine who then melts in his arms; or Stanley rape his sister-in-law Blanche du Bois while his wife is in the hospital giving birth to a child in *A Streetcar Named Desire.* Higher up the cultural food chain, young people can read of date rape in Homer or Jane Austen, watch it in *Don Giovanni* or *Rigoletto.*

The messages come early and often, and nothing in the feminist revolution has been able to counter them. A recent survey of sixth- to ninth-graders in Rhode Island found that a fourth of the boys and a sixth of the girls said it was acceptable for a man to force a woman to kiss him or have sex if he has spent money on her. A third of the children said it would not be wrong for a man to rape a woman who had had previous sexual experiences.

Certainly cases like Palm Beach, movies like *The Accused* and novels like Avery Corman's *Prized Possessions* may force young people to reexamine assumptions they have inherited. The use of new terms, like *acquaintance rape* and *date rape,* while controversial, has given men and women the vocabulary they need to express their experiences with both force and precision. This dialogue would be useful if it helps strip away some of the dogmas, old and new, surrounding the issue. Those who hope to raise society's sensitivity to the problem of date rape would do well to concede that it is not precisely the same sort of crime as street rape, that there may be very murky issues of intent and degree involved.

On the other hand, those who downplay the problem should come to realize that date rape is a crime of uniquely intimate cruelty. While the body is violated, the spirit is maimed. How long will it take, once the wounds have healed, before it is possible to share a walk on a beach, a drive home from work or an evening's conversation without always listening for a quiet alarm to start ringing deep in the back of the memory of a terrible crime?

QUESTIONS FOR ACTIVE READING

1. What are some of the definitions of *rape* that Gibbs presents? Why does she begin her article with nine paragraphs devoted to definitions?

2. Why do you think that she then writes, "The only way to capture the hard reality is to tell the story"? What effect do the narratives in the article have?

3. Find places where Gibbs discusses racism, sexism, anthropology, and psychology. How do these references to social, political, and scientific ideas contribute to the article?

QUESTIONS FOR THINKING CRITICALLY

1. Do you know someone who has been involved in a date rape situation? If so, describe this person's experience (without divulging his or her identity).

2. How can society protect the rights of both the accuser and the accused in rape cases to ensure that justice is served?

3. Imagine that you are the dean of students at your college. What actions would you take to address the problem of date rape? Explain your reasons for considering these actions.

If you can, discuss your responses to all these questions with classmates.

Taking a Problem-Solving Approach to Writing

Problem solving provides you with a framework that you can use in much of your writing. A problem-solving approach can assist you in generating ideas and organizing information for most subjects. For example, you can look at a writing assignment as a problem and use a modification of the five-step method as a way to work on it:

1. What exactly is the assignment? What is its purpose?

2. What are some alternative ways to complete it? Who is the obvious audience, and what other possible audiences should I consider?

3. What are the advantages and disadvantages of the alternatives? Am I prepared to change my subject or thesis if my initial approach doesn't work?

4. What is the best way for me to complete this assignment? How can I use conversations and peer review to gain additional perspectives?

5. After some drafting ask: How is my solution to the problem of the assignment working out?

Then, as you write any essay, you can use modifications of the problem-solving steps at any stage. Look at the thesis as a problem and ask the preceding questions about it. Look at any part of the paper and ask the questions. Actually, effective writers do this to some extent—perhaps less systematically—as they draft, plan, and revise. As you recall, Chapter 5 sets forth a similar pattern for approaching revision.

Research projects can also be seen and approached as problems. Just as you can apply a problem-solving approach to any writing assignment, so can you apply it to most research projects (see Chapter 14).

When you are asked to write a proposal, essay, or argument about solving a problem, as this chapter's Writing Project does, you can use the problem-solving method as a system of organization. The following principles for writing about problem solving may not apply to every instance, but they should help you convert answers to the questions in the problem-solving model into an effective essay.

1. Be aware of the needs of your audience. Your readers need specific details about background, history, special circumstances, and so forth, and they need to have this information presented in an order that they can understand. Begin your outline and draft by presenting this information in the clearest order you can devise. As you write and revise your essay, continually ask yourself, "Does my audience have all the information necessary to understand the point I am trying to make?"

2. Present all the information your audience needs in order to understand the problem before you begin to discuss alternative solutions.

3. Include a thesis statement indicating that you are going to discuss alternative solutions. If you are specifically writing an argument, be sure that your claim is debatable and that you give fair and equal consideration to opposing solutions.

4. Discuss each alternative solution by explaining what it would involve and by presenting its advantages and disadvantages. Provide enough specific information to allow your audience to see these advantages and disadvantages. Don't just say, "A program could be developed to help students see how to avoid date rape." Instead, begin a paragraph by saying: "Respected student leaders from honor societies and athletic teams could participate in a forum explaining how excessive drinking, certain drugs, and certain behaviors can lead to situations in which date rape might occur."

5. Present the alternative solutions in the order that will most help your audience comprehend them. In an argument, your rebuttal to each alternative should help your audience understand why you would select the one you did.

6. Conclude your essay by stating one solution, or some combination of solutions, and explain clearly why you chose it. If you have had time to implement the solution, describe whether or not it is working. If you have not yet implemented it, explain how you will determine whether or not it is working.

Writing Project: Proposing a Solution to a Problem

This chapter includes both readings and Thinking-Writing Activities that encourage you to familiarize yourself with the problem-solving model and the steps required for implementing it. Be sure to reread what you wrote for those activities, as you may be able to use some of that material when completing this project.

Write an essay in which you apply the five-step problem-solving method to a local, national, or international problem or to a personal problem. If you are analyzing a social problem, you will have to do some research and locate several articles that provide background information about and discussion of the problem. If you are analyzing a personal problem, you will enrich your paper by consulting some sources that pertain to it. Be sure to document all sources honestly and correctly in the format required by your instructor.

After you have drafted your essay, revise it to the best of your ability. Follow your instructor's directions about focus, length, scope, format, and so on.

Begin by considering the key elements in the Thinking-Writing Model in Chapter 1 on pages 7–9.

The Writing Situation

Purpose   You have a variety of purposes here. You can use this opportunity to learn about a major problem in order to arrive at the best possible solution—and thus become a better-informed citizen. You might be able to help solve the problem if you are involved in the situation. Also, you will be practicing the creative and critical thinking involved in the problem-solving model.

Audience   As usual, you will have several audiences for your paper. While working through the problem-solving model, you will be your own audience since in describing the problem and working through the alternative solutions, you will be determining the solution to the problem. As you begin to shape the answers to the model's questions into an essay, your audience will include readers other than yourself, so their needs should now occupy your attention.

Your classmates can be a valuable audience for peer review of a draft. They can react as intelligent readers who are not as knowledgeable as you are about the problem and its possible solutions but who can become interested as they read your description of it and your evaluation of the possible solutions. Finally, your instructor remains the audience who will judge how well you have analyzed the problem. As a writing teacher, he or she cares about a clear focus, logical organization, relevant details and examples, and accepted usage. Keep these factors in mind as you revise, edit, and proofread.

Subject   Problems are problems precisely because they are difficult to think about and to solve. Often this is true because we don't have enough accurate information to arrive at an intelligent solution. Working on this paper will encourage you to find good information and to think about viable alternative solutions. Since you will be deeply involved in the subject, select a problem that you care about, one that is challenging—but compelling—to write about.

Writer   This assignment provides you an opportunity to learn more about a problem that you care about but perhaps do not know enough about to propose a solid solution. You will use both online and print resources to increase your knowledge of the problem and give you the pleasure of having additional expertise about something significant. If your instructor asks or allows you to write about a personal problem, you might not have to do as much research, but you will have the opportunity to work out something that is of immediate concern. Equipped with the problem-solving model and the direction it provides, you should work as a confident writer as you complete this assignment.

The Writing Process

The following sections will guide you through the stages of generating, planning, drafting, and revising as you work on an essay about solving an important problem.

Try to be particularly conscious of both the critical thinking you do while working through the problem-solving model and the critical thinking and decision making you do as you revise.

Generating Ideas   You may find yourself in one of three situations:

1. If your instructor's directions specify that you must write about a particular local, national, or international problem, you must begin there. You might start by working through the problem-solving model and answering each question on the basis of your current knowledge. Then you will be able to see what additional information you need to know and thus will be aware of what to look for as you research the problem.

2. If your instructor's directions allow you to choose any important local, national, or international problem, you might begin by brainstorming (alone or with a group) a list of each of these types of problems. Then you can select the one that seems most important, the one that interests you most, or the one about which you are most informed.

3. If your instructor's directions allow you to write about a personal problem, you might begin by brainstorming a list of problems you now face. It might help to make three columns: school problems, work problems, and personal problems. Then you can pick one, preferably one that you have to solve soon and for which you would need to gather information to write about.

Whichever situation describes yours, once you have worked through the problem-solving model, you will almost certainly spot gaps in your information. Think about how much additional information you will need in order to evaluate each of the alternative solutions. Then locate that information, asking a librarian for assistance if necessary.

Once you have filled in all the gaps and selected a solution—and a means to determine whether it is working—you are ready to turn your attention to presenting your information to your audience.

Defining a Focus   Write a thesis statement that will make clear to your audience that you are going to explore a problem-solving situation. You might decide to write something like "After thinking about the problem carefully, I realize that I have only two possible choices." Or you might decide to name the possible choices: "Newton's possible solutions to its budget problem include raising more revenue, cutting the budget, or some combination of the two." You may even decide to announce your chosen solution in your thesis statement: "After carefully weighing the alternatives, raising more revenue while continuing to cut the budget appears to be the best choice."

Organizing Ideas   The five-step method for solving problems fits well with essay structure. Your description of the problem together with its necessary history and other background information will give you a working introduction which can include your thesis statement. Each of the alternative solutions, explained in as much detail as possible, along with its advantages and disadvantages, will provide one section of the body (one or more paragraphs). Your determination of the best solution and how it could be monitored will provide a conclusion.

Drafting   Begin with the easiest paragraph to draft. Keep your written answers to each part of the problem-solving model in front of you.

Remember to begin each section of the body with a topic sentence that names the alternative solution being considered. If you are discussing advantages or disadvantages in separate paragraphs, draft topic sentences that prepare your readers for that information—such as "Unfortunately, cutting the budget further will create serious disadvantages for many citizens." Then provide specific information.

You will, of course, have to determine the best order in which to arrange the section. Experiment until you find the one that seems most helpful to your audience.

Be sure to indicate the sources of your information. You do not have to use the correct citation format in a draft, but you do have to remind yourself exactly where you obtained the material so that you won't forget to cite it as you finish the paper.

In your conclusion, name the solution you have chosen. You may want to explain why you selected it if you think that will not be obvious to your audience. Remember to explain how you will evaluate the effectiveness of your solution.

Revising, Editing, and Proofreading   Use the step-by-step method in Chapter 6 on pages 152–154 to revise your essay and prepare a final draft.

The following essay shows how a student responded to this assignment—by writing about a social problem and citing according to Modern Language Association (MLA) format.

Student Writing

Joshua Bartlett's Writing Process

As a college student, Joshua witnessed firsthand the impact of irresponsible attitudes toward alcohol among his peers. Even though he and his classmates were required to participate in various "alcohol awareness" education programs as part of freshman orientation at their campus, Joshua knew that the programs were not engaging, urgent, or serious enough to get the attention of young people like himself. Because Joshua was writing a formal argument, and because he was required to use sources to provide information, Joshua did not include anecdotes from his own personal experience. Had he been writing an opinion piece for his campus newspaper, he might well have described a campus party in which a fellow student was seriously hurt in an alcohol-related incident; he might even have described his own experiences with binge drinking. Although that evidence would certainly be compelling, it might not be adequately objective for an academic audience—and you can imagine how it might undermine his credibility with his professor! Instead, Joshua provides objective evidence from a range of sources to support his well-thought-out approach to the problem of alcohol abuse on college campuses.

To structure his draft, Joshua used the Detailed Method for Solving Problems (pages 403–404).

Critical Thinking About Uncritical Drinking

by Joshua Bartlett

There is widespread agreement that excessive student drinking is a serious problem on many college campuses. However, there are different views on the causes of this problem and on the best solutions for it. In this paper I will present some perspectives on the problem of student drinking and conclude with suggestions on how to deal with this serious threat to student health and success.

Why do college students drink to excess? According to many experts, it is mainly due to the influence of the people around them. When most students enter college, they do not have a drinking problem. However, although few realize it, they are entering a culture in which alcohol is often the drug of choice, one that can easily destroy their lives. According to some estimates, 80 to 90 percent of the students on many campuses drink alcohol, and many of them are heavy drinkers (Engs 543). One study found that nearly 30 percent of university students consume more than 15 alcoholic drinks a week (Gerson A43). An additional study found that among those who drink at least once a week, 92 percent of the men and 82 percent of the women consume at least five drinks in a row, and half said they wanted to get drunk (Rosenberg 81).

The results of all this drinking are predictably deadly. Virtually all college administrators agree that alcohol is the most widely used drug among college students and that its abuse is directly related to emotional problems and violent behavior, ranging from date rape to death (Dodge, "Campus Crime" A33+; Leatherman A33). For example, at one university, a 20-year-old woman became drunk at a fraternity party and fell to her death from the third floor ("Clemson" A3). At another university, two students were killed in a drunk-driving accident after drinking alcohol at an off-campus fraternity house; the families of both students have filed lawsuits against the fraternity (Dodge, "Beer

Kegs Banned" A28). When students enter a college or university, they often become socialized into the alcohol-sodden culture of "higher education," at both formal and informal parties. The influence of peer pressure is enormous. Students often find it difficult to resist the pressures from their friends and fellow students to drink.

However, some observers of young people believe that, although peer pressure is certainly a factor in excessive college drinking, it is only one of a number of factors. They point out that the misuse of alcohol is a problem for all youth in our society, not just college students. For example, a recent study by the surgeon general's office shows that 1 in 3 teenagers consumes alcohol every week. This abuse leads to traffic deaths, academic difficulties, and acts of violence (Elson 64). Another study based on a large, nationally representative sample indicates that although college students are more likely to use alcohol, they tend to drink less per drinking day than nonstudents of the same age (Crowley 14); in other words, most college students who drink are more social drinkers than problem drinkers. One survey of undergraduate students found that college drinking is not as widespread as many people think (O'Hare 540). The conclusion from this data is that even though drinking certainly takes place on college campuses, it is no greater a problem than in the population at large.

Whatever the extent, the misuse of alcohol by college students is a serious situation with a number of probable causes. Certainly the influence of friends, whether in college or out, plays a role, as I've already discussed. But it is not the only factor. To begin with, there is evidence that family history is related to alcohol abuse. For example, one survey of college students found more problem drinking among students whose parents or grandparents had been diagnosed with alcoholism (Perkins and Berkowitz 237–240). Another study found that college students who come from families with high degrees of conflict display a greater potential for alcoholism (Pardeck 342–343).

Another important factor to consider in the misuse of alcohol by young people is advertising. A recent article entitled "It Isn't Miller Time Yet, and This Bud's Not for You" underscores the influence advertisers exert on the behavior of youth (Siler 52). By portraying beer drinkers as healthy, fun-loving, attractive young people, they create role models that many youths imitate. In the same way that cigarette advertisers used to encourage smoking among our youth—without regard for the health hazards—so alcohol advertisers try to sell as much booze as they can to whoever will buy it—no matter what the consequences.

A final factor in the abuse of alcohol is the people themselves. Although young people are subject to a huge number of influences, in the final analysis, they are free to choose what they want to do. They don't have to drink, no matter what the social pressures. In fact, many students resist these pressures and choose not to drink excessively or at all. In short, some students choose to think critically, while others choose to drink uncritically.

In order to encourage good judgment by more students and to minimize the causes of excessive drinking, I think that the following strategies could help solve the college alcohol problem. Only the last one has any disadvantages to be considered.

1. Colleges should have orientation and educational programs aimed at preventing alcohol abuse, and colleges should give top priority to campaigns against underage and excessive drinking.

2. Advertising and promotion of alcoholic beverages on college campuses and in college publications should be banned. Liquor distributors should not sponsor campus events. In addition, alcoholic beverage companies should be petitioned not to target young people in their ads.

3. Depending on the campus culture, colleges should ban or restrict alcohol use on campus and include stiff penalties for students who violate the rules.

4. Students at residential colleges should be able to live in substance-free housing, offering them a voluntary haven from alcohol, other drugs, tobacco, and peer pressure.

5. Colleges should create attractive alcohol-free clubs or pubs.

6. Colleges should ban the use of beer kegs, a symbol of cheap and easy availability of alcohol.

7. Fraternities should eliminate all alcohol-based contests or hazing torments.

8. Where possible, the on-campus drinking age should be reduced to 18 so that students won't be forced to move parties off-campus. At off-campus parties, there is no college control, and as a result, students tend to drink greater quantities and more dangerous concoctions.

Of course, this suggestion has the disadvantages of being in conflict with laws in many states or counties and also of seeming to encourage drinking by connecting it even more extensively with social events. But it has the advantages of control and of eliminating the attraction of what's forbidden.

In conclusion, alcohol abuse on college campuses is an extremely serious problem that is threatening the health and college careers of many students. As challenging as this problem is, I believe that it can be solved if students, teachers, and college officials work together in harmony and with determination to implement the suggestions made in this paper.

Works Cited

"Clemson Issues Ban on Parties Using Alcohol." <u>Chronicle of Higher Education</u> 31 Jan. 1990: A3.

Crowley, Joan E. "Educational Status and Drinking Patterns: How Representative Are College Students?" <u>Journal of Studies on Alcohol</u> 52.1 (1991): 10–16.

Dodge, Susan. "Campus Crime Linked to Students' Use of Drugs and Alcohol." <u>Chronicle of Higher Education</u> 17 Jan. 1990: A33+.

———"Use of Beer Kegs Banned by Some Colleges and National Fraternities." <u>Chronicle of Higher Education</u> 12 June 1991: A27–28.

Elson, John. "Drink Until You Finally Drop." <u>Time</u> 16 Dec. 1991 : 64.

Engs, Ruth C. "Family Background of Alcohol Abuse and Its Relationship to Alcohol Consumption Among College Students: An Unexpected Finding." <u>Journal of Studies on Alcohol</u> 51.6 (1990): 542–547.

Gerson, Mark. "30 Pct. of Ontario's Students Called 'Heavy Drinkers.'" <u>Chronicle of Higher Education</u> 12 April 1989: A43.

Leatherman, Courtney. "College Officials Are Split on Alcohol Policies; Some Seek to End Underage Drinking; Others Try to Encourage 'Responsible' Use." <u>Chronicle of Higher Education</u> 31 Jan. 1990: A33–35.

O'Hare, Thomas M. "Drinking in College: Consumption Patterns, Problems, Sex Differences and Legal Drinking Age." <u>Journal of Studies on Alcohol</u> 51.6 (1990): 536–541.

Pardeck, John T. "A Multiple Regression Analysis of Family Factors Affecting the Potential for Alcoholism in College Students." <u>Adolescence</u> 26.102 (1991): 341–347.

Perkins, H. Wesley, and Alan D. Berkowitz. "Collegiate COAs and Alcohol Abuse: Problem Drinking in Relation to Assessment of Parent and Grandparent Alcoholism." <u>Journal of Counseling and Development</u> 69.3 (1991): 237–240.

Rosenberg, Debra. "Bad Times at Hangover U." <u>Newsweek</u> 19 Nov. 1990: 81.

Siler, Julie Flynn. "It Isn't Miller Time Yet, and This Bud's Not for You." <u>Business Week</u> 24 June 1991: 52.

Alternative Writing Projects: Community Problems, Community Solutions

1. Prepare a concise PowerPoint presentation that addresses a specific campus or community problem and that proposes a specific solution. Your presentation should consist of no more than ten slides—about the time you would have to present your concerns at a public forum such as a student governance board or town council meeting. Plan to have two slides for each of the five steps of the Flexible Approach to Problem Solving in Figure 12.1. Your main purpose here is to be as concise as possible while issuing a call to action.

2. Apply the five-step problem-solving method to a local, national, or international problem that has already been successfully solved. You will be writing primarily in the past tense, and your purpose will be to describe *why* a particular solution worked so well. Your particular focus will be on step 5 of the process, Test the Solution, and your critical analysis will be focused on evaluation.

13

Constructing Arguments

Writing to Persuade

" I got into direct
confrontation with
everybody I love. "

—Lauryn Hill

Critical Thinking Focus: Using reasons, evidence, and logic

Writing Focus: Convincing an audience

Reading Theme: Arguments about important issues

Writing Project: Arguing a position on a significant issue

Principles of Argument

People who study communication, argument, and rhetoric believe that much of what we say, write, and post online can be defined as *argument* because most statements seek listeners' or readers' agreement with the ideas being presented. Unless someone is just saying "Hmmmm" or "Hello" or is asking a question only to obtain information, the purpose of his or her statement usually is to make a point, to convince the audience of its validity, and often to bring about change or action. Essays, letters, stories, poems, movies, web sites—and even paintings and clothes—can be considered arguments or have argumentative purposes.

This chapter is devoted to argument, even though most of your previous writing has had argumentative characteristics. Some writing is supposed to be predominantly argumentative, and you need to know how to create it and how to analyze it. Arguing effectively is essential to academic and professional success as well as to establishing your personal ethic. In addition, because both politicians and advertisers use argumentative techniques, you need to understand both valid and fallacious arguments in order to evaluate claims that people want you to accept.

THINKING-
WRITING
ACTIVITY

Analyzing Argumentative Writing

1. Select an essay or blog entry that you have written that you believe has an argumentative purpose. What is your thesis or claim? What specific evidence do you present? Who are your audiences? Does the paper advocate for any change or action? What is it?

2. Select a reading from a previous chapter that you consider argumentative. What is its claim? What evidence does it present? Who are its audiences? What change or action does it seek?

This chapter will introduce concepts related to argument, provide readings and Thinking-Writing Activities to help you grasp them, and conclude with a Writing Project that asks you to write a logical, well-organized argument for a position that is important to you. The chapter will also explore ways to construct effective arguments and to evaluate arguments.

FOUR QUALITIES
OF A CRITICAL THINKER
Philosopher Peter Singer

Curious   "Thought experiments" are used by scientists and philosophers to explore possibilities that might not otherwise be ethically or physically tested. As rigorously planned and carefully controlled as laboratory experiments, thought experiments allow the curious mind to explore its own limits. The Australian philosopher and ethicist Peter Singer, who teaches at Princeton University, uses thought experiments to explore such provocative social issues as animal rights, euthanasia, and the redistribution of wealth. One such thought experiment Singer has pursued proposes that our close genetic cousins the great apes (gorillas, chimpanzees, and orangutans) are entitled to "personhood" as defined by the United Nations.

Open-minded   Philosophers, as the great Socrates noted before being put to death by the Athenians, are "gadflies" that pique society from its complacency. To "speak truth to power" is also the role the pacifist religious group the Quakers define for themselves. Peter Singer's provocative, rigorous thinking challenges all of us to live ethically, in ways that do indeed shake the

comfortable material foundations of our culture. His call for ethical treatment of animals in his book *Animal Liberation*—most infamously, as a kind of thought experiment, by comparing the relative worth of an animal's life with that of a severely handicapped human infant—enraged many with the clarity of its moral distinctions. More recently, in a leading article in the *New York Times Sunday Magazine*, Singer called for a radical redistribution of personal wealth that far exceeds what most of us consider "charity." Singer's application of rigorous critical thinking to the most profound social problems (such as euthanasia, stemcell research, *in vitro* fertilization, and global poverty) spotlights the closed-minded approach of many prominent politicians and activists while urging all of us to open our minds to difficult questions.

Knowledgeable   Singer's philosophy is identified with Utilitarianism, a belief system which holds that the moral worth of an action depends on its consequences for other human beings. Singer's radical approach to Utilitarianism

Classical Concepts of Argument

The concepts that guide logical argument are central to Western culture. Articulated by the philosophers and rhetoricians of ancient Greece and Rome, they have been studied and applied for more than two thousand years. Even though emotions, gut reactions, and intuition cannot be brushed aside—because they are so human—logical thinking and the resulting structured arguments are expected in business, government, and scholarship. Therefore, as a college composition student, you have both practical and historical reasons for giving attention to principles of argument or rhetoric.

The Greek philosopher Aristotle, in his famous work the *Rhetoric* and in other writings on logic, is the source of many concepts basic to our ideas of argument. But even Aristotle, more than three hundred years B.C.E., was responding to earlier works on rhetoric; and to this day, those who have followed him have modified and redefined his ideas and those of other classical rhetoricians. Those concepts include *ethos*, the character of the speaker or writer; *pathos*, the effect on the audience; and *logos*, the logic and substance of an argument. All three are powerful aspects of any argument. You

extends beyond humans to all animals, including those species most commonly used by humans for food and for medical experimentation. However, Singer is not so rigid in his philosophy as to refuse to acknowledge the occasional benefits of animal research. In 2006, he outraged many animal rights activists when he publicly stated that a research experiment seeking a cure for Parkinson's disease involved fewer than 100 monkeys yet directly and positively impacted the lives of 40,000 human Parkinson's sufferers was a justifiable experiment. Although this view is not inconsistent with his arguments in *Animal Liberation*, some radical activists would rather abolish all animal experiments than ask the specific moral questions Singer suggests. In an interview with *The Daily Princetonian*, Singer reiterated that fundamental question: "You should ask yourself: Do I think this experiment is so important that I would be able to perform it on a human being at a similar mental level if that alternative were open to me?"

Creative Like Temple Grandin (see pages 191–195 in Chapter 7), Singer's work in *Animal Liberation* is revolutionary not only in that it argues for the ethical treatment of animals (ethical as compared to the way humans treat each other)

but in the great imaginative and empathic leap required to describe animal consciousness. Both Grandin and Singer understand that, in order to argue effectively for better treatment of animals, they needed to make the consciousness and the self-awareness of animals recognizable to a human audience. Neither Grandin nor Singer relies on the creative writer's strategy called "personification," familiar to most of us from children's stories and movies like *Babe* or *Charlotte's Web*. Instead, Singer and Grandin rely on objective science and experiential observation to advance stunning new insights into how animals think, and why humans must be more aware and protective of them.

Online Study Center
Peter Singer
Visit the Online Study Center for *Critical Thinking, Thoughtful Writing* at *college.hmco.com/pic/ chaffeeCTTW4e* to learn more about Peter Singer.

should try to identify them in arguments that others address to you, and you should work hard to achieve effectiveness with each in arguments that you write.

Responsible writers try to present themselves as knowledgeable, reasonable, trustworthy, and sensitive to the tone appropriate to the situation—that is, to achieve their desired *ethos*. Critical thinkers are able to build clear and logical discussions, avoid fallacious reasoning, and handle opposing viewpoints courteously but firmly—that is, achieve their desired *logos*. A good combination of *logos* and *ethos* will engage audiences and elicit thoughtful responses—that is, achieve the desired *pathos*.

Some other centuries-old concepts are the techniques for generation or discovery of ideas, the arrangement of sections of an argument, the thinking methods of deduction and induction, techniques for refutation, and moral concerns about the use of rhetorical power for honorable ends.

Links to the Thinking-Writing Model   The classical rhetoricians were concerned with oral communication; literacy for all, print, and electronics were yet to come. Speech is, of course, still essential to communication, both face to face and via electronic media. This book concentrates on writing, but the ancient concepts have never gone out of use, and they function well to promote effective writing. The topics in the Thinking-Writing Model (pages 7–9 in Chapter 1) that is the foundation of this book demonstrate contemporary applications of many classical principles.

Notice how subject, purpose, audience, and writer connect in multiple ways with the concepts of *logos, pathos*, and *ethos*. If *logos* means both content and the logic of its presentation, *logos* connects with the Thinking-Writing Model's topics of subject, defining a thesis, and organizing ideas as well as with thinking critically. *Pathos* connects, of course, with the Thinking-Writing Model's audience and purpose; *ethos*, with the writer and also with the editing and proofreading stages of revising since a well-finished paper gives a good impression of its writer.

The classical concepts of *discovery* and *arrangement* are clearly connected to the Thinking-Writing Model's notions of thinking creatively, generating ideas, organizing ideas, and drafting.

Responsible Rhetoric   Today, the words *argument* and *rhetoric* are regularly used in conversation and in the media differently from the ways in which they are used in this chapter. Popularly, *argument* often means "a quarrel," and *rhetoric* is often used to mean "insubstantial or misleading language" (which is connected to the classical concerns about the use of rhetorical power for honorable ends). In this chapter, *rhetoric* means "the use of the best means of persuasion." We will discuss argument throughout the chapter and define the term on page 458.

Modern Concepts of Argument

In the twenty-first century, much attention has been paid to argument, at least partly because both mass media and education have extended their reaches. More communication and analyses of it from different points of view continue to provide new ways of thinking about arguments. Three important modern approaches are the *Toulmin method*, analyzing the effects of electronic communication, and various consensus-building strategies.

Toulmin's Method   College composition students are often introduced to some concepts that have developed from the work of the British professor of philosophy Stephen Toulmin. Professor Toulmin's ideas about argument can be applied to almost any argument, no matter how it is constructed. Concepts important to the Toulmin method are *claim* and *qualified claim, grounds, warrants*, and *backings*.

You already understand *claim* because *thesis, main point*, and *conclusion* are other ways to say it. You already understand *grounds* because it means *reasons, evidence, support, examples*, and *data*. You have established a thesis and provided support for it in most papers that you have written for this course.

As you improved your ability to develop a good thesis and studied Chapter 8's material on definition and classification, you were learning about qualified claims or qualifiers. A *qualified claim* is an accurately worded claim, one that establishes the category to be discussed. A qualified claim is not exaggerated or overly general. For example, you might not want to claim that "*Teenagers* should not be allowed to drive after midnight." Instead, you might claim that "People *under eighteen years* of age should not be allowed to drive after midnight." That way you would be acknowledging the probable differences in experience and maturity between a sixteen-year-old and an eighteen- or nineteen-year-old and showing that the overly general word *teenager* needs qualification. Properly qualified claims produce effective arguments.

Warrants are the assumptions, principles, premises, and beliefs that are the foundations of most arguments. This is an important concept to understand because warrants are not always stated. However, warrants provide the connection between a claim and its grounds, and they enable the acceptance or rejection of an argument. Here's a simple example:

Claim: People should brush and floss their teeth regularly.

Grounds: Dentists tell us that brushing and flossing will help prevent tooth decay and gum disease.

Warrants: People do not want their teeth to fall out. They do not want to have toothaches or ugly decayed teeth. People do not want drilling, fillings, and dentists' bills.

Backings are larger principles that support warrants. They are the foundations of the foundations. A backing for the warrants about brushing and flossing is the generally accepted principle of self-interest. People are concerned about their own health, appearance, and finances; people are concerned about situations that affect them. Therefore, the backing of the principle of self-interest supports the warrants about what people don't want, which support and connect the claim and grounds about dental hygiene.

This use of the word *warrant* is related to its use in law enforcement—a warrant for an arrest or a search warrant, which authorizes actions. The warrants of an argument are also related to the sources of beliefs (see Chapters 3 and 11). In addition, warrants are related to the premises used in deductive reasoning, which you will study later in this chapter.

Just as you need to understand the sources of your beliefs and those of others, you need to understand the warrants behind the arguments that you make and that people present to you. You need to recognize them when they are stated as part of an argument and search for them if they are not stated.

Looking at these U.S. Army recruitment materials should help you understand warrants. Can you see some assumptions, principles, beliefs—or warrants—that are behind the approaches taken by the poster and by the web site as they try to convice young people to enlist?

I Want *You* for U.S. Army

BY JAMES MONTGOMERY FLAGG (1877–1960)

Born in New York in 1877, James Montgomery Flagg had an illustrious career as an illustrator for both books and magazines, but he is especially remembered today as the creator of the famous Uncle Sam recruiting poster. Flagg made his first sale to a well-known magazine at the age of twelve, and by fifteen had joined the staffs of *Life* and *Judge* magazines. Among his best-known illustrations were those for the *Jeeves* novels of P.G. Wodehouse. *Leslie's* Magazine asked him to paint "Uncle Sam" for its July 4, 1916, issue. When World War I broke out, the U.S. government asked him to create a recruiting poster featuring that figure. Flagg created forty-five other posters for the government during that war. In 1980, Flagg was elected to the Society of Illustrators Hall of Fame.

QUESTIONS FOR ACTIVE READING

1. What is your reaction to the figure of Uncle Sam? How do you read the gesture he is making? At whom is he pointing?

2. What is your reaction to the verbal text of the poster? Is it intimidating? Commanding?

3. Who was the "you" he wanted? In 1917, who would Uncle Sam not have been recruiting?

QUESTIONS FOR THINKING CRITICALLY

1. What are some assumptions, principles, beliefs—or warrants—that provide a foundation for the argument presented by this poster?
2. Why are warrants about service and patriotism powerful?
3. What is the meaning or symbolism of the fact that Uncle Sam appears to be an older white man?

www.goarmy.com

U.S. ARMY

The United States Army, the oldest branch of the U.S. Military, has its origins in the Continental Army commanded by George Washington during the Revolutionary War. During the 1800s, administration was centralized and the army became more professional, with career officers and standard operating procedures. The army has been responsible, together with the other branches of the armed services, for national defense as well as for certain policing functions within the country. Today the army is staffed with volunteers, so recruitment efforts are extremely important in order to maintain a force large enough for any contingency.

QUESTIONS FOR ACTIVE READING

1. What are the demographics in the two images shown on the web site? How do they compare to the 1917 poster?

2. What does the idea of "Paths of Strength" suggest to you?

3. While both this and the 1917 poster are recruitment devices, what different appeals do they make to potential enlistees? Consider the web site's use of "leverage" and "skills."

QUESTIONS FOR THINKING CRITICALLY

1. What are some assumptions, principles, beliefs—or warrants—that provide a foundation for the argument presented by this web site? Visit the U.S. Army web site at www.goarmy.com to gather additional information for your analysis.

2. Why are warrants for self-development powerful? Can you identify any backings for the warrants you found?

3. List the warrants you found for the poster and the web site. See if you and your classmates found the same ones.

For additional examples of how visuals can be used to provoke, persuade, and argue, see Thinking Critically About Images on pages 2-1 to 2-8.

Argument and Electronic Media   There is currently much speculation about the effects of electronic communication on arguments. Of course, different kinds of electronic technologies raise different questions. Obviously, podcasting transmits spoken arguments, and television uses both sound and visuals to produce its well-known impact on audiences. Computers do so many things that analysis is difficult—but exciting. Visuals, sounds, and texts can be combined in countless ways, so distinctions among written, pictorial, and spoken arguments are blurred.

Many characteristics of online communication can affect arguments. The movement of linking means that logical connections are not always made. The speed at which ideas are transmitted and the rapidity with which some information can change can cause confusion and raise questions about credibility. Many people tend to write more informally in email than on paper, and such informality can change the tone of an argument for better or for worse. The rapid transmission of email can quickly conclude an argument or cause it to go on longer.

On the other hand, many Internet texts are simply posted versions of printed material or have been composed in a traditional manner. You need to be aware of the ways in which electronic and written communications differ as well as the ways in which argumentative concepts operate similarly in various media.

More Links to the Thinking-Writing Model   Just as the concepts of classical rhetoric connect with components in the Thinking-Writing Model, so do the modern concepts. A claim, especially a qualified claim, clearly relates to defining a thesis. Grounds are important for generating and organizing ideas. Warrants and backing connect significantly with audience, purpose, and the writer. Writers need to understand their own assumptions and basic beliefs as they develop arguments in order to think critically about what they are presenting. Also, since assumptions and basic beliefs can differ in various communities, writers need to consider how the warrants beneath an argument might affect their audiences. Consensus-building approaches relate most obviously to reaching an audience but also pertain to purposes and to organizing ideas.

Achieving Mutual Understanding   Some people believe that the purpose of argument is to coerce or to "win." As we have seen in this book, though, critical thinkers strive to develop the most informed understanding, which involves trying to fully appreciate other perspectives. Instead of attempting to prove others wrong, a more desirable purpose is to arrive at a clear and mutual understanding about the issue being discussed. Sometimes people are so far apart in their convictions that agreement cannot be reached and an impasse (or worse) occurs. At other times people "agree to disagree" and work around their differences; but if agreement does come, good feelings can result in progress, problem solving, or other desired achievements. By thinking critically, you can inspire others to think critically as well so that all parties are working together to achieve the clearest understanding rather than splintering into adversarial factions. In the cartoon below, the man on the right seems to be pursuing conflict rather than mutual understanding. What are the disadvantages of such an approach? Can you think of some more constructive strategies that he could use?

"*I shall now punch a huge hole in your argument.*"

Considering Other Points of View   People do not argue about things on which they agree, nor do they argue about concepts that are accepted as facts. For example, it's not likely that an argument would arise over the relative lengths of a meter and a yard. A measuring tape takes care of the question. However, people do argue about whether the United States should adopt the metric system. Arguments develop because people have different opinions about issues.

You should not ignore opposing points of view when you are making an argument. Sometimes, people will ignore other ideas and present one-sided cases—as in most advertisements, some sermons, many political statements, and attempts at pushing proposals through. But in reasoned arguments, you should address varying ideas in order to demonstrate your grasp of the issue and also to try to achieve mutual understanding and, if possible, consensus or agreement.

GUIDELINES FOR ADDRESSING OTHER POINTS OF VIEW

1. *Restate the other claim to show that you understand it*. This is often easier to do in a face-to-face discussion than in writing, but it is important in any argument. Sometimes misunderstandings can be uncovered by this technique. Restatements can also lead to finding common ground. A restatement should be made in a nonjudgmental, respectful tone.

2. *Find areas of agreement, or common ground, at the outset of the argument*. This, too, is sometimes easier to do in a face-to-face discussion than in writing. It is a technique often used in negotiations and mediation. However, in a written argument, you should try whenever you can to establish common ground with those who have other beliefs about the issue that you are addressing. Often identifying warrants can lead parties to find areas of agreement. When people see that they agree about some parts of an issue, they can establish mutual respect and then examine their differing opinions carefully.

3. *Identify which differences are important and which are trivial*. This, too, is more easily done when people talk with each other, but it is also something that can be attempted in written argument. Here, too, identifying warrants sometimes clarifies the significance of some parts of an argument.

4. *Concede points that you cannot uphold*. Sometimes you will have to concede that some of your opponents' ideas are so strong that you cannot counter them, even if you do not agree with them.

5. *Compromise*. At times, accepting a middle position or a partial achievement of your purpose is better than arguing for its complete achievement.

6. *Rebut*. This means to refute or to present opposing evidence. Rebuttal often seems necessary. It is part of the debate tradition and is important in legal arguments, but it maintains adversarial positions. If you have to rebut an opposing point, do so courteously.

Thinking Critically About Images
Visual Persuasion

The images in this color portfolio were created as persuasive rhetoric. To be effective, their creators kept in mind audience and purpose, and they also drew upon such rhetorical strategies as *ethos, logos,* and *pathos;* satire; awareness of audience; and a nuanced sense of the different types of meanings. The following images are all "public service advertisements," created for various nonprofit or governmental advocacy groups by professional advertising agencies who often work for a reduced fee or even for free. Public service announcements (PSAs) appear on television and on the radio; in magazines and newspapers; and, increasingly, as web sites, podcasts, YouTube clips, and other news media outlets. They work to *persuade* people to take a stand, to change a behavior, or to participate in community and civic life. Unlike other kinds of written arguments, obviously, an effective PSA has a very limited amount of time or space in which to make its point and has a great deal of competition for your attention.

Each of the PSAs that follows draws upon strategies used by critical readers and thoughtful writers to create effective, brief, attention-getting persuasive arguments. In your academic and professional career, you will often be called upon to present information using several different kinds of media and combining text and visual images (and, increasingly, sound and video) in innovative and effective ways. Your instructor for this course might ask you to create, alone or as a collaborative project, a PSA that addresses a specific issue discussed in a reading elsewhere in this book.

Most of the PSAs that follow were created by the Ad Council. Since 1942, this nonprofit collective of major advertising agencies has worked to deliver messages related to public health, community life, and educational issues to the broadest possible audience. Some Ad Council campaigns that you might remember include Smokey Bear's "Only you can prevent forest fires," an American Indian approaching a polluted creek as a single tear rolls down his face, the slogans "Friends don't let friends drive drunk" and "A mind is a terrible thing to waste,"and, of course, the talking crash test dummies. A link to the Ad Council's site can be found at the Online Study Center.

"WHEN I HAVE AN ASTHMA ATTACK I FEEL LIKE A FISH WITH NO WATER."

—JESSE, AGE 5

ATTACK ASTHMA. ACT NOW.
 1-866-NO-ATTACKS ♻EPA
WWW.NOATTACKS.ORG

Room to Breathe

Childhood asthma is an American urban epidemic, with an estimated 5.5 children under the age of 15 afflicted. There is no cure for asthma, but with medical care and parental education, the condition can be managed.

THINKING CRITICALLY ABOUT THE IMAGE

1. Chapter 6 explores the ways in which effective writers use figurative language to craft their message. What specific figurative strategy is featured in this public service announcement? Why is this strategy persuasive?

2. This asthma education and prevention campaign also featured television and radio spots, which you can view at the web site listed above. Shown here is a version of the campaign created specifically for magazines. In what kinds of magazines would you expect this campaign to appear, and why? Who is the primary audience for this campaign?

Spoiled Yappy Dog for President?

The Federal Voting Assistance Program, which traditionally helps United States armed forces personnel and American citizens working outside of the United States to vote in federal elections, has turned its attention in recent years to promoting domestic voter turnout among 18- to 24-year-olds. In 2006, the FVAP's "Pay Attention and Vote" campaign used a web site (above), instant messenger icons, podcasts, YouTube spots, and other nontraditional media to reach out to this demographic.

THINKING CRITICALLY ABOUT THE IMAGE

1. How would you describe the overall tone of this web site? Why would this approach be effective for younger voters?

2. In what ways is a web page more interactive than a print ad (such as the "Attack Asthma" campaign on the previous page)?

3. If you are in this campaign's target demographic, does this web site persuade you to "pay attention" and to take action? Why, or why not?

No Musician Left Behind?

In an era of high-stakes testing on basic skills, arts education has been severely cut back or even eliminated in many public school districts. Americans for the Arts, which sponsored this public service advertisement, is a nonprofit group that advocates greater public and government support for and sponsorship of community-based arts programs.

THINKING CRITICALLY ABOUT THE IMAGE

1. Who is the target audience for this campaign, and how does it get that audience's attention?

2. What persuasive strategies does the text of this ad use, and what kind of action does it urge the audience to take?

3. The argument made by this campaign depends on a clear warrant. In your own words, what is that warrant? What backing is provided for that warrant? (See Chapter 13, pages 449–450 for more information about warrants and backing.)

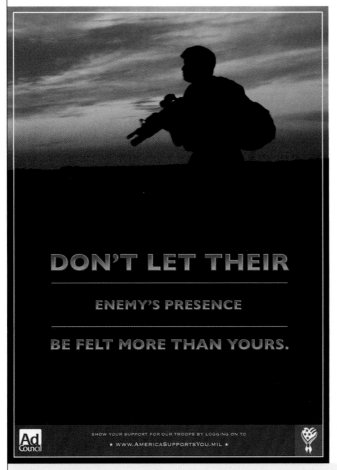

DON'T LET THEIR

ENEMY'S PRESENCE

BE FELT MORE THAN YOURS.

SHOW YOUR SUPPORT FOR OUR TROOPS BY LOGGING ON TO
★ WWW.AMERICASUPPORTSYOU.MIL ★

All He Can Be

In late 2004, the U.S. Department of Defense began the "America Supports You" initiative, designed to boost the morale of troops and their families by offering civilians opportunities to show their support. The television, radio, print, and online ads direct people to a web site (www.AmericaSupportsYou.Mil) where they can learn about ways to support military families.

THINKING CRITICALLY ABOUT THE IMAGE

1. Chapter 4 explores different types of meaning and how they apply to images as well as words. In your own words, describe the perceptual meaning of this image and how it relates to the connotative meaning of words like *enemy*.

2. Does this ad make a specifically political argument? What is its persuasive message?

3. Chapter 8 discusses how to use concepts to classify. Review pages 247–251, and then visit the America Supports You web site. In a brief essay, develop concepts that describe the different kinds of suggestions for troop support offered at the site, and classify the suggestions according to those concepts.

Trees Don't Grow On ... Trees ...

The National Parks Conservation Association is a private advocacy group that for almost ninety years has raised funds for, and awareness of, the preservation of American national parkland. This print ad campaign appeared in national magazines in 2006.

THINKING CRITICALLY ABOUT THE IMAGE

1. What is the visual pun on which the effectiveness of this ad depends? That is, what kind of visual genre or format does it "borrow" to make its point?

2. How does the connotative meaning of this image—the visual pun on which it is based—enhance the urgency of its message?

3. Chapter 10 discusses causal relationships. What kind of causal relationship(s) does the imagery in this advertisement suggest?

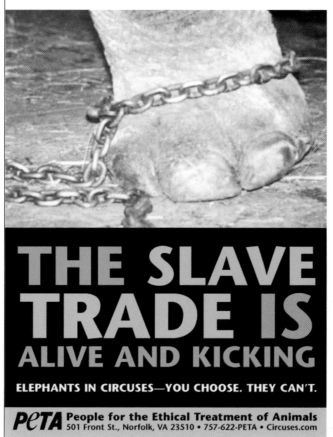

THE SLAVE TRADE IS ALIVE AND KICKING

ELEPHANTS IN CIRCUSES—YOU CHOOSE. THEY CAN'T.

PeTA **People for the Ethical Treatment of Animals**
501 Front St., Norfolk, VA 23510 • 757-622-PETA • Circuses.com

They Never Forget

People for the Ethical Treatment of Animals (PETA) is an animal-rights advocacy group that opposes all forms of animal exploitation and abuse—including the eating of meat, the use of animals for medical and other experiments, the wearing of leather and fur, and the captivity of animals solely for entertainment purposes. PETA also educates pet owners in caring for their animals and organizes relief efforts for animals abandoned during natural catastrophes such as Hurricane Katrina.

THINKING CRITICALLY ABOUT THE IMAGE

1. This particular ad makes a striking—and perhaps controversial—analogy. What is that analogy? How effective is this strategy for getting attention and persuading an audience to take action?

2. What is it about the composition of this photograph that makes it a particularly effective choice for this argument? Describe, in detail, as many nuances of the photograph as you can. What is the main issue of this ad's argument, and what specific supporting reasons and evidence does this photograph provide?

Your brother turns eight years old only once.
But you got high, came home and wrecked his party.
Weed can make you do stupid things like that.

freevibe.com

|r|e|g|r|e|t|
THE ANTI-DRUG.

Dude, Where's My Present?

The federal Office of National Drug Control Policy creates educational materials and public service announcements in a variety of media. In 1998, with bipartisan support, Congress created the National Youth Anti-Drug Media Campaign with the goal of preventing and reducing youth drug use.

THINKING CRITICALLY ABOUT THE IMAGE

1. How can you tell that this ad is specifically targeted towards younger people?

2. Does this advertisement rely on *logos, ethos,* or *pathos*—or some combination of these elements? Explain your answer, making reference to specific components of this advertisement.

7. *Be sensitive to different argumentative philosophies.* Some cultures, some groups, and some individuals prefer indirect methods of argumentation while others want to get to the point quickly. Sometimes a direct approach is seen as rude or overly aggressive; sometimes an indirect approach is seen as weak, sneaky, or confusing. In the United States, directness is often considered as the best approach. If your audience is from a different culture, however, be sure that you understand that culture's argumentative style.

THINKING-
WRITING
ACTIVITY

Establishing Agreement

1. Find a classmate who disagrees with you about something—for example, the quality of a specific television show, a political principle, or a controversy at your college. Each of you should then write a brief statement about your position. Next, read each other's statements.

2. See if you can establish some areas of agreement. Can you identify warrants for your position and for your classmate's? Where might you compromise? Determine whether any differences are not important. Do either of you have to concede a point?

Analyzing the Audience You learned long ago that you should speak and write differently to different audiences. You use one kind of vocabulary and tone with your friends and another with your grandparents. You write formally in a job application letter and informally in an email to your sister describing what you did last weekend.

The suggestions for completing every Writing Project in this book include some discussion of your audience because it is one of the major components of any writing situation and therefore is prominently featured in the Thinking-Writing Model. However, consideration of audience is especially important when you are writing an argumentative paper, particularly if you hope to effect some change or action. Also, remember that you may have more than one audience. Here are some questions to ask yourself about the audiences for any argument you write:

- Who is interested in this issue?
- What concerns do these interested people have?
- What is their level of education or expertise?
- What related issues interest them?
- How much time might they give to reading my argument?
- Who can do something about the situation?
- Who is opposed to my point of view?

- What are the opposing claims?
- What format, tone, or method of presentation will be effective with this audience?

Can you think of other questions to ask about audiences?

Going Too Far   Paying attention to audiences does not mean telling an audience only what it wants to hear or manipulating ideas just to reach a certain audience. Some advertisers and politicians mislead audiences in such ways. Pandering to an audience is one of the ways in which rhetoric can be misused. Responsible writers and speakers accommodate their audiences honestly.

Recognizing Arguments

Two Friends Argue: Should Marijuana Be Legalized?

Consider the following dialogue about whether marijuana should be legalized. Have you participated in such exchanges? In what ways do dialogues like this differ from written argument? How do such dialogues provide a starting point for written arguments?

DENNIS: Have you read about the medical uses of marijuana—that people who have cancer, AIDS, and some other diseases might be helped by smoking? I think some doctors are prescribing it, and some states may be changing their laws. This might change people's thinking more than all those discussions about unenforced laws, unjust punishments, and victimless crimes that have been going on since my uncles were in college.

CAROLINE: Well, I agree that we need to think about drug laws. But I hope you agree that we have to be careful. Drugs pose a serious threat to the young people of our country. Look at all the people who are addicted to drugs, who have their lives ruined, and who often die at an early age of overdoses. And think of all the crimes people commit to support their drug habits. So I don't know if anything that's illegal now should be legalized, . . . and the laws should be enforced.

DENNIS: That's ridiculous. Smoking marijuana is nothing like using drugs such as heroin or even cocaine. It follows that smoking marijuana should not be against the law if it's harmless and maybe even helpful to some sick people.

CAROLINE: I don't agree. Although marijuana may not be as dangerous as some other drugs, it does affect things like a driver's ability to judge distances. And smoking it surely isn't good for you. And I don't think that anything that is a threat to your health should be legal.

DENNIS: What about cigarettes and alcohol? We know that they are dangerous. Medical research has linked smoking cigarettes to lung cancer, emphysema, and heart disease. Alcohol damages the liver and also the brain. Has anyone ever proved that marijuana is a threat to our health? And even if it does turn out to be somewhat unhealthy, it's certainly not as dangerous as cigarettes and alcohol.

CAROLINE: That's a good point. But to tell you the truth, I'm not so sure that cigarettes and alcohol should be legal. And in any case, they are legal. The fact that cigarettes and alcohol are bad for your health is not reason to legalize another drug that can cause health problems.

DENNIS: Look—life is full of risks. We take chances every time we cross the street or climb into our cars. In fact, with all the irresponsible drivers on the road, driving could be a lot more hazardous to our health than any of the drugs around. Many of the foods we eat can kill. For example, red meat contributes to heart disease, and artificial sweeteners can cause cancer. The point is, if people want to take chances with their health, that's up to them. And many people in our society like to mellow out with marijuana. I read somewhere that over 70 percent of the people in the United States think that marijuana should be legalized.

CAROLINE: There is a big difference between letting people drive cars and letting them use dangerous drugs. Society has a responsibility to protect people from themselves. People often do things that are foolish if they are encouraged to or given the opportunity. Legalizing something like marijuana encourages people to use it, especially young people. It follows that many more people would use marijuana if it were legalized. It's like society saying "This is all right—go ahead and use it."

DENNIS: I still maintain that marijuana isn't dangerous. It's not addictive—like heroin is—and there is no evidence that it harms you. Consequently, anything that is harmless should be legal.

CAROLINE: Marijuana may not be physically addictive like heroin, but I think that it can be psychologically addictive because people tend to use more and more of it over time. I know a number of people who spend a lot of their time getting high. What about Carl? All he does is lie around and get high. This shows that smoking it over a period of time definitely affects your mind. Think about the people you know who smoke a lot—don't they seem to be floating in a dream world? How are they ever going to make anything of their lives? As far as I'm concerned, a pothead is like a zombie—living but dead.

DENNIS: Since you have had so little experience with marijuana, I don't think that you can offer an informed opinion on the subject. And anyway, if you do too much of anything, it can hurt you. Even something as healthy as exercise can cause problems if you do too much of it. But I sure don't see anything wrong with toking up with some friends at a party or even getting into a relaxed state by yourself. In fact, I find that I can even concentrate better on my school work after taking a little smoke.

CAROLINE: If you believe that, then marijuana really has damaged your brain. You're just trying to rationalize your drug habit. Smoking marijuana doesn't help you concentrate—it takes you away from reality. And I don't think that people can control it. Either you smoke and surrender control of your life, or you don't smoke because you want to retain control. There's nothing in between.

DENNIS: Let me point out something to you. Because marijuana is illegal, organized crime controls its distribution and makes all the money from it. If marijuana were legalized, the government could tax the sale of it—like cigarettes and alcohol—and use the money for some worthwhile purpose. For example, many states have legalized gambling and use the money to support education. In fact, the major tobacco companies have already copyrighted names for different marijuana brands—like "Acapulco Gold." Obviously they believe that marijuana will soon become legal.

CAROLINE: The fact that the government can make money out of something doesn't mean that they should legalize it. We could also legalize prostitution or muggings and then tax the proceeds. Also, even if the cigarette companies are prepared to sell marijuana, that doesn't mean that selling it makes sense. After all, they're the ones who are selling us cigarettes. . . .

Can you think of other views on the subject of legalizing marijuana? Can you think of other subjects about which such dialogues are taking place now?

The previous discussion illustrates two people's engaging in dialogue, the systematic exchange of ideas. Discussing issues with others encourages you to be mentally active, to ask questions, to view issues from different perspectives, to develop reasons that support conclusions, and to write convincingly.

This chapter focuses on the last quality of thinking critically—supporting claims with reasons—because when we offer reasons to support a conclusion, we are presenting an argument, the essence of most college and business writing. An *argument* is a form of thinking in which certain statements (reasons or evidence) are offered to support another statement (a conclusion or a claim).

In the dialogue, Dennis presents the following argument for legalizing marijuana:

Reason: Marijuana might help some people who have serious diseases.

Reason: Marijuana isn't dangerous like heroin and cocaine.

Reason: Governments could tax the sale of marijuana as they do cigarettes and alcohol.

Claim: Marijuana should be legalized.

Expanding the definition of *argument*, we can define the main ideas that make up an argument. *Reasons, evidence*, or *grounds* are statements that support another statement (a conclusion, claim, or thesis), justify it, or make it more probable. The *claim, thesis*, or *conclusion* is a statement that explains, asserts, or predicts on the basis of statements (known as reasons) that are offered as evidence to support it.

The type of thinking that uses argument—presenting reasons to support conclusions—is known as *reasoning*, and it is a type of thinking explained throughout this book. We are continually trying to explain, justify, and predict through the process of reasoning, and often we must present such thinking in writing.

Of course, our reasoning—and that of others—is not always correct. The reasons someone offers may not really support the claim they are intended to, a conclusion may not really follow from the reasons stated, or the reasons may be questionable or wrong. These difficulties are illustrated in a number of the arguments contained in the previous discussion on marijuana.

Nevertheless, whenever we accept a conclusion as likely or true on the basis of certain reasons, or whenever we offer reasons to support a conclusion, we are using arguments—even if our reasoning is weak or faulty and needs improvement.

Let's return to the discussion about marijuana. After Dennis presents one argument, Caroline presents another, giving reasons that lead to a conclusion that conflicts with the one Dennis has offered.

Reason: Drugs pose a very serious threat to the young people of our country.

Reason: Many crimes are committed to support drug habits.

Claim: As a result, society has to have drug laws and enforce them to convince people of the seriousness of the situation.

Which of Dennis's or Caroline's arguments do you see as reasonable? Which seem weak or faulty?

English, like other languages, provides guidance in our efforts to identify reasons and conclusions. Certain key words, or cue words, signal that a reason is being offered to support a conclusion or that a conclusion is being drawn on the basis of certain reasons. After you read the following list, go back to the dialogue and see how and when Dennis and Caroline use these words.

The following are some commonly used cue words for reasons and conclusions.

USEFUL
WORDS FOR
RECOGNIZING
AND WRITING
ARGUMENTS

Cue Words Signaling Reasons

since	in view of
for	first, second
because	in the first (second) place
as shown by	may be inferred from
as indicated by	may be deduced from
given that	may be derived from
assuming that	for the reason that

Cue Words Signaling Conclusions

therefore	then
thus	it follows that
hence	thereby showing
so	demonstrates that
(which) shows that	allows us to infer that
(which) proves that	suggests very strongly that
implies that	you see that
points to	leads me to believe that
as a result	allows us to deduce that
consequently	

Of course, identifying reasons, claims, and conclusions involves more than looking for cue words. The words and phrases just listed do not always signal reasons and conclusions, and in many cases people present arguments without using cue words. Cue words, however, do alert us that an argument is being offered. Careful use of cue words helps us to write effective arguments.

THINKING-
WRITING
ACTIVITY

Analyzing a Dialogue

Write responses to the previous dialogue. Then share your responses with classmates and note where you agree and disagree.

1. Review the discussion and underline cue words that signal when Dennis and Caroline are giving reasons or announcing conclusions.

2. Identify one argument in the dialogue that you find convincing and one that seems unconvincing. Write your reasons for your opinions, referring to specific places in the dialogue.

The following two essays discuss the issue of whether drugs should be legalized. The first passage is by essayist and novelist Gore Vidal. The second is by *New York Times* editor and columnist A. M. Rosenthal.

"Drugs"

BY GORE VIDAL (b. 1925)

An amazingly prolific writer of novels, short stories, plays, and essays, Gore Vidal holds a unique place in American life and letters. Among his many publications are the satiric novels *Myra Breckinridge* and *Live from Golgotha*, the play *Visit to a Small Planet*, and the screenplays for *The Catered Affair* and *Suddenly Last Summer*. He won the National Book Award in 1993 for *United States: Essays, 1952–1992*. Often compared to both Henry James and Mark Twain, two vastly different writers, Vidal is known for his satiric wit, his humor, and his willingness to say what he thinks without worrying about the consequences.

It is possible to stop most drug addiction in the United States within a very short time. Simply make all drugs available and sell them at cost. Label each drug with a precise description of what effect—good and bad—the drug will have on the taker. This will require heroic honesty. Don't say that marijuana is addictive or dangerous when it is neither, as millions of people know—unlike "speed," which kills most unpleasantly, or heroin, which is addictive and difficult to kick.

For the record, I have tried—once—almost every drug and liked none, disproving the popular Fu Manchu theory that a single whiff of opium will enslave the mind. Nevertheless many drugs are bad for certain people to take and they should be told why in a sensible way.

Along with exhortation and warning, it might be good for our citizens to recall (or learn for the first time) that the United States was the creation of men who believed that each man has the right to do what he wants with his own life as long as he does not interfere with his neighbor's pursuit of happiness. (That his neighbor's idea of happiness is persecuting others does confuse matters a bit.)

This is a startling notion to the current generation of Americans. They reflect a system of public education which has made the Bill of Rights, literally, unacceptable to a majority of high school graduates who now form the "silent majority"—a phrase which that underestimated wit Richard Nixon took from Homer who used it to describe the dead.

5   Now one can hear the warning rumble begin: If everyone is allowed to take drugs, everyone will and the GNP will decrease, the Commies will stop us from making everyone free, and we shall end up a race of zombies, passively murmuring "groovy" to one another. Alarming thought. Yet it seems most unlikely that any reasonably sane person will become a drug addict if he knows in advance what addiction is going to be like.

Is everyone reasonably sane? No. Some people will always become drug addicts just as some people will always become alcoholics, and it is just too bad. Every man, however, has the power (and should have the legal right) to kill himself if he chooses. But since most men don't, they won't be mainliners either. Nevertheless, forbidding people things they like or think they might enjoy only makes them want those things all the more. This psychological insight is, for some mysterious reason, perennially denied by our governors.

It is a lucky thing for the American moralist that our country has always existed in a kind of time-vacuum: We have no public memory of anything that happened before last Tuesday. No one in Washington today recalls what happened during the years alcohol was forbidden to the people by a Congress that thought it had a divine mission to stamp out Demon Rum—launching, in the process, the greatest crime wave in the country's history, causing thousands of deaths from bad alcohol, and creating a general (and persisting) contempt among the citizenry for the laws of the United States.

The same thing is happening today. But the government has learned nothing from past attempts at prohibition, not to mention repression.

Last year when the supply of Mexican marijuana was slightly curtailed by the Feds, the pushers got the kids hooked on heroin and deaths increased dramatically, particularly in New York. Whose fault? Evil men like the Mafiosi? Permissive Dr. Spock? Wild-eyed Dr. Leary? No.

10   The Government of the United States was responsible for those deaths. The bureaucratic machine has a vested interest in playing cops and robbers. Both the Bureau of Narcotics and the Mafia want strong laws against the sale and use of drugs because if drugs are sold at cost, there would be no money in it for anyone.

If there was no money in it for the Mafia, there would be no friendly playground pushers, and addicts would not commit crimes to pay for the next fix. Finally, if there was no money in it, the Bureau of Narcotics would wither away, something they are not about to do without a struggle.

Will anything sensible be done? Of course not. The American people are as devoted to the idea of sin and its punishment as they are to making money—and fighting drugs is nearly as big a business as pushing them. Since the combination of sin and money is irresistible (particularly to the professional politician), the situation will only grow worse.

QUESTIONS FOR ACTIVE READING

1. State Vidal's thesis or claim in one sentence. Where did he place it? Is this placement effective?
2. Identify at least two specific reasons that he gives to support his thesis.
3. Can you identify any warrants and backings for his arguments?
4. Vidal is known for his satire. Which, if any, sentences do you think are not intended to be taken literally? Why do you think so?

QUESTIONS FOR THINKING CRITICALLY

1. Do you agree with Vidal's argument that drugs should be legalized? Why or why not?
2. Do you agree with Vidal's comparison of the Bureau of Narcotics and the Mafia? How do you think agents for the Bureau would react to this comparison? How might members of the Mafia react?
3. What can you infer about Vidal's attitude toward American politics?

"The Case for Slavery"

BY A. M. ROSENTHAL (1922–2006)

Born in Sault Ste. Marie, Ontario, A. M. Rosenthal came to New York as a small child and became a reporter for the *New York Times* while still in college. After covering the then-new United Nations, he served as a foreign correspondent in India, Switzerland, Japan, and Poland. He received the Pulitzer Prize for his reporting from Poland in 1960. He has also won several Overseas Press Club awards, Front Page prizes, and a variety of other awards for his books and magazine articles. He was the author of "On My Mind," a column for the *New York Times* and was a contributing writer for several news and political periodicals.

Across the country, a scattered but influential collection of intellectuals is intensely engaged in making the case for slavery.

With considerable passion, these Americans are repeatedly expounding the benefits of not only tolerating slavery but legalizing it:

It would make life less dangerous for the free. It would save a great deal of money. And since the economies could be used to improve the lot of the slaves, in the end they would be better off.

The new antiabolitionists, like their predecessors in the nineteenth century, concede that those now in bondage do not themselves see the benefits of legalizing their status.

5   But in time they will, we are assured, because the beautiful part of legalization is that slavery would be designed so as to keep slaves pacified with the very thing that enslaves them!

The form of slavery under discussion is drug addiction. It does not have every characteristic of more traditional forms of bondage. But they have enough in common to make the comparison morally valid—and the campaign for drug legalization morally disgusting.

Like the plantation slavery that was a foundation of American society for so long, drug addiction largely involves specifiable groups of people. Most of the enchained are children and adolescents of all colors and black and Hispanic adults.

Like plantation slavery, drug addiction is passed on from generation to generation. And this may be the most important similarity: Like plantation slavery, addiction can destroy among its victims the social resources most valuable to free people for their own betterment—family life, family traditions, family values.

In plantation-time America, mothers were taken from their children. In drug-time America, mothers abandon their children. Do the children suffer less, or the mothers?

10   Antiabolitionists argue that legalization would make drugs so cheap and available that the profit for crime would be removed. Well-supplied addicts would be peaceful addicts. We would not waste billions for jails and could spend some of the savings helping the addicted become drug-free.

That would happen at the very time that new millions of Americans were being enticed into addiction by legalization—somehow.

Are we really foolish enough to believe that tens of thousands of drug gang members would meekly steal away, foiled by the marvels of the free market?

Not likely. The pushers would cut prices, making more money than ever from the ever-growing mass market. They would immediately increase the potency and variety beyond anything available at any Government-approved narcotics counters.

Crime would increase. Crack produces paranoid violence. More permissiveness equals more use equals more violence.

15   And what will legalization do to the brains of Americans drawn into drug slavery by easy availability?

Earlier this year, an expert drug pediatrician told me that after only a few months babies born with crack addiction seemed to recover. Now we learn that stultifying behavioral effects last at least through early childhood. Will they last forever?

How long will crack affect neurological patterns in the brain of adult crack users? Dr. Gabriel G. Nahas of Columbia University argues in his new book, *Cocaine: The Great White Plague*, that the damage may be irreversible. Would it not be an act of simple intelligence to drop the legalization campaign until we find out?

Then why do a number of writers and academicians, left to right, support it? I have discussed this with antidrug leaders like Jesse Jackson, Dr. Mitchell Rosenthal of Phoenix House, and William J. Bennett, who search for answers themselves.

Perhaps the answer is that the legalizers are not dealing with reality in America. I think the reason has to do with class.

20   Crack is beginning to move into the white middle and upper classes. That is a tragedy for those addicted.

However, it has not yet destroyed the communities around which their lives revolve, not taken over every street and doorway. It has not passed generation to generation among them, killing the continuity of family.

But in ghetto communities poverty and drugs come together in a catalytic reaction that is reducing them to social rubble.

The antiabolitionists, virtually all white and well-to-do, do not see or do not care. Either way they show symptoms of the callousness of class. That can be a particularly dangerous social disorder.

QUESTIONS FOR ACTIVE READING

1. State Rosenthal's thesis or claim in one sentence. Where did he place it? Is this placement effective?
2. Identify at least two specific reasons that he gives to support his thesis.
3. Can you identify any warrants and backings for his argument?
4. What impression does Rosenthal convey of himself? How is this similar or different from the impression conveyed by Vidal?

QUESTIONS FOR THINKING CRITICALLY

1. Do you agree with Rosenthal's argument that drugs should not be legalized? Why or why not?
2. Do you agree with Rosenthal's point that differences of opinion on this topic have to do with class? How might someone counter that point?

Arguments as Inferences

When you construct arguments, you are constructing views of the world by means of your ability to infer. As you saw in Chapter 11, inferring is a thinking process used to reason from what one already knows (or believes to be the case) to acquire new knowledge or beliefs. This is usually what you do when you construct arguments: work from reasons you know or believe to draw conclusions based on them.

Just as you can use inferences to make sense of different types of situations, you can also construct arguments for different purposes. As already noted, some people believe in using arguments to coerce or to "win." A more desirable goal is to use arguments to clarify issues, develop mutual understanding, and if possible, bring about agreement or consensus on the issue being discussed. Notice how you can work toward agreement when you construct arguments to do any of the following: decide, explain, predict, persuade.

Constructing Arguments to Decide

Reason: Throughout my life, I've always been interested in all kinds of electricity.

Reason: There are many attractive job opportunities in the field of electrical engineering.

Claim: Electrical engineering would be a good major for me.

Audience: Myself, my parents, my academic adviser, the scholarship office

Constructing Arguments to Explain

Reason: I was delayed leaving my house because my dog needed emergency walking.

Reason: There was an unexpected traffic jam caused by motorists slowing down to view an overturned chicken truck.

Claim: Therefore, I couldn't help being late for our appointment.

Audience: The person waiting for me

Constructing Arguments to Predict

Reason: Some people will always drive faster than the speed limit allows, no matter whether the limit is 55 or 65 mph.

Reason: Car accidents are more likely to occur at higher speeds.

Claim: A reinstated 65 mph speed limit will result in more accidents.

Audience: Legislators, voters, drivers

Constructing Arguments to Persuade

Reason: Chewing tobacco can lead to cancer of the mouth and throat.

Reason: Young people sometimes begin chewing tobacco because they see ads that feature sports heroes they admire doing it.

Claim: Ads for chewing tobacco should be banned.

Audience: Parents, voters, legislators, advertising agencies, media executives

Evaluating Arguments

To construct good arguments, you must be skilled at evaluating the effectiveness, or soundness, of arguments already constructed. You must investigate the components of an argument to determine the soundness of the argument as a whole.

1. How true are the reasons being offered to support the conclusion?

2. To what extent do the reasons support the conclusion, claim, or thesis—or to what extent does the conclusion follow from the reasons offered?

Truth: How True Are the Supporting Reasons?

The first aspect of an argument that you must evaluate is the truth of the reasons being used to support a conclusion. Ask yourself these questions:

* What specific evidence is the writer offering to illustrate each reason?
* Are any reasons consistent with my own experience?
* Are the reasons based on reliable sources?
* Are the reasons relevant to the subject of the argument?

You use these questions and others like them to analyze the reasons offered and to determine how true they seem to be. As you saw in Chapter 11, evaluating the kinds of beliefs used as reasons in arguments is a complex challenge.

Validity: Do the Reasons Support the Claim or Conclusion?

In addition to determining whether the reasons are true, evaluating arguments involves investigating the relationship between the reasons and the claim or the conclusion (which becomes the thesis of a piece of writing that argues a position on an issue).

When the reasons support the conclusion in such a way that the conclusion follows from them, you have a *valid argument*. If, however, the reasons do not support the conclusion—that is, if the conclusion does not follow from the reasons being offered—you have an *invalid argument*. Remember that the words *valid* and *true* do not have the same meaning. You must first evaluate the truth of a reason, then determine its validity.

One way to focus on the concept of *validity* is to assume that all the reasons in an argument are true, then try to determine how probable they make the conclusion. The following is an example of one type of valid argument.

Reason: Anything that is a threat to our health should not be legal.

Reason: Marijuana is a threat to our health.

Conclusion: Therefore, marijuana should not be legal.

This is a valid argument because if we assume that the reasons are true, its conclusion does necessarily follow from them.

Of course, we may not agree that either or both of the reasons are true; in that case, we would not agree with the conclusion. Nevertheless, the structure of the argument is valid. This particular form of thinking is known as *deduction*.

Here is a different type of argument.

Reason: As part of a project in my social science class, we selected one hundred students in the school to be interviewed. We took special steps to ensure that these students were representative of the student body as a whole (total students: 4,386). We asked the students whether they thought that the United States should actively try to overthrow foreign governments that it disapproves of. Of the one hundred students interviewed, eighty-eight said that the United States should definitely not be involved in such activities.

Conclusion: We can conclude that most students in this school believe that the United States should not be engaged in attempts to actively overthrow foreign governments that it disapproves of.

This is a persuasive argument because if we assume that the reason is true, that reason provides strong support for the conclusion. In this case, the key part of the reason is the statement that the one hundred students selected were representative of the entire student population at the school. To evaluate the truth of the reason, we might want to investigate the procedure used to select the one hundred students in order to determine whether this sample was in fact representative of all the students. (Notice that the conclusion carefully said "in this school." It did not imprecisely say "most students.")

This particular form of thinking is an example of *induction*.

Soundness: Is the Argument Both True and Valid?

When an argument includes both true reasons and a valid structure, the argument is considered sound. When an argument has either false reasons or an invalid structure, however, the argument is considered unsound.

Figure 13.1 reminds us that in terms of arguments, *truth* and *validity* are not identical concepts. An argument can have true reasons and an invalid structure or have false reasons and a valid structure. In both cases the argument is unsound. Consider the following argument:

Reason: Professor Davis believes that megadoses of vitamins can cure colds.

Reason: Davis is a professor of computer science.

Conclusion: Megadoses of vitamins can cure colds.

This argument is obviously not valid: even if we assume that the reasons are true, the conclusion does not follow. Professor Davis's expertise with computers does not provide her with special knowledge about nutrition and medicine. This invalid thinking is neither structurally nor factually acceptable. It is clearly not a sound argument. Now, consider this argument:

Reason: For a democracy to function most effectively, the citizens should be able to think critically about the major social and political issues.

Reason: Education plays a key role in developing critical thinking abilities.

Conclusion: Therefore, education plays a key role in ensuring that a democracy is functioning most effectively.

FIGURE 13.1   Sound and Unsound Arguments

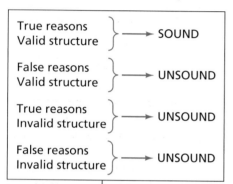

A good case could be made for the soundness of this argument because the reasons are persuasive and the argument structure is valid. Of course, someone might counter that one or both of the reasons are not completely true, which illustrates an important point about the arguments we construct and evaluate. Many of the arguments we encounter in life fall somewhere between complete soundness and complete unsoundness because often we are not sure if our reasons are completely true. Throughout this book, we have found that developing accurate beliefs is an ongoing process and that our beliefs are subject to clarification and revision. As a result, the conclusion of any argument can be only as certain as the reasons supporting the conclusion.

The following two articles present different points of view about "end of life" issues. A variety of topics are now receiving attention: passive euthanasia, or nontreatment; active euthanasia, or mercy killing; assisted suicide; the work of Dr. Kevorkian (nicknamed "Dr. Death"); the hospice movement (termed "Dr. Dignity"); the "right to die" laws of the state of Oregon and of the Netherlands.

These articles use different argumentative approaches. The first gives a human example, uses description, and employs *pathos*. The second, taken from the web site of the Hemlock Society, emphasizes logical argument, using many thinking patterns discussed in this book: contrast, comparison, definition, and causal analysis. It also refers to the fallacies *false dichotomy* and *slippery slope*.

"In No Hurry for Next Leg of the Journey"

BY DAVID GONZALEZ

Before joining the *New York Times* in 1990, David Gonzalez wrote for *Newsweek* from 1983 to 1990. A native of the Bronx, he often featured locations there in the "About New York" column he wrote in the *Times* from 1995 to 1999. He then became Caribbean and Central American bureau chief for the *Times* and, while based in Miami, reported on the political and social struggles in

Haiti and the changes in Cuba after the fall of the Soviet Union, as well as other issues through-out Central America. He returned to New York and writes the "Citywide" column for the paper as well as other news and feature articles. He has received numerous awards, including Columbia University's Mike Berger Award in 1992.

The waning afternoon sunlight slipped into the rooms of Calvary Hospital in the Bronx. Outside, the trees looked like propped-up sticks, gray, crooked and ready for winter. Inside, it was warm and quiet, in anticipation of a bigger chill. Michael Burke lay in his bed, the latest stop in a medical journey that started in September with treatment at another hospital for a cancer that spread from his colon to his lung and brain.

"The doctors think I'm terminal," he said. "I think I'm terminal."

Calvary Hospital bills itself as the country's only specialty hospital for adults in the final stages of advanced cancer. It is not a hospice, since its patients require constant medical attention to stabilize them and ease their pain. Doctors tend to nearly every aspect of a patient's physical and emotional comfort as well as helping families that are emotionally battered by the disease.

Doctors at Calvary, which started almost 100 years ago in a Greenwich Village house, see their work as a counterpoint to those who advocate "a definitive medical response" to terminal illness. In plain English, they offer the dying patient an alternative to assisted suicide. It's not a place that Dr. Jack Kevorkian, who was ordered this week to stand trial on murder charges for his role in a suicide shown on television, has ever visited.

Mr. Burke, 45, a mechanical contractor, understands how frustration and despair drive some people to suicide, even if they have received the best care. But he does not consider that an option, and he is alarmed by Dr. Kevorkian's increasingly brazen attempts to force the issue.

"He seems seriously aggressive about it," Mr. Burke said. "But what constitutes the envelope of what he considers candidates for euthanasia would become bigger and bigger. I think people need to make it difficult for guys like that."

Calvary operates under the auspices of the Roman Catholic Archdiocese of New York, so its opposition to suicide hews to church teaching. Its patients—200 on any given day—represent many faiths. In rare cases, critically ill patients arrive at the hospital asking for a quick end. More common are feelings of depression or emotional suffering, which, if not addressed by doctors, psychiatrists and social workers, could lead to desperate yearnings.

"Depression is more painful than physical pain," said Dr. Michael Brescia, the hospital's medical director. "Emotional suffering is the absence of love. This is a time when people have to say final farewells to their children. There are no more holidays. No future. You're not in this life, you're on the outside looking in. Everybody else has a life and you don't have one. Most people, if they ask for suicide, it's from the emotional aspects of this disease."

Those emotional hardships, doctors said, aren't made any easier by the difficulties patients have in persuading their health maintenance organizations to allow them to seek appropriate care in other hospitals, or at least let them check into Calvary when death is near. Dr. James Cimino, director of Calvary's palliative care institute, said the medical run-around has been exploited by proponents of assisted suicide, who present euthanasia as a dignified response to the indignities of the health care bureaucracy.

10   "Kevorkian forced us as a society to ask why people want to die prematurely," Dr. Cimino said. "But we should have confronted it before."

He knows that other doctors—good, well-meaning ones—also support euthanasia. But each day he sees patients who resist an early demise. "Maybe it's something about the nature of the person that they have this suffering, yet they don't request suicide," he said. "I don't want to get into the philosophy of that."

But Michael Burke does.

"Kevorkian is assuming there's nothing out there after this," he said. "I assume there is. I think that's where we part company."

He said that as long as he was comfortable—and he was—he had no problem. Suicide, he said, would be unfair to his wife and two children.

15   "I wouldn't want them to believe Daddy had the option of pushing this button and leaving," he said. "I'm not trying to squeeze every last moment. But if I can live for a week and see my son one more time, I would. As opposed to seeing Kevorkian this afternoon. Not that I think they would let him in the door here."

He gave a small smile and a thumbs-up sign. The gesture was his own definitive response.

QUESTIONS FOR ACTIVE READING

1. What is the central claim or thesis of Gonzalez's argument? Where did he place it? Is this placement effective?

2. How does he develop his thesis? What kind of evidence does he use?

3. What warrants and backings underlie his argument?

QUESTIONS FOR THINKING CRITICALLY

1. Although Calvary Hospital is not a hospice, its philosophy of easing the pain of dying patients and their families is practiced by hospices. Have you ever known anyone who entered into hospice care? What was that person's experience with hospice?

2. If given a terminal diagnosis, would you seek hospice care for yourself or for a loved one? Why or why not?

"Hospice Care or Assisted Suicide: A False Dichotomy"

BY JOHN L. MILLER

John L. Miller believes in the value of hospice care but also believes that it may not be for everyone. In the following article, reprinted from *American Journal of Hospice and Palliative Care* and later available on the Hemlock Society's web site (www.hemlock.org), Miller argues for certain forms of physician-assisted suicide. He refers both to Dr. Kevorkian, nicknamed "Dr. Death" because he has assisted in patient suicides, and to the hospice program, nicknamed "Dr. Dignity."

For the past few months, I have been reading, with great interest, the editorials and updates regarding the "Dr. Dignity" program. I would like to offer a different perspective. The view expressed here is one which comes from within the hospice movement, but which supports legal reforms to allow physician-assisted suicide.

Specifically, the legal reforms I am referring to would require many important safeguards which Dr. Kevorkian does not implement. A responsible assisted suicide would require free and repeated requests by the patient, with a substantial interval between requests. The involvement of a third party in a suicide ethically requires us to make sure the suffering is not temporary, or due to lack of information or obtainable (and desired) treatment. Informed consent, confirmed by two independent medical practitioners, would be required only after all available alternatives have been offered and explored. The fine details of these conditions are, of course, much debated. This article, however, looks not at these details, but at the ethical justification for such a position.

To begin, I applaud the promotion of hospice care in the media. Promoting compassionate palliative care to the general public is essential, especially if one believes that physician-assisted suicide should be made available in the context of offering choices.

But the "Dr. Dignity" program does not promote hospice care as just a choice. It promotes it as the only moral choice and, in doing so, sets up a false dichotomy. If one were to believe the editorials in this journal, one might mistakenly conclude that all proponents of legal reform were either historically naive, ignorant of hospice and palliative care, or both. And while some people may be guilty of this lack of information, many others are not.

5   Many people who have devoted their lives to the care of the dying are not opposed to physician-assisted suicide. Such people believe it should be available as one of several options, and, therefore, do not believe that promoting hospice[s] and advocating for the availability of regulated physician-assisted suicide are contradictory goals.

Understanding this position begins with an understanding of how and why assisted suicide and euthanasia differ. Not surprisingly, most people in the general public do not know the difference between the two terms; opponents of assisted suicide often deliberately obscure these differences by using the terms interchangeably.

But, many people support legalized assisted suicide for the same reason that they oppose euthanasia: the first offers us life choices and power over our own bodies, while the second takes control and choices away from us. Hospice care also offers people an essential choice, and so on we campaign to make it available, and to make it better.

The problem with hospice care, however, is that in spite of our best public relations efforts, it doesn't always take away people's pain, and it isn't always wanted.

Parallels are often drawn between this debate and the one on abortion rights. These parallels are indeed apt. And since the war of words is as confusing there as it is here, let's blow away the fog: Mainstream proponents of legalized, assisted suicide advocate for its availability not because they are pro death, but because they believe in a person's right to control his/her life, and the right of a person to a death which s/he feels is dignified (even if we don't agree that it is).

10   In the assisted suicide debate, opponents sometimes use logical fallacies and historical misinformation to point fear at the wrong menace. It is easy to quell dissent in this way.

Take the argument, for instance, that assisted suicide will lead to euthanasia, eugenics, or even genocide. For a "slippery slope" argument to be valid, there must be a connection between an initial minor social ill and a potentially more serious one—an ill which, when amplified incrementally, creeps up on us and finally, has catastrophic, societal results. This connection usually exists because the minor social ill is of the same kind as the more serious one, and because taking one step makes the next one easier.

In this case, it is not valid to link assisted suicide to the more serious threat of euthanasia, eugenics, and genocide simply because they all involve third parties in the death of another person. One of these things is not like the others. To link them in this way is as ridiculous as saying that electing a government to make state decisions leads to fascism. Just because both involve state rule doesn't mean that giving a government power inevitably leads to its absolute power. A slippery slope to fascism happens when the checks which make governments representative and accountable are subtly removed, one by one.

Fear of a societal erosion of personal autonomy is a valid concern. The response must be to give people more choices, not fewer; more autonomy, not less. The legal reforms I offer for debate move us further away from fascism, not towards it.

If assisted suicide were an act, which in some small way diminished a person's power of self-determination, then one might make an argument that allowing such an act pushes us down a slippery slope towards more serious violations of this kind. The slow whittling away of self-determination can creep up on us, if we don't watch out.

15   And so, concerns should be expressed when laws which erode people's rights are created, or when existing rights legislation is revoked. Concern should be expressed when states give power to medical practitioners to override informed consent.

In remembering history, let's remember that this is exactly what occurred in Nazi-occupied Europe. Under the Nazis, "physician-assisted suicide" was never any such thing. It was always murder, the taking of someone's life against his/her will. Doctors assisted in these murders in a context where Jews and other minorities had no rights of any kind, and where neither quality of life, nor life itself were valued.

It is indeed conceivable that personal freedoms may be eroded in North America. But the top of the slippery slope is not assisted suicide. If anything, the "slope" is the loss of personal autonomy, and it exists already. We are teetering on the edge, and proponents of assisted suicide are reaching out to help pull us back up, not to push us down.

If, in North America, the right to control our bodies and our lives is further eroded in any significant way, physician-assisted suicide would certainly never become available. Women's reproductive rights would also be targets (they already are), as would informed consent in any medical decision, including one involving hospice care.

Dressing up hospice care is a panacea, and the only moral alternative to physician-assisted suicide is unhelpful, and inaccurate.

20   This issue is not simplistic. Reforms must happen in a context where we continue to promote alternatives, where we understand that several things can be true at the same time. Hospice care is wonderful for some. Physician-assisted suicide is a valid choice for others. People will always seek to influence the vulnerable and the sick. With freedoms come responsibilities.

Disabled rights activists, and indeed those of us in the hospice movement, know that it is not just the state which can coerce people to make unwanted or unnecessary choices. Family members, friends, [and] peers can also put subtle pressures on loved ones to choose a path which is better for the well person than for the sick.

But these pressures work both ways, unfortunately. Just as there are those who pressure people they love to end it all, there are also those who push people unduly to "hang on until the end." Knowing when to step back, knowing when to move forward, finding this balance in supporting the dignity of those we care for—this is the precious challenge with which we are all entrusted in hospice care.

We must be wary of the danger of falling to the extremes. At one end, are those who value life at all cost—even at the expense of quality. At this end, preventing another person from ending his/her life regardless of the circumstances is seen as acceptable. At the other end are those who put quality of life first, but who also believe that they can know how good or bad someone else's life is. People who think this way can be equally dangerous, because they feel no qualms about either pressuring us to end our life if they feel we are too miserable, or pressuring us to hang on, if they decide for us that our life is still worth living.

When we fall to the extremes, we take choices away from those who[m] we believe we are helping. But, there is a middle ground. When we aim for that middle ground, we all win.

QUESTIONS FOR ACTIVE READING

1. What is the central claim or thesis of Miller's argument? Where did he place it? Is this placement effective?

2. How does he develop his thesis? What kind of evidence does he use?

3. What warrants and backings underlie his argument?

QUESTIONS FOR THINKING CRITICALLY

1. Have you ever known anyone who chose physician-assisted suicide? How would you feel if a loved one chose it?

2. Miller refers to the fallacies *false dichotomy* and *slippery slope*. What do these terms mean? Do you think he uses them correctly here?

3. Gonzalez focused on a particular patient while Miller argued historical, political, and ethical issues. Which technique is more effective? Why?

Forms of Argument

Arguments occur in many forms, but two major thinking methods—deduction and induction—provide the foundations for most arguments and also influence the organizational structure of arguments. They can be seen as (1) moving from general principles to specific applications and (2) moving from specific examples to general conclusions. Deduction and induction are seldom applied in "pure" or textbook ways in real-life arguments. Instead, they often are compressed or combined, so recognizing and analyzing their uses can sometimes be difficult. In fact, some teachers and students feel that studying them separately is more a mental exercise than a practical activity. However, as a critical thinker, a writer of arguments, and an analyst of arguments, you need to understand these principles.

Deductive Reasoning

The deductive argument is the one most commonly associated with the study of logic. Though it has a variety of valid forms, they all share one characteristic: if you accept the supporting reasons (also called *premises*) as true, you must also accept the conclusion as true. A *deductive argument* is an argument form in which one reasons from premises that are known or assumed to be true to a conclusion that necessarily follows from these premises. For example, consider the following famous deductive argument:

Reason/Premise: All persons are mortal.

Reason/Premise: Socrates is a person.

Conclusion: Therefore, Socrates is mortal.

In this example of *deductive reasoning*, accepting the premises of the argument as true means that the conclusion necessarily follows; it cannot be false. Many deductive arguments, like this one, are structured as *syllogisms*, an argument form that consists of two supporting premises and a conclusion. There are also, however, a large number of invalid deductive forms, one of which is illustrated in the following defective syllogism:

Reason/Premise: All persons are mortal.

Reason/Premise: Socrates is a person.

Conclusion: Therefore, all persons are Socrates.

This example is deliberately absurd, but people do shift terms in these ways and think things such as "all tall people should play basketball" just because basketball players are usually tall. Despite the variety of invalid deductive structures, once you become aware of the concept of *validity*, you should be able to detect invalidity.

One way to do this is through the application of a general rule. Whenever we reason by using the form illustrated by the valid Socrates syllogism, we are using the following argument structure:

Premise: All A (people) are B (mortal).

Premise: S is an A (Socrates is a person).

Conclusion: Therefore, S is B (Socrates is mortal).

This basic argument form is valid no matter what terms are included. For example:

Premise: All politicians are untrustworthy.

Premise: Bill White is a politician.

Conclusion: Therefore, Bill White is untrustworthy.

Notice again that with any valid deductive form, if we assume that the premises are true, we must accept the conclusion. Of course, in this case it is unlikely that the first premise is true.

Although we are not always aware of doing so, we use this basic type of reasoning whenever we apply a general rule. For instance:

Premise: All eight-year-old children should be in bed by 9:30 P.M.

Premise: You are an eight-year-old child.

Conclusion: Therefore, you should be in bed by 9:30 P.M.

Often we present this kind of reasoning in an abbreviated form called an *enthymeme*, which assumes the first premise: You should be in bed by 9:30 because you're an eight-year-old child; Bill White is a politician, so he's untrustworthy.

Describe an example from your own experience in which you use this deductive form, both as a syllogism and as an enthymeme.

Other Deductive Forms

Deductive arguments, or syllogisms and enthymemes, come in many other forms, most of which have been named by logicians. At some point in your college education, you should consider taking a course in critical thinking or logic to learn about as many kinds of reasoning as you can. This chapter provides only an introduction.

Affirming the Antecedent

Premise: If I have prepared thoroughly for the final exam, I will do well.

Premise: I prepared thoroughly for the exam.

Conclusion: Therefore, I will do well on the exam.

When we reason like this, we are using the following argument structure:

Premise: If A (I have prepared thoroughly), then B (I will do well).

Premise: A (I have prepared thoroughly).

Conclusion: Therefore, B (I will do well).

Like all valid deductive forms, this form is valid no matter what specific terms are included. For example:

Premise: If the Democrats register 20 million new voters, they will win the presidential election.

Premise: The Democrats have registered more than 20 million new voters.

Conclusion: Therefore, the Democrats will win the presidential election.

As with other valid argument forms, the conclusion will be true if the reasons are true. Although the second premise in this argument expresses information that can be verified, the first premise would be more difficult to establish.

Denying the Consequent

Premise: If Michael were a really good friend, he would lend me his car for the weekend.

Premise: Michael refuses to lend me his car for the weekend.

Conclusion: Therefore, Michael is not a really good friend.

When we reason in this fashion, we are using the following argument structure:

Premise: If A (Michael is a really good friend), then B (He will lend me his car).

Premise: Not B (He won't lend me his car).

Conclusion: Therefore, not A (He's not a really good friend).

Again, like other valid reasoning forms, this form is valid no matter what subject is being considered. As always, the truth of the premises must be evaluated.

Disjunctive Syllogism

Premise: Either I left my wallet on my dresser, or I have lost it.

Premise: The wallet is not on my dresser.

Conclusion: Therefore, I must have lost it.

When we reason in this way, we are using the following argument structure:

Premise: Either A (I left my wallet on my dresser) or B (I have lost it).

Premise: Not A (I didn't leave it on my dresser).

Conclusion: Therefore, B (I have lost it).

This valid reasoning form can be applied to any number of situations and still yield accurate results. For example:

Premise: Either your stomach trouble is caused by what you are eating, or it is caused by nervous tension.

Premise: You tell me that you have been very careful about your diet.

Conclusion: Therefore, your stomach trouble is caused by nervous tension.

To determine the accuracy of the conclusion, we must determine the accuracy of the premises. If they are true, then the conclusion must also be true.

All of the preceding basic argument forms can be found not only in informal daily conversations but also at more formal levels of thinking. They appear in academic disciplines, in scientific inquiry, in debates on social issues, and so on. Many other argument forms—both deductive and inductive—also constitute human reasoning. By sharpening your understanding of these ways of thinking, you will be better able to make sense of the world by constructing and evaluating effective arguments.

THINKING-
WRITING
ACTIVITY

Evaluating Deductive Arguments

Analyze the following brief arguments by completing these steps.

1. Summarize the reasons and conclusions given.
2. Identify which, if any, deductive argument forms are being used.
3. Evaluate the truth of the reasons that support the conclusion.

For if the brain is a machine of ten billion nerve cells and the mind can somehow be explained as the summed activity of a finite number of chemical and electrical reactions, [then] boundaries limit the human prospect—we are biological and our souls cannot fly free. —Edward O. Wilson, *On Human Nature*

The extreme vulnerability of a complex industrial society to intelligent, targeted terrorism by a very small number of people may prove the fatal challenge to which Western states have no adequate response. Counterforce alone will never suffice. The real challenge of the true terrorist is to the basic values of a society. If there is no commitment to shared values in Western society—and if none are imparted in our amoral institutions of higher learning—no increase in police and burglar alarms will suffice to preserve our society from the specter that haunts us—not a bomb from above but a gun from within. —James Billington, "The Gun Within"

To fully believe in something, to truly understand something, one must be intimately acquainted with its opposite. One should not adopt a creed by default, because no alternative is known. Education should prepare students for the "real world" not by segregating them from evil but by urging full confrontation to test and modify the validity of the good. —Robert Baron, "In Defense of Teaching Racism, Sexism, and Fascism"

The inescapable conclusion is that society secretly wants crime, needs crime, and gains definite satisfactions from the present mishandling of it! We condemn crime; we punish offenders for it; but we need it. The crime and punishment ritual is a part of our lives. We need crimes to wonder at, to enjoy vicariously, to discuss and speculate about, and to publicly deplore. We need criminals to identify ourselves with, to envy secretly, and to punish stoutly. They do for us the forbidden, illegal things we wish to do and, like scapegoats of old, they bear the burdens of our displaced guilt and punishment—"the iniquities of us all." —Karl Menninger, "The Crime of Punishment"

Inductive Reasoning

The preceding section focused on deductive reasoning, an argument form in which one reasons from premises that are known or assumed to be true to a conclusion that follows necessarily from the premises. This section introduces *inductive reasoning*, an argument form in which one reasons from premises or instances that are known or assumed to be true to a conclusion that is supported by the premises but does not necessarily follow from them.

When you reason inductively, your premises, instances, or data provide evidence that makes it more or less probable (but not certain) that the conclusion is true. The following statements are examples of conclusions reached through inductive reasoning. As you read them, think about how the data might have been obtained and what arguments could be based on each statement.

1. A recent Gallup poll reported that 74 percent of the American public believes that abortion should remain legal.

2. On the average, a person with a college degree will earn over $830,000 more in his or her lifetime than a person with just a high school diploma.

3. The outbreak of food poisoning at the end-of-year school party was probably caused by the squid salad.

4. The devastating disease AIDS is caused by a particularly complex virus that may not be curable.

5. The solar system is probably the result of an enormous explosion—a "big bang"—that occurred billions of years ago.

Each of the first two statements is an example of inductive reasoning known as *empirical generalization*—a general statement about an entire group made on the basis of observing some members of the group. The final three statements are examples of *causal reasoning*—a form of inductive reasoning which claims that an event (or events) is the result of the occurrence of another event (or events).

Causal Reasoning

You were introduced to causal analysis in Chapter 10 and also to the fallacies that can result if causes are not analyzed logically. Review pages 333–336 to recall the characteristics of this pattern of induction.

Causal reasoning is the backbone of the natural and the social sciences. It is also central to the *scientific method*, which operates on the assumption that the world is constructed in a complex web of causal relationships that can be discovered through systematic investigation. You apply the scientific method in your science courses.

Empirical Generalization

An important tool used by both natural and social scientists is empirical generalization. Have you ever wondered how the major television and radio networks can predict election results hours before the polls close? These predictions are made possible by using *empirical generalization*, a form of inductive reasoning which is defined as "reasoning by examining a limited sample to reach a general conclusion based on that sample."

Network election predictions, as well as public opinion polls that are conducted throughout a political campaign, are based on interviews with a select number of people. Ideally, pollsters would interview everyone in the "target population" (in this case, voters), but doing this, of course, is hardly practical. Instead, they select a relatively small group of individuals from the target population, known as a "sample," who they have determined will adequately represent the group as a whole. Pollsters believe that they can then generalize the opinions of this smaller group to the target population.

There are three key criteria for evaluating inductive arguments:

- Is the sample known?
- Is the sample sufficient?
- Is the sample representative?

Is the Sample Known?   An inductive argument is only as strong as the sample on which it is based. For example, sample populations described in vague terms—such as "highly placed sources" or "many young people interviewed"—provide a treacherously weak foundation for generalizing to larger populations. In order for an inductive argument to be persuasive, the sample population should be explicitly known and clearly identified. Natural and social scientists take great care when selecting members of sample groups. They also make information on members of the sample groups available to outside investigators who may wish to evaluate and verify the results.

Is the Sample Sufficient?   The second criterion for evaluating inductive reasoning is to consider the size of the sample. It should be large enough to provide an accurate sense of the group as a whole. In the polling example discussed earlier, we would be concerned if only a few registered voters had been interviewed, and the results of the interviews were then generalized to a much larger population. Overall, the larger the sample, the more reliable the inductive conclusions. Natural and social scientists have developed precise guidelines for determining the size of the sample needed to achieve reliable results. For example, poll results are often accompanied by a qualification such as "These results are subject to an error factor of ± 3 percentage points." This means that if the sample reveals that 47 percent of those interviewed prefer candidate X, we can reliably state that 44 to 50 percent of the target population prefers candidate X. Because a sample is usually a small portion of the target population, we can rarely state that the two match each other exactly—there must always be some room for variation. The exceptions to this are situations in which the target population is completely homogeneous. For instance, tasting one cookie from a bag of cookies is usually enough to tell us whether or not the contents of the entire bag are stale.

Is the Sample Representative?   The third crucial element in effective inductive reasoning is the representativeness of the sample. If we are to generalize with confidence from the sample to the target population, we have to be sure the sample is
similar in all relevant aspects to the larger group from which it is drawn. For
instance, in the polling example, the sample population should reflect the same percentage of men and women, of Democrats and Republicans, of young and old, and
so on, as exists in the target population. It is obvious that many characteristics—such
as hair color, favorite food, and shoe size—are not relevant to the comparison. The
better the sample reflects the target population in terms of relevant qualities, however, the better the accuracy of the generalizations. On the other hand, when the
sample does not represent the target population—for example, if the election
pollsters interviewed only females between the ages of thirty and thirty-five—the
sample is termed *biased*, and any generalizations about the target population will
be highly suspect.

How do we ensure that the sample is representative of the target population?
One important device is *random selection*, a selection strategy in which every member of the target population has an equal chance of being included in the sample. For
example, the various techniques used to select winning lottery tickets are supposed
to be random—each ticket is supposed to have an equal chance of winning. In
complex cases of inductive reasoning—such as polling—random selection is often
combined with the confirmation that all the important categories in the population
are adequately represented. For example, an election pollster would want to ensure
that all significant geographical areas are included and then would randomly select
individuals from within those areas to compose the sample.

Understanding the principles of empirical generalization is crucial to effective
thinking because we are continually challenged to evaluate this form of inductive
thinking in our lives. In addition, when writing about political or social issues,
we often use the results of inductive investigations, so we should be able to determine their accuracy and relevance.

THINKING-
WRITING
ACTIVITY

Analyzing Empirical Generalization

Review the following examples of empirical generalizing. Select two and then
evaluate the quality of the thinking by answering the following questions.

1. Is the sample known?
2. Is the sample sufficient?
3. Is the sample representative?
4. Do you believe that the conclusions are likely to be accurate? Why or why not?
5. What are some arguments that might be based on your answers?

In a study of a possible relationship between pornography and antisocial
behavior, questionnaires went out to 7,500 psychiatrists and psychoanalysts

whose listing in the directory of the American Psychological Association indicated clinical experience. Over 3,400 of these professionals responded. The result: 7.4 percent of the psychiatrists and psychologists had cases in which they were convinced that pornography was a causal factor in antisocial behavior, an additional 9.4 percent were suspicious, 3.2 percent did not commit themselves, and 80 percent said they had no cases in which a causal connection was suspected.

A survey by the Sleep Disorder Clinic of the VA hospital in La Jolla, California (involving more than one million people), revealed that people who sleep more than ten hours a night have a death rate 80 percent higher than those who sleep only seven or eight hours. Men who sleep fewer than four hours a night have a death rate 180 percent higher, and women with less [than four hours'] sleep have a rate 40 percent higher. This might be taken as indicating that too much and too little sleep cause death.

In a recent survey, twice as many doctors interviewed stated that if they were stranded on a desert island, they would prefer X Aspirin to Extra Strength Y.

Being a general practitioner in a rural area has tremendous drawbacks—being on virtual 24-hour call 365 days a year, patients without financial means or insurance, low fees in the first place, inadequate facilities and assistance. Nevertheless, America's small-town G. P.s seem fairly content with their lot. According to a survey taken by *Country Doctor*, fully 50 percent wrote back that they "basically like being a rural G. P." Only 1 in 15 regretted that he or she had not specialized. Only 2 out of 20 rural general practitioners would trade places with their urban counterparts, given the chance. And only 1 in 30 would "choose some other line of work altogether."

More Fallacies: Forms of False Reasoning

As we pointed out in Chapter 10, certain forms of reasoning are not logical. These types of pseudoreasoning (false reasoning) are often termed *fallacies:* arguments that are not sound because of various errors in reasoning. Fallacious reasoning is sometimes used to influence others. It seeks to persuade not on the basis of sound arguments and critical thinking but rather on the basis of emotional and illogical factors. Sometimes fallacious reasoning is used inadvertently. However, it is always dangerous, so it is important to recognize it as well as to avoid using it. Detecting fallacious reasoning is a significant factor in evaluating sources of beliefs, the concept discussed in Chapter 11.

In Chapter 8, we explored the way in which we form concepts through the interactive process of generalizing (identifying the common qualities that define the boundaries of the concept) and interpreting (identifying examples of the concept). This process is similar to the process involved in constructing empirical generalizations as we seek to reach a general conclusion based on a limited number of examples and then apply this conclusion to other examples. Although generalizing and interpreting are useful in forming concepts, they also can lead to fallacious ways of thinking, including hasty generalization, sweeping generalization, false dilemma, begging the questions, and red herring.

Hasty Generalization

Consider the following examples of reasoning. Do you think the arguments are sound? Why or why not?

- My boyfriends have never shown any real concern for my feelings. My conclusion is that men are insensitive, selfish, and emotionally superficial.
- My mother always gets upset over insignificant things. This leads me to believe that women are very emotional.

In both of these cases, a general conclusion has been reached that is based on a very small sample. As a result, the reasons provide very weak support for the conclusions. It does not make good sense to generalize from one or a few individuals to all men or all women. The conclusion is *hasty* because the information is not adequate enough to justify the generalization.

Sweeping Generalization

Whereas the fallacy of hasty generalization deals with errors in the process of generalizing, the fallacy of *sweeping generalization* stems from difficulties in the process of interpreting. Consider the following examples of reasoning. Do you consider the arguments sound? Why or why not?

- Vigorous exercise contributes to overall good health. Therefore, vigorous exercise should be practiced by recent heart-attack victims, people who are out of shape, and women in the last month of pregnancy.
- People should be allowed to make their own decisions, providing that their actions do not harm other people. Therefore, people who are trying to commit suicide should be left alone to do as they please.

In both of these cases, generalizations that are true in most cases have been deliberately applied to examples that are clearly intended to be exceptions to the generalizations because of their special features. Of course, the use of a sweeping generalization motivates us to clarify the generalization, rephrasing it to exclude examples, like those given here, that have special features. For example, the first generalization could be reformulated as "Vigorous exercise contributes to the overall good health of most people *except* recent heart-attack victims, people who are out of shape, and women who are about to give birth." Sweeping generalizations become dangerous when they are accepted without critical analysis.

Examine the following examples of sweeping generalizations. In each case (a) explain why it is a sweeping generalization and (b) reformulate the statement to make it a legitimate generalization.

1. A college education stimulates you to develop as a person and prepares you for many professions. Therefore, all people should attend college, no matter what career interests them.

2. Drugs such as heroin and morphine are addictive and therefore qualify as dangerous drugs. This means that they should never be used, even as painkillers in medical situations.

3. Once criminals have served time for the crimes they have committed, they have paid their debt to society and should be permitted to work at any job they choose.

False Dilemma

The fallacy of the *false dilemma*—also known as the *either/or* fallacy and the *false dichotomy* fallacy—occurs when one is asked to choose between two extreme alternatives without being able to consider additional options. For example, we may say, "You're either for me or against me." Sometimes giving people only two choices on an issue makes sense ("If you decide to swim the English Channel, you'll either make it or you won't"). At other times, however, viewing a complicated situation in such extreme terms can result in a serious oversimplification.

The following statements are examples of false dilemmas. After analyzing the fallacy in each case, suggest different alternatives than those being presented.

> *Example:* "Everyone in Germany is a National Socialist—the few outside the party are either lunatics or idiots." (Adolf Hitler, quoted by the *New York Times*, April 5, 1938)

> *Analysis:* Hitler was saying that Germans who were not Nazis were lunatics or idiots. By limiting the classification of the population to these three categories, Hitler was simply ignoring all the people who did not qualify as Nazis, lunatics, or idiots.

1. "America—love it or leave it!"

2. "She loves me; she loves me not."

3. "Live free or die."

4. "If you're not part of the solution, you're part of the problem."

5. "If you know about a BMW, you either own one or you want to."

Begging the Questions

This fallacious approach presents a circular argument that restates the claim in different words and so "begs off," or sidesteps, the important questions involved.

Example: Tough antidrug laws reduce drug use by making usage a criminal act.

Analysis: This begs the question of the effectiveness of prohibiting a substance and of punishment for its use.

Red Herring

Here is another way of moving the discussion away from a basic issue. This colorful expression comes from an old practice of dragging a very dead fish on the ground in front of young hunting dogs to teach them to follow a scent.

Example: Speculating about whether the governor will be re-elected as you analyze the environmental impact of a proposed new highway

Analysis: Who is governor may well affect legislation authorizing the highway, but this matter has little to do with analyzing environmental data.

Fallacies of Relevance

Many fallacious arguments try to gain support by appealing to factors that have little or nothing to do with the arguments. In these cases, false appeals substitute for sound reasoning and a critical examination of the issues. Such appeals are known as fallacies of *relevance*.

Appeal to Authority In Chapters 3 and 8, we explored the ways in which we sometimes use various authorities to establish our beliefs or to prove our points. At that time, we noted that to serve as a basis for beliefs, authorities must have legitimate expertise in the area in which they are advising—for example, an experienced mechanic could diagnose your car's problem. However, people occasionally appeal to authorities who are not qualified to give an expert opinion. Consider the reasoning in the following advertisements. Do you think the arguments are sound? Why or why not?

- Hi. You've probably seen me out on the football field. After a hard day's work crushing halfbacks and sacking quarterbacks, I like to settle down with a cold, smooth Maltz beer.
- SONY. Ask anyone.
- Over 11 million women will read this ad. Only 16 will own the coat.

Each of these arguments is intended to persuade us of the value of a product through the appeal to various authorities. In the first case, the authority is a well-known sports figure; in the second, the authority is large numbers of people; in the third, the authority is a select few, so the appeal is to our desire to be exclusive ("snob appeal"). Unfortunately, none of these authorities offers legitimate expertise about the product. Football players are not beer experts, large numbers of people are often misled, and exclusive groups of people are frequently mistaken in their beliefs. To evaluate authorities properly, we have to ask:

> What are the professional credentials on which the authorities' expertise is based?

> Is their expertise in the area on which they are commenting?

Appeal to Pity   Consider the reasoning in the following arguments. Do you think the arguments are sound? Why or why not?

* I know that I haven't completed my term paper, but I really think that I should be excused. This has been a very difficult semester for me. I caught every kind of flu that came around. In addition, my brother has a drinking problem, and this has been very upsetting for me. Also, my dog died.

* I admit that my client embezzled money from the company, Your Honor. However, I would like to bring several facts to your attention. He is a family man with a wonderful wife and two terrific children. He is an important member of the community. He is active in his church, coaches a Little League baseball team, and has worked very hard to be a good person who cares about people. I think that you should take these things into consideration when handing down your sentence.

In each of these arguments, the reasons offered to support the conclusions may indeed be true, yet they are not relevant to the conclusion. Instead of providing evidence that supports the conclusion, the reasons are designed to make us feel sorry for the person involved and therefore to agree with the conclusion out of sympathy. Although these appeals can often be effective, the arguments are not sound. The validity of a conclusion can only be established by reasons that support and are relevant to the conclusion.

Appeal to Fear   Consider the reasoning in the following arguments. Do you consider the arguments sound? Why or why not?

* I don't think you deserve a raise. After all, there are many people who would be happy to have your job at the salary you are currently receiving. I would be happy to interview some of these people if you really think that you are underpaid.

* If you continue to disagree with my interpretation of *The Catcher in the Rye*, I'm afraid it may affect the grade on your paper.

In both of these arguments, the conclusions being suggested are supported by an appeal to fear, not by reasons that provide evidence for the conclusions. In the first case, the threat is that if you do not forgo your salary demands, your job may be in jeopardy. In the second case, the threat is that if you do not agree with the teacher's interpretation, you may receive a low grade. In neither instance are the real issues—Is a salary increase deserved? Is the student's interpretation legitimate?—being discussed. People who appeal to fear to support their conclusions are interested only in prevailing, regardless of which position might be more justified.

Appeal to Ignorance   Consider the reasoning in the following arguments. Do you find the arguments sound? Why or why not?

- You say that you don't believe in God. But can you prove that an omnipotent spirit doesn't exist? If not, then you have to accept the conclusion that it does in fact exist.
- Greco Tires are the best. No others have been proved better.

When this argument form is used, the person offering the conclusion is asking his or her opponent to *disprove* the conclusion. If the opponent is unable to do so, the conclusion is asserted to be true. This argument form is not valid because it is the task of the person proposing the argument to prove the conclusion. The fact that an opponent cannot disprove it offers no evidence that the conclusion is justified.

Appeal to Personal Attack   Consider the reasoning in the following arguments. Do you think the arguments are valid? Why or why not?

- Senator Smith's opinion about a tax cut is wrong. It's impossible to believe anything he says since he left his wife for that model.
- How can you have an intelligent opinion about abortion? You're not a woman, so this is a decision that you'll never have to make.

This argument form has been one of the fallacies most frequently used through the ages. Its effectiveness results from ignoring the issues of the argument and focusing instead on the qualities of the person presenting it. Trying to discredit the other person is an effort to discredit the argument—no matter what reasons are offered. This fallacy is also referred to as the *ad hominem* argument (which means drawing attention "to the man" rather than to the issue) and as *poisoning the well* (since the speaker is trying to ensure that any water drawn from the opponent's well will be regarded as undrinkable).

The effort to discredit can take two forms, as illustrated in the preceding examples. The fallacy can be *abusive* by directly attacking the credibility of an opponent. In addition, the fallacy can be *circumstantial* by claiming that a person's circumstances, not character, render his or her opinion so biased or uninformed that it cannot be treated seriously. Another example of the circumstantial form would be disregarding the views on nuclear-plant safety that were presented by an owner of a nuclear plant.

Appeal to Popular Opinion or the Bandwagon   You are probably familiar with this "everybody else is doing it" appeal. Children use it while trying to convince parents to allow questionable activities and purchases. However, it is not absent from adult situations. Political and advertising campaigns often use the result of surveys to influence voters or consumers:

- Awww, Dad, I really need a new iPod. Everyone else in my class has one! Puuuhhhleeeeze . . .
- 58 percent of registered voters surveyed say that they will vote for Green Party nominee Edward Norton last week. Let's all get to the polls to send a message to the incumbents that we support Norton and his proposals for change!
- Well-dressed women will want pin-striped suits for fall!

This appeal can be effective because even thoughtful adults gravitate towards fashions in clothing and home furnishings, and voters want to support the policies and candidates with whom they agree. A certain amount of conformity is essential to a stable society, but clear thinkers are aware of the attraction of a "bandwagon" before they jump on.

THINKING-WRITING ACTIVITY

Analyzing Fallacies

1. Find in advertisements, political statements, or other arguments that you have encountered, examples of two or three false appeals. Write a brief explanation of why you think the appeal is not warranted. Look for the following fallacies:

   - Appeal to authority
   - Appeal to pity
   - Appeal to fear
   - Appeal to ignorance
   - Appeal to personal attack
   - Appeal to popular opinion

2. Share the fallacies you have found with classmates and also examine the ones they have identified.

3. Write a few sentences explaining how you can avoid using fallacies in your own writing.

Analyzing well-known arguments to see how they use deduction, induction, evidence *(logos), ethos, pathos,* appeals—and perhaps fallacious reasoning—is a challenging activity and one that can help you with your own arguments. Read the Declaration of Independence and the Declaration of Sentiments and Resolutions, which follow, and Martin Luther King Jr.'s speech, "I Have a Dream" (see pages 165–169 in Chapter 6). Then answer the questions that follow the readings.

The Declaration of Independence

In Congress, July 4, 1776
The unanimous declaration of the thirteen
United States of America

When in the course of human events, it becomes necessary for one people to dissolve the political bands which have connected them with another, and to assume among the powers of the earth, the separate and equal station to which the Laws of Nature and of Nature's God entitle them, a decent respect to the opinions of mankind requires that they should declare the causes which impel them to the separation.

We hold these truths to be self-evident, that all men are created equal, that they are endowed by their Creator with certain unalienable rights, that among these are life, liberty and the pursuit of happiness. That to secure these rights, governments are instituted among men, deriving their just powers from the consent of the governed. That whenever any form of government becomes destructive of these ends, it is the right of the people to alter or to abolish it, and to institute new government, laying its foundation on such principles and organizing its powers in such form, as to them shall seem most likely to effect their safety and happiness. Prudence, indeed, will dictate that governments long established should not be changed for light and transient causes; and accordingly all experience hath shown, that mankind are more disposed to suffer, while evils are sufferable, than to right themselves by abolishing the forms to which they are accustomed. But when a long train of abuses and usurpations, pursuing invariably the same object evinces a design to reduce them under absolute despotism, it is their right, it is their duty, to throw off such government, and to provide new guards for their future security. Such has been the patient sufferance of these Colonies; and such is now the necessity which constrains them to alter their former systems of government. The history of the present King of Great Britain is a history of repeated injuries and usurpations, all having in direct object the establishment of an absolute tyranny over these States. To prove this, let facts be submitted to a candid world.

He has refused his assent to laws, the most wholesome and necessary for the public good.

He has forbidden his Governors to pass laws of immediate and pressing importance, unless suspended in their operation till his assent should be obtained; and when so suspended, he has utterly neglected to attend to them.

He has refused to pass other laws for the accommodation of large districts of people, unless those people would relinquish the right of representation in the Legislature, a right inestimable to them and formidable to tyrants only.

He has called together legislative bodies at places unusual, uncomfortable, and distant from the depository of their public records, for the sole purpose of fatiguing them into compliance with his measures.

He has dissolved representative houses repeatedly, for opposing with manly firmness his invasions on the rights of the people.

He has refused for a long time, after such dissolutions, to cause others to be elected; whereby the legislative powers, incapable of annihilation, have returned to the people at large for their exercise; the State remaining in the meantime exposed to all the dangers of invasion from without and convulsions within.

He has endeavoured to prevent the population of these States; for that purpose obstructing the laws of naturalization of foreigners; refusing to pass others to encourage their migration hither, and raising the conditions of new appropriations of lands.

He has obstructed the administration of justice, by refusing his assent to laws for establishing judiciary powers.

He has made judges dependent on his will alone, for the tenure of their offices, and the amount and payment of their salaries.

He has erected a multitude of new offices, and sent hither swarms of officers to harass our people, and eat out their substance.

He has kept among us, in times of peace, standing armies without the consent of our legislatures.

He has affected to render the military independent of and superior to the civil power.

He has combined with others to subject us to a jurisdiction foreign to our constitution, and unacknowledged by our laws; giving his assent to their acts of pretended legislation.

For quartering large bodies of armed troops among us.

For protecting them, by a mock trial, from punishment for any murders which they should commit on the inhabitants of these States.

For cutting off our trade with all parts of the world.

For imposing taxes on us without our consent.

For depriving us, in many cases, of the benefits of trial by jury.

For transporting us beyond seas to be tried for pretended offences.

For abolishing the free system of English laws in a neighbouring Province, establishing therein an arbitrary government, and enlarging its boundaries so as to render it at once an example and fit instrument for introducing the same absolute rule into these Colonies.

For taking away our Charters, abolishing our most valuable laws, and altering fundamentally the forms of our governments.

For suspending our own Legislatures, and declaring themselves invested with power to legislate for us in all cases whatsoever.

He has abdicated government here, by declaring us out of his protection and waging war against us.

He has plundered our seas, ravaged our coasts, burnt our towns, and destroyed the lives of our people.

He is at this time transporting large armies of foreign mercenaries to complete the works of death, desolation and tyranny, already begun with circumstances of cruelty and perfidy scarcely paralleled in the most barbarous ages, and totally unworthy the head of a civilized nation.

He has constrained our fellow citizens taken captive on the high seas to bear arms against their country, to become the executioners of their friends and brethren, or to fall themselves by their hands.

He has excited domestic insurrections amongst us, and has endeavoured to bring on the inhabitants of our frontiers, the merciless Indian savages, whose known rule of warfare, is an undistinguished destruction of all ages, sexes, and conditions.

30   In every stage of these oppressions we have petitioned for redress in the most humble terms: our repeated petitions have been answered only by repeated injury. A prince whose character is thus marked by every act which may define a tyrant is unfit to be the ruler of a free people.

Nor have we been wanting in attention to our British brethren. We have warned them from time to time of attempts by their legislature to extend an unwarrantable jurisdiction over us. We have reminded them of the circumstances of our emigration and settlement here. We have appealed to their native justice and magnanimity, and we have conjured them by the ties of our common kindred to disavow these usurpations, which would inevitably interrupt our connections and correspondence. They too have been deaf to the voice of justice and of consanguinity. We must, therefore, acquiesce in the necessity, which denounces our separation, and hold them, as we hold the rest of mankind, enemies in war, in peace friends.

We, therefore, the Representatives of the United States of America, in General Congress assembled, appealing to the Supreme Judge of the world for the rectitude of our intentions, do, in the name, and by the authority of the good people of these Colonies, solemnly publish and declare, That these United Colonies are, and of right ought to be Free and Independent States; that they are absolved from all allegiance to the British Crown, and that all political connection between them and the State of Great Britain, is and ought to be totally dissolved; and that as Free and Independent States, they have full power to levy war, conclude peace, contract alliances, establish commerce, and to do all other acts and things which Independent States may of right do. And for the support of this declaration, with a firm reliance on the protection of Divine Providence, we mutually pledge to each other our lives, our fortunes, and our sacred honor.

Declaration of Sentiments and Resolutions

BY ELIZABETH CADY STANTON (1815–1902)

A leading suffragist of the nineteenth century, Elizabeth Cady Stanton was born in Jamestown, New York. Her father was a judge, and while working as his assistant, Stanton became aware of the extent of male dominance in the eyes of the law. She married an abolitionist, in spite of her parents' concerns, and together they crusaded to change racial and gender inequities. She organized the first Women's Rights Convention in Seneca Falls, New York, in 1848. In 1851, she formed a working relationship with Susan B. Anthony that united them for the rest of their lives. Stanton ran for Congress in 1866 and cofounded *The Revolution,* a suffragist newspaper, in 1868. Today, she is revered by feminists as an early leader in the fight for equality.

When, in the course of human events, it becomes necessary for one person of the family of man to assume among the people of the earth a position different from that which they have hitherto occupied, but one to which the laws of nature and nature's God entitle them, a decent respect to the opinions of mankind requires that they should declare the causes that impel them to such a course.

We hold these truths to be self-evident: that all men and women are created equal; that they are endowed by their Creator with certain inalienable rights; that among these are life, liberty, and the pursuit of happiness; that to secure these rights governments are instituted, deriving their just powers from the consent of the governed. Whenever any form of government becomes destructive of these ends, it is the right of those who suffer from it to refuse allegiance to it, and to insist upon the institution of a new government, laying its foundation on such principles, and organizing its powers in such form, as to them shall seem most likely to effect their safety and happiness. Prudence, indeed, will dictate that governments long established should not be changed for light and transient causes; and accordingly all experience hath shown that mankind are more disposed to suffer, while evils are sufferable, than to right themselves by abolishing the forms to which they were accustomed. But when a long train of abuses and usurpations, pursuing invariably the same object evinces a design to reduce them under absolute despotism, it is their duty to throw off such government, and to provide new guards for their future security. Such has been the patient sufferance of the women under this government, and such is now the necessity which constrains them to demand the equal station to which they are entitled.

The history of mankind is a history of repeated injuries and usurpations on the part of man toward woman, having in direct object the establishment of an absolute tyranny over her. To prove this, let facts be submitted to a candid world.

He has never permitted her to exercise her inalienable right to the elective franchise.

5   He has compelled her to submit to laws, in the formation of which she had no voice.

He has withheld from her rights which are given to the most ignorant and degraded men—both natives and foreigners.

Having deprived her of this first right of a citizen, the elective franchise, thereby leaving her without representation in the halls of legislation, he has oppressed her on all sides.

He has made her, if married, in the eye of the law, civilly dead.

He has taken from he all right in property, even to the wages she earns.

10   He has made her, morally, an irresponsible being, as she can commit many crimes with impunity, provided they be done in the presence of her husband. In the covenant of marriage, she is compelled to promise obedience to her husband, he becoming, to all intents and purposes, her master—the law giving him power to deprive her of her liberty, and to administer chastisement.

He has so framed the laws of divorce, as to what shall be the proper causes, and in case of separation, to whom the guardianship of the children shall be given, as to be wholly regardless of the happiness of women—the law, in all cases, going upon a false supposition of the supremacy of man, and giving all power into his hands.

After depriving her of all rights as a married woman, if single, and the owner of property, he has taxed her to support a government which recognizes her only when her property can be made profitable to it.

He has monopolized nearly all the profitable employments, and from those she is permitted to follow, she receives but a scanty remuneration. He closes against her all the avenues to wealth and distinction which he considers most honorable to himself. As a teacher of theology, medicine, or law, she is not known.

He has denied her the facilities for obtaining a thorough education, all colleges being closed against her.

15 He allows her in Church, as well as State, but a subordinate position, claiming Apostolic authority for her exclusion from the ministry, and, with some exceptions, from any public participation in the affairs of the Church.

He has created a false public sentiment by giving to the world a different code of morals for men and women, by which moral delinquencies which exclude women from society are not only tolerated, but deemed of little account in man.

He has usurped the prerogative of Jehovah himself, claiming it as his right to assign for her a sphere of action, when that belongs to her conscience and to her God.

He has endeavored, in every way that he could, to destroy her confidence in her own powers, to lessen her self-respect, and to make her willing to lead a dependent and abject life.

Now, in view of this entire disfranchisement of one-half the people of this country, their social and religious degradation—in view of the unjust laws above mentioned, and because women do feel themselves aggrieved, oppressed, and fraudulently deprived of their most sacred rights, we insist that they have immediate admission to all the rights and privileges which belong to them as citizens of the United States.

20 In entering upon the great work before us, we anticipate no small amount of misconception, misrepresentation, and ridicule; but we shall use every instrumentality within our power to effect our object. We shall employ agents, circulate tracts, petition the State and National legislatures, and endeavor to enlist the pulpit and the press in our behalf. We hope this Convention will be followed by a series of Conventions embracing every part of the country.

Resolutions

Whereas, The great precept of nature is conceded to be, that "man shall pursue his own true and substantial happiness." Blackstone in his Commentaries remarks, that this law of Nature being coeval with mankind, and dictated by God himself, is of course superior in obligation to any other. It is binding over all the globe, in all countries and at all times; no human laws are of any validity if contrary to this, and such of them as are valid, derive all their force and all their validity, and all their authority, mediately and immediately, from this original; therefore,

Resolved, That such laws as conflict, in any way, with the true and substantial happiness of woman, are contrary to the great precept of nature and of no validity, for this is "superior in obligation to any other."

Resolved, That all laws which prevent woman from occupying such a station in society as her conscience shall dictate, or which place her in a position inferior to that of man, are contrary to the great precept of nature, and therefore of no force or authority.

Resolved, That woman is man's equal—was intended to be so by the Creator, and the highest good of the race demands that she should be recognized as such.

Resolved, That the women of this country ought to be enlightened in regard to the laws under which they live, that they may no longer publish their degradation by declaring themselves satisfied with their present position, nor their ignorance, by asserting that they have all the rights they want.

Resolved, That inasmuch as man, while claiming for himself intellectual superiority, does accord to woman moral superiority for it is preeminently his duty to encourage her to speak and teach, as she has an opportunity, in all religious assemblies.

Resolved, That the same amount of virtue, delicacy, and refinement of behavior that is required of woman in the social state, should also be required of man, and the same transgressions should be visited with equal severity on both man and woman.

Resolved, That the objection of indelicacy and impropriety, which is so often brought against woman when she addresses a public audience, comes with a very ill-grace from those who encourage, by their attendance, her appearance on the stage, in the concert, or in feats of the circus.

Resolved, That woman has too long rested satisfied in the circumscribed limits which corrupt customs and a perverted application of the Scriptures have marked out for her, and that it is time she should move in the enlarged sphere which her great Creator has assigned her.

Resolved, That it is the duty of the women of this country to secure to themselves their sacred right to the elective franchise.

Resolved, That the equality of human rights results necessarily from the fact of the identity of the race in capabilities and responsibilities.

Resolved, therefore, That, being invested by the Creator with the same capabilities, and the same consciousness of responsibility for their exercise, it is demonstrably the right and duty of woman, equally with man, to promote every righteous cause by every righteous means; and especially in regard to the great subjects of morals and religion, it is self-evidently her right to participate with her brother in teaching them, both in private and in public, by writing and by speaking, by any instrumentalities proper to be used, and in any assemblies proper to be held; and this being a self-evident truth growing out of the divinely implanted principles of human nature, any custom or authority adverse to it, whether modern or wearing the hoary sanction of antiquity, is to be regarded as a self-evident falsehood, and at war with mankind.

[At the last session Lucretia Mott offered and spoke to the following resolution:]
Resolved, That the speedy success of our cause depends upon the zealous and untiring efforts of both men and women, for the overthrow of the monopoly of the pulpit, and for the securing to women an equal participation with men in the various trades, professions and commerce.

QUESTIONS FOR ACTIVE READING

1. What is the thesis of each of these arguments? Where is it stated in each of these arguments?
2. How does the Declaration of Independence use deduction and induction? Identify the premises and the conclusion in the second paragraph. Comment on the effectiveness of this deliberate use of these basic reasoning methods.
3. How does the Declaration of Sentiments and Resolutions use induction to support the central claim? What are the effects of its parallels with the Declaration of Independence?

QUESTIONS FOR THINKING CRITICALLY

1. In your library or on the Internet, locate a copy of Martin Luther King Jr.'s "Letter from Birmingham Jail." What differences in approach do you see between it and "I Have a Dream" (pages 165–169) What about the tone or *ethos?* Can you identify the warrants and qualifiers in King's arguments?
2. These political arguments address profound questions about human rights. What in these arguments could be applicable to arguments that you might write about academic or business issues? What might not be applicable?
3. How would you define *liberty* and *the pursuit of happiness?* Is it possible, in your current circumstances, to achieve either liberty or happiness? To what extent is the state responsible for guaranteeing *liberty* and *the pursuit of happiness*, according to your definition of both terms?

Deductive and Inductive Reasoning in Writing

As pointed out earlier in this chapter, writers and speakers seldom use deductive or inductive reasoning solely or purely. In their arguments, conclusions reached by induction become premises for deductions; statements that are premises are asserted but not demonstrated, as in the opening sentences of the Declaration of Independence. Deductively developed paragraphs interact with inductively developed ones, as in Gould's "Evolution as Fact and Theory" in Chapter 11.

However, deduction is used obviously when a definition or principle is established by the writer, and the point of the paper or paragraph is to claim that the subject being discussed fits the definition or demonstrates the principle. If the readers agree with the definition and also agree that the subject fits it, the claim is proved for whatever purpose the writer has. Political science, literature, philosophy, theology, psychology, and law are among the many fields that employ deductive arguments in this way.

Inductive reasoning is reflected in two ways in writing. One is structural. When a writer chooses to present instances of evidence first, leading readers to the claim presented as a conclusion, the paragraph or paper is organized inductively. Composition instructors tend to steer students away from using this technique to structure entire papers since great skill is needed to keep readers with the argument. The sections Organizing Ideas and Revising in the Writing Projects have asked you to think carefully about where you state your thesis or claim for this reason. It is usually more effective to use a deductively based structure.

A reflection of inductive reasoning that is often used in writing occurs when the writer makes a claim in a topic sentence or thesis statement, then simply exemplifies it. The writer is asking the readers to re-enact the inductive process that led him or her to make the claim. Notice how the list of evils alleged to have been committed by the British government functions this way in the Declaration of Independence. Notice how regularly you use this technique, and how often much of what you read uses it, too.

In addition, deduction often appears in the abbreviated form of the enthymeme (see page 475), and induction is commonly presented through the small sample of the example, the inference, and the anecdote. These practices are neither wrong nor fallacious. Writers cannot take the time or space to state all the premises of every deduction or to give multiple instances to support each idea. However, critical thinkers need to understand these reductions so that claims and evidence can be evaluated. Deduction and induction, the basic reasoning methods, are at work in various ways in what we write and read.

Principles for Writing Responsible Arguments

The following principles for writing responsible arguments are fundamental to the Western tradition of logical, structured argument. Always be sure to follow them as well as you can.

PRINCIPLES
FOR WRITING
RESPONSIBLE
ARGUMENTS

1. Formulate and qualify the thesis statement carefully. Place it purposefully. Use deductive and inductive approaches as appropriate to develop and support the thesis.

2. Provide a context for the thesis; give reasons for its importance. These might be warrants.

3. Provide sound evidence, or grounds, presented clearly and specifically.

(Continued)

4. Acknowledge and demonstrate understanding of other points of view. Grant validity to any point when it is justified. To strengthen your argument, refute courteously points with which you disagree.

5. Use the thinking/organizing patterns in Part Two. Arguments often rely on definitions. Causes of a situation and the effects of a proposal are often vital to an argument. Narratives and chronologies are often effective. Contrasts, comparisons, and analogies illuminate your points.

6. Don't use fallacious reasoning.

7. Be aware of your tone. You want to sound reasonable, thoughtful, and polite as you argue your points.

8. Remember that the conclusion to an argument is extremely important. Restate the thesis or claim with a suggestion, a call for action, a decision, or further thought.

Writing Project: Arguing a Position on a Significant Issue

This chapter has emphasized the importance of the basic concepts and terminology connected with argument because reasoned argument leading to mutual understanding, concensus, or agreement is the foundation of a democratic society and also is often the key to success in personal, academic, and business activities.

Because so much college and professional writing is argumentative, this Writing Project asks you to concentrate on the two central elements of argument: establishing a clear thesis and providing sound evidence for it. In addition, you should be particularly careful to be logical, to avoid fallacious statements, to consider your audience, and to present yourself as a reasonable, well-informed proponent of your claims.

Write an essay in which you argue logically for a position on an issue that you consider significant. Use print sources, electronic sources, and—if possible—an interview with an informed individual to support your claims. Follow your instructor's directions regarding the number and range of sources, length of the paper, and academic format for citation of sources. Be sure to follow exactly the model in your handbook when you complete your paper in MLA, APA, or other appropriate format. Consult Chapter 14 and the appendix in this book.

On a page separate from your paper, identify the audience to whom you are addressing your argument and explain why members will benefit from understanding your position. Also, either within the paper or in an accompanying note, explain why this issue is important to you so that your classmates and instructor, as they help you revise your drafts, can be aware of the nature of your expertise and any possible biases.

This chapter has included both readings and Thinking-Writing Activities that encourage you to think about argument. Be sure to reread what you wrote for those activities; you may be able to use some of the material for this Writing Project.

Begin by considering the key elements in the Thinking-Writing Model in Chapter 1 on pages 7–9.

The Writing Situation

Purpose   Your primary purpose is to write an argument that will persuade your intended audience to agree with your claim or thesis. As you work toward that goal, you will have to think critically about a subject that you care about and clarify or modify your view of it, which is another useful purpose.

Audience   The audience is a major concern in any argument. A successful writer understands the characteristics and attitudes of his or her audience. When you develop an argument, you must have a specific audience in mind. Although pandering dishonorably to the audience by distorting evidence or by using flattery is bad rhetoric, an arguer still should be aware of the makeup of the audience and accommodate its members' needs. Some factors to consider are knowledge (an expert audience needs less background than an uninformed one does), age (younger and older people often have different points of view), roles (people have various roles and respond differently as those roles change), relationships (an audience of peers can be approached differently than another kind of audience), and the emotional level of the issue and situation (a highly charged situation should be approached differently than a calm one would be).

Subject   Whenever you argue for a position about which you are concerned, you are addressing an important subject. In addition, the techniques of argument themselves constitute a subject that merits much attention because argument has such importance in people's lives.

Writer   If you have been using sources for other projects, you should be comfortable incorporating other people's ideas into your writing and documenting them appropriately. A new role for you may be that of the good rhetorician, the responsible arguer; if you use your developing critical thinking abilities, you will manage that role well.

The Writing Process

The following sections will guide you through the stages of generating, planning, drafting, and revising as you develop your argument.

Generating Ideas

- You may be involved with an issue because of your sex, ethnicity, or field of study or through some organization in which you participate. Or you may be concerned about a problem at your college, in your community, in your country, or elsewhere in the world. If so, you should have no problem deciding what to write about.

- If no issue comes quickly to mind, look around your campus and community to see what problems exist or what changes could be made.
- Be attentive to various print, broadcast, and online news outlets. Talk with friends, family members, and professors about significant issues.
- Think about questions in your areas of interest: your favorite college subjects, sports, entertainment, food, cars, the environment, architecture. Some of these questions may pertain to serious issues; some might be more lighthearted; many will merit a reasoned argument.
- Freewrite about one or two of your concerns. See how many issues or positions you can come up with in five minutes.

Defining a Focus   After selecting an issue to write about, draft a thesis statement that describes the position that you will argue. Be sure that the statement states your points accurately; it may be a complex sentence. Then share it with classmates to profit from their responses. Revise it on the basis of their feedback.

Organizing Ideas   Your argument should probably be set up in the traditional "no-fail" structure: introduction, thesis, evidence, handling of other views, summing up, conclusion/recommendation for action. However, you may be able to use some other arrangement effectively.

Notice how your material adapts itself to various thinking patterns. Use them firmly to clarify your points.

Select and place material from your sources carefully. Connect source material smoothly with your ideas by introducing and commenting on it.

Drafting   Begin with the easiest part to write, which for this paper might be the beginning since you have been thinking so much about your thesis and its context.

However, never get stymied by trying to compose a beginning. Draft sections in any order that works for you. You might want to draft the paragraphs that present your evidence, then consider what inductive or deductive methods you should use.

- Sometimes copying a draft or parts of it and revising one version while retaining another is productive. That way, if a revision is not satisfactory, you have preserved the earlier version.
- Sometimes writers need to start over by making a new file for a revised version.
- Sometimes it helps to scroll down or up and to rewrite a paragraph or section. Then you can use the better version and delete the weaker one.

Be sure to keep track of publication information for all sources. Note abbreviated titles, authors, and pages in your draft. Then, when you revise, you can cite the sources in the required format. Be sure to use quotation marks or indenting in your draft whenever you quote.

Revising, Editing, and Proofreading   Use the Step-by-Step method in Chapter 6 on pages 152–154 to revise your essay and prepare a final draft.

GUIDELINES FOR REVISING AN ARGUMENT

❑ Is my claim clearly stated and adequately qualified?

❑ Do I provide adequate evidence to support the validity of my claim? Have I correctly cited and documented the sources of that evidence?

❑ Are any of my statements fallacious? Have I double-checked my argument for fallacies?

❑ Should I clearly state the warrants for my argument, or should I leave them unstated?

❑ Have I appropriately established my *ethos* (the impression my audience will have of me) and *pathos* (the effect my argument will have on my audience)?

❑ Have I considered, and included, other points of view? Does my argument clearly prove why my claims are more logical, sensible, useful, or appealing than the opposition's viewpoints?

Student Writing

Josephine Cimino's Writing Process

Part-time student Josephine Cimino makes use every day of critical thinking and problem-solving strategies. As a mother of two who also holds a full-time job, Cimino has multiple responsibilities that require her to make thoughtful decisions no matter how difficult or pressing the circumstances. Her reasoning abilities and careful, logical thinking are evident in the following argument. Although she recognized that the issue of cell phones in schools is not as obviously urgent as the human rights issues addressed by Elizabeth Cady Stanton and Martin Luther King Jr.—or as difficult and problematic as the issues of rape and alcohol abuse discussed in Chapter 12—Cimino chose an issue that was of close personal interest. This allows her to clearly establish her *ethos* (as a working parent) and to visualize a specific audience (other parents of school-age children). Josephine began with the exercise on page 465, Constructing Arguments to Persuade, as a way of structuring her thinking about this issue.

Reason: For many working parents, cell phones allow them to keep track of their children's whereabouts and safety.

Reason: Because of the increasing use of cell phones, there are very few public pay telephones available either on school grounds or at places like athletic fields where students go after school.

Claim: Students should be allowed to carry cell phones on school grounds and during after-school activities.

Audience: Other parents who might not be aware of current efforts to make cell phones illegal on school grounds.

Cellular Phones in Public Schools

by Josephine R. Cimino

As one half of a two-income domestic partnership, I find it very difficult to keep track of my son's, my husband's and my own activities. I can only imagine how much harder it is for families with more children. My husband's job requires him to travel, often out of state. As a very concerned and involved parent, I am left with the task of keeping track and assuring the safety of our child. My son is now in high school, and his day is filled with school, sports, and other extracurricular activities.

He went to a high school football game not too long ago, and I did not have to worry about him because one of his friend's parents was going to give him a ride home. When he got home, he said one of his other friends was caught using a cellular phone to call his parents to pick him up. Unfortunately, the assistant principal saw and confiscated the phone. The student was automatically suspended for ten days for violating Maryland law and school policy. I was so perturbed by this incident that I spoke with a school administrator, Mrs. Shenk, who stated she agreed that the law should be changed. In fact, she had given her daughter, a senior in high school, a cell phone to keep in her car. The administrator admitted that her daughter kept the cellular phone hidden at all times to avoid detection by other school administrators or teachers.

A law was enacted in Maryland in 1989 banning cellular phones and pagers from school grounds and school-related activities (Shen M3). According to a Montgomery County Public Schools regulation, if a student is caught using a cellular phone, the phone is confiscated, and the student is automatically suspended for ten days. In addition, for a second offense, the school is obliged to notify the police. Further, the student can also be expelled if the use of the cell phone was related to any criminal activity (Regulation). According to Shen, violation of the law is a misdemeanor, punishable by a fine of as much as $2500, and a maximum six-month imprisonment (M1).

Various news reports state that some educators and lawmakers have been opposed to the use of cellular phones on school grounds and at school-related activities due to the perception in the late 1980's and early 1990's that cellular phones were used for drug and other illegal activities. According to Mrs. Shenk, some educators and opponents of cellular phones think that cell phones will cause undue disruption in the schools because of the ringing of phones and kids talking on the phones inappropriately. She further states that another argument against cell phones is the possible loss or theft of cell phones by other students. Further, she states, cell phones can also distract students from their school-related activities and their studies.

I do not agree with the current Maryland law. I believe that this law has been surpassed by the electronic age and the availability of cellular phones. I believe that students in the middle schools and high schools should be allowed to carry cellular phones on school grounds and be allowed to use them before and after classes. Further, I believe that students should be allowed to carry and use cellular phones at school-related activities as long as the use is not related to something illegal.

The reasons for having cell phones available to students in schools are compelling. First of all, cell phones are a real time-saver for busy working parents with several children who need to be in several places. Parents do not have to wait around for activities to finish. The children can call when they are ready to be picked up, or to say that they are staying longer and need to be picked up later. Parents still spend an inordinate amount of time in their cars waiting for their children to finish their activities. If children are allowed to have cell phones, parents can use their time more productively. An example is my son's friend at the football game. His parents were probably doing errands or eating dinner, rather than waiting in the parking lot. They probably used their time for something they wanted or needed to do, other than just waiting for their son.

The availability and accessibility of regular pay phones in schools and on school grounds are sadly lacking. There is only one pay phone outside of my son's high school building, and there are no pay phones available near the football field, the basketball courts, or the soccer field. The school is often closed when games are played during the evening hours; therefore, the pay phones inside cannot be accessed. The students often have to wait in long lines to use the one pay phone available on school grounds to call their parents.

Another reason why students should be allowed to have cell phones is so parents can keep track of their children. Parents like me want to know what their children are doing at all times. I, for one, want to know where my son is so that I can be assured that everything is going the way it should. If he tells me he is going home with another child, I want to know for sure that this is what he is doing and that there are no hitches in the plans. I do not want him to be stranded somewhere because his plans fell apart. Parents should be able to call their children after school is over to confirm their schedules and activities.

Finally, students should be allowed to have cellular phones for safety reasons. With the current prevalence of abductions, kidnappings, and school violence, students should be allowed the safety net of having a cellular phone. It would be easy to dial 911 in case of an accident, or if the safety of the child was in question. Students should be able to call parents in case of a dead car battery after a school activity, or if a ride home fell through, or they are separated from friends during a football game. Numerous news reports said that some students were able to call their parents during the Columbine shooting in Colorado. Parents were assured that their children were still alive and able to talk to them about what was happening.

Incidents like the Columbine shooting and other reports of abductions and kidnappings on the way to and from school force parents to think of safety first and to minimize the consequences if a child is caught using the cell phone during school-related activities. Most parents would rather have their kids safe than take the risk of their being harmed.

Earlier this year, a bill was introduced unsuccessfully to change the current laws regulating cellular phones in public schools (Shen M1). However, on April 26, 2000, the School Board of Montgomery County gave the principals in all Montgomery County public schools the discretion of suspending students from one to ten days, instead of the previous automatic ten-day suspension (MCPS–Board). Obviously educators and school administrators agreed that the law needed changing by this revision of county policy. This is a good start, but is not enough to keep our children safe.

Parents, as advocates for the safety of children, should continue efforts to convince lawmakers to change the current law. Students should be allowed to use and carry cell phones in schools and during school activities under strict guidelines. If these guidelines are not followed, then those students should suffer the consequences. Students should not be punished for wanting to be safe and to be in contact with their parents. The safety of our children should be our foremost priority.

Works Cited

Montgomery County Public Schools. "Board Endorses Reduced Penalty for Use of Cellular Phones, Approves Non-Recommended Reductions to

FY2001 Operating Budget Request." MCPS Media Announcement.
26 April 2000 <http//filemaker.mcps.k12.md.us>.

---."Regulation—Portable Communication Devices COG-RA." 26 April 2000
<http//www.mcps.k12.md.us>.

Shen, Fern. "Rules on Cell Phones Decried." <u>Washington Post</u> 17 February
2000: M1+.

Shenk, Susan. Personal interview. 2 January 2000.

Alternative Writing Project: The Pursuit of Happiness

Early women rights activists, including Elizabeth Cady Stanton, modeled much of
their rhetoric, style, and evidence for their Declaration of Sentiments and Resolutions on the original American Declaration of Independence. Both documents
assert—or warrant—that the "pursuit of happiness" is an "unalienable right." In a
well-argued essay, define the concept of *happiness* as it relates to a specific aspect of
your academic or professional life. Are you currently in that state of happiness, and
if so, argue for its adoption by other students or others in your career field. Is there
something or someone impeding your "unalienable right" to this specific kind of
happiness? Argue, perhaps by drawing up a list of injustices as the framers of the
Declaration of Independence did against King George, that this obstacle to your specific pursuit of happiness is unfair and unjust. Your final argument may draw upon
as many of the rhetorical strategies and specific appeals to audience that appear in
both of these Declarations.

Thinking About Research

Writing About Investigations

Knowledge
Creativity
Curiosity

> " *If we would have new knowledge, we must get a whole world of new questions.* "
>
> —Susanne K. Langer

Critical Thinking Focus: Deciding what information to look for, what to use, and how to present it

Writing Focus: Completing a research paper

Writing Project: A research project

Rewards of Research

When you work on your college research projects, you are participating in one of humanity's oldest and most productive efforts. You can easily come up with an endless list of scientific, technical, historical, and social investigations that have made our lives richer and safer. Conducting good research can also be rewarding for you. It can contribute to your success in college and, often, to your progress in a career. As you continue your studies, you will do several kinds of research, including retrieving and understanding what others have discovered, synthesizing and connecting others' discoveries, connecting others' discoveries with your own ideas, and formulating new concepts and theories yourself. Each of these activities is rewarding in itself, and each is also an important component in research as an extensive human activity.

Critical and creative thinking are parts of all aspects of research. The concepts discussed in every chapter of this book also pertain to research. As people seek information, they constantly deal with *perceptions, beliefs, perspectives, processes, causes, comparisons, contrasts, analogies, definitions,* and *arguments.* Research often involves *making decisions* and *problem solving*. Researchers present *reports, inferences,* and *judgments.*

In addition, like writing, research is often a recursive process rather than a linear one. One source will lead to another, new questions will arise, a creative insight will illuminate a topic, or a critical analysis will change the direction of a project.

This chapter introduces and explains strategies for using researched information in academic papers. An appendix to this book provides guidelines for using the Modern Language Association (MLA) documentation style and the American Psychological Association (APA) documentation style. Your instructor and your campus or local librarians can provide you with additional information.

Starting with Questions

Researchers begin with a question. Researchers are in pursuit of answers. Student researchers are often assigned a topic by their instructors, and asking questions about it is usually an effective approach because questions can help a researcher find a focus and can stimulate inquiry. Questions can help in various ways.

Questions That Identify Your Topic

If you are choosing your own topic, ask yourself questions:

- What interests me most within the guidelines for this project?
- What within the guidelines pertains to my college major or my future career?

THINKING-
WRITING
ACTIVITY

Developing Research Questions

1. Identify a field of study that interests you. Then write two or three questions about specific issues in that field.

2. If you can, show your questions to a professor or graduate student in the field. Ask her or him if these questions have been answered or if researchers are still working on them.

3. Share your questions with classmates. See if they have additional questions that pertain to this field of study.

- What affects my life or the lives of people close to me?
- What affects my community?
- What topics can I find material about in my college library and on the Internet?

Questions That Focus Your Topic

After you have selected a broad topic, or if your instructor has assigned a topic, you can use questions to focus it into a manageable and interesting topic. (Notice how many of these questions use the thinking patterns discussed in previous chapters of this book.)

- What are the issues involved in a topic? How are they defined? (Chapter 8)
- What are some different perspectives on the issues? (Chapter 9)
- Who is the audience for my research?
- What did people believe about my topic in previous historical periods? (Chapter 11)
- How have theories about it changed? (Chapter 11)
- What caused it? (Chapter 10)
- What problems are connected with it? How might they be solved? (Chapter 12)
- What is my purpose for conducting this research?
- What are future concerns about it likely to be?

The specific question that you want to investigate can be called a *research question*.

FOUR QUALITIES
OF A CRITICAL THINKER
Journalist Samantha Power

Curious   All research begins with a question, a desire to know more about a particular subject. Sometimes, curiosity requires courage as well, especially when the research question might lead to difficult, challenging, even dangerous inquiry. Lawyer, journalist, and human-rights activist Samantha Power is devoted to bringing the worst humanitarian crimes of recent years to international attention, including the mid-1990s genocides in Rwanda (see student Chris Buxton-Smith's paper on the subject, p. 537) and Bosnia. Power began work on her 2003 book *A Problem from Hell: America and the Age of Genocide*, after a visit to Bosnia prompted the question: why? "Not only why does this happen," she explained in an interview, "because all the time there are gaps between promise and practice, but what are the stories that we're telling ourselves such that we're living with this dissonance without experiencing it as dissonance?"

Open-minded   Researchers begin with a question, but like all critical thinkers and thoughtful writers, they consider alternative perspectives and anticipate, even expect, to be surprised by their discoveries. As she researched her book, Power tried to unravel not only the deep hatreds that led to genocide around the world, but also the inabilities and unwillingness of leaders in America and Western Europe to intervene. Her balanced but critical consideration of politics

THINKING-
WRITING
ACTIVITY

Identifying Research Questions

1. In your own words, write the research question(s) that might have inspired some of the student or professional writers included in this book.

2. What strategies did these writers use to develop their research questions?

Searching for Information

Finding Electronic and Print Sources in the Library

You are probably accustomed to using an online search engine to connect you with all kinds of information. However, you should use the resources of your college's computer center or library to help you learn the best ways to use these resources. Most college libraries provide guides to their resources. Some instructors or departments require completion of a workbook or physical or online attendance at library orientation sessions. You should take every opportunity to improve your ability to use your college library and the Internet.

and good intentions contributed to Power's book being awarded a Pulitzer Prize.

Knowledgeable A history major at Yale, Power described her education as "eclectic, it was basically just learning how to read books in a critical way. And as I said, learning how to write." Her first job after graduation was as a research assistant for the Carnegie Endowment for International Peace, where she became aware of ethnic cleansing in Bosnia and traveled to that war-torn nation as a freelance journalist.

Creative Whether working in a quiet library or dodging bullets in a war zone, the most thoughtful researchers are constantly trying to find new solutions to old problems or new approaches to difficult questions. An interviewer asked Samantha Power how concerned students could get involved

with human rights issues. "You don't have to go and join a human rights organization to be a human rights professional," she noted. "There are all kinds of ways in which, once you've decided that you're going to stand on that side of the line, and that you're always going to be attentive to the human consequences of whatever your policies are."

Online Study Center
Samantha Power
Visit the Online Study Center for *Critical Thinking, Thoughtful Writing* at *college.hmco.com/pic/ chaffeeCTTW4e* to learn more about Samantha Power.

Your library uses computers in at least four ways to direct you to source material:

1. The library's holdings are *cataloged* via a computer program, so the best way for you to find books, articles, videos, and DVDs is to learn to use the terminals in your library.

2. Most college libraries subscribe to *databases* such as Expanded Academic ASAP and National Newspapers that contain whole texts of articles from newspapers, magazines, and specialized journals, so a good way for you to find solid information is to learn to use whatever service your library has. The library provides databases that cannot be accessed on most home computers.

3. Your library probably has a *collection of CD-ROMs* containing encyclopedias, books, poems, and visuals.

4. Computer terminals available to library patrons allow you to access the Internet and use various search engines to find an infinite variety of material.

THINKING-
WRITING
ACTIVITY

Learning About Your Library

1. Go to you college or community library. Find out how to access its holdings and learn what Internet services it provides.

2. Write a paragraph explaining what your library can do for you and how to use its computers. Also, explain how you would go about obtaining print sources.

Primary and Secondary Sources

Researchers find valuable information in both *primary* and *secondary* sources. Primary sources include original documents such as letters, texts of speeches, or governmental resolutions; works of literature such as novels, stories, poems, plays, and autobiographies; and firsthand reports of experiments, observations, or interviews by the persons who conducted them. Secondary sources comment on other sources. Examples are literary criticism, biographies, studies of historical events, and any synthesis or analysis of other sources.

You should use primary sources as much as possible and try to compare secondary sources with the primary sources on which they comment to be sure that interpretations seem valid.

Collecting Information from Experts and from the Field

In addition to obtaining material from print and electronic sources, you can get information from people who have expertise on your subject. Also, you can go to places or events that are important to your research questions and conduct field research, where you observe and carefully document what goes on.

Interviews   Conducting an interview can be a valuable way to obtain information. Your creativity and critical abilities will be well used in an interview. Here are some guidelines for interviewing:

1. Identify the person with whom you wish to talk and then make an appointment with that person.

2. Carefully develop—and write out—the questions you will ask. You might want to email them to the interviewee ahead of time so that he or she will be able to prepare thorough responses.

3. Be careful as you record the interview. If you want to tape the interview, you must ask permission. If you are writing down the responses or keying them into a laptop computer, you must be sure to be accurate.

4. Do not take up too much of your interviewee's time, and—of course—give appropriate thanks.

5. Use and cite the material from an interview as you would any other source (see the MLA appendix, page 547 for guidelines). It should be effectively integrated into your paper where it works best to develop the points that you are making.

6. If you can, give your interviewee a draft of your paper to show how you have presented the material and be willing to heed suggestions if any are offered.

7. Provide the person interviewed with a copy of the completed paper and thank him or her again.

Questionnaires   Using questionnaires is another way to obtain information from people, but they are difficult to design well. If you want to gather information with a questionnaire, you should review the material on inductive reasoning and empirical generalization in Chapter 13 on pages 478–480. As a beginning researcher, you should only ask a few questions, perhaps no more than three or four.

Also, think about these concerns:

1. What exactly is the issue about which you want people's opinions? Define it very clearly.

2. How can you state questions to obtain unambiguous information? Sometimes "yes-no" or "two-way" questions are best since they elicit specific responses. However, sometimes yes-no questions are frustrating because people do not want to respond in such a limited way.

3. If you do not ask yes-no questions, how can you obtain possible responses in a small number of consistent categories that pertain to the information you want? Do you want choices? Do you want to construct a scale?

4. Can the responses be easily tabulated?

5. How many people can you poll in the time that you have and with the methods that you want to use? Will that group provide a representative sample appropriate for the scope of your project?

6. How will you use the results? How can you report them accurately, clearly identifying the characteristics and numbers of those who responded?

7. How can you use caution when drawing conclusions?

Questionnaires can be administered in several ways: by face-to-face polling; by mailing forms with a stamped, addressed return envelope; or by email. Practically speaking, a first attempt should focus on a small group—for example, asking the people on your block about a community issue or asking the students in one of your classes about a campus or political issue.

If you know someone experienced in questionnaire use—such as a social science professor, a public health researcher, or a journalism major—you might ask that person to help you craft your instrument. Also, test your questions on a few close friends or family members to see what kinds of answers you get. Then, after revising any questions that need adjusting, pose them to your selected group.

☀ *Online Study Center*
Additional Resources for Questionnaire Use
Visit the Online Study Center for this book at *college.hmco.com/pic/chaffeeCTTW4e* to find additional resources on questionnaires.

Field Research   Observations provide firsthand data and are often used in art history, sociology, education, environmental studies, medicine, and other branches of science. If you want to conduct field research, you should review Chapter 7 to remind yourself about factors that might affect your perceptions and Chapter 9 to recall different perspectives that you might take as an observer, either consciously or unconsciously. You should consider the following principles when you conduct an observation:

1. Identify a place, situation, or object that pertains to your research question.

2. Ask permission from an appropriate person if the site is reserved for use by a specific group such as a class, a club, or a religious assembly.

3. Select a good time to go to your observation site.

4. Do not become involved in any of the activities that you have come to observe.

5. Be as unobtrusive as possible. The presence of an observer often alters the dynamics of a situation.

6. If you are observing an object such as a painting, statue, building, or element of nature, try to study it at different times of day or under varying circumstances. In your write-up, accurately report the circumstances under which you made your observations.

7. Note your observations carefully.

8. Present your observations as objectively as possible. State any inferences and judgments carefully and separate them from your reporting of information obtained through your senses.

THINKING-
WRITING
ACTIVITY

Interviews Questionnaires, and Observations

1. Interview one of your instructors about using firsthand (or "primary") sources of information. Ask him or her about how observations, questionnaires, and interviews are used in his or her field. Ask how these instruments should be designed and what pitfalls to avoid.

2. Write a paragraph or two about what you have learned from the interview.

Using Information

Finding material is relatively easy. Dealing with it is the challenging part. You must evaluate the information that you have found, which involves active and critical reading. You must use critical thinking to select what you will use, and then save, copy, or take notes from it carefully. Writing your paper involves all the interrelated elements of the Thinking-Writing Model. In addition, you must integrate and cite source material in a prescribed academic format, which may at first seem difficult. Most important, you must present information accurately and honestly.

Evaluating Sources for a Research Project

All material found during research has to be evaluated. Sometimes evaluation is easy—a source may be so obviously good that you know you will use it, or it may be so clearly weak or irrelevant to your inquiry that you know you will not need it.

Here are some guidelines for deciding whether print and online material will be useful to you. These guidelines are an abbreviated version of the material in Chapter 11 on pages 366–368. Also, you may want to consult Chapters 3 and 11 to think again about some of the ways in which your beliefs have been formed since beliefs have a strong influence on evaluation.

These basic questions can help to judge information and sources:

1. *How reliable is the source?*

   • What kind of text is this? an editorial, a report, an advertisement?
   • Who is its intended audience? Is this audience important to the text's point of view?

- When was it written? Is the date relevant to my research question?
- Is it a primary or secondary source?

2. *How knowledgeable or experienced is the author?*
   - What credentials does the person who provided this information have?
   - If the person is not an expert, under what circumstances did she or he provide the information?

3. *What specific ideas are being presented?*
   - What is the main point, claim, or thesis?
   - What reasons or evidence support the information? Does anything about it seem false?
   - Does anything seem to have been left out?
   - Are interests, purposes, and intended audiences apparent?
   - If an argument is presented, can you identify its warrants?

Material found on the Internet needs to be carefully evaluated. Online texts of articles from well-known publications have undergone a review or editorial process before being printed and posted online. If a newspaper, magazine, or journal is known for publishing sound material, then an article from its online version is probably reliable. However, if the publication is considered biased or shallow, then you must examine the article more carefully.

Material from individual web sites needs special scrutiny. The following checklist will help you develop a healthy skepticism.

GUIDELINES FOR EVALUATING THE RELIABILITY OF A WEB SITE

Criterion 1: Authority

❑ Is it clear who sponsors the site and what the sponsor's purpose is in maintaining it?

❑ Is it evident who wrote the material and what the author's qualifications for writing on this topic are?

❑ If the material is protected by copyright, is the name of the copyright holder given?

❑ Is there a way to verify the legitimacy of the page's sponsor; that is, is there a phone number or postal address to contact for more information? If there is, don't hesitate to send a letter or email or to phone. You may even end up with more information for your project.

❑ If you recognize the source and are sure that it is operating the site, you are likely to be on solid ground. But don't forget that some of the people running sites are trying to confuse you, that sites on a particular topic often carry opposing messages, and that hackers can sometimes commandeer legitimate sites.

❑ A *tilde* in the web site's address (as in ~ jdoe) often indicates a personal home page, not one sponsored by an organization or institution. Another clue that a site is a personal page is when the address includes the name of a common Internet service provider—such as *geocities, tripod,* or *members.aol.com.*

❑ If you come across unfamiliar topics or web site authors, run their names through a search engine to see what other people have said about them.

Criterion 2: Accuracy

❑ Are the sources of any factual information clearly listed so that they can be verified in another source?

❑ Has the sponsor provided a link to other sites and sources—such as product reviews or reports filed with government organizations—that can be used to verify the sponsor's claims? Even better, does the site contain some references to print and other offline sources?

❑ Is statistical data in graphs and charts well labeled and easy to read?

❑ Is the information free of grammatical, spelling, and typographical errors? These kinds of errors sometimes indicate a lack of quality control and can also produce inaccuracies in the information.

Criterion 3: Objectivity

❑ For any given piece of information, is the sponsor's motivation for providing it evident?

❑ Is the information content obviously separated from any advertising or opinion content?

❑ Is the sponsor's point of view presented in a clear manner with well-supported arguments?

❑ If the site is not objective, does it at least take opposing points of view into account?

Criterion 4: Currency

❑ Is the material recent enough to be relevant to your project?

❑ Are there any indications that the material is kept up-to-date? On a browser such as Netscape Navigator, you can click on View and Page Info to see when the site was last revised.

❑ If the site contains charts and graphs, do you see statements indicating when the data were gathered?

❑ Is there an indication that the site has been completed and is not still being developed?

Online Study Center
A Guide to Critical Thinking About What You See on the Web
Visit the Online Study Center for this book at *college.hmco.com/pic/chaffeeCTTW4e* for a guide to critical thinking about what you see on the web.

THINKING-
WRITING
ACTIVITY

Evaluating Print and Web Sources

1. After you have found a print source, ask the evaluative questions above and then write your answers.

2. Go to an Internet site and evaluate it according to the web guidelines. Then write your answers.

3. Examine your answers to the previous two questions. How will they influence your possible use of these sources?

Moving from Questions to Thesis

The next step in your research is to move from your research questions to a thesis for your research paper. The guidelines for all of this book's Writing Projects include suggestions for identifying a focus and defining a thesis. Reviewing these suggestions will help you when you are writing a research paper.

Some research papers take an informative position; others are strongly argumentative. This distinction will depend on your purpose, the traditions of the discipline in which you are writing the paper, and your instructor's goals for the assignment. Be sure that you understand whether your instructor wants your paper to be informative or argumentative.

THINKING-
WRITING
ACTIVITY

Going from Questions to Thesis

1. Select one of the questions that you wrote for the Thinking-Writing Activity: Developing Research Questions on page 505. Then find or imagine some answers to it. Next, write at least one thesis statement that answers it or makes a claim about an answer to it.

2. Look at the questions and statements that two or three of your classmates created for this Thinking-Writing Activity. Identify the statements that seem clearest and have the most potential to be developed into solid papers.

Understanding Plagiarism and Using Information Ethically

Plagiarism is presenting another person's ideas or words as your own. There are two good reasons not to plagiarize. The first is honesty. Most people do not want to be fakes; they want to be honest, and so they do not want to steal others' ideas and work without giving credit. The second is that plagiarism can bring severe penalties, both in college and at work.

In college writing, two kinds of plagiarism are possible. One is deliberate and dishonorable—the willful copying of all or part of another student's paper or all or part of a source. Buying a paper from a service is also plagiarism because a student who does this is taking credit for someone else's words, ideas, and effort.

The other kind of plagiarism is accidental and happens when a student does not know how to document properly. Once you understand that you must always signal where any material from a source begins and ends and that you must always make clear who said something and where it was said, you should be able to avoid accidental plagiarism. The sections in this chapter on Taking Notes, The Logic Behind Documentation Formats, and Tips on Avoiding Plagiarism will help.

A *fabrication* is a deliberately false or invented statement. It presents as true something that is made up or distorted, such as an event that did not happen, a statement that was not made, a misleading addition or omission of words or data, a listing of a source that was not used. Some writers are tempted to fabricate or falsify if they do not have real information that they need in order to make a point or create a desired effect. Yet readers must be able to trust the material that is presented in academic work and in responsible media.

Fabrication is different from making a mistake, which unfortunately almost everyone does occasionally, but not deliberately. A fabrication is different from a hypothesis or hypothetical example, which should be identified as such.

GUIDELINES
FOR
AVOIDING
PLAGIARISM

❑ Remember that all material from any source must be documented in some way. Downloaded items, web sites, email, interviews, illustrations, DVDs, videos, films, broadcasts, lectures, books, articles—anything that is not drawn from your own experience, observation, or creativity—must be cited appropriately.

❑ Learn the different methods of citation used in various writing situations. In college, you may need to use different formats in papers written for different classes. These disciplinary formats are explained in guides to research and handbooks. At work, you will give credit to others as expected in your occupation. In writing done for community activities, you will probably cite information informally, just stating that a person, article, or report said something.

❑ Be sure to present quoted material (exact words) in quotation marks, indented, or in some other indicative way, depending on the format that you are using.

❑ Remember that copied-and-pasted material, paraphrases, summaries, and short extracts, even of less than a sentence, all must be cited. Other people's ideas must be documented as well as their exact words.

❑ Be sure to indicate in all drafts where source material is from so that you do not lose track of it as you revise and edit.

(Continued)

❑ Signal where material from others begins and where it ends. Learn to do this in a variety of ways, as appropriate to the writing situation.

❑ Take pride in presenting your own thinking and distinguish your ideas clearly from those of your sources.

❑ Be careful to capture all bibliographic material as you download, photocopy, and take notes so that you can easily provide documentation. Be sure to record authors' full names, exact titles, publication information, dates, page numbers, URLs, and other access items.

❑ Consult with your instructors and writing center tutors about citing sources when you are drafting your researched writing.

❑ When in doubt, cite.

THINKING-
WRITING
ACTIVITY

Plagiarism in the News

1. Read carefully your college's statements about plagiarism. Does your college have an honor code? If so, what does it say about plagiarism? Write a few sentences giving your responses to these statements.

2. Search for information about Stephen Glass, Jayson Blair, Janet Cook, James Frey, Stephen Ambrose, or Doris Kearns Goodwin. Find out what any of these writers are reported to have fabricated or plagiarized, what they said about their situations, and what happened to them.

3. What can college students learn from the experience of these professionals?

Share your responses to these questions with classmates and see how your ideas are similar or different.

Taking Notes

Although photocopying and downloading have made note taking less necessary than it was in previous eras, researchers still need to have methods for deciding what to note, highlight, or underline; for accurately recording content and bibliographic information; and for integrating source material thoughtfully into their own written work.

Deciding When to Take Notes

Sometimes you can easily see that certain parts of an article, book, or web site relate to your research question or working thesis. Naturally, in such cases, you will then note the material or photocopy, highlight, or download it. However, at other times, you may not be sure what to select from a source.

Your critical reading abilities will come into play here. Before you even think about taking notes, you should read an entire article. If you are consulting a book, read the whole book—if possible—or skim it, consult the index, and read the chapters that contain information related to your topic. Look for headings, topic sentences, chapter titles—all the elements that point out what the writer is discussing. As you read through, jot down page numbers or mark passages that strike you in some way, but you really should not take notes until you have a grasp of the entire piece.

After getting an overview of the work, you need to go back and select specific points that pertain to your question or thesis. If you're not sure how the material relates, note it! At this stage, you want too much information instead of too little. Highlighting and underlining are forms of note taking because you are choosing information.

Quoting and Paraphrasing

Another decision that you have to make while taking notes is when to quote (using exact words) or to paraphrase (restating). Highlighting and underlining are forms of quoting. There are only two rules:

1. When you quote, put all of the quoted material inside quotation marks in your notes so that you will never forget that these are the author's exact words. Then you will know that anything else in your notes that is not in quotation marks is paraphrased.

2. Be accurate.

The following are some guidelines for quoting:

- If the author has said something in a distinctive way, quote or highlight it.
- If the author has said something complicated and/or technical, quote or highlight it.
- If the author has said something controversial, quote or highlight it.
- When in doubt, quote the author's words in your notes. You can decide if you would rather paraphrase them later when you are writing your paper.
- If you know that you only want a summary of a source or an indication of what it says, paraphrase it.

Here are examples of a full note and the paraphrased version:

Quoted note: "A Kampala journalist named Michael Wakabi told me that Kampala has become a 'used culture.' The cars are used—they arrive from Japan with broken power windows and air conditiong, so Ugandan drivers bake in the sun. Used furniture from Europe lines the streets in Kampala. The Ugandan Army occupies part of neighboring Congo with used tanks and aircraft from Ukraine. And the traditional Ugandan dress made from local cotton, called gomesi, is as rare as the mountain gorilla. To dress African, Ugandans have to have money."—Packer 58.

Paraphrased note: The economy of Uganda is ruined by exploitation—local industries and culture are almost extinct. Nothing is fabricated or produced in Uganda anymore; most consumer goods are rejects from Western countries. Because native Ugandan products are so rare, only wealthy Ugandans can have them.—Packer 58.

The author's full name and all publication information will be on a bibliography card or list (see pages 519–520).

Characteristics of Effective Note-Taking Systems

Good note-taking systems include:

- accuracy in recording material
- accuracy in recording full bibliographic information
- differentiation between quoted and paraphrased material
- indication of the source from which a specific note is taken
- indication of the section of a paper to which a specific note pertains
- capacity to rearrange notes to put material into the appropriate sections of a paper

The traditional technique of using note cards has all of these characteristics. Other methods can accomplish the same tasks, but researchers need to use care to separate noted items and to find a way to sort information in order to insert it in its logical place in the paper. If, like many students today, you only use note cards when you cannot photocopy or download a source, you need to think carefully about ways to develop a method that will provide you with the benefits of the note-card system.

The traditional system has two parts: a note card for each piece of information and a bibliographic card for every source.

Note Cards   Each note card contains only one item of information. The act of selecting specific items motivates you to think carefully about what *you* are looking for in order to present your ideas in the paper. Figure 14.1 shows an example of a note card.

You indicate clearly on the card whether the material is quoted by using quotation marks or whether it is paraphrased by not using the marks. You also briefly identify the source on the card and note the section or subtopic of your paper to which the information pertains. As you begin drafting, arrange the cards in groups according to the places in the paper where that information will be used. Citation of sources is easy because each card records its source.

Author of source

Descriptive heading or subtopic

FIGURE 14.1 | Note Card

Direct quotation begins and ends with quotation marks

Carter, Stephen L.   his own definition of integrity

"Integrity, as I will use the term, requires three steps: discerning what is right and what is wrong; acting on what you have discerned, even at personal cost; and saying openly that you are acting on your understanding of right and wrong."

507

Page where quotation was found

FIGURE 14.2   Bibliography Card

Carter, Stephen L. "The Insufficiency of Honesty."
Great Writing. Ed. Harvey S. Weiner and Nora Eisenberg.
3rd ed. San Francisco: McGraw, 2002. 507–512.

Bibliographic Cards   A good note-taking system includes a set of bibliography cards (or a list) which provides the full publication information for each source. You arrange the cards alphabetically by author or title when preparing your Works Cited list.

Figure 14.1 shows the bibliography card for the source of the quotation illustrated in Figure 14.2.

Look at the Works Cited list for one of the documented student papers in this book or consult your handbook. Then ask yourself: Is this source recorded in the MLA Works Cited–list format? Is it a book, a periodical, or an Internet source? Why will it be easy for this student to insert this source into her Works Cited list?

Using Your Computer to Take Notes   Computers can be used in many ways for note taking. Simply by using a word-processing program, you can enter notes in appropriate files or under specific headings, and by pasting, copying, or using other combining methods, you can put the information into the part of your paper where you want it. You should double- or triple-space so that you can see items clearly, write changes interlinearly on printouts, and cut pages up to rearrange material. You can compile a Works Cited (MLA) or References (APA) list by using an alphabetizing program or simply by copying or pasting.

Most students use combinations of note taking and recording methods—card- or paper-based systems when necessary, electronic-based ones when possible. Probably the most unwieldy system—and one to avoid—is writing page after page of notes in a notebook, on both sides of the paper, without leaving spaces for notes to be annotated or cut apart and rearranged. You should avoid using any technique that does not allow you to review and organize material easily.

THINKING-
WRITING
ACTIVITY

Learning About the Methods of Experienced Note Takers

1. Ask one of your instructors or a successful upper-division student how he or she takes notes, keeps records of sources, and arranges source material for use in a paper. Ask also about the advantages and disadvantages of the system.

2. Write a paragraph summarizing what you have learned. Then share what you have written with classmates and see what systems they have learned about.

THINKING-
WRITING
ACTIVITY

Creating Your Own Note-Taking Methods

1. If you have previously worked on research projects, write an explanation of your own note-taking and record-keeping processes. How do you use your computer to complete tasks? What do you do that is effective? What do you need to improve?

2. Share your system with your classmates and learn about their systems. Does a classmate have a technique that you would like to adopt?

Summarizing

You will often need to summarize what a source says, either as a way of taking notes or as a way of inserting information into your paper. Your critical reading abilities will serve you well when you write a summary. Here are some guidelines:

- A summary is by definition short. An article or book chapter might be summarized in five or six sentences.

- A summary presents major points, not introductory material or multiple examples. It might give one necessary example.

- A summary should state the main point or the thesis clearly, probably at the beginning.

- A summary does not include your commentary on or evaluation of the material. You can comment later as you introduce summarized material into your paper or after you have included it.

  Comment or evaluation: "This article discussed a major breakthrough. . . ."
  Summary: "It says . . ."
  Comment or evaluation: "This book takes a stand that is no longer accepted. . . ."
  Summary: "It claims . . ."

- Signal that you are presenting summarized material. One way to begin a summary is to state the main point. Signal words such as *The article says . . . He points out . . . or She concludes . . .* are helpful throughout a summary.

- Usually a summary paraphrases a source, but if you quote special words, graceful phrases, or entire sentences, be sure to use quotation marks.

- A summary is accurate.

The following is a professionally written summary of the article "Hospice Care or Assisted Suicide: A False Dichotomy" that appears in Chapter 13 on pages 470–473.

In this paper, the author argues that making assisted suicide available is not a contradictory position to espousing hospice care. He draws on historical and political examples to explain the ethical basis for this assertion. By defining the issue at stake as one of personal autonomy (the loss or gain thereof), the author challenges the argument that making assisted suicide available leads to a slippery slope toward euthanasia, eugenics, or genocide. He asserts that narrowing choices by preventing people from seeking assistance in suicide is more likely to lead us down the slippery slope toward coercive medical and state intervention in our lives.

THINKING-
WRITING
ACTIVITY

Learning to Summarize

1. Write a four- or five-sentence summary of one of the sources that you evaluated for the Thinking-Writing Activity: Evaluating Print and Web Sources on page 514.

2. If you can, ask a classmate to read the source and then comment on whether your summary seems accurate.

Preparing an Annotated Bibliography

One technique that can help you evaluate your sources is writing an annotated bibliography. Your research librarian can show you annotated bibliographies about many subjects, either as books, as indexes, or online.

Sometimes instructors will ask students to create an annotated bibliography as a part of a research project. An *annotated bibliography* is a list of sources with a brief summary of and some evaluative comments about each one.

A student who was researching genocide in Rwanda made the entries shown in the example in Figure 14.3 on page 523. His instructor had required students to prepare an annotated bibliography of several sources before drafting their research papers.

THINKING-
WRITING
ACTIVITY

Creating an Annotated Bibliography

1. Find three sources that pertain to one of the questions that you used in a previous Thinking-Writing Activity or to a paper that you are writing.

2. After you have read the sources carefully, create an annotated bibliography in which you list full bibliographic information. Also, summarize each source in one or two sentences and comment in one or two sentences about what each source's value would be in a paper about the subject.

FIGURE 14.3   Sample Annotated Bibliography Entries

Carter, Stephen L. "The Insufficiency of Honesty." <u>Great Writing</u>. Ed. Harvey
    S. Weiner and Nora Eisenberg. 3rd ed. San Francisco: McGraw, 2002.
    507–512.

    In this essay, Carter provides a very detailed definition of integrity and
a thoughtful discussion of applications of the concept of integrity to difficult
real-world situations.
    These examples helped me see that I could connect the concept of
integrity with the United States' and United Nations' lack of response to the
atrocities in Rwanda. This essay will be central to my paper because I want
to show that integrity demanded that they intervene.

United Nations General Assembly. "Convention on the Prevention and
    Punishment of The Crime of Genocide." 1948. 5 Dec. 2005. <http://
    www.hrweb.org/legal/genocide.html>.

    The 19 articles of this United Nations document state clearly that genocide
is a political as well as a moral crime. It specifies genocidal acts, such as
killing a group's members, aiming to destroy a group, preventing birth of or
taking its children, and causing physical and mental harm that will prevent
a group from maintaining its way of life.
    This primary document provides valuable context and support for my
paper's thesis. I will use it to show that in addition to the moral obligation
to intervene in Rwanda, there was a contractual obligation as well.

Integrating Source Material

Research has often been described as an endless conversation. The formats in which academic work is presented reflect the metaphor of research as conversation by indicating who is saying what.

The most important point to remember is that *you* are the person presenting the information in your paper. You are, in effect, participating in a conversation with your sources and your readers. Your paper is not just a series of quotations and paraphrases from sources; instead, it is a presentation of your ideas about the issue and your thinking about what your sources have said.

Introducing Sources

An extension of the notion of research as conversation is seeing a research paper as analogous to a dignified television or radio talk show or a panel discussion about a current issue. Think of yourself as a talk-show host as you write a paper that uses source material. Just as the host sets up the discussion, you will provide a context and a clear purpose for presenting the material that you have found. Just as the host introduces each guest to the audience, you will select sources your audience will be interested in and respect. Just as the host helps the guests interact, you will point out the connections and oppositions between and among your sources. And just as the host wraps the show up, you will conclude your paper in an effective manner.

To be considerate of your audience, you will need to know how academic writers introduce a source into a paper. Here are some techniques:

- *Use the name of the author, especially a significant writer or scholar:*
  "Elizabeth Cady Stanton wrote that 'it is the duty of the women of this country to secure to themselves their sacred right to the elective franchise.'"

- *Use the name of the publication:*
  "A *New York Times* article provides guidelines for evaluating information found on the Web. It says . . ."

- *Establish a context:*
  "Students now receive much advice about how to decide whether information found on the Internet is likely to be good or useless. For example, an article in the *New York Times* provides a list of hints and warnings. This article says . . ."

- *Indicate your purpose for presenting the information.* This is part of the research conversation. You are talking about the source. In the following passage, a student has commented in his own voice both before and after paraphrasing from a source.

Student

Integrity is at the heart of my position on this situation. According to Stephen L. Carter in his essay "The Insufficiency of Honesty," integrity is much more than acting or appearing noble when dealing with a situation.

Source

He says that there are three steps in defining the degree of one's integrity. These are "discerning what is right and what is wrong; acting on what you have discerned, even at personal cost; and saying openly you are acting on your understanding of what is right and what is wrong" (507).

Student

Obviously the massacre of 800,000 innocent people is inherently wrong; having knowledge that a massacre of 800,000 people is about to occur is inherently wrong, and not acting on this legitimate intelligence is painfully misguided. It is completely devoid of any semblance of integrity.

Establishing Your Voice

You will use your own voice in your research writing to fulfill several purposes. First, as just explained, you will always signal in some way that you are introducing source material into your paper. In addition, as the author of a paper, not just a complier of other people's ideas, you might

- *Comment on what sources say.* You should indicate your purpose for including the source material in the paper. You could express agreement or disagreement with particular sources. You might explain which sources you consider most important to the points you are making in the paper. Providing such commentary is an important part of your role as "host."
- *Synthesize what sources say.* You should discuss ways in which sources relate to each other. You might point out a chronological sequence of concepts or explain how theories differ from each other. You could show how sources agree.
- *Present your own thinking.* You have established a thesis for your paper, and, of course, you will present ideas to support it. You might explain why you agree with one source or a group of sources or why you differ from them all and have your own claim to put forth. You might present ideas that have come from your experiences, your observations, your interpretations, or your creative thinking.

You need to clarify when you are speaking in order to be credited for your ideas and comments, just as you must indicate when your sources are speaking so that proper credit is given to them.

Your voice should be easily identifiable as long as you have indicated where all source material begins and ends. Then everything else is either your commentary, your synthesis, or your own thinking. Often, you will want to use words or phrases to show that you are commenting—such as "Therefore," "A consideration of these concepts shows . . .," or "Another significant idea is . . ."

Choosing Pronouns

If your instructor agrees, you could simply present some of your comments and ideas as first-person statements: "I want to suggest . . ."; "After analyzing these reports, I decided . . ."; "I believe . . ." However, there is an academic tradition that discourages the use of the first person singular pronoun (*I*) in order to suggest an objective and impersonal point of view. This tradition is stronger in some disciplines than in others. You should ask your instructors about the preferred pronoun use in research papers and also look at pronoun use in academic journals in the fields in which you are studying.

Also be careful about using *we*. Be sure you identify who "we" is—people sometimes use the word to mean society at large, the citizens of a particular country, or the readers of a particular newspaper or magazine. However, your readers should never have to assume. In addition, the second person (*you*) is rarely used in academic writing.

THINKING-
WRITING
ACTIVITY

Clarifying Who Is Talking

1. Look at the student paper at the end of this chapter, at other documented papers in this book, or at a research paper in your handbook. Notice how the student writers introduce other people's ideas into their papers. Then write a paragraph about what you have observed. Quote some different ways in which these student writers bring sources into their papers.

2. Notice how the writers clarify what their own thinking is about the source material or about the point that the source is being used to support. Identify two specific places where student writers are speaking in their own voices.

Think about how this activity might help you to write your next documented paper and to avoid creating a paper that is just a string of quotations and paraphrases of others' ideas.

The Logic Behind Documentation Formats

Reasons for Documentation

Two principles underlie academic documentation formats:

- Readers have to know *who* says something.
- Readers have to know *where* something is said.

All academic formats provide this information in logical systems whether they use parentheses, endnotes, or footnotes. Different disciplines use different formats, but they are all based on these two principles. Your handbook or guide to research will explain most of the formats, such as those adopted by the American Psychological Association (APA), the Council of Science Editors (CSE), and the Modern Language Association (MLA). Also, these associations maintain web sites on which you can find the most current format models. Guidelines to the MLA and APA styles are in this book's appendix.

Researchers clarify who said something and where it was said for a number of reasons:

- *To give credibility to a paper.* The strength or weakness of source materials helps readers judge the strength or weakness of a research project and its presentation.
- *To help readers and other researchers learn more.* Proper documentation can direct readers to sources so that they can find out more about a subject than what is presented in a paper.
- *To give credit where credit is due.* Research papers combine many people's ideas. Democracy tells us that each person is important. Giving appropriate credit shows respect for the human being who expressed the idea being used. Further, out of self-respect, researchers and writers want their own ideas to be credited to them just as much as they want to acknowledge others' ideas.
- *To observe the courtesies of conversation.* If research is a millennia-long conversation, the courtesies of conversation are in order. People take turns speaking during a conversation; sometimes points are recapped; often questions are asked and answered. It is usually important to know who is speaking in a conversation.
- *To avoid plagiarism.*

THINKING-WRITING ACTIVITY

Citing and Paraphrasing

Students usually know that quoted material of a sentence or more must be documented. However, students sometimes have difficulty understanding that paraphrases and quotations of short, "apt phrases" must also be cited. Read the following passage that was written by Lynn Z. Bloom and appears on page 90 of the eighth edition of *The Essay Connection*, published by Houghton Mifflin in 2007:

> *Original passage:* "Narratives have as many purposes, as many plots, as many characters as there are people to write them. You have but to examine your life, your thoughts, your experiences, to find an unwritten library of narratives yet to tell."

Why is this use acceptable?

1. Lynn Bloom points out that all people have stories worth telling if they will just look into their lives and experiences where they will "find an unwritten library of narratives." (90)

(Continued)

Why could this use be seen as plagiarism by some or as an error in punctuation by others. What do you think?

2. Each person's life can be seen as holding an unwritten library of narratives. (Bloom 90)

   Where do you see plagiarism here?

3. Storytelling may be one of the defining characteristics of the human species. Stories come in countless forms, and have been told in various ways by almost everybody who has ever lived. Indeed, narratives have as many purposes, as many plots, as many characters as there are people to tell them.

Using Common Knowledge

It is usually not necessary to document information that is considered "common knowledge," or things that "everybody" knows. Common knowledge is often factual, such as the fact that hijacked planes piloted by terrorists crashed into the World Trade Center on September 11, 2001. Well-known sayings like "Haste makes waste" are usually not documented, nor are accepted concepts like consuming large amounts of high-calorie food will cause most people to gain weight. However, discussions of facts or well-known ideas are not common; they are produced by individuals and must be documented.

In addition, common knowledge is not universally common. Different cultures, different time periods, different academic disciplines, and different occupations all have their own common knowledge and often do not see ideas from other groups or eras as well known. Therefore, you need to be cautious about presenting something as common knowledge and perhaps consult with your instructor. If in doubt, document. It is better to overcite than to plagiarize.

The Logic of MLA Style

The MLA system is used in this book because it is widely used in English classes and the humanities. To understand how it works, look at the paper at the end of this chapter or at a model in your handbook or guide to research.

1. First, note that at the end of a paper, there is a list of Works Cited, with the sources listed alphabetically according to *author*, or if no author is given, according to the *title* of the source. Full bibliographic information is given in this list so that it does not have to be provided in the parenthetical citations within the body of the paper.

2. Next, look at the places within the paper where sources are cited. Note that when material has been taken from a source, the last name or an abbreviated title under which it is listed in Works Cited is given—either when the material

is introduced or in parentheses at the end of its use. The number of the page on which the material can be found is given in parentheses at the end of the quotation or paraphrase. The parentheses signal the end of the source material.

3. If a source does not have a page number, then a number cannot be given, so you must otherwise signal that use of the source has ended. Many online documents do not show page numbers, so you must be careful to indicate where your use of such a source ends.

THINKING-
WRITING
ACTIVITY

Explaining the MLA System

1. Look again at the documented paper in this chapter or in your handbook. Then write an explanation of how the MLA system works as illustrated in that paper. Explain the relationship between the Works Cited list and the parenthetical citations.

2. Next, explain the MLA system to a classmate. Then tell your classmate why you believe the reasons for documentation are important. See if she or he agrees.

Working Thoughtfully on Research Projects

Much of the work you do to produce a research paper is similar to what you do when you write from your own resources. However, research projects often involve some special steps and concerns, including scheduling a significant amount of time, planning your paper carefully, using a specified academic format, and, often, consulting with librarians and with your instructor.

Time

No one needs to tell you that you cannot just sit down and write up the results of a research project in a short hour spent at your keyboard. Reading, evaluating, selecting, noting, commenting on, and arranging material demands the use of critical and creative thinking processes that usually cannot be hurried.

Using a library can involve waiting for help from a librarian, learning to use the computerized catalog, searching the shelves for material, seeing interesting material that doesn't pertain to your paper, and, of course, having to read, evaluate, copy, take notes, and think about what you've found. College libraries are pleasant places where time is usually well spent—and where you will spend much time while working on a research project.

Deciding on the scope of a project, working though research questions, narrowing a topic, interviewing knowledgeable persons, and revising and qualifying a thesis all take time.

Therefore, you should make a schedule when you begin a research project. You must complete the project within the time frame that your instructor allows. Instructors usually give weeks or months for research projects, but it is amazing how quickly that time evaporates and how suddenly deadlines are staring you in the face. Start as soon as you are given the assignment. Block out time to work on it regularly. Be sure to follow any time line that your instructor establishes.

One instructor gives her students this checklist:

Research Project Checklist		
	Due Date	*Date(s) Completed*
Decide on focus	_____	_____
Develop research questions	_____	_____
Locate and evaluate sources (ongoing)	_____	_____
Select and read sources (ongoing)	_____	_____
Identify useful sources; take notes	_____	_____
Develop thesis	_____	_____
Develop working outline	_____	_____
Draft sections of paper	_____	_____
Conference with instructor	_____	_____
Draft(s) of complete paper	_____	_____
Peer review	_____	_____
Revise, edit, and proofread paper	_____	_____
Hand in completed paper and all required material	_____	_____

Remember that this checklist makes research seem more linear and less recursive than it usually is.

Planning and Outlining

Since research papers are often longer than essays or reports, planning and outlining are important steps. You will probably have to gather information before you can see what shape your paper will take, but as soon as you can, you will want to block out the sections of the paper and make a working outline (to be changed as the paper develops). If your instructor requires that a formal outline be submitted with your finished paper, look at the paper at the end of this chapter or consult your handbook for a model. Some word-processing programs include formal outlines in their formatting options, so your computer might help you create an outline.

Formats and Models

You must use an accepted academic documentation format when you write a research paper for a college class. You cannot be creative about documentation. You must follow the models exactly. You should also familiarize yourself with the style, design, and format your instructor requires for the presentation of your research paper.

Collaboration

The research conducted in business, at large laboratories, and by think tanks and professional organizations is often done by teams. Therefore, to give students this experience, some instructors may assign team projects in college classes. But even if the project that you will be working on will be an individual effort, other people can provide much help. You will want to work with your instructor, the librarians, computer experts, and your classmates as much as you can as you complete your research. See Chapter 6, pages 153–154 for using peer response groups as a revising strategy.

Writing Project: A Research Paper

This chapter emphasizes the reasoning behind many of the activities that occur while you are engaged in research. The Thinking-Writing Activities should help you find and use information. Be sure to reread what you wrote for those activities.

Following all instructions given by your instructor, complete a research project and write a well-documented paper in which you report and discuss your findings.

Begin by considering the key elements in the Thinking-Writing Model in Chapter 1 on page 7–9.

The Writing Situation

Purpose   Your two major purposes for research are to learn as much as you can about your topic and then to present your thinking about your findings in an effective paper. Also, you can improve your ability to use your college library and the Internet. You can also become more skilled at using and better understanding academic formats.

ZITS   *BY JERRY SCOTT AND JIM BORGMAN*

As tempting as this "mental blender" approach to research might appear, there is at this time no substitute for research based on thoughtful exploration, effective planning, productive collaboration, and above all, critical thinking.

In addition, you will further develop your critical and creative thinking abilities as you apply almost every concept presented in this book to your research project.

Audience   If your classmates are working on similar projects, they will be an excellent audience for your finished paper as well as for drafts. If your research topic is about a social or political issue, your audience might include people beyond your college. Perhaps you can find a way to share what you've learned at a community forum; in a newspaper, newsletter, or listserv; or on a web site. Your instructor remains the audience who will judge how well you have shaped your research question, investigated possible answers, discussed what you have found, and documented your paper in the required academic format.

Subject   Obviously, you should be interested in the subject of your research so that your work will be a pleasure rather than a chore. If the subject is significant in your life or connected with one of your favorite academic fields, you should be able to think of a stimulating research question. If the subject has been assigned and, perhaps, is not among your interests, do everything you can to connect it to your interests. Ask questions about it, read as widely as you can, and consult web sites. You will almost surely find issues within any subject that you can relate to your own concerns.

Writer   If you've already worked on research projects in previous classes, you should feel confident as you undertake this one, but you should be willing to improve your abilities throughout the entire process. Be your most efficient self by setting up a schedule, working steadily, and meeting all deadlines. Don't hesitate to ask for help from librarians, computer room staff, and your instructor.

Remember the talk-show analogy presented in this chapter: you are the host, in charge of the paper. Comment on what you discover during your investigation; present your own thinking and keep yourself in the paper as much as is appropriate to the subject, to the traditions of the discipline in which you are working, and to your assignment.

The Writing Process

Much of the material already presented in this chapter relates to generating ideas, finding a focus, and defining a thesis as you work on a research project. You should review it before you begin your paper.

Generating Ideas

* As you use the technique of asking questions about your subject, look again at the questions presented in Chapter 4 (pages 90–93). Apply as many of those questions as you can.
* Brainstorm and freewrite as you begin your research project, just as you would do when writing a paper from your own experience. "Talk to yourself" on paper about what you want to investigate and what you want to say about the topic.
* Use the thinking patterns discussed in Chapters 7 to 10 as ways to find ideas. Ask yourself about any processes involved in your subject. Describe important objects connected with it. Think about similarities and differences within it. Identify causal relationships. Define important terms. And be sure to write down what the thinking patterns show you.
* Before you decide on a limited focus, read widely about your subject. Consult encyclopedias and web sites to get background information and ideas.

Defining a Thesis or Making a Claim   As you turn your research question (or questions) into a tentative thesis statement or claim, you need to be sure that your thesis or claim reflects the rhetorical purpose of your paper. Are you explaining, describing, or presenting different points of views? In that case, you will need to create a thesis statement. Or are you arguing for a specific position? For a researched argument, you will need to match and support a claim.

Notice how the documented student papers in Chapters 8 and 10 explain their topics. Notice how Joshua Bartlett's paper in Chapter 12 and the paper in Chapter 13 argue for specific changes. Notice how the paper in this chapter argues for a claim.

Draft more than one possible thesis statement or claim and then decide which one best serves your purposes. Remember that you may refocus your paper as you draft and revise it, so you should be open to reshaping your thesis statement or claim as you rework the paper.

Organizing Ideas   Research papers, are usually divided into logically distinguished sections. As you organize your paper, you need to think about how the material that you have found pertains to different aspects of the topic. And in an interactive process, as your research develops, the material you find will suggest different points that you may want to develop.

For example, if you are researching changes in beliefs about healthy diets, you might divide your paper chronologically or according to food groups, depending on what you decide to emphasize. If you are researching homelessness in a community in order to present an overview of it to an audience of relatively affluent young people, your paper might include almost equally developed sections on the estimated numbers of homeless people, the causes of homelessness, and the programs to help the homeless. If your purpose is to argue for improved programs, your paper might have a short introductory section on the numbers and causes and well-developed sections on various options for helping the homeless.

If you have used note cards and classified them according to the aspect of your topic to which they contribute, you can easily arrange and rearrange them as you incorporate information into your draft. If you have taken notes on your computer, you can print files and/or copy and organize. If you have assembled printouts and photocopies of articles and pages, you'll need to identify the parts of your paper where this information belongs and sort it appropriately. If you have a combination of downloaded material, photocopies, and written notes—which is likely—you will need to put them in logical piles or arrange them near your keyboard in a way that will help you to incorporate information and keep track of where every item came from.

Outlines are usually necessary planning tools for long research papers. You should draft working outlines several times during your research process. If your instructor requires a formal outline, you can write one at the end of your planning, after you have completed a draft or after you finish the paper. A formal outline will provide a good measure of the organization of your paper.

Drafting   Drafting a research paper differs from drafting a personal paper in one important way: you must remember to indicate within the draft where source material begins, where it ends, where it is from, and whether it is quoted or paraphrased. In a draft, citation formats and wordings of the signals that indicate a source do not have to be perfect. You can polish these up when you revise and edit, but to avoid accidental plagiarism, you must keep track of this material as you draft.

One decision you will have to make during drafting is whether to quote, paraphrase, or summarize source material. This is not always an easy choice. You do not want to quote too much, yet you do need to report what sources say. You should read documented papers and articles in your fields of interest in order to develop a sense of how experienced academic writers use their sources. Notice how these writers use short quotations, long quotations, paraphrases, and summaries.

The following are some guidelines for deciding what to quote, paraphrase, or summarize.

* You probably should quote if what a source has said is worded in a special way, is complicated or technical, or is controversial.

- If you are still learning about the field that your sources are discussing, you might need to quote more than an expert would.
- You should not use many long quoted passages. If you include a lot of lengthy quotations, you may end up compiling a small anthology instead of writing a paper.
- Remember that you do not have to quote whole sentences; often a few words will suffice. Example: In contrasting facts and theories, Stephen Jay Gould calls facts "the world's data" and theories "structures of ideas that explain and interpret facts." (page 381 in Chapter 11)
- You might want to quote fairly extensively in an early draft and then ask your classmates, writing center tutors, or instructor for help with shortening quotations and paraphrasing.
- *Paraphrasing*, or restating another's ideas in your own words, requires a good vocabulary and well-developed critical reading skills. Ask yourself as you are drafting: "Let's see. What is this source saying? How do these ideas help develop my paper?" Then write your answers and see how they might help you to incorporate the source into your paper.
- You use *summaries* to show the main points of an article, section, chapter, book, or Internet source. Remember to explain the significance of the summarized material.

Remember that you must always signal the beginning and end of source use and cite appropriately, whether you are quoting, paraphrasing, or summarizing.

You should remain aware of your talk-show host role as you comment on what you have used from your sources. You will probably need to draft your statements several times as you reread your notes and sources and rethink what you want to say.

Revising, Editing, and Proofreading   Use the Step-by-Step Method in Chapter 6 on pages 152–153 to revise your essay and prepare a final draft.

Annotated Student Research Paper with Outline and Drafts

The paper on pages 538–546 was written for an English composition course that emphasizes exposition, argument, and research. A sequence of reading and writing assignments led up to the paper assignment. Students responded to each other's drafts during two peer review sessions. Chris Buxton-Smith describes how he thought about his writing situation and writing process.

Chris Buxton-Smith's Writing Situation

Purpose   Midway through the semester, our instructor gave us an assignment for which we were to choose one of several concepts and write an argument of at least six pages, using a minimum of four sources. The essay was to address a specific concept in order to argue for or against a particular act or position. Among the concepts were *masculinity, femininity, racism*, and *integrity*, as well as a whole slew of others that pertained to readings we had been assigned throughout the semester. The purpose was to demonstrate our understanding of the concept and our proficiency at writing a strong argumentation paper. After some thought, I saw that I might be able to choose a subject that, since my late teens, I had always wanted to write about: the Rwandan Genocide that left nearly a million ethnic Tutsis dead.

Audience   I identified my audience as my classmates, who could also be regarded as a portion of the general American public, most of whom were in the dark about the atrocities that occurred in 1994 in the African country of Rwanda. Many Americans had not been aware that a genocide was occurring, even under the watchful eye of the world press. In class, after a peer review, classmates were awed by the fact that such things could occur in this seemingly modern world where almost a million people were scratched from existence in only one hundred days, in spite of the potential of United States military power and the possibility of diplomacy by the United Nations. I wanted to open my audience's eyes.

Subject   When I started, I was torn between [writing on one of the suggested] concepts and [determining] how I could effectively apply one to a pertinent subject in which I had great interest. I knew I could take the easier route and write a straightforward essay addressing one of the concepts in a one-dimensional fashion. Instead, I chose a pair that had a number of controversial details to discuss. I opted for the concept of *integrity* and how it applied to the United States' and the United Nations' involvement, or lack thereof, in the Rwandan Genocide. In the end, I was able to connect the two in a way that met the demands of the assignment.

Writer   After reading about the situation that occurred in Rwanda in a book called *We Wish to Inform You That Tomorrow You Will be Killed with Your Families* by Phillip Gourevitch, I became haunted by the subject of modern-day mass genocide. I tried to write the paper in a state of sort of suspended ignorance in order to keep an open mind since I had already read the book on Rwanda, and I had preconceived emotions about the subject. When I began researching, I tried to check those emotions at the door and allow myself to remain open to a fresh perspective. But, in the end, my research reinvigorated my anger and confusion about how genocides still occur.

Chris's Writing Process

Brainstorming   The process I used to write this paper was relatively straightforward. Using techniques of which I had prior knowledge and new ones that I learned in class, I set about writing. The first step was to brainstorm. Using this technique, I was able to come up with numerous ideas, no matter the quality, and choose from among them a subject that I could combine with a concept given by our instructor. Even the most outlandish idea was not subject to disposal. I found brainstorming very helpful because I wrote down possible subjects to think about.

Finding a focus   After brainstorming for a while, I set about choosing a concept and subject. In choosing *integrity*, I found myself with a general concept that needed to be narrowed down to address a specific aspect or act of integrity. At first, I thought integrity would be difficult to write about; but in combination with the subject of Rwanda, everything began to come together.

Researching   My next steps, and perhaps the most important ones, were researching my subject and finding quality sources to use. Since I had two topics which I had to bring together, I needed to find sources about each and combine them. Using books, periodicals, and online resources, I was able to dredge up enough information in what I thought were legitimate sources.

Organizing   Generating a working outline was a very important step in my writing process. Since so much information is usually contained amidst the clutter of notes, I found it very helpful to filter out information and organize it in a fashion that was easily viewable when I sat down to write my first draft. Honestly, though, my outline was rather sparse because I found myself really getting into freewriting about the subject. Sometimes, when one has strong feelings about a subject, the words just flow. Eventually, I was able to trim my content down and develop clear paragraphs.

Drafting and revising   As I said, my drafting process consists of a lot of freewriting in confluence with my outline. I took the items in the outline, wrote topic sentences explaining them, and developed the paragraphs accordingly. Often, I found myself with too much content. So I tried to streamline each sentence, omitting redundant ideas. Oddly enough, this seemingly redundant material often proved valuable in later paragraphs when I thought I was stuck—but then saw that those points fit in.

Finishing   After a peer review session, I set about typing my final draft, using peer input combined with extra proofreading. I took into account everything I had learned about writing an argument and using sources. In addition, I added heartfelt conviction to a subject that I believe needed to be addressed.

Chris's Working Outline

```
Lest We Forget Rwanda

  I. Introduction/thesis

 II. Integrity

     • Integrity and Rwanda

     • Definition

III. Background

     • Conflict between the two ethnicities

     • Revolution and power struggle

     • Rise of Hutu power
```

IV. World awareness

- Initially world not aware
- America's stance on war and intervention
- U.N. resolution

V. Genocide

- Definition of *genocide*
- Goal of the Hutu government regarding Tutsis
- U.N. and U.S. viewed conflict as a civil war

VI. Civil war

VII. Misinformation/ignoring intelligence

- Hutu security official's fax

VIII. Intervention

IX. Lack of morality/integrity

X. Conclusion/thesis

Sample Annotated Research Paper

Chris Buxton-Smith "Lest We Forget About Rwanda"

1"

1/2"

Buxton-Smith 1

Chris Buxton-Smith

Instructor McMahon

English 1A

5 December 2005

Double space
paper

Center title

Lest We Forget About Rwandam

Indent 1/2"
(5 spaces)

Introduction

What would you do if one night while lying awake in bed, on the verge
of sleep, you hear a blood-curdling scream from the house of your elderly
next-door neighbor? Would you stand by and let the cries go unheeded, or
would you attempt to remedy the situation by intervening? Hopefully, if

1"

1"

1"

Buxton-Smith 2

you had some sense of integrity, moral fortitude, even an inkling of benevolence for your fellow human beings, you would assist your elderly neighbor. This comparison is a microcosm of a situation that occurred in the African country of Rwanda. According to Philip Gourevitch—author, journalist, and the editor of <u>The Paris Review</u>, "In Rwanda, in the course of 100 days in the spring and early summer of 1994, 800,000 people were put to death in the most unambiguous case of state-sponsored genocide in an attempt to exterminate a category of humanity, a people, since the Nazi Holocaust of the Jews of Europe" (<u>Triumph</u>). This massacre was one of the most expeditious and brutally efficient genocides in terms of the number of people that were killed in a relatively short period of time.

The question I must pose is: Should the United States and the United Nations have, as a matter of integrity, intervened in the situation? Understandably, many would say no. The U.S. is not the police force of the world, and the U.N. must adhere to a strict set of guidelines before it embarks on any peacekeeping mission. Many people feel that the two bodies must allow countries to carry out and conduct their own internal affairs whenever possible. I agree; but where do we draw the line that allows a nation to maintain its political sovereignty when its government sponsors the massacre of a portion of its own population? My answer is that America and the United Nations did, as a matter of integrity, have a moral obligation to intervene in the Rwandan massacre.

Integrity is at the heart of my position on this situation. Law professor and author Stephen L. Carter observes in his essay "The Insufficiency of Honesty" that integrity is more than acting nobly when dealing with a situation. He says that there are three steps in defining the degree of one's integrity. These are "discerning what is right and what is wrong; acting on what you have discerned, even at personal cost; and saying openly you are acting on your understanding of what is right and what is wrong" (507). Obviously the massacre of 800,000 innocent people is inherently wrong;

Background information; source identified, quotation of four lines or fewer not indented.

Research question

Background information; preview of specific points

Statement of thesis or claim; answer to research question

Warrants

Page number given; essay source

Boxton-Smith 3

having knowledge that a massacre of 800,000 people is about to occur is
inherently wrong, and not acting on this legitimate intelligence is
painfully misguided. It is completely devoid of any semblance of integrity.

Background
information

In order to understand the birth of the complex conflict between the
two native ethnic groups in Rwanda, the Hutus and the Tutsis, it is necessary to have some background on the matter. Rwanda is located in central
Africa, surrounded by Burundi, the Democratic Republic of the Congo,
Tanzania, and Uganda.

Before the Germans and then the Belgians colonized Rwanda, there was
little racial distinction or tension between the two groups; what tension
there was, was due to the disproportionate distribution of economic wealth
and political power. Gourevitch explains: "Until the late 19th century,
which is to say, until European colonization, Tutsis (the minority) represented the aristocratic upper classes; Hutus were the peasant masses."
Then, when the Europeans arrived, they used the pre-existing socioeco-
nomic situation as a skeleton for the new colonial government that was
implemented. They "took this traditional structure and made it even more

Source quoted,
paraphrased, and
quoted; online
source—no page
numbers

extreme and more polarized into an almost apartheid-like system. And
ethnic identity cards were issued, and Tutsis were privileged for all things,
and Hutus were really made into a very oppressed mass" (Triumph).

Rwanda gained independence from Belgium in 1962. Then, Gourevitch
reports, a revolution occurred. After years of oppression, the Hutus finally
gained power over the Tutsis. They took over the country's government
institutions and infrastructure; this new-found power, coupled with resentment towards their Tutsi counterparts, began a new era of Hutu power
movements. With this new era came the social oppression of the once powerful Tutsis. There was " . . . a Hutu dictatorship running through the
'60s, the '70s, the '80s, and into the mid '90s. Throughout that period,
there was systematic political violence used to maintain this Hutu power"

Source worked
into a sentence

(Triumph).

Buxton-Smith 4

Source
paraphrased and
cited

According to Gourevitch, this violence climaxed when the slaughter of the Tutsis began in 1994, after Hutu President Habyarimana was killed when his plane was apparently shot down. Habyarimana was engaged in peace talks sanctioned by the U.N. in order to establish a cease fire between the rival groups, which—it has been suggested—militant Hutu leaders did not want. These militant leaders incited the massacre by building ethnic hatred of the Tutsis and saying that the Tutsis had killed the president (<u>Triumph</u>).

Student writer
synthesizing
information that
is generally
accepted

Initially, the world was not well informed about the situation in Rwanda because conflicting stories from inside sources, chaos within the country, and biased intelligence from within the Hutu regime clouded the brutal reality of the situation. The United States and the United Nations had been aware of some escalating violence and tension between the groups, but they seem to have shrugged it off as a conflict limited to within the Rwandan border. They did not intervene.

Warrants

America's involvement in international conflicts has long been the topic of heated bipartisan and civilian debate, ranging from general support for the "World Wars" to heavy protest against the Vietnam War. U.S. involvement in a sovereign nation's war with another country, or with a country's civil war, is drastically different from U.S. involvement in a government-sponsored genocide like the one that occurred in Rwanda. However, both America's stance on genocide and the action required when it is occurring are clear. On December 9, 1948, the U.S., as a member of the United Nations, adopted a resolution, specifically resolution 260(III), which states as follows: "The contracting parties confirm that genocide, whether committed in time of peace or in time of war, is a crime under international law which they undertake to prevent and to punish" (United Nations). Not only did America and the U.N. have a moral obligation to assist with the situation in Rwanda; they had a contractual obligation as well.

Buxton-Smith 5

As a result of the European Holocaust of the 1930s and 40s, the word genocide was coined; it means "'the destruction of a nation or of an ethnic group' and implies the existence of a coordinated plan aimed at total extermination" (Destexhe, quoting Raphael Lemkin). This describes the goal of the Hutu government, Gourevitch claims, especially officials with close ties to the recently assassinated president. With no evidence, they blamed Tutsi extremists for the assassination, using it as a rallying call for Hutu militias to take up arms against their Tutsi neighbors. For decades, intermittent massacres had been occurring at the hands of Hutu extremists with the full knowledge of the government. To the rest of the world, including the United States, this appeared to be nothing more than a decades-long power struggle between two ethnic parties vying for political control; in essence, a civil war (Triumph).

United Nations and United States foreign policy dictate that, unless crimes against humanity are being committed, it is a violation of a nation's sovereignty to intervene in a civil war. A civil war, according to The American Heritage Dictionary of the English Language: Fourth Edition is "1. A war between factions or regions of the same country. 2. A state of hostility or conflict between elements within an organization." This seemed like what was occurring in Rwanda, but in reality the Tutsis had no political power or influence; they had no representatives in the government because the rule was totalitarian under the Hutu party. However, "much of the reporting said, 'The civil war has been renewed in Rwanda.' But a civil war involves two or more armies fighting one another—a rebel army and a government army. And it means that soldiers fight soldiers. The objective is to defeat the other party" (Gourevitch Triumph). Under this premise, the United Nations and the United States did not intervene.

Unfortunately, the premise upon which the U.S. and the U.N. did not intervene was not simply a case of misinformation; rather, it was a case of

Source using a source

Synthesis of material; source worked into sentence

Buxton-Smith 6

ignoring viable intelligence from a legitimate source within the Hutu
regime. Gourevitch reports that on January 14, 1994, a Hutu security advisor
sent a fax to the United Nations intelligence office alerting U.N. officials to

Source
paraphrased and
cited

the situation he knew was about to occur. This Hutu official was in the
upper echelon of the party and was aware that his government was about to
sponsor a massacre against unarmed Tutsi civilians. The official stated in
his fax that he been hired by the now-deceased president's political party to
train the Interahamawe, a Hutu power militia, in order to orchestrate the
extermination of the Tutsis (Triumph). No one listened.

Only after the killings of a small contingent of Belgian U.N. peacekeep-
ers and the identification of large arms caches, did the U.N. define the
situation as genocide:

Material omitted
(…)

> By early June, the Secretary-General of the U.N.—and even, . . . the
> French Foreign Minister—had taken to describing the slaughter in
> Rwanda as "genocide." But the U.N. High Commissioner for Human
> Rights still favored the phrase "possible genocide," while the Clinton

Four lines or more
quoted, indented;
no quotation
marks.

> administration actually forbade unqualified use of the g-word. The
> official formulation approved by the White House was: "acts of
> genocide may have occurred." (Gourevitch Genocide)

The U.S., after suffering a recent humiliation in the peacekeeping mission
of Somalia, chose not to intervene. In addition, officials may have wanted
to appear "respectful" of a sovereign nation's boundaries and its affairs
within those boundaries.

Not only was there no intervention by the U. S., but little attention
was paid by the U. S. government to the genocide in Rwanda. In her
Pulitzer Prize–winning book "A Problem from Hell": America and the Age of
Genocide, Samantha Power states, "It is shocking to note that during the
entire three months of the genocide, Clinton never assembled his top policy
advisors to discuss the killings." Power offers this explanation: "Rwanda

generated no sense of urgency and could safely be avoided by Clinton at no political cost" (366). America and the United Nations, a country and an organization built upon the idea of maintaining freedom and integrity in regards to the civilized world, chose to ignore the desperate cries for help from an African nation on the brink of disaster.

Clearly, both the United States and the United Nations, in their failure to intervene, lacked any sense of integrity regarding the massacre in Rwanda; moral and lawful obligation deemed it necessary that action be taken. Because no action was taken, they subsequently violated standards and ethics upon which the frames of both bodies were built. Stephen L. Carter states this about the Rwanda situation in an article in Christianity Today:

> In cases of genocide, we often hear opponents of unilateral action say that it is up to the world community to act. But this argument touches only expediency, not morality. We can well imagine a war that is morally imperative even though every country in the world lines up against it. We can also imagine a war that is morally prohibited even though every country supports it. If protecting a people against the ravages of their own sovereign is indeed a matter of moral urgency, one cannot shirk it on the ground that others do not agree. ("Defending")

It is true that the U.N. was created to be an organization where collective decisions lead to unified action in regards to world affairs; but when those collective decisions and their subsequent actions become mired in a political bog of allegiances and futile hopes of letting the situation run its course, action must be taken to preserve the sanctity of morality and the safety of the world. Carter again makes a poignant statement on the issue when he says that "the morality of humanitarian intervention has nothing to do with whether others agree that the action is appropriate" ("Defending").

Summing up

Buxton-Smith 8

Our country and our world now have the blood of over 800,000 innocent men, women, and children on their hands because people with bureaucratic allegiances and obligations could not see past the red tape hindering their views of the reality in the Rwanda situation. In 1848, the American philosopher and author Henry David Thoreau—angered by the Mexican War—wrote this about American integrity: "This American government,— what is it but a tradition, though a recent one, endeavoring to transmit itself unimpaired to posterity, but each instant losing some of its integrity." The mistakes of the past should not cement our reactions towards events of the future. In times of peril, we must not let past actions cloud our response to imminent threats of human barbarity and depravity.

As one nation and a part of one world, the United States cannot turn a deaf ear to the cries of a people under duress. The United Nations and the United States must remain vigilant towards maintaining the integrity of the rules and the laws that they have established, through consistent enforcement of resolutions like that of resolution 260 (III), lest we forget about those one hundred terrible days in Rwanda.

Conclusion; restatement of the claim or thesis

Restatement of title

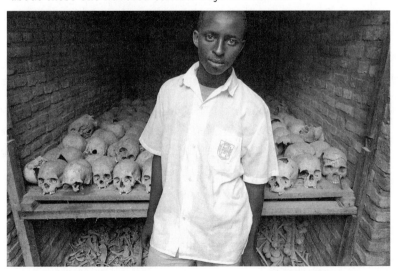

Fig. 1   Rwandan boy in front of skulls from Rwandans massacred during the genocide.

Buxton-Smith 9

Works Cited

Carter, Stephen. L. "Defending Our Neighbor." <u>Christianity Today</u> Nov. 2004.
     15 Nov. 2005 <http://christianitytoday.com/ct/2004/011/29.82.html>.

"The Insufficiency of Honesty." <u>Great Writing</u>. Ed. Harvey S. Weiner and
     Nora Eisenberg. San Francisco: McGraw, 2002. 507–512.

"Civil war." <u>The American Heritage Dictionary of the English Language</u>.
     4th ed. Boston: Houghton Mifflin, 2000. 1 Dec. 2005
     <www.bartleby.com/61/>.

Destexhe, Alain. <u>The Crime of Genocide</u>. 1995. 15 Nov. 2005
     <http://www.pbs.org/wgbh/pages/frontline/shows/rwanda/reports/
     destexhe.html>.

Gourevitch, Philip. <u>Genocide in Rwanda</u> as quoted in "Glimpses of Tyranny
     and Resistance" 2003. 10 Nov. 2005 <http://www.aft.org/pubs/reports/
     american_educator/fall2003/glimpses.html>.

————. <u>The Triumph of Evil</u>. 1996. 10 Nov. 2005 <http://www.pbs.org/
     wgbh/pages/frontline/shows/evil/interviews/gourevitch.html>.

Power, Samantha. <u>A Problem from Hell: America and the Age of
     Genocide</u>. New York: Perennial, 2003.

"Rwanda." TheFreeDictionary.Com. 1 Dec. 2005. <http://www
     .thefreedictionary.com/_/viewer.aspx?path=hm&name=A4rwanda>.

"The Rwandan Genocide through Photographs." <u>Rwanda</u> 1 Dec. 2005
     <http://emileelime.tripod.com/id5.html>.

Thoreau, Henry David. <u>The Columbia World of Quotations</u>. New York:
     Columbia University Press, 1996. 20 Nov. 2005
     <www.bartleby.com/66/>.

United Nations General Assembly. "Convention on the Prevention and
     Punishment of the Crime of Genocide." 1948. 15 Nov. 2005
     <http://www.hrweb.org/legal/genocide.html>.

Electronic publication; simultaneous print publication

Article in print anthology

Electronic version of print dictionary

Online posting of television program

Book

Web site

Appendix
MLA and APA Documentation Styles

Modern Language Association Style

Careful documentation and a complete works-cited list provide readers with full information on sources cited in the paper. (See The Logic of MLA Style, Chapter 14, pages 527–528 for information on in-text citations.)

To be useful to readers, citations must be clear and consistent. Therefore, very specific rules of documentation have been devised and must be applied.

Quick Reference

Using the following formats, begin preparing your works-cited entries as soon as you begin taking notes.

- A book by one author

  Author's last name, first name. *Book title.* Additional information. City of publication: Publishing company, publication date.

- An article by one author

  Author's last name, first name. "Article title." *Periodical title* Date: inclusive pages.

Citation Format

Most research writing in English and other humanities courses uses the documentation format described in Joseph Gibaldi's *MLA [Modern Language Association] Handbook for Writers of Research Papers,* sixth edition (New York: MLA, 2003). This documentation format, known as MLA style, is simple, clear, and widely accepted.

Accuracy and Completeness

Because works-cited entries direct readers to sources used in research writing, they must be as complete as possible and presented in a consistent and recognizable format. If the following guidelines do not cover a source you want to use, consult the *MLA Handbook,* your instructor, or a reference librarian.

547

What to Include in MLA Citations

MLA citations present information in an established order. When combining forms (to list a translation of a second edition, for example), follow these guidelines to determine the order of information:

1. *Author(s).* Use the name or names with the spelling and order shown on the title page of a book or on the first page of an article, without degrees, titles, or affiliations. If no author (individual or organization) is named, list the work by title in the works-cited entry.

2. *Title.* List titles from part to whole: the title of an essay (the part) before the book (the whole), the title of an article before the periodical title, an episode before the program, or a song before the compact disc. Use complete titles, including subtitles, no matter how long they are.

3. *Additional information.* In the order noted next, include any of the following information listed on the title page of the book or on the first page of an article: editor, translator, compiler, edition number, volume number, or name of series.

4. *Facts of publication.* For a book, find the publisher's name and the place of publication on the title page and the date of publication on the copyright page (immediately following the title page). Use the publisher's name in abbreviated form (numerous samples are present throughout the appendix), use the first city listed if more than one is given, and use the most recent date shown. When a city is outside the United States, include an abbreviation for the country, if necessary for clarity. For a periodical, find the volume number, issue number, and date on the masthead (at the top of the first page of a newspaper or within the first few pages in a journal or magazine, often in combination with the table of contents).

5. *Page numbers.* When citing a part of a book or an article, provide inclusive page numbers without page abbreviations. Record inclusive page numbers from one to ninety-nine in full form (8–12, 33–39, 68–73); inclusive numbers of one hundred or higher require at least the last two digits and any other digits needed for clarity (100–02, 120–36, 193–206).

Format for MLA Works-Cited List

The MLA Works-Cited list follows these general formatting guidelines:

- Begin the first line of each entry at the left margin and indent subsequent lines one-half inch (five spaces).
- Invert the author's name so that it appears with the last name first (to alphabetize easily). If sources are coauthored, list additional authors' names in normal, first-last order.
- Italicize or underline titles of full-length works (the meaning is the same), but do not underline the period that follows the title. Be consistent throughout the paper.

- Separate major sections of entries (author, title, and publication information) with periods and one space, not two. When other forms of end punctuation are used (when titles end with question marks or exclamation points, for example), the period may be omitted.
- Double-space all entries; do not insert additional space between entries.

Annotations

Annotations are sometimes used to clarify for readers the value of sources or to provide additional information. Typically, these comments assess the quality of the source, describe the source's condition or availability, or provide additional clarification. In most student writing, annotations usually evaluate a source's value for the research project by highlighting its special features.

Present an annotation in one or more complete sentences. It follows the citation's closing period and retains the citation's indention pattern and line spacing, as in this sample.

> National Commission on Excellence in Education. *A Nation at Risk: The Imperative for Educational Reform.* Washington: GPO, 1983. With its aggressively critical tone, this small publication by the NCEE launched the educational reform movement that is affecting our schools today.

Books

Book by one author

> Monmonier, Mark. *Rhumb Lines and Map Wars: A Social History of the Mercator Projection.* Chicago: U of Chicago P, 2004.

(The letters *U* and *P,* without periods, abbreviate *University* and *Press.*)

Book by two or more authors

Authors' names appear in the order in which they are presented on the title page, which may or may not be alphabetical. A comma follows the initial author's first name; second and third authors' names appear in normal order.

> Fainaru-Wada, Mark, and Lance Williams. *Game of Shadows: Barry Bonds, BALCO, and the Steroids Scandal That Rocked Professional Sports.* New York: Gotham, 2006.

When a book has four or more authors, include only the first author's name in full form; substitute *et al.* (meaning "and others," not italicized), for the names of additional authors.

> McDaniel, Susan H., et al. *Family-Oriented Primary Care: A Manual for Medical Providers.* 2nd ed. New York: Springer, 2004.

Book with no author

When no author is named, list the work by title. Alphabetize books listed by title using the first important word of the title, not the articles *a, an,* or *the.*

MLA Style

> *UPI Stylebook and Guide to Newswriting.* 4th ed. Sterling, VA: Capital Books, 2004.

Multiple works by the same author

When citing multiple works by the same author, present the first citation completely. Subsequent entries, alphabetized by title, are introduced by three hyphens and a period. Coauthored works require full names and are alphabetized after those with single authors.

> Ehrenreich, Barbara. *Bait and Switch: The (Futile) Pursuit of the American Dream.* New York: Metropolitan Books, 2005.
>
> ---. *Nickel and Dimed: On (Not) Getting By in America.* New York: Henry Holt, 2002.
>
> Ehrenreich, Barbara, Elizabeth Hess, and Gloria Jacobs. *Re-Making Love: The Feminization of Sex.* Garden City: Anchor-Doubleday, 1986.

(Notice that the publisher of the last selection includes a two-part name: the imprint and the major publisher; see "An Imprint," page 552, for an additional sample).

Book with an organization as author

When an organization is both the author and the publisher, present the name completely in the author position and use an abbreviation in the publisher position.

> American Psychological Association. *Publication Manual of the American Psychological Association.* 5th ed. Washington: APA, 2001.

Edition other than the first

The edition number, noted on the title page, follows the title of the book. When a book also has an editor, translator, or compiler, the edition number follows that information. Edition numbers are presented in numeral-abbreviation form (2nd, 3rd, 4th).

> Bjelajac, David. *American Art: A Cultural History.* 2nd ed. Upper Saddle River, NJ: Prentice-Hall, 2004.

Reprint

A reprint, a newly printed but unaltered version of a book, is identified as such on the title page or copyright page. The original publication date precedes the facts of publication, and the date of the reprinted edition follows the publisher's name.

> Joyce, James. *Ulysses.* 1992. Mineola, NY: Dover, 2002.

Multivolume work

A multivolume work may have one title, or it may have a comprehensive title for the complete work and separate titles for each volume. When you use the entire set of volumes, use the collective title and note the number of volumes. If volumes are published over several years, provide inclusive dates (2000–02); if the work is still in progress, include the earliest date, a hyphen, one space, and the closing period (1999–.).

> *The Norton Anthology of American Literature.* Ed. Nina Baym. 6th ed. 5 vols. New York: W. W. Norton, 2002.

To emphasize a single volume, first cite the volume as a separate book. Then add the volume number, the collection title, and the total number of volumes.

Ramazani, Jahan, Richard Ellman, and Robert O'Clair, eds. *Modern Poetry.* 3rd ed. New York: W. W. Norton, 2003. Vol 1 of *The Norton Anthology of Modern and Contemporary Poetry.*

Work in a collection

To cite a work in a collection, include the name of the selection's author, the title of the specific selection (appropriately punctuated), the collection title, publication facts, and the inclusive page numbers for the selection (without page abbreviations). To cite more than one selection from the collection, prepare separate citations (see Multiple Selections from the Same Collection, which follows).

Foster, Roy. "Something of Us Will Remain: Sebastian Barry and History." *Out of History: Essays on the Writings of Sebastian Barry.* Ed. Christina Hunt Mahony. Washington, DC: The Catholic U of America P, 2006. 183–97.

Previously published work in a collection

To indicate that a selection has been previously published, begin the citation with original facts of publication. *Rpt.,* meaning "reprinted," begins the second part of the citation, which includes information about the source you have used.

Sloan, Gary. "Sleuthing Patriotic Slogans." *Alternet* 10 Apr. 2003. Rpt. in *The Thomson Reader: Conversations in Context.* Ed. Robert P. Yagelski. New York: Wadsworth, 2006. 323–26.

Multiple selections from the same collection

To cite several selections from the same collection, prepare a citation for the complete work—beginning either with the editor's name or with the collection title. Additional references begin with the author of the individual selection and its title. However, instead of providing full publication information, include the editor's name or a shortened version of the title; provide inclusive page numbers for the selection. Notice that all citations are alphabetized.

Denman, Peter. "From Rhetoric to Narrative: The Poems of Sebastian Barry." Mahony 9–23.

Mahony, Christina Hunt, ed. *Out of History: Essays on the Writings of Sebastian Barry.* Washington, DC: The Catholic University of America P, 2006.

Roche, Anthony. "Redressing the Irish Theatrical Landscape: Sebastian Barry's *The Only True History of Lizzie Finn.*" Mahony 147–65.

Article in an encyclopedia or other reference work

Use an author's name when it is available. If only initials are listed with the article, match them with the name from the list of contributors. Well-known reference books require no information other than the title, edition number (if any), and date. Citations for less well-known or recently published reference works include full publication information. Page numbers are not needed when a reference work is arranged alphabetically.

DeGregorio, William. "Zachary Taylor." *The Complete Book of U.S. Presidents.* 6th ed. New York: Gramercy, 2005. 175–86.

(Because the articles on presidents are arranged chronologically, not alphabetically, page numbers are required.)

> Angermüller, Rudolph. "Salieri, Antonio." *The New Grove Dictionary of Music and Musicians.* 2001 ed.

(This twenty-volume set is extremely well known and consequently needs no publication information.)

When no author's name or initials appear with an article, begin with the title, reproduced to match the pattern in the reference book. Other principles remain the same.

> "Socrates" *Encyclopedia of Ancient Greece.* Ed. Nigel Wilson. New York: Routledge, 2006.

Work in a series The name of a series (a collection of books related to the same subject, genre, time period, and so on) is typically found on a book's title page and should be included just before the publishing information. Abbreviate the word *Series* (*Ser.*) if it is part of the series title.

> Yang, Gua-ja. *Contradictions.* Trans. Stephen Epstein and Kim Mi-Young. Cornell East Asia Ser. Ithaca: Cornell UP, 2005.

When a volume in a series is numbered, include both the series name and the number, followed by a period.

> Audubon, John James. *The Audubon Reader.* Everyman's Library 284. New York: Knopf, 2006.

Imprint An imprint is a specialized division of a larger publishing company. When an imprint name and a publisher name both appear on the title page, list them together (imprint name first), separated by a hyphen and no additional spaces.

> Atwood, Margaret. *The Tent.* New York: Talese-Doubleday, 2006.

(Nan A. Talese is the imprint, which is shortened to *Talese;* Doubleday is the publisher.)

Translation A translator's name must always be included in a citation for a translated work because he or she prepared the version that you read. To emphasize the original work (the most common pattern), place the abbreviation *Trans.* (for "translated by," not italicized) and the translator's name after the title (but following editors' names, if the translator translated the entire work).

> Allende, Isabel. *Zorro: A Novel.* Trans. Margaret Sayers Peden. New York: Harper Collins, 2005.

If selections within a collection are translated by different people, then each translator's name should follow the appropriate selection.

Freixis, Laura. "Absurd Ending:" Trans. John R. King. *Short Stories in Spanish: New Penguin Parallel Texts*. Ed. John R. King. New York: Penguin, 2001. 143–62.

(This citation indicates that John R. King was both translator and editor.)

Preface, introduction, foreword, epilogue, or afterword

To cite material that is separate from the primary text of a book, begin with the name of the person who wrote the separate material, an assigned title (if applicable) in quotation marks, a descriptive title for the part used (capitalized but not punctuated), the title of the book, the name of the book's author (introduced with *By,* not italicized), publication facts, and inclusive page numbers for the separate material. Note that most prefatory or introductory material is paged using lowercase roman numerals.

Updike, John. Introduction. *Walden*. By Henry David Thoreau. Ed. J. Lyndon Shanley. Princeton: Princeton UP, 2004, ix–xiii.

Pamphlet

When a pamphlet contains clear and complete information, it is cited like a book. When information is missing, use these abbreviations: *N.p.* for "No place of publication," *n.p.* for "no publisher," *n.d.* for "no date," and *N. pag.* (with a space between the abbreviations) for "no page."

Depression and Spinal Cord Injury. Seattle: UW Medicine, 2005. N. pag.

Dissertation

A citation for an unpublished dissertation begins with the author's name, the dissertation title in quotation marks, the abbreviation *Diss.* (not italicized), the name of the degree-granting school (with *University* abbreviated), and the date.

Wentland, Meghan Pontbriand. "Terrorists and Terrorism: Representations of Violence in 'Troubles' Fiction." Diss. Catholic U of America, 2004.

A published dissertation is a book and should be presented as such. However, include dissertation information between the title and the facts of publication.

Sacred writings

A citation for a sacred writing follows a pattern similar to that of any other book, with several notable variations. First, titles of sacred writings (the parts or the whole) are neither placed in quotation marks nor italicized; they are capitalized only. Second, full facts of publication are not required for traditional editions. When appropriate, include additional information according to the guidelines for the element.

The Bhagavad Gita. Trans. Juan Mascaró. New York: Penguin, 1962.

(Include translators when appropriate.)

The Holy Bible.

(This citation is for the King James version of the Bible, the traditional edition.)

The New Oxford Annotated Bible. Ed. Herbert G. May and Bruce M. Metzger. Rev. Standard Version. New York: Oxford UP, 1973.

(This citation provides full information, highlighting a version other than the King James and the editorial work that it includes.)

Government-Civic Documents

A citation for *Congressional Record* is exceedingly brief: the italicized and abbreviated title, *Cong. Rec.*, the date (presented in day-month-year order), and the page number. Page numbers used alone indicate Senate records; page numbers preceded by an *H* indicate records from the House of Representatives.

> *Cong. Rec.* 7 April 2006. 3380.

> *Cong. Rec.* 6 April 2006. H1566.

Information to describe a government document is generally presented in this order: (1) country, state, province, or county; (2) government official, governing body, sponsoring department, commission, center, ministry, or agency; (3) office, bureau, or committee; (4) the title of the publication, italicized; (5) if appropriate, the author of the document, the number and session of Congress, the kind and number of the document; (6) the city of publication, the publisher, and the date.

When citing more than one work from the same government or agency, use three hyphens and a period to substitute for identical elements.

> United States. Cong. Senate. Committee on Energy and Natural Resources. 107th Cong., 2nd sess. 2002. Washington: GPO, 2003.

> ---. Dept. of Education. *Alcohol, Other Drugs, and College: A Parent's Guide.* Washington: GPO, 2000.

> ---. Dept. of Health and Human Services. *Steps to a Healthier US.* Washington: GPO, 2005.

(The Government Printing Office, the publisher of most federal documents, is abbreviated to save space.)

Periodicals

To cite an article in a monthly magazine, include the author's name, the article's title in quotation marks, the magazine's name (italicized), the month (abbreviated) and year, and the inclusive pages of the article (without page abbreviations).

> Teague, Matthew. "Double Blind: The Untold Story of How British Intelligence Infiltrated and Undermined the IRA." *The Atlantic* Apr. 2006: 53–62.

(Note that the period comes before the closing quotation marks of the article's title, that one space [but no punctuation] separates the periodical title and the date, and that a colon separates the date and the pages.)

MLA Style

Article in a weekly magazine

A citation for an article in a weekly or biweekly magazine is identical to that for a monthly magazine, with one exception: the publication date is presented in more detailed form, in day-month-year order (with the month abbreviated).

> Conley, Kevin. "How High Can You Go? The Roller Coaster's New Golden Age." *The New Yorker* 30 Aug. 2005: 48–55.

Article in a journal with continuous paging

A journal with continuous paging numbers issues sequentially for the entire year. For this kind of journal, place the volume number after the journal title, identify the year in parentheses, follow it with a colon, and then list page numbers.

> Fry, Prem S., and Dominique L. Debats. "Sources of Life Strengths as Predictors of Late-Life Mortality and Survivorship." *International Journal of Aging and Human Development* 62 (2006):303–34.

Article in a journal with separate paging

For a journal that pages each issue separately, follow the volume number with a period and the issue number (without spaces).

> Brittan, Alice. "The Diarist, the Cryptographer, and *The English Patient*." *PMLA* 121.1 (2006): 200–13.

Article in a newspaper

A citation for a newspaper resembles that for a magazine: it includes the author's name, article title (in quotation marks), newspaper title (italicized), the date (in day-month-year order, followed by a colon), and inclusive pages.

However, when a newspaper has editions (*morning, evening, national*), they must be identified. After the year, place a comma and describe the edition, abbreviating common words.

When sections of a newspaper are designated by letters, place the section letter with the page number, without a space (*A22, C3, F11*). If sections are indicated by numerals, place a comma after the date or edition (rather than a colon), include the abbreviation *sec.* (not italicized), the section number, a colon, a space, and the page number (*sec. 1: 22, sec. 3: 2, sec. 5: 17*).

> Callender, David. "Amid Scandals, Still No Sign of Campaign Reform." *Capital Times* (Madison, WI) 15 Dec 2005: A1.

When an article continues in a later part of the paper, indicate the initial page, use a comma, and then add the subsequent page. If the article appears on more than three separated pages, list the initial page, followed by a plus sign (*22+, A17+, sec. 2: 9+*).

Weekly newspapers are cited just like daily newspapers.

> Keefe-Feldman, Mike. "Heart of Noise." *Washington City Paper* 7 Apr. 2006, 31+.

Editorial

The citation for an editorial resembles that for a magazine or newspaper article, with one exception: the word *Editorial* (not italicized), with a period, follows the title of the essay.

> Herbert, Bob. "George Bush's Trillion-Dollar War." Editorial. *New York Times* 23 Mar. 2006, natl. ed: A25.

Letter to the editor

Include the author's name, the word *Letter* (not italicized), the name of the publication (magazine, journal, or newspaper), and appropriate facts of publication. Do not record descriptive, attention-getting titles that publications, not authors, supply.

> Alexie, Sherman. Letter. *Harper's* Dec. 2005: 6.

Review

Begin with the author's name and the title of the review (if one is provided). The abbreviation *Rev. of* (not italicized) follows, Publication information ends the citation, incorporating elements required for different kinds of sources.

> Gleiberman, Owen. "The High Drama." Rev. of *Traffic*, dir. Steven Soderbergh. Perf. Benicio Del Toro, Catherine Zeta-Jones, Don Cheadle, and Michael Douglas. *Entertainment Weekly* 5 Jan. 2001: 45–46.

Nonprint Sources

If you have difficulty finding the information to document nonprint sources clearly, ask your instructor or a librarian for help.

Lecture or speech

A citation for a formal lecture or speech includes the speaker's name, the title of the presentation (in quotation marks), the name of the lecture or speaker series (if applicable), the location of the speech (convention, meeting, university, library, meeting hall), the city, and the date in day-month-year order.

> Courtright, Robert. "The Carpe Diem Poem." Class Lecture. George Mason University. McLean, VA. 11 Apr. 2006.

> Doyle, Roddy. "An Evening with Roddy Doyle." Seattle Arts and Lectures. Seattle, WA. 15 Nov. 2004.

(For class lectures, provide as much of this information as possible: speaker, title of lecture in quotation marks, a descriptive title, the school, the city, and the date.)

> Bush, George W. State of the Union Address. United States Capitol. 31 Jan. 2006.

Work of art

When an artist titles his or her own work, include this information: artist's name; the title (italicized); the museum, gallery, or collection where the work of art is housed; and the city (and country if needed for clarity).

> Cézanne, Paul. *Houses along a Road.* The Hermitage, St. Petersburg, Russia.

When an artist has not titled a work, use the title that art historians have given to it (without quotation marks), followed by a brief description of the work. The rest of the citation is the same.

> Madonna and Child with Cherubim. Bas-relief in marble. Vatican Library, Vatican City.

MLA Style

Map, graph, table, or chart

A map, graph, table, or chart is treated like a book. If known, include the name of the author, artist, designer, scientist, person, or group responsible for the map, graph, table, or chart. Then include the title (italicized), followed by a separately punctuated descriptive title. Also include any other necessary information.

> Pope, C. Arden. *Children's Respiratory Hospital Admissions.* Graph.

Cartoon

Begin with the cartoonist's name, the title of the cartoon in quotation marks, and the word *Cartoon* (not italicized), followed by a period. Then include the citation information required for the source.

> Rees, David. "Get Your War On." Cartoon. *Rolling Stone* 11 Dec. 2003: 36.

Film

To cite a film as a complete work, include the title (italicized), the director (noted by the abbreviation *Dir.,* not italicized), the studio, and the date of release. If you include other people's contributions, do so after the director's name by using brief phrases (*Screenplay by, Original score by*) or abbreviations (*Perf.* for "performed by," *Prod.* for "produced by") to clarify their roles. Indicate a nonfilm format—VHS, DVD, or laserdisc—before the studio name. If a film is released by two studios, include both names, separated by a hyphen.

> *Ray.* Dir. Taylor Hackford. Perf. Jamie Foxx, Regina King. Universal Pictures, 2004.

To emphasize the contribution of an individual (rather than the film as a whole), place the person's name first, followed by a comma and a descriptive title (beginning with a lowercase letter). The rest of the citation follows normal patterns.

> Allen, Woody, dir. *Anything Else.* Perf. Jason Biggs, Christina Ricci. Dream-Works SKG, 2003.

> "Flunky File Clerk." *American Splendor.* Dir. Robert Pulcini and Shari Springer Berman. Perf. Paul Giamatti. DVD. HBO Video, 2003.

Television broadcast

List a regular program by the title (italicized), the network (CBS, CNN, Fox), the local station (including both the call letters and the city, separated by a comma), and the broadcast date (in day-month-year order).

Include other people's contributions after the program title, using brief phrases (*Written by, Hosted by*) or abbreviations (*Perf.* for "performed by," *Prod.* for "produced by") to clarify their roles.

> *The Sopranos.* Perf. James Gandolfini and Edie Falco. HBO. 15 Apr. 2006.

To cite a single episode of an ongoing program, include the name of the episode in quotation marks before the program's title. Other elements are presented in the same order as used for a regular program.

> "Two Weeks Out." *The West Wing.* Perf. Alan Alda, Jimmy Smits, and Richard Schiff. NBC. WRC, Washington, DC. 19 Mar. 2006.

List special programs by title, followed by traditional descriptive information. If a special program is part of a series (for example, Hallmark Hall of Fame, Great Performances, or American Playhouse), include the series name without quotation marks or italics immediately preceding the name of the network.

The Sleeping Beauty. Composed by Peter Ilich Tchaikovsky. Choreographed by Marius Petipa. Perf. Viviana Durante and Zoltan Solymosi. Great Performances. PBS. WFYI, Indianapolis. 24 Dec. 1995.

Radio broadcast A citation for a radio broadcast follows the same guidelines as those for a television broadcast.

The War of the Worlds. CBS Radio. WCBS, New York. 30 Oct. 1938.

Recording A citation for a recording usually begins with the performer or composer, followed by the title of the recording (italicized except for titles using numerals for musical form, key, or number), the recording company, and the copyright date.

The Beatles. *Let It Be . . . Naked.* Capitol/Apple, 2003.

Davis, Miles. *The Cellar Door Sessions 1970.* 6 discs. Sony, 2005.

To cite a single selection from a recording, include the selection title in quotation marks followed by the title of the complete recording. All else remains the same.

Springsteen, Bruce. "Silver Palomino." *Devils and Dust.* Sony, 2005.

To cite liner notes, the printed material that comes with many recordings, list the name of the writer and the description *Liner notes* (not italicized), followed by a period. The rest of the citation follows normal patterns.

Kooper, Al. Liner notes. *Bob Dylan: No Direction Home: The Soundtrack [The Bootleg Series Vol. 7].* 2 Discs. Sony, 2005.

Interview A citation for a personally conducted interview includes the name of the person interviewed, the type of interview (personal or telephone), and the interview date.

Heller, William. Personal interview. 5 Feb. 2006.

A citation for a broadcast or printed interview includes the name of the person interviewed, the descriptive title *Interview* (not italicized), and information necessary to describe the source.

Holloway, Dave. Interview. *Larry King Live.* CNN. 11 Apr. 2006.

Transcript A transcript of a program is presented according to the source of the original broadcast, with clarifying information provided.

Adler, Margot. "Letters Offer Glimpse of Life in Nazi Labor Camps." *All Things Considered.* Natl. Public Radio. 7 Mar. 2006. Transcript.

Questionnaire or survey

A citation for a personally conducted questionnaire or survey begins with your name (since you are the author of the questions and compiler of the results) and then includes a descriptive title and the date (which may be inclusive) on which you gathered your information. For additional clarity, you may include information about the location of your work.

> Greene, Erika. Survey. Terre Haute: Indiana State U. 30 Jan. 2006.

Electronic Sources

Businesses, organizations, government agencies, and publishers of all kinds have transferred many of their print-based documents to subscription databases, CD-ROMs, the Internet, online video broadcasts, and other electronic formats.

As you gather citation information for Internet and other electronic sources, you must be both resourceful and patient because the patterns of electronic publication are less consistent than those of traditional print publication. Your goal should be to gather the most complete set of data possible to describe each electronic source, following the patterns described in this section.

Online scholarly project or information database

To cite an entire online scholarly project or information database, present available information in this order: the title of the project or database, italicized; the editor or compiler, if identified, introduced with the abbreviation *ed.* or *comp.* (not italicized); the version number, if applicable; the date of electronic posting or the date of the most recent update; the name of the sponsoring organization or institution, if identified; the date you accessed the site; and the electronic address (URL), in angle brackets.

> *ProQuest*. 2006. ProQuest Company. 10 Apr. 2006. <http://
> proquest.umi.com/pqdweb/>.

> *The Victorian Web*. Ed. George P. Landow. 2005. Brown U. 11 Apr. 2006.
> <http://www.victorianweb.org>.

To cite a selected source—article, illustration, map, or other—from an online scholarly project or information database, begin with the name of the author (or artist, compiler, or editor) of the individual source, if appropriate; the title of the source, punctuated appropriately (quotation marks for articles, italics for charts, and so on); and print information if the source reproduces a print version. Continue the citation with the name of the online project or database and other required information. However, use the URL of the specific source, not the general address for the project or database, in angle brackets.

> Cody, David. "Queen Victoria." *Victorian Web*. 2005. Brown U. 11 Apr. 2006.
> <http://www.victorianweb.org>.

> Cooke, Bill. "Fatal Attraction." *Astronomy* 34.5 (2006): 46–52. *ProQuest*. 2006.
> ProQuest Company. 20 Apr. 2006 <http://proquest.umi.com>.

Web site

To cite a web site, including blogs, podcasts, and video, provide the name of the author, editor, or host, if any; the title of the site, italicized; the date of electronic posting or the date of the most recent update; the name of the organization or institution, if any, affiliated with the site; the date you accessed the site; and the URL, in angle brackets. As the variety of online content, such as podcasts and v-casts, increases, new academic citation guidelines will be issued. For the purposes of your papers, it is most important that you provide your reader with enough information to locate and verify the site, and that you properly acknowledge any ideas or content that you find online.

> *ABA Law Student Division.* 5 Jan. 2002. American Bar Association. 11 Jan. 2002 <http://www.abanet.org/lsd/home.html>.

> *UNICEF.* 7 Jan. 2002. United Nations. 12 Jan. 2002 <http://www.unicef.org/>.

> Atrios. "Unpopular President." *Escaton.* 24 Apr. 2006. Weblog. <http://atrios.blogstop.com/>.

> ABC News. *The Afternote.* 22 Apr. 2006. Podcast. 24 April 2006. <http://abcnews.go.com/ThisWeek/>.

Online book

To cite an online book that has a corresponding print version, first prepare a standard citation describing the print version. Then provide additional information required for a scholarly project or information database, if applicable; the date you accessed the site; and the specific URL of the book, not the general project or database, in angle brackets.

> Tarkington, Booth. *Gentle Julia.* New York: Doubleday, 1922. *Project Gutenberg.* Apr. 2006. U of Illinois. 26 Apr. 2006 <http://www.gutenberg.org/etext/18259>.

To cite an online book that is available only in electronic form, provide the name of the author or editor; the title, italicized; the date of electronic posting or the date of the most recent update; the name of the sponsoring organization or institution, if provided; the date you accessed the site; and the URL of the book, not the project or database, in angle brackets.

> Buxhoeveden, Sophie. *The Life and Tragedy of Alexandra Feodorvna, Empress of Russia.* 2004. *Russian History Website.* 20 Apr. 2006. <http://www.alexenderpalace.org/alexandra/>.

Article in an online encyclopedia or reference source

To cite an article from an online encyclopedia or reference source, provide the author of the entry, if there is one; the title of the entry exactly as it appears in the source ("Paige, Satchel"); the name of the reference work, italicized; the date of electronic posting or the date of the most recent update; the date you accessed the site; and the URL for the specific article, not the general reference, in angle brackets.

> Coney, Peter. "Plate Tectonics." *Encarta Online Encyclopedia.* 2006. 4 Apr. 2006 <http://encarta.msn.com/encyclopedia_761554623/Plate_Tectonics.html>.

Online government document

To cite an online version of a government document—book, report, proceedings, brochure, or other—first provide the information required for the print source. Then continue the citation with the information appropriate to the electronic source, whether it is a scholarly project, an information database, or a web site.

United States. Cong. Budget Office. *China's Growing Demand for Oil and Its
Impact on U.S. Petroleum Markets.* Washington: GPO, 2006. Cong. Budget
Office. 26 Apr. 2006 <http://www.cbo.gov/ftpdocs/71xx/doc7128/
04-07-ChinaOil.pdf>.

Article in an online magazine

To cite an article in an online magazine, provide the name of the author, if appropriate; the title of the article, in quotation marks; the name of the magazine, italicized; the date of electronic publication or the date of the most recent update; the date on which you accessed the article; and the URL of the specific article, not the general magazine site, in angle brackets.

O'Neill, Hugh. "You Say You Want a Resolution?" *Men's Health.com* 9 Jan. 2001.
11 Jan. 2002 <http://www.menshealth.com/health/resolution.html>.

Article in an online journal

To cite an article in an online journal, provide the name of the author, if appropriate; the title of the article, in quotation marks; the name of the journal, italicized; the volume and issue number; the year of publication, in parentheses; the date on which you accessed the article; and the URL of the specific article, not the general journal site, in angle brackets.

Cramer, Kenneth M., and Lynn A. Perrault. "Effects of Predictability, Actual
Controllability, and Awareness of Choice on Perceptions of Control."
Current Research in Social Psychology 11.8 (2006). 20 Apr. 2006
<http://www.uiowa.edu/%7Egrpproc/crisp/crisp.html>.

Article in an online newspaper

To cite an article in an online newspaper, provide the name of the author, if appropriate; the title of the article, in quotation marks; the name of the newspaper, italicized; the date of electronic publication or the date of the most recent update; the date on which you accessed the article; and the URL of the specific article, not the general newspaper site, in angle brackets.

Rodriguez, Cindy. "Amid Dispute, Plight of Illegal Workers Revisited." *Boston
Globe* 9 Jan. 2001. 10 Jan. 2002 <http://www.boston.com/dailyglobe2/
010/nation/amid_dispute_plight_of_illegal_workers_revisited+.shtml>.

Online transcript of a lecture or speech

To cite the transcript of a lecture or speech, first provide the information required for a lecture or speech. Then include the word *Transcript,* not italicized; the date of electronic publication or the date of the most recent update; the date on which you accessed the transcript; and the URL of the specific transcript, not the general site, in angle brackets.

King, Martin Luther, Jr. Nobel Peace Prize Acceptance Speech. Nobel Prize
Ceremony. Oslo, 10 Dec. 1964. Transcript. 2001. 31 Jan. 2002
<http://www.stanford.edu/group/king>.

Work of art online

To cite a work of art online, provide the name of the artist, if known; the assigned title of the work of art, italicized, or the common name of the work of art, not italicized; a phrase describing the artistic medium; the museum, gallery, or collection where the work is housed; the city; the date on which you accessed the work of art; and the URL of the specific work of art, not the general site, in angle brackets.

> Picasso, Pablo. *Les Demoiselles d'Avignon.* Oil on canvas. Museum of Modern Art. New York. 30 June 2002 <http://www.moma.org/docs/collection/paintsculpt/C40.htm>.

Online map, graph, table, or chart

To cite a map, graph, table, or chart online, first provide the information required for the kind of visual element. Then continue the citation with the information appropriate to the electronic source, whether it is a scholarly project or an information database or a web site.

> "New York City Subway Route Map." Map. 5 Mar. 2000. New York City Subway Resources. 9 Jan. 2002 <http://www.nycsubway.org/maps/route/>.

Online cartoon

To cite a cartoon online, provide the name of the cartoonist, if known; the assigned title of the cartoon, in quotation marks; the word *Cartoon,* not italicized; the source, italicized; the date of electronic publication or the date of the most recent update; the date on which you accessed the cartoon; and the URL of the cartoon, not the general site, in angle brackets.

> Steiner, Peter. "Don't Anybody Move: This Is a Merger." Cartoon. *Cartoonbank.* 10 Jan. 2001. 13 Jan. 2001 <k.com/cartoon_closeup.asp?/mscssid=2BGLVUGOU7S92MD000GPBQXMNAB6808>.

Online film or filmclip

To cite an online film or filmclip, first provide the information required for a film. Then include the name of your electronic source, italicized; the date of electronic publication or the date of the most recent update; the date on which you accessed the film or filmclip; and the URL of the film or filmclip, not the general site, in angle brackets.

> *Reefer Madness.* Dir. Louis J. Gasnier. 1938. *The Sync.* 2000. 22 Apr. 2002 <http://www.thesync.com/ram/reefermadness.ram>.

Online transcript of a television or radio broadcast

To cite an online transcript of a television or radio broadcast, first provide the information required for a television or radio broadcast. Then include the word *Transcript,* not italicized; the date on which you accessed the transcript; and the URL of the transcript, not the general site, in angle brackets.

> "Inside the World of Polygamy." *Larry King Live.* CNN, Washington. 15 Apr. 2006. Transcript. 25 Apr. 2006 <http://transcripts.cnn.com/TRANSCRIPTS/0604/15/lkl.01.html>.

Online recording

To cite an online recording of previously released material, first provide the information required for a traditional recording. Then include the date of electronic publication or the date of the most recent update; the date on which you accessed the recording; and the URL of the recording, not the general site, in angle brackets.

To cite an online recording that has not been previously released, provide the name of the recording artist; the title of the selection; and performance information such as concert locations and dates, recording studios, locations, or other relevant information. Then provide information about your source for the recording, whether a database or a web site.

> Dylan, Bob. "Yea! Heavy and a Bottle of Bread." New York City, 11 Nov. 2002. 20 Apr. 2006 <http://bobdylan.com/performances>.

CD-ROM sources

Because Internet sites provide researchers with more easily updated materials than do CD-ROMs, most libraries are phasing out CD-ROMs from their collections. However, you may still need to cite a CD-ROM source.

If a CD-ROM source reproduces material available in print form, begin the citation with full print information: author (or editor), title, and facts of publication. If the material is not available in print form, begin the citation with identifying information: author, if given; title, italicized; and the date of the material, if appropriate. Next, citations for both kinds of materials include the title of the publication, italicized; the description *CD-ROM,* not italicized; the city, if known, and name of the company that produced the CD-ROM; and the date of electronic publication.

> *The Baseball Encyclopedia: The Complete and Definitive Record of Major League Baseball.* CD-ROM. New York: Macmillan, 1996.

> Becklake, Sue. *All about Space.* Illus. Sebastian Quigley. CD-ROM. New York: Scholastic Reference, 1998.

Email interview

To cite an email interview, include the name of the person you interviewed; the phrase *Email interview,* not italicized; and the date of the email posting.

> Lublin, Robert. Email interview. 1 Mar. 2006.

Online posting

To cite an online posting to a forum or discussion group, provide the name of the author, if known; the official title of the posting, in quotation marks; or a descriptive title, without quotation marks; the phrase *Online posting,* not italicized; the date of electronic publication or the date of the most recent update; the name of the forum or discussion group; the date on which you accessed the posting; and the URL of the posting, not the general forum or discussion site, in angle brackets.

> Bailey, Buddy. "What's Wrong with My Miniature Roses?" Online Posting. 22 Apr. 2006. Miniature Roses Forum. 26 Apr. 2006. <http://forums .gardenweb.com/forums/load/rosesmin/msg0422021712641.html?4>.

> **Online Study Center**
> **Creating a Works-Cited Page**
> Visit the Online Study Center for this book at *College.hmco.com/pic/chaffeeCTTW 4e* for more information on creating a works-cited page.

American Psychological Association Style

In fields such as psychology, education, public health, and criminology, researchers follow the guidelines given in the *Publication Manual of the American Psychological Association*, fifth edition (Washington: APA, 2001) to document their work. Like MLA style, APA style encourages brevity in documentation, uses in-text parenthetical citations of sources, and limits the use of numbered notes and appended materials.

Paper Format

Title page Include a descriptive title, your name, and your affiliation (course or university), with two spaces between elements; center this information left to right and top to bottom. In the upper-right corner, include the first few words of the paper's title, followed by five spaces and the page number (without a page abbreviation). Two lines below, at the left margin, type the words *Running head* (not italicized), a colon, and a brief version of the title (no more than fifty letters and spaces) in all capital letters. The title page is always page 1.

Abstract On a separate page following the title page, type the label *Abstract* (capitalized but not italicized). Two lines below, include an unindented paragraph describing the major ideas in the paper; it should contain no more than 120 words.

Introduction Include a paragraph or series of paragraphs to define the topic, present the hypothesis (or thesis), explain the method of investigation, and state the theoretical implications (or context).

Body Incorporate a series of paragraphs to describe study procedures, results obtained, and interpretations of the findings.

In-text documentation In parentheses, include the author and date for summaries and paraphrases; include the author, date, and page number for quotations and facts.

List of sources Cite sources used in the paper in a listing titled "References."

Appendix Include related materials (charts, graphs, illustrations, and so on) that cannot be incorporated into the body of the paper.

Manuscript Format

Fonts

Use any standard font with serifs (cross lines on the ends of individual letters). Sans serif fonts like Helvetica are used only for labeling illustrations, not for text. Use italics to identify titles of complete, separately published works.

Spacing

All elements of the paper are double-spaced.

Margins

Use one-inch margins at the top and bottom and on the left and right. Indent paragraphs five to seven spaces; indent long quotations five spaces.

Paging

Put the first two or three words of the title (no more than fifty letters and spaces) in the upper-right corner; after five spaces, include the page number without a page abbreviation.

Headings

Whenever possible, use headings to label divisions and subdivisions of the paper.

Number style

Express numbers one through nine (and zero) in words and all other numbers in numeral form. When numbers are used for comparisons, all must appear in numeral form.

Citation Format

The following samples illustrate a number of basic citation forms. If you are using other kinds of sources, consult the APA style guide.

Reference List Format

Book by one author

Monmonier, M. (2004). *Rhumb lines and map wars: A social history of the Mercator Projection.* Chicago: University of Chicago Press.

(Use initials for the author's first name. After the author's name, place the publication date in parentheses, followed by a period. Capitalize only the first word of the title and of the subtitle and any proper nouns and proper adjectives. Spell out the names of university presses. For other publishers, retain only the words *Books* and *Press*.)

Book by two or more authors

Fainaru-Wada, M., & Williams, L. (2006). *Game of shadows: Barry Bonds, BALCO, and the steroids scandal that rocked professional sports.* New York: Gotham.

(Invert the names of all authors. Insert an ampersand [&] before the last author's name.)

Book with an organization as author

American Psychological Association. (2001). *Publication manual of the American Psychological Association* (5th ed.). Washington: Author.

(When the organization is also the publisher, use the word *Author* [not italicized] in the publisher position.)

Edition other than the first

Bjelajac, D. (2004). *American art: A cultural history* (2nd ed.). Upper Saddle River, NJ: Prentice Hall.

(Insert information about the edition in parentheses, following the title but before the period.)

Work in a collection

Foster, R. (2006). Something of us will remain: Sebastian Barry and history. In C. H. Mahony (Ed.), *Out of history: Essays on the writings of Sebastian Barry* (pp. 183–197). Washington: The Catholic University of America Press.

(Do not enclose the title of a short work in quotation marks. *In,* not italicized, introduces its source. Provide the editor's name, the abbreviation *Ed.* [capitalized, not italicized, and placed in parentheses] followed by a comma, the collection title, and inclusive page numbers for the short work [given in parentheses]. Abbreviate *pages.*)

Article in a monthly magazine

Teague M. (2006, April). Double blind: The untold story of how British intelligence infiltrated and undermined the IRA. *The Atlantic 297*, 53–62.

(Give the year of publication followed by a comma and the month and day [if any]. When appropriate, follow the magazine title with a comma, one space, the volume number, and another comma [all italicized]. Do not use a page abbreviation.)

Article in a journal with separate paging

Brittan, A. (2006). The diarist, the cryptographer, and *The English Patient. PMLA: Publications of the Modern Language Association of America, 121*(1), 200–213.

(Italicize the name of the journal, the comma that follows it, and the volume number. The issue number [or numbers] in parentheses immediately follows the volume number; no space separates them; the issue number is *not* italicized. No abbreviation for pages accompanies the inclusive page numbers.)

Article in a newspaper

Callender, D. (2005, December 15). Amid scandals, still no sign of campaign reform. *The Capital Times* (Madison, Wisconsin), p. 1:1.

(Invert the date. Do not include information about the edition or section. When sections are indicated by letters, present them along with the page numbers with no intervening space.)

Lecture or speech

Doyle, R. (2004, November 15). *An evening with Roddy Doyle.* Lecture presented for Seattle Arts and Lectures. Seattle, Washington.

(Italicize the title of the speech. Follow the title with the name of the sponsoring organization and the location, separated by commas.)

APA Style

Nonprint materials

Allen, W. (Director). (2003). *Anything else* [motion picture]. United States: Dream-Works SKG.

(List entries by the name of the most important contributor [director, producer, speaker, and so on]; note the specific role in full in parentheses following the name. Identify the medium [motion picture, slide show, tape recording] in brackets after the title. The country of origin precedes the name of the production company.)

Electronic Sources

Online scholarly project, information database, or web site

Cody, D. (2005). Queen Victoria. Victorian Web. Providence: Brown University. Retrieved April 11, 2006, from http://www.victorianweb.org

(To cite an online scholarly project, information database, or professional web site, include the author, if known, and the date in parentheses; the title of the source without special punctuation [followed by the date if there is no author]; the name of the project, database, or web site; and a retrieval statement.)

Article in an online encyclopedia or reference source

Children in foster care. (2004). [Chart]. *Infoplease almanac.* Retrieved April 10, 2006, from http://www.infoplease.com/

(To cite an article from an online encyclopedia or reference source, provide the author of the entry, if there is one, and the date in parentheses; the title of the entry exactly as it appears in the source, without special punctuation [followed by the date if there is no author]; the name of the reference work, italicized; facts of publication, if the source first existed in print form; and the retrieval statement.)

Article in an online magazine

Wheelright, J. (2001, January). Betting on designer genes. *Smithsonian, 31.* Retrieved October 18, 2001, from http://www.smithsonianmag.sr.edu/smithsonian/issues01/jan01/gene.html

(To cite an article in an online magazine, provide the name of the author, if appropriate; the date in parentheses; the title of the article; the name of the magazine and volume number, italicized; and the retrieval statement.)

Article in an online journal

Cramer, K., & Perrault, L. (2006). Effects of predictability, actual controllability, and awareness of choice on perceptions of control. *Current Research in Social Psychology, 11*(8). Retrieved April 20, 2006, from http://www.uiowa.edu/%7Egrpproc/crisp/crisp.html

(To cite an article in an online journal, provide the name of the author, if appropriate; the date in parentheses; the title of the article; the name of the journal

Article in an online newspaper

Rodriguez, C. (2001, January 9). Amid dispute, plight of illegal workers revisited. *Boston Globe.* Retrieved November 10, 2001, from http://www.boston.com/dailyglobe2/010/nation/Amid_dispute_plight_of_illegal_workers_revisited+.html

(To cite an article in an online newspaper, provide the name of the author, if appropriate; the date of publication in parentheses; the title of the article; the name of the newspaper, italicized; and the retrieval statement.)

CD-ROM sources

Welmers, W. E. (2003). African languages. *The new Grolier multimedia encyclopedia.* Retrieved from Grolier database (Grolier, CD-ROM, 2003 release).

(To cite a CD-ROM source, provide the name of the author, if given; the release date; the title of the selection, without special punctuation; the CD-ROM title, italicized; and a special CD-ROM retrieval statement, which includes the publisher's name, without special punctuation, and, in parentheses, the name of the database; the description *CD-ROM,* not italicized; the release date; and an item number, if applicable.)

Online posting

Whinney, K. (2001, January 11). Discussion of *A clockwork orange.* Message posted to Book Lovers' Discussion, archived at http://www.Whatamigoingtoread.com/book.asp?bookid=6395

(To cite an online posting to a forum or discussion group, provide the name of the author, if known; the official or descriptive title of the posting; the phrase *Message posted to,* not italicized; the name of the forum or discussion group; the phrase *archived at,* not italicized; and the URL.)

Text Citation Format

One author

Greybowski (1995) noted that . . .

Or:

In a recent study at USC (Greybowski, 1995), participants were asked to . . .

Multiple authors: first citation

Cadrillo, Thurgood, Johnson, and Lawrence (1967) found in their evaluation . . .

Multiple authors: subsequent citations

Cadrillo et al. (1967) also discovered . . .

Corporate authors: first citation

. . . a close connection between political interests and environmental issues (Council on Environmental Quality [CEQ], 1981).

Corporate authors: subsequent citations

. . . in their additional work (CEQ, 1981).

Quotations Within the Text

First option

She stated, "The cultural awareness of a student depends, by implication, on the cultural awareness of the parents" (Hermann, 1984, p. 219).

Second option

Hermann (1984) added that "enrichment in our schools is costly and has little bearing on the later lives of the students" (pp. 230–231).

Third option

"A school's responsibility rests with providing solid educational skills, not with supplementing the cultural education of the uninterested," stated Hermann (1984) in her summary (p. 236).

Credits

Chapter 1: Page 7: © Scott Adams/Dis. By United Feature Syndicate, Inc; page 11: from *My American Journey* by Colin Powell with Joseph E. Persico, copyright © 1995 by Colin L. Powell. Used by permission of Random House, Inc.; page 18: from *Writing Down the Bones* by Natalie Goldberg, © 1986. Reprinted by arrangement with Shambhala Publications, Inc., Boston. www.Shambhala.com.

Chapter 2: Page 25: Photo by Cameron Davidson; page 36: Copyright © 1998 by Julia Alvarez. From *Something to Declare*, published by Plume, an imprint of Penguin Group (USA), in 1999 and originally in hardcover by Algonquin Books of Chapel Hill. Reprinted by permission of Susan Bergholz Literary Services, New York. All rights reserved.

Chapter 3: Page 53: Time Life Pictures/Getty Images; page 54: © The New Yorker Collection 1998 Frank Cotham from cartoonbank.com. All rights reserved; page 58: Joe Raedle/ Getty Images News; page 62: from *An American Childhood* by Annie Dillard, pp. 147–149. Copyright © 1987 by Annie Dillard. Reprinted by permission of HarperCollins Publishers; page 64: from *Leonardo's Mountain of Clams and the Diet of Worms* by Stephen Jay Gould, Copyright © 1998 by Turbo, Inc. Used by permission of Harmony Books, a division of Random House, Inc.; page 71: excerpted from "The Case Against Choice," By Jane Smiley, *Harper's* Magazine. Copyright © 1995 by Harper's Magazine. All rights reserved. Reproduced from the June issue by special permission; p. 75. Copyright © 2004 by Mansueto Ventures LLC. Reproduced with permission of Mansueto Ventures LLC via Copyright Clearance Center.

Chapter 4: Page 87: Diego Goldberg/Sygma/Corbis; page 95: Brenda Ann Kenneally/Corbis; page 101: from Alan Lightman, "Spellbound by the Eternal Riddle, Scientists Revel in Their Captivity," *New York Times*, November 11, 2003, Science Times Section. Copyright © 2003 by The New York Times Co. Reprinted with permission; page 104: "The Six Myths of Creativity," by Bill Breen, *Fast Company*, December 2004; page 114: Dave Wobser/Great Lakes & Seaway Shipping News.

Chapter 5: Page 119: Bettmann/Corbis; page 130: from Sara Corbett, "The Lost Boys," The New York Times Upfront, Copyright © by Scholastic Inc. and the New York Times. Reprinted by permission of Scholastic Inc.

Chapter 6: Page 147: from The Autobiography of Malcolm X by Malcolm X and Alex Haley, Copyright © 1964 by Alex Haley and Malcolm X. Copyright © 1965 by Alex Haley and Betty Shabazz. Used by permission of Random House, Inc;

page 154: Donald Murray, "The Maker's Eye: Revising Your Own Manuscripts." Reprinted by permission of the author; page 159: "If You Can't Master English, Try Globish," by Mary Blume, International Herald Tribune Online, April 22, 2005. Copyright © 2006, I.H.T./iht.com. Reprinted by permission; page 165: Reprinted by arrangement with The Heirs to the Estate of Martin Luther King Jr., c/o Writers House as agent for the proprietor New York, NY. Copyright 1963 Martin Luther King Jr., copyright renewed 1991 Coretta Scott King; page 170: from "Beslan Atrocity: They're Terrorists—Not Activists," by Daniel Pipes, New York Sun, September 7, 2004. Reprinted with permission of Daniel Pipes.

Chapter 7: Page 187: Eric Robert/Corbis; page 189: © Image Bank/Getty Images; page 191: from "Animal Feelings," in *Animals in Translation: Using the Mysteries of Autism to Decode Animal Behavior*, Temple Grandin and Catherine Johnson, 2005, pp. 88–93. Reprinted with permission of the authors; page 198: "The Learning Curve" as it appeared in *The New Yorker*, January 28, 2002 and published in a slightly different version in Complications: A Surgeon's Notes on an Imperfect Science as "Education of a Knife" by Atul Gawande. Copyright 2002 by Atul Gawande. Reprinted by permission of Henry Holt and Company, LLC.

Chapter 8: page 215: Harry Borden; page 224: from "Choosing Clothes, but Not Husbands," by Joseph Berger, The New York Times, November 28, 2004. Copyright © 2004 by The New York Times Co. Reprinted with permission; page 228: Copyright © 1986 by Scott Russell Sanders; first appeared in The North American Review; from *The Paradise of Bombs*; reprinted by permission of the author and the author's agents, the Virginia Kidd Agency, Inc.; page 234: "My Papa's Waltz," Copyright © 1942 by Hearst Magazines, Inc., from *The Collected Poems of Theodore Roethke* by Theodore Roethke. Used by permission of Doubleday, a division of Random House, Inc.; page 236: first published in Granta 41, September 1, 1992. Copyright © 1992 by Louise Erdrich, permission of The Wylie Agency; page 240: from Richard Cohen, "Men and Their Hidden Feelings" *Washington Post* Writers Group, 1983. Copyright © 1983, The Washington Post Writers Group. Reprinted with permission; page 243: from Carol Tavris, "How Friendship Was Feminized," The New York Times, May 28, 1997. Copyright © 1997 *The New York Times*. Reprinted by permission; page 246: "Girl" from *At the Bottom of the River* by Jamaica Kincaid. Copyright © 1983 by Jamaica Kincaid. Reprinted by permission of Farrar, Straus and Giroux, LLC; page 248: From *Pulp!* Used by permission of Louis Hellman.

Chapter 9: page 267: Wikimedia Foundation/Creative Commons; page 268: © Scott Adams/Dis. By United Feature Syndicate, Inc.; page 269: © John Jonik from cartoonbank.com. All rights reserved; page 271: from "They Shoot Helicopters, Don't They? How Journalists Spread Rumors During Katrina," by Matt Welch, http://www.reason.com/0512/co.mw.they.shtml. Reprinted with permission of Reason Foundation; page 275: from Brian Thevenot, "Myth-Making in New Orleans," American Journalism Review, December/January 2006. Reprinted courtesy of American Journalism Review; page 282: from Russell R. Dynes and Haviden Rodriguez, "Finding and Framing Katrina: The Social Construction of Disaster," http://understandingkatrina.ssrc.org/Dynes_Rodriguez/pf/. Reprinted with permission of the authors; page 290: From The New York Times, February 22, 1965. Copyright © 1965 by The New York Times Co. Reprinted with permission; page 291: Reprinted by permission from Life 3/5/61. © 1965 Times Inc.; page 291: Copyright © 1965. Reprinted by permission of the New York Post; page 292: Paragraph on the assassination of Malcolm X, Associated Press, February 22, 1965. Reprinted by permission of the Associated Press; page 292: Excerpt from the Amsterdam News, February 27, 1965/Reprinted by permission of the New York Amsterdam News; page 311: from "A Natural Disaster, and a Human Tragedy," by Ted Steinberg, The Chronicle of Higher Education, September 23, 2005, http://chronicle.com/free/v52/i05/05b01101.htm. Reprinted with permission of the author; page 320: Reprinted with permission of Jennifer Wade.

Chapter 10: Page 327: Mike Segar/Reuters; page 333: © B. Stitzer/PhotoEdit; page 338: Richard Corliss and Michael D. Lemonick, "How to Live to Be 100," Time Magazine, August 30, 2004, pp. 40–49. Copyright © 2004 Time Inc. Reprinted by permission.

Chapter 11: Page 359: AP Photo/Joseph W. Jackson III; page 363: from "For Katrina Evacuee, Getting Help Is a Full-Time Job," by Nicholas Confessore, New York Times, March 8, 2006, p. B4. Copyright © 2006 by The New York Times Co. Reprinted with permission; page 369: Alan Lightman, "Is the Earth Round or Flat?" Reprinted by permission of the author; page 380: "Evolution as Fact and Theory" by Stephen Jay Gould, Discover Magazine, 1981. Reprinted by permission of the author; page 386: Frank & Ernest. © Thaves/Dist. by Newspaper Enterprise Association, Inc.

Chapter 12: Page 399: Farjana K. Godhuly/AFP/Getty Images; page 415: © The New Yorker Collection 1998 Frank Cotham from cartoonbank.com. All rights reserved; page 417: Baltimore Sun, "Hopkins Targets Campus Racism: Diversity Training, Other Steps Planned," by Sumathi Reddy, November 3, 2006. Copyright © 2006 by Baltimore Sun Company. Reproduced with permission of Baltimore Sun Company via Copyright Clearance Center; page 420: "Young Hate" by David Shenk. David Shenk (dshenk@bigfoot.com) is a writer living in Brooklyn. This article originally appeared in the February 1990 issue of CV Magazine; page 421 (top): Jeff Kowalsky/AFP/Getty Images; (bottom) Chris Chung/The Press Democrat; page 427: Nancy Gibbs, "When Is It Rape?" Time Magazine, June 3, 1991. Copyright © 1991 Time Inc. Reprinted by permission.

Chapter 13: Page 447: © Derek Goodwin; page 450: Library of Congress; page 451: www.goarmy.com. Reprinted with permission; page 453: © The New Yorker Collection 1998 Bernard Schoenbaum from cartoonbank.com; page 460: "Drugs" by Gore Vidal, Copyright © 1970 by Gore Vidal, from Homage to Daniel Shays: Collected Essays by Gore Vidal. Used by permission of Random House, Inc.; page 462: from "The Case for Slavery," by A. M. Rosenthal, New York Times, 1989. Copyright © 1989 by The New York Times Co. Reprinted with permission; page 468: From "In No Hurry for Next Leg of Journey," by David Gonzalez, New York Times, 1998. Copyright © 1998 by The New York Times Co. Reprinted with permission; page 470: Miller JL: "Hospice Care or Assisted Suicide: A False Dichotomy," American Journal of Hospice & Palliative Care, May/June 1997.

Chapter 14: Page 507: Paul Hawthorne/Getty Images; page 532: Zits Partnership, King Features Syndicate; page 545: Gianluigi Guercia/AFP/Getty Images.

Insert 1: Page 1-2: Antony Njuguna/Reuters/Corbis; page 1-3: Getty Images News; page 1-4: © Patrick Robert/Corbis; page 1-5: Faleh Kheiber/Reuters/Corbis; page 1-6: © Reza/Webistan/Corbis; page 1-7: © Andrew Holbrooke/ Corbis; page 1-8: Mark Wilson/Getty Images; page (8): Mario Tama/Getty Images News.

Insert 2: Page 2-2: EPA/The Ad Council: page 2-3: Americans for the Arts/The Ad Council: page 2-4: www.payattention.org; page 2-5: U.S. Department of Defense/The Ad Council, page 2-6: National Parks Conservation Association/The Ad Council: page 2-7: Courtesy, PETA; page 2-8: National Youth Anti-Drug Media Campaign.

Index

Tips for Evaluating the Reliability of a Web Site

This method is presented in more detail in Chapter 14.

1. AUTHORITY

- ❑ Are the sponsor's identity and purpose clear?
- ❑ Are the author's identity and qualifications evident?
- ❑ If the material is copyrighted, who is the copyright holder?
- ❑ Is there a way to verify the legitimacy of the site's sponsor?
- ❑ Don't forget that some of the people running sites are trying to confuse you.
- ❑ Look for clues that indicate a personal home page.
- ❑ Run unfamiliar topics or author names through a search engine.

2. ACCURACY

- ❑ Are sources of factual information clearly listed?
- ❑ Has the sponsor provided links that can be used to verify the sponsor's claims?
- ❑ Is statistical data well labeled and easy to read?
- ❑ Is the information free of grammatical errors, spelling errors, and typos?

3. OBJECTIVITY

- ❑ Is it evident why the sponsor is providing each piece of information?
- ❑ Is the information content separate from advertising or opinion?
- ❑ Is the sponsor's point of view presented clearly with well-supported arguments?
- ❑ If the site is not objective, does it account for opposing points of view?

4. CURRENCY

- ❑ Is the material recent enough to be relevant to your project?
- ❑ Are there any indications that the material is kept up to date?
- ❑ Do you see statements indicating where data for charts and graphs were gathered?
- ❑ Is there an indication that the site is complete and not still being developed?